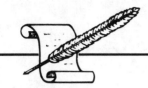

HISTORIC
DOCUMENTS
OF
1990

Cumulative Index, 1986-1990
Congressional Quarterly Inc.

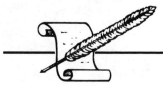

HISTORIC

DOCUMENTS

OF

1990

Congressional Quarterly Inc.
1414 22nd St. N.W., Washington, D.C. 20037

The Library of Congress cataloged the first issue of this title as follows:

Historic documents.   1972—
       Washington. Congressional Quarterly Inc.

       1. United States — Politics and government — 1945— — Yearbooks.
2. World politics — 1945— —Yearbooks. I. Congressional Quarterly Inc.

E839.5H57   917.3'03'9205   72-97888

ISBN 0-87187-563-2

ISSN 0892-080X

PREFACE

Historic Documents of 1990 carries through the nineteenth year the project Congressional Quarterly began with *Historic Documents of 1972.* The purpose of this continuing series is to give students, librarians, journalists, scholars, and others convenient access to documents of basic importance in the broad range of world affairs.

Each document is preceded by an introduction that provides background information and, when relevant, an account of continuing developments during the year. We believe that these introductions will become increasingly useful as memories of current times fade in the future.

The year 1990 was filled with dramatic events worldwide. Americans may remember it as the year of the Gulf crisis leading to war with Iraq. For Germans it was the year of unification, bringing East and West Germany into a single nation. In Britain 1990 marked the end of Margaret Thatcher's decade as prime minister.

Soviet cooperation in the United Nations enabled the United States to win Security Council approval of a dozen resolutions condemning Iraq's armed seizure of Kuwait and to assemble a coalition of military and economic forces to punish Saddam Hussein. But as economic and political problems intensified inside the Soviet Union, recent reforms were cast in jeopardy and Mikhail S. Gorbachev appeared beholden to a conservative hierarchy he had previously managed to circumvent. *Foreign Affairs* magazine observed that "the shape of the post-Cold War order was far more uncertain at the end of the year than at the beginning."

Africa's last colony, Namibia, declared its independence in ceremonies attended by Prime Minister F. W. de Klerk of South Africa, whose country had long controlled it in defiance of the United Nations. In South Africa itself, more racial barriers fell at de Klerk's urging. To the joyous acclaim of black South Africans, Nelson R. Mandela left prison—a free man for the first time in twenty-seven years—and resumed his leadership of a fragmented anti-apartheid movement. He later made a triumphal tour of the United States.

In Latin America, dictatorships on the political left (Nicaragua) and right (Chile) peacefully handed over control to democratically elected presidents. Gen. Augusto Pinochet surrendered power in Chile after nearly two decades of military rule, and in Nicaragua a decade of Marxist rule ended with the election and inauguration of Violeta Barrios de Chamorro over Sandinista incumbent Daniel Ortega.

At home, the nation conducted its decennial census and counted fewer than 250 million people, slightly below official estimates, prompting cries of an "undercount" in the big cities. The economy entered a recession in all but official designation. Tax revenues shrank but the costs of closing down and bailing out bankrupt savings institutions moved steadily upward. In the closing days of the 101st Congress, President George Bush and the Democratic leadership ended a protracted budget disagreement. Voters elected a new Congress, largely unchanged from the old one, with Democratic majorities in both houses.

Junk-bond king Michael R. Milken, who personified the Wall Street boom of the 1980s, was sent to prison. But a prison sentence imposed on Iran-contra figure Oliver L. North was removed by a federal appeals court. Abortion foes continued to mount vigorous campaigns in state legislatures, but the governors of Idaho and Louisiana—who both professed to oppose abortion—vetoed restrictive laws.

Such topics of national and international significance are presented in texts of official statements, Supreme Court decisions, reports, presidential news conferences, speeches, and special studies. In our judgment, the documents chosen for this volume will be of lasting interest. Where space limitations prevent reproduction of a full text, excerpts provide essential details.

Hoyt Gimlin, Editor
Washington, D.C., February 1991

How to Use This Book

The documents are arranged in chronological order. If you know the approximate date of the report, speech, statement, court decision, or other document you are looking for, glance through the titles for that month in the table of contents.

If the table of contents does not lead you directly to the document you want, turn to the index at the end of the book. There you may find references not only to the particular document you seek but also to other entries on the same or a related subject. The index in this volume is a five-year cumulative index of *Historic Documents* covering the years 1986-1990.

The introduction to each document is printed in italic type. The document itself, printed in roman type, follows the spelling, capitalization, and punctuation of the original or official copy. Where the full text is not given, omissions of material are indicated by the customary ellipsis points.

CONTENTS

January

CONTENTS

February

March

Veto of Idaho Bill Restricting Abortions

April

Soviet Admission of Katyn Massacre

Supreme Court on Tax Increase

Supreme Court on Child Pornography

Milken's Guilty Plea

Chamorro Inaugural in Nicaragua

Final Court Action on America's Cup Race

May

June

July

CONTENTS

August

September

December

CONTENTS

January

HAVEL'S ADDRESS TO NATION AND U.S. CONGRESS

January 1 and February 21, 1990

Vaclav Havel, the celebrated writer who moved from prison to the presidency of Czechoslovakia during 1989, began his fifth day in office with a New Year's address to his fellow citizens. Vowing "not to lie" to them as his Communist predecessors had done, Havel told the people they all shared the blame for the wretched conditions from four decades of tyranny.

"Our country is not prospering," Havel said, introducing a list of economic and environmental woes. "We have become morally ill, because we have become accustomed to saying one thing and thinking another." He said "all of us" became "accustomed to the totalitarian system, accepted it as an inalterable fact, and thereby kept it running." To shun all responsibility for the past not only would be wrong, Havel said, but also would detract from the need for each person to "act on his own initiative, freely, sensibly and quickly" to assure that freedom is retained and hardship overcome.

Havel did not exclude himself from these indictments, but he could justly have done so. He was often called the conscience of his country. For more than a decade, he had attacked the ruling regime in plays and other writings that were banned at home but published abroad. For his acts of defiance, Havel went to prison three times, spending almost five years there.

His last arrest—though without imprisonment—came only two months before he was unanimously selected president by a newly constituted Parliament and formally installed December 28. Havel thus became Czechoslovakia's first non-Communist head of state since the mysterious

3

death of President Jan Masaryk in 1948. Havel insisted he would retain the presidency only until national elections were held in June. (Communist Concessions in Czechoslovakia, Historic Documents of 1989, p. 635) *But the new Parliament that was chosen that month promptly re-elected him to the office by a vote of 234 to 50. Havel said the votes against him were proof that democracy was flourishing in Czechoslovakia.*

Havel's New Year's Day address drew favorable attention in other East European countries emerging from Soviet control, and in the Western press. Newsweek *columnist Meg Greenfield called the speech "profound and brilliant." Havel's sudden ascent from an oft-jailed dissident writer to president bestowed celebrity status on him at home and abroad.*

He traveled to the United States in February and received a hero's welcome. Still unaccustomed to pinstriped suits and wary of conforming to stereotypes, Havel declared himself an intellectual first and a politician second. He wrote his own speeches—a practice almost obsolete in American public life. During two days in Washington, he impressed America's senior politicians with his moral authority and his concern for the rights of mankind in modern society.

Address to U.S. Congress

In an address to a joint session of Congress February 21, the Czech president appealed for help—not so much for his country as for its past oppressor, the Soviet Union. Instead of asking for massive aid or a continued U.S. military presence in Europe—as was expected—Havel urged the United States to lead by the example of its democracy and to help the Soviet Union "on its irreversible but immensely complicated road to democracy."

While in Washington, Havel couched his appeal in broad philosophical terms, but with an element of pragmatism. Czech officials accompanying him said they were aware that the United States by itself could not propel Eastern Europe out of the Third World status into which it had fallen during Communist domination. Recognizing federal budget limits, Havel traveled to New York City in search of private investments to help transform his country's stagnant Communist economy into a vibrant one based on capitalism.

Within a week of his speech to Congress, Havel was in Moscow publicly expressing gratitude for seven Soviet dissidents who in 1968 had dared to protest the Kremlin's use of tanks and troops to crush a democratic movement that flourished briefly in Czechoslovakia that year—a liberalization known as the Prague Spring. Continuing with high-profile acts of symbolism, Havel arranged for West German president Richard von Weizsäcker to visit Prague on March 15, the anniversary of Hitler's invasion of Czechoslovakia in 1939. Weizsäcker expressed contrition about the German past, and Havel responded by equating anti-German feeling in Czechoslovakia to anti-Semitism. He expressed the hope that Europeans could cast aside bitter memories and leave the continent free of recriminations.

From Dramatist to Dissident

Amid his numerous scheduled appearances, Havel found time to visit places he had known during a brief stay in Manhattan in 1968, when his play The Memorandum *ran on Broadway. Another visit—to the Fifth Avenue offices of Helsinki Watch, a volunteer organization that monitors human rights abuses in the world—left him visibly touched. "I feel I am here as a friend among friends," the Czech president was quoted as saying to the staff. "I know very well what you did for us, and perhaps without you, our revolution could not be."*

Soon after Havel returned home from New York in 1968, Soviet military forces invaded Czechoslovakia, abruptly ending the Prague Spring. He was out of a theater job in Prague. He continued to write for publications abroad, but his public role shifted to politics. He became a principal organizer of Charter 77, a dissident group organized in 1977 to try to compel the Czechoslovak government to abide by the human rights provisions of the Helsinki Accords, an international treaty signed by Czechoslovakia and thirty-four other nations.

The first of Havel's prison sentences followed his initial work with Charter 77. Even in confinement, he managed to gather material for his writings in protest of arbitrary power. In Technical Notes on My House-Arrest, *Havel reported that, when he asked police what the charges were against him, he "was only told that they had no instructions to pass such information on to me." Prison correspondence with his wife, published in English as* Letters to Olga, *provided many readers previously unacquainted with the author's works a personal and somber look at the life of a dissident in Communist-controlled Eastern Europe.*

Following are texts of speeches by President Vaclav Havel to his nation on January 1, 1990, and to the U.S. Congress on February 21, in English translation by the State Department:

HAVEL'S NEW YEAR'S ADDRESS TO THE NATION

Dear fellow citizens. For the past 40 years on this day you have heard my predecessors utter different variations on the same theme, about how our country is prospering, how many more billion tons of steel we have produced, how happy we all are, how much we trust our government, and what beautiful prospects lie ahead of us. I do not think you proposed me to this office for me, of all people, to lie to you.

Our country is not prospering. The great creative and spiritual potential of our nation is not being used to its full potential. Whole sectors of industry are producing things in which no one is interested, while the things we need are in short supply.

The state, which calls itself a state of the working people, is humiliating and exploiting the workers. Our outdated economy is squandering energy, of which we are in short supply. A country which could once be proud of the standard of education of its people spends so little on education that today it occupies 72nd place in the world. We have laid waste [the water] and soil, the rivers and the forests that our forefathers bequeathed to us, and we have the worst environment in the whole of Europe today. Adults in our country die earlier than in most other European countries.

Allow me to tell you about a little personal experience of mine. Flying to Bratislava recently, I found time during various meetings to look out of the window. What I saw was the Slovnaft [oil refinery] complex and the Petrzalka suburb immediately beyond it. That view was enough for me to understand that four statesmen and politicians had not even looked, or did not even want to look out of the windows of their planes. None of the statistics available to me would have enabled me to understand more quickly or more easily the situation we have gotten ourselves into.

But not even all of that is the most important thing. The worst thing is that we are living in a decayed moral environment. We have become morally ill, because we have become accustomed to saying one thing and thinking another. We have learned not to believe in anything, not to have consideration for one another, and only to look after ourselves. Notions such as love, friendship, compassion, humility, and forgiveness have lost their depth and dimension, and for many of us they merely represent some kind of psychological idiosyncrasy, or appear to be some kind of stray relic from times past, something rather comical in the era of computers and space rockets. Few of us managed to cry out that the powerful should not be all-powerful, and that the special farms which produce ecologically sound and high-quality foodstuffs for them should send their produce to the schools, children's hostels, and hospitals, since our agriculture is not yet able to offer this to everyone.

The previous regime, armed with its arrogant and intolerant ideology, denigrated man into a production force and nature into a production tool. In this way it attacked their very essence and the relationship between them. It made talented people who were capable of managing their own affairs and making an enterprising living in their own country into cogs in some kind of monstrous, ramshackle, shell machine whose purpose no one can understand. It can do nothing more than slowly but surely wear itself down, and all the cogs in it.

When I talk about a decayed moral environment, I do not mean merely those gentlemen who eat ecologically pure vegetables and do not look out of their airplane windows. I mean all of us, because all of us have become accustomed to the totalitarian system, accepted it as an inalterable fact, and thereby kept it running. In other words, all of us are responsible, each to a different degree, for keeping the totalitarian machine running. None of us [were] merely a victim of it, because all of us helped to create it together.

Why do I mention this? It would be very unwise to see the sad legacy of the past 40 years as something alien to us, handed down to us by some distant relatives. On the contrary, we must accept this legacy as something which we have brought upon ourselves. If we can accept this, then we will understand that it is up to all of us to do something about it. We cannot lay all the blame on those who ruled us before, not only because this would not be true, but also because it could detract from the responsibility each of us now faces—the responsibility to act on our own initiative, freely, sensibly and quickly.

Let us not delude ourselves: not even the best government, the best parliament, or the best president can do much on their own, and it would be profoundly unjust to expect them alone to put everything right. Freedom and democracy, after all, mean that we all have a part to play and bear joint responsibility. If we can realize this, then all the horrors which the new Czechoslovak democracy has inherited will suddenly cease to appear so terrible. If we can realize this, hope will return to our hearts.

In putting right the general state of affairs, we already have a sound footing on which to build. The recent times, and especially the last 6 weeks of our peaceful revolution, have shown what an enormous generally human, moral, and spiritual charge and what high standards of civic maturity lay dormant in our society under the mask of apathy that had been forced upon it. Whenever anyone, talking to me, began to put categorical labels on our people, I always pointed out that society is a very mysterious creature, and that it is never wise to trust only the particular fact that it is presenting to you. I am glad to have been proven right.

Throughout the world, people are surprised that the acquiescent, humiliated, skeptical Czechoslovak people who apparently no longer believed in anything suddenly managed to find the enormous strength in the space of a few weeks to shake off the totalitarian system in a completely decent and peaceful way. We ourselves are also surprised at this, and we ask where the young people, in particular, who have never known any other system, find the source of their aspirations for truth, freedom of thought, political imagination, civic courage, and civic foresight? How is it that their parents, the generation which was considered lost, also joined in with them? How is it even possible that so many people immediately grasped what had to be done, without needing anyone else's advice or instructions?

I think that this hopeful aspect of our situation today has two main reasons. Above all, man is never merely a product of the world around him, he is always capable of striving for something higher, no matter how systematically this ability is ground down by the world around him. Secondly, the humanistic and democratic traditions—which are often spoken about in such a hollow way—nonetheless lay dormant somewhere in the subconscious of our nations and national minorities, and were passed on quietly from one generation to the next in order for each of us to discover them within us when the time was right, and to put them into practice.

Of course, for our freedom today we also had to pay a price. Many of our people died in prison in the fifties, many were executed, thousands of human lives were destroyed, hundreds of thousands of talented people were driven abroad. Those who defended the honor of our nations in the war were prosecuted, as were those who resisted totalitarian government, and those who simply managed to remain true to their own principles and think freely. None of those who paid the price in one way or another for our freedom today should be forgotten. Independent courts should justly assess the appropriate guilt of those responsible, so that the whole truth about our recent past comes out into the open.

Neither should we forget that other nations paid an even higher price for their freedom today, and thus they also paid indirectly for us too. The rivers of blood which flowed in Hungary, Poland, Germany, and recently also in such a horrific way in Romania, as well as the sea of blood shed by the nations of the Soviet Union, should not be forgotten, primarily because all human suffering affects every human being. But more than that, they must not be forgotten because it was these great sacrifices which weaved the tragic backcloth for today's freedom or gradual liberation of the nations of the Soviet bloc, and the backcloth of our newly charged freedom too.

Without the changes in the Soviet Union, Poland, Hungary, and the GDR[German Democratic Republic—East Germany], the developments in our country could hardly have happened, and if they had happened, they surely would not have had such a wonderful peaceful character. The fact that we had favorable international conditions, of course, does not mean that anyone was helping us directly in those weeks. For centuries, in fact, both our nations [reference to Czechs and Slovaks] have risen up by themselves, without relying on any help from more powerful states or big powers.

This, it seems to me, is the great moral stake of the present moment. It contains the hope that in the future we will no longer have to suffer the complex of those who are permanently indebted to someone else. Now it is up to us alone whether this hope comes to fruition, and whether our civic, national, and political self-confidence reawakens in a historically new way.

Self-confidence is not pride. Quite the contrary. Only a man or a nation self-confident in the best sense of the word is capable of listening to the voice of others, accepting them as equal to oneself, forgiving their enemies, and regretting one's own mistakes. As such people, let us try to introduce self-confidence into the life of our community and as nations into our conduct on the international arena. Only thus shall we regain self-respect and respect for each other, as well as the respect of other nations. Our state should never again be a burden or a poor relation to anyone else. Although we have to take a great many things and learn many things from others, we must do this, after a long period of time, as equal partners who also have something to offer.

Our first president [Thomas G. Masaryk] wrote "Jesus and not Caesar." In this he followed up both on philosopher-writer Peter Chelcicky [1390-1460] and [Moravian churchman-educator John Amos] Komensky [1592-1670]. This idea has once again been reawakened in us. I dare say that perhaps we even have the possibility of spreading it further, thus introducing a new factor in both European and world politics. Love, desire for understanding, the strength of the spirit and of ideas can radiate forever from our country, if we want this to happen. This radiation can be precisely what we can offer as our very own contribution to world politics.

Masaryk founded his politics on morality. Let us try, in a new time and in a new way, to revive this concept of politics. Let us teach both ourselves and others that politics ought to be a reflection of the aspiration to contribute to the happiness of the community and not of the need to deceive or pillage the community. Let us teach both ourselves and others that politics does not have to be the art of the possible, especially if this means the art of speculating, calculating, intrigues, secret agreements, and pragmatic maneuvering, but that it also can be the art of the impossible, that is the art of making both ourselves and the world better.

We are a small country, but nonetheless we were once the spiritual crossroads of Europe. Is there any reason why we should not be so again? Would this not be another contribution through which we could pay others back for the help we will need from them?

The home Mafia—those who do not look out of their airplane windows and eat specially-fed pigs—are still alive, true, and make trouble from time to time, but they are no longer our main enemy, and international Mafias are even less of an enemy. Our worst enemy today is our own bad qualities—indifference to public affairs, conceit, ambition, selfishness, the pursuit of personal advancement, and rivalry—and that is the main struggle we are faced with.

We are going into free elections, and an election battle. Let us not allow that battle to sully the still clean face of our gentle revolution. Let us ensure that we do not lose the sympathy of the world, which we won so rapidly, equally rapidly by getting bogged down in a tangle of skirmishes for power. Let us not allow the aspiration to look after ourselves to flourish once again under the noble attire of the aspiration to serve the general cause.

Now the issue really is not which party, club, or group wins the elections. The issue now is that the elections are won by those who are best in the moral, civic, political, and specialist sense. The future policy and the prestige of our state will depend on what kind of personalities we select and subsequently elect to our representative bodies.

Dear fellow citizens. By your will 3 days ago, as conveyed by Federal Assembly deputies, I became president of this republic. You rightly expect me to mention the tasks which I see as your president lie ahead of us.

The first is to make use of all my powers and my influence to ensure that we all come soon and with dignity to the ballot box in free elections and that this journey of ours to this historic milestone is a decent and peaceful one.

My second task is to watch over to ensure that we come to these elections as two truly sovereign nations which respect each other's interests, national identity, religious traditions, and each other's symbols. As a Czech occupying the presidential office, who was sworn in by an important Slovak, who is also close to me, I feel after the various bitter experiences the Slovaks experienced in the past a special duty to watch over to ensure that all interests of the Slovak nation are respected and that the access to any state office, including the highest one, is never closed to it in the future.

As my third task I regard my support for everything that will lead to a better position for children, the elderly, women, the sick, those involved in heavy manual work, members of ethnic minorities, and in general all citizens who are worse off than others for whatever reason. Better food or hospitals must no longer be the privilege of the powerful but must be offered to those who need them most.

As the supreme commander of the defense forces, I intend to guarantee that the defense capability of our state will no longer be a pretext for anyone to thwart courageous peace initiatives, including the shortening of military service, establishing a system of alternative military service, and generally making military life more humane.

Our country has many prisoners who, although they have committed serious crimes and have been sentenced for them, have had to pass through a decayed system of justice which has infringed their rights, despite the goodwill of certain investigating judges and, in particular, certain lawyers. They have to live in prisons which do not seek to awaken everything that is good in each of us, but on the contrary humiliate people, and destroy them in both body and mind.

In the light of this fact, I have decided to declare a relatively wide amnesty. I also ask prisoners to understand that 40 years of mistakes in investigation, the administration of justice, and imprisonment cannot be put right overnight, and to understand that all the hastily drawn-up changes will nonetheless take a certain time. By rioting in the prisons, they will not help either this society or themselves.

I then ask the public not to be afraid of the prisoners released, not to aggravate their lives, but to help them in a Christian spirit after their return among us to find in themselves what prisons have failed to find in them—the ability to repent and desire to live orderly lives.

My honorable task is to strengthen the authority of our country in the world. I would like other states to respect us for our show of understanding, tolerance, and love of peace. I would be happy if Pope John Paul II and the Dalai Lama of Tibet visited our country even for a single day before the elections take place. I would be happy if our friendly relations with all nations were strengthened. I would be happy if we succeeded even before the elections take place to establish diplomatic relations with the Vatican and Israel. I would like to contribute to peace also by the brief visit tomorrow to our two mutually related neighbors, the GDR and the FRG [Federal Republic of Germany—West Germany]. I shall not forget our other neighbors either: fraternal Poland, Hungary, and Austria, which are becoming increasingly close to us.

I would like to conclude by saying that I want to be a president of action rather than words, a president who not only looks out of the windows of his airplane carefully, but one, above all, who is consistently present among his fellow citizens and listens to them carefully.

Perhaps you are asking what kind of republic I have in mind. My reply is this: a republic which is independent, free, and democratic, with a prospering economy and also socially just—in short a republic of the people which serves the people, and is therefore entitled to hope that the people will serve it too. I have in mind a republic of people with a well-rounded education, because without such people none of our problems—can be tackled.

One of my most distinguished predecessors began his first speech by quoting Comenius. Allow me to end my first speech with my own paraphrase of the same statement: people, your government has returned to you!

HAVEL'S ADDRESS TO A JOINT SESSION OF CONGRESS

My advisors have advised me, on this important occasion, to speak in Czech. I don't know why. Perhaps they wanted you to enjoy the sweet sounds of my mother tongue.

The last time they arrested me, on October 27 of last year, I didn't know whether it was for two days or two years.

Exactly one month later, when the rock musician Michael Kocab told me that I would probably be proposed as a presidential candidate, I thought it was one of his usual jokes.

On the 10th of December 1989, when my actor friend Jiri Bartoska, in the name of the Civic Forum, nominated me as a candidate for the office of President of the Republic, I thought it was out of the question that the parliament we had inherited from the previous regime would elect me.

Twelve days later, when I was unanimously elected President of my country, I had no idea that in two months I would be speaking in front of this famous and powerful assembly, and that what I say would be heard by millions of people who have never heard of me and that hundreds of politicians and political scientists would study every word I say.

When they arrested me on October 27, I was living in a country ruled by the most conservative Communist government in Europe, and our society slumbered beneath the pall of a totalitarian system. Today, less than four months later, I am speaking to you as the representative of a country that has set out on the road to democracy, a country where there is complete freedom of speech, which is getting ready for free elections, and which wants to create a prosperous market economy and its own foreign policy.

It is all very strange indeed.

But I have not come here to speak of myself or my feelings, or merely to talk about my own country. I have used this small example of something I know well, to illustrate something general and important.

We are living in very odd times. The human face of the world is changing so rapidly that none of the familiar political speedometers are adequate.

We playwrights, who have to cram a whole human life or an entire historical era into a two-hour play, can scarcely understand this rapidity ourselves. And if it gives us trouble, think of the trouble it must give to political scientists, who spend their whole lives studying the realm of the probable.

Let me try to explain why I think the velocity of the changes in my country, in Central and Eastern Europe, and of course in the Soviet Union itself, has made such a significant impression on the face of the world today, and why it concerns the fate of us all, including you Americans. I would like to look at this, first from the political point of view, and then from a point of view that we might call philosophical.

Twice in this century, the world has been threatened by a catastrophe; twice this catastrophe was born in Europe, and twice you Americans, along with others, were called upon to save Europe, the whole world and yourselves. The first rescue mission—among other things—provided significant help to us Czechs and Slovaks.

Thanks to the great support of your President [Woodrow] Wilson, our first president, Tomas Garrigue Masaryk, could found our modern independent state. He founded it, as you know, on the same principles on which the United States of America had been founded, as Masaryk's manuscripts held by the Library of Congress testify.

At the same time, the United States was making enormous strides. It became the most powerful nation on earth, and it understood the responsibility that flowed from this. Proof of this are the hundreds of thousands of your young citizens who gave their lives for the liberation of Europe, and the graves of American airmen and soldiers on Czechoslovak soil.

But something else was happening as well: the Soviet Union appeared, grew, and transformed the enormous sacrifices of its people suffering under totalitarian rule, into a strength that, after World War Two, made it the second most powerful nation in the world. It was a country that rightly gave people nightmares, because no one knew what would occur to its rulers next and what country they would decide to conquer and drag into their sphere of influence, as it is called in political language.

All of this taught us to see the world in bipolar terms, as two enormous forces, one a defender of freedom, the other a source of nightmares. Europe became the point of friction between these two powers and thus it turned into a single enormous arsenal divided into two parts. In this process, one half of the arsenal became part of that nightmarish power, while the other—the free part—bordering on the ocean and having no wish to be driven into it, was compelled, together with you, to build a complicated security system, to which we probably owe the fact that we still exist.

So you may have contributed to the salvation of us Europeans, of the world and thus of yourselves for a third time: you have helped us to survive until today—without a hot war this time—but merely a cold one.

And now what is happening is happening: the totalitarian system in the Soviet Union and in most of its satellites is breaking down and our nations are looking for a way to democracy and independence. The first act in this remarkable drama began when Mr. Gorbachev and those around him, faced with the sad reality of their country, initiated their policy of "perestroika" [reform]. Obviously they had no idea either what they were setting in motion or how rapidly events would unfold. We knew a lot about the enormous number of growing problems that slumbered beneath the honeyed, unchanging mask of socialism. But I don't think any of us knew how little it would take for these problems to manifest themselves in all their enormity, and for the longings of these nations to emerge in all their strength. The mask fell away so rapidly that, in the flood of work, we have literally no time even to be astonished.

What does all this mean for the world in the long run? Obviously a number of things. This is, I am firmly convinced, an historically irreversible process, and as a result Europe will begin again to seek its own identity without being compelled to be a divided armory any longer. Perhaps this will create the hope that sooner or later your boys will no longer have to stand on guard for freedom in Europe, or come to our rescue, because Europe will at last be able to stand guard over itself. But that is still not the most important thing: the main thing is, it seems to me, that these revolutionary changes will enable us to escape from the rather antiquated straitjacket of this bipolar view of the world, and to enter at last into an era of multipolarity. That is, into an era in which all of us—large and small—former slaves and former masters—will be able to create what your great President [Abraham] Lincoln called "the family of man." Can you imagine what a relief this would be to that part of the world which for some reason is called the Third World, even though it is the largest?

I don't think it's appropriate simply to generalize, so let me be specific:

1) As you certainly know, most of the big wars and other conflagrations over the centuries have traditionally begun and ended on the territory of modern Czechoslovakia, or else they were somehow related to that area. Let the Second World War stand as the most recent example. This is understandable: whether we like it or not, we are located in the very heart of Europe, and thanks to this, we have no view of the sea, and no real navy. I mention this because political stability in our country has traditionally been important for the whole of Europe. This is still true today. Our government of national understanding, our present Federal Assembly, the other bodies of the state and I myself will personally guarantee this stability until we hold free elections, planned for June. We understand the terribly complex reasons, domestic political reasons above all, why the Soviet Union cannot withdraw its troops from our territory as quickly as they arrived in 1968. We understand that the arsenals built there over the past twenty years cannot be dismantled and removed overnight. Nevertheless, in our bilateral negotiations with the Soviet Union, we would like to have as many Soviet units as possible moved out of our country before the elections, in the interests of political stability. The more successful our negotiations, the more those who are elected in our places will be able to guarantee political stability in our country even after the elections.

2) I often hear the question: how can the United States of America help

us today? My reply is as paradoxical as the whole of my life has been: you can help us most of all if you help the Soviet Union on its irreversible, but immensely complicated road to democracy. It is far more complicated than the road possible to its former European satellites. You yourselves know best how to support, as rapidly as possible, the non-violent evolution of this enormous, multi-national body politic towards democracy and autonomy for all of its peoples. Therefore, it is not fitting for me to offer you any advice. I can only say that the sooner, the more quickly, and the more peacefully the Soviet Union begins to move along the road towards genuine political pluralism, respect for the rights of nations to their own integrity and to a working—that is a market—economy, the better it will be, not just for Czechs and Slovaks, but for the whole world. And the sooner you yourselves will be able to reduce the burden of the military budget borne by the American people. To put it metaphorically: the millions you give to the East today will soon return to you in the form of billions in savings.

3) It is not true that the Czech writer Vaclav Havel wishes to dissolve the Warsaw Pact tomorrow and then NATO [North Atlantic Treaty Organization] the day after that, as some eager nationalists have written. Vaclav Havel merely thinks what he has already said here, that for another hundred years, American soldiers shouldn't have to be separated from their mothers just because Europe is incapable of being a guarantee of world peace, which it ought to be, in order to make some amends, at least, for having given the world two world wars. Sooner or later Europe must recover and come into its own, and decide for itself how many of whose soldiers it needs so that its own security, and all the wider implications of that security, may radiate peace into the whole world. Vaclav Havel cannot make decisions about things it is not proper for him to decide. He is merely putting in a good word for genuine peace, and for achieving it quickly.

4) Czechoslovakia thinks that the planned summit conference of countries participating in the Helsinki process [of guaranteeing human rights] should take place soon, and that in addition to what it wants to accomplish, it should aim to hold the so-called Helsinki Two conference earlier than 1992, as originally planned. Above all, we feel it could be something far more significant than has so far seemed possible. We think that Helsinki Two should become something equivalent to the European peace conference, which has not yet been held; one that would finally put a formal end to the Second World War and all its unhappy consequences. Such a conference would officially bring a future democratic Germany, in the process of unifying itself, into a new pan-European structure which could decide about its own security system. This system would naturally require some connection with that part of the globe we might label the "Helsinki" part, stretching westward from Vladivostok all the way to Alaska. The borders of the European states, which by the way should become gradually less important, should finally be legally guaranteed by a common, regular treaty. It should be more than obvious that the basis for such a treaty would have to be general respect for human rights, genuine political pluralism and genuinely free elections.

5) Naturally we welcome the initiative of President [George] Bush, which was essentially accepted by Mr. [Mikhail S.] Gorbachev as well, according to which the number of American and Soviet troops in Europe should be radically reduced. It is a magnificent shot in the arm for the Vienna disarmament talks and creates favorable conditions not only for our own efforts to achieve the quickest possible departure of Soviet troops from Czechoslovakia, but indirectly as well for our own intention to make considerable cuts in the Czechoslovak army, which is disproportionately large in relation to our population. If Czechoslovakia were forced to defend itself against anyone, which we hope will not happen, then it will be capable of doing so with a considerably smaller army, because this time its defense would be—not only after decades but even centuries—supported by the common and indivisible will of both its nations and its leadership. Our freedom, independence and our new-born democracy have been purchased at great cost, and we will not surrender them. For the sake of order, I should add that whatever steps we take are not intended to complicate the Vienna disarmament talks, but on the contrary to facilitate them.

6) Czechoslovakia is returning to Europe. In the general interest and in its own interest as well, it wants to coordinate this return—both politically and economically—with the other returnees, which means, above all, with its neighbors the Poles and the Hungarians. We are doing what we can to coordinate these returns. And at the same time, we are doing what we can so that Europe will be capable of really accepting us, its wayward children. Which means that it may open itself to us, and may begin to transform its structures—which are formally European but de facto Western European—in that direction, but in such a way that it will not be to its detriment, but rather to its advantage.

7) I have already said this in our parliament, and I would like to repeat it here, in this Congress, which is architecturally far more attractive: for many years, Czechoslovakia—as someone's meaningless satellite—has refused to face up honestly to its co-responsibility for the world. It has a lot to make up for. If I dwell on this and so many important things here, it is only because I feel—along with my fellow citizens—a sense of culpability for our former responsible passivity, and a rather ordinary sense of indebtedness.

8) Last but not least, we are of course delighted that your country is so readily lending its support to our fresh efforts to renew democracy. Both our peoples were deeply moved by the generous offers made a few days ago in Prague at the Charles University, one of the oldest in Europe, by your Secretary of State, Mr. James Baker. We are ready to sit down and talk about them.

Ladies and gentlemen, I've only been president for two months and I haven't attended any schools for presidents. My only school was life itself. Therefore I don't want to burden you any longer with my political thoughts, but instead I will move on to an area that is more familiar to me, to what I would call the philosophical aspect of those changes that still concern everyone, although they are taking place in our corner of the world.

As long as people are people, democracy in the full sense of the word will always be no more than an ideal; one may approach it as one would a horizon, in ways that may be better or worse, but it can never be fully attained. In this sense you too are merely approaching democracy. You have thousands of problems of all kinds, as other countries do. But you have one great advantage: you have been approaching democracy uninterruptedly for more than two hundred years, and your journey towards that horizon has never been disrupted by a totalitarian system. Czechs and Slovaks, despite their humanistic traditions that go back to the first millenium, have approached democracy for a mere twenty years, between the two world wars, and now for the three and a half months since the 17th of November of last year.

The advantage that you have over us is obvious at once.

The communist type of totalitarian system has left both our nations, Czechs and Slovaks—as it has all the nations of the Soviet Union and the other countries the Soviet Union subjugated in its time—a legacy of countless dead, an infinite spectrum of human suffering, profound economic decline, and above all enormous human humiliation. It has brought us horrors that fortunately you have not known.

At the same time, however—unintentionally, of course—it has given us something positive: a special capacity to look, from time to time, somewhat further than someone who has not undergone this bitter experience. A person who cannot move and live a somewhat normal life because he is pinned under a boulder has more time to think about his hopes than someone who is not trapped in this way.

What I am trying to say is this: we must all learn many things from you, from how to educate our offspring, how to elect our representatives, all the way to how to organize our economic life so that it will lead to prosperity and not to poverty. But it doesn't have to be merely assistance from the well-educated, the powerful and the wealthy to someone who has nothing and therefore has nothing to offer in return.

We too can offer something to you: our experience and the knowledge that has come from it.

This is a subject for books, many of which have already been written and many of which have yet to be written. I shall therefore limit myself to a single idea.

The specific experience I'm talking about has given me one great certainty: consciousness precedes Being, and not the other way around, as the Marxists claim.

For this reason, the salvation of this human world lies nowhere else than in the human heart, in the human power to reflect, in human meekness and in human responsibility.

Without a global revolution in the sphere of human consciousness, nothing will change for the better in the sphere of our Being as humans, and the catastrophe towards which this world is headed, whether it be ecological, social, demographic or a general breakdown of civilization, will be unavoidable. If we are no longer threatened by world war, or by the danger that the absurd mountains of accumulated nuclear weapons might blow up the world, this does not mean that we have definitively won. We are in fact far from definitive victory.

We are still a long way from that "family of man"; in fact, we seem to be receding from the ideal rather than drawing closer to it. Interests of all kinds: personal, selfish, state, national, group and, if you like, company interests still considerably outweigh genuinely common and global interests. We are still under the sway of the destructive and vain belief that man is the pinnacle of creation, and not just a part of it, and that therefore everything is permitted. There are still many who say they are concerned not for themselves, but for the cause, while they are demonstrably out for themselves and not for the cause at all. We are still destroying the planet that was entrusted to us, and its environment. We still close our eyes to the growing social, ethnic and cultural conflicts in the world. From time to time we say that the anonymous megamachinery we have created for ourselves no longer serves us, but rather has enslaved us, yet we still fail to do anything about it.

In other words, we still don't know how to put morality ahead of politics, science and economics. We are still incapable of understanding that the only genuine backbone of all our actions—if they are to be moral—is responsibility. Responsibility to something higher than my family, my country, my firm, my success. Responsibility to the order of Being, where all our authority is indelibly recorded and where, and only where, they will be properly judged.

The interpreter or mediator between us and this higher authority is what is traditionally referred to as human conscience.

If I subordinate my political behavior to this imperative mediated to me by my conscience, I can't go far wrong. If on the contrary I were not guided by this voice, not even ten presidential schools with two thousand of the best political scientists in the world could help me.

This is why I ultimately decided—after resisting for a long time—to accept the burden of political responsibility.

I'm not the first, nor will I be the last, intellectual to do this. On the contrary, my feeling is that there will be more and more of them all the time. If the hope of the world lies in human consciousness, then it is obvious that intellectuals cannot go on forever avoiding their share of responsibility for the world and hiding their distaste for politics under an alleged need to be independent.

It is easy to have independence in your program and then leave others to carry that program out. If everyone thought that way pretty soon no one would be independent.

I think that you Americans should understand this way of thinking. Wasn't it the best minds of your country, people you could call intellectuals, who wrote your famous Declaration of Independence, your Bill of Human Rights and your Constitution and who—above all—took upon themselves the practical responsibility for putting them into practice? The worker from Branik in Prague that your President referred to in his State of the Union message this year is far from being the only person in Czechoslovakia, let alone in the world, to be inspired by those great documents. They inspire us all. They inspire us despite the fact that they are over two hundred years old. They inspire us to be citizens.

[*Speaking English*] When Thomas Jefferson wrote that, "Governments are instituted among Men deriving their just Powers from the Consent of the Governed," it was a simple and important act of the human spirit.

What gave meaning to the act, however, was the fact that the author backed it up with his life. It was not just his words, it was his deeds as well.

I will end where I began: history has accelerated. I believe that once again, it will be the human mind that will notice this acceleration, give it a name, and transform those words into deeds.

Thank you.

COAL STRIKE SETTLEMENT
January 1, 1990

On New Year's Day Secretary of Labor Elizabeth Dole announced that a settlement had been reached in the long and bitter strike by the United Mine Workers of America (UMWA) against the Pittston Coal Group, and the parent Pittston Company, at coal mines in Virginia, West Virginia, and Kentucky. The striking miners ratified the new work contract by a vote of 1,247 to 734, the union reported February 20, ending a work stoppage that began the previous April 5.

During that period, miners in neighboring states walked off their jobs at various times to show sympathy for the Pittston strikers. As many as 44,000 miners engaged in those "wildcat" (unauthorized) work stoppages. A rally in support of the strike drew some 12,000 miners to the statehouse in Charleston, West Virginia, on June 11.

At or near Pittston facilities, strikers and their sympathizers used roadblocks and other measures to stall the delivery of coal mined by replacement workers. Coal trucks often were tied up in traffic by vehicles moving with deliberate slowness. The trucks' windshields frequently were smashed by rocks as they moved across picket lines or along mountain roads. In the end, the union incurred tens of millions of dollars in court fines for strike-law violations, and hundreds of strikers were arrested.

In October, after the two sides had engaged in months of fruitless bargaining, Secretary Dole persuaded UMWA president Richard L. Trumka and Pittston Company chairman Paul W. Douglas to let a federal mediator, W. J. Usery, Jr., direct the negotiations. After sixty-two days of negotiation, the agreement was reached. "Truly this is a victory for collective bargaining," Usery said. He appeared with Dole, Trumka, and Douglas at a news conference in Washington, D.C., where the labor secretary made her January 1 announcement.

"For us," Trumka said on behalf of the union, "this is Thanksgiving Day." He and several other labor leaders, including AFL-CIO president Lane Kirkland, hailed the outcome as a victory for the union. Douglas's comment was more circumspect. He spoke of the "mutual achievement of mutual objectives" but cautioned that agreement "would require an enormous amount of human and other forms of cooperation that you cannot just write down on a piece of paper."

Union Prestige at Stake

A settlement that provided some of the UMWA's demands—as this one did—was considered crucial to the credibility of the 150,000-member miners' union and to Trumka. This test of prestige extended even to the AFL-CIO, which in October had readmitted the UMWA after its forty-two years of self-imposed exile. The union severed the ties in 1947 in a dispute between its boss, John L. Lewis, and the parent organization's leadership.

Underlining the union's reaffiliation with the AFL-CIO, the announcement of the strikers' approval of the new contract with Pittston was made at the annual AFL-CIO meeting in Bal Harbour, Florida, in the presence of Dole, Kirkland, Trumka, and Usery. At a news conference the previous day, Kirkland said, referring to the strike's outcome, "We have achieved our objectives."

The strikers had walked off their jobs after working fourteen months without a contract. Pittston had refused to accept a new four-year contract negotiated in 1988 between the Bituminous Coal Operators Association and the UMWA. It was signed by most of the other companies involved. The most contentious issue was health care. Pittston said it could not afford to continue paying the full cost of health care for active, retired, and disabled miners.

New Contract's Major Terms

Under the new contract, the company agreed to pay all health-care charges incurred by the miners, pensioners, and their families. Technically, individuals would pay the first $1,000, but in practical terms they would pay nothing. The company agreed to offset that amount with $500 bonuses every six months. The contract also called for a pay raise of $1.20 an hour to reach a top wage scale of $17.52 within three years.

The company was obligated to hire UMWA members, including those on layoff, for four of every five jobs at new operations at nonunion subsidiaries and at mines previously uncovered by contract. Pittston's subcontractors who operate on its property were required to fill nineteen of every twenty new jobs with UMWA members.

Pittston, in turn, won a concession from the union to substitute "flex-time" options for the standard eight-hour, five-day week. These options would enable the company to keep shifts operating all hours except during the daytime on Sundays.

> *Following is the text of Secretary of Labor Elizabeth Dole's announcement at a news conference in Washington, D.C., January 1, 1990, of a settlement in the strike by the United Mine Workers of America against the Pittston Coal Group and its parent corporation, the Pittston Company:*

It gives me great personal pleasure to announce that the labor dispute between the Pittston Coal Company and the United Mine Workers of America, has, at long last, been settled. Bill [W. J.] Usery, [Jr.], our supermediator, has indicated to me, that of the more than 800 disputes he's mediated or negotiated, this was the toughest.

As you may recall, on October 13, I went down to the coal fields of southwest Virginia to meet with coal miners, their families and representatives of Pittston. I felt the time was ripe for decisive action, and called the parties to meet with me in my office the following day. At that meeting, I told Paul [W.] Douglas, chief executive officer of Pittston, and Rich [Richard L.] Trumka, president of the United Mine Workers, of my desire to use my good offices to facilitate the collective bargaining process and hopefully to resolve this troubling dispute. They agreed with my decision to appoint a supermediator, and several days later agreed with my choice of former Secretary of Labor Bill Usery for that job.

For the past few months, Bill, Paul, Rich, and their negotiators have been hard at work, meeting, on some occasions, literally around the clock. There was one mammoth 96-hour session just before Christmas. And today, we can rejoice in their accomplishments, and express our heartfelt thanks for their dedication and their persistence.

I know that all parties would agree with me in saying that today's settlement is a victory for the collective bargaining process—a process, which, over the years, has resulted in protection for all workers, stronger businesses and greater cooperation between management and labor.

I also know that both Pittston and the United Mine Workers join with me in heartfelt thanks to Bill Usery for his diligence, patience, and perseverance. Frankly, this dispute would have tested the mettle of any seasoned labor negotiator, but I never doubted that Bill would meet his stated objective to have an agreement by the holidays. I also want to applaud the dedication of the mediators of the Federal Mediation and Conciliation Service for their efforts in these negotiating sessions. Their assistance has been invaluable.

And today's settlement is a very special holiday gift for all parties involved—a gift for the Pittston Company, which can now move forward and work toward a productive future and a supportive work environment; and a gift for the workers, their families, and their communities, who have faced 9 months of a bitter labor dispute.

One of the difficult issues in this dispute was the long-term security of the pension and health care benefits of the miners and their families. But the issue is larger than this particular dispute, and I am committed to addressing it, to help fashion a solution on an informed and deliberate basis. Therefore, I will soon appoint a secretarial commission, which will review all aspects of the pension and health care issue and make recommendations to me for dealing with it.

During this holiday season, it is fitting, indeed, to remember the words from the Book of Isaiah: "Come, let us reason together." The timeless strength of these words can be seen in the victory we celebrate today.

My congratulations, and the nation's as well, go to all the parties involved for their successful efforts to reason together.

SUPREME COURT ON
TENURE REVIEW DISCLOSURE
January 9, 1990

The Supreme Court unanimously held January 9 that assertions of academic freedom did not exempt the University of Pennsylvania from having to disclose confidential information that concerned a teacher's tenure, in an antidiscrimination case. The university, supported by several other academic institutions and the American Association of University Professors, argued that such assessments of a teacher's ability by faculty colleagues would suffer if the deliberations ceased to be confidential.

The case, University of Pennsylvania v. Equal Employment Opportunity Commission, *was brought by the EEOC on behalf of Rosalie Tung, an associate professor at the university's Wharton School of Business, who was denied tenure in 1985. Tung, a Chinese-American, formally complained to the commission that she was a victim of illegal discrimination on the basis of race, sex, and national origin. She alleged that her department chairman had sexually harassed her and negatively evaluated her work to the university's Personnel Committee after she resisted his advances.*

Moreover, Tung contended that she was recommended for tenure by a majority of the faculty members of her department and that her qualifications were "equal to or better than" those of five colleagues who received more favorable treatment. Tung said she discovered by her own effort that the Personnel Committee attempted to justify its decision to deny her tenure "on the ground that the Wharton School is not interested in China-related research." The explanation, she asserted, was "simply their way of saying they do not want a Chinese-American,

23

Oriental, woman in their school." Tung subsequently went to the University of Wisconsin, where she won tenure as a professor and director of its International Business Center.

Question of Academic Freedom

Investigating her complaint, the EEOC was refused information it requested from the University of Pennsylvania. The commission issued a subpoena compelling the university to turn over a list of tenure file documents. University officials responded by asking that "confidential peer review information" be excluded from the list. The commission refused and obtained an enforcement order from the federal district court in Philadelphia, where the university is located.

The university appealed the enforcement order to the U.S. Court of Appeals for the Third Circuit, also in Philadelphia, but the appellate court upheld the order. On further appeal, the Supreme Court agreed to review the matter. Justice Harry A. Blackmun wrote the opinion.

The Court strongly rejected the university's argument that academic freedom provided the institution a special shield against the disclosure of peer-review material. The argument turned on interpretations of the First Amendment and the rules of evidence for federal courts. The university insisted that both the amendment and the rules required the EEOC to state a more specific need for the subpoenaed material than it had done. The Court held that the commission had only to show that its need for the files was "relevant" to its investigation.

Blackmun wrote that while the Court was aware of the importance of confidentiality in the peer-review process, "The costs that ensue from disclosure . . . constitute only one side of the balance." He added: "As Congress has recognized, the costs associated with racial and sexual discrimination in institutions of higher learning are very substantial. Few would deny that ferreting out this kind of invidious discrimination is a great if not compelling governmental interest." Blackmun went on to say that "if there is a 'smoking gun' to be found that demonstrates discrimination in tenure decisions, it is likely to be tucked away in peer review files."

As for the First Amendment's protection of academic freedom, Blackmun drew a sharp distinction between the government efforts to determine whether discrimination occurred and government attempts "to control or direct the content of the speech on campus." Moreover, he rejected the argument that if professors could not be assured of confidentiality in their assessment of a colleague's scholarly fitness, candor would suffer, and the university's ability to make informed choices in its hiring of faculty members would be impaired. Blackman wrote, "Not all academics will hesitate to stand up and be counted when they evaluate their peers."

On-Campus Impact of the Ruling

Many were dismayed by the Supreme Court's decision. David Merkowitz, director of public affairs for the American Council on

Education, which represents about 1,500 colleges and universities, said the ruling might "inhibit the willingness of some people to be frank or even participate in the [peer review] process." James O. Freeman, president of Dartmouth College, said that because of litigation in various tenure decisions, "[T]here is certainly more fear among faculty members who are asked to evaluate a faculty member's work."

In 1986, for example, a federal appeals court ordered Franklin and Marshall College in Pennsylvania to give the EEOC the tenure and promotion files of thirty-two faculty members for an investigation into a faculty member's complaint of discrimination. No evidence was found.

The Chronicle of Higher Education *reported that for several years some states had forbidden tenure review secrecy at academic institutions that received public financial support. However, the amount of material that was routinely made public varied from institution to institution. In some instances, only summaries of information, containing no names, would be provided upon request. The University of Pennsylvania, a privately funded school, had no disclosure requirement. Shelley Green, the university's counsel who argued its case before the Supreme Court, said that the Court's decision "did not dictate any change in policy" at the school.*

In fact, the decision was narrowly drawn. It did not, for example, address the question of whether an individual acting on his own initiative could compel such a disclosure. However, the Court's unanimity in the University of Pennsylvania case suggested that the justices might be inclined to expand their ruling in future tenure-review cases. James N. Rosse, provost of Stanford University, said, "The Supreme Court has given us reason to question our expectations of preserving confidentiality."

> *Following are excerpts from Justice Harry A. Blackmun's opinion in* University of Pennsylvania v. Equal Opportunity Commission, *issued January 9, 1990, upholding the commission's right to obtain confidential tenure-review files from the university in order to investigate a discrimination claim:*

<u>No. 88-493</u>

University of Pennsylvania, Petitioner *v.* Equal Employment Opportunity Commission	On writ of certiorari to the United States Court of Appeals for the Third Circuit

[January 9, 1990]

JUSTICE BLACKMUN delivered the opinion of the Court.

In this case we are asked to decide whether a university enjoys a special privilege, grounded in either the common law or the First Amendment, against disclosure of peer review materials that are relevant to charges of racial or sexual discrimination in tenure decisions.

I

The University of Pennsylvania, petitioner here, is a private institution. It currently operates 12 schools, including the Wharton School of Business, which collectively enroll approximately 18,000 full-time students.

In 1985, the University denied tenure to Rosalie Tung, an associate professor on the Wharton faculty. Tung then filed a sworn charge of discrimination with respondent Equal Employment Opportunity Commission (EEOC or Commission). App. 23. As subsequently amended, the charge alleged that Tung was the victim of discrimination on the basis of race, sex, and national origin, in violation of § 703(a) of Title VII of the Civil Rights Act of 1964, 42 U. S. C. § 2000e-2(a), 78 Stat. 255, as amended, which makes it unlawful "to discriminate against any individual with respect to his compensation, terms, conditions, or privileges of employment, because of such individual's race, color, religion, sex, or national origin."

In her charge, Tung stated that the Department Chairman had sexually harassed her and that, in her belief, after she insisted that their relationship remain professional, he had submitted a negative letter to the University's Personnel Committee which possessed ultimate responsibility for tenure decisions. She also alleged that her qualifications were "equal to or better than" those of five named male faculty members who had received more favorable treatment. Tung noted that the majority of the members of her Department had recommended her for tenure, and stated that she had been given no reason for the decision against her, but had discovered of her own efforts that the Personnel Committee had attempted to justify its decision "on the ground that the Wharton School is not interested in China-related research." This explanation, Tung's charge alleged, was a pretext for discrimination: "simply their way of saying they do not want a Chinese-American, Oriental, woman in their school."

The Commission undertook an investigation into Tung's charge, and requested a variety of relevant information from petitioner. When the University refused to provide certain of that information, the Commission's Acting District Director issued a subpoena seeking, among other things, Tung's tenure-review file and the tenure files of the five male faculty members identified in the charge. Petitioner refused to produce a number of the tenure-file documents. It applied to the Commission for modification of the subpoena to exclude what it termed "confidential peer review information," specifically, (1) confidential letters written by Tung's evaluators; (2) the Department Chairman's letter of evaluation; (3) documents reflecting the internal deliberations of faculty committees considering applications for tenure, including the Department Evaluation Report summarizing the deliberations relating to Tung's application for tenure;

and (4) comparable portions of the tenure-review files of the five males. The University urged the Commission to "adopt a balancing approach reflecting the constitutional and societal interest inherent in the peer review process" and to resort to "all feasible methods to minimize the intrusive effects of its investigations."

The Commission denied the University's application. It concluded that the withheld documents were needed in order to determine the merit of Tung's charges. The Commission found: "There has not been enough data supplied in order for the Commission to determine whether there is reasonable cause to believe that the allegations of sex, race and national origin discrimination is true." The Commission rejected petitioner's contention that a letter, which set forth the Personnel Committee's reasons for denying Tung tenure, was sufficient for disposition of the charge. "The Commission would fall short of its obligation" to investigate charges of discrimination, the EEOC's order stated, "if it stopped its investigation once [the employer] has ... provided the reasons for its employment decisions, without verifying whether that reason is a pretext for discrimination." The Commission also rejected petitioner's proposed balancing test, explaining that "such an approach in the instant case ... would impair the Commission's ability to fully investigate this charge of discrimination." The Commission indicated that enforcement proceedings might be necessary if a response was not forthcoming within 20 days.

The University continued to withhold the tenure-review materials. The Commission then applied to the United States District Court for the Eastern District of Pennsylvania for enforcement of its subpoena. The court entered a brief enforcement order.

The Court of Appeals for the Third Circuit affirmed the enforcement decision. Relying upon its earlier opinion in *EEOC* v. *Franklin and Marshall College* (1985), the court rejected petitioner's claim that policy considerations and First Amendment principles of academic freedom required the recognition of a qualified privilege or the adoption of a balancing approach that would require the Commission to demonstrate some particularized need, beyond a showing of relevance, to obtain peer review materials. Because of what might be thought of as a conflict in approach with the Seventh Circuit's decision in *EEOC* v. *University of Notre Dame du Lac,* and because of the importance of the issue, we granted certiorari limited to the compelled-disclosure question.

II

As it had done before the Commission, the District Court, and the Court of Appeals, the University raises here essentially two claims. First, it urges us to recognize a qualified common-law privilege against disclosure of confidential peer review materials. Second, it asserts a First Amendment right of "academic freedom" against wholesale disclosure of the contested documents. With respect to each of the two claims, the remedy petitioner seeks is the same: a requirement of a judicial finding of particularized necessity of access, beyond a showing of mere relevance, before peer review materials are disclosed to the Commission.

A

Petitioner's common-law privilege claim is grounded in Federal Rule of Evidence 501. This provides in relevant part:

> "Except as otherwise required by the Constitution ... or provided by Act of Congress or in rules prescribed by the Supreme Court ... , the privilege of a witness ... shall be governed by the principles of the common law as they may be interpreted by the courts of the United States in the light of reason and experience."

The University asks us to invoke this provision to fashion a new privilege that it claims is necessary to protect the integrity of the peer review process, which in turn is central to the proper functioning of many colleges and universities. These institutions are special, observes petitioner, because they function as "centers of learning, innovation and discovery."

We do not create and apply an evidentiary privilege unless it "promotes sufficiently important interests to outweigh the need for probative evidence . . . ." *Trammel* v. *United States* (1980). Inasmuch as "[t]estimonial exclusionary rules and privileges contravene the fundamental principle that 'the public ... has a right to every man's evidence,' " quoting *United States* v. *Bryan* (1950), any such privilege must "be strictly construed."

Moreover, although Rule 501 manifests a congressional desire "not to freeze the law of privilege" but rather to provide the courts with flexibility to develop rules of privilege on a case-by-case basis, we are disinclined to exercise this authority expansively. We are especially reluctant to recognize a privilege in an area where it appears that Congress has considered the relevant competing concerns but has not provided the privilege itself. Cf. *Branzburg* v. *Hayes* (1972). The balancing of conflicting interests of this type is particularly a legislative function.

With all this in mind, we cannot accept the University's invitation to create a new privilege against the disclosure of peer review materials. We begin by noting that Congress, in extending Title VII to educational institutions and in providing for broad EEOC subpoena powers, did not see fit to create a privilege for peer review documents.

When Title VII was enacted originally in 1964, it exempted an "educational institution with respect to the employment of individuals to perform work connected with the educational activities of such institution." Eight years later, Congress eliminated that specific exemption by enacting § 3 of the Equal Employment Opportunity Act of 1972. This extension of Title VII was Congress' considered response to the widespread and compelling problem of invidious discrimination in educational institutions. The House Report focused specifically on discrimination in higher education, including the lack of access for women and minorities to higher ranking (*i.e.*, tenured) academic positions. Significantly, opponents of the extension claimed that enforcement of Title VII would weaken institutions of higher education by interfering with decisions to hire and promote faculty members. Petitioner therefore cannot seriously contend that Congress was oblivious to concerns of academic autonomy when it abandoned the exemption for educational institutions.

The effect of the elimination of this exemption was to expose tenure determinations to the same enforcement procedures applicable to other employment decisions. This Court previously has observed that Title VII "sets forth 'an integrated, multistep enforcement procedure' that enables the Commission to detect and remedy instances of discrimination." *EEOC* v. *Shell Oil Co.* (1984), quoting *Occidental Life Ins. Co.* v. *EEOC* (1977). The Commission's enforcement responsibilities are triggered by the filing of a specific sworn charge of discrimination. The Act obligates the Commission to investigate a charge of discrimination to determine whether there is "reasonable cause to believe that the charge is true." If it finds no such reasonable cause, the Commission is directed to dismiss the charge. If it does find reasonable cause, the Commission shall "endeavor to eliminate [the] alleged unlawful employment practice by informal methods of conference, conciliation, and persuasion." If attempts at voluntary resolution fail, the Commission may bring an action against the employer.

To enable the Commission to make informed decisions at each stage of the enforcement process, § 2000e-8(a) confers a broad right of access to relevant evidence:

> "[T]he Commission or its designated representative shall at all reasonable times have access to, for the purposes of examination, and the right to copy any evidence of any person being investigated ... that relates to unlawful employment practices covered by [the Act] and is relevant to the charge under investigation."

If an employer refuses to provide this information voluntarily, the Act authorizes the Commission to issue a subpoena and to seek an order enforcing it. § 2000e-9 (incorporating 29 U. S. C. § 161).

On their face, § 2000e-8(a) and § 2000e-9 do not carve out any special privilege relating to peer review materials, despite the fact that Congress undoubtedly was aware, when it extended Title VII's coverage, of the potential burden that access to such material might create. Moreover, we have noted previously that when a court is asked to enforce a Commission subpoena, its responsibility is to "satisfy itself that the charge is valid and that the material requested is 'relevant' to the charge ... and more generally to assess any contentions by the employer that the demand for information is too indefinite or has been made for an illegitimate purpose." It is not then to determine "whether the charge of discrimination is "well founded" or "verifiable."

The University concedes that the information sought by the Commission in this case passes the relevance test set forth in *Shell Oil*. Petitioner argues, nevertheless, that Title VII affirmatively grants courts the discretion to require more than relevance in order to protect tenure-review documents. Although petitioner recognizes that Title VII gives the Commission broad "power to *seek* access to all evidence that may be 'relevant to the charge under investigation,'" it contends that Title VII's subpoena enforcement provisions do not give the Commission an unqualified right to *acquire* such evidence. This interpretation simply cannot be reconciled with the plain language of the text of § 2000e-8(a), which states that the Commission *"shall ... have* access" to "relevant" evidence (emphasis added). The provision can be read only as giving the Commission a right to obtain that evidence, not a mere license to seek it.

Although the text of the access provisions thus provides no privilege, Congress did address situations in which an employer may have an interest in the confidentiality of its records. The same § 2000e-8 which gives the Commission access to any evidence relevant to its investigation also makes it "unlawful for any officer or employee of the Commission to make public in any manner whatever any information obtained by the Commission pursuant to its authority under this section prior to the institution of any proceeding" under the Act. A violation of this provision subjects the employee to criminal penalties. To be sure, the protection of confidentiality that § 2000-8(e) provides is less than complete. But this, if anything, weakens petitioner's argument. Congress apparently considered the issue of confidentiality, and it provided a modicum of protection. Petitioner urges us to go further than Congress thought necessary to safeguard that value, that is, to strike the balance differently from the one Congress adopted. Petitioner, however, does not offer any persuasive justification for that suggestion.

We readily agree with petitioner that universities and colleges play significant roles in American society. Nor need we question, at this point, petitioner's assertion that confidentiality is important to the proper functioning of the peer review process under which many academic institutions operate. The costs that ensue from disclosure, however, constitute only one side of the balance. As Congress has recognized, the costs associated with racial and sexual discrimination in institutions of higher learning are very substantial. Few would deny that ferreting out this kind of invidious discrimination is a great if not compelling governmental interest. Often, as even petitioner seems to admit, disclosure of peer review materials will be necessary in order for the Commission to determine whether illegal discrimination has taken place. Indeed, if there is a "smoking gun" to be found that demonstrates discrimination in tenure decisions, it is likely to be tucked away in peer review files. The Court of Appeals for the Third Circuit expressed it this way:

> "Clearly, an alleged perpetrator of discrimination cannot be allowed to pick and choose the evidence which may be necessary for an agency investigation...."

Moreover, we agree with the EEOC that the adoption of a requirement that the Commission demonstrate a "specific reason for disclosure," beyond a showing of relevance, would place a substantial litigation-producing obstacle in the way of the Commission's efforts to investigate and remedy alleged discrimination. A university faced with a disclosure request might well utilize the privilege in a way that frustrates the EEOC's mission. We are reluctant to "place a potent weapon in the hands of employers who have no interest in complying voluntarily with the Act, who wish instead to delay as long as possible investigations by the EEOC." *EEOC* v. *Shell Oil Co.*

Acceptance of petitioner's claim would also lead to a wave of similar privilege claims by other employers who play significant roles in furthering speech and learning in society. What of writers, publishers, musicians, lawyers? It surely is not unreasonable to believe, for example, that confidential peer reviews play an important part in partnership determinations at some law firms. We perceive no limiting principle in petitioner's argument. Accordingly, we stand behind the breakwater Congress has established: unless specifically provided otherwise in the statute, the EEOC may obtain "relevant" evidence. Congress has made the choice. If it dislikes the result, it of course may revise the statute.

Finally, we see nothing in our precedents that supports petitioner's claim. In *United States* v. *Nixon* (1974), upon which petitioner relies, we recognized a qualified privilege for Presidential communications. It is true that in fashioning this privilege we noted the importance of confidentiality in certain contexts:

> "Human experience teaches that those who expect public dissemination of their remarks may well temper candor with a concern for appearances and for their own interests to the detriment of the decisionmaking process."

But the privilege we recognized in *Nixon* was grounded in the separation of powers between the Branches of the Federal Government. "[T]he privilege can be said to derive from the supremacy of each branch within its own assigned area of constitutional duties. Certain powers and privileges flow from the nature of enumerated powers; the protection of the confidentiality of Presidential communications has similar constitutional underpinnings." . . . [P]etitioner's claim of privilege lacks similar constitutional foundation. . . .

B

. . . [P]etitioner characterizes its First Amendment claim as one of "academic freedom." Petitioner begins its argument by focusing our attention upon language in prior cases acknowledging the crucial role universities play in the dissemination of ideas in our society and recognizing "academic freedom" as a "special concern of the First Amendment." *Keyishian* v. *Board of Regents* (1967). In that case the Court said: "Our Nation is deeply committed to safeguarding academic freedom, which is of transcendent value to all of us and not merely to the teachers concerned." . . . Petitioner places special reliance on Justice Frankfurter's opinion, concurring in the result, in *Sweezy* v. *New Hampshire* (1957), where the Justice recognized that one of "four essential freedoms" that a university possesses under the First Amendment is the right to "determine for itself on academic grounds *who may teach*" (emphasis added).

Petitioner contends that it exercises this right of determining "on academic grounds who may teach" through the process of awarding tenure. A tenure system, asserts petitioner, determines what the university will look like over time. "In making tenure decisions, therefore, a university is doing nothing less than shaping its own identity."

Petitioner next maintains that the peer review process is the most important element in the effective operation of a tenure system. A properly functioning tenure system requires the faculty to obtain candid and detailed written evaluations of the candidate's scholarship, both from the candidate's peers at the university and from scholars at other institutions. These evaluations, says petitioner, traditionally have been provided with express or implied assurances of confidentiality. It is confidentiality that ensures candor and enables an institution to make its tenure decisions on the basis of valid academic criteria.

Building from these premises, petitioner claims that requiring the disclosure of peer review evaluations on a finding of mere relevance will undermine the existing process of awarding tenure, and therefore will result in a significant infringement of petitioner's First Amendment right of academic freedom. As more and more peer evaluations are disclosed to the EEOC and become public, a "chilling effect" on candid evaluations and discussions of candidates will result. And as the quality of peer review evaluations declines, tenure committees will no longer be able to rely on them. "This will work to the detriment of universities, as less qualified persons achieve tenure causing the quality of instruction and scholarship to decline." Compelling disclosure of materials "also will result in divisiveness and tension, placing strain on faculty relations and impairing the free interchange of ideas that is a hallmark of academic freedom." The prospect of these deleterious effects on American colleges and universities, concludes petitioner, compels recognition of a First Amendment privilege.

In our view, petitioner's reliance on the so-called academic freedom cases is somewhat misplaced. In those cases government was attempting to control or direct the *content* of the speech engaged in by the university or those affiliated with it. In *Sweezy*, for example, the Court invalidated the conviction of a person found in contempt for refusing to answer questions about the content of a lecture he had delivered at a state university. Similarly, in *Keyishian*, the Court invalidated a network of state laws that required public employees, including teachers at state universities, to make certifications with respect to their membership in the Communist Party. When, in those cases, the Court spoke of "academic freedom" and the right to determine on "academic grounds who may teach" the Court was speaking in reaction to content-based regulation. . . .

Fortunately, we need not define today the precise contours of any academic-freedom right against governmental attempts to influence the content of academic speech through the selection of faculty or by other means, because petitioner does not allege that the Commission's subpoenas are intended to or will in fact direct the content of university discourse toward or away from particular subjects or points of view. Instead, as noted above, petitioner claims that the "quality of instruction and scholarship [will] decline" as a result of the burden EEOC subpoenas place on the peer review process.

Also, the cases upon which petitioner places emphasis involved *direct* infringements on the asserted right to "determine for itself on academic grounds who may teach." In *Keyishian,* for example, government was attempting to *substitute* its teaching employment criteria for those already in place at the academic institutions, directly and completely usurping the discretion of each institution. In contrast, the EEOC subpoena at issue here effects no such usurpation. The Commission is not providing criteria that petitioner *must* use in selecting teachers. Nor is it preventing the University from using any criteria it may wish to use, except those—including race, sex, and national origin—that are proscribed under Title VII. . . .

That the burden of which the University complains is neither content-based nor direct does not necessarily mean that petitioner has no valid First Amendment claim. Rather, it means only that petitioner's claim does not fit neatly within any right of academic freedom that could be derived from the cases on which petitioner relies. In essence, petitioner asks us to recognize an *expanded* right of academic freedom to protect confidential peer review materials from disclosure. Although we are sensitive to the effects that content-neutral government action may have on speech, and believe that burdens that are less than direct may sometimes pose First Amendment concerns, we think the First Amendment cannot be extended to embrace petitioner's claim.

First, by comparison with the cases in which we have found a cognizable First Amendment claim, the infringement the University complains of is extremely attenuated. . . .

Indeed, if the University's attenuated claim were accepted, many other generally applicable laws might also be said to infringe the First Amendment. In effect, petitioner says no more than that disclosure of peer review materials makes it more difficult to acquire information regarding the "academic grounds" on which petitioner wishes to base its tenure decisions. But many laws make the exercise of First Amendment rights more difficult. For example, a university cannot claim a First Amendment violation simply because it may be subject to taxation or other government regulation, even though such regulation might deprive the university of revenue it needs to bid for professors who are contemplating working for other academic institutions or in industry. We doubt that the peer review process is any more essential in effectuating the right to determine "who may teach" than is the availability of money. . . .

In addition to being remote and attenuated, the injury to academic freedom claimed by petitioner is also speculative. As the EEOC points out, confidentiality is not the norm in all peer review systems. Moreover, some disclosure of peer evaluations would take place even if petitioner's "special necessity" test were adopted. Thus, the "chilling effect" petitioner fears is at most only incrementally worsened by the absence of a privilege. Finally, we are not so ready as petitioner seems to be to assume the worst about those in the academic community. Although it is possible that some evaluators may become less candid as the possibility of disclosure increases, others may simply ground their evaluations in specific examples and illustrations in order to deflect potential claims of bias or unfairness. Not all academics will hesitate to stand up and be counted when they evaluate their peers.

The case we decide today in many respects is similar to *Branzburg* v. *Hayes.* In *Branzburg,* the Court rejected the notion that under the First Amendment a reporter could not be required to appear or to testify as to information obtained in confidence without a special showing that the reporter's testimony was necessary. Petitioners there, like petitioner here, claimed that requiring disclosure of information collected in confidence would inhibit the free flow of information in contravention of First Amendment principles. In the course of rejecting the First Amendment argument, this Court noted that "the First Amendment does not invalidate every incidental burdening of the press that may result from the enforcement of civil or criminal statutes of general applicability." We also indicated a reluctance to recognize a constitutional privilege where it was "unclear how often and to what extent informers are actually deterred from furnishing information when newsmen are forced to testify before a grand jury." . . . We were unwilling then, as we are today, "to embark the judiciary on a long and difficult journey to . . . an uncertain destination."

Because we conclude that the EEOC subpoena process does not infringe any First Amendment right enjoyed by petitioner, the EEOC need not demonstrate any special justification to sustain the constitutionality of Title VII as applied to tenure peer review materials in general or to the subpoena involved in this case. Accordingly, we need not address the Commission's alternative argument that any infringement of petitioner's First Amendment rights is permissible because of the substantial relation between the Commission's request and the overriding and compelling state interest in eradicating invidious discrimination.

The judgment of the Court of Appeals is affirmed.

It is so ordered.

BOSTON MAYOR'S REMARKS ON STUART MURDER HOAX

January 10, 1990

"It seems that we—all of us—have been the victims of a cruel hoax,"
Boston mayor Raymond L. Flynn said in a State of the City broadcast
address January 10. He referred to the shooting death of Carole Stuart, a
pregnant white woman said by her husband to have been murdered by a
raspy voiced black man dressed in a jogging suit. The murderer, Charles
Stuart said, invaded their car as they stopped for traffic in the predomi-
nantly black Mission Hill area of South Boston while enroute to their
suburban home from a city hospital's childbirthing class. The shootings
on the night of October 23, 1989, aroused emotions and heightened racial
tensions in Boston as few other incidents had done in recent years.

By chance, a network TV camera crew was on hand and recorded the
grisly scene of the couple's arrival at a hospital—he badly wounded but
somehow steering their car to the emergency entrance and she, her head
blasted open, slumped in the opposite seat. Carole Stuart died, and
seventeen days later so did their son who had to be delivered two months
prematurely. The wounded father survived after two operations and six
weeks in the hospital.

Her funeral was attended by, among hundreds of others, several
prominent politicians, including Flynn and Michael S. Dukakis, the
governor of Massachusetts. Her death elicited a great outpouring of grief
and anger throughout the community and the nation. Flynn promptly
assigned all available detectives to the case. The police soon turned up a
suspect named William Bennett, a thirty-nine-year-old black man who
had spent thirteen years in prison for crimes that included shooting a
police officer. According to the police, Bennett had bragged to his young

nephew that he had robbed the Stuarts and taken their jewelry.

Already in custody on charges of robbing a video store, Bennett was placed in a lineup as soon as Charles Stuart was well enough to go to the police station. Stuart said Bennett looked like the man who robbed and shot them. There the investigation stood until Charles Stuart's younger brother Matthew, twenty-three, began to tell quite a different story of what had happened the night of October 23, first to friends and family members and on January 3 to the police.

His tale implicated himself and Charles in the murder—for reasons that remained murky. Matthew Stuart said it was to collect Mrs. Stuart's insurance money, although there was evidence suggesting that the husband did not want a child and had a romantic attachment to another woman. Matthew had become so depressed about his involvement that a friend feared he was contemplating suicide. It was his brother who committed suicide instead. Charles Stuart's body was pulled from the icy Mystic River on January 4; he left behind a note saying that "all the allegations have taken all my strength."

Through his lawyer, Matthew Stuart said he had aided his brother on the night of the shooting—that by arrangement he met Charles and took from him Carole's handbag and a handgun, and dumped both in the Pines River north of Boston. Police divers recovered both the purse and the gun; it was determined to be the murder weapon. The new evidence suggested that Charles Stuart had shot himself deliberately to throw off the police investigation but had accidentally wounded himself more severely than he intended.

The new story created a sensation. Many blacks expressed outrage that many men in the Mission Hill area had been stopped and frisked by the police in their search for a suspect. Some black leaders asserted that the crime had falsely indicted the black community. Flynn visited Bennett's mother to apologize for the suspicion that fell on her son, and the mayor devoted about half of his twenty-two minute State of the City address to pleading with the people to overcome the harm that had been done to race relations, the city's good name, and especially that of Mission Hill.

Flynn defended his action in ordering "an aggressive police response" as something "any mayor would have done." But he said that he, too, was a victim of the "sinister hoax." Saying "it's hard to know what specifically happened," the mayor promised a full investigation. A Suffolk County grand jury received evidence about the complex case and undertook to determine just what role Matthew Stuart had in the shooting.

He and other members of the Stuart family also were called before the grand jury. Even if they had known about the crime but not reported it to the police, they appeared immune to prosecution. In defining the crime of "accessory after the fact," Massachusetts law provides exemptions for a spouse or close blood relatives. They may not be punished as accessories to the crime on the ground that otherwise they might be put in an untenable position of testifying against a family member.

Prosecutors were also foiled in their attempt to compel Charles

Stuart's lawyer, John T. Dawley, to testify before a grand jury, whose investigation of the case had bogged down. The Massachusetts Supreme Court ruled November 4 that attorneys were not free to divulge their clients' secrets even after the clients were dead. Suffolk County district attorney Newman Flanagan said that he would reconvene the grand jury and present unspecified "new evidence."

> *Following are excerpts from Boston mayor Raymond L. Flynn's State of the City address, broadcast January 10, 1990:*

... Every year about this time, I give this State of the City address. To be honest with you, the speech I am going to give tonight is much different than the one I had prepared last week—because of the recent events that have shocked the city. And so the beginning of this speech is what I've been hearing throughout the city for the past six days.

Sunday night—I couldn't sleep, and so I was driving around the city, as I often do. I went into Dunkin Donuts in North Station at about one a.m. to get a cup of coffee. Some guys working all night were in there on their coffee break. They were talking about the day's N.F.L. football games. I asked them about the games, since I hadn't been able to watch them myself. And they filled me in on the scores....

I started to leave. But then I stopped and turned around. I want back to them, and told them I was preparing this address. And I asked them: "What do you think I should say about the Stuart case?"

The guy with the hat, who was black, said: "Hey, Mayor. Just tell the people that an honest mistake was made by everybody. Just tell them that we're doing O.K. in Boston and we're proud of our city."

And you know, I think he's right. We are doing O.K. We are proud of Boston. And I think everyone feels that way.

But Charles Stuart—he took us all in.

Now, I have spent a lot of my time in the last six days on Boston's streets, in coffee shops, and in many homes. And I must report with more than a little sadness, that the state of the city—or better, the *mood* of the city—ranges from disbelief, to cynicism, to anger.

It seems that we—all of us—have been the victims of a cruel hoax. Of course, I have to add that after the events that have unfolded in the last six days, it's hard to know what specifically happened. The district attorney is actively pursuing the criminal investigation. He informs me that he will soon present evidence to the grand jury. I would support the investigation of any allegations of civil rights violations which are brought to the attention of law enforcement officials. But in addition, it is important that there be a review by people with the highest reputations for integrity and insight to identify the broader lessons to be learned from this event.

But as we now understand things, it appears that Charles Stuart has perpetrated a giant fraud on this city. He hurt everyone—especially the residents of Mission Hill and the Greater Roxbury neighborhoods.

Charles Stuart told us that a black man killed his pregnant wife and shot him. And the most evil thing about this awful fraud was that it hurt the heart and the soul of a city that has worked so hard to break down the racial barriers that for years divided it. It will take weeks, maybe even months, to fully understand what occurred here. But the way to the truth is through honest reflection.

I want to start by re-stating what we thought took place. We thought that a gunman invaded a car in which a man and his pregnant wife were leaving childbirth classes at one of our hospitals. We thought that this couple was kidnapped and shot. We thought that the person who did it was at large in our neighborhoods. And we wanted him caught before anyone else was hurt.

When I ordered an aggressive police response, I think I did what any mayor would have done. I wanted to send a strong signal—as strong as I could—to show the city's outrage, and to show that we would not tolerate such an act.

Was I wrong? You know, I don't think so. An unthinkable crime was committed. But it turned out we were all victims of a sinister hoax. And we were all hurt—especially the residents of the good Mission Hill community. Last night at a powerful and moving service in Mission Church, we were urged to transform our hurt and our anger into healing—through patience and sensitivity.

But there was one person missing last night—the person who owes us the biggest apology. In hindsight, we were all wrong to accept too readily his version of this crime—because it fit with at least some of the common stereotypes about society. Sadly, it made too much sense—to all of us. It became a crime story that played nationally—because it fit so neatly with our national tragedy of racial discord.

Well, we must address those fears, that anger, and those stereotypes directly—if we are going to learn from this experience, and if we are going to move Boston forward.

I'd like to take a moment here to bring up another very difficult time for the city of Boston—because I think it holds some lessons for us now. Fifteen years ago, the busing story in Boston was also national news. For those who went through it, it was a terribly wrenching time. Many wrongs were committed. Mindless violence occurred. Many thoughtless statements were made.

I was deeply offended by the sweeping characterization of all residents of my neighborhood as racists. I knew that that wasn't true. But just as today, the stereotype was accepted. And as I walked the streets of South Boston, and saw the pain my neighbors were feeling from these accusations, my frustrations were enormous.

It made me angry. Back then, it was my neighborhood that was the victim of stereotyping—of the same mindless, thoughtless bias, of the same rush to judgment that today victimizes Mission Hill and the Greater Roxbury community. And that experience made me re-double my commitment—both as a private individual and as a public official—to do all I could to see that each resident—and every neighborhood—of this city was treated fairly—and with dignity and respect.

As I said at the Morningstar Baptist Church, the Sunday following the Stuart shooting: "No one group or community should be singled out because of the actions of a few."

Well, it is for others to judge my record. But in the six years I have been mayor, I have worked as hard as I know how, to meet that goal. Frankly though, this Stuart incident—for the moment anyway—has set that effort back. It has temporarily created new tensions and new doubts in the city. And it has generated considerable hostility.

How people perceive their city is very important. And so is the way *others* portray it. Countless residents of Boston have told me in recent days that they think it was easier for people to believe Charles Stuart's story because of the too frequent negative portrayal of the minority community in the city's print and electronic media.

Well, I am urging that those news organizations on whom we rely for our understanding of events around us re-examine their approach to the coverage of news—about our working class neighborhoods, about our young people, and about our entire city. And I urge the media to work with us to show the many positive things that are taking place in our neighborhoods every day—so that believing in stereotypes doesn't come so easy in the future.

The Stuart case isn't what the city of Boston is about today. Because Boston is a much different city than it was ten or fifteen years ago. And we can't let a single incident—no matter how terrible—set us back. But neither can we stand still. The unity of a city is a very fragile thing. And the healing process is never over—it just goes on and on and on.

And we will go on. We have a city to run. We have parks to fix for our kids, streets to clean, education to improve and good health care to provide for our elderly. We have to continue to work hard—and work together. . . .

Now, our greatest accomplishment has been to use the city's economic prosperity to build bridges of opportunity, between our strong downtown economy and our neighborhoods. Thanks to our linkage policies, houses for first-time homebuyers now stand where vacant lots used to be. Thanks to our first-in-the-nation jobs policies, Boston residents, minorities, and women are working in decent jobs that they never would have had access to just ten years ago.

We will continue to fight for economic justice and fairness—so that people in all of our neighborhoods get the same chances that we all want—for homeownership, for jobs, and for business opportunities.

And we are succeeding. According to a study just released and funded by the Rockefeller Foundation, family poverty has decreased by one third in Boston. And another recent study found that there has been a dramatic decrease in welfare cases in Boston, compared to the rest of the state. . . .

And we will continue to use our resources to move this city forward by continuing to fight homelessness by creating more affordable housing, by

further committing ourselves to the young people of our city with the help
of our business community, by working with our public school parents and
our school committee for a better school system for our children, by
developing new strategies to meet the challenges of a new regional and
international economy.

And after a year of healthy—and frankly, sometimes heated—dialogue
with the city's leading bankers, we are on the verge of launching a four
hundred million dollar private sector investment plan that will put more
working families into affordable homes at lower interest rates, more
businesses and jobs into community commercial districts, and more bank
branches into under-served neighborhoods. . . .

. . . The issue of neighborhood investment isn't black or white—it's
green. . . .

I want to end tonight with something that President Kennedy said that
I'm afraid applies to us here, today, in Massachusetts. It went something
like this: "The people who sell us short have substituted fear—for faith in
our future. They are caught up in their own disbeliefs and doubts about
our ability to build a better, stronger America."

Well, I say now is no time for doubt. It's a time for faith—in ourselves
and in our city. It's a time to work even harder to unite behind the dreams
we all share, and to keep building strong families and strong
neighborhoods.

There will always be challenges. But we've come too far to turn back.
And there are too many people who need our help. Now is no time to think
about the past. It's a time to move forward. It's a time for leading, and it's
a time for healing. It's a time for caring about each other and respecting
one another. It's a time to assure our young people they have nothing to
fear from the future. Now is a time to dream. And now is a time to dare.

GOVERNOR WILDER'S
INAUGURAL ADDRESS
January 13, 1990

L. Douglas Wilder, the first black to be elected governor of any state in the Union, assumed the Virginia governorship in a brief oath-taking ceremony January 13. In his inaugural address that followed, Wilder, a Democrat, struck essentially the same notes that had carried him to a narrow victory at the polls the previous November 7.

Before an inaugural crowd of 30,000 well-wishers gathered at Richmond's Capitol Square, and a throng of television cameras, the new governor spoke of himself as "a son of Virginia" who represented a "new mainstream" of politics in the Old Dominion. He emphasized that he intended to serve the interests of all Virginians, black and white. The fact that his election made history, he suggested, was only incidental to his purposes of promoting a politics of inclusion.

P. B. S. Pinchback, a former slave, had served briefly as acting governor of Louisiana in the Reconstruction era after the Civil War, but his role did not nullify Wilder's claim to being the first of his race to win a governor's job through the ballot box. Wilder's low-key approach to his historic accomplishment did not dilute the drama of his inauguration. There in the former capital of the Confederacy was the grandson of a slave taking the oath of office, eightieth in a line of governors that included many distinguished figures in state and national history— including the commonwealth's first governor, Patrick Henry. Moreover, Wilder was assuming an office that only a generation earlier had been used to promote "massive resistance" to public school desegregation.

The oath was administered by Lewis F. Powell, Jr., a retired justice of the U.S. Supreme Court. The new governor, only a few days short of his

41

fifty-ninth birthday, had grown up in a poor home in still-segregated Richmond. He attended a black college and saw combat duty in the Korean War. Returning home as a decorated veteran, Wilder embarked on a career in law and politics. His business and professional record was not without flaws. He was reprimanded by the Virginia Supreme Court in 1978 for "unexcused, unreasonable and inordinate procrastination" in handling a client's case. He did not always pay his taxes on time, and his investment property was cited several times as rundown by community groups and Richmond officials.

But in politics, Wilder started compiling a string of electoral "firsts"— in 1969 becoming the first black elected to the Virginia Senate after Reconstruction and in 1985 winning the post of lieutenant governor, the first statewide office in the South won by a black since that post-Civil War era.

A Close Election

The mainstream image and a measured personal manner that Wilder cultivated was a "formula" that also worked elsewhere for two other prominent black Democratic candidates on November 7, who, like Wilder, faced a white voting majority. New York City and Seattle elected their first black mayors—David N. Dinkins and Norman B. Rice, respectively.

In Virginia's biggest turnout (1,787,131 ballots) in a nonpresidential election, Wilder won 6,741 more votes than his Republican opponent, J. Marshall Coleman, a former attorney general of the state with a record of civil-rights support. Because black voters constitute only about one-fifth of the state's electorate, Wilder had to hold 95 percent of the black vote and win about 40 percent of the white vote. This he did, according to postelection analyses, but his ability to capture white votes turned out to be weaker than preelection surveys had indicated.

The opinion polls had pointed to a comfortable winning margin of 5 percent to 10 percent. Instead, it was only a fraction of 1 percent, suggesting to some analysts that many voters who had indicated no discomfort at the thought of voting for a black man actually balked at doing so when they entered the voting booth. However, Wilder said in a news conference after the election that he did not consider race a factor in the close election.

Many black Americans greeted Wilder's election as a breakthrough that had long eluded them. From far and near they traveled to Richmond for the inauguration and formed a clear majority among his well-wishers.

Demographics of the "New Dominion"

In statewide voting, a black candidate must appeal to a large segment of the white voters. Demographic changes in recent years have made this task less difficult than formerly. In Virginia the votes of rural "Byrd Democrats"—following in the tradition of the late Harry F. Byrd, a former governor and U.S. senator—and the financial backing of conserva-

tive Richmond bankers and lawyers no longer assured election to state-wide offices.

The political epicenter had been shifted by hefty population growth in the Northern Virginia suburbs of Washington, D.C., in metropolitan Richmond, and in the urban Tidewater region embracing Norfolk, Virginia Beach, Plymouth, Hampton, and Newport News. Many of the newcomers were from the Northeast and Midwest. Wilder carried the "New Dominion" handily, winning about 60 percent of the vote in Northern Virginia and 55 percent in the Tidewater. But Wilder received slightly fewer than half of the votes cast in metropolitan Richmond and fewer still elsewhere in "Old Virginia."

However, the race question in voting patterns was distorted by two nonracial issues. One was abortion. Wilder strongly supported abortion rights, while Coleman retreated uncertainly from his previous prolife position. According to exit polls and other election analyses, Wilder's strong stand appealed to many women voters in the populous suburbs who otherwise might have voted Republican.

The other issue, a coal strike in southwestern Virginia, undoubtedly cost Wilder votes. Gov. Gerald L. Baliles, whom Wilder served as lieutenant governor, was unpopular in that region. Strikers bitterly resented the governor's use of the state police to keep pickets from blocking trucks hauling coal from the mines.

Wilder's Political Climb

The lieutenant governorship, a largely ceremonial post, served Wilder as a springboard to the state chief executive's office—just as it had served his two immediate Democratic predecessors, Baliles and Charles S. Robb. (Virginia governors, elected to four-year terms, are ineligible to succeed themselves.) As a legislator and lieutenant governor, Wilder often was at odds with both Robb and Baliles, but he drew their support in his gubernatorial race. Moreover, Wilder represented himself as a man attuned to their middle-of-the-road brand of politics, which had found favor with voters and generally with the press. He stressed fiscal conservatism during the election campaign and continued the theme upon becoming governor.

Two days after his inauguration, Wilder opened the state General Assembly with an address described by political commentators as a study in conservatism. He endorsed an expanded use of the death penalty, spoke out against tax increases, and proposed to trim budget recommendations that Baliles had made before leaving office.

Wilder had moved a long way from the firebrand style that characterized the early years of his political career. Entering an all-white state Senate, he had made himself all the more conspicuous by sporting an Afro hair style, wearing bold plaid suits, and making fiery speeches on behalf of black causes—sometimes in strong denunciation of traditions his colleagues considered almost sacred. Gradually Wilder ceased being an outspoken foe of the establishment and worked within it to achieve his aims, although he sometimes reverted to old habits of cutting down an opponent in debate. As Wilder's approach moved from confrontation to conciliation, his political effectiveness grew.

As a candidate for governor, Wilder portrayed himself as one who was building on revered Virginia traditions. In his inaugural speech, he approvingly invoked the names of Jefferson, Madison, and Mason and suggested that his election represented a triumph for their ideas of freedom. Wilder said: "We mark not a victory of party or the accomplishments of an individual, but the triumph of an idea—an idea as old as America." In that regard, he wanted the "young people of this Commonwealth" to know that it would be possible to lift oppression, end discrimination, overcome disability, and learn that "poverty need not be binding."

> *Following are excerpts from the inaugural address of Governor L. Douglas Wilder of Virginia, delivered January 13, 1990, in Richmond:*

Four years ago, I stood on this spot to assume the second highest office in the Commonwealth. Today, because of your faith in our efforts, I stand before you as Chief Executive of this state. And now—in keeping with the sanctioned privilege extended to all Governors—it is my honor to address the people of this Commonwealth, and to express to my fellow citizens the profound gratitude and deep sense of purpose that I feel in fulfilling your expectations.

Candor and honesty would have me admit to you that I was not blessed with the foresight to know that this moment was in the offing when I stood here in 1985. Having been tested in the political crucible of trial and cross-examination, I have been rendered a verdict by having had delivered unto me the greatest outpouring of votes ever accorded any candidate for this great office. For that, I shall be eternally grateful. And—be assured—I shall demonstrate that gratitude during the next four years by being a Governor who will be beholden to but one special interest: the welfare of Virginians, *all* Virginians.

But my gratitude is not of such recent origin. It is said "To whom much is given, much shall be expected." I will be the first to admit that I have been the beneficiary of much through no endeavors of my own. While I have indeed worked hard and performed to the best of my abilities, I have also had a few breaks along the way.

Indeed, in every walk—in every period of my life—there have been many more deserving and justly entitled to the fruits that wholesome opportunities present. And yet, for many, those chances never came and the bell of fulfillment never tolled for them. Providence indeed has directed my course. And I shall remain ever mindful of my good fortune.

In recent years, Virginia too has been blessed with good fortune. The progress and the prosperity we have enjoyed during this period has enabled us to reclaim the respected achievements of times past.

In looking to our accomplishments in education, economic development, the environment, employment, housing, or transportation, we find that Virginia ranks among those states in the vanguard of forward looking movement. Not surprisingly, the ensuing pride in seeing our state climb in rank among our sister states in the nation and in preeminence among the Southern states, cause Virginians everywhere to feel good about our cause, our mission, and our success in forging Virginia's New Mainstream. . . .

Cicero in parting observation, noted that, "A Commonwealth is not any collection of human beings . . . but an assembly of people joined in agreement on justice and partnership for the common good, and a community where civility must reign and all must live peacefully together." And we know what happened to Cicero's Rome which could *not* pass on the heritage of its past to the people of its future. But we *have* done so; we *can* do so. And we *shall* do so.

These are times when the people of our state and of our country can feel the resurgence of the dominance of the individual spirit which proves daily to be unconquerable. Whirlwinds of rebellion shake all shores where tyranny once ruled, and we are redeemed in our deeply held and treasured beliefs in the development of the high possibility of every individual who breathes the sweetness of liberty's air.

At this time—and in the place where so many great names in American history have trod—we renew this celebration of freedom in the full and certain knowledge that with it comes great responsibility.

Without question, much tighter economic times which loom in the days ahead will test to the fullest our ability to make hard decisions, to lead, and to govern.

But progress will be possible.

Opportunity can be expanded.

Freedom can be increased.

Resources employed in the past for the finer things in life can be—and will *have* to be—deployed for the more serious of our needs.

For we know that freedom is but a word for the man or woman who needs and cannot find a job.

Freedom—as it has been written—is a dream deferred when it "Dries up like a raisin in the sun, and stinks like rotten meat."

Freedom is meaningless when a woman's right to choose is regulated outside the dictates of her own faith and conscience.

Freedom is impotent when there is intolerance to those who hold moral and political beliefs different from our own.

Freedom is restricted when labor and management cannot reach agreements.

Freedom is impossible for the uneducated who try to live in today's complex world.

Freedom is restrained for business and industry when our network of transportation is allowed to deteriorate.

Freedom for the police is denied when their resources are unduly limited.

Freedom for the people is assaulted when lawful authority is abused.

Freedom for the next generation is mortgaged when we destroy our environment.

And—as has been proven throughout recorded history—freedom is no where to be found when the people are overtaxed and overregulated.

As we salute the idea of freedom today, let us pledge to extend that same freedom to others tomorrow.

Let us fulfill the perfect promise of freedom and liberty left as a legacy for us by those who founded this Commonwealth.

And let us likewise be thankful that—while our country gave birth to a freedom long denied and delayed for *all* who loved freedom—the belief in these dreams held by those forebears was passed from generation to generation, and spawned the seeds that propagated the will and the desire to achieve.

We are on hallowed ground today, and the steps we take from this place must be steps of honor. The words we issue must be words of wisdom. The laws we pass must be laws of mercy and justice. And the faith we possess must be true to the Almighty.

In meeting these challenges—and they will be difficult—I ask your help and that of God. I do not shrink from the enormity of the task. In six million Virginians, there is endless courage and enormous strength—in the coming years, we will need it all. . . .

We must set priorities in the coming years.

Specifically, we must be partners in working toward a revived economy—a healthy and thriving economy that provides equal opportunity for all Virginians. While the flow may have slowed, Virginia's New Mainstream is far from drying up. It shall be the task of this administration to ensure that a rising tide of prosperity and opportunity is possible in the future.

Some describe conditions in our Commonwealth today in dismal terms. And yet, one must question the resolve and the reserve of those who are not called upon to make sacrifices greater than those who have preceded us.

Despite our economic slowdown, we are living in the best of times. And they *can* be even better. And they *will* be better.

If you will forgive me . . . a moment of nostalgia . . .

We mark today not a victory of party or the accomplishments of an individual, but the triumph of an idea—an idea as old as America; as old as the God who looks out for us all.

It is the idea expressed so eloquently from this great Commonwealth by those who gave shape to the greatest nation ever known . . . Jefferson, Madison, Mason, and their able colleagues. . . . The idea that shows forth in the concepts of freedom and opportunity—not only in Virginia—but more recently in the fresh, new winds of Eastern Europe and the tumult of Panama.

If these words about freedom are to be heard at all today, I hope they will be heard by the young people of this Commonwealth. I want them to know:

that oppression can be lifted;

that discrimination can be eliminated;

that poverty need not be binding;

that disability can be overcome;

And that offer of opportunity in a free society carries with it the requirement of hard work, the rejection of drugs and other false highs, and a willingness to work with others whatever their color or national origin.

We have come far, but we have far to go.

We have done much, but we have much to do.

I ask for your energy; for your understanding; for your dedication; for your patience; and—yes—for your prayers.

Four years ago, I said to the people of Virginia that I was proud to be a Virginian. . . . [T]hat pride . . . lifts my voice and my spirit to proclaim, "I am a son of Virginia."

I thank you all. And may God be ever with us.

STATE OF THE UNION ADDRESS
AND THE DEMOCRATIC RESPONSE

January 31, 1990

President George Bush delivered his first State of the Union address January 31, proclaiming a "new era in the world's history." In a nationally televised speech before a joint session of Congress, the president underscored how much the world had changed in the past year. He spoke especially of communism's crumbling in Europe, depicting the events as "singular moments in history" that separate all that had come before from all that would follow.

Surprisingly, Bush responded to the "new era" of East-West relations by proposing reductions in American and Soviet military forces in Europe below levels that were already being discussed by the two sides. (Bush-Gorbachev Summit Remarks and Documents, p. 331) In domestic affairs, the president proposed no bold legislative ventures. The goals he identified for his second year in office—notably, improving the schools and environment—could be endorsed by almost any politician.

Bush's reluctance to push daring programs belied the political strength he had gained in his relations with Congress. Tapping into one of the most immediate sources of his recent surge in popularity, Bush began his address by using world affairs rather than domestic politics as the backdrop for his first year in office. He announced that U.S. troops committed to the invasion of Panama in December 1989, one of the most popular U.S. military ventures in years, would be home by the end of February. Polls indicated that public approval of his work had risen to 80 percent, the highest since he had entered the White House. (Bush Announces Invasion of Panama, Historic Documents of 1989, p. 701)

Bush further strengthened his hand with Congress soon after the

49

lawmakers opened the second session of the 101st Congress in January. He unexpectedly managed to muster enough votes to sustain his veto of the 1989 legislation that would have given Chinese students in the United States statutory protection from being returned to China against their will. Bush insisted that he could accomplish the same purpose through his executive authority.

Although the president had been in office slightly more than a year, it was his first State of the Union address. His predecessor, Ronald Reagan, had delivered the 1989 address before leaving the presidency. (State of the Union Address, Historic Documents of 1989, p. 57) The speech's can-do optimism was vintage Bush, but he seemed most at ease when he spoke of the birth of his twelfth grandchild. "When I held the little guy for the first time," the president said, "the troubles at home and abroad seemed manageable and totally in perspective."

Speech's Upbeat Tone

His upbeat tone contrasted with the ominous message delivered to Congress two days earlier by Richard G. Darman, director of the presidential Office of Management and Budget (OMB). In an introduction to the administration's $1.2 trillion budget for fiscal year 1991, Darman warned that government resources could be gobbled up by future liabilities, which he characterized as hidden "Pacmen," a reference to a computerized arcade game.

"Someone ought to take that budget and introduce it to the State of the Union speech," said House Majority Whip William H. Gray III, D-Pa. "The budget walks one way, and the speech another."

Bush spoke to Congress mainly about noncontroversial themes. He hailed the progress of prodemocracy forces abroad, set goals for improving higher education, spoke of requesting $2 billion in new spending for environmental protection, and asked for a Domestic Policy Council review of recommendations for bringing "the staggering costs of health care under control." His speech was a paean to American values that Democrats could deflate only by saying that Bush's feel-good words and style were not matched by legislative specifics and hard cash in his budget.

In an otherwise conciliatory address, Bush opened partisan wounds only when he turned his attention to budget and tax policy. When he promised to balance the federal budget by 1993 while adhering to his campaign pledge of no new taxes, Republicans in the audience jumped to their feet in a thunderous standing ovation, while Democrats remained seated. A similar party line was drawn in audience reaction when Bush restated his support for cutting federal taxes on capital gains.

Treading around a freshly laid tax-policy land mine, Bush alluded to his opposition to a new proposal by Sen. Daniel Patrick Moynihan, D-N.Y., to cut Social Security payroll taxes. "The last thing we need to do is mess around with Social Security," Bush said, expressing a formulation that all sides on the tax issue could applaud.

Moving to counter criticism that he was not doing enough as the "education president," Bush outlined school goals that were drafted by him and governors of the states at an "education summit" conference in Charlottesville, Virginia, in September 1989. The aims included making American students competent in math and science. (Education Summit, Historic Documents of 1989, p. 601)

Democrats' Criticism

Democrats in Congress had criticized Bush's budget for what they considered timid cuts in defense spending. But the president defused that criticism with his surprise offer to make cuts in military forces in Europe larger than the United States previously had advocated at international talks at Vienna. He proposed that each side reduce its troop strength in central Europe to 195,000, and to 225,000 on the entire continent. That would constitute a reduction of 80,000 American troops and 370,000 to 380,000 Soviet troops in Europe.

In delivering the Democrats' response to Bush's speech, House Speaker Tom S. Foley of Washington took the lead in a partywide effort to portray Bush's leadership as a series of well-meaning gestures lacking practical commitment. "You can't become the education president, with all the problems we face in this area, by proposing a meager 2 percent increase in the education budget." Senate Majority Leader George J. Mitchell, D-Maine, echoed that sentiment. "It will be up to Congress to produce the deeds to match the president's words," he said.

Bush's first State of the Union address also presented a first for Foley, whose response was his first televised address on behalf of the Democrats since he became Speaker in 1989, succeeding Rep. Jim Wright, D-Texas.

> *Following are texts of President George Bush's State of the Union address to Congress and a national television audience on January 31, 1990, and the response by House Speaker Tom S. Foley on behalf of congressional Democrats. (The bracketed headings have been added by Congressional Quarterly to highlight the organization of the text.):*

STATE OF THE UNION ADDRESS

Mr. President, Mr. Speaker, members of the United States Congress:

I return as a former president of the Senate and a former member of this great House. And now, as president, it is my privilege to report to you on the State of the Union.

Tonight, I come not to speak about the "state of the government," not to detail every new initiative we plan for the coming year, nor to describe every line in the budget. I'm here to speak to you and to the American people about the State of the Union, about our world, the changes we've seen, the challenges we face—and what that means for America.

There are singular moments in history, dates that divide all that goes before from all that comes after. Many of us in this chamber have lived much of our lives in a world whose fundamental features were defined in 1945. And the events of that year decreed the shape of nations, the pace of progress, freedom or oppression for millions of people around the world.

Nineteen forty-five provided the common frame of reference—the compass points of the postwar era we've relied upon to understand ourselves. And that was our world—until now. The events of the year just ended—the revolution of '89—have been a chain reaction, changes so striking that it marks the beginning of a new era in the world's affairs.

Think back—think back just 12 short months ago to the world we knew as 1989 began.

One year—one year ago, the people of Panama lived in fear, under the thumb of a dictator. Today democracy is restored—Panama is free.

Operation "Just Cause" has achieved its objective. The number of military personnel in Panama is now very close to what it was before the operation began. And tonight, I am announcing that well before the end of February the additional numbers of American troops, the brave men and women of our armed forces who made this mission a success, will be back home.

A year ago in Poland, Lech Walesa declared that he was ready to open a dialogue with the Communist rulers of that country. And today, with the future of a free Poland in their own hands, members of Solidarity lead the Polish Government.

A year ago, freedom's playwright, Vaclav Havel, languished as a prisoner in Prague. And today, it's Vaclav Havel—president of Czechoslovakia. And one year ago, Erich Honecker of East Germany claimed history as his guide. He predicted the Berlin Wall would last another hundred years. Today, less than one year later, it's the wall that's history.

Remarkable events, events that fulfill the long-held hopes of the American people—events that validate the longstanding goals of American policy, a policy based on a single, shining principle: the cause of freedom.

America—not just the nation, but an idea, alive in the minds of people everywhere. As this new world takes shape, America stands at the center of a widening circle of freedom—today, tomorrow and into the next century. Our nation is the enduring dream of every immigrant who ever set foot on these shores and the millions still struggling to be free. This nation, this idea called America, was and always will be a new world. Our new world.

At a workers' rally—in a place called Branik on the outskirts of Prague—the idea called America is alive. A worker, dressed in grimy overalls, rises to speak at the factory gates. He begins his speech to his fellow citizens with these words, words of a distant revolution: "We hold these truths to be self-evident: that all men are created equal, that they are endowed by their Creator with certain unalienable rights, that among these are life, liberty and the pursuit of happiness."

[Goals for America]

It's no secret that, here at home, freedom's door opened long ago. The cornerstones of this free society have already been set in place: Democracy. Competition. Opportunity. Private investment. Stewardship. And, of course, leadership. And our challenge today is to take this democratic system of ours—a system second to none—and make it better—a better America. Where there's a job for everyone who wants one. Where women working outside the home can be confident their children are in safe and loving care, and where government works to expand child-care alternatives for parents. Where we reconcile the needs of a clean environment and a strong economy. Where "Made in the U.S.A." is recognized around the world as the symbol of quality and progress. And where every one of us enjoys the same opportunities to live, to work and to contribute to society. And where, for the first time, the American mainstream includes all of our disabled citizens. Where everyone has a roof over his head—and where the homeless get the help they need to live in dignity. Where our schools challenge and support our kids and our teachers—and where all of them make the grade. Where every street, every city, every school and every child is drug-free. And, finally, where no American is forgotten. Our hearts go out to our hostages, our hostages who are ceaselessly on our minds and in our efforts.

That's part of the future we want to see, the future we can make for ourselves. But dreams alone won't get us there. We need to extend our horizon, commit to the long view. Our plans for the future start today.

In the tough competitive markets around the world, America faces great challenges and great opportunities. We know that we can succeed in the global economic arena of the '90s, but to meet that challenge we must make some fundamental changes—some crucial investment in ourselves.

[Invest in America]

Yes, we are going to invest in America. This administration is determined to encourage the creation of capital—capital of all kinds. Physical capital—everything, from our farms and factories to our workshops and production lines, all that is needed to produce and deliver quality goods and quality services. Intellectual capital—the source of ideas that spark tomorrow's products. And, of course, our human capital—the talented work force we'll need to compete in the global market.

Let me tell you: If we ignore human capital, we lose the spirit of American ingenuity, the spirit that is the hallmark of the American worker. That would be bad. The American worker is the most productive worker in the world.

We need to save more. We need to expand the pool of capital for the new investments that mean more jobs and more growth. And that's the idea behind a new initiative I call the Family Savings Plan, which I will send to Congress tomorrow.

We need to cut the tax on capital gains. Encourage risk-takers—

especially those in our small businesses—to take those steps that translate into economic reward, jobs and a better life for all of us.

We'll do what it takes to invest in America's future. The budget commitment is there. The money is there. It's there for Research and Development, R&D—a record high. It's there for our housing initiative—HOPE—to help everyone from first-time home buyers to the homeless. The money's there to keep our kids drug-free: 70 percent more than when I took office in 1989. It's there for space exploration. And it's there for education—another record high.

And one more thing. Last fall at the education summit, the governors and I agreed to look for ways to help make sure kids are ready to learn—the very first day they walk into that classroom. And I've made good on that commitment—by proposing a record increase in funds, an extra half a billion dollars, for something near and dear to all of us: Head Start.

[Education Goals, Environmental Needs]

Education is the one investment that means more for our future because it means the most for our children. Real improvement in our schools is not simply a matter of spending more. It is a matter of asking more—expecting more—of our schools, our teachers, of our kids and our parents and ourselves. That's why tonight I am announcing America's education goals—goals developed with enormous cooperation from the nation's governors. And, if I might, I'd like to say I'm very pleased that Governor [Booth] Gardner [D-Wash.] and Governor [Bill] Clinton [D-Ark.], Governor [Terry E.] Branstad [R-Iowa], Governor [Carroll A.] Campbell [Jr., R-S.C.], all of whom were very key in these discussions, these deliberations, are with us here tonight.

● By the year 2000, every child must start school ready to learn.

● The United States must increase the high school graduation rate to no less than 90 percent.

● And we're going to make sure our schools' diplomas mean something. In critical subjects—at the fourth, eighth and 12th grades—we must assess our students' performance.

● By the year 2000, U.S. students must be first in the world in math and science achievement.

● Every American adult must be a skilled, literate worker and citizen.

● Every school must offer the kind of disciplined environment that makes it possible for our kids to learn—and every school in America must be drug-free.

Ambitious aims? Of course. Easy to do? Far from it. But the future's at stake. This nation will not accept anything less than excellence in education.

These investments will keep America competitive. And I know this about the American people: We welcome competition. We'll match our ingenuity and energy, our experience and technology, our spirit and enterprise, against anyone. Let the competition be free—but let it also be fair. America is ready.

Since we really mean it, and since we are serious about being ready to meet that challenge, we're getting our own house in order. We've made real progress. Seven years ago, the federal deficit was 6 percent of our gross national product—6 percent. In the new budget I sent up two days ago, the deficit is down to 1 percent of gross national product.

That budget brings federal spending under control. It meets the Gramm-Rudman target, brings that deficit down further, and balances the budget by 1993—with no new taxes. And let me tell you, there's still more than enough federal spending. For most of us, $1.2 trillion is still a lot of money.

And once the budget is balanced, we can operate the way every family must when it has bills to pay. We won't leave it to our children and our grandchildren. Once it's balanced, we will start paying off the national debt.

And there's something more. There's something more we owe the generations of the future: stewardship, the safekeeping of America's precious environmental inheritance.

It's just one sign of how serious we are, we will elevate the Environmental Protection Agency to Cabinet rank. Not more bureaucracy, not more red tape—but the certainty that here at home, and especially in our dealings with other nations, environmental issues have the status they deserve.

This year's budget provides over $2 billion in new spending to protect our environment, with over $1 billion for global change research. And a new initiative I call "America the Beautiful," to expand our national parks and wildlife preserves and improve recreational facilities on public lands. And something else—something that will help keep this country clean, from our forest land to the inner cities, and keep America beautiful for generations to come: the money to plant a billion trees a year.

And tonight, let me say again to all the members of the Congress: The American people did not send us here to bicker. There is work to do, and they sent us here to get it done. And once again, in a spirit of cooperation, I offer my hand to all of you, and let's work together to do the will of the people. Clean air. Child care. The Educational Excellence Act. Crime and drugs. It's time to act. The farm bill. Transportation policy. Product-liability reform. Enterprise zones. It's time to act together.

[Social Security, Health Care]

And there's one thing I hope we will be able to agree on. It's about our commitments. And I'm talking about Social Security. To every American out there on Social Security, to every American supporting that system today and to everyone counting on it when they retire: We made a promise to you, and we are going to keep it.

We rescued the system in 1983—and it's sound again. Bipartisan arrangement. Our budget fully funds today's benefits, and it assures that future benefits will be funded as well. And the last thing we need to do is mess around with Social Security.

There's one more problem we need to address. We must give careful consideration to the recommendations of the health care studies under way now, and that's why tonight, I am asking Dr. Sullivan, Lou Sullivan, secretary of health and human services, to lead a Domestic Policy Council review of recommendations on the quality, accessibility and cost of our nation's health care system. I am committed to bring the staggering costs of health care under control.

The state of the Government does indeed depend on many of us in this very chamber. But the State of the Union depends on all Americans. We must maintain the democratic decency that makes a nation out of millions of individuals. And I have been appalled at the recent mail bombings across this country. Every one of us must confront and condemn racism, anti-Semitism, bigotry and hate. Not next week, not tomorrow, but right now—every single one of us.

The state of the Union depends on whether we help our neighbor—claim the problems of our community as our own. We've got to step forward when there's trouble, lend a hand, be what I call a point of light to a stranger in need. We've got to take the time after a busy day to sit down and read with our kids, help them with their homework, pass along the values we learned as children. And that's how we sustain the state of the Union. Every effort is important. It all adds up. It's doing the things that give democracy meaning. It all adds up to who we are and who we will be.

Let me say that so long as we remember the American idea, so long as we live up to the American ideal, the State of the Union will remain sound and strong.

And to those who worry that we've lost our way, well, I want you to listen to parts of a letter written by James Markwell, Private First Class James Markwell, a 20-year-old Army medic of the 1st Battalion, 75th Rangers. It's dated December 18th, the night before our Armed Forces went into action in Panama. It's a letter servicemen write—and hope will never be sent. And sadly, Private Markwell's mother did receive this letter. She passed it along to me out there in Cincinnati.

And here is some of what he wrote: "I've never been afraid of death, but I know he is waiting at the corner. I have been trained to kill and to save, and so has everyone else. I am frightened of what lays beyond the fog, and yet, do not mourn for me—revel in the life that I have died to give you. But most of all, don't forget the Army was my choice—something that I wanted to do. Remember I joined the Army to serve my country and insure that you are free to do what you want and live your lives freely."

Let me add that Private Markwell was among the first to see battle in Panama and one of the first to fall. But he knew what he believed in. He carried the idea we call America in his heart.

I began tonight speaking about the changes we've seen this past year. There is a new world of challenges and opportunities before us. And there is a need for leadership that only America can provide. Nearly 40 years ago, in his last address to the Congress, President Harry Truman predicted such a time would come. He said: "As our world grows stronger, more united, more attractive to men on both sides of the Iron Curtain, then inevitably there will come a time of change within the communist world." Today, that change is taking place.

For more than 40 years, America and its allies held communism in check and ensured that democracy would continue to exist. Today, with communism crumbling, our aim must be to ensure democracy's advance, to take the lead in forging peace and freedom's best hope, a great and growing commonwealth of free nations. And to the Congress and to all Americans, I say it is time to acclaim a new consensus at home and abroad, a common vision of the peaceful world we want to see.

Here in our own hemisphere, it's time for all the people of the Americas, North and South, to live in freedom. In the Far East and Africa, it is time for the full flowering of free governments and free markets that have served as the engine of progress. It is time to offer our hand to the emerging democracies of Eastern Europe, so that continent, for too long a continent divided, can see a future whole and free. It's time to build on our new relationship with the Soviet Union, to endorse and encourage a peaceful process of internal change toward democracy and economic opportunity.

[Troop Reduction in Europe]

We are in a period of great transition, great hope, yet great uncertainty. We recognize that the Soviet military threat in Europe is diminishing, but we see little change in Soviet strategic modernization. Therefore, we must sustain our own strategic offense modernization and the strategic defense initiative. But the time is right to move forward on a conventional arms control agreement to move us to more appropriate levels of military forces in Europe, a coherent defense program that ensures the U.S. will continue to be a catalyst for peaceful change in Europe. I've consulted with leaders of NATO—and in fact I spoke by phone with [Soviet] President [Mikhail S.] Gorbachev just today.

I agree with our European allies that an American military presence in Europe is essential and that it should not be tied solely to the Soviet military presence in Eastern Europe. But our troop levels can still be lower. So tonight I am announcing a major new step, for a further reduction in U.S. and Soviet manpower in Central and Eastern Europe to 195,000 on each side. This level—reflects the advice of our senior military advisers. It's designed to protect American and European interests and sustain NATO's defense strategy. A swift conclusion to our arms control talks—conventional, chemical and strategic—must now be our goal. And that time has come.

Still, we must recognize an unfortunate fact: In many regions of the world tonight, the reality is conflict, not peace. Enduring animosities and opposing interests remain. Thus the cause of peace must be served by an America strong enough and sure enough to defend our interests and our ideals. It's this American idea that for the past four decades helped inspire this Revolution of '89.

Here at home and in the world, there's history in the making and history to be made. Six months ago, early in this season of change, I stood at the gates of the Gdansk Shipyard in Poland at the monument to the fallen workers of Solidarity. It's a monument of simple majesty. Three tall crosses rise up from the stones. And atop each cross, an anchor, an ancient symbol of hope.

The anchor in our world today is freedom—holding us steady in times of change, a symbol of hope to all the world. And freedom is at the very heart of the idea that is America. Giving life to that idea depends on every one of us. Our anchor has always been faith and family.

In the last few days of this past momentous year, our family was blessed once more, celebrating the joy of life when a little boy became our 12th grandchild. When I held the little guy for the first time, the troubles at home and abroad seemed manageable and totally in perspective.

Now, I know you're thinking: That's a grandfather talking. Well, maybe you're right. But I've met a lot of children this past year, across this country and everywhere from the Far East to Eastern Europe. All kids are unique. Yet all kids are alike: the budding young environmentalists I met this month, who joined me exploring the Florida Everglades; the Little Leaguers I played catch with in Poland, ready to go from Warsaw to the World Series. Even the kids who are ill or alone—and God bless those boarder babies, born addicted to drugs, coping with problems no child should have to face. But, you know, when it comes to hope and the future, every kid is the same—full of dreams, ready to take on the world, all special because they are the very future of freedom. To them belongs this new world I've been speaking about.

And so tonight I'm going to ask something of every one of you. Let me start with my generation, with the grandparents out there. You are our living link to the past. Tell your grandchildren the story of struggles waged at home and abroad, of sacrifices freely made for freedom's sake. And tell them your own story as well—because every American has a story to tell.

And parents, your children look to you for direction and guidance. Tell them of faith and family. Tell them we are One Nation under God. Teach them that of all the many gifts they can receive, liberty is their most precious legacy. And of all the gifts they can give, the greatest is helping others.

And to the children and young people out there tonight: With you rests our hope, all that America will mean in the years and decades ahead. Fix your vision on a new century—your century. On dreams we cannot see. On the destiny that is yours—and yours alone.

And, finally, let all Americans—all of us together here in this chamber, the symbolic center of democracy—affirm our allegiance to this idea we call America. And let us all remember that the State of the Union depends on each and every one of us.

God bless all of you, and may God bless this great nation, the United States of America.

FOLEY'S DEMOCRATIC RESPONSE

Good evening.

I'm Tom Foley, the Speaker of the House. Earlier tonight, you may have seen me sitting behind President Bush as he delivered his address.

The first time I was present for a State of the Union message, I was a young staff member working here in the Capitol for one of the giants of the United States Senate, Scoop [Henry M.] Jackson of Washington state. It was the cold winter of 1962—a few months after the Berlin Crisis—and President Kennedy spoke eloquently, to the Congress and to the country, of the "burden and the glory of freedom."

Today, as we begin a new decade, we join together to celebrate the glory of a new era of freedom. This new era is not a coincidence or an accident. Its coming is due in large measure to those who carried the burden for nearly half a century—presidents and people alike, defenders and dissenters, Congresses and administrations from Harry Truman to George Bush.

In a special way, the credit goes to successive generations of young Americans, the 25 million who have served in the armed forces since World War II and the 350,000 who have been wounded or lost their lives.

And in the end, the credit goes to all the American people, who have paid the cost and stayed the course of a Cold War that was the longest conflict in American history, and perhaps the most fateful conflict in American history, modern history.

Some doubted it could ever end, except in defeat or in flames. But we as a nation met John Kennedy's challenge to "persevere, to look beyond our own shores and ambitions"—and so we have helped, in Ronald Reagan's words, "to turn the tide of history away from totalitarian darkness and into the warm sunlight of human freedom."

The events are still unfolding, and the Old World's new revolution of hope is still unfinished. But this is a time of honor and pride for America, and for free men and women everywhere.

We have a continuing obligation to fulfill—an obligation to those who struggle on, from South Africa to China. Who could ever forget the bravery of one Chinese student, who stood all alone in the front of a tank near Tiananmen Square and stopped it? We Democrats believe it was wrong for the Bush administration to yield to pressure from a communist dictatorship in Beijing; it was wrong for the president to veto a bill that would have safeguarded Chinese students in America from being sent back to their homeland's reign of repression. One lesson of the past 45 years is that no Congress and no president should be timid in the defense of freedom.

There's another, underlying truth in the ferment sweeping the globe. We are perhaps near the end of a great struggle, but we are certainly not at the end of history.

The 1990s will be a period of profound and continuing change. This new decade marks more than a division of time, and it will lead to more than a new century. For there are new realities to be grasped, new challenges to be met, and very different battles to be won.

In the 1990s and well into the next century, the central challenge for America will be economic, not military. The greatest test of our strength will be our classrooms, not our missile silos. The gravest threat will come not from any nation's attempt at world domination, but from every nation's complicity in the worldwide destruction of the environment.

This period of vast change will be a period of fundamental choice. Much of what the president said tonight I agree with. Some of what he said I disagree with.

But my purpose here is not to debate point by point. I'm here to tell you what we, as Democrats, believe, where we stand, the values we hold, the vision we have and the choices we face.

First, we believe that we must renew our economic capacity and regain control of our economic destiny.

Today, the America that invented the computer chip and the VCR has seen its market share shrink or vanish in both products.

We are falling dramatically behind in new technologies, such as high-definition television.

As Democrats, we're not satisfied with a trend that has seen this nation drop from first to sixth in standard of living. We're not satisfied to be told that within 10 years the average West German worker may earn 150 percent as much as the average American worker. We're not satisfied to have American students rank near the bottom of the industrial nations in math and science. We will set a national goal of making our schools once again the best in the world by the year 2000.

On this issue, the president's words seem to agree with us, but his actions say something else. You can't become the education president, with all the problems we face in this area, by proposing a meager 2 percent increase in the education budget. That's a fact. And for all the talk, that's exactly what the president proposes to do.

We also believe that American corporations have a responsibility and should have the opportunity to re-invest in America. We believe that the wave of corporate mergers and leveraged buyouts is a waste of resources. It leaves Wall Street raiders with large sums of money in their pockets, and it leaves our companies overburdened with debt and weakened in competing for world markets.

This issue represents another real difference between us and the Republicans. For too many years, their policies have encouraged debt and quick profit instead of investment and long-term growth. The result: The amount of private resources put into research and development has fallen in real dollars.

It's imperative to reverse the trend and to secure America's place on the frontiers of enterprise and invention.

At the same time, we must demand that nations trading with us give our products an equal chance in their markets—products ranging from innovations of the service sector to the abundant harvest of American agriculture.

Make no mistake about it—we favor expanding trade, but we reject the idea of one-way free trade. We believe this nation should be in the business of exporting the goods our workers make, not the jobs our workers need.

We also believe in encouraging a rise in savings, which have collapsed to a record low during the 1980s. The Republicans say they want to do this by cutting the capital gains tax, a cut which would give 80 percent of the benefits to the richest 1 percent of Americans. Instead, we are fighting to restore IRAs, so middle-income families can save as much as $2,000 a year tax free and then use the money for their own retirement, or as a down payment on a first home.

We took on the struggle against the capital gains proposal when the odds were against us. We won last year, and this year we will do all we can to make sure that the greatest part of any tax cut, of any kind, goes to those of you who live on a paycheck—not just the few who have the highest incomes, the largest stock portfolios and, by the way, the potential for the biggest tax shelters.

This issue goes to the heart of the reason we are Democrats: Above all else, we stand with you, the people who go to work and pay the taxes. It is your cause to which we are committed, and your side on which we fight.

So we will also fight for the most effective clean-air bill, even though that may offend entrenched and powerful interests.

We will fight for child care, so that working parents don't have to choose between their family's standard of living and their children's standard of care.

We will fight for campaign finance reform. We disagree with the administration's opposition to limits on campaign spending. Let's be blunt about it. Don't we all know there is simply too much money being raised and being spent in American politics?

And there is another issue on which we have only just begun to fight: this administration's practice of misusing the Social Security trust fund to hide the size of the federal budget deficit.

Social Security involves more than a trust fund; it involves the basic bond of trust between our people and our government. From the beginning, Social Security has been the Democratic Party's proudest achievement. We reject the suggestion of some Republicans to privatize the system. They say that's a new idea. We think it's the same old bad idea, another version of the repeated Republican attempt to undermine Social Security.

Finally, as Democrats, we believe that there are areas where the government simply does not belong. We will continue to defend a woman's right to choose, for we are convinced that politicians cannot and should not attempt to make the choice.

But we also believe government can have a positive role—not to dominate, but to help people improve their own lives.

The reason we have so many homeless in America today is not because government has cared too much, but because government has cared too little. We have to do better than that, on a whole range of critical needs.

We will seek to secure the right of all our children to learn in better schools and to earn a better life.

We will seek to secure the civil rights of all our people. We can't celebrate freedom abroad and then deny freedom at home.

We are also committed to the strongest possible attack on the drugs that are attacking our society and our families. On this we are all united. Narcotics destroy the children of Democrats and Republicans alike.

One of my first jobs was as a deputy prosecutor in my hometown of Spokane, Washington. I believed then and I believe now in enforcing the law, not in legalizing drugs. We won't win this struggle overnight or in a few months or even over a year or two.

But together we can begin to reclaim our streets and our schools and our neighborhoods.

Let me say it again: We will work with the president wherever and whenever we can. On some issues, we will have differences because we care deeply about certain principles and about the people who have been the abiding concern of the Democratic Party. Today, we Democrats stand, as we have before, for working families. We stand for both economic justice and economic opportunity. For protecting the environment. For senior citizens and the soundness of Social Security.

And, where we must, we will disagree with the administration. We will stand our ground when that is the only way to stand for you.

Above all else, we have high ambitions for America in the 1990s. We cannot be content to be bystanders, riders on the storm of history. For we are living in one of those rare seasons of change that come to few generations. We are being challenged by countries who say America is in decline, that we can never again be the best in the world marketplace. We do not accept that. We reject those who assume that Americans aren't smart enough or disciplined enough or tough enough to rise to the moment.

We were in the 1940s, and we saved the postwar world. Now we must strengthen our own country. The time has come for America to help herself, to rebuild, to re-energize, to reinvigorate our hopes, to gather together our talents and to reclaim our place in the world.

In the short span of this decade, we have a long way to move as a nation. Let us resolve that on that day when America enters the 21st century, we shall be first—first economically, first in education and science, first in human decency and human rights.

Thank you, God bless you, God bless our country.

Good night.

February

DE KLERK AND MANDELA
ON SOUTH AFRICAN CHANGES
February 2, 10, 11, and June 26, 1990

Nelson Mandela, possibly the world's most famous prisoner, gained his freedom February 11 to the joyous acclaim of his fellow black South Africans. As he had been when he went to prison twenty-seven-and-a-half years earlier, he emerged an outspoken foe of South Africa's white minority rule and apartheid, the system of legally imposed racial segregation.

Mandela's release had been expected ever since President F. W. de Klerk used his victory over the autocratic P. W. Botha in the September 1989 national elections to promise "a totally changed South Africa . . . free of domination or oppression." (South African President's Inaugural Address, Historic Documents of 1989, p. 545) *He repeatedly defied the traditions of his National party, which instituted apartheid in 1948. The new president soon permitted the first anti-apartheid street demonstrations in three decades and opened to all people bathing at beaches previously reserved for whites. Furthermore, de Klerk promised to dismantle the Separate Amenities Act, a basic law of apartheid. On June 19 Parliament voted its repeal.*

In October 1989 de Klerk freed several longtime political prisoners, including Walter Sisulu, who was second only to Mandela in the leadership of the outlawed African National Congress (ANC) at the time of Mandela's arrest and imprisonment August 5, 1962. Mandela, charged with sabotage and plotting to overthrow the government, was convicted at his trial two years later and drew a life sentence.

In addressing a new session of Parliament on February 2, de Klerk stunned critics and supporters alike by announcing plans to negotiate with anti-apartheid organizations on a new constitutional order for South Africa. He lifted the ban on thirty-six political organizations, including the ANC, the country's biggest black nationalist group. Moreover, the president said additional political prisoners would be freed, including Mandela—whose release would come as quickly as arrangements could be made.

Having met with Mandela December 13, de Klerk commented to Parliament that the imprisoned leader "has declared himself willing to make a constructive contribution to the peaceful political process in South Africa." After meeting with Mandela again on February 9, de Klerk announced the next day that his release would follow on February 11.

Mandela Freed, Leadership Resumed

At 4:14 p.m. on that day, the gray-haired, seventy-one-year-old prisoner stepped from a car that carried him just beyond the last guard post at Victor Vester Prison and into a throng of 5,000 black and white people chanting his name. He smiled gently and thrust his right arm outward in the black nationalist salute. With his wife, Winnie, at his side, Mandela made his way through a police corridor to another official vehicle that took him to Cape Town, forty miles away.

From the balcony of the Cape Town City Hall, in his first public speech in nearly three decades, Mandela called on his followers at home and abroad not to relax their pressure on the South African government to bring about democratic changes. "We have waited too long for our freedom," he told a cheering crowd of possibly 250,000 and a world-wide television audience. A delayed but uncensored broadcast of the speech was shown on the state-controlled South African television service.

"Today, I wish to report to you that my talks with the government have been aimed at normalizing the political situation in our country," Mandela added. "We have not as yet begun discussing the basic demands of the struggle."

From the moment of Mandela's release it was clear that he would be the principal spokesman and negotiator for black South Africans. This role became formalized March 2 when he was elected deputy president of the ANC, making him effectively its leader because illness had disabled the seventy-two-year-old president, Oliver N. Tambo.

Even as leader and spokesman, however, Mandela was unable to bring peace and solidarity to the black nationalist movement. His plea to warring black factions in Natal to throw their guns and knives into the sea went unheeded. The strife there was described as inter-tribal violence between the Zulus, the largest of South Africa's twelve ethnic groups, and the Xhosas, the second largest group. Since 1985, the ANC had sought to assert control over all anti-apartheid forces, but in Natal it encountered strong resistance.

ANC-Government Negotiations

Delegations led by de Klerk and Mandela concluded three days of talks May 4 by reporting progress toward undertaking full-scale negotiations on the nation's future. The two sides jointly announced they would work together to curb a wave of political violence. Mandela hinted that the ANC would renounce its longtime endorsement of an armed guerrilla struggle.

On May 8, de Klerk lifted the government's state of emergency in all but Natal province, where political violence had claimed more than 3,000 black lives in the past three years and was continuing. The emergency decree giving the government extraordinary powers to quell dissent through bannings, detention without trial, and news censorship had been imposed in June 1986. That move had triggered a wave of South African disinvestment by European and American corporations.

De Klerk lifted the decree upon his return from a visit to Western Europe where, according to press reports, he sensed a willingness by some host governments to consider lifting economic restrictions they had imposed on South African trade and investment. A study released in May by the Investor Responsibility Research Center in Washington concluded that the South African economy was 20 to 35 percent smaller than it would have been if sanctions had not been in effect. However, the study found that South Africa was much less vulnerable to sanctions than it had been in the past.

News analysts suggested that, additionally, de Klerk was attempting to lessen the impact of a European and American tour that Mandela had begun. In Paris, the black leader welcomed the lifting of the state of emergency but said it did not change his mind about sanctions. Throughout his trip, Mandela urged national leaders to maintain the sanctions until South African government and society were opened fully to blacks.

"Both de Klerk and Mandela are in a bidding war for international opinion," said Pauline Baker, a senior associate at the Carnegie Endowment for International Peace. At stake were sanctions, economic aid for the ANC, the moral support of the world community, and other cards to be played at the negotiating table.

Mandela's U.S. Visit

President George Bush invited both de Klerk and Mandela to visit the United States. Mandela began an eight-city tour of the United States June 20, attracting huge crowds especially from the black American community in New York, Washington, Boston, Atlanta, Miami, Detroit, Los Angeles, and Oakland. In New York, Mandela began his American visit with a ticker tape parade down Broadway and later addressed the United Nations General Assembly. He paid tribute to the late Martin Luther King, Jr., in Atlanta and received a warm welcome from labor officials in Detroit. Only in Miami and Washington did his visit elicit sour notes.

In an otherwise well-received address to a joint session of Congress on

June 26 and in a visit with President George Bush at the White House the previous day, Mandela drew some criticism for not renouncing armed forces in the struggle against apartheid. "I call on all elements in South African society to renounce violence and armed struggle," Bush said in his remarks of greeting.

Mandela did not respond directly but indicated elsewhere that he was not prepared to renounce an armed struggle until the anti-apartheid battle was won. He told Congress that despite recent reforms in South Africa, "we have yet to arrive at the point when we can say that South Africa is set on an irreversible course" toward democracy. He asked that U.S. economic sanctions be maintained until that time comes.

The 1986 sanctions law, which Congress passed over President Ronald Reagan's veto, specified actions that the South African government had to take to have it repealed. They included releasing Mandela from prison and legalizing the ANC. But only some of the nearly 1,000 political prisoners had been released, and Natal was still subject to the emergency decree. While Congress appeared unready to lift the sanctions, neither it nor President Bush seemed willing to provide the ANC economic aid, as Mandela sought.

De Klerk visited Washington in September and drew praise from Bush, who called his reforms "irreversible." Bush told de Klerk that if his government continued to dismantle apartheid, he would try to persuade Congress to modify or suspend the U.S. sanctions against South Africa. In meetings with congressional leaders, de Klerk said he was determined to build an American-like constitutional democracy based on the principle of "one man, one vote."

> *Following are excerpts from President F. W. de Klerk's address to Parliament February 2, 1990, and the text of his February 10 announcement of Nelson Mandela's release from prison, both from the South African government; Mandela's speech in Cape Town upon being released February 11, as reported in the American press; and excerpts from his address to a joint session of the U.S. Congress, June 26, as recorded in the* Congressional Record:

DE KLERK ADDRESS TO PARLIAMENT

The general election on September the 6th, 1989, placed our country irrevocably on the road of drastic change. Underlying this is the growing realization by an increasing number of South Africans that only a negotiated understanding among the representative leaders of the entire population is able to ensure lasting peace.

The alternative is growing violence, tension and conflict. That is unacceptable and in nobody's interest. The well-being of all in this country is linked inextricably to the ability of the leaders to come to terms with one another on a new dispensation. No-one can escape this simple truth.

On its part, the Government will accord the process of negotiation the highest priority. The aim is a totally new and just constitutional dispensation in which every inhabitant will enjoy equal rights, treatment and opportunity in every sphere of endeavour—constitutional, social and economic. . . .

The season of violence is over. The time for reconstruction and reconciliation has arrived. . . .

Practically every leader agrees that negotiation is the key to reconciliation, peace and a new and just dispensation. However, numerous excuses for refusing to take part, are advanced. Some of the reasons being advanced are valid. Others are merely part of a political chess game. And while the game of chess proceeds, valuable time is being lost.

Against this background I committed the Government during my inauguration to giving active attention to the most important obstacles in the way of negotiation. Today I am able to announce far-reaching decisions in this connection.

I believe that these decisions will shape a new phase in which there will be a movement away from measures which have been seized upon as a justification for confrontation and violence. The emphasis has to move, and will move now, to a debate and discussion of political and economic points of view as part of the process of negotiation.

I wish to urge every political and community leader, in and outside Parliament, to approach the new opportunities which are being created, constructively. There is no time left for advancing all manner of new conditions that will delay the negotiating process.

The steps that have been decided, are the following:

- The prohibition of the African National Congress, the Pan Africanist Congress, the South African Communist Party and a number of subsidiary organisations is being rescinded.
- People serving prison sentences merely because they were members of one of these organisations or because they committed another offence which was merely an offence because a prohibition on one of the organisations was in force, will be identified and released. Prisoners who have been sentenced for other offences such as murder, terrorism or arson are not affected by this.
- The media emergency regulations as well as the education emergency regulations are being abolished in their entirety.
- The security emergency regulations will be amended to still make provisions for effective control over visual material pertaining to scenes of unrest.
- The restrictions in terms of the emergency regulations on 33 organisations are being rescinded. . . .
- The conditions imposed in terms of the security emergency regulations on 374 people on their release, are being rescinded and the regulations

which provide for such conditions are being abolished.

- The period of detention in terms of the security emergency regulations will be limited henceforth to six months. Detainees also acquire the right to legal representation and a medical practitioner of their own choosing.

These decisions by the Cabinet are in accordance with the Government's declared intention to normalise the political process in South Africa without jeopardising the maintenance of the good order. They were preceded by thorough and unanimous advice by a group of officials which included members of the security community.

Implementation will be immediate and, where necessary, notices will appear in the Government Gazette from tomorrow.

The most important facets of the advice the Government received in this connection, are the following:

- The events in the Soviet Union and Eastern Europe, to which I have referred already, weaken the capability of organisations which were previously supported strongly from those quarters.
- The activities of the organisations from which the prohibitions are now being lifted, no longer entail the same degree of threat to internal security which initially necessitated the imposition of the prohibitions.
- There have been important shifts of emphasis in the statements and points of view of the most important of the organisations concerned, which indicate a new approach and a preference for peaceful solutions.
- The South African Police is convinced that it is able, in the present circumstances, to combat violence and other crimes perpetrated also by members of these organisations and to bring offenders to justice without the aid of prohibitions on organisations.

About one matter there should be no doubt. The lifting of the prohibition on the said organisations does not signify in the least the approval or condonation of terrorism or crimes of violence committed under their banner or which may be perpetrated in the future.... Violence from whichever source, will be fought with all available might. Peaceful protest may not become the springboard for lawlessness, violence and intimidation. No democratic country can tolerate that....

On the state of emergency I have been advised that an emergency situation, which justifies these special measures which have been retained, still exists. There is still conflict which is manifesting itself mainly in Natal, but as a consequence of the countrywide political power struggle. In addition, there are indications that radicals are still trying to disrupt the possibilities of negotiation by means of mass violence.

It is my intention to terminate the state of emergency completely as soon as circumstances justify it and I request the co-operation of everybody towards this end....

Our country and all its people have been embroiled in conflict, tension and violent struggle for decades. It is time for us to break out of the cycle of violence and break through to peace and reconciliation. The silent majority is yearning for this. The youth deserve it.

With the steps the Government has taken it has proven its good faith and the table is laid for sensible leaders to begin talking about a new dispensation, to reach an understanding by way of dialogue and discussion.

The agenda is open and the overall aims to which we are aspiring should be acceptable to all reasonable South Africans.

Among other things, those aims include a new, democratic constitution; universal franchise; no domination; equality before an independent judiciary; the protection of minorities as well as of individual rights; freedom of religion; a sound economy based on proven economic principles and private enterprise; dynamic programmes directed at better education, health services, housing and social conditions for all.

In this connection Mr. Nelson Mandela could play an important part. The government has noted that he has declared himself to be willing to make a constructive contribution to the peaceful political process in South Africa.

I wish to put it plainly that the Government has taken a firm decision to release Mr. Mandela unconditionally. I am serious about bringing this matter to finality without delay. The Government will take a decision soon on the date of his release. Unfortunately, a further short passage of time is unavoidable.

Normally there is a certain passage of time between the decision to release and the actual release because of logistical and administrative requirements. In the case of Mr. Mandela there are factors in the way of his immediate release, of which his personal circumstances and safety are not the least. He has not been an ordinary prisoner for quite some time. Because of that, his case requires particular circumspection.

Today's announcements, in particular, go to the heart of what Black leaders—also Mr. Mandela—have been advancing over the years as their reason for having resorted to violence. The allegation has been that the Government did not wish to talk to them and that they were deprived of their right to normal political activity by the prohibition of their organisations.

Without conceding that violence has ever been justified, I wish to say today to those who argued in this manner:

- The Government wishes to talk to all leaders who seek peace.
- The unconditional lifting of the prohibition on the said organisations places everybody in a position to pursue politics freely.
- The justification for violence which was always advanced, no longer exists. . . .

Therefore, I repeat my invitation with greater conviction than ever: Walk through the open door, take your place at the negotiating table together with the Government and other leaders who have important power bases inside and outside of Parliament.

Henceforth, everybody's political points of view will be tested against their realism, their workability and their fairness. The time for negotiation has arrived. . . .

DE KLERK ANNOUNCEMENT OF MANDELA'S RELEASE

In pursuance of my opening address to Parliament, I am now in a position to announce that Mr. Nelson Mandela will be released at the Victor Verster Prison on Sunday, 11 February 1990, at about 3 p.m.

Yesterday evening I met with Mr. Mandela in Cape Town, together with Ministers [Gerrit] Viljoen and [Kobie] Coetzee. During the meeting Mr. Mandela was informed of the government's decision regarding his release.

We would all like Mr. Mandela's release to take place in a dignified and orderly manner. To attain this, government officials are at the moment involved in discussions with parties concerned in order to afford them the opportunity to make suitable arrangements.

Two issues were also raised during the discussions between me and Mr. Mandela, namely the state of emergency and the position of persons serving sentences for politically motivated crimes, as well as those who have committed such crimes and who are now outside the country.

I stressed the importance of creating conditions which would enable me to lift the state of emergency without jeopardizing the maintenance of law and order. Regarding the position of persons involved in politically motivated crimes, I indicated that while this is a matter that should be dealt with in negotiations, exploratory discussions could take place in the meantime.

I want to emphasize that there can no longer be any doubt about the government's sincerity to create a just dispensation based on negotiations. I call upon Mr. Mandela and all other interested parties to make their contribution towards a positive climate for negotiations.

The eyes of the world are presently focused on all South Africans. All of us now have an opportunity and the responsibility to prove that we are capable of a peaceful process in creating a new South Africa.

MANDELA'S SPEECH

Amandla! Amandla! i-Afrika, mayibuye! [Power! Power! Africa it is ours!]

My friends, comrades and fellow South Africans, I greet you all in the name of peace, democracy and freedom for all. I stand here before you not as a prophet but as a humble servant of you, the people.

Your tireless and heroic sacrifices have made it possible for me to be here today. I therefore place the remaining years of my life in your hands.

On this day of my release, I extend my sincere and warmest gratitude to the millions of my compatriots and those in every corner of the globe who have campaigned tirelessly for my release.

I extend special greetings to the people of Cape Town, the city to which, which has been my home for three decades. Your mass marches and other forms of struggle have served as a constant source of strength to all political prisoners.

I salute the African National Congress. It has fulfilled our every expectation in its role as leader of the great march to freedom.

I salute our president, Comrade Oliver Tambo, for leading the A.N.C. even under the most difficult circumstances.

I salute the rank-and-file members of the A.N.C. You have sacrificed life and limb in the pursuit of the noble cause of our struggle.

I salute combatants of Umkonto We Sizwe [Spear of the Nation], like Solomon Malhangu and Ashley Kriel, who have paid the ultimate price for the freedom of all South Africans.

I salute the South African Communist Party for its steady contribution to the struggle for democracy. You have survived 40 years of unrelenting persecution. The memory of great Communists like Moses Kotane, Yusuf Dacoo, Bram Fischer and Moses Madidha will be cherished for generations to come.

I salute General Secretary Joe Slovo, one of our finest patriots. We are heartened by the fact that the alliance between ourselves and the party remains as strong as it always was.

I salute the United Democratic Front, the National Education Crisis Committee, the South African Youth Congress, the Transvaal and Natal Indian Congresses. And Cosatu. And the many other formations of the mass democratic movement.

I also salute the Black Sash and National Union of South African Students. We note with pride that you have acted as the conscience of white South Africans. Even during the darkest days in the history of our struggle, you held the flag of liberty high. The large-scale mass mobilization of the past few years is one of the key factors which led to the opening of the final chapter of our struggle.

I extend my greetings to the working class of our country. Your organized stance is the pride of our movement. You remain the most dependable force in the struggle to end exploitation and oppression.

I pay tribute—I pay tribute to the many religious communities who carried the campaign for justice forward when the organizations of our people were silenced.

I greet the traditional leaders of our country. Many among you continue to walk in the footsteps of great heroes like Hintsa and Sekhukhuni.

I pay tribute to the endless heroes of youth. You, the young lions. You the young lions have energized our entire struggle.

I pay tribute to the mothers and wives and sisters of our nation. You are the rock-hard foundation of our struggle. Apartheid has inflicted more pain on you than on anyone else. On this occasion, we thank the world—we thank the world community for their great contribution to the anti-apartheid struggle. Without your support our struggle would not have reached this advanced stage.

The sacrifice of the front-line states will be remembered by South Africans forever.

My salutations will be incomplete without expressing my deep appreciation for the strength given to me during my long and lonely years in prison by my beloved wife and family.

I am convinced that your pain and suffering was far greater than my own.

Before I go any further, I wish to make the point that I intend making only a few preliminary comments at this stage. I will make a more complete statement only after I have had the opportunity to consult with my comrades.

Today the majority of South Africans, black and white, recognize that apartheid has no future. It has to be ended by our own decisive mass actions in order to build peace and security. The mass campaigns of defiance and other actions of our organizations and people can only culminate in the establishment of democracy.

The apartheid destruction on our subcontinent is incalculable. The fabric of family life of millions of my people has been shattered. Millions are homeless and unemployed.

Our economy—our economy lies in ruins and our people are embroiled in political strife. Our resort to the armed struggle in 1960 with the formation of the military wing of the A.N.C., Umkonto We Sizwe, was a purely defensive action against the violence of apartheid.

The factors which necessitated the armed struggle still exist today. We have no option but to continue. We express the hope that a climate conducive to a negotiated settlement would be created soon so that there may no longer be the need for the armed struggle.

I am a loyal and disciplined member of the African National Congress. I am, therefore, in full agreement with all of its objectives, strategies and tactics.

The need to unite the people of our country is as important a task now as it always has been. No individual leader is able to take all these enormous tasks on his own. It is our task as leaders to place our views before our organization and to allow the democratic structures to decide on the way forward.

On the question of democratic practice, I feel duty bound to make the point that a leader of the movement is a person who has been democratically elected at a national conference. This is a principle which must be upheld without any exceptions.

Today, I wish to report to you that my talks with the Government have been aimed at normalizing the political situation in the country. We have not as yet begun discussing the basic demands of the struggle.

I wish to stress that I myself had at no time entered into negotiations about the future of our country, except to insist on a meeting between the A.N.C. and the Government.

Mr. de Klerk has gone further than any other Nationalist president in taking real steps to normalize the situation. However, there are further steps as outlined in the Harare Declaration that have to be met before negotiations on the basic demands of our people can begin.

I reiterate our call for inter alia the immediate ending of the state of emergency and the freeing of all, and not only some, political prisoners.

Only such a normalized situation which allows for free political activity can allow us to consult our people in order to obtain a mandate. The people need to be consulted on who will negotiate and on the content of such negotiations.

Negotiations cannot take place—negotiations cannot take up a place above the heads or behind the backs of our people. It is our belief that the future of our country can only be determined by a body which is democratically elected on a nonracial basis.

Negotiations on the dismantling of apartheid will have to address the overwhelming demand of our people for a democratic nonracial and unitary South Africa. There must be an end to white monopoly on political power.

And a fundamental restructuring of our political and economic systems to insure that the inequalities of apartheid are addressed and our society thoroughly democratized.

It must be added that Mr. de Klerk himself is a man of integrity who is acutely aware of the dangers of a public figure not honoring his undertakings. But as an organization, we base our policy and strategy on the harsh reality we are faced with, and this reality is that we are still suffering under the policies of the Nationalist Government.

Our struggle has reached a decisive moment. We call on our people to seize this moment so that the process toward democracy is rapid and uninterrupted. We have waited too long for our freedom. We can no longer wait. Now is the time to intensify the struggle on all fronts.

To relax our efforts now would be a mistake which generations to come will not be able to forgive. The sight of freedom looming on the horizon should encourage us to redouble our efforts. It is only through disciplined mass action that our victory can be assured.

We call on our white compatriots to join us in the shaping of a new South Africa. The freedom movement is the political home for you, too. We call on the international community to continue the campaign to isolate the apartheid regime.

To lift sanctions now would be to run the risk of aborting the process toward the complete eradication of apartheid. Our march to freedom is irreversible. We must not allow fear to stand in our way.

Universal suffrage on a common voters roll in a united democratic and nonracial South Africa is the only way to peace and racial harmony.

In conclusion, I wish to go to my own words during my trial in 1964. They are as true today as they were then. I wrote: I have fought against white domination, and I have fought against black domination. I have cherished the idea of a democratic and free society in which all persons live together in harmony and with equal opportunities.

It is an ideal which I hope to live for and to achieve. But if needs be, it is an ideal for which I am prepared to die.

[The following portion was delivered in Xhosa.]

My friends, I have no words of eloquence to offer today except to say that the remaining days of my life are in your hands.

[He continued in English.] I hope you will disperse with discipline. And not a single one of you should do anything which will make other people to say that we can't control our own people.

MANDELA ADDRESS TO CONGRESS

... Our people demand democracy. Our country, which continues to bleed and suffer pain, needs democracy. It cries out for the situation where the law will decree that the freedom to speak of freedom constitutes the very essence of legality and the very thing that makes for the legitimacy of the constitutional order.

It thirsts for the situation where those who are entitled by law to carry arms, as the forces of national security and law and order, will not turn their weapons against the citizens simply because the citizens assert that equality, liberty and the pursuit of happiness are fundamental human rights which are not only inalienable but must, if necessary, be defended with the weapons of war.

We fight for and visualize a future in which all shall, without regard to race, color, creed or sex, have the right to vote and to be voted into all elective organs of state. We are engaged in struggle to ensure that the rights of every individual are guaranteed and protected, through a democratic constitution, the rule of law, an entrenched bill of rights, which should be enforced by an independent judiciary, as well as a multi-party political system.

Mr. Speaker, we are acutely conscious of the fact that we are addressing an historic institution for whose creation and integrity many men and women lost their lives in the war of independence, the civil war and the war against nazism and fascism. That very history demands that we address you with respect and candor and without any attempt to dissemble.

What we have said concerning the political arrangements we seek for our country is seriously meant. It is an outcome for which many of us went to prison, for which many have died in police cells, on the gallows, in our towns and villages and in the countries of Southern Africa. Indeed, we have even had our political representatives killed in countries as far away from South Africa as France.

Unhappily, our people continue to die to this day, victims of armed agents of the state who are still determined to turn their guns against the very idea of a nonracial democracy. But this is the perspective which we trust Congress will feel happy to support and encourage, using the enormous weight of its prestige and authority as an eminent representative of democratic practice.

To deny any person their human rights is to challenge their very humanity. To impose on them a wretched life of hunger and deprivation is to dehumanise them. But such has been the terrible fate of all black persons in our country under the system of apartheid. The extent of the deprivation of millions of people has to be seen to be believed. The injury is made that more intolerable by the opulence of our white compatriots and the deliberate distortion of the economy to feed that opulence.

The process of the reconstruction of South African society must and will also entail the transformation of its economy. We need a strong and growing economy. We require an economy that is able to address the needs of all the people of our country, that can provide food, houses, education, health services, social security and everything that makes human life human, that makes life joyful and not a protracted encounter with hopelessness and despair.

We believe that the fact of the apartheid structure of the South African economy and the enormous and pressing needs of the people, make it inevitable that the democratic government will intervene in this economy, acting through the elected parliament. We have put the matter to the business community of our country that the need for a public sector is one of the elements in a many-sided strategy of economic development and restructuring that has to be considered by us all, including the private sector.

The ANC [African National Congress] holds no ideological positions which dictate that it must adopt a policy of nationalisation. But the ANC also holds the view that there is no self-regulating mechanism within the South African economy which will, on its own, ensure growth with equity.

At the same time, we take it as given that the private sector is an engine of growth and development which is critical to the success of the mixed economy we hope to see in the future South Africa. We are accordingly committed to the creation of the situation in which business people, both South African and foreign, have confidence in the security of their investments, are assured of a fair rate of return on their capital and do business in conditions of stability and peace.

We must also make the point very firmly that the political settlement and democracy itself, cannot survive, unless the material needs of the people, the bread and butter issues, are addressed as part of the process of change and as a matter of urgency. It should never be that the anger of the poor should be the finger of accusation pointed at all of us because we failed to respond to the cries of the people for food, for shelter, for the dignity of the individual.

We shall need your support to achieve the post-apartheid economic objectives which are an intrinsic part of the process of the restoration of the human rights of the people of South Africa. We would like to approach the issue of our economic cooperation not as a relationship between donor and recipient, between a dependent and a benefactor.

We would like to believe that there is a way in which we could structure this relationship so that we do indeed benefit from your enormous resources in terms of your capital, technology, all-round expertise, your enterprising spirit and your markets. This relationship should however be one from which your people should also derive benefit, so that we who are fighting to liberate the very spirit of an entire people from the bondage of the arrogance of the ideology and practice of white supremacy, do not build a relationship of subservient dependency and fawning gratitude.

One of the benefits that should accrue to both our peoples and to the rest of the world, should surely be that this complex South African society, which has known nothing but racism for three centuries, should be transformed into an oasis of good race relations, where the black shall to the white be sister and brother, a fellow South African, an equal human being, both citizens of the world. To destroy racism in the world, we, together, must expunge apartheid racism in South Africa. Justice and liberty must be our tool, prosperity and happiness our weapon.

Mr. Speaker, distinguished representatives of the American people, you know this more than we do that peace is its own reward. Our own fate, borne by a succession of generations that reach backward into centuries, has been nothing but tension, conflict, and death. In a sense we do not know the meaning of peace except in the imagination. But because we have not known true peace in its real meaning; because, for centuries, generations have had to bury the victims of state violence, we have fought for the right to experience peace.

On the initiative of the ANC, the process toward the conclusion of a peaceful settlement has started. According to a logic dictated by our situation, we are engaged in an effort which includes the removal of obstacles to negotiations. This will be followed by a negotiated determination of the mechanism which will draw up the new constitution.

This should lead to the formation of this constitution-making institution and therefore the elaboration and adoption of a democratic constitution. Elections would then be held on the basis of this constitution and, for the first time, South Africa would have a body of lawmakers which would, like yourselves, be mandated by the whole people.

Despite the admitted commitment of President de Klerk to walk this road with us, and despite our acceptance of his integrity and the honesty of his purposes, we would be fools to believe that the road ahead of us is without major hurdles. Too many among our white compatriots are steeped in the ideology of racism to admit easily that change must come.

Tragedy may yet sully the future we pray and work for if these slaves of the past take up arms in a desperate effort to resist the process which must lead to the democratic transformation of our country. For those who care to worry about violence in our country, as we do, it is at these forces that they should focus their attention, a process in which we are engaged.

We must contend still with the reality that South Africa is a country in the grip of the apartheid crime against humanity. The consequences of this continue to be felt not only within our borders but throughout Southern

Africa which continues to harvest the bitter fruits of conflict and war, especially in Mozambique and Angola. Peace will not come to our country and region until the apartheid system is ended.

Therefore we say we still have a struggle on our hands. Our common and noble efforts to abolish the system of white minority domination must continue. We are encouraged and strengthened by the fact of the agreement between ourselves, this Congress as well as President Bush and his administration that sanctions should remain in place. Sanctions should remain in place because the purpose for which they were imposed has not yet been achieved.

We have yet to arrive at the point when we can say that South Africa is set on an irreversible course leading to its transportation into a united, democratic, and nonracial country. We plead that you cede the prerogative to the people of South Africa to determine the moment when it will be said that profound changes have occurred and an irreversible process achieved, enabling you and the rest of the international community to lift sanctions.

We would like to take this opportunity to thank you all for the principled struggle you waged which resulted in the adoption of the historic comprehensive Anti-Apartheid Act which made such a decisive contribution to the process of moving our country forward toward negotiations. We request that you go further and assist us with the material resources which will enable us to promote the peace process and meet other needs which arise from the changing situation you have helped to bring about.

The stand you took established the understanding among the millions of our people that here we have friends, here we have fighters against racism who feel hurt because we are hurt, who seek our success because they too seek the victory of democracy over tyranny. And here I speak not only about you, Members of the U.S. Congress, but also of the millions of people throughout this great land who stood up and engaged the apartheid system in struggle, the masses who have given us such strength and joy by the manner in which they have received us since we arrived in this country.

Mr. Speaker, Mr. President, Senators and Representatives; we went to jail because it was impossible to sit still while the obscenity of the apartheid system was being imposed on our people. It would have been immoral to keep quiet while a racist tyranny sought to reduce an entire people into a status worse than that of the beasts of the forest. It would have been an act of treason against the people and against our conscience to allow fear and the drive toward self-preservation to dominate our behavior, obliging us to absent ourselves from the struggle for democracy and human rights, not only in our country but throughout the world.

We could not have made an acquaintance through literature with human giants such as George Washington, Abraham Lincoln and Thomas Jefferson and not been moved to act as they were moved to act. We could not have heard of and admired John Brown, Sojourner Truth, Frederick Douglass, W. E. B. DuBois, Marcus Garvey, Martin Luther King, Jr., and others—we could not have heard of these and not be moved to act as they were moved to act. We could not have known of your Declaration of Independence and not elected to join in the struggle to guarantee the people life, liberty and the pursuit of happiness.

We are grateful to you all that you persisted in your resolve to have us and other political prisoners released from jail. You have given us the gift and privilege to rejoin our people, yourselves and the rest of the international community in the common effort to transform South Africa into a united, democratic and nonracial country. You have given us the power to join hands with all people of conscience to fight for the victory of democracy and human rights throughout the world.

We are glad that you merged with our own people to make it possible for us to emerge from the darkness of the prison cell and join the contemporary process of the renewal of the world. We thank you most sincerely for all you have done and count on you to persist in your noble endeavors to free the rest of our political prisoners and to emancipate our people from the larger prison that is apartheid South Africa.

The day may not be far when we will borrow the words of Thomas Jefferson and speak of the will of the South African Nation. In the exercise of that will by this united nation of black and white people, it must surely be that there will be born a country on the southern tip of Africa which you will be proud to call a friend and an ally, because of its contribution to the universal striving toward liberty, human rights, prosperity and peace among the peoples.

Let that day come now. Let us keep our arms locked together so that we form a solid phalanx against racism to ensure that that day comes now. By our common actions let us ensure that justice triumphs without delay. When that has come to pass, then shall we all be entitled to acknowledge the salute when others say of us, blessed are the peacemakers.

Thank you for your kind invitation to speak here today and thank you for your welcome and the attention you have accorded our simple message.

Thank you.

PRESIDENT'S ECONOMIC REPORT, ECONOMIC ADVISERS' REPORT
February 6, 1990

Hailing an economic expansion in its eighth year, President George Bush and his Council of Economic Advisers (CEA) presented their first annual economic reports to Congress on February 6. While outlining a generally conservative economic course, the reports spelled out a philosophy differing sharply from the supply-side and monetarist principles that guided the Reagan administration.

Bush, in a six-page message, credited the "longest peacetime expansion on record" to American firms and workers who had "created more than 20 million jobs." In their 275-page report, his advisers struck a markedly optimistic note by predicting that the expansion would continue. They said that chances of a recession did not increase "as the period of expansion" ran on.

Sticking closely to Republican belief in free markets and rejecting close management of the economy, the report said that regulation may be required only "where competitive private markets do not exist or cannot function." Moreover, whereas the Reagan administration had often criticized the independent Federal Reserve Board, which controls monetary policy, the Bush economists wrote that by attempting to pursue a "forward-looking policy consistent over time," the Federal Reserve Board "appears to have achieved" a high degree of credibility.

President's Advisers

The CEA in the Bush administration quickly won greater prominence than it had in the Reagan administration. The Wall Street Journal *commented that Michael Boskin "stands out as the first chairman of the*

Council of Economic Advisers to have the president's ear since Alan Greenspan. . . ." Chairman of the Federal Reserve Board Greenspan headed the council in Gerald Ford's presidency. Boskin, on leave from Stanford University, replaced Beryl W. Sprinkel, a monetarist, as council chairman. The Journal said Boskin had "transformed his post, which had atrophied into irrelevance, into a potent force." The other new CEA members were John B. Taylor and Richard L. Achmalensee.

Importing Skilled Workers?

Pointing to an increasing need in the United States for skilled workers, the CEA report said the Bush administration might consider an immigration policy aimed for the first time at admitting skilled workers into the country. The proposal would represent a sharp break with traditional U.S. policies that encouraged immigration for such humanitarian reasons as the reunion of families and the resettlement of refugees. In recent years, only about one-tenth of all immigrants were admitted specifically because of their education or skills. The report argued that more jobs required workers with higher levels of education and training than were currently available.

Projections and Recommendations

Decrying a low national savings rate, the council recommended special tax-exempt family savings accounts and other measures to help spur economic growth. The U.S. rate of saving in the 1980s was well below that of other industrial countries and its own average over the previous thirty years. By international standards, the economists wrote, saving performance in the United States was "abysmal."

The report said a higher rate of national saving (saving by households, businesses, and government) would reduce the cost of investment funds to American firms. A lower cost of capital, in turn, would encourage investment and enhance productivity.

The CEA urged a reexamination of such federal government policies as double taxation that, the report said, were biased toward consumption and against saving. The council also strongly recommended the reduction of the federal budget deficit and restoration of the capital gains tax differential as ways to help enhance savings. In his report, Bush said a capital gains tax cut would "stimulate saving and investment throughout the economy."

The Council of Economic Advisers predicted a 2.6 percent increase in real gross national product (GNP) from the fourth quarter of 1989 to the fourth quarter of 1990. For the same period, the council projected a 4.1 percent increase in inflation.

However, in mid-year the Bush administration issued a gloomier forecast, predicting lower GNP growth (2.2 percent) and higher inflation (4.8 percent). Those later estimates were closer than the previous one to forecasts by the Congressional Budget Office and many private econo-

mists. Several yardsticks of business activity pointed to a slowdown nationally.

Following are excerpts from the Economic Report of the President and the Annual Report of the Council of Economic Advisers, both issued February 6, 1990, by the White House:

ECONOMIC REPORT OF THE PRESIDENT

To the Congress of the United States:

The United States enters the 1990s as a prosperous nation with a healthy and dynamic economy. Our living standards remain well above those of other major industrialized nations, and our prosperity is spread widely. Since 1982, American firms and workers have produced the longest peacetime expansion on record and created more than 20 million jobs. The containment of inflation during this long economic expansion is a milestone in postwar U.S. history.

In 1989, we regained our position as the world's leading exporter and retained our position as the world's leading job creator, with the fraction of the population employed reaching its highest level ever. In all, 2½ million jobs were created in 1989. The unemployment rate fell to levels not seen since the early 1970s, as did jobless rates for blacks and teenagers. The unemployment rate for Hispanics was the lowest since 1980, when the United States began regularly reporting it.

We have proven to the world that economic and political freedom works. After years of economic decline, the people of Eastern Europe are turning toward free markets to revive economic growth and raise living standards. I remain strongly committed to aiding the efforts of these brave men and women to transform their societies—and thereby to change the world.

Despite our successes, we cannot be satisfied with simply sustaining the strong record of the 1980s. We must improve on that record, deal with inherited problems, and meet the new challenges and seize the new opportunities before us.

Goals and Principles

The primary economic goal of my Administration is to achieve the highest possible rate of sustainable economic growth. Achieving this goal will require action on many fronts—but it will permit progress on many more. Growth is the key to raising living standards, to leaving a legacy of prosperity for our children, to uplifting those most in need, and to maintaining America's leadership in the world.

To achieve this goal, we must both enhance our economy's ability to grow and ensure that its potential is more often fully utilized than in previous decades. To these ends, as explained in the *Report* that follows, my Administration will:

- Reduce government borrowing by slowing the growth of Federal spending while economic growth raises revenue until the budget is balanced, and reduce the national debt thereafter;
- Support a credible, systematic monetary policy program that sustains maximum economic growth while controlling and reducing inflation;
- Remove barriers to innovation, investment, work, and saving in the tax, legal, and regulatory systems;
- Avoid unnecessary regulation and design necessary regulatory programs to harness market forces effectively to serve the Nation's interest; and
- Continue to lead the world to freer trade and more open markets, and to support market-oriented reforms around the world.

In advancing these principles, we must be both ambitious and realistic. There is room to improve, and there is much to be done to prepare for the next century. We must not fear to dream great dreams. But we must not fail to do our homework; the American people are ill-served by promises that cannot be kept.

Macroeconomic Prospects and Policies

The economy's performance during 1989, the seventh·year of economic expansion, has set the stage for healthy growth in the 1990s. Growth in national output was more·moderate in 1989 than the very rapid pace in 1988 and 1987. But, in sharp contrast to most past periods of low unemployment and high capacity utilization, inflation was kept firmly in check. Measured broadly, the price level rose 4.1 percent during 1989, down from 4.5 percent during 1988.

If my budget proposals are adopted, and if the Federal Reserve maintains a credible policy program to support strong noninflationary growth, the economy is projected to expand in 1990 at a slightly faster pace than in 1989. Growth is projected to pick up in the second half of the year and to continue at a strong pace as the level of output rises to the economy's full potential.

Fiscal and monetary policies should establish credible commitments to policy plans aimed at maximizing sustainable growth over the long run. A steady hand at the helm is necessary to produce rapid and continuous increases in employment and living standards.

My budget proposals reflect a strong commitment to the principles of the Gramm-Rudman-Hollings law, which has helped reduce the Federal deficit from 5.3 percent of GNP in fiscal 1986 to 2.9 percent in fiscal 1989. That is why I insisted last fall that the Congress pass a clean reconciliation bill and stood by the sequestration order that resulted from my strict adherence to the Gramm-Rudman-Hollings law.

I have also proposed a fundamental new rule for fiscal policy that would ensure that projected future Social Security surpluses are not spent for other purposes but are used to build the reserves necessary to guarantee the soundness of Social Security. Moreover, it would transform the Federal

Government from a chronic borrower, draining savings away from private investment, to a saver, providing funds for capital formation and economic growth by reducing the national debt.

I remain strongly committed to the principles of low marginal tax rates and a broad tax base developed in the Economic Recovery Tax Act of 1981 and the Tax Reform Act of 1986. Steady adherence to these principles reduces government's distorting effect on the market forces that drive economic growth.

I strongly support the Federal Reserve's goal of noninflationary growth and share with them the conviction that inflation must be controlled and reduced in a predictable fashion. Accelerating inflation not only erodes the value of families' savings; it produces economic imbalances and policy responses that often lead to recessions.

The United States is part of an increasingly integrated global economy, in which domestic fiscal and monetary policies affect the economies of other nations, though the main impacts are on the domestic economy. My Administration remains committed to participating actively in the valuable process of coordinating macroeconomic policies internationally.

Encouraging Economic Growth

As we begin the 1990s, a central focus of my economic policies will be to build on the successes of the 1980s by creating an environment in which the private sector can serve as the engine that powers strong, noninflationary economic growth.

America's continued economic progress depends on the innovation and entrepreneurship of our people. I will therefore continue to press for a permanent research and experimentation tax credit, for increased Federal support of research with widespread societal benefits and that private firms would not have adequate incentives to undertake, for removal of regulatory and legal barriers to innovation, and for a lower tax rate on capital gains.

We must remove impediments to saving and investment in order to enhance the economy's growth potential. The fiscal policy I described earlier will raise national saving. In addition, I have asked the Congress to enact the Savings and Economic Growth Act of 1990, which contains a comprehensive program to raise household saving across the entire income spectrum. This program would help American families plan for the future and, in the process, make more funds available to finance investment and spur productivity, thus raising living standards, enhancing competitiveness, and expanding employment opportunities.

One of my highest legislative priorities this year is to reduce the capital gains tax rate. This tax reform would promote risk-taking and entrepreneurship by lowering the cost of capital, thereby encouraging new business formation and creating new jobs. A capital gains tax cut would stimulate saving and investment throughout the economy.

Government can encourage economic growth but cannot manage it. I remain strongly opposed to any sort of industrial policy, in which the government, not the market, would pick winners and losers. Second-guessing the market is the way to raise government spending and taxes, not living standards.

The growth of our Nation's labor force is projected to slow in the 1990s, and demands for skilled workers are expected to continue to increase. These developments will shift attention away from worries about the supply of jobs that have haunted us since the 1930s and toward new concerns about the supply of workers and skills.

We cannot maintain our position of world leadership or sustain rapid economic growth if our workers lack the skills of their foreign competitors. As I demonstrated last fall at the Education Summit, the Federal Government can lead in improving the inadequate performance of our elementary and secondary schools. Because school systems must be held accountable for their students' performance, the Nation's Governors and I have developed ambitious national education goals. To meet these goals, we must give students and parents the freedom to choose their schools, and we must give schools the flexibility to meet their students' needs.

More disadvantaged Americans must be brought into the economic mainstream, not just to enhance our Nation's economic growth, but as a matter of simple decency. To this end, I have supported legislation to open new opportunities for the disabled, increased assistance to the homeless, helped implement welfare reform, proposed more effective job training programs, and introduced initiatives that will bring jobs and better housing to depressed inner cities. I have proposed substantial increases in spending for Head Start to prepare children from disadvantaged families for effective learning.

Those who cannot read and write cannot participate fully in the economy. Mrs. Bush and I will continue to support the difficult but important struggle to eliminate adult functional illiteracy.

Regulatory Reform

The improved performance of U.S. markets that were deregulated during the 1980s showed clearly that government interference with competitive private markets inflates prices, retards innovation, slows growth, and eliminates jobs. But in some cases, well-designed regulation can serve the public interest.

My proposals for reform of food safety regulation and the Clean Air Act follow the two key principles that apply in these cases: the goals of regulation must balance costs and benefits; and the methods of regulation must be flexible and cost-effective. One of my top legislative priorities is to improve the Clean Air Act in a way that preserves both a healthy environment and a sound economy.

When confronted with a threat to the solvency of our thrift institutions, my Administration moved swiftly to resolve the crisis. We must continue to reform the regulation of financial institutions and markets to preserve the soundness of the U.S. financial sector while encouraging innovation and competition.

The Global Economy

The 1980s have underscored the increased importance of global economic events in shaping our lives. We have all been touched by the movements toward political and economic freedom in Eastern Europe. We have been impressed by the rapid growth of market-oriented Asian economies. And we have great expectations for the movement in the European Community toward a single, open market by 1992.

Reductions in trade barriers between nations have raised living standards around the world. Investment has become more globally integrated, as citizens of other countries recognize the great strength and potential of our economy, and as Americans continue to invest abroad. . . .

America will continue to lead the way to a world of free, competitive markets. Increased global competition is an opportunity for the United States and the world, not a threat. But we cannot remain competitive by avoiding competition. My Administration will therefore continue to resist calls for protection and managed trade. To serve the interests of all Americans, we must open markets here and abroad, not close them. I will strongly resist any attempts to hinder the free international flows of investment capital, which have benefited workers and consumers here and abroad. And my Administration will work to reduce existing barriers to international investment throughout the world.

My highest trade policy priority is the successful completion this year of the current Uruguay Round of negotiations, aimed at strengthening and broadening the General Agreement on Tariffs and Trade (GATT). Successful completion of these negotiations will expand the world's gains from free and fair trade and raise living standards in all nations.

Looking Ahead

When I look back on the 1980s, on what the American people have accomplished, it is with pride. And when I look forward to the 1990s, it is with hope and optimism. Our excellent economic health will allow us to build on the successes of the 1980s as we prepare for the next century. Clearly, there is much work to be done. But with the economic principles and policies that I have proposed, I am confident that the United States can enjoy strong, sustainable economic growth and use the fruits of that growth to raise living standards, solve longstanding problems, deal with new challenges, and make the most of new opportunities.

THE ANNUAL REPORT OF THE
COUNCIL OF ECONOMIC ADVISERS

Building on Success

In 1989, the U.S. economy marked its seventh consecutive year of economic growth, the longest peacetime expansion on record and the second longest expansion in U.S. history. The American economy has created more than 20 million new jobs since 1982. The average unemployment rate in 1989 was at its lowest level since 1973 and was lower than in any major European country. America's standard of living, as measured by per capita income, is the highest of any major industrialized country in the world, fully one-third higher than that of West Germany or Japan. In 1989, exports reached an all-time high, and the United States once again became the world's leading exporter. Moreover, unlike any other expansion since World War II, inflation has been contained, laying a solid foundation for continued strong growth in the 1990s.

The successes of the 1980s stand in sharp contrast to economic performance in the 1970s, when inflation soared and unemployment simultaneously increased. In that earlier decade, tax rates climbed for a growing segment of the population. Productivity growth collapsed. Government interference in private markets escalated. The result was an inefficient economy and stagnant living standards. . . .

The Current Expansion and Future Prospects

The economy's performance during 1989 has set the stage for a continuation of the expansion into the 1990s. Adjusting for the rebound in farm production from the 1988 drought, real (inflation-adjusted) gross national product (GNP) rose 1.9 percent during the year, well below the strong pace of 1987 and 1988. Significantly, pressures for increased inflation evident in 1988 were contained. The broadest measure of economy-wide inflation, the GNP fixed-weighted price index, rose by 4.1 percent during 1989, down from 4.5 percent in 1988 and about the same as in 1987.

Continued growth in employment and income in 1989 provided new economic opportunities. A substantially better balance between domestic spending and domestic production was achieved. Growth in government purchases slowed, while net exports and business investment grew more rapidly. Both government and household saving rates rose. These patterns have provided a foundation for sustained strong economic growth.

The Administration's outlook is contingent on implementation of the President's proposals to reduce the Federal budget deficit steadily to zero by fiscal 1993 and to reduce the national debt thereafter. It is also contingent on the Federal Reserve maintaining a credible monetary policy program to support strong noninflationary growth. With these policies, the Administration projects that the U.S. economy will enjoy sustained growth in 1990 at a slightly faster pace than in 1989. Real growth is expected to pick up in the second half of 1990 relative to the first half. In 1991, the economy's growth rate is expected to increase further, as the level of output rises to its full potential; the growth rate is then anticipated to return gradually to its longer run expected potential pace of about 3 percent. Inflation is anticipated to remain close to its 1989 rate in 1990, and then to decline gradually in later years.

The remarkable length of the current expansion, by itself, does not increase the likelihood of an imminent recession. To be sure, occasional episodes of economic contraction will occur in the future. Adverse external events cannot be ruled out, even in the near term. But with the right economic policies in place, expansions in the future can be longer than expansions in the past. The success in containing inflation in this expansion offers an important protection against future recessions. Since World War II, sharp increases in inflation have usually caused policy responses or private sector imbalances that have led to a recession. . . .

Fiscal Policy

The Administration's commitment to the principles of the Gramm-Rudman-Hollings law, clearly demonstrated by the President's actions last fall, constitutes an important step toward a credible and systematic fiscal policy. Moreover, the Administration supports the principle that any supplemental spending increase in the current fiscal year must be offset by decreases in other parts of the budget.

The Administration has proposed a *new rule for fiscal policy* that would extend the Gramm-Rudman-Hollings law by requiring the Federal Government to maintain a balanced non-Social Security budget after 1993. The projected future surpluses in Social Security could not be spent for other purposes but would be devoted to building reserves through a proposed Social Security Integrity and Debt Reduction Fund. This rule would reduce the national debt, free up substantial funds for private capital formation, and increase economic growth. Higher growth would not only protect the integrity of Social Security by increasing the resources available to cope with the retirement of the baby-boom generation, but would also raise national output to meet other private and public needs and wants.

The Administration remains committed to the principles of low marginal tax rates and a broad tax base developed in the Economic Recovery Tax Act of 1981 and the Tax Reform Act of 1986. Steady adherence to these principles reduces tax-induced distortions of private incentives and increases the economy's growth potential.

Monetary Policy

Monetary policy should be designed and credibly committed to sustaining strong economic growth and macroeconomic stability while predictably controlling inflation. Changes in the relationship between the monetary aggregates and the economy have made it difficult to be precise or mechanical in designing monetary policy.

Nevertheless, it is important both to state clearly the basic intentions of monetary policy and to recognize the long-run significance of the monetary aggregates as an anchor for price stability. The Federal Reserve generally increases interest rates when inflationary pressures appear to be rising and lowers interest rates when inflationary pressures are abating and recession appears to be more of a threat. Judgment about such factors as inflationary expectations is of course required to determine the degree of inflationary pressures and the size of the appropriate interest rate response. But, the demonstrated consistency of the Federal Reserve's behavior is evolving into a monetary policy procedure with a considerable degree of credibility. That credibility has been enhanced by the strong record of achievement built in the 1980s. The Administration firmly supports the Federal Reserve's goal of strong noninflationary growth and believes that continued vigilance in controlling inflation is necessary. . . .

Investment and Technology

In order to enhance the economy's long-run health, the Federal Government should aim for a prosperity marked by a high ratio of investment to GNP through policies that reduce obstacles to both saving and investment. U.S. investment in physical capital increased in the 1980s, but it remains low by international standards. . . .

A key item on the Administration's economic agenda, reducing the tax rate on capital gains, will enhance all types of investment. Cutting the capital gains tax rate will lower the cost of investment funds and thus stimulate investment. Much of the reward to entrepreneurial activity, such as generating new technology and bringing it to the market, comes in the form of an increase in the value of businesses. Reducing the capital gains tax rate will thus reward these efforts and encourage invention and innovation.

The Administration has recommended substantial increases in Federal investment in research that has broad relevance and that would be underfunded by the private sector alone. Basic research builds the knowledge base on which technological progress depends and augments the ability of U.S. universities to train the scientists and engineers in whose hands the Nation's technological future rests. In order to enhance incentives for private investment in the Nation's intellectual capital, the Administration also proposes to make permanent the research and experimentation tax credit and will work to remove unnecessary legal and regulatory barriers to innovation.

But the Administration remains strongly opposed to any sort of industrial policy, which would involve second-guessing private investment decisions by selecting particular firms, industries, or commercial technologies for favorable tax treatment or direct subsidies. History provides strong support for the view that private market participants, who have profits and jobs at stake, have sharper incentives and better information than government decisionmakers and, as a consequence, make sounder investment decisions. . . .

National Saving

Business, households, and governments all save at a lower rate in the United States than their counterparts in other advanced economies. Moreover, during the 1980s, the U.S. national saving rate—the sum of what households, businesses, and governments save—was substantially below its average over the previous three decades. A higher rate of national saving will reduce the cost of investment funds to U.S. firms. A lower cost of capital will, in turn, encourage investment, enhance productivity, and spur growth.

The most direct and important step that can be taken to increase U.S. national saving is to reduce the Federal budget deficit. The Administration's new rule for fiscal policy, discussed above, will eliminate the budget deficit and then reduce the national debt. The Administration's program for increasing national saving also includes policies to increase private saving by reducing the tax rate on capital gains and by establishing Family Savings Accounts to encourage saving for pre-retirement objectives. . . .

Investing in America's Future

A major challenge of the 1990s will be to increase the rate at which the productive capacity of the U.S. economy grows. Increasing the rates of growth of productive capacity and living standards will require higher rates of saving and investment. Yet longstanding tax, spending, and regulatory policies impede national saving and investment. Partly, if not entirely, because of these government policies, Americans save and invest a smaller fraction of gross national product (GNP) than their counterparts in other industrialized countries.

The Federal Government cannot, alone, produce dramatic increases in capacity growth. But it can foster an environment conducive to rapid long-term economic growth. *The President is committed to maintaining America's economic leadership, and has thus made it a central element of his economic program to remove impediments to saving, investment, and innovation.* . . .

Technological Progress and Economic Growth

Technological change has played a central role in economic growth. Many famous innovations—in agriculture, textile manufacture, transportation, communications, and electronics—have played an important role in economic growth and have led to a transformation of society over the past two centuries. The combined effect of a host of less visible minor improvements in product designs and production techniques has been equally important. There is a role for government policy in financing technological progress because the full benefits of research are rarely captured solely by the firm or individual undertaking the research. Rather, additional benefits accrue to society as a whole. Because these additional benefits cannot be captured as part of the private-sector return, there is a natural tendency for private markets to do too little research and development from society's broader viewpoint. The Federal Government can offset this tendency through policies to raise national spending on research and development. . . .

The Role of Government

For basic research, the difference between the benefits to society and the returns to those who perform the research is often particularly large. Basic research frequently increases knowledge that has wide application. Because it is usually difficult or inefficient to keep advances in basic research secret, the benefits accrue broadly. Private firms must weigh the costs and risks of a potential investment in basic research against the modest fraction of the total expected social benefit that they generally receive, and thus tend strongly to underinvest in basic research. Moreover, basic research contributes to the strength of universities, which train scientists and engineers for the private sector, as well as for our national defense. *The Federal Government has a key role in supporting basic research.*

Although industry performs about three-quarters of all R&D in the United States, the Federal Government plays an enormous role in science and technology. It provides 47 percent of the funds for R&D, most of which is undertaken by industry and universities. The Federal Government carries out R&D at many facilities, accounting for 11 percent of national R&D spending. It helps to finance the education of scientists and engineers. It protects the intellectual property rights of innovators through the patent system and laws dealing with copyrights, trademarks, and trade secrets. It encourages private innovation through a 20-percent income tax credit for research and experimentation (R&E) and by allowing most R&D expenses to be deducted for tax purposes immediately rather than spread over several years.

Strengthening the U.S. Research Base

The Administration has proposed a broad program of initiatives that will strengthen the Nation's basic research base and enhance private-sector incentives to translate this knowledge into productive innovations.

Improving the Legal Environment. The Administration has advanced important proposals to improve the legal environment for innovation. First, the Administration is aggressively pursuing improved international protection of intellectual property. The current negotiations in the Uruguay Round of the General Agreement on Tariffs and Trade (GATT) are an important forum for developing better international rules. Negotiations on intellectual property rights are also being conducted in the World Intellectual Property Organization and in trilateral talks with the European Community and Japan.

Second, the Administration has proposed reform of product liability laws. The current product liability system, with 50 different State laws, generates excessive litigation, increases the cost of doing business in the United States, and discourages innovation, particularly in the form of new products. The Administration supports the adoption of uniform product liability standards based on three principles of fairness: the right of an innocent person to fair compensation for actual damages; liability based on responsibility for harm and not ability to pay; and encouragement of alternatives to costly litigation. The proposed changes to product liability laws would maintain incentives to produce safe products, but would restore balance to the tort system and reduce uncertainty—particularly for new products.

Third, the Administration supports continued elimination of unwarranted regulation. Deregulation can spur innovation as well as lower prices. New telephone equipment was rapidly introduced after deregulation of the market. Airlines created more efficient route structures after deregulation. Lives are extended and research is accelerated by the expedited approval of drugs for acquired immune deficiency syndrome (AIDS).

Deregulation also requires a continuous reexamination of existing regulatory policies in light of new technologies. Antitrust regulation, in particular, must be sensitive to changes in technology and in international competition. Unnecessary and burdensome regulations must not be allowed to stifle new products and processes.

Restoring the Capital Gains Tax Differential. Although applied research and development have high average rates of return, they are also quite risky. The high cost of capital such risk produces is a particularly onerous burden for new ventures and small businesses, which have only limited access to traditional sources of finance. Much of the return to entrepreneurs and their backers who bring new products to market—particularly through startup ventures—comes through increasing the value of the business. Reducing the tax rate on capital gains will reward those who bring successful ideas to market and will help provide a climate that encourages businesses to invest in new technologies and products.

Because capital gains are taxed only when assets are sold, the current high tax rate discourages the sales of assets and locks in investors. Reducing the tax rate on capital gains will free these investors to search for more productive new investments.

The Administration has proposed restoring a capital gains tax differential such as existed before the Tax Reform Act of 1986. Most major foreign competitors tax long-term capital gains less heavily than ordinary income, if they tax them at all. A lower tax rate on capital gains will encourage entrepreneurs to take risks to advance themselves by creating wealth for others: new firms hiring new workers producing new products for new markets here and abroad. Reducing the capital gains tax rate will encourage innovation and, by increasing investment, hasten the adoption of these innovations. . . .

Policy Toward Saving

The saving performance of the United States reflects, in part, longstanding features of Federal Government policy. Large, persistent Federal budget deficits directly reduce national saving. Many types of personal saving are taxed twice, once when the income is earned and again when the returns on the saving are received. Inflation increases taxable returns to capital without affecting real returns; these extra taxes further penalize saving and investment. For businesses, returns to corporate equity, particularly dividends, are taxed at both the corporate and individual levels. These and other policies need to be reexamined as part of any effort to increase national saving. Current policies are biased toward consumption—whether in the household, business, or government sector—and against saving.

National saving reflects the actions of the three principal sectors of the economy. Household saving is the result of the spending decisions by individuals and families; business saving reflects decisions by firms to retain after-tax profits; and government saving is the outcome of the political debate over revenue measures and spending priorities.

Government policy should focus on national saving. National saving determines the amount of domestic funds available for investment, affects the cost of capital, and influences the balance of trade. Policies toward saving must be analyzed both for each sector of the economy—household, business, government—and for the Nation as a whole. Policymakers must be especially careful not to develop incentives to raise private saving at the expense of public borrowing, thereby simply transferring a portion of the low national saving rate from the private to the public sector.

Government Saving

The single most direct way for the government to increase national saving is to continue to reduce the Federal budget deficit. Some economists argue that reducing Federal deficits would not succeed in raising national saving because private savers would recognize the increased government saving and feel a corresponding reduction in their need to save. In this view, private saving adjusts to offset changes in government saving. This argument is both flawed and inconsistent with the evidence. For example, in the early 1980s, household saving fell even as Federal deficits rose. Because there is no offsetting decrease in private saving, reduced deficits will increase the pool of domestic funds available for private investment. To raise national saving effectively, however, deficit reduction should not be attained by increasing disincentives for private saving or by reducing government investment.

The Gramm-Rudman-Hollings Act was designed to reduce the deficit each year, reaching a balanced budget in 1993. The Administration remains firmly committed to deficit reduction. The Federal Government must end its role as a chronic borrower and stop draining the Nation's scarce savings pool.

Deficit reduction is not enough in view of the likely future demands that the retirement of the baby-boom generation will place on the Social Security system and, indeed, on the whole economy. The Administration proposes to establish a Social Security Integrity and Debt Reduction Fund to safeguard projected surpluses in the Social Security trust funds and to reduce the national debt. Reducing the national debt will increase the pool of domestic saving, reduce the current account deficit, lower the cost of capital, spur investment and productivity growth, and lead to higher future living standards. This proposal would prevent the use of Social Security receipts to finance other spending, reduce the legacy of public debt, and leave a more secure fiscal status to future generations.

Household Saving

Household saving is the most familiar component of national saving. Because the saving decision reflects so many individual goals, however, fostering household saving is a difficult policy task. Households save as a precaution against accident, illness, or loss of job. For these purposes, savings must be sufficiently liquid to meet unexpected needs. Households also save to purchase homes and big-ticket durable goods and to pay future educational expenses. These saving goals are particularly important for young families who have few assets and relatively little financial flexibility. People also save to help finance their retirement and to leave bequests to their heirs. For these long-term goals, security or the rate of return to saving may dominate considerations of liquidity.

The overall household saving rate can change even when all individuals have the same proclivity to save over their lifetimes. One source of change in overall saving is change in the age structure of the population. Because of the baby-boom generation, those under 35 have constituted an unusually large fraction of the working population over the past 15 years. Young people typically save relatively little of their income, which explains part of the overall decline in saving. As the baby-boom generation ages, the household saving rate will rebound somewhat.

The response of household saving to changes in the rate of return on saving is a critical issue, because tax policy directly affects the rate of return. But increases in the rate of return have two opposing effects on saving. Higher rates of return lower the price of future consumption, thus increasing the incentive to save. Higher rates also reduce the amount of saving required to achieve a given level of future consumption, thereby reducing the incentive to save. Although this area is being actively researched and debated, empirical studies on balance suggest that saving increases modestly with higher rates of return.

Several options are available to allow savers to earn the untaxed rate of return for retirement purposes, but such options are not typically available for shorter term saving goals. Pensions, Keogh and 401(k) plans, and, for those eligible, deductible individual retirement accounts (IRAs) all permit individuals to deduct their contributions, with both contributions and earnings taxed only upon withdrawal.

Another form of tax-preferred savings account would not allow deductions for contributions. Withdrawals of both contributions and earnings, however, would be tax free. If a taxpayer is in the same tax bracket at the time of contribution and at withdrawal, such accounts would offer the same rate of return as deductible IRAs. As long as households realize this fact, their spending would be the same under either type of account.

Individual Retirement Accounts. IRAs represent one means to reduce the double taxation of saving and reduce the bias against saving. The degree to which this incentive is successful depends in part upon the limit for contributions to the IRA. Higher contribution limits increase the number of households who receive a saving incentive, because the pre-tax rate of return will apply to their last dollar saved. Higher contribution limits therefore raise private saving.

Deductible IRAs and pensions lower the distortion produced by tax treatment of retirement saving and are a valuable contribution to the climate for saving. Because of penalties for early withdrawal, however, they are not an attractive vehicle for savers with intermediate saving goals. The inaccessibility of savings in IRAs and pensions prior to retirement restricts their usefulness for these purposes. To address this issue, the Administration proposes easing the withdrawal requirements on IRAs to permit savers to use these funds for first-time home purchases.

Family Savings Accounts. To further reduce the bias against saving, especially for families with pre-retirement savings objectives, the Administration proposes creating a Family Savings Account (FSA). Contributions to FSAs would be nondeductible, but earnings on contributions would be exempt from income tax. Annual contributions to an FSA could be up to $5,000 for married couples and $2,500 for single people. FSAs would be limited to married couples with incomes below $120,000, singles with incomes below $60,000, and heads of households with incomes below $100,000. If contributions were held for at least 7 years, both the original contribution and all earnings could be withdrawn without tax. Withdrawals made in the first 3 years would be subject to both ordinary income tax and a 10-percent excise tax on the earnings alone. Earnings included in withdrawals made after 3 years, but before the 7-year period, would be subject to ordinary income tax.

The enhanced liquidity of the FSA provided by the shorter holding period is an important addition to policy toward saving. It is particularly valuable for families who wish to save for such pre-retirement objectives as a child's education or a down payment on a home. Further, the contribution limits are more generous than for existing IRAs. FSAs will increase household saving. Moreover, they are best viewed as part of the larger program to reduce the bias against saving in the United States.

Social Security. The most important Federal Government policy toward retirement is the Social Security program. Its effect on personal saving has been the object of intense study and controversy among economists. Individuals can substitute Social Security for retirement saving. In addition, Social Security reduces the riskiness of retirement consumption because benefits are indexed for inflation and are paid until the death of both the worker and spouse. As such, they are essentially government insurance of a constant base level of consumption. These effects may reduce private saving.

Until recently, Social Security ran on a pay-as-you-go basis, with current workers' payroll taxes paying current retirees' benefits. As a result, no government saving was available to offset any reduction in private saving, suggesting that Social Security reduced national saving. After many studies and opinions, the weight of the evidence suggests that Social Security modestly reduced saving in the postwar period. However, reforms enacted in 1983 will produce substantial government saving in the future. As discussed above, the expected increase in government saving will be an important contribution to national saving, and the Administration has proposed policies to ensure that the integrity of projected future Social Security surpluses is protected.

Business Saving

Corporate saving typically accounts for well over one-half of gross private saving, yet most debate regarding saving—whether among policy-makers, academics, members of the press, or the public at large—focuses on either household saving or government saving. Businesses save out of earnings, by retaining and reinvesting some profits within the business rather than paying them out as dividends or share repurchases. The impact on business saving of a particular policy therefore depends criti-cally on its effects on the level of earnings and on the incentive to pay them out.

By increasing the incentive to retain earnings, a lower capital gains tax rate will increase business saving. For shareholders, the return to retained earnings comes in the form of higher stock prices, which are taxed at the capital gains rate. Therefore, retained earnings are taxed both when the corporate income is earned and again when the gains are received. Lower capital gains tax rates will both reduce the pressure to pay dividends and increase the incentive for equity finance. Both effects increase retained earnings.

Under current law, dividends are also taxed twice, once when the income is earned by the corporation and again when it is paid out to shareholders. Eliminating the double taxation of corporation income—which can be accomplished in a variety of ways—has a theoretically uncertain effect on business saving. It would increase equity finance, but corporations would have a reduced incentive to retain their earnings.

Even if business saving is reduced slightly, however, total private saving might not fall. Eliminating the double taxation of dividends and lowering the tax rate on capital gains would increase the rate of return to household savers. Personal saving may increase in response by enough to offset any decline in business saving. Moreover, shareholders may change their saving in direct response to changes in business saving—they may see through the so-called corporate veil. If corporations save less for their shareholders, the shareholders can compensate by increasing their household saving. The available evidence indicates that a reduction in business saving is indeed offset—at least in part—by an increase in household saving. Shareholders consume only part of the higher payouts.

Share repurchases, takeovers, and leveraged buyouts have increased dramatically in recent years; net equity issues by U.S. nonfinancial corporations have been negative in each year since 1984. The effect of these repurchases on the corporate debt-to-equity ratio has been mitigated by the rise in the market value of equity over the same period. Still, the increasing trend to debt finance makes it more likely that the net effect of removing the tax bias against equity finance would be to increase private saving.

Removing Impediments to Saving

The Administration's proposals are a comprehensive approach to reducing the current policy bias against saving by households, businesses, and government.

- Reducing the Federal budget deficit is the most reliable policy to increase national saving. The Administration proposes to go further, establishing the Social Security Integrity and Debt Reduction Fund and using it to safeguard projected surpluses in the Social Security trust funds, to reduce the national debt, and to help finance increased investment and spur growth.
- Restoring the capital gains tax differential, as proposed by the Administration, will increase saving by both households and businesses.
- Establishing Family Savings Accounts (FSAs) will further reduce the bias against saving. The enhanced liquidity of the FSA is particularly valuable for families who wish to save for such pre-retirement objectives as a child's education or a down payment on a home. . . .

Human Resources in the 1990s

The sustained economic expansion of the 1980s has produced remarkable growth in employment and increased economic opportunity. As the Nation looks ahead to the 1990s, new challenges demand attention. Some have forecast that labor shortages—especially among skilled workers—will dominate the next decade and may limit the potential for economic growth. Based on the experience of past decades, however, the remarkably flexible U.S. labor market should—if left to itself—respond well to these new challenges. But continued growth will require increased labor mobility investment in the skills and knowledge of the work force. . . .

Skills and Education: Investing in Human Resources

A modern growing economy requires an educated and flexible labor force. The median years of schooling acquired by young adults (aged 25 to 29) rose steadily in this country to an historic high in 1976 of 12.9 years. But there has been no increase since then, while the need for a more highly skilled labor force continues to grow. Raising the quality of education in elementary and secondary schools is at least as important as increasing years of schooling. Higher achievement among students of every age will better prepare tomorrow's workers for productive employment. The Federal Government can play an important leadership role in stimulating improvement in the education and training of U.S. workers, but it is important to recognize that the primary responsibility for this task resides in State and local governments and in the private sector.

The Growing Need for Skilled Labor

The demand for more highly educated labor has increased steadily for many decades in the United States.... [T]he share of jobs in occupations requiring greater education has expanded. In 1970, 21 percent of the work force were in white-collar jobs (professional, administrative, managerial, and technical occupations). By 1988, 28 percent of workers held these jobs. Correspondingly, the share of blue-collar jobs (production, craft, operative, labor, and agricultural work) fell from 40 percent to 31 percent. The share of sales, clerical, and service jobs rose slightly, and there was a shift toward more skilled jobs within these categories.

These occupational changes have been closely related to the declining share of employment in traditional manufacturing industries and the rising share in service-producing industries. In contrast to the stereotype of service-sector jobs as low-skilled labor, the growing service sector in general contains a higher percentage of jobs requiring more education. Fully 24 percent of workers in the service-producing sectors of the economy held a college degree in 1980, while only 20 percent had no high school diploma. In contrast, only 11 percent of the workers in the goods-producing sectors held college degrees, while 30 percent had not completed high school.

As the economy continues to shift toward services, the need for skilled labor will continue to rise. The Bureau of Labor Statistics predicts that the fastest employment growth between now and the year 2000 will occur in white-collar occupations, where 57 percent of all workers are college graduates and 97 percent are high school graduates. Blue-collar occupations, where only 5 percent are college graduates and 71 percent are high school graduates, will continue to shrink....

Labor Shortages, Worker Mobility, and Immigration

As the U.S. economy enters the 1990s, concerns are growing about the effects of possible labor shortages on production and wages. Employers in some areas of the country report a shortfall of entry-level workers and are paying wages well above the minimum wage to attract new employees. Other firms report difficulties in hiring suitably trained employees for more skilled positions.

In many cases, limited supplies of workers with particular skills or in particular geographic areas have developed from changes in the labor force, forcing employers to intensify their efforts to attract new workers. In other cases, uneven patterns of economic growth and technological change have altered the skill requirements or location of jobs, resulting in labor shortages for employers in growing areas or industries and job losses among workers whose skills have become obsolete or who find themselves in areas with few job opportunities.

Most of the time the labor market has readily and naturally resolved such imbalances. Employers perceiving a labor shortage have often raised wages to attract workers, encouraging new entry or geographic mobility. Other firms have relocated to areas with a greater supply of available workers, coupled lower hiring standards with remedial and on-the-job training, or targeted nontraditional sources of labor such as older workers and the handicapped. Immigration has also been an important source of new workers in particular industries and occupations.

Labor markets typically do not experience long-run imbalances, but gradually adjust to changes in supply and demand. Governments can help the market to adjust more promptly and efficiently by avoiding or easing regulations that inhibit labor mobility and restrict the use of alternative sources of labor. . . .

Immigration

When labor market mobility is insufficient to eliminate area- or industry-specific labor shortages, employers often turn to immigrants. Throughout U.S. history, economic growth and job opportunities have drawn millions of foreign-born persons to this country, both legally and illegally. Of course, factors influencing immigration include family ties and the freedoms offered by the United States. But whatever their motivation for coming to America, immigrants traditionally have adapted well to the U.S. labor market and have contributed significantly to long-run U.S. economic growth.

Between 1980 and 1988, legal immigration averaged 580,000 persons per year—about one-quarter of 1 percent of the U.S. population. This rate of immigration was above the pace of the 1970s, but well below the average immigration rate prior to 1921, when numerical restrictions on immigration were first introduced. Efforts to control illegal immigration, estimated by the U.S. Census Bureau to have added between 100,000 and 300,000 illegal aliens each year in the first half of the 1980s, led to the Immigration Reform and Control Act of 1986. This act restricted the employment opportunities of illegal aliens by imposing penalties on employers who hired them, but offered legal immigrant status to aliens who were in the United States before 1982.

Do immigrants take jobs that would otherwise go to U.S. workers and depress wages in particular areas and occupations? The many case studies of this question provide no conclusive answer, and disagreement over the existence and magnitude of any effects continues to be widespread. However, one recent study of 120 cities between 1970 and 1980 found that, on average, an increase in the number of immigrants equal to 1 percent of a city's population (more than four times the annual rate of immigration to the United States as a whole) had a negligible effect on the employment status of less-skilled native workers and reduced their wage rates only about 1 percent over that 10-year period.

Moreover, numerous studies suggest that the long-run benefits of immigration greatly exceed any short-run costs. The unskilled jobs taken by immigrants in years past have often complemented the skilled jobs typically filled by the native-born population, increasing employment and income for the population as a whole.

Currently, U.S. immigration policy is based primarily on the humanitarian principles of family reunification and refugee resettlement. Fewer than 10 percent of immigrants in recent years were admitted because of their skills. Less skilled immigrants will clearly continue to be a valuable resource for employers. Yet, with projections of a rising demand for skilled workers in coming years, the Nation can achieve even greater benefits from immigration by augmenting this traditional emphasis on family reunification with policies designed to increase the number of skilled immigrants. Immigrants with more education or training will likely make the greatest contributions to the U.S. economy, suggesting that basic skill levels could be one guide to admitting new immigrants under a skill-based criteria. . . .

Homelessness and Housing. This Administration has proposed expanded funding and new programs to address the problem of homelessness and housing affordability among low-income families. One of the more visible problems in urban areas in the 1980s has been homelessness. Not only is homelessness a social problem, but it is also a barrier to effective participation in the labor market. Reliable estimates of the homeless population are difficult to obtain, and few national estimates have been made. An extensive recent study estimated that 500,000 to 600,000 persons were homeless in the United States over a given week in 1987, while approximately double that number experienced homelessness at some point during that year. As the study acknowledges, however, no one knows exactly how many homeless people there are in the United States.

The homeless population is generally composed of at least three distinguishable groups. First, there are those who have a history of serious mental illness. Although estimates vary, most studies indicate that around one-third of the homeless population are mentally disabled. This group is often the most difficult to reach and the least likely to use temporary shelters and care facilities. Second, homeless families, primarily low-income women and children, constitute about one-quarter of the homeless, and tend to be actually on the streets for the shortest period of time before they enter the public assistance system. The remainder of the homeless are predominantly single men between the ages of 20 and 50. Many of these men work intermittently; some receive food stamps or small payments from State assistance programs; many have ongoing problems with alcohol or other drugs.

Changes in urban housing markets are often cited as an important cause of homelessness, along with the deinstitutionalization of the mentally disabled, drug abuse, spouse abuse, and other problems. Rising rents and land prices and the rejuvenation of downtown areas have displaced low-income populations. The availability of boarding houses and rooms for rent, typically used by poor single adults, has diminished in most cities. In some areas, rent control, restrictive building codes, and zoning regulations also may have decreased the stock of low-income housing.

The President has proposed programs that will provide housing assistance and supportive services to the most troubled homeless individuals as part of his HOPE initiative (discussed below). The Administration also supports full funding of the Stewart B. McKinney Homeless Assistance Act. Passed in 1987, the McKinney Act was the first legislation to authorize major direct Federal expenditures for emergency food, shelter, counseling, and other services for the homeless. For the past 3 fiscal years, the Congress has appropriated less money than it authorized, a situation the Administration seeks to rectify in its proposed 1991 budget.

Homelessness is a serious issue, but housing affordability is the dominant housing problem confronting most poor. It is estimated that more than 40 percent of the poor paid more than one-half of their income for housing in 1985. The Administration continues to emphasize housing vouchers or other tenant subsidies as the most efficient way to address low-income housing needs.

The Administration has also proposed a major new program, Homeownership and Opportunity for People Everywhere (HOPE), to expand housing opportunities for the poor. This proposed legislation includes tax incentives to encourage greater construction and rehabilitation of low-income housing and to encourage savings for down payments; opportunities for residents of federally subsidized housing projects to have more voice over their housing, through tenant management and potential tenant-purchase plans; and 50 Housing Opportunity Zones that would establish Federal-local partnerships in metropolitan jurisdictions to remove barriers to affordable housing. . . .

The Economy and the Environment

Economic prosperity and environmental quality are widely regarded as two of this Nation's most important goals. Some view these as competing goals and argue that economic growth begets environmental degradation. Increasingly, however, this conventional wisdom is being questioned, and a new consensus is emerging that economic growth and environmental quality need not be incompatible. Indeed, economic growth and environmental quality are in many respects complementary. For example, economic growth provides the opportunity for firms to invest in new facilities that are cleaner and more efficient. It is no coincidence that the wealthy societies are the ones that are both willing and able to devote substantial resources to environmental protection.

Compatibility between economic growth and environmental improvement is far from automatic, however; it depends on selection of appropriate goals and careful design of regulatory programs. Environmental goals must balance the associated benefits and costs. The public interest is best served when government provides a framework that creates incentives for the private sector to seek out the most cost-effective way to meet its regulatory goals. Government should not be in the business of picking environmental protection technologies and imposing them on firms, their workers, and their customers. . . .

Global Environmental Issues

Like environmental problems at the local or national level, global environmental problems arise because actions taken 'by one individual have unintended adverse effects on another. Global environmental problems are complicated by the fact that the individuals involved live in many nations. Because one nation cannot impose its wishes on another, international cooperation is required to solve such problems. Differences across countries—in income, natural resource endowments, population, sensitivity to particular environmental changes, and the political strength of environmental movements—mean that countries inevitably have different views on these issues. At the Paris Summit in July 1989, the President joined other heads of state in recognizing the need for cooperation in addressing global environmental concerns. The President has also encouraged international organizations to facilitate international cooperation to solve global environmental problems.

Stratospheric ozone depletion and possible climate change are two global issues that may affect the economy and the environment far into the next century. To evaluate the impact of a policy course chosen today, the impact it will have on the economic well-being of both current and future generations and its environmental impact must be assessed.

Scientific evidence of possible stratospheric ozone depletion is stronger than scientific evidence of possible global warming, although significant uncertainties surround both. There uncertainties extend to environmental and economic as well as scientific aspects of these two issues. Because policymakers must understandably make decisions before information on such issues is complete, the government has an important role to play in supporting basic scientific and economic research that can reduce critical uncertainties in the meantime.

Even when uncertainty cannot be eliminated, identifying a probable range of effects can inform policy choice. For example, a consensus that changes in global climate will lead to at most a small rise in sea level over the next 60 years would make a policy response to protect high-value coastal areas more feasible than if a large rise were expected. Finally, because the regulatory agenda is often influenced by public perceptions that may not accurately reflect available knowledge, the government also has a responsibility to educate the public.

Stratospheric Ozone Depletion

Ozone in the upper layer of the Earth's atmosphere (the stratosphere) provides an essential screen from the Sun's ultraviolet rays. In recent years, evidence has mounted that the stratospheric ozone layer is being depleted. Several chemical compounds, most notably chlorofluorocarbons (CFCs) and bromofluorocarbons (halons) have been identified as sources of the increased atmospheric concentrations of chlorine and bromine that cause ozone depletion. These chemical compounds have long atmospheric lifetimes, so that even if their production were halted immediately, elevated concentrations of chlorine and bromine would persist for decades before subsiding. If production is phased out by 2000, current chlorine concentrations would be likely to increase by 50 percent and then decline slowly to one-half of current levels by 2080. Without any production curtailment, these concentrations would rise indefinitely. . . .

Costs of Protecting the Ozone Layer. Preliminary estimates place the U.S. costs of a phaseout of CFCs and halons by 2000 at $2.7 billion over the next decade if the schedule of intermediate reductions currently incorporated in the Montreal Protocol is maintained. Acceleration of this schedule would drive compliance costs upward significantly. These cost estimates reflect a substitution strategy involving conservation, process changes, and the use of more expensive substitute compounds. The availability of substitutes is critical to avoid economic disruption.

The United States is using transferable allowances to implement the reductions required under the protocol in a cost-effective manner. Manufacturers and importers of CFCs and halons will receive permits in proportion to their base period market shares. As supply is restricted, rising prices will encourage users with available low-cost substitutes to switch, leaving remaining supplies for high-value uses. This approach avoids unnecessary direct regulation of end-use applications, while ensuring compliance with U.S. obligations to reduce production and consumption. Moreover, because there are significant economies of scale in the production of CFCs and halons, the use of permit transfers to concentrate production in a small number of facilities during the phasedown has the potential to increase efficiency on the supply side. Allowing for this kind of flexibility on the international level would yield further cost savings.

Global Climate Change

Greenhouse gases (carbon dioxide, methane, CFCs, and nitrous oxide, among others) absorb heat that radiates from the Earth's surface and send some of the heat downward, warming the climate. Many scientists believe that fossil fuel burning, certain agricultural practices, deforestation, and other human activities that increase the atmospheric concentration of greenhouse gases will alter the global climate. Scientists are much less confident of the magnitude, timing, location, and character of the greenhouse-induced warming. Many argue that no warming has yet occurred despite a substantial increase in greenhouse emissions; some contend that appreciable future warming is unlikely. Others strongly dispute these views.

Computer models of the Earth's climate system are a principal tool of global climate research. Economic models of energy supply and demand provide the future emissions projections used as input by the climate models. Economic models can also be used to assess the cost and growth impacts of policy actions to change the future emissions profile. . . .

CHANCELLOR KOHL'S RESPONSE TO RABBI ON GERMAN UNITY
February 9 and 28, 1990

West German chancellor Helmut Kohl, responding to a letter from an American rabbi on behalf of surviving victims of the Holocaust, insisted that a reunified Germany would not pose new dangers to Jews or to the world. In his reply to Rabbi Marvin Hier, dean of the Simon Wiesenthal Center for Holocaust Studies in Los Angeles, Kohl made perhaps his most extensive remarks about Nazi crimes and the extent of present-day German responsibility since his address September 1, 1989, on the fiftieth anniversary of the beginning of World War II. (Kohl on German Remorse, Historic Documents of 1989, p. 487)

Kohl, the political leader of the drive for reuniting East and West Germany, said he understood the anxiety among survivors of the Nazi era, 1933-1945, but he insisted that the fears of a reunited Germany were misplaced. "The very respect for the untold suffering inflicted on those people [the victims] in the name of Germany and by Germans demands such understanding," he wrote. On the other hand, he suggested that "such anxiety" is rooted in the past and not the present.

In a letter dated February 9 Rabbi Hier wrote the chancellor that the fears were not irrational. "The fears are real," Hier said, "because those who bear the scars of the last 'unified Germany' do not see their concerns being addressed in the current reunification discussions between world leaders."

The rabbi said that "not a single word is said publicly" as to how East Germans, "cut off from the real world for more than forty years," could be educated about the Nazi era "to prevent their ignorance of the past from negatively affecting the course of the future."

The recently deposed Communist regime in East Germany took the position that Communists were the first Germans to oppose Hitler and thus were his first victims. Many of the men who later became East German leaders served time in Nazi prisons. They asserted they had no responsibility for the Holocaust, the murder of some 6 million European Jews and throngs of others in Nazi slave camps.

East Germany's Formal Apology

After East Germany held its first free elections March 18, a new democratic government took office April 12, and the East German Parliament immediately issued a formal apology on behalf of the East German people "for the humiliation, expulsion and murder of Jewish women, men and children." The statement added: "We feel sadness and ashamed as we acknowledge this burden of German history." The statement was approved by the six main factions in Parliament and by a vote of 379 to 0, with 21 abstentions.

The same declaration also conceded East German guilt in helping the Kremlin crush a democratic movement in Czechoslovakia in 1968 and pledged that East Germany had no territorial claims on Poland. As for the Jews of the world, the document asked for their forgiveness. It asked "the people of Israel to forgive us for the hypocrisy and hostility of official East German policies toward Israel and the persecution and degradation of Jewish citizens also after 1945 in our country."

East Germany pledged "to contribute as much as possible to the healing of mental and physical suffering of survivors and to provide just compensation for material losses." An Israeli Foreign Ministry official, Michael Shiro, was quoted as saying that the declaration met Israel's conditions for establishing formal relations with East Germany—a willingness to admit responsibility for the Holocaust and to pay reparations.

In his letter to Rabbi Hier, Chancellor Kohl contended that the East German people, although living under a restrictive regime that ignored the Holocaust, were not isolated from the outside world. "[D]ue to diverse links, especially via television, they had a very clear picture of what was happening in the free part of Germany and in the world," he said. West Germans, Kohl asserted, were instructed about the "causes and consequences" of the Nazi era in schools and universities and by the press and churches. And he expressed "deep disappointment" that many opponents of reunification had not taken note of what had been done in his country.

Had the East Germans actually been cut off from the West, Kohl added, "it would surely be an additional argument" in favor of bringing the two groups together again. He said that unification would result in the educational institutions in the East adopting the curricula of the West. Moreover, having overcome a communist dictatorship, the East Germans were "immune to any new totalitarian temptations," he reasoned.

Germany's Postwar Division

Germany was divided into two political spheres in the aftermath of World War II, roughly along a line where the conquering Soviet and Western allied armies met in the war's final days. Separate republics, the larger Federal Republic of Germany in the west and the smaller German Democratic Republic in the east, formally came into being in 1949—the former linked to the West militarily and economically, and the latter subservient to Moscow until 1989.

Amid other political upheavals instigated by Soviet leader Mikhail S. Gorbachev's new policies, the East German Communist party in 1989 was forced to jettison its top leaders and dismantle physical barriers that long had kept East Germans apart from West Germans. (Berlin Wall and Reunification, Historic Documents of 1989, p. 625)

In the March 18 election, East Germans rejected what remained of the Communist leadership and supported a cluster of conservative parties that endorsed prompt reunification. The new government that took office April 12 was headed by Prime Minister Lothar de Maiziere, whose Democratic Christian Union was the leading party in a six-party "grand coalition." During the three months preceding the election, Kohl campaigned for reunification in East Germany. He did not acknowledge that he had crossed into a separate state or was campaigning in a foreign election. Typically, he was introduced to the campaign crowds not as the chancellor of West Germany but as the "chancellor of our German fatherland." Political analysts in Germany and abroad construed the voting as a mandate for Kohl to proceed rapidly toward merging East Germany's 17 million people into the larger and far more prosperous West German republic.

Josef Joffe, a columnist for the West German newspaper Suddeutsche Zeitung, wrote in the New York Times that "East Germans behaved like any 'normal' democratic electorate: they voted their pocketbook." The message of the conservatives, Joffe wrote, was not so much the nationalistic message "Deutschland über alles [Germany over all]" as "Deutsche mark über alles [German money over all]." The East Germans wanted to share in a prosperity that West Germany had long enjoyed but which had eluded the East under communism.

Return of the German Question

Despite the apparent permanence of the two Germanys during four decades of formal separation, the "German question"—how and when they might rejoin as a single entity—never entirely disappeared. West Germany's first chancellor, Konrad Adenauer, placed reunification at the top of his government's political goals. "It is self-evident," he said in 1956, "that reunification is our great national concern, and our hopes are directed towards its realization." Adenauer's policy was to deny the legality of Germany's postwar division.

In the 1960s Chancellor Willy Brandt shifted West German policy from antagonism to accommodation with East Germany and its Soviet over-seers. In the era of détente between Moscow and Washington, Brandt's government recognized East Germany as a sovereign entity. However, he never formally abandoned the goal of reunification, insisting that East and West Germany were merely "two states within the German nation."

With renewal of Cold War tensions in the 1980s, the German question all but disappeared from view until the very end of the decade. By then the Gorbachev era was in full flower, and the so-called Soviet bloc nations of Eastern Europe—including East Germany—began slipping out of Moscow's orbit.

Unease Among Germany's Allies

The growing prospect of a reunited Germany created mixed reactions in Moscow and Western capitals. Most of West Germany's allies cautiously reaffirmed their commitment to the principle of German self-determination but stopped short of unconditionally endorsing a merger. Poland wanted assurance that a united Germany would not attempt to claim some prewar German territory that had become Polish at the war's end.

The foreign ministers of West Germany, the United States, Britain, France, and the Soviet Union met in Ottawa, Canada, February 13 and agreed on a two-stage unification process. First the two Germanys would discuss the details of a merger and then meet with the other four countries to iron out matters relating to postwar security issues—such as whether a united Germany would remain in the North Atlantic Treaty Organization (NATO) or declare its neutrality.

A Wall Street Journal/NBC News poll conducted early in March indicated that 75 percent of Americans favored German reunification. However, many expressed concern over the economic strength of a bigger Germany. Among the World War II generation and Jewish Americans were fears of a German military resurgence. Jews, in particular, were far more troubled than the general population about reunification.

As expressed by Rabbi Hier in his letter to Chancellor Kohl, the victims of Nazism feared that "the consequences [of reunification] may lead to a weak 'Deutsche memory' "—a German forgetfulness of the past. Hier suggested, among other things, that the study of the Nazi era be required in German schools and become the subject of government-sponsored television and radio programs, that an official agency be set up to monitor hate groups, and that restitution to families of the Nazi victims be made in East Germany as it was in West Germany.

> Following are the texts of the letter from Rabbi Marvin Hier to Chancellor Helmut Kohl of West Germany, dated February 9, 1990, and the chancellor's reply, dated February 28, as made public by the Simon Wiesenthal Center in Los Angeles:

RABBI'S LETTER TO KOHL

Dear Chancellor Kohl:

My concerns are about the dramatic events that are reshaping the world and which have impacted on the body politic as we have known it for the past four decades. I must tell you, I am not among those in the cheering section applauding the rush towards German reunification. However, if that is the inevitable course, let us at least place on record our concerns.

You are undoubtedly aware, Mr. Chancellor, the great fear that German reunification brings to the community of victims of Nazism. It is not an irrational fear or the kind that one explains away as the recurring nightmares of victims who remain locked into their past and lose all perspective of present reality.

The fears are real because those who bear the scars of the last "unified Germany" do not see their concerns being addressed in the current reunification discussions between world leaders. They open their papers each day and read about proposals concerning the demilitarization of armed forces; about the external alliances of the two Germanys; about monetary union and the rate of exchange of the Deutsche Mark.

All very legitimate, but not a single word is said publicly about the great internal questions of how to educate millions of people who have lived under an oppressive regime and have been cut off from the real world for more than forty years and how to prevent their ignorance of the past from negatively affecting the course of the future.

To the victims of Nazism, Mr. Chancellor, it is not the potential weakness of the Deutsche Mark that is critical, but the consequences that may lead to a weak 'Deutsche memory'.

Therefore, I think it appropriate to raise important points that should be discussed candidly and openly in an attempt to reassure those who bear the scars of Nazism that a united Germany will never again heed the call of a dictator.

1) The establishment of a National Education Task Force that would introduce the Holocaust as a subject of high priority in German textbooks so that school-children would gain a first-hand knowledge of the truth of the Third Reich. This would ensure that East German children would understand the events and learn the lessons of the Holocaust.

2) The establishment of a Federal agency to monitor hate groups similar to the U.S. Drug Enforcement Agency empowered to analyze and collect data from all hate groups and to prosecute vigorously those who violate the law (a similar Bill calling for such national monitoring of hate crimes just passed the U.S. Senate). Such a national agency would be free from local and intra-provincial politics.

3) The continuation of the special relationship with the State of Israel

and the establishment of close cultural and educational contacts, particularly in East Germany where contact between the people in East Germany and the State of Israel was forbidden.

4) The convening in 1992, on the 50th anniversary of the Wannsee Conference [of Nazi leaders who planned a systematic extermination of Jews], of a government-sponsored conference to which world leaders would be invited to discuss the lessons and implications of the Wannsee Conference.

5) The establishment of a government commission to prevent the future de-Judaization of Nazi concentration camps and other Holocaust sites in East Germany, particularly Ravensbruck and Buchenwald, and to explore the possibilities of building a major museum and learning center attached to those sites that would depict the horrors of Nazism and become a major resource for East German citizens.

6) The banning of terrorist organizations whose avowed views are dismantlement and destruction of the State of Israel. Such organizations have enjoyed respectability in East Germany.

7) The organizing of a cultural exchange program between the government of Germany and Jewish organizations around the world to promote exhibitions, exchange of artists and musicians, particularly in the areas where such contacts have been forbidden in the past.

8) A government commitment to undertake the sponsorship of special television and radio programs on the subject of memory and reconciliation.

9) The negotiating and completion of a protocol of 'Veidergutmachung', restitution payments to the families of the victims of Nazism similar to the program established by West Germany immediately after the Second World War.

10) A government commitment to revitalize former synagogues and Jewish centers of learning throughout the territory of East Germany.

Mr. Chancellor, an open and candid discussion of these points on all levels of German society, while not allaying all the fears, would, at least, show the world that the architects of the German reunification movement are sensitive to the lessons of history.

As the Soviet poet Yevtushenko said in a recent poem, "... one cannot be a half guard with the cardinal, and simultaneously half a king's musketeer. There is no semi-fatherland, nor can we fathom semi-conscience; half freedom is the trek to jail, and saving our fatherland halfway would fail."

I look forward to your response to these suggestions and the possibility of meeting with you in Washington.

Cordially,

Rabbi Marvin Hier

KOHL'S LETTER TO RABBI

Dear Rabbi Hier,

First of all, I would like to stress that I understand the anxiety expressed by some victims of the National Socialist [Nazi] dictatorship in view of the prospect of German unity. The very respect for the untold suffering inflicted on those people in the name of Germany and by Germans demands such understanding.

On the other hand, it needs to be asked whether such anxiety is essentially justified, whether its roots lie not only in the past but also in the present. In this respect, our views evidently differ.

I cannot conceal my deep disappointment at how little many opponents of German unity take note of the fact that for decades now especially the young generation in the free part of Germany has been informed without any taboos of the causes and consequences of the National Socialist tyranny: in schools, universities, church or other educational institutions and the media.

It has probably also escaped your notice that in our Penal Code precisely those "crimes of hatred" whose combating you recommend to me are punishable with fines or prison sentences. In this connection I need only mention the dissemination of propaganda of anti-constitutional organizations, instigation of the people, incitement to racial hatred or defamation of National Socialist victims, especially by denial of the Holocaust.

To my mind there is no doubt that these provisions will also apply in a united Germany; this certainly does not require any special demand!

Such means of suppression are of course not sufficient on their own. Relentless political measures to combat right-wing extremism as well as the intensive public information campaign will be continued; this, too, does not require any special demand.

The vast majority of young people in Germany are fully aware of the inestimable value of a free democracy. Together with their peers in France, Britain or Italy, in Poland, Czechoslovakia or Hungary, they already regard themselves as equal citizens of a united Europe founded on freedom, human rights and self-determination. They deserve our sympathy and encouragement, not our distrust and discouragement.

Your anxiety appears to rest in part on the assumption that the people in the GDR [German Democratic Republic—East Germany], unlike their fellow-countrymen in the Federal Republic of Germany [West Germany], have until now not been given any opportunity to learn from the past. That is not correct, but even it were true, it would surely be an additional argument in favour of the Germans coming together at last in common freedom! After all, the unification of the two states will also result in the syllabuses for schools, universities and other educational institutions in the present-day GDR being adapted to the standards prevailing in the Federal Republic.

The Germans in the GDR do not seek unity for reasons of chauvinism, but because they want to live in peace and freedom together with their compatriots in the Federal Republic of Germany. By peaceful means they have overcome a dictatorship which ignored their fundamental rights and which, by invoking an allegedly "anti-fascist" ideology, sought to impress on them a distorted view of history.

The people in the GDR have had enough of this. They feel they were lied to and cheated. Often risking considerable disadvantages for themselves, they fought against the lack of freedom and truth. To my mind this makes them especially immune to any new totalitarian temptations. The same applies to the Poles, Hungarians, Czechs or Slovaks. We who have for a long time been fortunate enough to live in freedom and prosperity can take the courage of those people and nations as an example. As a German and European I take pride in what happened in the Eastern part of our continent in 1989.

All peace-loving people in the world welcomed that development as a victory of the ideals embodied in, for example, the American Declaration of Independence of 1776 and the American Constitution of 1787. I would therefore have expected you to express in your letter at least some words of joy at the fact that, after decades of repression by a dictatorship imposed on them, 16 million Germans at last secured their freedom. This alone is a manifestation of their democratic maturity.

Furthermore, throughout that lengthy period the people in the GDR were by no means isolated from the rest of the world, as you assert, being evidently unaware of the actual conditions in Germany. In fact, due to diverse links, especially via television, they had a very clear picture of what was happening in the free part of Germany and in the world.

To me, learning from the historical experiences of this century also means not repeating the mistake of forcing the Germans into psychological isolation. This would be but grist to the mill of right-wing extremists. Wise, responsible and far-sighted men and women in the United States, Israel and other countries fully realized why they reached their hand out to the Germans in the Federal Republic after 1945 and invited them to participate actively in building a community of free nations—here I have in mind above all the European Community and the Atlantic Alliance.

President George Bush fully follows that splendid tradition, and I am deeply indebted to him for this. Only recently such an eminent figure as Lord Weidenfeld pronounced himself in the same spirit. The recent remarks made by Simon Wiesenthal on the German Question were also particularly prudent and helpful.

The majority of Germans in East and West are today well aware that they can secure a common future in peace, freedom and prosperity only if they are firmly anchored in the Western community of values. Ever since I have been a politician I have combated those who advocate that Germany go it alone and follow separate chauvinistic paths. This entitles me to warn against any tendencies today to exclude the Germans as a whole as equal partners from the community of free nations.

It is high time for the positive things that have happened in Germany since 1945 to be discussed more intensively in the United States. I feel that an alarming lack of information exists in this respect. For example, do you realize that the Federal Republic of Germany has for decades maintained particularly close and good relations with the state of Israel and has for years been the only one of the twelve members of the European Community to stand up actively and without restriction for Israel's interests as regards its existence, freedom and security? One should tell the truth always and everywhere—in this I concur with you. But it must be the whole truth, and not just parts of it.

A copy of this letter is being sent to Simon Wiesenthal.

Yours sincerely,

Helmut Kohl

DRUG SUMMIT AGREEMENTS
AT CARTAGENA, COLOMBIA
February 15, 1990

President George Bush met February 15 with the presidents of Bolivia, Colombia, and Peru in Cartagena, Colombia, and joined them in signing a pact pledging a united attack on illegal drugs. The three South American countries, the principal suppliers of cocaine to the U.S. market, had come under U.S. pressure to clamp down on the illicit trade. They, in turn, insisted they needed American military and economic aid to control drug trafficking and to entice farmers to switch from growing coca—the raw material for cocaine—to other crops.

The "drug summit" sought to address those issues in a main document, the Declaration of Cartagena, signed by all four leaders—presidents Bush, Virgilio Barco Vargas of Colombia, Jaime Paz Zamora of Bolivia, and Alan Garcia Perez of Colombia—and in separate agreements between the United States and each of the other countries. "The multilateral agreement we have just signed opened a new era in this struggle against drugs," the host president, Barco Vargas declared at a news conference attended by the four leaders immediately after their day-long meeting. "It is the first time that we developed a common scheme for common action," Barco added.

In a separate meeting with news reporters later that day, President Bush expressed a similar thought. "[W]e've committed ourselves to the first common comprehensive international drug control strategy," he said. "We in fact created the first anti-drug cartel." He alluded to an international cartel of drug lords who operated with relative impunity in and around the Colombian city of Medellin, and conducted terrorist campaigns against their enemies throughout the country.

A spate of assassinations and bombings threatened to undermine the Colombian government during the summer of 1989. Among the murder victims was Luis Carlos Galan, the expected leading candidate in the 1990 presidential election. Within hours of Galan's death, President Barco Vargas ordered a crackdown on the drug lords. They fought back with more killings and bombings in Colombia's major cities.

Colombia's Appeals for Help

In September, the Colombian president appeared before the United Nations General Assembly in New York and appealed to the world community for assistance. (Bush's Drug-War Speech, Colombian Leader's UN Appeal, Historic Documents of 1989, p. 499) Bush had already ordered that U.S. military equipment be sent to Colombian soldiers and police involved in the "drug war," and later he asked Congress to consider authorizing a large, long-term plan of economic and military aid for the three countries.

By early in 1990, Barco's fight against the Medellin drug cartel was showing signs of success. The drug lords, in an apparent plea for leniency, sent the government a message saying it had won the war. That message followed a statement by President Barco Vargas saying that he was "not inflexible" in his opposition to a negotiated settlement. However, the drug war appeared far from over.

Although terrorism had abated, the four leaders met amid heavy security in the Naval Academy of Cartagena. Thousands of Colombian soldiers guarded the city's streets and the airport 60 miles away at Barranquilla, where Bush landed and transferred from his official jetliner to a fleet of U.S. Marine Corps helicopters. They flew to the conference site at treetop level and conducted a series of high-speed maneuvers to foil any possible attack. Colombian and U.S. warships patrolled offshore while U.S. counterterrorist units and underwater "frogmen" guarded land and sea approaches to the naval academy.

U.S. Military Force and Money

The summit statements steered clear of the controversial issue of how U.S. military forces might be used to deter drug smuggling off the South American coasts. However, the presence of two U.S. warships near Colombia during the summit and the deployment of AWACS radar planes to Puerto Rico then and in subsequent weeks led to speculation that U.S. military interdiction efforts were being stepped up. According to a Pentagon official, by March, 40 percent of AWACS operations worldwide were being devoted to anti-drug operations.

More significant, according to participants and observers, was the summit's emphasis on the equal role the four nations shared in fighting the drug crisis. The Andean leaders and many members of Congress had said Bush placed too much importance on interdiction and law enforcement and not enough on treatment and prevention in the United States. In a key communiqué from the conference, Bush agreed that it was "clear that to be fully effective, supply reduction efforts must be accompanied by significant reductions in demand."

At the meeting, Bush did not go beyond his proposals to give the three nations $2.2 billion in military and economic assistance over the next five years. The budget he sent Congress in January requested fiscal assistance of $423 million in fiscal year 1991, up from $217 million in 1990. That request included a sixfold increase in economic aid, to $209 million, but it was still less than what the three nations sought.

Peruvian president Garcia Perez, nevertheless, praised the agreement for what he called a change in "basic tactics" from "a military, a police concept" to "an economic and social issue." Even critics of the administration's anti-drug policies praised Bush's efforts to work out a joint strategy with the South American leaders. "Just his going [to the conference] is a tremendous success and an invaluable contribution to improving our relationship with those countries," said Charles B. Rangel, D-N.Y., chairman of the House Select Committee on Narcotics Abuse and Control. "These countries are economic basket cases," Rangel added. "If you really eliminated the coca trade in Bolivia and Peru, those two countries would go under." In testimony before the Senate Judiciary Committee on January 18, Bolivia's ambassador to the United States, Jorge Crespo-Velasco, said that 40,000 workers in his country were involved in the coca-cocaine industry and that coca was the nation's most important crop.

Global production of opium poppies, coca, marijuana, and hashish soared in 1989, according to a report released by the State Department March 1. The report attributed part of the increase to the fact that "corruption undermined enforcement efforts, and a number of governments still failed to exhibit a serious commitment to reducing drug production and trafficking." Worldwide drug abuse also increased substantially, the department said, as higher yields pushed drug traffickers to aggressively seek out new markets.

Following are the text of the Declaration of Cartagena, signed February 15, 1990, in Cartagena, Colombia, by the presidents of Bolivia, Colombia, Peru, and the United States, committing these countries to a united attack on illicit drugs; and White House Fact Sheets on separate U.S. agreements with Bolivia, Colombia, and Peru:

DECLARATION OF CARTAGENA

The Parties [to the agreement] consider that a strategy which commits the Parties to implement or strengthen a comprehensive, intensified anti-narcotics program must address the issues of demand reduction, consumption and supply. Such a strategy also must include understandings regarding economic cooperation, alternative development, encouragement of trade and investment, as well as understandings on attacking the traffic in illicit drugs, and on diplomatic and public diplomacy initiatives.

The Parties recognize that these areas are interconnected and self-reinforcing. Progress in one area will help achieve progress in others. Failure in any of them will jeopardize progress in the others. The order in which they are addressed in the document is not meant to assign to them any particular priority.

Economic cooperation and international initiatives cannot be effective unless there are concomitant, dynamic programs attacking the production of, trafficking in and demand for illicit drugs. It is clear that to be fully effective, supply reduction efforts must be accompanied by significant reduction in demand. The Parties recognize that the exchange of information on demand control programs will benefit their countries.

The Parties recognize that the nature and impact of the traffic in and interdiction of illicit drugs varies in each of the three Andean countries [Bolivia, Colombia, and Peru] and cannot be addressed fully in this document. The Parties will negotiate bilateral and multilateral agreements, consistent with their anti-narcotics efforts, specifying their responsibilities and commitments with regard to economic cooperation and intensified enforcement actions.

Understandings Regarding Economic Aspects and Alternative Development

The Parties recognize that trafficking in illicit drugs has a negative long-term impact on their economies. In some of the Parties, profits from coca production and trade from illicit drug trafficking contribute, in varying degrees, to the entry of foreign exchange and to the generation of employment and income. Suppression of coca production and trade will result in significant, immediate, and long-term economic costs that will affect, in various ways, each of the Andean countries.

The President of the United States will request Congress to authorize new funds for the program during fiscal years 1991 to 1994, in order to support the Andean Parties' efforts to counteract the short- and long-term socio-economic impact of an effective fight against illicit drugs. This contribution by the United States would be made within the framework of actions against drug trafficking carried out by the Andean Parties. The Andean Parties reiterate the importance of implementing or strengthening sound economic policies for the effective utilization of such a contribution. The United States is also prepared to cooperate with the Andean Parties in a wide range of initiatives for development, trade and investment in order to strengthen and sustain long-term economic growth.

Alternative development, designed to replace the coca economy in Peru and Bolivia and illicit drug trafficking in all the Andean Parties, includes the following areas of cooperation. In the short term, there is a need to create and/or to strengthen social emergency programs and balance of payments support to mitigate the social and economic costs stemming from substitution. In the medium and long term, investment programs and measures will be needed to create the economic conditions for definitive substitution of the coca economy in those countries where it exists or of that sector of the economy affected by narcotics trafficking. It is necessary to implement programs to preserve the ecological balance.

Alternative Development and Crop Substitution

In order to foster increased employment and income opportunities throughout the entire productive system and implement or enhance a sound economic policy to sustain long-term growth, the United States will support measures aimed at stimulating broad-based rural development, promoting non-traditional exports, and building or reinforcing productive infrastructure. The Parties, in accordance with the respective policies of Bolivia, Colombia, Peru and the United States, shall determine the economic assistance required to ensure sound economic policies and sustain alternative development and crop substitution, which in the medium term will help replace the income, employment and foreign exchange in the countries in which these have been generated by the illegal coca economy. The United States is prepared to finance economic activities of this kind with new and concessional resources.

In order to achieve a complete program of alternative development and crop substitution, the Parties agree that in addition to the cooperation provided by the United States, economic cooperation, as well as greater incentives to investment and foreign trade from other sources, will be needed. The Parties will make concerted efforts to obtain the support of multilateral and other economic institutions for these programs, as the three Andean Parties implement or continue sound economic policies and effective programs against drugs.

The Parties are convinced that a comprehensive fight against illicit drug traffic will disrupt the market for coca and coca derivatives and will reduce their prices. As success is achieved in this fight, those employed in growing coca and in its primary processing will seek alternative sources of income either by crop substitution or by changing jobs. The Parties will work together to identify alternative-income activities for external financing. The United States is ready to consider financing of activities such as research, extension, credit and other agricultural support services and support of private-sector initiatives for the creation of micro-enterprises and agro-industries.

The United States will also cooperate with the Andean Parties to promote viable domestic and foreign markets to sell the products generated by alternative development and crop substitution programs.

Mitigation of the Social and Economic Impact of the Fight Against Illicit Drug Trafficking

As the Andean Parties implement or continue to develop effective programs of interdiction of the flow of illicit drugs and of crop eradication, they will need assistance of the fast disbursement type to mitigate both small- and large-scale social and economic costs. The Parties will cooperate to identify the type of assistance required. The United States is prepared to provide balance of payments support to help meet foreign exchange needs. The United States will also consider funding for emergency social programs, such as the successful one in Bolivia, to provide employment and other opportunities to the poor directly affected by the fight against illicit drugs.

Trade Initiatives, Incentives to Exports and Private Foreign Investment

An increase in trade and private investment is essential to facilitate sustained economic growth and to help offset the economic dislocations resulting from any effective program against illicit drugs. The Parties will work together to increase trade among the three Andean countries and the United States, effectively facilitating access to the United States market and strengthening export promotion, including identification, development and marketing of new export products. The United States will also consider providing appropriate technical and financial assistance to help Andean agricultural products comply with the admission requirements.

The Parties may consider the establishment of economic and investment policies, as well as legislation and regulations to foster private investment. Where favorable conditions exist, the United States will facilitate private investment in the three Andean countries, taking into account the particular conditions and potential of each.

Understandings Regarding Attacking Illicit Drugs

The Parties reaffirm their will to fight drug trafficking in a comprehensive manner attacking all facets of the trade: production, transportation and consumption. Such comprehensive action includes the following:

- Preventive actions to reduce consumption and therefore demand.
- Control and law enforcement activities against illegal cultivation, processing, and marketing of illicit drugs.
- Control of essential chemicals for the production of illegal drugs and the means used for their transport.
- Seizure, forfeiture, and sharing of illegal proceeds and property used in committing narcotics-related crimes.
- Coordination of law enforcement agencies, the military, prosecutors and courts, within the framework of national sovereignty of each of the Parties.
- Actions to bring about a net reduction in the illegal cultivation of coca.

The Parties undertake to engage in an ongoing evaluation of their cooperation, so that the President of the United States, as appropriate, may request Congress to provide additional assistance to the Andean Parties.

Given that the Parties act within a framework of respect for human rights, they reaffirm that nothing would do more to undermine the war on drugs than disregard for human rights by participants in the effort.

Prevention and Demand

The Parties undertake to support development and expansion of programs on comprehensive prevention, such as preventive public education in both rural and urban areas, treatment of drug addicts, and information to encourage the public opposition to illegal drug production, trade and consumption. These programs are fundamental if the drug problem is to be successfully confronted.

The Parties recognize that prevention efforts in the four countries will benefit from shared information about successful prevention programs and from bilateral and multilateral cooperation agreements to expand efforts in this field.

To this end, the Parties undertake to contribute economic, material and technical resources to support such comprehensive prevention programs.

Interdiction

A battle against an illicit product must focus on the demand for, production of and trade in that product. Interdiction of illegal drugs, as they move from producer to consumer, is essential. The Parties pledge to step up efforts within their own countries to interdict illegal drugs and to increase coordination and cooperation among them to facilitate this fight. The United States is ready to provide increased cooperation in equipment and training to the law enforcement bodies of the Andean Parties.

Involvement of the Armed Forces of the Respective Countries

The control of illegal trafficking in drugs is essentially a law enforcement matter. However, because of its magnitude and the different aspects involved, and in keeping with the sovereign interest of each State and its own judicial system, the armed forces in each of the countries, within their own territory and national jurisdictions, may also participate. The Parties may establish bilateral and multilateral understandings for cooperation in accordance with their interests, needs and priorities.

Information Sharing and Intelligence Cooperation

The Parties commit themselves to a greater exchange of information and intelligence in order to strengthen action by the competent agencies. The Parties will pursue bilateral and multilateral understandings on information and intelligence cooperation, consistent with their national interests and priorities.

Eradication and Discouragement of Illicit Crops

Eradication can play an essential part in the anti-drug fight of each country. In each case, eradication programs have to be carefully crafted, measuring their possible effect on total illicit drug production in each country; their cost-benefit ratio relative to other means of fighting illicit drugs; whether they can be most effective as voluntary or compulsory programs or a combination of the two; and their probable political and social consequences.

The Parties recognize that to eradicate illicit crops, the participation of the growers themselves is desirable, adopting measures that will help them obtain legal sources of income.

New economic opportunities, such as programs for alternative development and crop substitution, shall be fostered to help to dissuade growers from initiating or expanding illegal cultivation. Our goal is a sustained reduction in the total area under illegal cultivation.

Eradication programs must safeguard human health and preserve the ecosystem.

Control of Financial Assets

The Parties agree to identify, trace, freeze, seize, and apply other legal procedures for the disposition of drug crime proceeds in their respective countries, and to attack financial aspects of the illicit drug trade. In accordance with their respective laws, each of the Parties will seek to adopt measures to define, catagorize, and criminalize money laundering, as well as to increase efforts to implement current legislation. The Parties agree to establish formulas providing exception to banking secrecy.

Forfeiture and Sharing of Illegal Drug Proceeds

The Parties pledge to implement a system for forfeiture and sharing of illegal drug profits and assets, and to establish effective programs in this area.

In United States cases related to forfeiture of property of illegal drug traffickers where Bolivia, Colombia, and Peru provide assistance to the United States Government, the Government of the United States pledges to transfer to the assisting government such forfeited property, to the extent consistent with United States' laws and regulations. The Parties will also seek asset sharing agreements for Bolivia, Colombia, and Peru, with other countries.

Control of Essential Chemicals Used in the Production of Illicit Drugs

The control in the United States of the export of chemical substances used in the processing of cocaine is vital. In addition, there is a need for greater control of the import and domestic production of such substances by the Andean Parties. Joint efforts must be coordinated to eliminate the illicit trade in such substances.

The Parties agree:

- to step up interdiction of the movements of essential chemicals that have already entered the country, legally or illegally, and are being diverted for illegal drug processing. This includes controlling choke points as well as establishing investigative and monitoring programs in close cooperation with all the Parties' law enforcement agencies.

- to further develop an internal system to track essential chemicals through sale, resale and distribution to the end user.
- to cooperate bilaterally and multilaterally to provide each other with information necessary to track domestic and international movements of essential chemicals for the purpose of controlling their sale and use.
- to support the efforts under the Organization of American States (OAS) auspices to develop and implement a regional inter-American agreement on essential chemicals.

Control of Weapons, Planes, Ships, Explosives and Communications Equipment Used in Illegal Drug Trafficking

Illicit drug trafficking is heavily dependent on weapons, explosives, communications equipment, and air, maritime and riverine transportation throughout the illicit cultivation and the production and distribution process.

The Parties agree:

- to strengthen controls over the movement of illegal weapons and explosives and over the sale, resale and registration of aircraft and maritime vessels in their respective countries, which should be carried out by their own authorities.

The Parties agree to establish within their own territory control programs that include:

- the registration of ships and aircraft;
- the adoption of legal standards that permit effective forfeiture of aircraft and vessels;
- controls on pilot licenses and training;
- registration of airfields in their respective countries;
- development of control measures over communications equipment used in illegal drug trafficking to the extent permitted by their respective laws and national interests.

The United States agrees to work with the Andean Parties to stem weapons exports from the United States to illegal drug traffickers in the three Andean nations.

Legal Cooperation

The Parties pledge to cooperate in the sharing of instrumental evidence in forms admissible by their judicial proceedings. The Parties also agree to seek mechanisms that permit the exchange of information on legislation and judicial decisions in order to optimize legal proceedings against the traffic in illicit drugs.

The Parties recognize the value of international cooperation in strengthening the administration of justice, including the protection of judges, judicial personnel, and other individuals who take part in these proceedings.

123

Understandings Regarding Diplomatic Initiatives and Public Opinion

The scourge of illicit drug trafficking and consumption respects no borders, threatens national security, and erodes the economic and social structures of our nations. It is essential to adopt and carry out a comprehensive strategy to promote full awareness of the destructive effects of illegal production, illicit trafficking and the improper consumption of drugs....

Strengthening Public Opinion in Favor of Intensifying the Fight Against Illegal Drug Trafficking

Public awareness should be enhanced also by means of active and determined diplomatic action. The parties pledge to strengthen plans for joint programs leading to the exchange of ideas, experiences, and specialists in the field. The Parties call upon the international community to intensify a program of public information stressing the danger of drug trafficking in all of its phases. In this regard, the Parties undertake to give active support to Inter-American public awareness and demand reduction programs, and will support the development of a drug prevention education plan at the Inter-American meeting in Quito this year.

Economic Summit

The 1989 Economic Summit in Paris established a Financial Action Task Force to determine how governments could promote cooperation and effective action against the laundering of money gained through illegal drug trafficking.

The United States will host the next Economic Summit on July 9-11, 1990, in Houston. The United States will use this opportunity to seek full attention on a priority basis to the fight against illegal drug trafficking.

The Parties call upon the Economic Summit member countries, and on the other participants in the Financial Action Task Force, to give greater emphasis to the study of economic measures which may help to reduce drug trafficking. In particular, the Parties call upon the Economic Summit countries to take the steps necessary to ensure that assets seized from illicit drug trafficking in Bolivia, Colombia and Peru are used to finance programs of interdiction, alternative development and prevention in our countries.

Multilateral Approaches and Coordination

The Parties intend to coordinate their actions in multilateral economic institutions in order to ensure for Bolivia, Colombia and Peru, broader economic cooperation within the framework of a sound economic policy.

Report to the UN Special Session on Illicit Trafficking in Drugs

The United Nations has recognized that the problem of drug trafficking presents a grave threat to the security of the states and economic stability.

It has called for a Global Action Plan and it has convened a Special Session, February 20-23, 1990, to discuss the magnitude of this problem. This will be a proper occasion to reiterate the need to bring into force as quickly as possible the UN Convention Against Illicit Traffic in Narcotic Drugs and Psychotropic Substances, which provides for energetic measures against illegal drug trafficking, while recognizing the ancestral and traditional uses of coca leaf.

The Parties request that consideration be given during the Special Session to the inclusion of the cooperative efforts outlined in this document to develop concrete programs for strengthening multilateral responses to the drug problem, as recommended in Resolution No. 44/141 of the United Nations General Assembly.

Report to the OAS Meeting of Ministers and CICAD

The Organization of American States has called an Inter-American meeting of Ministers responsible for national narcotics programs, to be held on April 17-20, 1990 in Ixtapa, Mexico. The parties urge that the meeting of Ministers and the Inter-American Drug Abuse Control Commission (CICAD) give priority to the understandings set forth in this document and lend support to their early implementation within the context of regional cooperation against drugs.

Madrid Trilateral Meeting

The Parties stress the importance of the document issued by the Trilateral Meeting in Madrid and the efforts undertaken in Europe, particularly the participation of the European Community, with a view to adopting specific policies and initiatives against illicit trafficking of drugs.

World Ministerial Summit to Reduce Demand for Drugs and to Combat the Cocaine Threat

The Parties note with satisfaction the convening of a World Ministerial Summit to Reduce Demand for Drugs and to Combat the Cocaine Threat, to be held on April 9-11, 1990 in London. This meeting will serve to highlight the role demand reduction must play in the international community's efforts to reduce the trade in illicit drugs and will underline the social, economic and human costs of the trade. The Parties agree to coordinate their action and future strategies in this area. . . .

Demarches to Transit Countries

Through specialized agencies of the United Nations such as the Heads of National Law Enforcement Agencies, our countries participate in important coordination efforts. The Parties undertake to strengthen cooperation with transit countries on interdiction of traffic in illicit drugs.

World Conference Against Illicit Drug Trafficking

In order to progress towards the goals agreed upon at the Cartagena Summit, the Parties call for a world conference in 1991 to strengthen international cooperation in the elimination of improper consumption, illegal trafficking and production of drugs.

Follow-Up Meeting to the Cartagena Summit

In order to follow up on progress of agreements arising under the foregoing understandings, the Parties agree to hold a high level follow-up meeting within a period of not more than six months.

WHITE HOUSE FACT SHEET ON THE BOLIVIA-UNITED STATES ESSENTIAL CHEMICALS AGREEMENT

The U.S. and Bolivia signed a bilateral agreement on essential chemicals today. William J. Bennett, Director of the Office of National Drug Control Policy, signed on behalf of the United States, and Minister of Foreign Affairs Carlos Iturralde signed on behalf of Bolivia.

The agreement:

- specifies certain information to be collected by the parties and provides for information sharing, mutual cooperation, and the coordination of investigative and enforcement efforts with respect to essential chemicals;
- requires parties to promptly investigate the intended consignee or destination to confirm that the essential chemicals will be used solely for legitimate purposes;
- requires the enactment of domestic legislation, where necessary, to implement the agreement, including the ability to seize illicit shipments of essential chemicals;
- obligates the parties to invite key nations and international organizations to join these efforts and to support them fully;
- is consistent with and complements the Organization of American States' proposed Inter-American Drug Abuse Control (CICAD) agreement on precursor and other chemicals.

The agreement complements existing U.S. legislation and should provide us with additional tools to control movement and usage of those chemicals key to the processing of illicit drugs.

The Declaration of Cartagena reaffirms the need to enhance cooperation in the areas of monitoring, investigation, and enforcement with respect to illicit shipments of essential chemicals. . . .

WHITE HOUSE FACT SHEET ON THE PERU-UNITED STATES EXTRADITION AGREEMENT

The United States and Peru signed an exchange of notes on extradition today. Secretary of State James A. Baker III signed on behalf of the

United States. Guillermo Larco Cox, Prime Minister and Foreign Minister, signed on behalf of Peru.

This exchange of notes will:

- confirm our bilateral commitment to extradition;
- confirm explicitly that narcotics trafficking and related drug offenses are incorporated by reference in the 1899 United States-Peru Extradition Treaty.

This agreement represents the mutual desire of our countries to try to enhance effective law enforcement cooperation and to recognize the importance of the return of fugitives to stand trial as part of this effort.

The exchange of notes should lead to further discussions between the two Governments with respect to extradition and the return of fugitives generally.

WHITE HOUSE FACT SHEET ON THE BOLIVIA- AND PERU-UNITED STATES PUBLIC AWARENESS MEASURES MEMORANDUMS OF UNDERSTANDING

The United States signed two bilateral public awareness measures memorandums of understanding today in Cartagena, one with Bolivia and one with Peru. Secretary of State James A. Baker III signed both agreements on behalf of the United States. Minister of Foreign Affairs Carlos Iturralde signed on behalf of Bolivia. Guillermo Larco Cox, Prime Minister and Foreign Minister, signed on behalf of Peru.

These understandings will promote concrete measures reflecting the Declaration of Cartagena's emphasis on the need to raise public awareness and support for the measures we need to take to combat drug trafficking and consumption by:

- encouraging collaboration on initiatives to build public support for countering narcotics production, distribution, and use;
- recognizing that cross-fertilization of ideas, experience, and activities is essential to the success of counternarcotics efforts;
- encouraging parties to establish and share the International Narcotics Information Network (ININ), a computerized data base, so that antidrug activities can be made easily obtainable to those needing this information;
- promoting joint cosponsorship of mass media projects that promote the sharing of information about drug problems and solutions in the four countries.

The United States is discussing the possibility of similar understandings with other countries.

WHITE HOUSE FACT SHEET ON THE PERU-UNITED STATES TAX INFORMATION EXCHANGE AGREEMENT

The United States and Peru signed a tax information exchange agreement (TIEA) today. Secretary of State James A. Baker III signed on behalf of the United States. Guillermo Larco Cox, Prime Minister and Foreign Minister, signed on behalf of Peru.

This agreement will:

- permit the exchange of tax records, bank statements, and other information in order to uncover illicit drug profits, trace drug money-laundering, and generally to further civil and criminal tax investigations;
- encourage prosecution for tax evasion as an effective way to put drug dealers behind bars;
- improve tax compliance, through exchanges of technical know-how, development of new audit techniques, identification of new areas of noncompliance, and joint studies of noncompliance areas.

The agreement is responsive on a bilateral basis to the pledge in the Declaration of Cartagena to tighten monitoring of financial transactions. We are discussing similar arrangements with other countries.

WHITE HOUSE FACT SHEET ON THE BOLIVIA-UNITED STATES WEAPONS EXPORT CONTROL MEMORANDUM OF UNDERSTANDING

The United States and Bolivia signed a weapons export control memorandum of understanding today. Secretary of State James A. Baker III signed on behalf of the United States. Minister of Foreign Affairs Carlos Iturralde signed on behalf of Bolivia.

The memorandum of understanding will help diminish the flow of U.S. light arms and other items to drug traffickers in the Andean countries by providing a framework for:

- the Department of State's Office of Munitions Control to condition issuance of a U.S. firearms export license upon the presentation of an import certificate validated by the importing government;
- subsequent discussions that will specify the weapons and other items to be covered by the understanding.

The U.S. Government is also working domestically to suppress the flow of smuggled arms, which are an important part of the narcotics trafficking problem. We are pursuing discussions with other governments also concerned about limiting the flow of U.S. weapons to illegitimate end users in the Andean countries.

HUMAN RIGHTS REPORTS
February 21 and July 10, 1990

"The year 1989 may very well go down in history books as a watershed year regarding the worldwide cause of human rights." In those words the State Department introduced its latest annual analysis of human rights conditions around the world. The volume, "Country Reports on Human Rights Practices for 1989," was submitted to Congress—as required by law—and publicly released February 21, 1990.

"Revolutionary changes in Bulgaria, Czechoslovakia, the German Democratic Republic [East Germany], and Romania left Albania as the only totalitarian regime left intact in Europe by year's end," the State Department authors wrote. They added that those events in what were once known as Soviet satellite countries "tended to overshadow remarkable steps" taken by the Soviet Union itself in the direction of an open society. Examining the human rights situation in 169 countries, they concluded that "the positive trends are unmistakable, making the setbacks all the more stark."

Among the setbacks were China's bloody suppression of student-led protests in June 1989, and recurrences of civil strife and religious or ethnic violence on every continent—in Northern Ireland, Israeli-occupied territories, Sri Lanka, Colombia, and El Salvador, to name but a few of the troubled places. (China's Protest and Repression, Historic Documents of 1989, p. 275)

Amnesty International, in issuing its "1990 Report" on July 10, said: "Thousands of people were imprisoned, tortured and killed in 1989 by governments seeking to repress or control ethnic and nationalist tensions in their country." Many of those tensions, it added, were "rooted in the movement and dislocation of people in the past: the mass migrations of people fleeing oppression or seeking economic survival, and the redrawing of national borders by colonial powers or in the aftermath of wars. The result is that many of today's nation-states encompass different population groups, each with an identity and a history of its own."

In Eastern Europe, not all changes were benign. As Soviet controls were loosened, old ethnic enmities flared up. Smoldering hatreds sometimes turned to violence in minority Hungarian communities in Romania and in ethnic Turkish communities in Bulgaria. Czechoslovakia's new president, Vaclav Havel, endured a storm of protest for apologizing to a German minority in Czechoslovakia who were dispossessed of their homes and property in the aftermath of World War II. In Yugoslavia, out from under Moscow's control since 1948 but still under Communist rule, unrest continued in the Kosovo province where repeated crackdowns by the central government on ethnic Albanians drew charges of gross human rights violations.

Middle East Violence

The State Department's monitoring of the Palestinian uprising in the West Bank and Gaza recorded more violent deaths there in 1989 than in 1988. The department's report said: "The human rights situation in the occupied territories remains a source of deep concern to the United States." According to the report, 432 Palestinians were killed in the conflict, 304 of them by Israeli security forces and settlers, and 128 by other Palestinians. Thirteen Israeli soldiers and civilians were killed by Palestinians during the year.

The Israeli government criticized the document for accusing its security forces of abusing Arab human rights—causing avoidable deaths and injuries in the occupied territories, deporting Arab residents, destroying property, and using firearms excessively. Moshe Raviv, a deputy director general at the Foreign Ministry in Jerusalem, said the report failed to show that "everything we are doing arises from Arab violence." But another Israeli official, Brig. Gen. Amnon Strashnov, the chief military prosecutor, said he accepted most of the facts in the report. Amnesty International, in its report, said "thousands of Palestinians were beaten while in the hands of Israeli forces or were tortured or ill-treated in detention centres."

Both the State Department and Amnesty International painted a grim picture of conditions in nearby Iraq. "Iraq's human rights record remained abysmal in 1989," the State Department said. "Effective opposition to government policy [of President Saddam Hussein] is stifled; the intelligence services engage in extensive surveillance and utilize ... torture and summary execution to deal with antiregime activities." Amnesty International said that not only did torture of political prisoners remain widespread but thousands of persons had "disappeared" and presumably had been killed.

The State Department also deplored the state of human rights in Syria. *Middle East Watch,* an independent human rights monitoring group, said in a special report it issued September 13 on Syria: "... [T]he United States government regularly expresses concern over human rights violations in Syria. When it comes to action, however, the U.S. record has been abysmal." The *Middle East Watch* report, "Human Rights in Syria," accused Syrian president Hafez Assad and his government of carrying on a systematic campaign of terrorism—including killings and torture—against his political opponents. "Under a longtime state of emergency," the report said, "security forces routinely arrest citizens without charges, torture them during interrogation and imprison them without trial for political reasons." The report contended that the government killed at least 10,000 people in the early 1980s.

"If the past forty years are anything to go by," it said, "little can be expected from Washington in the event of any future human rights outrage by the Assad regime, and perhaps less than ever following the warming of relations produced by shared hostility to Saddam Hussein." The report was issued five days before Secretary of State James A. Baker III called on Assad in Damascus. The visit was interpreted as an effort to coordinate U.S. and Syrian pressure on Hussein to withdraw from Kuwait. (Iraqi Invasion of Kuwait, p. 533)

Hope for South Africa and Mexico

For South Africa, the scene of human rights violations on a massive scale over the years, both reporting organizations expressed cautious hope for improvement under President F. W. de Klerk, who took office in 1989. He relaxed several controls on racial separation, released some political prisoners, and opened formal discussions with some of the country's black leaders. However, the State Department noted that "the main legislative pillars of apartheid remained in place in 1989." The suppression of human rights, sometimes with violence, had not disappeared. (De Klerk and Mandela on South African Changes, p. 65)

Similarly in Mexico, a new government brought hope that an improvement in human rights conditions would follow. Soon after President Salinas de Gortari assumed office in December 1988 he announced the creation of a Directorate of Human Rights in the Interior Ministry and issued the first in a series of pardons for certain prisoners who had been detained for "socially and politically motivated offenses." But much was still left undone, the Amnesty International report made clear. The State Department noted that paramilitary bands and local police controlled by political bosses and landlords were often accused of oppressing and even murdering Mexican peasant activists.

Following are excerpts from Amnesty International's "1990 Report," issued July 10, 1990, for the year 1989; and from the State Department's "Country Reports on Human Rights Practices for 1989," publicly released February 21, 1990:

AMNESTY INTERNATIONAL

Introduction

Thousands of people were imprisoned, tortured and killed in 1989 by governments seeking to repress or control ethnic and nationalist tensions in their country. The repressive measures have, in many cases, served to entrench bitter conflicts, dimmed prospects for dialogue and added to the toll of suffering and death. . . .

Many of the world's ethnic and nationalist tensions are rooted in the movement and dislocation of people in the past: the mass migrations of people fleeing oppression or seeking economic survival, and the redrawing of national borders by colonial powers or in the aftermath of wars. The result is that many of today's nation-states encompass different population groups, each with an identity and a history of its own. . . .

In Somalia, gross human rights violations have occurred against a background of clan-related tensions. The Somali National Movement (SNM), whose membership is mainly from one northern clan, has been fighting the government since 1980. Members of the clan—the Issaq—have been targeted for arrest, torture and extrajudicial execution either in reprisal for SNM activities or on suspicion of having links with the organization. Many Issaq areas, including the northern capital of Hargeisa, have been devastated by intensified fighting since 1988. Hundreds of thousands of people have fled to Ethiopia and Djibouti to seek refuge from reprisals by the Somali army, which is dominated by other clans. Many Issaqs have been imprisoned for criticizing the government's policies towards the north or for simply being Issaq. Most were released in a general amnesty declared in early 1989 but further arrests took place later in the year. Some 46 prisoners in Mogadishu, all of them Issaq and including children, were massacred by soldiers in July. A rebellion by Ogadeni clan members in the army led to similar reprisals against Ogadeni in the southwest in late 1989. In addition, Somalis living in neighboring Kenya were also targeted for arbitrary arrest by the Kenyan authorities in late 1989 on account of their ethnic origin.

In Ethiopia, there has been armed opposition in several parts of the country for the past three decades by groups fighting for territorial independence or against the central government on the basis of regional or ethnic identity. Many people from these areas, particularly those from Eritrea, Tigray, Wollega and Hararghe, have been imprisoned and often tortured on suspicion of having links with the Eritrean People's Liberation Front or other Eritrean groups, the Tigray People's Liberation Front or the Oromo Liberation Front. Some have been adopted as prisoners of conscience as they were imprisoned for their regional or ethnic origin and not for any proven advocacy of armed opposition. Several were released in 1989 after many years in detention without trial, but others remained in prison.

In Sudan, members of ethnic groups from the south have been tortured and killed by members of the armed forces and government-backed militias. The government has responded to the activities of the Sudan People's Liberation Army (SPLA), which draws most of its support from southern ethnic groups, by supporting several tribal militias from other ethnic groups loyal to the government. After a lull in mid-1989 due to a cease-fire, killings of villagers by government soldiers and militia increased in October, while government officials continued to dismiss raids on civilians as "tribal fighting". Members of the Dinka, Nuber, Nuer and Shilluk communities, displaced by fighting in the south, have been victims of gross human rights violations solely because of their ethnic origin. In July, three weeks after a new military government took power, at least 34 Dinka and Luo people were killed by soldiers in the southern town of Wau, apparently as a reprisal after a soldier was injured. Southerners living in the north have also been targeted. In October soldiers reportedly took some 42 Dinka and Nuba people from police custody in Khartoum and extrajudicially executed them. Troops and militias have extrajudicially executed thousands of men, women and children from Dinka and other non-Arab ethnic groups since the outbreak of civil war in 1983.

In Sri Lanka, reports of "disappearances", extrajudicial executions, arbitrary arrests and torture escalated in the 1980s against a background of an armed Tamil secessionist movement based in the northeast. Human rights violations continued in the northeast after July 1987 when Indian forces took over responsibility for security in the area. In the south, opposition to the government increased among the majority Sinhalese following the Indo-Sri Lanka accord, and since mid-1987 a militant Sinhalese group has engaged in extensive killings of civilians. New legislation and special emergency powers adopted in the early 1980s to combat Tamil secessionist movements have been used since 1987 against the Sinhalese militants in the south, where Sri Lankan security forces have committed widespread human rights violations. The legislation allows long-term incommunicado detention without charge or trial and throughout 1989 provided for security forces to dispose of bodies without post-mortem or inquest, facilitating extrajudicial executions by enabling security forces to kill with effective impunity. In 1989 thousands of people were reported to have "disappeared" following arrest or to have been extrajudicially executed by the regular Sri Lankan security forces or paramilitary forces believed to be associated with them.

In the state of Punjab in India, hundreds of non-combatant Sikh civilians have been victims of human rights abuses since armed conflict between Sikh groups and government forces escalated in 1984. "Encounter killings"—deliberate extrajudicial executions in so-called confrontations staged by the police—have continued to be reported in the region. Elderly people and children have been among those subjected to arbitrary arrest, particularly in the Batala District, in apparent attempts by the authorities to intimidate the population. Government forces have also beaten village elders in public and women have been raped by the police. Civilian detainees have been tortured by police and paramilitary forces. Most reports of torture have been received from the three western districts bordering Pakistan. Several Sikhs have "disappeared" from detention.

In Myanmar (formerly Burma), army units on counter-insurgency duties have executed and tortured indigenous peasants in remote and mountainous areas where armed opposition groups are active. The peasants living in areas controlled by the insurgents, and the members of the principal insurgent groups themselves, are not ethnic Bamans (Burmans); they are members of a variety of ethnic groups such as the Kayin, Shan and Mon. The opposition groups have been waging a guerrilla war against the central government since the country gained independence from the United Kingdom (UK) in 1948.

Since 1975, when Indonesian forces invaded East Timor and claimed it as Indonesia's 27th province, there have been repeated reports of serious human rights violations against the East Timorese, who are predominantly of Malay and Melanesian origin. In 1989, despite a heavily publicized "opening" of the island to tourism and commerce, reports of unfair trials, torture in police and military custody, political killings and "disappearances'" continued to emerge.

In the UK [United Kingdom], armed groups from both the minority Catholic and majority Protestant communities in Northern Ireland have continued to resort to violence in support of their demands. In attempting to deal with perpetrators of politically motivated violent acts, the UK Government has failed to allay public concern that its agents have operated outside the rule of law. A series of fatal shootings by security forces has given rise to serious allegations of an official policy allowing suspected members of armed groups, mainly the Catholic-based Irish Republican Army (IRA), to be deliberately killed rather than arrested. The official procedures for investigating such killings have failed to clarify fully the facts of these cases, and the government has rejected calls for an independent judicial inquiry. In two separate cases involving bomb attacks carried out in 1974 by the IRA in England, people were sentenced to life imprisonment mainly or solely on the basis of uncorroborated confessions which the prisoners claimed had been obtained through threats and ill-treatment while they were held incommunicado. The "Guildford Four", convicted in 1975 for bomb attacks, were released in October 1989 after new evidence emerged that the police had lied to the courts about the confession statements. The "Birmingham Six", convicted in 1975 for bomb attacks, remained in prison at the end of the year.

But even in countries where movements have expressed nationalist or ethnic aspirations using mainly peaceful methods, people have been subjected to human rights abuses.

In the USSR, for example, there was a dramatic upsurge of unrest and political organization among national groups in 1989. In some cases the Soviet authorities responded with the forcible dispersal of non-violent demonstrations, the banning of meetings and the arrest of organizers, who were then held for up to several months before being released. Such incidents were reported in Armenia, Azerbaidzhan, Byelorussia and Moldavia. In April, 20 people died when special troops broke up a peaceful demonstration in the Georgian capital Tbilisi. Around 3,000 were said to have been injured, most by the effects of gas. In October an unarmed crowd of about 1,000 people in the western Ukraine was charged repeatedly by police and special troops, who allegedly beat and kicked children and adults indiscriminately. The crowd was protesting against police disruption of a folk festival. Several dozen of the injured needed hospital treatment.

In Yugoslavia, troops were sent into Kosovo province in February 1989 in response to a general strike by ethnic Albanians who were protesting against constitutional changes limiting the province's autonomy. Clashes led to at least 24 deaths, and several hundred ethnic Albanians were administratively detained for up to four months without charge or trial. Many later alleged that they had been savagely beaten while held incommunicado. Over 1,000 others were summarily sentenced to up to two months' imprisonment; others were held for trial on charges of "counter-revolutionary activities".

In China, demonstrations by Tibetans demanding independence were broken up in March 1989 by Chinese troops and martial law was imposed in the Tibetan capital Lhasa. Tens of Tibetan demonstrators were believed to have been shot dead during the violent confrontations and more than 1,000 were subsequently arrested. There were many reports of Tibetans being tortured in detention, including severe beating, electric shocks and suspension by the arms for long periods.

If tensions between different groups degenerate into intercommunal violence, the duty of the authorities is to keep the peace. All too often, however, governments themselves abandon the rule of law and instead of maintaining order, resort to trampling on the human rights of a section of their citizens.

In Burundi, tension between the ruling minority Tutsi and the Hutu, who make up 80 percent of the population, erupted into intercommunal fighting in mid-1988 with many Tutsi killed by Hutu. Thousands of unarmed Hutu were subsequently massacred by the Tutsi-dominated armed forces. By the end of 1989 the massacres had not been investigated and more than 40 Hutu arrested in mid-1988 had not been brought to trial.

Intercommunal violence was also the context for government security forces committing human rights abuses in Mauritania. In the wake of disturbances between Senegalese and Mauritanians in April 1989, which led to hundreds of deaths in Mauritanian and Senegalese cities, thousands of black Mauritanians were expelled to neighbouring Senegal. In the process of these expulsions, the predominantly Beïdane (Arabic-speaking) Mauritanian police and army arbitrarily detained, tortured or killed many black Mauritanians. The Mauritanian Government rejected Amnesty International's concern about these abuses and accused the organization of taking Senegal's side.

In several countries, it has been stated official policy to deprive certain ethnic or national groups of their civil and political rights. The most extreme example of this has been the *apartheid* system in South Africa, where the Constitution itself has denied the black majority population political rights and the state has persistently abused its powers to maintain a society based on racial inequality. Widespread opposition to *apartheid* has been met by emergency powers, first introduced on a nationwide scale in June 1986 and renewed annually since then. These have been used to detain many thousands of government opponents without charge or trial. Prisoners have frequently been ill-treated in detention and hundreds of political opponents of the government have been placed under restriction orders, sometimes including house arrest. Judicial death sentences have been imposed disproportionately on the black population by an almost entirely white judiciary: 97 percent of the 1,070 people hanged in the country between 1980 and 1988 were black. In 1989 at least 60 people were executed; two of them were white.

Populations living under occupation by a foreign power are particularly liable to human rights abuses. In addition to the existence of human rights standards, there is a separate body of international law designed specifically to regulate the conduct of occupying powers. However, as has been shown in the Israeli-Occupied Territories, governments do not always respect these standards and laws.

Israel occupied the West Bank and Gaza Strip—areas populated by Palestinian Arabs—in 1967. In the two years since December 1987, when an uprising against the occupation and in support of an independent Palestinian state began, hundreds of Palestinians have been killed by Israeli forces, including possible victims of extrajudicial executions and some who may have died as a result of torture. Thousands have been beaten and about 9,000 have been administratively detained without charge or trial.

Ethnic minorities or national groups have faced varying degrees of human rights abuses in other parts of the world. In Chad, members of the Hadjeraï ethnic group have been persecuted. More than 180 Hadjeraïs were believed to have been held in secret detention since mid-1987: reportedly many of them have been tortured and some may have died. At least 200 members of the Zaghawa ethnic group were detained after April 1989. Many of those held were arrested arbitrarily because of their ethnic origin.

Kurds have faced extreme and widespread human rights violations. The Kurds were denied a state of their own by the European colonial powers after the break-up of the Ottoman Empire in the 1920s. The territory heavily populated by Kurds is now divided between Iraq, Iran, Turkey, Syria and the USSR.

In Iraq, Kurds have been systematically subjected to human rights abuses. In 1988 Kurdish towns and villages were attacked from the air with chemical weapons and bombs and whole communities were rounded up and shot. Tens of thousands of Kurds fled the country. Members of Kurdish opposition groups were among thousands of political prisoners, including possible prisoners of conscience, who remained in detention throughout 1989 without charge or trial, or after summary trials. They were also among those reportedly tortured while in detention. Of the thousands of detainees who had "disappeared" in previous years, 8,000 Barzani Kurds remained unaccounted for. Information was received in October 1989 of the "disappearance" of 353 Kurds after their arrest in 1988 in Duhok Province following chemical weapons attacks in the area by Iraqi Government forces. The majority were civilians, mainly farmers, and included 52 children. In the same month, reports were received about the "disappearance" of several Kurds from Bahark resettlement camp outside Arbil city. In addition, seven Kurds who gave themselves up to the authorities after an amnesty had been declared in February were executed in April 1989.

In Iran, hundreds of members of opposition groups fighting for Kurdish autonomy have been among thousands of political prisoners subjected to unfair trials, torture and execution since the 1979 revolution. In a wave of secret executions that began in August 1988 and continued until January 1989, over 2,000 political prisoners were executed. Among the victims were members of Kurdish opposition parties.

In Turkey, the government's policy has been to deny the existence of Kurds as an ethnic minority. It has also refused them the right to pursue their own culture. Several thousand members of Kurdish organizations have been imprisoned, among them many prisoners of conscience. One was sentenced in 1988 to seven years' imprisonment for speaking in Kurdish when defending himself in court. Kurds have also figured prominently in reports of torture in Turkish police stations and jails, in accounts of unfair political trials, and in lists of prisoners on death row.

In neighbouring Bulgaria, the pattern was similar, although the target was the Turkish minority. Until December the government denied Turks their ethnic identity and forbade the use of the Turkish language. Hundreds of ethnic Turks were imprisoned or banished for resisting the policy, and large numbers remained in prison in 1989. In May 1989 security forces killed several ethnic Turks during and after peaceful demonstrations protesting the assimilation campaign. Others died as a result of beatings, which were reportedly widespread and indiscriminate.

Suppression of cultural rights has also led to widespread abuses in Guatemala. When a council of indigenous communities was set up in 1988 to campaign for the rights of Indian communities, the people involved quickly became the target of death threats, "disappearances" and extrajudicial executions. Overwhelming evidence linked members of the official security forces with the abuses, acting either in uniform or clandestinely in the guise of "death squads". In April 1989 uniformed soldiers seized four men from their homes apparently because of their membership of the council. Their whereabouts were unknown at the end of 1989.

In several countries, ethnic groups are treated as less than equal and their rights as more expendable than those of others. Neither law enforcement agencies nor the judicial system give them adequate protection under the law.

In Brazil, many members of indigenous communities—Indians—have been killed trying to defend their land and communities from incursions by ranchers and mining and timber companies, often with the acquiescence or collusion of local governmental authorities. Indians are theoretically offered greater protection under the law than peasants, but in practice, as with peasants, the authorities have persistently failed to guarantee their legal rights or adequately investigate violent assaults on them and bring those responsible to justice. No progress had been made in bringing to trial non-Indian settlers accused of ambushing and killing 14 members of the Ticuna tribe in 1988. Several Yanomami men, women and children have been killed by miners since the incursion into their lands began in 1986. Ill-treatment by military police of Indians, such as the Macuxi in Roraima and Ticuna in Amazonas state, has also been reported.

A pattern of abuse of members of underprivileged groups also continued in India, where many victims of torture were members of tribal communities or scheduled castes (known as "harijans" or, formerly, "untouchables"). Although India's Constitution gives these people special protection, in practice they are particularly vulnerable to ill-treatment at the hands of the police. For example, many victims of torture and rape in police custody belong to these communities, particularly in the state of Bihar. In early 1989, 20 members of the Pardhi tribal community were held for several weeks in Maharashtra in unacknowledged detention. As in other cases, a local magistrate refused to hear their complaints of torture and one of them died in custody. Over 50 people died in police custody in India in 1989 in suspicious circumstances: a similar figure to that recorded in previous years. Most were poor and many were members of such underprivileged groups. Relatives and others alleged that they had been tortured to death. Those responsible were not known to have been brought to justice.

In 1989 Amnesty International campaigned against the death penalty and executions throughout the world. This terrible and final punishment tends to be inflicted mostly on the vulnerable members of a society— including members of racial or ethnic minorities. In the United States of America, evidence suggested that the death penalty continued to be used in a racially biased manner, with death sentences being more often imposed in cases where the murder victim was white.

It is not Amnesty International's role to take a position on the difficult and vexed questions of national independence, regional and cultural autonomy, and territorial integrity, nor does it take sides in any of the complex disputes which form the background to the human suffering described in this report. The organization sees its role as constantly reminding governments and public opinion that there are international standards set for the protection of human rights which all governments are bound to observe, irrespective of the circumstances. Where governments or government-like bodies fail to respect these standards, Amnesty International will do all that it can to bring the human rights violations to world attention and to prevent further abuses from occurring.

Mexico

... The new administration of President Salinas de Gortari, who assumed office in December 1988, embarked on a series of measures with the stated intention of "modernizing" the country. Some of these related to human rights. In February President Salinas announced the first in a series of pardons for certain prisoners detained for "socially and politically motivated offences" as a step towards "national reconciliation".... By November several hundred prisoners had been released, many of them indigenous people thought to have been arrested in the context of land disputes, as well as other long-term prisoners held for politically motivated offences.

In February a Directorate of Human Rights was set up within the Interior Ministry. One of its main functions was to receive complaints of human rights abuses. The head of the Directorate, Luis Ortíz Monasterio, stated that cases of detainees alleged to have "disappeared" in the 1970s and early 1980s would be "analysed on a case-by-case basis, in an attempt to resolve the matter to the satisfaction of all parties involved". He and several other officials—including a state attorney general—acknowledged that torture occurred although they denied that it was deliberate policy. They criticized the use of initial statements taken by police as the "queen of proofs" (compelling evidence) against suspects because of the risk that it may have been obtained through coercion. In November torture was made a state crime in Chihuahua, punishable with between two and 10 years' imprisonment. Local bishops and other human rights activists had reported numerous cases of torture in the state, and by the end of the year several police agents had been detained and accused of killing two men in September and October allegedly through torture. ...

In April the Attorney General's Office of the Federal District asked the courts to issue arrest warrants against five judicial police agents accused of causing the death in custody of Octavio Hernández Pérez the same month. Reports indicated that he had died as a result of blows to the head and other parts of the body. The outcome of the investigations into his death was not known. The head of the Federal District Judicial Police acknowledged initially that the police "went too far" during the interrogation.

In May the president of the Mexican Bar Association called on the judicial police in Mexico state to end the use of torture and the practice of holding detainees incommunicado. The Attorney General of the Republic was reported as saying in September that an investigation would be carried out into the ill-treatment of detainees and that anyone found responsible would be brought to justice.

Although the authorities promised to investigate cases of "disappearances" from the 1970s and early 1980s, no progress was reported by the end of the year....

Reports of killings, mostly in the context of land disputes, were received from the states of Michoacán, Puebla, Oaxaca, Veracruz, Hidalgo, Chiapas and Chihuahua. ..

In a few other cases investigations into killings led to the imprisonment of those allegedly responsible, although most cases remained unclarified. . . .

Amnesty International welcomed the new measures taken by the government concerning the release of prisoners and the announcement that "disappearances" would be investigated on a case by case basis, but continued to press for information about the outcome of the investigations. . . . In October a response was received from the Foreign Ministry informing Amnesty International of steps taken by the government regarding human rights and stating its intention to respond at a later date to the specific issues raised in the letter.

South Africa

P. W. Botha resigned as State President and was replaced in July by F. W. de Klerk. The National Party was returned to power in September with a reduced majority following a general election, from which the majority black population was excluded. The election took place in the face of a defiance campaign organized by the Mass Democratic Movement (MDM), a broad coalition of anti-*apartheid* groups. During the campaign the number of arrests and allegations of police brutality increased.

The newly elected administration relaxed controls on demonstrations and released eight long-term political prisoners, including Walter Sisulu, former Secretary-General of the banned African National Congress (ANC). These government measures coincided with a reduction in violent activities by the ANC. However, the high level of violence continued in Natal between supporters of Chief Gatsha Buthelezi's Inkatha movement, a conservative KwaZulu "homeland"-based organization, and supporters of the United Democratic Front (UDF), a broad coalition of anti-*apartheid* organizations. . . .

At the beginning of the year, at least 1,000 critics and opponents of the government were held without charge or trial under the emergency regulations. Many prisoners of conscience were among them, including the leading UDF member Mutile Henry Fazzie and his wife, Ethesia Buyiswa Fazzie. Like many others, the couple had been held continuously since 1986. Most of these detainees were released in the first half of the year following a wave of hunger-strikes by emergency detainees protesting their continued imprisonment. Mutile Henry Fazzie and Ethesia Buyiswa Fazzie were among those released in May. . . .

Political detainees held without trial were reportedly tortured, although official restrictions on media coverage of detention and prison conditions obscured the extent to which torture occurred. In March a witness at an inquest in the case of Caiphus Nyoka, a student leader who died in 1987 after being shot by police during his arrest, described being tortured by police at Daveytown police station. Exodus Guguletu Nyakane, who was with Caiphus Nyoka when the police arrested him at Caiphus Nyoka's home, said he had been shut in a locker containing tear-gas, been partially suffocated with a cloth, had boiling water poured down his back and been given electric shocks. The inquest court rejected his testimony. It also ruled that the police, who had shot Caiphus Nyoka nine times after bursting into the bedroom where he was sleeping, had acted in self-defence and were not criminally liable for his death. The police told the court that they had believed Caiphus Nyoka to be armed. No substantial evidence was produced in court to support this claim. . . .

The death penalty continued to be used extensively, although the number of executions declined significantly from previous years. At least 60 people were hanged at Pretoria Central Prison. An unknown number of executions were also carried out in the nominally independent "homelands". In October the authorities in the Transkei "homeland" announced a moratorium on executions, pending consideration of abolishing the death penalty.

In May, 14 of the 26 defendants tried in connection with a politically motivated killing at Upington were sentenced to death. Like 12 people sentenced to death in June in connection with a similar case in Ciskei, the defendants were convicted and sentenced on the basis of the "common purpose" doctrine. This maintains that people present at the time of a killing may be considered culpable even without proof of their direct participation in the crime. Appeals were pending in both cases at the end of 1989. . . .

United Kingdom

Armed groups from both the minority Catholic and the majority Protestant communities in Northern Ireland continued to resort to violence in support of their demands. Republican armed groups such as the IRA are opposed to the British presence in Northern Ireland and fight for a united Ireland. Members of security forces, loyalist leaders and civilians have been killed as a result of IRA attacks, mainly in Northern Ireland but also in England and continental Europe. Loyalist armed groups, notably the Ulster Volunteer Force (UVF) and the Ulster Freedom Fighters, want Northern Ireland to remain a part of the UK. Their acts of violence are mainly directed against the Catholic population. It was reported that during 1989, 54 people were killed by the IRA, 19 by loyalist groups, and four by the security forces.

The government continued to derogate from those articles of the European Convention on Human Rights and the International Covenant on Civil and Political Rights which state that anyone arrested has the right to be brought promptly before a judge. This right was violated in cases where people had been arrested under the Prevention of Terrorism Act, which allows suspects to be held for up to seven days without judicial supervision.

In September the Police Complaints Authority (PCA) brought disciplinary charges against the senior police officer who led inquiries into disturbances at London's Broadwater Farm estate in 1985. The *in camera* disciplinary hearing had not taken place by the end of the year. The charges followed an investigation supervised by the PCA into complaints about police behaviour during the interrogation of juveniles charged with the murder of a police officer who was killed during the riot. The PCA stated that it would not make public the findings of its investigation.

Four prisoners sentenced to life imprisonment in 1975 for IRA pub bombings in Guildford and Woolwich, known as the "Guildford Four", were released in October. The Court of Appeal quashed their convictions after it was shown that the four had been wrongly convicted because of police malpractice, including lying to the courts about confessions. The government then set up an inquiry, headed by a former senior judge, into the circumstances of the convictions and into the reasons it took so long for crucial information to be disclosed. The inquiry was also to look into wider policy issues, such as the use of uncorroborated confessions as the basis for prosecution, the adequacy of safeguards for suspects in terrorist cases, and the procedures used to investigate possible miscarriages of justice. . . .

Inquests into the deaths of six unarmed people killed in 1982 by the security forces in Northern Ireland had still not been completed at the end of the year. Of these, the inquest into the deaths of Gervaise McKerr, Eugene Toman and Sean Burns, which began in November 1988, was adjourned because of an appeal to the Court of Appeal. It was further postponed in January 1989 after the government appealed against the judgment of the Court of Appeal to the House of Lords. The appeal was not resolved during 1989, delaying inquests into some 17 killings by members of the security forces.

A police inquiry, carried out between 1984 and 1986 by senior police officers John Stalker and Colin Sampson, found evidence that police officers had conspired to pervert the course of justice after the 1982 killings. However, the report of the inquiry continued to be withheld from the public on grounds of "national security". . . .

During a meeting held in April Amnesty International told the Secretary of State for Northern Ireland about its concern over the lack of thorough investigations into disputed killings by security forces in Northern Ireland and the fact that results of investigations were not made public. Amnesty International renewed its call for the government to establish a full judicial inquiry into disputed killings in Northern Ireland, focusing in particular on the procedures used to investigate such incidents and on legislation governing the use of lethal force. It also expressed concern that inquests into the disputed killings of 1982 had still not been completed. . . .

STATE DEPARTMENT

China

. . . The human rights climate in China deteriorated dramatically in 1989. On March 5-7, People's Armed Police (PAP) used indiscriminate and excessive force in suppressing demonstrations in Lhasa, Tibet, killing scores of persons. These killings and other serious human rights abuses, however, were dwarfed when the leadership ordered the People's Liberation Army (PLA) and other security forces to suppress forcefully a peaceful, student-led movement seeking greater freedom for China's people. At least several hundred, and possibly thousands, of people were killed in Beijing on June 3-4. The Beijing massacre was followed by a drastic, country-wide crackdown on participants, supporters, and sympathizers. Thousands were arrested and about a score are known to have been executed, following trials which fell far short of international standards, for alleged crimes committed during the unrest. There have also been persistent but unconfirmed reports of numerous unannounced executions. At year's end the crackdown was still continuing. The Government attempted to defend its actions by a massive disinformation campaign, expulsion and harassment of foreign journalists, a ban on the sale of books by dissidents, and the jamming of the Voice of America and some other foreign radio stations. Virtually all internationally recognized human rights discussed in this report are restricted, many of them severely....

There were credible reports of numerous raids on university campuses, private residences, workers' dormitories, think tanks, and hotels in the weeks following the June 3-4 massacre by both the PLA and various security bureaus. Large numbers of persons who participated in or supported the spring demonstrations were detained. While most of these detentions occurred soon after the June massacre, the crackdown continued months later. When universities reopened, returning students were investigated, and some students were detained by security forces. The Government acknowledges that some students, such as Liu Gang, Zho Fengsuo, Ma Shaofang, and others on the list of 21 most wanted, have been arrested; however, it has not publicly charged, or acknowledged holding, the majority of students reportedly detained whose whereabouts are unknown. Some workers at a computer firm that supported deposed CCP General Secretary Zhao Ziyang, journalists from Beijing-based newspapers, and intellectuals also remain unaccounted for. Since announcing a total of about 2,500 detentions by the end of June, the Government has refused to comment on the number of additional detentions since that time or to provide any information on those detained....

Reports of torture and degrading treatment of persons detained for committing so-called counterrevolutionary crimes have been persistent and consistent. Many Chinese citizens who participated in the demonstrations suffered beatings and other forms of ill-treatment in police efforts to extract information about others who may have been involved....

In 1989 the number of persons accused of political offenses rose dramatically as a result of the spring demonstrations. The number of people initially detained and the number who remain under detention has not been released. Estimates of the number of detainees after June 4 vary from the 2,500 officially announced in late June to over 100,000 according to some journalists and human rights groups. Western press reports in December quoted "well-informed" government sources as putting the figure at 10,000....

Colombia

Despite Colombia's strong democratic traditions, it has suffered from social unrest and an extraordinary level of violence for most of the past 40 years. The main causes of the violence and the concomitant human rights abuses are political extremists of both the left and the right, and the enormously wealthy narcotics traffickers, with the latter being the single largest cause in 1989. There have also been significant abuses by individual members of the army and police in responding to violence from these other sources.

The extreme left includes several armed guerrilla groups which use terrorism and narcotics trafficking to achieve their goal of violently overthrowing the democratic Government. The extreme right is composed of disparate elements, including a number of "self-defense" groups which were originally formed by rural landowners to defend against guerrilla attacks and which have degenerated into vigilante squads that assassinate, torture, and massacre people believed to have links with leftist political figures or the guerrillas. In areas where traffickers are powerful, these groups are often allied with the traffickers. The traffickers control enormous illicit enterprises which utilize extreme violence in attempts to bend the Colombian political and judicial systems to their own purposes. The major traffickers have achieved virtual immunity from prosecution by threatening, kidnaping, and murdering judges, government officials, political leaders, and their families. The relationships among the traffickers and between traffickers and rightwing elements or guerrillas are complex. . . .

Colombia has one of the highest murder rates in the world, and its police and judicial systems lack the resources to investigate and prosecute most of these crimes, making it difficult to separate political and nonpolitical murders. Nevertheless, the figure of 324 confirmed political killings in Colombia from January through August 1989 provided by the Bogota-based group Centro de Investigaciones y Educacion Popular (CINEP)—a Jesuit-affiliated social research institution which follows the human rights situation—seems reasonably accurate. This is a significant drop from the 706 political killings recorded by CINEP during the same period in 1988. CINEP labeled an additional 1,069 murders as possible political killings, compared to 1,145 during the same period in 1988. These numbers exclude deaths in combat. Narcotics-related killings increased some 140 percent during this period for a total of 129. . . .

In October [1989] Amnesty International (AI) issued a report on Colombia in which it charged that government security forces were directly responsible for thousands of extrajudicial killings and also suggested that the traffickers and their allies operate with government support. Clearly, Colombia, whose democratic system is under assault by narcotics traffickers and political extremists, has a serious human rights problem. AI's assertion that the high command of the security forces has adopted a deliberate policy of gross human rights violations was rejected as inaccurate and misleading by Colombians with a wide variety of political views as well as by local and international human rights groups. Two other reports issued in late 1989, one by the Lawyers Committee for Human Rights and the other by the Washington Office on Latin America (WOLA), assert that persons connected to the Government or security forces have links to violence. An Americas Watch (AW) report of April 1989 was "certain" that the Government was not behind any of the killings but was not prepared to absolve the military or political leadership. In any case, AW held the Government indirectly responsible for the murders by failing to fully protect all its citizens.

In 1989 senior military and police officials initiated a campaign to expel officers believed to be cooperating with armed rightwing groups. While never condoning such cooperation, in previous years the highest officials of the Government had not taken effective steps to recognize and stop it. In the first 8 months of 1989, however, 84 officers were dismissed from the armed forces, according to Attorney General Alfonso Gomez Mendez, most of them for association with narcotics traffickers, cooperation with armed rightist groups, and violations of human rights. In one of the most publicized cases, the army high command removed and retired Lieutenant Colonel Luis Bohorquez, the top military commander in the Magdalena Medio region, who was accused of supporting the armed rightwing groups which dominate the region. In April the Government announced the formation of a 1,000-man special police force devoted exclusively to combating rightist groups. Despite the Government's efforts, however, there likely are members of the police and army who continue to participate in extrajudicial killings. Punishment for human rights abuses within the military judicial system seldom extends beyond dismissal from the service. In 1989 the Supreme Court upheld the right of civilian courts to try military personnel in a wide variety of situations. In the immediate future, however, there appears to be little prospect of effective action by judges of the weak civilian judicial system. . . .

El Salvador

As the [Farabundo Marti Front for National Liberation—FMLN] insurgency gathered strength in the early 1980's, members of the security forces repeatedly violated the human rights of their fellow citizens and were unquestionably involved in widespread death squad activities. Although abuses continue, successful investigation and prosecution efforts now mean that military personnel, including officers, cannot count themselves immune to prosecution. In March 1989 the military turned over two officers, three noncommissioned officers, and six soldiers to civilian authorities for prosecution resulting from the September 1988 massacre of 10 civilians in San Sebastian. In May an active duty officer in the armed forces was found guilty and sentenced for the 1987 murder of three men. In January 1990, Colonel Guillermo Alfredo Benavides Moreno, Commandant of the Military Academy and Overall Commander of units providing security to the Academy area, along with two lieutenants, a sub-lieutenant, and five other soldiers, was held in custody and charged with the slayings of six Jesuit priests, a housekeeper, and her daughter on the campus of the University of Central America on November 16. . . .

The judicial process continued to be hindered by archaic procedures, inadequate facilities, intimidation of judges, and corruption. The FMLN's assassination of the Attorney General in April was an additional blow. Unfortunately, there was little progress in the prosecution of some key human rights cases during 1989. Although the military leadership showed somewhat greater cooperation in investigations of reported human rights abuses by members of the military, this attitude was not reflected in the lower ranks of the ESAF [Armed Forces of El Salvador], where cooperation with civilian investigators is, at best, erratic or problematic.

. . . Discerning a trend or pattern in the level of such violence is always difficult, the more so in 1989 with a guerrilla offensive beginning in November. . . .

The November FMLN offensive precluded a satisfactory count of political killings through the end of the year. Through August, the number of deaths reported in the Salvadoran press which may have been politically motivated averaged 17 per month; this compares with a monthly average of 19 in 1988, 23 in 1987, 22 in 1986, 28 in 1985, 64 in 1984, 140 in 1983, 219 in 1982, 444 in 1981, and 750 in 1980. Given the isolation of some rural areas, it is likely that the press does not report the full number of civilian deaths. . . .

In 1989 various groups charged that formal paramilitary death squads were operating again. Not since 1984, however, have there been any publicly acknowledged death squad killings by ultra-rightwing groups, as there were in earlier years. While some human rights groups continue to attribute certain political killings to "death squads," many of these deaths are likely the result of individual acts of rightwing vigilantism rather than of organized paramilitary death squads as existed before 1984. . . .

During the November FMLN offensive, the guerrillas took positions in the working class neighborhoods north and east of San Salvador, using innocent civilians as shields against Army and Air Force counterattacks. The FMLN set up fortified positions in civilian housing complexes and used private homes as command headquarters or sniper posts. In many instances, confirmed by diplomatic officials and the international media, the guerrillas did not allow the civilian residents to evacuate these areas. This tactic was designed to provide a shield and maximize the number of civilian casualties in order to blame the ESAF for those casualties.

The Embassy estimates, based on death reports and visits to hospital and emergency organizations, that there were between 200 and 400 civilian deaths in the capital during the fighting and between 1,500 and 3,000 civilians wounded. Most of the wounded received minor injuries and only 600 to 700 required hospitalization. Most casualties were the result of heavy street fighting and the use of infantry weapons such as small arms, machine guns, grenades, and mortars; few casualties seem to have been caused by aerial bombardment.

Charges of indiscriminate bombing by the Air Force during the FMLN urban offensive were not borne out. An Americas Watch (AW) report noted that in three San Salvador neighborhoods visited "the civilians had the impression that helicopter strafing and bombing were aimed principally at guerrilla emplacements." The ESAF followed its existing Rules of Engagement (ROE) regarding close air support during the offensive. The ROE allows for air support in populated areas only when the mission is to "retard or dissuade" terrorist activities. According to Embassy reports and eyewitness civilian accounts, the Air Force made efforts to target helicopter strafing, rocketing, and bombings at guerrilla emplacements, which resulted in few civilian casualties. However, despite initial ESAF denials, the ESAF did drop several bombs on guerrilla positions in San Salvador and San Miguel. Both 500 and 250 pound bombs were employed. These attacks caused some civilian casualties....

Guatemala

Violence in Guatemala decreased in the first 2 years of the new civilian Government's tenure in comparison with the levels of the early 1980's. In 1989, however, the country saw a resurgence of violence and terrorism, much of it politically inspired. A coup attempt in May 1989 by disaffected military and ex-military personnel sought, among other things, to oust reformist Defense Minister General Gramajo. Departing from past practice, the Government moved to prosecute the plotters. In November, seven were found guilty. Five were sentenced to 10 years, two to 2 years in prison. With foreign aid, the Government made efforts to continue to professionalize the police and the judiciary in order to increase their ability to investigate and prosecute crimes. However, the Goverment, hampered by a week [sic] criminal justice system, was unable to check the determined efforts of antidemocratic elements and criminals to create an environment of chaos and a lack of effective government control. There continued to be credible reports of security forces personnel and political extremists engaging in extrajudicial killings, disappearances, and other serious abuses. Few, if any, of the perpetrators of such actions were apprehended, tried, and convicted. Throughout the year, the Communist guerrillas increased their campaign of violence, which included destruction of public and private property, robbery, forced recruitment and labor, murder, and indiscriminate use of landmines. Drug-related crime and corruption also rose in 1989, and evidence grew of guerrilla involvement in the cultivation and trafficking of opium. Terrorists launched a series of bombings in the latter half of the year directed at television and electrical transmission towers, the telephone company, retail stores, political party headquarters, and the offices of two human rights groups. A series of kidnapings and brutal murders took place in August and September, including those of a group of evening students at the University of San Carlos in Guatemala City.

Police statistics showed about 2,000 murders countrywide, nearly the same as in 1988. Critics charge that these figures understate killings in those areas with minimal police presence or where residents refused to report incidents. While most killings appeared to result from personal vendettas or other criminal activities, an unknown but probably relatively small number were politically motivated. It is impossible, however, to determine the exact number.

There is no evidence that extrajudicial killings were part of the Government's counterinsurgency or anticrime actions, or that top government officials ordered or condoned them. However, as stated publicly by the Defense and the Interior Ministers at the height of the wave of violence which swept the country over the summer, persons in the security forces as well as extremist political groups engaged in extrajudicial killings. Authorities failed to investigate effectively and bring to trial the perpetrators of these crimes. Particularly troubling was the failure, with few exceptions, to detain or prosecute those perpetrators who were likely to have been connected with the security forces. In this regard, the Washington-based International Human Rights Law Group asserted in a July report that the police were unwilling to investigate a case aggressively when the military was thought to be involved. . . .

The media reported frequent discoveries of bodies, often with signs of torture or post-mortem mutilation. While many were not identified, a number were persons who had arrest and conviction records, leading some to conclude that vigilante groups were involved in some killings in which the perpetrators likely had access to police, court, and prison data. There were credible reports that, during the summer, an average of four bodies of teenaged males were found daily in Guatemala City, bound and shot once in the back of the head. . . .

Guerrillas were involved in extrajudicial killings in rural areas. Reliable reports indicate uniformed guerrillas murdered relatives of army personnel in the area between Patulul, Suchitepequez, and Pochuta, Chimaltenango in April. Guerrillas killed a deputy mayor in San Marcos department, the Huehuetenango deputy military zone commander, and, in Quiche, two repatriated refugees: Mateo Juan Baltazar, an alternate delegate to the National Dialogue (set up under the National Reconciliation Commission established under the Esquipulas II accords), and his brother.

Uniformed, machinegun-bearing guerrillas of the Revolutionary Organization of the People in Arms (ORPA) temporarily seized the town of Acatenango, Chimaltenango, where, according to the press and an eyewitness, they publicly murdered an already disarmed policeman. Uniformed guerrillas also briefly took San Miguel Duenas, near Antigua, held a forced meeting of the inhabitants, and killed a small child when his parents tried to run a roadblock in their vehicle.

Army personnel in rural areas were credibly reported to have engaged in extrajudicial killings of persons suspected of guerrilla sympathies or drug smuggling, particularly in San Marcos and . . . Peten. . . .

Iraq

Iraq's human rights record remained abysmal in 1989. Effective opposition to government policy is stifled; the intelligence services engage in extensive surveillance and utilize extralegal means, including torture and summary execution, to deal with antiregime activity. The civil rights of Iraqi citizens continue to be sharply limited, and Iraqis do not have the right to change their government. The freedoms of speech and press and of assembly and association are virtually nonexistent. Other important human rights problems include continuing disappearances and arbitrary detentions, lack of fair trial, widespread interference with privacy, excessive use of force against Kurdish civilians, and an almost total lack of worker rights. In addition to the repressive domestic controls that predate the war with Iran, tight wartime controls, including travel restrictions, remain in effect despite the August 1988 cease-fire with Iran.

An armed Kurdish insurgency continued in 1989, but at a reduced level. Although there were no allegations that the Government used chemical weapons against Kurdish civilians in 1989, as it did in 1988, in its efforts to crush the rebellion, it continued to violate the human rights of elements of the Kurdish population. The Government announced in June that in its campaign to suppress the rebellion it has pursued a program since 1987 of establishing a depopulated security zone along the full length of Iraq's borders with Iran and Turkey. Under this program, the Government has destroyed villages within a 30-kilometer-wide zone and relocated approximately 500,000 Kurdish and Assyrian inhabitants into more easily controlled and protected towns, cities, and newly constructed settlements in traditional Kurdish areas. . . .

For years execution has been an established Iraqi method for dealing with perceived political and military opponents of the government, including, but not limited to, members of the outlawed Da'wa organization (an Iran-supported fundamentalist Shi'a Muslim group that has engaged in acts of international terrorism). In some cases, a family only learns that one of its members has been executed when the security services return the body and require the family to pay a fine.

Amnesty International (AI), in its presentation before the U.S. Subcommission on the Prevention of Discrimination and Protection of Minorities in August, stated that it had received allegations that some 80 army deserters were executed in December 1988 and charged that the Government executed 11 of its Kurdish opponents in March and April 1989.

In its February report, "Iraq: Children: Innocent Victims of Political Repression," AI stated that it receives allegations of hundreds of executions in Iraq each year. AI cited the case of 29 Kurdish children and youths allegedly executed in January 1987. In addition, AI, in its 1989 Report covering 1988, cited allegations that hundreds of civilians, including women and children, were executed at Tanjaro Military Garrison, Sulaimaniya province. Independent information to confirm the allegations cited in AI reports is not available. . . .

In its 1989 Report, AI stated that the routine torture and ill-treatment of prisoners continued to be widely reported. It said the victims included detainees below the age of 18 who were reportedly beaten, whipped, given electric shocks, and deprived of food. The Government categorically denied any use of torture against children as an official policy or as a practice, and stated its readiness to consider fully any individual allegation with a view to bringing perpetrators to justice. Impartial observers have so far been unable to look into these allegations.

While the Constitution and legal code provide for the' rights of citizens and place checks on police powers in such areas as arrest, detention, imprisonment, and search, these provisions have virtually no weight in political or national security cases, although they are generally respected in ordinary criminal cases. Security police not only make arbitrary arrests but also secretly detain suspects, whose fate sometimes becomes known only after they have been executed. Security charges have included espionage, treason, and conspiracy against Iraq, often in collaboration with unnamed foreign enemies.

The relocation of 500,000 Kurdish villagers to other areas of Kurdistan since 1987 may be considered a form of internal exile. The Government declared in June 1989 that it was creating an uninhabited security zone to ensure the safety and security of citizens in the border regions (who were subjected to shelling and military operations during the war with Iran) and to provide better services to the villagers.

Although the Government has ceased expelling Iraqis of supposed Iranian descent, most of the few remaining Iranians have been imprisoned or live under the fear of deportation or incarceration. Spouses of Iraqis of Iranian origin are required to obtain a divorce or suffer the same consequences. Moreover, other Iraqis, whose grandparents are shown not to be of Iraqi origin, are subject to arbitrary detention and deportation. . . .

Israel

Torture is forbidden by Israeli law, and Israeli authorities assert they do not condone its use in the occupied territories. IDF orders forbid the use of force after the detention of a suspect and the cessation of violent resistance. Nevertheless, reports continue of harsh and demeaning treatment of prisoners and detainees, as well as allegations of beatings of suspects and detainees, including beating during house searches, which is contrary to IDF rules. At least 10 deaths can be attributed to beatings. Palestinians and international human rights groups claim that other cruel practices—including enforced standing in one position for prolonged periods, hooding, sleep deprivation, and cold showers—have continued since being confirmed in the 1987 report of the Landau judicial commission. . . .

According to IDF figures, 9,138 Palestinians were being held in IDF prison facilities as of January 1, 1990. Two military detention centers were added to the nine existing facilities. . . .

Administrative detention for alleged security reasons without formal charges was widespread in 1989. Israel maintains that administrative detention is used only against persons engaged in activities threatening security; however, in a number of cases persons appear to have been detained for nonviolent political activities. While the number of administrative detainees at any one time varies, IDF figures indicate that the number was 1,271 as of January 1, 1990. Most were detained under a 6-month order, although many orders have been renewed for a second or third time. In August the maximum length of detention under orders was extended to 12 months. . . .

. . . Since 1967, there have been episodic but sometimes intense outbreaks of violence within the occupied territories, reflecting Palestinian opposition to the occupation. In December 1987, there was a dramatic outburst of civilian unrest and violence. This has continued throughout 1989 and has been far more widespread and intensive than at any time heretofore. This has led to a severe crackdown by the Israeli Defense Forces (IDF).

The human rights situation in the occupied territories remains a source of deep concern to the United States. Overall, there were more Palestinian deaths in 1989 than in 1988. A total of 432 Palestinians were killed in intifada-related violence in 1989, of whom 304 were killed by Israeli security forces and settlers and 128 by other Palestinians; 13 Israelis, soldiers and civilians, were killed by Palestinians during 1989. . . .

This unrest and violence, known as the intifada, has as its minimum goal the end of the Israeli occupation, a goal strongly supported by Palestinians in the West Bank and Gaza. The leadership of the uprising, known as the United National Leadership of the Uprising (UNLU), attempts to direct and coordinate intifada activities. As it developed, groups of young people which have formed in individual localities but are loosely associated with each other and coordinate their tactics have, throughout the occupied territories, enforced business shut-downs and strikes, and directed attacks at Israeli military patrols and Israeli travelers, particularly settlers, whose cars are routinely pelted with stones. Occasionally firebombs have been thrown. The security forces have responded with tear gas, rubber and plastic bullets, and metal bullets.

Israeli occupation authorities have sought to end the intifada through widescale arrests, detention, raids on homes in which suspects were thought to reside, and more severe forms of punishment, including deportation. The rules of engagement of the Israeli Defense Forces provide for the use of force in case of self-defense in life-threatening situations, in the arrest of a suspect to a crime if the suspect resists, and dispersing a violent riot which endangers public order or the safety of soldiers. The rules allow the use of live fire only as a last resort and under defined procedures in these circumstances. The guidelines for the use of force stipulate that once force is no longer needed, it should no longer be applied. The Government of Israel makes clear to all forces serving in the occupied territories the need to adhere to the rules of engagement. However, violations of these rules have resulted in death and injuries. Only a relatively small number of such incidents have resulted in prosecution, and the sentences meted out have tended to be light.

An important aspect of the situation in the occupied territories in 1989 has been the significant increase in violence by Palestinians directed at other Palestinians. This has taken a number of forms, including assassinations, other acts of violence, and threats of violence. This took place in an environment influenced by some statements by various Palestinian leaders and the Unified Command promoting violence (e.g., a call by one UNLU leaflet to use knives, hatchets, and Molotov cocktails), tough Israeli security measures, the breakdown in law enforcement against conventional crime, and factional differences among Palestinians. The Unified Command has not disassociated itself from the phenomenon of intra-Palestinian violence but has sought to curb that element not under its control.

The strength of the Islamic fundamentalist Hamas movement has contributed to this intra-Palestinian violence and atmosphere of intimidation. Hamas opposes any reconciliation with Israel, and it would appear that its appeal, albeit still limited to a minority of the Palestinian population, has also shaped intra-Palestinian tensions.

Israel's open, democratic society enables widespread access to data on and investigations of human rights in the territories, notwithstanding IDF restraints applied there. Israel has designated officials in the Ministry of Defense with whom U.S. officials discuss specific allegations of human rights violations. . . .

BUSH AND GOVERNORS'
STATEMENTS ON EDUCATION GOALS
February 25 and 26, 1990

Five months after their historic education "summit" meeting in September 1989, the nation's governors and members of the Bush administration—including the president—produced a longer and more detailed agenda to address the perceived crisis in American schooling.

After intense negotiations the National Governors' Association (NGA) formally endorsed the agenda with its approval of the "National Education Goals" at a meeting in Washington, D.C., February 25. The document builds on a plan outlined at the 1989 summit in Charlottesville, Virginia, at which the governors and Bush administration officials called for making "America's educational performance second to none in the 21st century." Their three primary aims were to produce students (1) whose later work capabilities would enhance the U.S. competitive position in the international economy, (2) who would have a greater understanding of their civic responsibilities, and (3) who would have the skills to cope with rapid changes in the workplace and the world. (Statements at the Education Summit, Historic Documents of 1989, p. 561)

The 1990 statement repeated ambitious education goals, to be achieved in twenty years, that President George Bush announced in his 1990 State of the Union Address (State of the Union Address and Democratic Response, p. 49), and also listed twenty-one specific "target" areas for reform that the governors identified.

"Dramatic Turning Point"

The lengthy process of hammering out the agreement was undertaken by a small group that included Roger B. Porter, the administration's domestic policy adviser; John H. Sununu, White House chief of staff; Richard G. Darman, director of the Office of Management and Budget; Govs. Bill Clinton of Arkansas and Carroll A. Campbell, Jr., of South Carolina, cochairmen of the NGA education task force; Gov. Terry E. Branstad of Iowa, chairman of the NGA; and Gov. Booth Gardner of Washington. Clinton and Gardner are Democrats; Campbell and Branstad are Republicans. Secretary of Education Lauro F. Cavazos attended few of the policy meetings.

Meeting with the governors at the White House February 26, Bush said, "Never before have the President of the United States and the Governors joined together in a partnership and long-term commitment on a single issue."

Several thorny questions remained, including the amount of available funding and who would be responsible for overseeing the reforms. "I'm worried about this being a hollow exercise if education continues to be only 2 percent of [the federal] budget," said Gov. Roy Romer of Colorado. In a similar vein, a fellow Democrat, Gov. James J. Blanchard of Michigan, said: "I think our national leaders are being too timid in terms of the budget. It's nice to have an 'A' for attention, but we need an 'A' for results."

Porter, the administration's chief negotiator with the governors, disagreed. "There's not going to be any fight over the issue of money," he said. "If it's going to take more money, we're going to support that. But we're not looking to change the fundamental balance regarding the respective roles of state and local and federal governments [in setting education policy]." Despite funding differences, the administration and governors pledged to be flexible on the spending issue.

On the question of oversight, participants could not reach agreement on the type of group that would monitor progress toward achieving the goals or to whom it should report. However, the final statement reflected a consensus that a bipartisan committee would supervise "the process of determining and developing appropriate measurements and reporting on the progress toward meeting the goals." The NGA and the White House agreed to work together, and with others, to develop assessment strategies and to establish a panel that would review existing education regulations to see whether they could be made more flexible.

Reforms Face Obstacles

The 1990 effort to devise national education objectives was reminiscent of the situation in 1983, when Secretary of Education Terrel H. Bell issued a highly critical report of the nation's public school system, entitled "A Nation at Risk." Among that report's goals were to raise the high school graduation rate to more than 90 percent by 1990, raise scores on college admissions tests above the 1965 average, provide teachers with more competitive salaries, and make high school graduation requirements more stringent. To discuss implementing these goals, the adminis-

tration convened a forum that included governors, members of Congress, state legislators, chief state school officers, and college and university professors. But they were unable to agree on a comprehensive strategy. (Education Report, Historic Documents of 1983, p. 413)

"What's different today than what happened in 1983 is that you've got both the president of the United States and the 50 governors coming together on national goals and national strategies to address those goals," commented Milton Goldberg, director of the Education Department's Office of Research. "We didn't do that in 1983 and 1984."

Nonetheless, the move to enhance U.S. students' educational performance faced stiff obstacles. The National Assessment of Educational Progress (NAEP)—operated by the Educational Testing Service under contract to the U.S. Department of Education—released a report January 9, 1990, that showed few gains in student reading ability in almost two decades. Based on a test of 100,000 elementary, middle, and high school students, the report found that students at age nine and seventeen were reading slightly better in 1988 than were their counterparts sampled in 1971, but that thirteen-year-olds were reading at about the same level.

In a separate report on writing, a NAEP study of approximately 18,000 students in grades four, eight, and eleven found that performance remained low and had not changed significantly since 1974. A third NAEP report, released April 2, pointed to shortcomings in students' knowledge of American history and civics. Commenting on those studies, Secretary Cavazos said, "If anyone still doubts that it is time for change at an elemental, fundamental level, these data should be persuasive.... [O]ur educational system must be restructured. We need a revolution in teaching and learning."

> *Following are the text of "National Education Goals," released by the National Governor's Association February 25, 1990, and excerpts from President George Bush's remarks to governors at the White House the next day:*

STATEMENT ON EDUCATION GOALS

Introduction

At the historic education summit in Charlottesville five months ago, the President and the Governors declared that "the time has come, for the first time in U.S. history, to establish clear, national performance goals, goals that will make us internationally competitive." The six national education goals contained here are the first step in carrying out that commitment.

America's educational performance must be second to none in the 21st century. Education is central to our quality of life. It is at the heart of our economic strength and security, our creativity in the arts and letters, our invention in the sciences, and the perpetuation of our cultural values. Education is the key to America's international competitiveness.

Today, a new standard for an educated citizenry is required, one suitable for the next century. Our people must be as knowledgeable, as well trained, as competent, and as inventive as those in any other nation. All of our people, not just a few, must be able to think for a living, adapt to changing environments, and to understand the world around them. They must understand and accept the responsibilities and obligations of citizenship. They must continually learn and develop new skills throughout their lives.

America can meet this challenge if our society is dedicated to a renaissance in education. We must become a nation that values education and learning. We must recognize that every child can learn, regardless of background or disability. We must recognize that education is a lifelong pursuit, not just an endeavor for our children.

Sweeping, fundamental changes in our education system must be made. Educators must be given greater flexibility to devise challenging and inspiring strategies to serve the needs of a diverse body of students. This is especially important for students who are at risk of academic failure—for the failure of these students will become the failure of our nation. Achieving these changes depends in large part on the commitment of professional educators. Their daily work must be dedicated to creating a new educational order in which success for all students is the first priority, and they must be held accountable for the results.

This is not the responsibility of educators alone, however. All Americans have an important stake in the success of our education system, and every part of our society must be involved in meeting that challenge. Parents must be more interested and involved in their children's education, and students must accept the challenge of higher expectations for achievement and greater responsibility for their future. In addition, communities, business and civic groups, and state, local, and federal government each has a vital role to play throughout this decade to ensure our success.

The first step is to establish ambitious national education goals— performance goals that must be achieved if the United States is to remain competitive in the world marketplace and our citizens are to reach their fullest potential. These goals are about excellence. Meeting them will require that the performance of our highest achievers be boosted to levels that equal or exceed the performance of the best students anywhere. The performance of our lowest achievers must be substantially increased far beyond their current performance. What our best students can achieve now, our average students must be able to achieve by the turn of the century. We must work to ensure that a significant number of students from all races, ethnic groups, and income levels are among our top performers.

If the United States is to maintain a strong and responsible democracy and a prosperous and growing economy into the next century, all of our citizens must be involved in achieving these goals. Every citizen will benefit as a result. When challenged, the American people have always shown their determination to succeed. The challenge before us calls on each American to help ensure our nation's future.

National Goals for Education

Readiness

Goal 1: By the year 2000, all children in America will start school ready to learn.
Objectives:

- All disadvantaged and disabled children will have access to high quality and developmentally appropriate preschool programs that help prepare children for school.
- Every parent in America will be a child's first teacher and devote time each day helping his or her preschool child learn; parents will have access to the training and support they need.
- Children will receive the nutrition and health care needed to arrive at school with healthy minds and bodies, and the number of low birthweight babies will be significantly reduced through enhanced prenatal health systems.

School Completion

Goal 1: By the year 2000, the high school graduation rate will increase to at least 90 percent.
Objectives:

- The nation must dramatically reduce its dropout rate and 75 percent of those students who do drop out will successfully complete a high school degree or its equivalent.
- The gap in high school graduation rates between American students from minority backgrounds and their non-minority counterparts will be eliminated.

Student Achievement and Citizenship

Goal 3: By the year 2000, American students will leave grades four, eight, and twelve having demonstrated competency over challenging subject matter including English, mathematics, science, history, and geography, and every school in America will ensure that all students learn to use their minds well, so they may be prepared for responsible citizenship, further learning, and productive employment in our modern economy.
Objectives:

- The academic performance of elementary and secondary students will increase significantly in every quartile, and the distribution of minority students in each level will more closely reflect the student population as a whole.
- The percentage of students who demonstrate the ability to reason,

solve problems, apply knowledge, and write and communicate effectively will increase substantially.

- All students will be involved in activities that promote and demonstrate good citizenship, community service, and personal responsibility.
- The percentage of students who are competent in more than one language will substantially increase.
- All students will be knowledgeable about the diverse cultural heritage of this nation and about the world community.

Mathematics and Science

Goal 4: By the year 2000, U.S. students will be first in the world in mathematics and science achievement.
Objectives:

- Math and science education will be strengthened throughout the system, especially in the early grades.
- The number of teachers with a substantive background in mathematics and science will increase by 50 percent.
- The number of U.S. undergraduate and graduate students, especially women and minorities, who complete degrees in mathematics, science, and engineering will increase significantly.

Adult Literacy and Lifelong Learning

Goal 5: By the year 2000, every adult American will be literate and will possess the knowledge and skills necessary to compete in a global economy and exercise the rights and responsibilities of citizenship.
Objectives:

- Every major American business will be involved in strengthening the connection between education and work.
- All workers will have the opportunity to acquire the knowledge and skills, from basic to highly technical, needed to adapt to emerging new technologies, work methods, and markets through public and private educational, vocational, technical workplace, or other programs.
- The number of quality programs, including those at libraries, that are designed to serve more effectively the needs of the growing number of part-time and mid-career students will increase substantially.
- The proportion of those qualified students, especially minorities, who enter college; who complete at least two years; and who complete their degree programs will increase substantially.
- The proportion of college graduates who demonstrate an advanced ability to think critically, communicate effectively, and solve problems will increase substantially.

Safe, Disciplined, and Drug-Free Schools

Goal 6: By the year 2000, every school in America will be free of drugs and violence and will offer a disciplined environment conducive to learning.

Objectives:

- Every school will implement a firm and fair policy on use, possession, and distribution of drugs and alcohol.
- Parents, businesses, and community organizations will work together to ensure that schools are a safe haven for all children.
- Every school district will develop a comprehensive K-12 drug and alcohol prevention education program. Drug and alcohol curriculum should be taught as an integral part of health education. In addition, community-based teams should be organized to provide students and teachers with needed support.

Necessary Changes and Restructuring

These goals are ambitious, yet they can and must be achieved. However, they cannot be achieved by our education system as it is presently constituted. Substantial, even radical changes will have to be made.

Without a strong commitment and concerted effort on the part of every sector and every citizen to improve dramatically the performance of the nation's education system and each and every student, these goals will remain nothing more than a distant, unattainable vision. For their part, Governors will work within their own states to develop strategies for restructuring their education systems in order to achieve the goals. Because states differ from one another, each state will approach this in a different manner. The President and the Governors will work to support these state efforts, and to recommend steps that the federal government, business, and community groups and educators should take to help achieve these national goals. The nature of many of these steps is already clear.

The Preschool Years

American homes must be places of learning. Parents should play an active role in their childrens' early learning, particularly by reading to them on a daily basis. Parents should have access to the support and training required to fulfill this role, especially in poor, undereducated families.

In preparing young people to start school, both the federal and state governments have important roles to play, especially with regard to health, nutrition, and early childhood development. Congress and the administration have increased material and child health coverage for all families with incomes up to 133 percent of the federal poverty line. Many states go beyond this level of coverage, and more are moving in this direction. In addition, states continue to develop more effective delivery systems for prenatal and postnatal care. However, we still need more prevention, testing, and screening, and early identification and treatment of learning disorders and disabilities.

The federal government should work with the states to develop and fully fund early intervention strategies for children. All eligible children should have access to Head Start, Chapter 1, or some other successful preschool program with strong parental involvement. Our first priority must be to provide at least one year of preschool for all disadvantaged children.

The School Years

As steps are taken to better prepare children for schools, we must also better prepare schools for children.

This is especially important for young children. Schools must be able to educate effectively all children when they arrive at the schoolhouse door, regardless of variations in students' interest, capacities, or learning styles.

Next, our public education system must be fundamentally restructured to ensure that all students can meet higher standards. This means reorienting schools so they focus on results, not on procedures; giving each school's principal and teachers the discretion to make more decisions and the flexibility to use federal, state, and local resources in more productive, innovative ways that improve learning; providing a way for gifted professionals who want to teach to do so through alternative certification avenues, and giving parents more responsibility for their children's education through magnet schools, public school choice, and other strategies. Most important, restructuring requires creating powerful incentives for performance and improvement, and real consequences for persistent failure. It is only by maintaining this balance of flexibility and accountability that we can truly improve our schools.

The federal government must sustain its vital role of promoting educational equity by ensuring access to quality educational programs for all students regardless of race, national origin, sex, or handicapping condition. Federal funds should target those students most in need of assistance due to economic disadvantage or risk of academic failure.

Finally, efforts to restructure education must work toward guaranteeing that all students are engaged in rigorous programs of instruction designed to ensure that every child, regardless of background or disability, acquires the knowledge and skills necessary to succeed in a changing economy. In recent years, there has been an increased commitment to math and science improvement programs. The federal government should continue to enhance financial assistance to state and local governments for effective programs in these areas. Likewise, there has been a greater federal emphasis on programs that target youth at risk of school failure and dropping out. The federal government should continue to enhance funding and seek strategies to help states in their efforts to seek solutions to these problems.

Improving elementary and secondary student achievement will not require a national curriculum, but it will require that the nation invest in developing the skills and knowledge of educators and equipping our schools with up-to-date technology. The quality of teachers and teaching is essential to meeting our goals. We must have well-prepared teachers and we must increase the number of qualified teachers in critical shortage areas, including rural and urban schools, specialized fields such as foreign languages, mathematics and science, and from minority groups. Policies must attract and keep able teachers who reflect the cultural diversity of our nation. Policies that shape how educators are prepared, certified, rewarded, developed, and supported on the job must be consistent with efforts to restructure the education system and ensure that every school is capable of teaching all of our children to think and reason. Teachers and other school leaders must not only be outstanding, the schools in which they work must also be restructured to utilize both professional talent and technology to improve student learning and teacher- and system-productivity.

The After-School Years

Comprehensive, well-integrated lifelong learning opportunities must be created for a world in which three of four new jobs will require more than a high school education; workers with only high school diplomas may face the prospect of declining incomes; and most workers will change their jobs ten or eleven times over their lifetime.

In most states, the present system for delivering adult literacy services is fractured and inadequate. Because the United States has far higher rates of adult functional illiteracy than other advanced countries, a first step is to establish in each state a public-private partnership to create a functionally literate workforce.

In some countries, government policies and programs are carefully coordinated with private sector activities to create effective apprenticeship and job training activities. By contrast, the United States has a multilayered system of vocational and technical schools, community colleges, and specific training programs funded from multiple sources and subject to little coordination. These institutions need to be restructured so they fit together more sensibly and effectively to give all adults access to flexible and comprehensive programs that meet their needs. Every major business must work to provide appropriate training and educational opportunities to prepare employees for the twenty-first century.

Finally, a larger share of our population, especially those from working class, poor, and minority backgrounds, must be helped to attend and remain in college. The cost of a college education, as a percentage of median family income, has approximately tripled in a generation. That means more loans, scholarships, and work-study opportunities are needed. The federal government's role in ensuring access for qualified students is critical. At the same time, the higher education system must use existing resources far more productively than it does at present, and must be held more accountable for what students do or do not learn. The federal government will continue to examine ways to reduce students' increasing debt burden and to address the proper balance between grant and loan programs.

Assessment

National education goals will be meaningless unless progress toward meeting them is measured accurately and adequately, and reported to the

American people. Doing a good job of assessment and reporting requires the resolution of three issues.

First, what students need to know must be defined. In some cases, there is a solid foundation on which to build. For example, the National Council of Teachers of Mathematics and the Mathematical Sciences Education Board have done important work in defining what all students must know and be able to do in order to be mathematically competent. A major effort for science has been initiated by the American Association for the Advancement of Science. These efforts must be expanded and extended to other subject areas.

Second, when it is clear what students need to know, it must be determined whether they know it. There have been a number of important efforts to improve our ability to measure student learning at the state and national levels. This year for the first time, the National Assessment for Education Progress (NAEP) will collect data on student performance on a state-by-state basis for thirty-seven states. Work is underway to develop a national assessment of adult literacy. These and other efforts must be supported and strengthened.

The Governors urge the National Assessment Governing Board to begin work to set national performance goals in the subject areas in which NAEP will be administered. This does not mean establishing standards for individual competence; rather, it requires determining how to set targets for increases in the percentage of students performing at the higher levels of the NAEP scales.

Third, measurements must be accurate, comparable, appropriate, and constructive. Placement decisions for young children should not be made on the basis of standardized tests. Achievement tests must not simply measure minimum competencies, but also higher levels of reading, writing, speaking, reasoning, and problem-solving skills. And in comparing America's achievement with that of other countries, it is essential that international comparisons are reliable. In addition, appropriate, nationally directed research, demonstration projects, data collection, and innovation should be maintained and recognized as a set of core responsibilities of the federal government in education. That role needs to be strengthened in cooperation with the states.

The President and the Governors agree that while we do not need a new data-gathering agency, we do need a bipartisan group to oversee the process of determining and developing appropriate measurements and reporting on the progress toward meeting the goals.

A Challenge

These national educational goals are not the President's goals or the Governors' goals; they are the nation's goals.

These education goals are the beginning, not the end, of the process. Governors are committed to working within their own states to review state education goals and performance levels in light of these national goals. States are encouraged to adjust state goals according to this review, and to expand upon national goals where appropriate. The President and the Governors challenge every family, school, school district, and community to adopt these national goals as their own, and establish other goals that reflect the particular circumstances and challenges they face as America approaches the twenty-first century.

REMARKS TO MEMBERS OF THE NATIONAL GOVERNORS' ASSOCIATION

. . . I am very pleased to be with you on this occasion, an occasion which I believe will be viewed in years to come as a dramatic turning point for our country. You've come to Washington for this annual meeting with an uncommon agenda. Today we're launching a new era in education reform. Its focus: high expectations. Its hallmark: results. Its energy derived from the people of our great nation, who will insist on a world-class education for our kids. For the first time in America's history, we now have national education goals and objectives, goals that pave the way to a decade-long commitment to excellence in education for all Americans, goals that will guide us on the journey toward an American renaissance in education.

We made the commitment to develop national goals last fall there in Charlottesville, Virginia. Five months later, I'm glad to see that the spirit of cooperation and bipartisanship, so much in evidence there at Charlottesville, is still very much alive. That spirit has got to endure. And over the coming months and years, the spirit must serve as a signal to America that our commitment to these common goals remains unshakable, very strong, not for just today, not just tomorrow, but for the rest of the decade, to the year 2000, until we get the job done and get it done right.

You know, only a year or so ago, the notion of the President and the Governors agreeing on education goals was considered a bold step for America to take. Even now, there are some who say the goals we've established are too ambitious. I think they're mistaken. They've failed to appreciate the depth of our commitment to restructuring and change.

We've all been following the extraordinary events which have unfolded before our eyes in Eastern Europe over the last year, and there is a lesson in those events for all of us in this room and for all Americans. And that lesson is: When people unite behind common goals and demand the freedom to pursue their dreams, no system can stop them. And nothing will stop us.

There is nothing more important to the long-term stability and stature of America than establishing a first-class education system. Nothing is more important to a competitive America in the 21st century. Nothing is more important than the promise inherent in these goals that all children in America can realize their fullest potential and reach out for their dreams.

I want to see these goals posted on the wall in every school so that all who walk in—the parents, students, teachers—know what we're aiming for, so that everyone knows we have set for ourselves the goal that every child will be ready to learn from the first day they walk into the classroom; the goal of raising the graduation rate to 90 percent by making our schools meaningful, challenging, and relevant to the needs of our students; of setting high standards of achievement among our students, seeing that they leave the transition grades of 4, 8, and 12 having mastered the important subject matter; the goal of achieving first place in math and science among industrialized nations; of every American adult being skilled and literate, equipped to be a productive worker and a responsible citizen; and finally, the goal of every school in America being safe, disciplined, and drug free.

These goals and objectives have been developed with a great deal of energy and effort over these past 5 months and with the input of hundreds of citizens from all sectors of society. And I want to thank everyone who has participated in this process. Governor [Terry E.] Branstad [of Iowa] and the members of your Education Task Force, I thank you for your commitment, your dedication, and all the hundreds of hours of hard work—that as we acknowledge this first step, we've also got to recognize that hard work lies ahead.

Over the next few months, I know you'll be looking at strategies in your States which will move us forward to these goals, and strategies that will focus on measuring progress by results, by how well students are doing. One of the Governors encouraged me ... to encourage the people of this country to support State and local initiatives that have to do with making the educational system better. And certainly, I am prepared to do that, just as I am grateful to the Governors for their participation in setting these goals.

In the coming months, we'll work together with Congress on legislation to increase flexibility in Federal funding in return for enhanced accountability. And you, the Nation's Governors, have committed to break the bureaucratic shackles that smother innovation and stand guard over the status quo. Although the Federal Government traditionally has a limited role in education—and we all respect and acknowledge that it is the dynamism at the State and local level that achieves excellence—I promise you that this administration is determined to walk with you every step of the way.

When I next meet with my Cabinet, many of whom were with us there in Charlottesville, I'll ask each to work with our domestic policy adviser to devise strategies that can support your efforts and those of your communities in helping to achieve these goals. I will work with you to establish a bipartisan group to ensure that proper and constructive measurements of our educational performance are developed where they don't already exist. And this group is going to report to me each year on the progress we make.

And I'm calling on America's private sector to be a third party in this enterprise. We need to know from them what the workplace will need and expect of our citizens in the 21st century. And we need their talent and their commitment to help move this reform effort forward. And finally, I will do everything I can to provide the national leadership and energy to keep education in the forefront of America's domestic agenda.

The work ahead will not be easy. We're traveling uncharted waters. And never before have we as a nation set such goals for education. And never before have the Nation's leaders stepped forward to say we are willing to be held accountable for the results of this process. And never before have the President of the United States and the Governors joined together in a partnership and a long-term commitment on a single issue.

If we can accomplish just one thing today—and it may be the simplest and yet most valuable of all—it is to send a message to parents, teachers, community leaders, and every other American: These goals are not the Governors' goals. They're not the President's goals. They are the Nation's goals. And we are rejecting the status quo, raising our sights, investing our faith in the American people. And so, today I hope the Governors and the Cabinet will join me in extending a challenge to all Americans to adopt these goals as their own and to take aim now at the year 2000 and to enlist every ounce of American innovation, energy, resolve in the effort to achieve these education goals and prepare this nation for the challenges of a new century.

Thank you all very, very much for your superb cooperation.

March

1990 CENSUS PROCLAMATION
March 6, 1990

The nation again set out in 1990 to count its people and find where and how they live. The twenty-first decennial census, eight years in the planning, was formally authorized March 6 in a presidential proclamation fulfilling a constitutional requirement. In keeping with past custom, the Bureau of the Census designated April 1 Census Day. The count actually began a few days earlier and continued for several months in an effort to track down all residents and reduce a chronic "undercount" that long had plagued census-takings.

While much of the information was obtained from census forms mailed on or before March 23 to 88.5 million of the nation's 106 million households, the rest of it had to be ferreted out by census workers— enumerators—visiting or telephoning remote or unresponsive dwelling places. Thousands of enumerators made a special effort to count the homeless by devoting the night of March 20 to seeking out street people in shelters and alleyways.

The bureau employed about 425,000 permanent and temporary workers to carry out the 1990 Census of Population and Housing and to tabulate the findings. The cost of the entire undertaking, covering a ten-year period that ends in 1992, was likely to exceed the $2.6 billion that Congress had already authorized, making the 1990 census the costliest of all.

Census information provides a statistical portrait of the nation on the basis of which countless decisions are made that will affect nearly all Americans during the 1990s. Where people live at ten-year intervals determines which states gain or lose congressional seats. It also affects the allocation of federal and state funds to localities, plans for business locations and market strategies, school construction, social needs of the inner city, and many other matters.

The uses of national censuses have expanded enormously since the first one was conducted in 1790, only a year after the federal government was formed. The newly ratified Constitution required that the people be counted once each decade for the express purpose of apportioning the House of Representatives among the states on the basis of population. Although censuses have been put to many uses, the "apportionment count" has remained its central purpose. Federal law requires that the state-by-state count from the 1990 census be delivered to President George Bush by the end of the year and made available to Congress and the states in greater detail by April 1, 1991.

If past patterns hold true, other findings from the 1990 census will be published only months, even years, after the count. Not all of the data from the 1980 census had been issued when preparations for the 1990 census began in 1982—although that compilation was the most auto-mated of any census until that time.

Most households received the Census Bureau's short form, which asked only fourteen questions, including the names and some personal charac-teristics of the occupants, and their housing conditions. But 17 percent of the households received forty-five additional questions. The 1990 census questionnaire included a first—a space for the responding householder to designate an "unmarried partner." By matching the answers with the gender of the respondents, census analysts hope to be able to determine the homosexual population.

In all census answers, complete confidentiality is assured by law. After the answers are recorded, the names of the respondents are destroyed. However, as in past census-takings, many people remained reluctant to give out information. This reticence was believed to be especially true of illegal immigrants, who apparently feared that their answers might enable the government to discover their true identities and deport them.

The "Undercount" Dispute

Illegal immigration undoubtedly adds to the "undercount" that has plagued census takers. The inability to track down every individual, especially blacks and Hispanics in the inner cities, has led the bureau since 1950 to invoke statistical means of trying to calculate the size of the undercount. Demographers compare census results with statistics on births, deaths, immigration, and emigration to arrive at their estimates of the "true" population of various cities and the entire nation. The estimated undercount gradually declined from 4.4 percent in 1950 to 1.4 percent in 1980.

Nevertheless, it remained significant to cities and other localities where an undercount could mean huge losses in federal assistance apportioned on the basis of population. In 1990 some 5,300 municipalities apportioned on the basis of population. In 1990 some 5,300 municipalities complained to the Census Bureau that their people and dwellings had not been fully counted. The Census Bureau reported to the president December 26 a national count of 249,632,692, including almost a million federal civilian and military personnel and their dependents living overseas. Under a new law they were included in the 1990 total, for an increase of 23 million, or 10.2 percent, over the 1980 census. The bureau planned to determine by July 15, 1991, whether to revise the 1990 figure on the basis of continuing claims of undercount or other errors.

Recheck figures released by the bureau and government auditors at a congressional hearing September 25 indicated that the undercount was far less than many of the municipalities claimed. Census takers returned to areas where the undercount was considered likeliest. In visits to more than 15 million dwellings, they uncovered only 313,000 units missing from the original lists. New York City contended that as many as a million of its residents and 250,000 housing units were overlooked. An initial round of recanvassing in the city added 23,000 units; L. Nye Stevens, an official of the General Accounting Office, suggested that the figure might rise to 59,000 and increase the New York City population count by 140,000.

At the hearing before the House's Subcommittee on Census and Population, Census Director Barbara Everitt Bryant was questioned closely about the undercount complaints. "We sympathize with those officials who have to govern cities losing or not gaining population and a tax base," Dr. Bryant said. "But we should not be blamed for such changes. In effect, there should be no shooting of the proverbial messenger in anticipation of bad news."

Two Centuries of Census-Taking

From its very beginning, the nation's census-taking has been beset with problems. Federal marshals who took the 1790 census were obstructed by poor roads, marauding Indians, and a reluctance of some residents to answer the questions. President George Washington complained of an undercount in the 1790 census, which—in a letter he wrote Gouverneur Morris—he ascribed to the "religious scruples of some . . . fears of others that it [the census] was intended as the foundation of a tax . . . indolence of the people, and negligency of many of the [census] officers."

The first census reported 3,929,214 people in an area that now constitutes eighteen states—the original thirteen plus Maine, Vermont, Kentucky, and West Virginia (then part of Virginia). The total included no "untaxed" Indians, but 697,705 Negro slaves. They were counted separately for apportionment purposes. Until the Thirteenth Amendment outlawed slavery in 1865, each slave had three-fifths the numerical value of a free citizen when congressional districts were drawn.

As the territory and economy of the United States grew, so did the need for more information. The only age information collected in the 1790 census was a listing of males sixteen and older; the 1800 tabulation listed free white males and females in five age categories. A census of manufac-

tures (business) was first conducted in connection with the 1810 decennial census; later it was conducted separately.

In 1820 the census began to ask the occupation of each working householder. In the thirty years that had elapsed since the first census, the U.S. population had more than doubled, to 9,638,453. It was spread from Florida and Maine to the Rocky Mountains, embracing the vast territory of the Louisiana Purchase and new states of the upper Middle West. In 1860, on the eve of the Civil War, the westward surge continued. The population had risen to 31,443,321, eight times greater than in 1790.

The 1890 census, showing 62,947,717 Americans, inspired the historian Frederick Jackson Turner to declare in a celebrated paper that the frontier had closed. It was no longer possible, he said, to draw a contiguous line connecting territories where the population density was less than two persons per square mile. Sometime in the second decade of the twentieth century, the United States added its hundredth million person.

In the censuses of 1880 and 1890 some persons had to answer as many as 470 questions, the largest number ever requested. Census-takers asked, for example, if the origin of each homeless child had been "respectable"; whether each pauper was "habitually intemperate"; whether there were any idiots in the family and, if so, whether their heads were larger or smaller than average.

In 1902 Congress recognized the need for continuity in census work and set up in the Department of the Interior a permanent office. It later became the Bureau of the Census, in the Department of Commerce. But until 1930 Congress continued to write the census questions. A separate census of housing was combined with the population census of 1940. The 1960 census was the first in which the bureau tested questions in advance for clarity and relevance.

The 1920 census recorded 105,710,620 people. For the first time the census found that more Americans lived in urban than in rural areas, and many of the urban Americans were recent immigrants from southern and central Europe. More than one American in five was foreign-born or had at least one parent who was. That finding, according to some social historians, influenced a xenophobic revival in American politics and led to the passage of restrictive immigration laws. The laws were relaxed in the 1970s and 1980s, especially in regard to Asians and Latin Americans, but each census tends to produce findings that influence the nation's thinking.

> *Following is the text of President George Bush's proclamation of March 6, 1990, declaring that the 1990 Census of Population and Housing would be conducted throughout the United States:*

In 1790, barely a year after our Nation's government was established, the first Census of Population was taken by the United States Marshals under the direction of then-Secretary of State Thomas Jefferson. A total of 3.9 million residents were counted. This year, another census will be taken — the 21st in the history of the United States. Each decennial census has helped to chart the growth and change experienced by our vast country during the past 200 years.

The primary purpose for the census remains the same today as it was in 1790: to serve as the source of State population totals so that the number of seats in the House of Representatives can be properly apportioned among the States. Mandated by the Constitution, the use of census figures in guaranteeing representative government has been expanded over the years by the courts. It now includes the reshaping of voting district boundaries for State legislatures and local governments, as well.

Since our Nation's founding, the census has been a way of taking a "statistical snapshot" of our people and determining their number and location. Over the years, census information has become essential in the distribution of billions of dollars annually under Federal and State programs for such worthwhile purposes as education, health care, community development, transportation, and crime prevention. Government policymakers routinely use census data to make decisions on where to locate or expand public facilities and services, while business planners employ census numbers to devise strategies for the Nation's economic development.

Data from the 1990 census will serve as the basis for many of the Nation's official statistics during the coming decade. Leaders in government and the private sector will use the information it provides in making critical decisions as we prepare to enter the 21st century.

Abraham Lincoln once observed: "If we could just know where we are and whither we are tending, we could better judge what to do and how to do it." The census helps to provide us with such insight.

Now, Therefore, I George Bush, President of the United States of America, by virtue of the authority vested in me by the Constitution and laws of the United States, do hereby declare and make known that under the law it is the responsibility and obligation of every person who usually resides in the United States to take part in the 1990 Census of Population and Housing by truthfully answering all questions on the census forms applying to him or her and to each member of the household to which he or she belongs, and to the residence being occupied.

Every resident of the United States is hereby assured that the information provided in the census will be used solely for the purposes allowed by law. Only combined statistical summaries of answers to census questions are published. By law, individual and household answers cannot be released in any way that will identify or harm any person or household. Individual information collected will not be used for purposes of taxation, investigation, or regulation, or in connection with military or jury service, the compulsion of school attendance, the regulation of immigration, or the enforcement of any other Federal, State, or local law or ordinance.

In Witness Whereof, I have hereunto set my hand this sixth day of March, in the year of our Lord nineteen hundred and ninety, and of the Independence of the United States of America the two hundred and fourteenth.

George Bush

SECRETARY SULLIVAN'S PROPOSAL FOR NEW FOOD LABELING RULES
March 7, 1990

Dr. Louis W. Sullivan, Secretary of Health and Human Services (HHS), proposed March 7 that most foods sold in the marketplace bear labels clearly stating their nutritional value. His proposal would extend mandatory labeling far beyond existing requirements that apply only to food products containing vitamin additives or making specific health claims. About 30 percent of the $350 million worth of foods sold each year in American retail outlets came under those rules, according to the Food and Drug Administration (FDA), an agency within HHS that supervises the federal government's food labeling rules.

Another 30 percent of the foods bore nutritional labels that the processors placed on the cans and packages under a voluntary system that was adopted in 1973. Sullivan's proposal for mandatory labeling would apply both to the unlabeled and voluntarily labeled categories. In addition, the HHS secretary said information on the food containers should be explicit and understandable to the shopper.

"The grocery store has become a Tower of Babel, and consumers need to be linguists, scientists and mind readers to understand the many labels they see," Sullivan said in an address to the National Food Policy Conference in Washington, D.C., where he announced his labeling plan. The label information would include the amounts of saturated fat, fiber, and cholesterol in the food, as well as the percentage of its calories that come from fat. Such phrases as "low fat" and "high fiber" would have to be defined. A product could not use a "no fat" label, for instance, unless the specified number of grams of fat per unit of weight was below a certain level.

But the labels would no longer have to specify the amounts of vitamins such as thiamine, riboflavin, and niacin. Because diseases associated with those substances are rare, the government opted to omit them to provide space for the new information on food labels.

Legislation already had been introduced to require by law more stringent labeling practices than the secretary sought to impose by regulation. The legislative sponsors were two influential members of Congress, Rep. Henry A. Waxman, D-Calif., and Sen. Howard M. Metzenbaum, D-Ohio. "Congress can do a better job and faster through a change in the law than the [Bush] administration can do through a change in regulation," Waxman remarked after Sullivan announced his plan.

There were suggestions that the secretary's intent was to head off the legislation. But it was passed in October, shortly before Congress adjourned for the year, to take effect six months after the FDA writes detailed regulations to fulfill the law. Unlike Sullivan's proposals, the legislation would set a single, uniform national standard, preventing any state from imposing stricter rules on its own. The legislation had support from both the food industry and consumer groups. The health-claims issue became a matter of concern to both groups after the Reagan administration in 1987 abandoned an eighty-one-year-old ban on making such claims. A dispute between the FDA and the Office of Management and Budget created a stalemate over further regulation of the claims. During that time a proliferation of health claims created "food wars," which united the food industry and consumers in a drive for re-regulation.

In his speech, Sullivan said that "high on his agenda" was to urge Congress to modify the Delaney Clause, which prohibits the presence of any suspected carcinogenic substance in food or drugs. He said that scientific opinion holds that the prevailing "zero risk" standard was too severe and should be "negligible risk."

> *Following is the text of the address by Dr. Louis W. Sullivan, Secretary of Health and Human Services, to the National Food Policy Conference in Washington, D.C., March 7, 1990, in which he proposed to extend and clarify nutritional labeling of food products sold in American markets:*

This conference is timely and extremely important. Consumers are more health conscious than ever before. They are demanding accurate, credible and understandable information about food. We can and should take pride in the knowledge that Americans are adopting healthier eating habits. Mortality from heart disease alone has declined nearly 40 percent over the past 25 years, and healthier diets are primarily responsible for this progress. We must work tirelessly to advance policies that will foster even better eating habits.

Yet, as consumers shop for healthier foods, they encounter confusion and frustration. The grocery store has become a Tower of Babel, and consumers need to be linguists, scientists and mind readers to understand the many labels they see.

I'm sure all of us have encountered the mayhem. Some food labels are hard to read and understand. Vital information is missing, and frankly some unfounded health claims are being made in the marketplace.

It is a real mess. No wonder *Time* Magazine recently reported that "Barraged by conflicting nutritional advice and hyperbolic health claims for various foods, consumers are no longer sure what is good or what is bad for their bodies."

The time for clarity is here, or we risk wasting the opportunity to help educate consumers about health promotion through better eating habits. Millions of consumers are prepared to make lifestyle choices that will prolong and enhance their lives, if we can eliminate the confusion and uncertainty. We already have much of the scientific information that consumers need, as indicated in the Department's unprecedented *Surgeon General's Report on Nutrition and Health.*

In my brief time with you today, I'll outline the steps the Department of Health and Human Services is taking to help encourage greater clarity for the consumer and to encourage healthier dietary behavior. Specifically, I would like to talk about four issues:

- First, FDA's proposals for regulations on health messages;
- Second, the FDA's proposals for a Food Labeling Initiative;
- Third, the regulation of seafood; and
- Finally, changes that must be made in the Delaney Clause.

New Regulations About Health Messages

I am certain that we would all agree that health messages must be accurate, sound and fair. There has to be truth in labeling, and misrepresentations must be exposed and eliminated. That is why the FDA recently published its revised proposal on "health messages" for food products.

The regulation withdraws an earlier proposal that proved to be too permissive. It also seeks comment from the public on new ways to permit valid and reliable health messages. And it sets forth how the FDA is likely to exercise its enforcement discretion while the rule-making is underway. It provides guidance to companies interested in including health-related information on their food labels. At the same time, this revised proposal will make it easier to take action against food products that make unjustified health claims.

Food Labeling Initiative

Perhaps most important, this new proposal on health messages will complement a comprehensive food labeling initiative now underway in the Department of Health and Human Services.

Last June, I directed the FDA to consider sweeping changes in the way this country's food is labeled. I felt then, and I feel even more strongly now, that the time has come to re-examine and to improve our food labels.

The FDA promptly took up this challenge. After announcing its intent to undertake a thorough and exhaustive review of food labeling in the U.S., the FDA held four major public hearings across the Nation. All told, some 200 people testified at these national hearings, and more than 1,500 people participated in 50 local "consumer-exchange" meetings. This outpouring of oral testimony was supplemented by more than 2,000 written comments on the FDA's requests for comments on changes in the Nation's food labels.

We have examined the testimony and the comments, and an overwhelming consensus has emerged: It's time to move ahead in food labeling. After a careful review of all of the issues, we are prepared to take actions that, when carried out, will equal a comprehensive reform of the Nation's food labeling. Let me share those actions with you now.

To begin with, two principles will guide our approach:

- First, as we did with health messages, we will give priority to labeling changes that will have the greatest public health impact.
- Second, rather than wait for the perfect agreement on *all* aspects of the food label, we will enact reforms as each individual issue is resolved.

With this basic approach, we will initially focus on the extremely important area of nutrition labeling and propose:

- Mandatory nutrition labeling for most foods, and
- Revisions in labeling content.

Regarding mandatory labeling, we will propose mandatory nutrition labeling for most packaged foods. We know from a range of studies that nutrition labeling is the American consumer's primary source of information about what individual foods contain. According to current estimates, 60 percent of the sales of FDA-regulated packaged food already carries nutrition labeling. We will propose that nearly all of the U.S. food supply regulated by the Department of Health and Human Services be required to furnish nutrition labeling.

While there is broad consensus for mandatory requirements, any thoughtful proposal would have to provide for reasonable exceptions. We will propose to exempt products that have no nutritional content at all. Other products, such as foods produced by small operations like local retail bakeries, are likely to be exempted for economic reasons.

We're also placing high priority on the *content* of a food's nutrition label. Here, too, the time has come for a change. The current nutrition label content was adopted in 1973. That was seventeen years ago, and now we have much more information which consumers need, and want, to assist them in selecting healthier diets.

Accordingly, we would propose that requirements for nutrients, such as saturated fatty acids, cholesterol and fiber be added. This would go a long way toward helping Americans make healthy choices about their diets.

Less important information may also be deleted or made optional. For nutrients such as vitamins and minerals, this is likely to mean removing the requirement that labeling carry information about such nutrients as thiamine, riboflavin, and niacin.

While we are confident that our labeling requirements will be sufficiently comprehensive so that states and the food industry will be satisfied, we must be sensitive to the fact that some states may be interested in additional labeling information. Under our proposed regulations, states would be able to add to the information required, but they will not be able to subtract from the bedrock information mandated by the regulation.

Of course, when these regulations are proposed, as always, there will be a comment period during which time the public may voice any concerns or potential drawbacks. But you may rest assured that our bottom line is the same as yours — protection of the American consumer.

In time, we are also going to resolve several other matters, including food descriptors. FDA will formally define such health-related terms as "low fat" and "high fiber."

Also, over time we will be revising the format of the nutrition label, for consumers have told us that they want a nutrition label that is easier to understand. We will identify a variety of alternative formats, and then test market them with consumers to determine which format works best.

Taken as a whole, all of these changes and others I have not mentioned, represent a major, comprehensive revision of the food label.

To summarize, in one year, we expect to have proposals on several of the most important food labeling issues:

- For mandatory nutrition labeling and for revisions on nutrition labeling content, we expect to publish proposals by mid-year;
- For definitions of food descriptors and for regulations to enhance ingredient labeling, we expect to publish regulations by the end of the year; and
- For a final policy on health messages for foods and progress toward identifying a proposed new label format, we expect *Federal Register* notices in early 1991.

Seafood Safety Regulation

Now that I've sketched out for you our food labeling priorities, I'd like to mention briefly a couple of related food questions that are also high on my agenda — one has to do with seafood, the other with the Delaney Clause and the concept of "negligible" risk.

This Administration currently believes that seafood inspection is best done by the FDA, working together with the National Oceanic and Atmospheric Administration (NOAA). Of course, some have argued otherwise. But the FDA has a proven track record of successful regulation and years of experience, and has been successful in assuring that the Nation's seafood is safe for many years. The FDA's mandatory inspection program of facilities that handle seafood in interstate commerce has produced a seafood supply which is comparable in safety to meat and poultry.

According to current data, seafood is in fact the safest source of muscle protein available. Moreover, the rate of illness from seafood on a per-pound-consumed basis is *declining*. The FDA has achieved these results, I might add, at a fraction of the cost of continuous inspection programs.

Also, the FDA and NOAA have the expertise for the job. Seafood inspection requires highly specialized scientific expertise primarily because most of the associated health risks arise through microbiological or chemical contaminants.

I would be remiss if I failed to add that the FDA is *increasing* its seafood coverage, and that the budget submitted by President Bush for the coming Fiscal Year includes an increase of 14 million dollars. But this is predicated upon the seafood programs staying with the FDA through that budget year.

Proposed Changes to the Delaney Clause

Now let me turn to the issue of the Delaney Clause, and its impact on food safety issues.

The President's plan for pesticide residues, announced last fall, proposes that for residues in processed food, the Food, Drug, and Cosmetic Act should be amended so that the Delaney Clause does not apply. So we propose to add a tolerance threshold at a level where the public health is not threatened. The new standard for this threshold would be "negligible risk."

As you know, the Delaney Clause has been interpreted as requiring absolute safety — or zero risk — because it prohibits the presence of even negligible quantities of an added carcinogen. Thirty years ago when the clause was first enacted, such an interpretation was consistent with the science and knowledge of the day. But today it is not because we are able to detect chemical residues in our foods at parts per trillion or less.

Increased scientific understanding of the mechanism of carcinogenesis, along with increasingly sensitive analytical methodologies, have resulted in the development of sophisticated risk assessment techniques. Commensurately, this requires more sophistication by the public to understand this detailed information.

These advances have led scientists to conclude that, in some circumstances, substances shown to be carcinogenic in high-dose animal studies may not present a risk to human health under specified conditions of use.

Although the concept of "negligible risk" was proposed in the context of carcinogenic pesticide residues, Congress should also consider extending this standard to food and color additives as well. I call upon our elected representatives to replace an outdated, excessively rigid approach to regulation with an approach which maximizes rationality and choice.

Conclusion

In conclusion, I strongly believe that American consumers should have full access to information that will help them make informed choices about the food they eat. Simply put, the American consumer should be able to read and understand food labels. The consumer must be given reliable and vital information. The actions which I have outlined today will go a long way toward addressing the perplexity and frustration in the marketplace by making labels more clear and cogent.

I wish all of you success in your work at this vital conference. Thank you and God bless you.

LITHUANIAN DECLARATION OF INDEPENDENCE

March 11, 1990

Lithuania became the first among the Soviet Union's restive republics to declare itself a free and sovereign state. A newly elected Parliament, at its first meeting March 11, proclaimed the restoration of the independent Lithuanian republic that existed before it was forcibly annexed by the Soviet Union in 1940. (Baltic Freedom Statements, Historic Documents of 1989, p. 469)

The brief resolution asserted that Lithuania's declaration of independence of February 15, 1918, was never annulled and thus continued to be valid. By that reasoning, the past fifty years of Soviet control amounted to an illegal military occupation—although the document did not say so outright, as many Lithuanian politicians had. The vote on the resolution was unanimous, 124 to 0 with 9 abstentions and absentees.

At the same time, while thousands of cheering Lithuanians gathered outside the parliamentary building in Vilnius, the capital, the lawmakers named the leaders of a noncommunist government to negotiate their future relations with Moscow. At the head of the government and newly restored state, they placed Vytautas Landsbergis.

The soft-spoken, fifty-seven-year-old music professor had led the Sajudis pro-independence movement to victory in national elections February 24—the first multiparty balloting in Lithuania in seven decades. The Sajudis-dominated Parliament elected Landsbergis president over Algirdas Brazauskas, the Lithuanian Communist party leader whose popularity soared after his party broke with the Soviet Communist party in December 1989.

Agitation for political reform—eventually for independence—began in the Baltic states of Lithuania, Latvia, and Estonia in 1987 after Soviet president Mikhail S. Gorbachev called for a reevaluation of Stalin's nationalities policies, those dealing with the various peoples and constituent republics that make up the Soviet Union.

A demonstration by Lithuanians on February 16, 1988, to mark the seventieth anniversary of the birth of the republic, turned into a massive anti-Soviet protest. That spring the first unofficial political groups appeared, seizing on Gorbachev's encouragement of "grass roots" citizen initiatives to support his social and political programs.

That summer more demonstrations greeted the anniversary of the 1940 nonaggression pact between Stalin and Hitler that enabled Stalin to seize the independent Baltic republics. Pushed by the growing strength of Sajudis, Brazauskas endorsed Lithuanian as the official language of the state, and for the first time in decades on February 16, 1989, permitted public celebrations on Independence Day. A new constitution was approved. The cathedral in Vilnius was reconsecrated and the Catholic Church resumed a role long denied in public life. But try as they might, the Lithuanian Communists could not bring about reforms fast enough to blunt the Sajudis-led campaign for independence.

Gorbachev's Uncertain Response

The strength of the Lithuanian resolve apparently caught Moscow by surprise. After the Lithuanian Parliament proclaimed independence, Gorbachev waited two days to speak, calling the action "illegitimate and invalid" and vowing never to negotiate. The Soviet Congress of People's Deputies—in effect, the Soviet Parliament—similarly declared on March 15 that the declaration was not legally binding. Gorbachev nevertheless persuaded the Soviet Congress to pass a resolution that was much milder than what others originally proposed.

Gorbachev was aware that taking a hard-line stand against Lithuania would likely place his courtship of the West in jeopardy. At the same time, he was pressured to display a strong hand in Lithuania as a warning to other republics and to placate hard-liners in Moscow.

Lithuania's sister Baltic republics of Latvia and Estonia were also moving toward assertions of independence despite acts of intimidation from Moscow. On March 30 the Estonian Parliament passed a resolution that stopped short of being an outright declaration of independence but amounted to a notice to Moscow that the Estonian people had started on a gradual course of reclaiming their sovereignty. Similarly, the Latvian Parliament on May 4 declared the beginning of a transition period leading to the republic's independence. By mid-year, eleven of the Soviet Union's fifteen republics had formally asserted greater autonomy.

In Gorbachev's dealings with Lithuania, he mixed threats of force—which included sending Soviet tanks through the streets of Vilnius and the seizure of certain public buildings in the city—with promises of gradual autonomy within the Soviet system. When the Lithuanian government refused to yield, the Soviet leader gave a forty-eight-hour *warning and on April 13 began to cut the republic's supplies of oil and natural gas.*

American Policy Dilemma

For Western democracies—especially for the United States—this created a dilemma. On the one hand, American politicians had demanded freedom for the Baltic states ever since Stalin had absorbed them into the Soviet Union. For decades Congress had ritually passed resolutions condemning the Soviet occupation of the "captive nations." But the cheers for Lithuania's bold dash were distinctly muted in Washington and other Western capitals. Lithuania's action came at an embarrassingly inconvenient time for both the Soviet Union and the West. By insisting on immediate secession before Gorbachev was prepared to deal with it, the Lithuanians exposed his domestic difficulties, particularly his need to court the hard-line constituencies that opposed his economic and political reforms.

Having thrown his support behind Gorbachev at the Malta summit meeting in December 1989, President George Bush had an enormous stake in the Soviet leader's success at home and abroad. (Bush-Gorbachev on Malta, Bush on NATO, Historic Documents of 1989, p. 643) Bush's initial reaction to events in Lithuania was to warn Gorbachev not to intervene. But as the situation alternately tensed and eased, Bush said little and adopted what amounted to a hands-off approach. He declined to impose sanctions on the Soviet Union.

The United States, which has never recognized Soviet sovereignty over the Baltic republics, now refused to recognize Lithuanian independence. The U.S. stance brought an anguished outcry from Lithuanian president Vytautas Landsbergis. He said "This is Munich"—suggesting appeasement as British and French leaders had attempted with Hitler at a 1938 meeting in the German city—and charged that the Bush administration had "sold us out for larger interests."

Compromise After Long Standoff

After a sixteen-week standoff, Moscow and Vilnius reached a compromise that temporarily lifted the crisis just as the last of Lithuania's oil reserves were approaching empty. Moscow agreed to negotiate the issue and lift the economic boycott. The Lithuanian Parliament, in turn, voted June 29 to suspend its March 11 resolution of independence for one hundred days beyond the beginning of negotiations. The next day the Soviet oil pipeline to Lithuania was reopened, and early in August the negotiations opened in Moscow.

Following are a Lithuanian government translation of the resolution approved by the Lithuanian Parliament, March 11, 1990, asserting the continuing validity of the republic's declaration of independence, February 16, 1918, and an official translation of that document:

RESOLUTION ON
LITHUANIAN STATE RESTORATION

The Lithuanian Republic's Supreme Council, expressing the will of the Nation, resolves and solemnly proclaims the restoration of the exercise of sovereign powers which were constrained by a foreign force beginning in 1940.

The Lithuanian Council's February 16, 1918, Declaration of Independence and the May 15, 1920, resolution of the Constituent Assembly on the restoration of the democratic Lithuanian state were never annulled. They have full force and form the constitutional foundation of the Lithuanian State.

Lithuania's territory is whole and indivisible; no other state's constitution is in force on it.

The Lithuanian State guarantees human, civil and national community rights and recognizes the principle of inviolability of borders, as it is formulated in the 1975 European Conference on Security and Cooperation Helsinki Final Act.

As the voice of sovereign powers, the Lithuanian Republic's Supreme Council will seek to realize the State's complete sovereignty.

1918 DECLARATION OF INDEPENDENCE

The Council of Lithuania in its meeting on February 16, 1918, voted unanimously to address the governments of Russia, Germany, and other states with the following declaration:

The Council of Lithuania, sole representative of the Lithuanian people, in conformity with the recognized right to national self-determination, and in accordance with the resolution of the Lithuanian Conference held in Vilnius from September 18 to 23, 1917, hereby proclaims the restitution of the independent State of Lithuania, founded on democratic principles, with Vilnius as its capital, and declares the rupture of all ties which formerly bound this State to other nations.

The Council of Lithuania also declares that the foundation of the Lithuanian State and relations with other countries will be finally normalized by a Seimas, elected in a democratic way by the people of Lithuania.

The Council of Lithuania in informing (the nations addressed) to this effect kindly requests recognition of the independent State of Lithuania.

CHILEAN PRESIDENT'S
INAUGURAL ADDRESS
March 12, 1990

Gen. Augusto Pinochet surrendered power in Chile on March 11 to a democratically elected civilian president, Patricio Aylwin. The transition brought an end to a long and often bitter period of military rule in a nation known for its deep-rooted democratic and law-abiding tradition. It also marked the restoration of civilian government to South America's last remaining dictatorship.

Aylwin, 71, and Pinochet, 74, participated jointly in the inaugural ceremony in the half-finished new Congress building in the Chilean seaport of Valparaiso. The two men stood side by side in the plenary hall of the Congress as Gabriel Valdes, the president of the Senate, administered the oath of office to Aylwin and draped the red, white, and blue presidential sash over his shoulder. Pinochet handed Aylwin a star-shaped brooch symbolic of executive authority, which is believed to have been owned by Bernardo O'Higgins, the nation's liberator from Spain and handed down from president to president for more than a century and a half.

Valdes embraced Aylwin, who then turned and shook Pinochet's hand. The retiring president, who remains the head of the Chilean army, left the hall to a combination of cheers and jeers. Aylwin remained behind to swear in his twenty-member cabinet, drawn from a political spectrum ranging from Aylwin's centrist Christian Democrat party to the leftist Socialist party and other members of the seventeen-party coalition that brought the new government to power.

Aylwin left Valparaiso in a motorcade for the seventy-mile trip to Santiago, the capital and seat of the executive branch. Thousands greeted the new chief executive at La Moneda, the presidential palace, where he appeared on a balcony to address brief remarks to the crowd assembled in the open courtyard below. "What we have to do, we have to do together," Aylwin said. "Chile does not want any more violence. It does not want war. It wants peace." The following day Aylwin delivered his formal inaugural address at the National Stadium, where thousands of Chileans had been held during the 1973 coup that unseated Salvador Allende, Chile's last elected civilian president. The address expanded on the themes of reconciliation and national harmony after sixteen-and-a-half years of domination by the military.

Path Back to Civilian Rule

For most of the twentieth century, Chile enjoyed a reputation as one of Latin America's most steadfast democracies. The exceptions were the coups that overthrew an elected president, Arturo Alessandri, in the 1920s and a military dictator, Gen. Carlos Ibañez, in 1931. Both men were subsequently returned to power by the Chilean electorate. But for four decades, through the rigors of the Great Depression and World War II, Chile was a relative oasis of tranquility in a generally unstable Latin America.

In 1970, Salvador Allende Gossens, a Socialist, was chosen president although he received a bare plurality (36.6 percent) of the vote in a tightly contested three-man race. Tolerated—if not supported—at first by the centrist Christian Democrats, the majority party, and by the military, Allende soon alienated all but the far left of the country's political spectrum by his attempt to transform Chile's economic and political structures to a Marxist system. As the economy collapsed and inflation zoomed, the military rose on September 11, 1973, seizing control of the major cities and attacking the presidential palace in Santiago. Allende died in the revolt—whether by suicide or by execution is still unknown.

In 1973, Aylwin, a leader of the Christian Democrats and a prominent senator, was one of Allende's most outspoken critics. He and others welcomed the military intervention. But as the military regime's brutality surfaced, and Pinochet's determination to hold onto power became clear, Aylwin moved into opposition, forming in 1983 a multiparty coalition called the Democratic Alliance (AD). It attempted over the next five years to reach an accommodation with the government to end military rule.

Finally, in a plebiscite on October 5, 1988, the voters rejected a bid by Pinochet to remain in the presidency through 1997. The dictator conceded his defeat, opening the way to presidential and congressional elections in 1989. Aylwin, chosen as the opposition candidate in the elections, easily defeated Pinochet's hand-picked nominee, Hernan Buchi, a former minister of the economy. Aylwin received 55 percent of the vote, compared with Buchi's 29 percent, and 15 percent for Francisco Javier Errazuriz, an independent. Pinochet, pressed by his fellow officers and by the United States, accepted the popular mandate and called on Chileans to support their new president.

Economic and Political Challenges

Aylwin inherited the strongest economy in South America—the legacy of Pinochet's free-market philosophy—which was strongly influenced by University of Chicago academics. Aylwin, nonetheless, would need the continued support of Pinochet and the military, as well as the cohesion of the widely diverse political coalition that rode with him into power.

In 1988 economic growth in Chile was 7.4 percent, inflation was a relatively low 14.8 percent, and unemployment stood at 6.7 percent, in marked contrast to the crippled economies of Argentina, Brazil, and Peru. The high growth rates of recent years, however, were unevenly distributed. The gap between Chile's rich and poor accelerated during the Pinochet years. The richest 20 percent of the population had 59 percent of Chile's total income in 1989, while the poorest 20 percent had only 3.5 percent.

The Aylwin government faced strong popular expectations of improvement in such social areas as education and health, but at the same time there was a broad consensus to continue with Pinochet's free-market policies and the former government's open trading regime, which had held inflation in check and made Chile attractive to foreign investors.

The Aylwin coalition, lacking control of the national Congress, would have to reach agreement in the Senate with the political center-right, which supported Pinochet in the election. Mindful of this, Aylwin did not propose any drastic measures as he assumed power.

Between 8,000 and 15,000 people were executed and 2,000 disappeared during the Pinochet years, according to the Chilean Commission on Human Rights. Several hundred political prisoners remained in custody at the time Aylwin took office. One of his first acts was to pardon at least forty of the political detainees, with a promise to review other pending cases. It remained doubtful, however, that any of the military officers who committed human rights violations would be brought to justice. Pinochet, before leaving office, said, "If any of my people are touched, I will bring the entire constitutional process to a halt." Aylwin was expected to settle for the creation of public tribunals to find the truth about abuses without insisting on punishment for the guilty.

Such a moderate stance would not sit well with the political left. Before Aylwin's inauguration, a string of bombings served notice of potential turmoil ahead. A few days after the inaugural ceremony, a former Chilean Air Force general, Gustavo Leigh, an original member of the military junta that seized power in 1973, was shot and seriously wounded in an attack for which a Communist guerrilla group claimed responsibility. As Air Force chief, Leigh had ordered jets to fire rockets at the presidential palace where Allende was holding out against the military rebels during the 1973 uprising.

As an "act of unity and peace," Aylwin permitted Allende's followers to

*rebury him September 4 from an unmarked grave in an obscure cemetery
to a prominent place in Santiago. Tens of thousands of Chileans lined the
route of the funeral procession. At the gravesite, Aylwin said he hoped
that giving proper homage to Allende would help "bury violence and
intemperance forever."*

> *Following is the text of Patricio Aylwin's inaugural address,
> March 12, 1990, assuming the presidency of Chile, as pro-
> vided in English translation by the Chilean government:*

We are gathering here today with hope and joy. Hope, because at last we
begin, with fraternal spirit and a yearning for freedom and justice, a new
stage in our national life. Joy, because for the first time in 20 years we
begin walking a path that we ourselves chose consciously and freely. It has
not been imposed on us. It is the result of the free and sovereign will of the
Chilean people.

Today we celebrate a new daybreak. In this beautiful gathering, more
than celebrating the victory that was officially sanctioned during the
inauguration at Congress yesterday, we make public our firm commitment
to consolidate our national unity, seeking reconciliation among all Chileans
on the bases of mutual respect and the nonrestrictive reign of truth, law,
and justice.

This celebration is enhanced by the presence of our guests, leaders and
representatives of friendly countries. They are with us at this happy
moment as they were with us in solidarity during the days of persecution
and pain.

They joined our struggle with the asylum they generously granted all
exiled Chileans [applause], with their defense of the human rights of so
many fellow Chileans, and with their solidarity with our people's struggle
to recover democracy. In the name of our people, I now thank you, thank
you very much.

We would also like to add something else. You can rest assured that the
return of democracy in Chile will also mean that we will actively participate in all international cooperative efforts, that we may contribute to the
development of the people, to justice and peace among nations, and to the
reign of human rights in all countries of the world.

Millions of Chileans from one end of the nation to the other are with us
in this festivity. Others who live abroad, either voluntarily or because they
were forced to do so, have hopes for the restoration of democracy here. We
are conveying to them our fraternal greetings.

During the sad, hateful, and blind days when force prevailed over
reason, this stadium was for many countrymen a place of imprisonment
and torture. We would like to say to all Chileans and to the world that
never again will human dignity be violated. . . .

Today we are making a commitment to rebuild our democracy faithful
to the values we inherited from our forefathers, values which Cardinal
Silva Enriquez, a just man and a great friend of the Chilean people, to

whom we owe so much, described beautifully as the soul of Chile, the love for freedom, the rejection of all forms of oppression, the supremacy of the law over injustice, the supremacy of faith over any form of idolatry, tolerance of differing opinions, and the tendency not to exacerbate conflicts but to try to resolve them through agreement. These values will prevail among us again.

We have a beautiful and complex job ahead of us. We must restore a climate of respect and confidence among the Chilean people, no matter what their beliefs, points of view, activities, or the social class to which they belong; no matter whether they are civilians or military. Yes, gentlemen, yes fellow countrymen, no matter whether they are civilians or military, Chile is a single country. The innocent should not pay for the guilty.

We must be able to reconstruct the unity of the Chilean family, be they workers or businessmen, laborers or intellectuals. We must open paths for democratic participation so that everyone may cooperate in achieving well-being. We must do away with the great differences that divide us and especially must raise the living standards of the most needy sectors to respectable and human levels. We must safeguard the health of our fellow countrymen.

We must establish a fair relationship between those involved in the economic process. We must give our youths access to knowledge, job opportunities, and progress, which is in keeping with the time we are living in. We must grant our elderly the respect they deserve. We must promote the participation and enhance the role of the women in Chilean society. We must promote growth and safeguard the stability of our economy. We must improve the terms of our foreign trade. We must preserve the environment and our renewable natural resources. We must make our utmost contribution to Latin America's democratization, development and integration, and to the consolidation of world peace. In sum, we must implement the policies contained in the program that the coalition of the parties for democracy [CPPD] proposed to the country.

Although the job that lies ahead of us is beautiful and complex, and demands from us our utmost effort and enthusiasm as we undertake it we must be fully aware of the difficulties it will pose. We are going to face difficulties caused by the obstacles and restraints that the past regime has left us. There will be obstacles stemming from the very nature of the various issues, and there will also be others, no less important, which we created ourselves. Nobody ignores that the previous government tried to perpetuate itself in power. . . .

Those who exercised full power made an effort to the last day to reduce the power of the new democratic officials. Those who used the assets of the state as their absolute owners, without any limitations, found the way to take away as many assets as possible from the administration to which it constitutionally belongs, from the President of the Republic.

Many people are asking why we accepted these things. They do not hide their rejection of the cordial way in which the transfer of power was being conducted, while these events were taking place. While I am supporting the moral condemnation that such a conduct deserves, a condemnation which I am sure history will approve, I invite my countrymen to look at the other side of the issue.

We are happy with the peaceful path we took, without any emotional stress, to the Democratic Government. In order to avoid the limitations imposed by the former regime, should we have exposed our people to new violence, suffering, and loss of life?

We, the Chilean Democrats, decided to achieve democracy by defeating authoritarianism on its own playing field. This is what we did, accepting the benefits and costs involved.

I sincerely believe that the path we chose was the best possible one. Courtesy does not mean cowardice. I believe that most of the obstacles used to try to restrain us will not resist the weight of reason and the law. I trust that the national congress, disregarding differences among parties, will approve the necessary reforms to insure the normal and prompt operation of our new democracy. I am sure that our armed and security forces will fulfill their institutional duties if anyone dared, or is tempted, to employ force against the will of the people.

We will also have to overcome the natural problem involving issues. Our program is large, the requirements are many. There are many needs that have not been fulfilled for years that must be met. We will not be able to do everything at once. We will have to establish priorities. . . .

We must also resolve other difficulties: the problems within ourselves. I will call them the great temptations: the temptation to consume all our time in settling old accounts, the temptation to begin everything anew, and the temptation of power.

It is legitimate and just for people to want truth after a long period of an absolute and mysterious power, with so much suffering, and with public matters held as inaccessible secrets. We have said before, and we solemnly reiterate today, that the moral conscience of the nation demands that we find out the truth about the missing people, the truth about the horrendous crimes and other grave human rights violations that occurred during the dictatorship. We have also said, and I reiterate today, that we must face this delicate matter by reconciling the virtues of justice and prudence. After the responsibility for those crimes is determined, the time for pardon will arrive.

There are also other unjust matters that demand reparation and prompt correction. Today I have signed decrees pardoning numerous political prisoners.

In the coming days we will resolve other cases. I have sent to Congress the appropriate bills to resolve the problems of all political prisoners. We will also have to clarify matters that have never been explained well. Some of these matters involve the state patrimony and the national interest.

In this necessary exercise of justice, we must avoid the risks of reenacting the past. We must avoid our past conflicts: We must avoid spending endless hours in inquiries, recriminations, or witch hunts. We must not forget our duty to the future. I consider it my duty to ensure that all our time is not spent looking at the past. The spiritual health of the country demands that we find formulas to complete—in a reasonable period of time—the moral cleansing of the nation. The time will come when we will all be able to look at the future with trust, to reconcile ourselves, and to join efforts in the task of developing the country....

At this crucial time in our national life, I invite all of my countrymen to go deep into their minds to ask themselves how everyone can contribute to the great common task, and to be ready to assume their share of responsibility. The world is looking at us. The great leaders of our history demand that we act in a suitable manner. The future generations will judge our conduct. The task is beautiful: To build together the nation we want, free, just, and good for all Chileans. It is up to us countrymen.

SEABROOK NUCLEAR PLANT BEGINS OPERATIONS
March 15, 1990

The government on March 15 licensed the Seabrook nuclear reactor to begin commercial operations, closing out the longest-running challenge to any American nuclear power plant. The reactor's startup came five days later, eleven years behind schedule and nearly fourteen years after the plant's construction was begun at Seabrook, a hamlet on the New Hampshire coast. The first objections had come even earlier. Environmentalists and many nearby residents contended that the plant's location near crowded summer beaches and several sizable towns was unwise.

As early as January 1974, the state of Massachusetts began legal action to block construction. The state argued that it would be impossible to carry out an emergency evacuation of residents in nearby towns—including six Massachusetts towns within ten miles of the plant—in the event of a nuclear disaster. The Nuclear Regulatory Commission (NRC), the federal licensing agency, ruled that emergency planning did not need to be considered until the plant's owners sought an operating license after it was built. It was completed in July 1986.

All that time, and for the next decade and a half, Seabrook was a focal point of protesters voicing their concerns about the safety of nuclear power. Not all the protests were argued before the NRC and the courts. Some were large placard-waving demonstrations at the gates of the facility. In May 1977, during one of the largest demonstrations, some 2,000 protesters cut through barbed wire surrounding the plant and had to be forcibly evicted. Fourteen hundred were arrested by the end of the day.

Dukakis vs. Sununu

A year after the 1979 nuclear accident at Three Mile Island in Pennsylvania, the commission required states and localities within ten miles of a nuclear plant to submit plans for sheltering and evacuating people before the plant could be licensed. After the 1986 Chernobyl nuclear accident in the Soviet Union, Gov. Michael S. Dukakis of Massachusetts refused to submit plans, saying they were useless. His refusal had the effect of blocking a license until President Ronald Reagan November 18, 1988, issued an executive order permitting the federal government to draft emergency plans if local or state officials refused. A year later an NRC administrative panel approved a plan written by the utilities that owned Seabrook. That set the stage for the commission's approval. (Kemeny Commission Report on Three Mile Island Crisis, Historic Documents of 1979, p. 823; Chernobyl Nuclear Accident, Historic Documents of 1986, p. 383)

Even as the commission voted to award the long-sought license, protesters were arrested at Seabrook for trying to block the entrance to the plant. The commission's 3-0 vote was a victory for White House chief of staff John N. Sununu, who was governor of New Hampshire from 1983 to 1988 and pushed hard for the plant's completion and its licensing. When New Hampshire communities near Seabrook refused to submit evacuation plans, he ordered the state government to perform that task.

The commission's vote was taken March 1, with two of the five commissioners abstaining, but the licensing was delayed until March 14 to permit Massachusetts and two other opponents to file blocking motions with the U.S. Court of Appeals for the District of Columbia. The motions were denied, and on March 15 the Office of Nuclear Reactor Regulation issued the license. Voting for the license were commissioners Kenneth M. Carr, Thomas M. Roberts, and Kenneth C. Rogers. Commissioners Forrest J. Remick and James R. Curtiss excused themselves from voting.

Bankruptcy and Delay

The startup of Seabrook not only was eleven years behind schedule but had been attained at a cost of $6.45 billion, twelve times the original estimate. That estimate was for two reactors, one of which was canceled by the owners in 1984 after the expenditure of $800 million. The cost overruns created the first bankruptcy of a major investor-owned utility since the 1930s depression. The Public Service Company of New Hampshire, the principal shareholder among thirteen remaining owners of the plant, filed for bankruptcy January 28, 1988, after it was denied a 15 percent rate increase by the New Hampshire Supreme Court. Maine and Vermont utilities, under orders from state regulators, had sold their shares in Seabrook in 1986. At one time, as many as sixteen New England utilities were partners in the ownership arrangement.

In December 1989 the New Hampshire legislature approved a rate *increase, fulfilling a condition in a bankruptcy reorganization plan that enabled Northeast Utilities of Hartford, Connecticut, to acquire Public Service Company for $2.3 billion—the amount of Public Service's investment in Seabrook. Public Service's stake in Seabrook was then spun off into a separate entity controlled by the bankrupt company's creditors and stockholders, and bearing the Public Service name. The upshot of those legal and financial arrangements was that the license bore the name Public Service Company of New Hampshire. It became the 110th nuclear reactor to be licensed in the United States. Only four others were being planned or constructed.*

Sen. Edward M. Kennedy, D-Mass., a longtime foe of the Seabrook plant, called the commission a "rogue agency that lives by its own set of pro-industry rules." He said the vote was "the culmination of a long line of irresponsible 'public-be-damned' decisions by the NRC." Harold B. Finger, president of the U.S. Council for Energy Awareness, a group that campaigns for nuclear energy, had a contrasting view. "It will light the homes and run the factories of New England while emitting no greenhouse gases and while displacing 11 million barrels of oil every year."

Following is a press statement issued by the Nuclear Regulatory Commission on March 15, 1990, announcing its issue of an operating license to the owners of the Seabrook, New Hampshire, nuclear reactor:

The Nuclear Regulatory Commission's Office of Nuclear Reactor Regulation issued a license on March 15 to Public Service Company of New Hampshire (PSNH) and other owners authorizing full power operation of the Seabrook Station, Unit 1, located in Rockingham County, New Hampshire.

The NRC Commissioners granted approval of a full power license on March 1. The Commission placed a "courtesy" stay until March 14 to permit filing of stay motions with the U.S. Court of Appeals. A stay motion was denied on March 14.

The Seabrook Station is located on a site on the southeast coast of New Hampshire in the Town of Seabrook about 11 miles south of Portsmouth. Seabrook is 35% owned by PSNH. The other owners of the facility are 11 public and private New England utilities.

Unit 1, which is a pressurized water reactor and at full power will have an electrical output of about 1150 megawatts, was previously licensed for power testing up to five percent of full power on May 26, 1989.

An Atomic Safety and Licensing Board, which conducted a public hearing of safety and onsite emergency planning matters, initially issued a partial decision on March 25, 1987, that authorized the NRC's Director of Nuclear Reactor Regulation to issue a low-power license upon making required findings not at issue in the hearing. However, a license was not issued until May 26 because of stays by the Commission and the Atomic

Safety and Licensing Appeal Board and subsequent remands of a number of contentions, including the issue of a lack of a prompt notification system for Massachusetts communities within the plant's emergency planning zone.

An Atomic Safety and Licensing Board, which conducted a public hearing on offsite emergency matters, issued a decision on November 9, 1989, that authorized the NRC's Director of Nuclear Reactor Regulation to issue a full power license upon making findings not at issue in the hearing. After intervenors in the licensing proceeding requested that authorization of full power be stayed, the commission took review and decided on March 1 that its "immediate effectiveness" review supported allowing the Licensing Board's authorization of a full power license.

The owners of Seabrook allowed the application for an operating license for Unit 2 to expire October 31, 1988.

INDEPENDENCE OF
NAMIBIA
March 20 and 21, 1990

Namibia, the last colony in Africa, witnessed the arrival of independence March 21 with festivities marking the end of 106 years of colonial rule and twenty-three years of guerrilla warfare. In Windhoek, the capital, the long-awaited day was greeted at a midnight ceremony in a soccer stadium attended by thousands of cheering Namibians and a large gathering of foreign dignitaries. They included Secretary General Javier Perez de Cuellar of the United Nations, and President F. W. de Klerk of South Africa, the departing power.

Amid jubilant cheers, the South African flag was hauled down and replaced by the new blue, red, green, and gold flag of the Republic of Namibia. "In the name of our people, I declare that Namibia is forever free, sovereign and independent," said Sam Nujoma upon being sworn in as the new republic's first president. Nujoma, leader of the South-West Africa People's Organization (SWAPO), the main nationalistic movement, led his party to victory in elections conducted throughout Namibia in November 1989 under UN supervision. Some 7,900 UN personnel had been sent to Namibia to keep the peace and guarantee a fair election. They included a special UN force of 4,500 troops and 1,500 police officers from several countries.

"We extend a hand of friendship to our new neighbours," the South African president said in a speech preceding Nujoma's. The "season of violence has passed for Namibia and for the whole of Southern Africa," de Klerk added. He was congratulated on his speech by, among others, Yasir Arafat, leader of the Palestine Liberation Organization. Another honored guest was Nelson Mandela, leader of South Africa's most

*prominent black nationalist group, the African National Congress, who
had spent twenty-seven years in prison before his recent release by de
Klerk.* (De Klerk and Mandela on South African Changes, p. 65)

*Prominent among the guests were Secretary of State James A. Baker
III and Chester Crocker, an assistant secretary of state in the Reagan
administration who was the principal architect of a 1988 agreement that
led to Namibia's independence. In that agreement, South Africa pledged
to relinquish its control of Namibia, a territory it called South-West
Africa, in return for the withdrawal of Soviet-supplied Cuban troops from
neighboring Angola. That accord was worked out under UN sponsorship
in July 1988 and signed that December in New York by the foreign
ministers of South Africa, Angola, and Cuba.* (Angola-Namibia Peace
Accord, Historic Documents of 1988, p. 947)

*The cost of pursuing a military solution became intolerable to all
parties in the regional conflict. War-torn Angola ran up huge foreign
debts despite assistance from the Soviet Union, which became increasingly less inclined to continue its support. South Africa, plagued by U.S.
and some European economic sanctions in response to its apartheid
racial policies, was forced to make budget cuts and reduce its outlays in
Angola. Until 1988, South Africa maintained as many as 50,000 troops in
Namibia to counter SWAPO guerrillas, who often took refuge in Angola.*

Long Pursuit of Independence

*In 1915, South Africa seized control of Namibia from Germany, which
had declared it a protectorate in 1884 and a colony in 1890. After World
War I the League of Nations gave South Africa a mandate over the
territory. The UN, the league's successor organization, sought to replace
the South African mandate with its own in 1946, in the aftermath of
World War II. But South Africa defied the world organization for more
than four decades. Meanwhile, in 1966, SWAPO was formed and began its
guerrilla warfare. In 1978 the UN Security Council passed Resolution 435
that laid the groundwork for the 1988 political settlement in southern
Africa and Namibian independence.*

*At the Windhoek celebration, the UN secretary general told the
cheering crowd that "at long last" Namibia was taking "its rightful place
among the community of nations," marking the "triumph of the international rule of law." It became the 160th member of the United Nations.
De Cuellar further pledged that the United Nations would not abandon
Namibia in its "challenging task of nation-building."*

*Namibia, a country twice the size of California, occupied by only 1.5
million people, remained economically dependent on South Africa. Per
capita income was slightly more than $1,000 a year—high by African
standards. But Nujoma noted in his inaugural address that "more than
thirty per cent of our workforce is unemployed and an even larger
number is under-employed." Two-thirds of the people "are very poor by
our standards and by the standards of the world," he added.*

Devoting much of his speech to economic problems, Nujoma retreated from his previous espousal of all-out socialism and called for a "partnership between the state and the private sectors." He envisaged private enterprise as "an engine for growth and prosperity," and welcomed foreign investors.

Bush Welcomes New Nation

In Washington, President George Bush announced March 21 that the United States had established diplomatic relations with Namibia and lifted economic sanctions that had applied while it was under South African rule. Saying that Namibian independence had been brought about "in large measure by vigorous American diplomacy," Bush said the new nation would be "a full trading partner" of the United States.

Bush said he was "especially gratified that Namibia's Constituent Assembly has produced a constitution that is among the most democratic in Africa." Although SWAPO won 57 percent of the seats in the assembly, it had to negotiate with six other political parties in drawing up the constitution. That process, according to foreign political observers, resulted in a document expressing more democratic ideals than would have been expected if the drafting had been left solely to SWAPO.

Following are excerpts from the texts of speeches delivered in Windhoek, in celebration of Namibia's independence, by Secretary General Javier Perez de Cuellar of the United Nations and President F. W. de Klerk of South Africa, both on March 20, 1990, and by Sam Nujoma, Namibia's first president, on March 21 at his inauguration:

DE CUELLAR SPEECH

It is my honour and pleasure to address this distinguished gathering at a moment which is solemn as well as full of joy and hope. A new state is about to be born, and, at long last, to take its rightful place among the community of nations.

We gather in Windhoek tonight to celebrate the culmination of the struggle for national dignity and independence of many generations of Namibians. Numerous lives have been sacrificed in seeking the goal which has now been reached.

The whole world, especially Africa, rejoices with Namibia. What is a triumph for Namibia is a triumph for Africa and indeed for the principles that are enshrined in the Charter of the United Nations. . . .

Namibia has been the special concern of the United Nations from its earliest days. Indeed, the mandated status of Namibia was a product of the League of Nations. The historic process of decolonization which has so vigorously been promoted by our organization generated a new imperative for Namibia: the restoration to its people of their inalienable right to independence.

Every principal organ of the United Nations has been engaged in this great issue. The Security Council and the General Assembly kept faith with the people of this country. The Security Council adopted the landmark Resolution 435 which provided the basis for Namibia's independence today. The aspirations of Namibia have prompted countless acts of support and the dedicated work of the deliberative bodies of our organization. They have been reflected in the several advisory opinions of the International Court of Justice which dealt specifically with the status of Namibia. . . .

May I also mention the special meaning of the present occasion for me personally. When I assumed my responsibilities as secretary-general more than eight years ago, I said that I would make the subject of Namibia the highest priority for myself.

I am, therefore, filled with profound emotion and gratitude that this priority has been realized—by arduous effort, with frustrations and occasional setbacks in the past no doubt, but through a process which has fully vindicated the repute and effectiveness of the United Nations.

The independence of Namibia also marks the triumph of the international rule of law. The achievement bears eloquent testimony to the strength of the norms of democracy and human rights.

Moreover, the settlement process itself, and the transition to independence, confirm once again the fundamental importance of negotiation in the settlement of international disputes. . . .

Without the cooperation of all parties, in particular SWAPO [South-West Africa People's Organization] and South Africa, the transition process could not have been brought to a happy end. Such cooperation became a cornerstone for the whole edifice. I should like, Mr. President-elect, to express my deep appreciation to you for the support you gave at each critical juncture. I want you to know of our admiration for the statemanship with which you have transformed yourself from the dauntless leader of your party to the leader of your nation. My appreciation, Mr. State President, also goes to your South African government and to its administrator-general, advocate Louis Pienaar, for their support of the process of peaceful settlement once implementation has been decided upon.

I am sure that all represented here are unanimous in their hope that the Namibian experience may help to pave the way to peaceful and democratic solutions to other major problems of Southern Africa.

UNTAG [U.N. Transition Assistance Group] itself was a unique operation, bringing together eight thousand men and women from more than one hundred nations. Tonight, I pay public tribute to the efforts of my special representative, Mr. Martti Ahtisaari, and his deputy, Mr. Legwaila, and the force commander, General Prem Chand. UNTAG broke much new ground, and successfully supervised and controlled a step-by-step procedure leading to free and fair elections for a constituent assembly. In the process, it faced and overcame acute problems, political and practical. . . .

In the conviction that national reconciliation held the key for unlocking closed doors I invited the leadership of all the political parties to come together for the first time when I visited Namibia last July. Their response to this call and the degree to which they developed the concept of joint effort laid the basis for the success of the whole endeavour. The result was further consolidated by the impressive manner in which the constituent assembly went about its work, in a spirit of mutual respect and principled compromise. The assembly has adopted a constitution, by consensus, which is a model of democratic construction. The maturity and restraint displayed by the leadership of the people, coupled with their determination to exercise their right to self-determination, lent an exemplary character to the political process. They gave a remarkable lesson to the whole world in the effectiveness of democratic procedures.

With the completion of the implementation of Resolution 435, UNTAG's mandate to assist the independence process will draw to a close in just a few minutes. But the role of the United Nations and of the international community in assisting the government and people of independent Namibia will not cease.

I wish to pledge the full support of the United Nations to Namibia in the challenging task of nation-building. Preparations are already under way for me to convene a pledging conference to assist in mobilizing the necessary resources for the social and economic development of Namibia....

DE KLERK SPEECH

I stand here tonight as an advocate for peace. The season of violence has passed for Namibia and for the whole of Southern Africa.

The birth of the new, independent nation of Namibia is only minutes away. The thoughts of the nations of the world are with you now. And we, the nations of Southern Africa, share in the joy of the people of Namibia on this momentous occasion.

It has been a long and arduous road, spanning several generations. Many made the supreme sacrifice in this process and it is fitting that we should remember them tonight.

It is above all a moment of hope—hope that the future of this vast and beautiful land will bring peace, security and prosperity for its children.

The independence of Namibia marks the end of a chapter and the beginning of a new era, for the whole of the Southern African region....

Mr. President-Elect, I congratulate you on your election. The people of South Africa join me in wishing you and the people of the new Nation of Namibia prosperity and good fortune. We extend a hand of friendship to our new neighbours. Together we should seek to build a constructive and mutually rewarding relationship between our two countries. Good neighbourliness is in our mutual interest....

May Almighty God be with you and bless you.

NUJOMA INAUGURAL ADDRESS

... [W]e are welcoming the arrival of a new epoch in our country. Our nation is finally free and independent. The long suffering of our people is being replaced with happiness and joy. From this day on, our people will have the chance to shape their own future.

However, independence did not come on a silver platter. We fought and sacrificed for it. Namibia is achieving nationhood with a proud history of martyrdom. ...

The most recent phase of our history gives us reason to be confident that the Namibian people are indeed capable of marching forward in unison to consolidate our hard-won independence.

In November, the Namibian people came out in big numbers to register to vote in the independence elections and elect their representatives. In turn, the elected leadership took up the challenge with energy and a sense of mission to draft a Constitution that reflected the aspirations of all the Namibian people, thereby facilitating the arrival of this joyous day.

Seven parties participated in the drafting of the Constitution. The work was characterized by a spirit of national reconciliation. Today, with our Constitution serving as the fundamental law of the land and the guide to action, the door is now open for my distinguished colleagues and I to establish the first government of the Republic of Namibia.

In this spirit of national reconciliation, SWAPO [South-West Africa People's Organization], as we stated time and again, has no intention of ruling the government alone. Indeed, we have extended invitations to the other parties to join us in the great and challenging task of setting up a state machinery for the Republic. We must work together to build our nation. We must give all Namibians an opportunity to participate in the affairs of the country. In this connection, we are striving to achieve a balanced restructuring of the economy, the public service and to democratize our society.

Now that we have won our independence, we must focus our attention on economic development. We have inherited a lopsided and underdeveloped economy. We confront major economic difficulties. We are inheriting a budget deficit of R500 million [rands—the national currency] from the South African administration. Two-thirds of our population are very poor by our standards and by the standards of the world.

One of the most crippling legacies of colonialism is Namibia's mass unemployment. More than thirty per cent of our workforce is unemployed and an even larger number is under-employed. This robs so many Namibian families of the chance to live a decent life.

In addition, we rely heavily on imported foodstuff, such as, maize, rice and most of our fruits come from outside Namibia.

This large import bill causes higher prices, increases our budget deficit and deprives us of jobs in the agricultural sector. Most, if not all of this food can be grown right here on Namibian soil. In our fertile northern regions, unemployment is particularly high and work opportunities are few. Yet, with adequate capital and technical assistance, the northern regions could feed our nation.

The government is seriously looking into the use of hydroponics, a kind of irrigation that prevents water loss and increases agricultural output. We foresee our nation developing large-scale commercial farming. This will create more jobs and produce agricultural goods which have a great potential not only to feed our people, but also for export.

For the immediate future, we encourage people to remain on the land to pursue subsistence farming. The government stands ready to help through a variety of means, such as, our agricultural extension services, provisions for better equipment, training, transport and marketing.

There is still a long way to go before our country's resources are fully exploited to improve living conditions for our people. Indeed, there is enormous room for building our industrial base. Our raw materials are exported in an unprocessed form. We need to process our own diamonds, beef, karakul, fish and so on, thus serving our local markets and exporting to the world. The fishing industry alone has tremendous potential for expanding into new enterprises like canning and marketing. This is crucial for job creation and increasing national revenue.

Putting an emphasis on the development of industry will put Namibia on the road to true independence and create more jobs and opportunities for our jobless majority. . . .

Our young country will not be able to generate all the capital necessary for economic development. We welcome inflows of capital and technical know-how from abroad. Private investment will be needed to employ our workforce.

We are committed to a mixed economy. In this regard, we look forward to a good partnership between the state and the private sectors, because only through working together will our economy prosper. The state will increase investment into the development of water, energy and road infrastructures. These are critical for mining and other industries. The government seeks to enter into joint ventures with the private sector in the areas of fishing, large-scale farming and agroindustries.

However, we want to ensure a more dynamic role for the private sector. This sector should be an engine for growth and prosperity. We shall eliminate the laws which have long limited access to private sector production for the majority of Namibian households.

In addition, our emerging nation needs foreign investment. In this connection, we are formulating an investment code which will spell out our open and inviting attitude to investment and set out the kind of commitment that we would expect from investors towards our goal of national development.

We do not underestimate the difficulties on the road to economic independence. We need to reduce the deficit speedily. We must cut inefficiency and redundancy in administration. We must increase efficiency in tax collection. We must achieve the economic growth which will raise revenue without increasing overall tax rates. Together, as a united people, we can improve our production, our access to productive resources and our welfare. We can provide the basic services needed by our people....

Today, we have achieved the pre-condition for an economy and economic policy by and for Namibians. We have ended 106 years of colonial rule....

... [W]e express our deepest gratitude to the forces of international solidarity, those international organisations, non governmental organisations, and individuals who for so many years have stood by us in our struggle and lent us valuable material and moral support. We remain forever indebted to all of them....

Therefore, as a country which has enjoyed international support and solidarity during its struggle, Namibia will play an active role in international affairs.... We will promote friendship among nations. We will [sic] peace and economic cooperation among the countries of Southern Africa.

With regard to the situation in South Africa, we are encouraged by the fact that both the African National Congress and the government of South Africa have expressed their readiness to begin negotiations towards a non-racial and democratic South Africa. The fact that President de Klerk and Comrade Nelson Mandela are here with us today gives us hope that a solution will soon be found to end the unjust system of apartheid. We encourage this process and stand ready to help in whatever capacity requested.

In conclusion, I would like ... to pledge that the Cabinet and I will do our utmost to uphold the Constitution of the Republic. By the same token, I call upon all the Namibian people to jealously protect our hard-won independence and to defend the territorial integrity of the Republic. Let us celebrate with honour, dignity and confidence this great and solemn day.

SOVIET DISSIDENT ELENA BONNER'S REMARKS ON GORBACHEV'S AIMS

March 22, 1990

Elena Bonner, widow of Andrei Sakharov, the Soviet scientist and human rights advocate, gave a dissident's evaluation of leader Mikhail S. Gorbachev at a University of California forum March 22 in honor of her late husband. She said that in terms of the Soviet Union's internal political life, the reform-minded leader had accomplished "practically nothing at all." In a question period following her lecture at the Berkeley campus, Bonner said, "I have nothing against Gorbachev—it's just that Gorbachev has to be forced to do the job and not to create power for himself." She added that the West's "uncritical love of Gorbachev" is spoiling him.

Bonner noted that terms such as perestroika *(restructuring) and* glasnost *(openness), usually associated with Gorbachev, had all been used by Sakharov in his 1972 book* Memorandum to Leaders. *But she credited Gorbachev with sponsoring four important changes: (1) greater—albeit incomplete—freedom of expression; (2) release of many, though not all, prisoners of conscience; (3) greater freedom to travel and emigrate; and (4) withdrawal of Soviet troops from Afghanistan.*

She said the constitutional changes effected by Gorbachev in the last two years served only to increase his own power. She urged basic constitutional change to make clear the nature of "reconstruction" and to defend the rights of both individuals and "constituent" peoples of the Soviet Union. "Only the path of a new constitutional agreement between [Soviet] republics," Bonner said, "can keep our peoples from mutual slaughter." She specifically called upon the West to support the national movements of Lithuanians and Armenians. Bonner urged the creation of "something like a Marshall Fund" to help Poland, Czechoslovakia, and Hungary cope with their economic problems, but warned against aid to the Soviet Union unless there was political change.

Bonner's Career

Bonner had been intimately involved in political turmoil from an early age. When she was fourteen, her father, a member of the Armenian Communist party elite, was executed during a Stalinist purge in 1937. Her Jewish mother spent seventeen years in labor camps and exile. As a nurse in World War II, Bonner suffered a battle injury that resulted in a lifelong struggle against blindness. Nevertheless, she became a physician, writer, and lecturer. Her first marriage broke up as she joined the fledgling human rights movement during the 1960s. She helped to produce a publication that reported human rights abuses in the Soviet Union and was cofounder of a Helsinki Watch Group, organized to monitor Soviet compliance with the international agreement signed by the Soviet Union and other nations in 1975 in the Finnish capital and known as Helsinki Accords.

Her activism brought her into contact with Sakharov, whom she married in 1971. In 1975, while in Italy for an eye operation, she managed to go on to Oslo, Norway, to accept her husband's Nobel Peace Prize after Soviet authorities denied him permission to travel. During her husband's exile to Gorky from 1980 to 1984, she maintained contact with Western supporters and journalists. Throughout that time, the Soviet press portrayed her as a Zionist and an agent of the Central Intelligence Agency (CIA). The hate campaign prompted threats that drove Bonner's two children by her previous marriage, and her elderly mother, to emigrate to the United States.

After her own arrest and exile in 1984, Bonner received permission to travel to Boston for cardiac by-pass surgery in 1986, following repeated appeals and hunger strikes by Sakharov. Abiding by the condition that she not talk with reporters while in the United States at that time, during her recuperation Bonner wrote Alone Together, her harrowing account of the couple's exile. Finally, in response to years of international pressure, Bonner and Sakharov were granted freedom later that year. He died December 14, 1989.

Berkeley Event

At Bonner's lecture, Berkeley physicist Andrew Sessler noted Sakharov's *"very significant contributions"* to plasma physics, elementary particle physics, and cosmology. In another tribute, Czeslaw Milosz, a Lithuanian-born Polish writer and Nobel laureate in literature, observed that Sakharov was opposed to the institutions of his country and the most powerful police apparatus in the world. *"I don't know whether his refusal to compromise would have been possible without the love of Elena Bonner, who gave him her full support in danger,"* Milosz said. Bonner was presented with the Berkeley Citation, usually granted for *service to education but this time awarded for "memorable and coura-geous service to humanity and to upholding the highest ideals of freedom and human values."*

> *Following are excerpts from Elena Bonner's lecture at the University of California in Berkeley, March 22, 1990, in honor of her late husband, the Soviet scientist and dissident Andrei Sakharov. The text was made available, in transla-tion from Russian, by the university:*

I am deeply grateful for this special award being presented to me today—grateful to the university governors and administrators, and to all the students both graduate and undergraduate. Although it is my name that is written on this beautiful document, I share it with Andrei Sakharov just as we always shared our struggle for civil and human rights.

This is an occasion on which we have come together to honor and remember Andrei Sakharov, but you will forgive me if I do not speak about him personally, but rather about his social involvement, his work in defense of human rights and world peace.

I think that today it is particularly important to speak about the situation in our country, and in the countries of the so-called (and thank God now former) "Communist bloc," because the common future of all of us depends upon how events in that part of the world unfold; because it is more important now than ever before for people in the West—and particularly Western social and political figures—to have a concrete understanding of what exactly has changed and what should now be done. What I am about to say I do not consider to be the authoritative "last word" on the subject, but I will say what I think and how I view events.

Five years ago there began in our country a process which is usually called by the now world-famous term "perestroika." This word is usually associated with the name of Mikhail Gorbachev, but I would like to remind you that in his 1972 work *Memorandum To Leaders* Sakharov used all those words that have now simply become part of fashionable usage: "perestroika," "glasnost," "stagnation." In that work, alongside an assess-ment of the situation in the Soviet Union, he sketched out a clear, systematic plan—indicating what needed to be changed for our country to stop being a monster, terrifying the rest of the world, and for it to join the ranks of other democratic countries.

It seems to me that, having set "perestroika" in motion, Gorbachev passed through two phases: the first part of this five year period (two to three years) really did constitute a progressive move forward. During this time "glasnost" really did appear—not full "freedom of the press," but at least it now became permissible to talk about what had happened in the past—the tragic past of the country—and about those negative elements which persisted from the "stagnation" period. "Glasnost" gave the Soviet reader things that had only been published in the West, and in all of this it performed a great service.

A second point. The early "perestroika" years were notable for the release of a large number of prisoners of conscience. That does not mean that there are no more prisoners of conscience left in our country—there still are, and the struggle on that front must not stop. There is even one new prisoner, whose arrest (for a whole year—a year and two months even—he has been held in jail) is motivated by nothing other than that he is an Armenian leader of Popular Karabakh [Karabakh People's Committee]. His name is Manucharov—he's an elderly man, he served in the second world war and I would like to draw your attention to his fate.

The third change that "perestroika" brought is a change in the policies for leaving the country, both for emigration or in documentation process for visits to and from the Soviet Union, which has become much simpler. This is a very important, concrete step, because it has eased the plight of many separated families, friends and loved ones. And—this is a key point to note—all these three steps are achievements towards which people were struggling in the West as well, not just dissidents within the Soviet Union. Sakharov always used to insist on the need for freedom of information, on freedom for prisoners of conscience and the freedom to travel and emigrate.

The fourth important step taken in the "perestroika" period by Mikhail Gorbachev and his government was the withdrawal of Soviet troops from Afghanistan. The war there brought incalculable misery to the people of Afghanistan and who knows what its psychological consequences will be for the younger generation in our own country. And our government recently took one more step that was very difficult for it to make. It declared the war to have been an unjust war, a war that should never have even been begun, much less waged—, that is, the government admitted its own guilt for the war. I should point out that Sakharov played an important role in this decision. You have probably all seen the television clips where a young Afghan vet, who lived through the war in Afghanistan and lost both his legs, started to attack Sakharov (the young man was told to do so—he had been specially prepared). Those clips were broadcast all over the country and all around the world. Finally though, under great pressure from Sakharov and the huge mass of public opinion which gathered behind him, our government reluctantly took this decision, a decision which amounted to self-condemnation.

So now I have enumerated the four most important achievements of the first period of Gorbachev's rule. At the same time as this was going on, several steps were taken on the economic front—steps which turned out to be errors, and which seriously destabilized the financial and economic system of a state which has always had serious difficulties in coping with its economy.

And that is probably all one can say on the subject of positive steps. At least as regards internal policy. Because there were also some important changes in foreign policy. Particularly important is the change in real policy on disarmament. . . .

. . . [T]he disarmament process . . . brought Gorbachev great adulation in the West. And I would fully share the feelings of the West, were it not for other actions of Gorbachev which obscured his positive moves. In the country's internal political life Gorbachev has unfortunately accomplished very little, practically nothing at all. . . .

All the constitutional changes effected by Gorbachev over the last two years concerned only the potential for increasing the personal power of, first, the Chairman of the Supreme Soviet and, now, the President. . . . Our country needs a constitution which defends its citizens and their rights, which defends its constituent peoples. What we need is something like a "Bill of Rights," but for the moment all we have is a "Bill of the Rights of the State over Citizens, Peoples, Republics." We need a new ethnic-constitutional mechanism, in which no one people would have any more or less weight than any other. . . .

But Gorbachev has not made a single step along this path. During the 5 years of perestroika, apart from the first flawed economic reforms, not a single real attempt was made to change the people's continually worsening material conditions. And I am not exaggerating—the whole country was thunderstruck and dismayed when for the umpteenth time we were offered a Five Year Plan of development, with the promise of future well-being—a plan which was in no way conceptually different from the preceding thirteen Five Year Plans which brought us into poverty. Parallel with this plan, the shelves in stores have emptied, the ruble is undergoing spiralling inflation and the country is literally becoming impoverished and hungry. Ethnic conflicts are tearing the country apart—blood has been shed—and the overall number of victims in our country is no less than there was in Beijing's Tienanmen Square. . . .

It was said out loud at the first Congress of Soviets that 43 million people in our country live below the poverty line. That's below the Soviet poverty line of 70 rubles a month. But that figure is a total fabrication—people cannot live on that. Many deputies said that we had to do something immediately to improve the material situation of these people. And the whole country, following the Congress on television, thought that the corresponding decision would be taken. A few months later our rather idle press dug out and printed a story about how party functionaries were being promoted right across the board. And when deputies at the Supreme Soviet tried to tackle Gorbachev on this point he said that party people had a very hard job to do and that few people were willing to do it.

So that is my brief account of the internal situation in my country. When people in the West praise Gorbachev's actions—and I did say that in international policy there truly have been some real changes—the argument used usually runs like this: "Gorbachev did not use his tanks and invade Poland, Hungary or Czechoslovakia whereas Brezhnev did." It's true—he did not invade, but it is no merit of Gorbachev's that he did not. Rather it's his problem, because he cannot. Our army cannot do it, nor can our country as a whole. The army is in a state of psychological stress after the inglorious Afghan campaign. A large number of middle-ranking army officers—indeed the army in general—are finding it very hard to deal with the new attitude of the people towards them after the tragedy in Tbilisi, and the whole country is on the verge of breakup.

And that's why it was possible, thank God, for what happened in Eastern Europe to happen. On that path we have been outstripped by our Eastern neighbors. In Poland, Czechoslovakia, Hungary real political changes have occurred. I think that it is the West's task to create something like a Marshall Fund to help them cope with their economic problems. As for our country, I'm very doubtful as to whether aid today would be of any use. Without political change that aid will just vanish—as they say in Russia "it will turn to sand." Or—even worse—it will be used to fortify the still vigorous Party-bureaucratic apparatus. And that will not only slow down the process of democratic development within the country, but it will be a threat to the West as well. . . .

There are still two other particular issues that I consider very important and would like to mention. First of all, Lithuania today. It is quite possible that if the new union agreement which I was speaking about had been concluded a year or two ago then Lithuania would not have seceded. But now we have to deal with a fait accompli. I think that Lithuania was right to select its own path of development. For 45 years your government's position was that Lithuania, along with the other Baltic republics, was under occupation by the Soviet Union. For 45 years your country has been commemorating the national holidays of the Baltic republics. And that is why I simply cannot comprehend why today the U.S. administration, instead of officially recognizing Lithuania as an independent state, is restricting itself to meaningless announcements. It is of no importance whether or not Gorbachev gives assurances that he will or will not use force. But by international law, if you have been recognizing Lithuania as "occupied" then you should now recognize it as "independent." And I cannot understand the position of the United Nations on this question— total silence.

The second issue—Armenia. Armenia, which besides the tragic conflict with Azerbaijan had to undergo a terrifying earthquake. Armenia, whose international aid (the funds earmarked for quake relief) disappeared nobody knows where. A people in the throes of severe depression after the earthquake and the totally unjust and unjustifiable decision on Nagorno-Karabakh—that nation is in a terrible state. Today in the Armenian republic, out of a population of just over 30 million inhabitants, one million are homeless. Today the army is forcibly deporting Armenians from Karabakh, arguing that otherwise they cannot guarantee their safety against attacks by Azeris.

The Armenian people, which survived the ferocious genocide of 1915— an experience equally tragic for that small nation as the 1940s and their experiences in Germany were for the Jews. The Armenian nation is standing on the threshold of another genocide, and the world community is reacting to this much as it would to a minor ethnic conflict. I was struck by the behavior of the UN General Secretary, who happened to be in Moscow during those days when Armenians were being killed in Baku, when the tanks entered the city, and who said absolutely nothing. I call upon you all to help reach a just solution of the Nagorno-Karabakh problem. Today 80% of the population there is Armenian, but if the army continues to deport them, it may be that they'll be saying to us in a few years' time: "There's no problem—there are no Armenians."

That is all I have to say. . . .

VETO OF IDAHO BILL
RESTRICTING ABORTIONS
March 30, 1990

Idaho became a testing ground for the abortion issue after the Supreme Court ruled in July 1989 that some state regulation of abortion was permissible. No longer was the issue confined to the courts, as generally had been the situation after 1973 when the Supreme Court established a woman's right to an abortion in the landmark Roe v. Wade *decision.* (Supreme Court on Abortion, Historic Documents of 1973, p. 101)

Gov. Cecil D. Andrus, a Democrat and professed foe of abortion, stunned the anti-abortion movement by vetoing a bill passed by the Republican-controlled Idaho Legislature to restrict abortions. In his March 30 veto message, Andrus said the bill was too restrictive—and written purposely to invite a legal challenge that would provide the Supreme Court a new opportunity to overturn Roe. *The 1989 decision,* Webster v. Reproductive Health Services, *weakened but did not discard the 1973 ruling.* (Webster Abortion Case, Historic Documents of 1989, p. 365)

The Idaho bill was drafted largely by the National Right to Life Committee as model legislation intended to attract a five-member majority on the Court to reverse Roe. *The bill would have allowed abortions only when needed to save the life of the woman or to prevent serious damage to her physical health, when the fetus was deformed, or when pregnancy resulted from rape, or from incest if the victim was a minor.*

Abortion-rights activists threatened a nationwide boycott of Idaho potatoes, the state's largest cash crop, if Andrus signed the bill. The state tourism office reported it had received calls from out-of-state groups and individuals threatening to cancel their Idaho vacations.

The governor said in his veto message that it was not his duty to "engage in such speculation" as to whether "Idaho will face boycotts of our products." But, "It is my duty to face the specific issues presented in this bill," he added. "When all the rhetoric and emotion is set aside and the issues are examined in the cold glare of hard cases, these restrictions failed the test of reasonableness and compassion."

Andrus issued his message after the legislative session had ended, leaving no opportunity to override the veto. In his message, he cited the names of conservative legal scholars who backed his veto decision. Several political analysts thought the governor had handled the situation skillfully. He continued to be favored in his race for reelection and, in fact, easily won an unprecedented fourth term as governor.

Post-Webster Legislation

Although disappointed that the Supreme Court had not overturned the Roe decision, leaders of the anti-abortion movement were jubiliant nevertheless that Webster opened the way for state restrictions. However, their confidence turned to concern as pro-choice supporters mobilized as never before. Various women's organizations joined forces and countered with an effective campaign that seemed to neutralize the political advantage that the anti-abortion movement previously held. Many politicians retreated from pro-life positions, and some who stuck to those positions were rebuffed.

The Washington Post reported in mid-year, after most of the state legislative sessions were over, that the lawmakers in about forty states considered more than 300 abortion bills. But new restrictions had been enacted only in Pennsylvania, South Carolina, West Virginia, and the American territory of Guam. Pro-life advocates were bitterly disappointed in several states, including Idaho and Louisiana, where similarly restrictive legislation was vetoed.

At the time of its passage, the Idaho bill was considered the strictest to be approved by any state legislature in the wake of the Webster decision. That description was later applied to a Louisiana measure that twice drew Gov. Buddy Roemer's veto. Like Andrus, Roemer was a Democrat who said he opposed abortion. But he had vowed to veto any bill that made no exception for pregnancies resulting from rape or incest. The Louisiana Legislature handed him such a bill and he vetoed it July 6. After falling a few scant votes short of mustering a two-thirds majority to override Roemer's veto, the lawmakers promptly passed another bill making exceptions for rape, incest, and a woman's life being endangered by pregnancy. After weeks of uncertainty, Roemer vetoed that bill also.

At a news conference in Baton Rouge on the day of the second veto, July 27, Roemer said "common sense, common decency and respect for women" required broader exceptions than the revised bill made for victims of rape. The bill permitted abortions only if the crime was reported within seven days. Roemer said that he still considered himself "pro-life," but abortion foes denounced him and pledged to renew their efforts to place before the Supreme Court a restrictive state law that could serve as a test case.

They expressed hope that the July 20 resignation of Justice William J. Brennan, Jr., who was a defender of Roe, would result in a Supreme Court majority willing to overturn the decision. David H. Souter, President George Bush's nominee to succeed Brennan had not then expressed his views on abortion. But his apparent political conservatism made him more acceptable than Brennan to abortion foes. (Court on Parental Consent for Teenage Abortions, p. 387; Judge Souter's Testimony to Senate Judiciary Committee, p. 615)

Until the Souter nomination, anti-abortion advocates had focused their attention on finding another case that might win over Justice Sandra Day O'Connor, the "swing vote" in Webster. It was clear that a majority of the justices no longer considered abortion to be a fundamental right. But while O'Connor was willing to cast the decisive vote in the 5-4 majority opinion giving the states a voice in regulating abortion, she balked at the outright repudiation of Roe.

First Test in Florida

In the first legislative action on abortion after the Court spoke, Gov. Bob Martinez, an outspoken Republican foe of abortion, called the Florida Legislature into special session in October 1989 but could not push through any of his six anti-abortion measures. That same month Pennsylvania enacted a law to ban abortions after twenty-four weeks of pregnancy except to save the life of the woman or prevent irreversible impairment of her health.

More legislative action followed in 1990. James G. Blanchard, the Democratic governor of Michigan, on February 23 vetoed a bill that required women under eighteen years of age to get permission from one parent or a judge before having an abortion. However, the Republican governor of South Carolina, Carroll A. Campbell, Jr., on February 28 signed a similar bill applying to women under seventeen. The Supreme Court on June 26 ruled that states may impose such laws on minors, requiring them to notify at least one parent or obtain a judge's consent before having an abortion. West Virginia limited public funding for abortions.

The American territory of Guam on March 8 took the strongest action of any U.S. jurisdiction by reinstating a strict law that had been in existence before the 1973 Roe decision. It prohibited all abortions except in instances of extreme danger to the woman's health. The new law was promptly challenged in federal court, which enjoined its enforcement until the case could be decided by an appeals court.

Following is the text of a statement issued March 30, 1990, by Gov. Cecil D. Andrus of Idaho stating his reasons for vetoing the state Legislature's House Bill 625aa, which placed restrictions on abortion:

There is no more difficult, divisive issue in American life today than the issue addressed in House Bill 625aa. There can be no doubt that the feelings of individuals on both sides of the issue are deeply and honestly held. Good and decent Idaho people honestly and passionately disagree. For that reason, it is an issue that all of us must approach with respect, care and tolerance.

My position on abortion has always been very clear.

I personally oppose abortion and have so stated for all my years in public service, but I recognize that there are circumstances for which we must make exceptions. Therapeutic abortions are acceptable to me in the case of a mother's life being endangered by the pregnancy and in cases in which the pregnancy results from rape or incest.

There has been much speculation about how this legislation—if it becomes law—would affect the medical community, whether the legal sanctions are enforceable, and even whether Idaho will face boycotts of our state and our products. It is not my responsibility to engage in such speculation. It is my duty to face the specific issues presented in this bill. That is what I have done.

There is an old saying that "hard cases make bad law," but it is indeed the hard cases that we must examine when we consider House Bill 625aa.

What are we to do when a woman becomes impregnated as a result of a rape? This bill says that if, for some reason, she does not report that rape to law enforcement authorities within seven days of its having been committed, she violates the law if she terminates her pregnancy. This law would force the woman to compound the tragedy of the rape. In such a hard case, this woman would have no consideration under the edicts of House Bill 625aa. On the eighth day, she ceases to be the victim and becomes a criminal.

What are we to do in a circumstance in which a 12-year-old girl becomes pregnant as a result of incest? If, for whatever reason, she does not or cannot report the identity of the perpetrator to the authorities, she will violate the law if she or her family cause the pregnancy to be terminated. This law would demand that this 12-year-old girl, who has already been the victim of an unspeakable act, compound her tragedy. In this hard case, this young girl would receive no consideration under the edicts of House Bill 625aa. She would cease to be the victim and would become the criminal.

In short, House Bill 625aa does not provide any flexibility for a woman and her family in these difficult circumstances. The bill is drawn so narrowly that it would punitively and without compassion further harm an Idaho woman who may find herself in the horrible, unthinkable position of confronting a pregnancy that resulted from rape or incest. When all the rhetoric and emotion is set aside and the issues are examined in the cold glare of hard cases, these restrictions fail the test of reasonableness and compassion.

I am advised by legal scholars of both political parties that, in their opinion, there is not the remotest chance of this legislation's being found constitutional by the Supreme Court. The definition of "maternal health" and the reporting requirements for pregnancies resulting from rape and incest are too narrow to be accepted by any court. The civil enforcement provisions would be quickly struck down.

The media and the proponents of HB625aa continue to report that this bill provides for abortion if the pregnancy is the result of rape or incest or threatens the life of the mother. But practical application of the bill results in not providing for abortions in almost all circumstances.

The financial burden to Idaho will be excessive if we litigate this issue when we are told by legal scholars that there is little chance of prevailing. I have spoken at length with Professor Richard Wilkins of Brigham Young University Law School. He is a member of the Republican party, a pro-life advocate, and an attorney who worked on this issue for the Reagan Administration for nine years. He advises a veto. Professor James McDonald of the University of Idaho School of Law advises the same. As do many others.

Mr. Speaker, it is the legislative sponsors and those outside the legislative arena who pushed this proposal. They alone shoulder the responsibility for what they have produced. Many of the arguments I have outlined were well known while this proposal was under discussion. There were ample opportunities to address these issues, but all were shunted aside in the frenzy to pass a bill that, by the sponsors' own admission, was conceived outside of our state for the sole purpose of getting this issue back before the Supreme Court of the United States. I believe, and I am confident the people of Idaho believe, that we can make our own judgments on this terribly important issue without outside pressure and outside influence or threats.

When I consider what is right for Idaho, I must consider my own views and the needs of Idaho. This bill satisfies neither. It is not good legislation, and I cannot in good conscience affix my signature to it in passage. I did not take the oath of office of Governor of Idaho to lend my name to bad legislation. Therefore, I have vetoed HB 625aa and returned it to the House from which it came.

April

SOVIET ADMISSION
OF KATYN MASSACRE
April 13, 1990

Half a century after the disappearance of 15,000 captured Polish officers, the Soviet Union formally admitted what it had previously denied—that Stalin's secret police had killed thousands in the Katyn forest near Smolensk in western Russia. The official Soviet news agency Tass published a statement from the Kremlin on April 13 expressing "deep regret" for the Soviet act. Historical material had been "discovered," the statement said, that pointed "direct responsibility" to Levrenti Beria, the notorious secret police chief, and his deputy, Vsevolod Merkulov. After Stalin's death in March 1953, both men were executed for reasons unrelated to the massacre.

The admission came the same day Polish president Wojciech Jaruzelski met in Moscow with Soviet president Mikhail S. Gorbachev to discuss ways of improving relations between Moscow and the noncommunist government that Poland established in 1989. (Poland's New Era, Historic Documents of 1989, p. 523) Even during the long years that Poland was a Soviet vassal state, the officers' disappearance clouded the Moscow-Warsaw relationship.

"To speak about this [massacre] is not easy," Gorbachev was quoted as saying during a luncheon with Jaruzelski, "but it is necessary because it is only through truth that we find the road to genuine renewal and genuine mutual understanding." Jaruzelski responded that "for us [the Polish people], this was an unusually painful question." He received reams of documents that, Soviet officials said, listed the names of the dead officers and verified the complicity of Stalin and his secret police agency, the NKVD, forerunner of the present KGB.

The next day Jaruzelski visited the site of the mass grave near the village of Katyn, where the remains of some 4,500 of the Polish officers were discovered in 1943 by German soldiers during their invasion of Russia. On a visit to Katyn in November 1989, Polish prime minister Tadeusz Mazowiecki made clear that he held the Soviet Union responsible for the killings and demanded "moral" compensation for the deaths of all Poles at Soviet hands, including those who perished in labor camps.

According to Soviet affairs analysts, Gorbachev sought to make the apology more palatable to Kremlin hard-liners by offering it to Jaruzelski, a communist, rather than to Mazowiecki, a noncommunist. Although noncommunists gained control of the Polish government in 1989, Jaruzelski, as president, retained a modicum of the power he once held.

Mixed Polish Reaction

In Warsaw, government spokesman Malgorzata Niezabitowska said that the "crime" of fifty years ago "had an extremely painful influence on relations between our nations." He went on to say, "we are awaiting the elucidation of all blank spots in our common history, which for us Poles are symbolized by the Katyn crime."

"Gorbachev provided a final assessment of the [Katyn] issue," Jaruzelski told newsmen at the conclusion of his visit to Moscow. "I received a very extensive documentation connected with the tragedy. I think the documents will be of invaluable assistance to historians and of great value to families and relatives of the murdered officers." It was presumed that they would also throw light on the fate of captured officers whose bodies were not found at Katyn.

Lech Walesa, leader of Poland's anticommunist Solidarity movement, told the press that the "Soviet Union's admission of responsibility for the murder of 15,000 Polish officers is an act of moral justice long awaited by Polish society," but he added that "unsettled questions" remain. They included, Walesa said, compensation for the families of the victims and access to places in the Soviet Union "emotionally important to Poles."

Moscow's Longstanding Denial

The Kremlin had insisted that Nazis committed the massacre in 1941, when the Smolensk area fell to the invading German forces. After its recapture by Soviet forces later in the war, the London-based Polish government-in-exile sent investigators to the massacre site. They concluded that the killings took place in 1940 when the area was under Soviet control. The Russian army had captured the Polish officers when it joined Germany in an invasion of Poland in September 1939, touching off World War II. That collaboration between Hitler and Stalin was abruptly shattered the following summer with Germany's surprise invasion of Russia.

Stalin refused to accept the finding of the Polish exile government, and later broke relations with it, paving the way for the postwar communist *takeover of Poland. Some Poles and others have contended that Stalin ordered the killings to rid Poland of likely future leaders who might challenge his own designs on their nation.*

Until 1989, when Soviet control dissipated in Poland, a monument to the victims in Warsaw bore an inscription blaming the Germans. That inscription was then removed, leaving only the words "Katyn 1940" above the names of Kozielsk, Ostaskzhow, and Starobielsk, three prison camps where the Polish prisoners were held before they disappeared.

Following are excerpts from the official statement reported April 13, 1990, by the news agency Tass on Soviet responsibility for the murder of captured Polish military officers in 1940, as translated into English by the Polish government:

Recently Soviet archive workers and historians have discovered some documents concerning Polish soldiers who were imprisoned in the Kozelsk, Starobelsk and Ostashkov camps by the NKVD security police.

The documents indicate that 394 from about 15,000 Polish officers kept in the three camps were transferred to the Grazovetsk camp in April-May 1940. Most of them, however, were "turned over" to the NKVD administrations in the Smolensk, Voroshilovgrad and Kalinin regions and never mentioned in NKVD reports since.

The discovered archival materials point to direct responsibility of Beria, Merkulov and their subordinates for the crime committed in the Katyn forest.

Expressing deep regret over the Katyn tragedy, the Soviet side declares it one of the gravest crimes of Stalinism.

Copies of the discovered documents have been passed over to the Polish side. The search for archival materials continues. . . .

SUPREME COURT ON
TAX INCREASE
April 18, 1990

The Supreme Court ruled April 18 that a federal judge could order a local property tax increase to pay for school desegregation. In the case, Missouri v. Jenkins, *the Court's five-member majority said the judge's authority to direct an increase in taxes flowed from his power to devise remedies to the constitutional violation of school segregation.*

That view was heatedly challenged by the Court's four dissenters as an improper judicial intrusion into the affairs of local and state governments. Some legal scholars expressed surprise at a decision affirming a broad view of judicial power. A succession of civil rights decisions by the Court in 1989 limited legal redress for job discrimination and seemed to point the Court's direction in desegregation cases. (Supreme Court Rulings on Civil Rights Laws, Historic Documents of 1989, p. 321)

Justice Byron R. White moved away from his usual alignment with the Court's conservative majority to cast the pivotal vote in Missouri *and to write the decision. Justices William J. Brennan, Jr., Thurgood Marshall, Harry A. Blackmun, and John Paul Stevens concurred. A lengthy and often caustic dissenting opinion by Justice Anthony M. Kennedy was joined by Justices Sandra Day O'Connor, Antonin Scalia, and Chief Justice William H. Rehnquist.*

Kansas City Desegregation Case

This case arose from a 1977 lawsuit charging the state of Missouri with maintaining a segregated school system in a district that included much of Kansas City, Missouri, and parts of two neighboring communities. The schools in those areas, although previously integrated, had been left essentially black by white flight to the suburbs. U.S. District Court Judge Russell G. Clark in 1984 ruled in favor of the plaintiffs, a group of parents and children who were joined by the district school board.

During the next two years, the judge ordered the adoption of a broad and expensive plan for building, renovating, and equipping the district's schools so they could offer a superior education and serve as a "magnet" to attract white children. Clark ruled in 1987 that the state and the district should share the estimated cost of $500 million to $700 million for fulfilling the plan. To pay the district's share, school officials asked for higher property taxes, but local voters rejected a tax boost. After that, the judge stepped in and imposed a higher tax rate over the state's objection.

The state appealed, challenging the scope of the desegregation remedy, the allocation of the cost between it and the district, and the tax increase. The U.S. Eighth Circuit Court of Appeals in St. Louis rejected the state's arguments, upholding the desegregation plan, cost allocation, and a federal judge's authority to order a tax increase. But it said that instead of imposing the tax increase directly by order from the bench, the judge should in future situations of that kind order local authorities to raise the tax.

Kennedy's Strong Dissent

On appeal to the Supreme Court, the justices granted review only on the tax question but did not explain their reasons. They heard arguments in the case on October 20, 1989, and on April 18 unanimously struck down the tax increase Judge Clark had imposed. But in upholding the appellate court's approach—that the judge could order the school district to raise taxes—the justices split 5-4. In his dissent, Justice Kennedy said the distinction between the two approaches was a "convenient formalism."

Declaring that the "power of taxation is one that the Federal judiciary does not possess," Kennedy caustically added: "Today's casual embrace of taxation imposed by the unelected, life-tenured Federal judiciary disregards fundamental precepts for the democratic control of public institutions." Kennedy took the unusual step of reading a substantial portion of his dissenting opinion from the bench.

Arthur A. Benson II, attorney for a group of plantiffs in the case, called the decision "a victory for civil rights litigants." He further said in a press statement: "It affirms the principle that constitutional violations can and must be remedied, even if the remedy requires the constitutional violators to raise taxes, and whether or not their constituents are in favor of the new taxes." The school board president, Julia Hill, said she was "delighted" by the ruling.

However, Missouri's two Republican senators, John C. Danforth and Christopher S. Bond, were not pleased. Two days after the Court ruled, they introduced a proposed constitutional amendment in Congress to reverse the ruling. Their proposal specified that a court could not order or instruct a state or municipality to raise taxes. There appeared to be little congressional support for the amendment. Enactment would require approval by a two-thirds vote in the House and Senate, and ratification by three-fourths of the states.

Following are excerpts from the Supreme Court's 5-4 ruling, delivered April 18, 1990, in Missouri v. Jenkins, *affirming that federal judges may in special circumstances order local governments to increase taxes, and from the dissenting opinion by Justice Anthony M. Kennedy:*

No. 88-150

Missouri, et al., Petitioner *v.* Kalima Jenkins et al.	On writ of certiorari to the United States Court of Appeals for the Eighth Circuit

[April 18, 1990]

JUSTICE WHITE delivered the opinion of the Court.

The United States District Court for the Western District of Missouri imposed an increase in the property taxes levied by the Kansas City, Missouri, School District (KCMSD) to ensure funding for the desegregation of KCMSD's public schools. We granted certiorari to consider the State of Missouri's argument that the District Court lacked the power to raise local property taxes. For the reasons given below, we hold that the District Court abused its discretion in imposing the tax increase. We also hold, however, that the modifications of the District Court's order made by the Court of Appeals do satisfy equitable and constitutional principles governing the District Court's power.

[I-II omitted]

III

We turn to the tax increase imposed by the District Court. The State urges us to hold that the tax increase violated Article III, the Tenth Amendment, and principles of federal/state comity. We find it unnecessary to reach the difficult constitutional issues, for we agree with the State that the tax increase contravened the principles of comity that must govern the exercise of the District Court's equitable discretion in this area.

It is accepted by all parties, as it was by the courts below, that the imposition of a tax increase by a federal court was an extraordinary event. In assuming for itself the fundamental and delicate power of taxation the District Court not only intruded on local authority but circumvented it altogether. Before taking such a drastic step the District Court was obliged to assure itself that no permissible alternative would have accomplished the required task. We have emphasized that although the "remedial powers of an equity court must be adequate to the task, ... they are not unlimited," *Witcomb* v. *Chavis* (1971), and one of the most important considerations governing the exercise of equitable power is a proper respect for the integrity and function of local government institutions. Especially is this true where, as here, those institutions are ready, willing, and—but for the operation of state law curtailing their powers—able to remedy the deprivation of constitutional rights themselves.

The District Court believed that it had no alternative to imposing a tax increase. But there was an alternative, the very one outlined by the Court of Appeals: it could have authorized or required KCMSD to levy property taxes at a rate adequate to fund the desegregation remedy and could have enjoined the operation of state laws that would have prevented KCMSD from exercising this power. The difference between the two approaches is far more than a matter of form. Authorizing and directing local government institutions to devise and implement remedies not only protects the function of those institutions but, to the extent possible, also places the responsibility for solutions to the problems of segregation upon those who have themselves created the problems.

As *Brown* v. *Board of Education* (1955) observed, local authorities have the "primary responsibility for elucidating, assessing, and solving" the problems of desegregation. See also *Milliken* v. *Bradley* (1977). This is true as well of the problems of financing desegregation, for no matter has been more consistently placed upon the shoulders of local government than that of financing public schools. As was said in another context, "[t]he very complexity of the problems of financing and managing a ... public school system suggests that 'there will be more than one constitutionally permissible method of solving them,' and that ... 'the legislature's efforts to tackle the problems' should be entitled to respect." *San Antonio Independent School District* v. *Rodriguez* (1973) (quoting *Jefferson* v. *Hackney* (1972)). By no means should a district court grant local government *carte blanche,* ... but local officials should at least have the opportunity to devise their own solutions to these problems. ...

The District Court therefore abused its discretion in imposing the tax itself. The Court of Appeals should not have allowed the tax increase to stand and should have reversed the District Court in this respect. ...

IV

We stand on different ground when we review the modifications to the District Court's order made by the Court of Appeals. The Court of Appeals held that the District Court in the future should authorize KCMSD to submit a levy to the state tax collection authorities adequate to fund its budget and should enjoin the operation of state laws that would limit or reduce the levy below that amount.

The State argues that the funding ordered by the District Court violates principles of equity and comity because the remedial order itself was excessive. As the State puts it, "[t]he only reason that the court below needed to consider an unprecedented tax increase was the equally unprecedented cost of its remedial programs." We think this argument aims at the scope of the remedy rather than the manner in which the remedy is to be funded and thus falls outside our limited grant of certiorari in this case. As we denied certiorari on the first question presented by the State's petition, which did challenge the scope of the remedial order, we must resist the State's efforts to argue that point now. We accept, without approving or disapproving, the Court of Appeals conclusion that the District Court's remedy was proper. See *Cone* v. *West Virginia Pulp & Paper Co.* (1947).

The State has argued here that the District Court, having found the State and KCMSD jointly and severally liable, should have allowed any monetary obligations that KCMSD could not meet to fall on the State rather than interfere with state law to permit KCMSD to meet them. Under the circumstances of this case, we cannot say it was an abuse of discretion for the District Court to rule that KCMSD should be responsible for funding its share of the remedy. The State strenuously opposed efforts by respondents to make it responsible for the cost of implementing the order and had secured a reversal of the District Court's earlier decision placing on it all of the cost of substantial portions of the order. The District Court declined to require the State to pay for KCMSD's obligations because it believed that the Court of Appeals had ordered it to allocate the costs between the two governmental entities. Furthermore, if the District Court had chosen the route now suggested by the State, implementation of the remedial order might have been delayed if the State resisted efforts by KCMSD to obtain contribution.

It is true that in *Milliken* v. *Bradley,* we stated that the enforcement of a money judgment against the State did not violate principles of federalism because "[t]he District Court ... neither attempted to restructure local governmental entities nor ... mandat[ed] a particular method or structure of state or local financing." But we did not there state that a District Court could never set aside state laws preventing local governments from raising funds sufficient to satisfy their constitutional obligations just because those funds could also be obtained from the States....

We turn to the constitutional issues. The modifications ordered by the Court of Appeals cannot be assailed as invalid under the Tenth Amendment. "The Tenth Amendment's reservation of nondelegated powers to the States is not implicated by a federal-court judgment enforcing the express prohibitions of unlawful state conduct enacted by the Fourteenth Amendment."...

Finally, the State argues that an order to increase taxes cannot be sustained under the judicial power of Article III. Whatever the merits of this argument when applied to the District Court's own order increasing taxes, a point we have not reached ... a court order directing a local government body to levy its own taxes is plainly a judicial act within the power of a federal court. We held as much in *Griffin* v. *Prince Edward County School Bd.,* where we stated that a District Court, faced with a county's attempt to avoid desegregation of the public schools by refusing to operate those schools, could "require the [County] Supervisors to exercise the power that is theirs to levy taxes to raise funds adequate to reopen, operate, and maintain without racial discrimination a public school system...." *Griffin* followed a long and venerable line of cases in which this Court held that federal courts could issue the writ of mandamus to compel local governmental bodies to levy taxes adequate to satisfy their debt obligations....

The State maintains, however, that even under these cases, the federal judicial power can go no further than to require local governments to levy taxes *as authorized under state law*. In other words, the State argues that federal courts cannot set aside state-imposed limitations on local taxing authority because to do so is to do more than to require the local government "to exercise the power *that is theirs*." We disagree....

... Here the KCMSD may be ordered to levy taxes despite the statutory limitations on its authority in order to compel the discharge of an obligation imposed on KCMSD by the Fourteenth Amendment. To hold otherwise would fail to take account of the obligations of local governments, under the Supremacy Clause, to fulfill the requirements that the Constitution imposes on them. However wide the discretion of local authorities in fashioning desegregation remedies may be, "if a state-imposed limitation on a school authority's discretion operates to inhibit or obstruct the operation of a unitary school system or impede the disestablishing of a dual school system, it must fall; state policy must give way when it operates to hinder vindication of federal constitutional guarantees." *North Carolina State Bd. of Education* v. *Swann* (1971). Even though a particular remedy may not be required in every case to vindicate constitutional guarantees, where (as here) it has been found that a particular remedy is required, the State cannot hinder the process by preventing a local government from implementing that remedy.

Accordingly, the judgment of the Court of Appeals is affirmed insofar as it required the District Court to modify its funding order and reversed insofar as it allowed the tax increase imposed by the District Court to stand. The case is remanded for further proceedings consistent with this opinion.

It is so ordered.

JUSTICE KENNEDY, with whom THE CHIEF JUSTICE, JUSTICE O'CONNOR, and JUSTICE SCALIA join, concurring in part and concurring in the judgment.

In agreement with the Court that we have jurisdiction to decide this case, I join Part II of the opinion. I agree also that the District Court exceeded its authority by attempting to impose a tax. The Court is unanimous in its holding, that the Court of Appeals' judgment affirming "the actions that the [district] court has taken to this point" must be reversed. This is consistent with our precedents and the basic principles defining judicial power.

In my view, however, the Court transgresses these same principles when it goes further, much further, to embrace by broad dictum an expansion of power in the federal judiciary beyond all precedent. Today's casual embrace of taxation imposed by the unelected, life-tenured federal judiciary disregards fundamental precepts for the democratic control of public institutions. I cannot acquiesce in the majority's statements on this point, and should there arise an actual dispute over the collection of taxes as here contemplated in a case that is not, like this one, premature, we should not confirm the outcome of premises adopted with so little constitutional justification. The Court's statements, in my view, cannot be seen as necessary for its judgment, or as precedent for the future, and I cannot join Parts III and IV of the Court's opinion.

I

Some essential litigation history is necessary for a full understanding of what is at stake here and what will be wrought if the implications of all the Court's statements are followed to the full extent. The District Court's remedial plan was proposed for the most part by the Kansas City, Missouri, School District (KCMSD) itself, which is in name a defendant in the suit. Defendants, and above all defendants that are public entities, act in the highest and best tradition of our legal system when they acknowledge fault and cooperate to suggest remedies. But in the context of this dispute, it is of vital importance to note that the KCMSD demonstrated little concern for the fiscal consequences of the remedy that it helped design.

As the District Court acknowledged, the plaintiffs and the KCMSD pursued a "friendly adversary" relationship. Throughout the remedial phase of the litigation, the KCMSD proposed ever more expensive capital improvements with the agreement of the plaintiffs, and the State objected. Some of these improvements involved basic repairs to deteriorating facilities within the school system. The KCMSD, however, devised a broader concept for district-wide improvement, and the District Court approved it. The plan involved a variation of the magnet school concept. Magnet schools ... offer special programs, often used to encourage voluntary movement of students within the district in a pattern that aids desegregation.

Although we have approved desegregation plans involving magnet schools of this conventional definition. ... the District Court found this insufficient. Instead, the court and the KCMSD decided to make a magnet of the district as a whole. The hope was to draw new non-minority students from outside the district. The KCMSD plan adopted by the Court provided that "every senior high school, every middle school, and approximately one-half of the elementary schools in the KCMSD will become magnet schools by the school year 1991-92." The plan was intended to "improve the quality of education of all KCMSD students." The District Court was candid to acknowledge that the "long term goal of this Court's remedial order is to make available to *all* KCMSD students educational opportunities equal to or greater than those presently available in the average Kansas City, Missouri metropolitan suburban school district."

It comes as no surprise that the cost of this approach to the remedy far exceeded KCMSD's budget, or for that matter, its authority to tax. A few examples are illustrative. Programs such as a "performing arts middle school," a "technical magnet high school" that "will offer programs ranging from heating and air conditioning to cosmetology and robotics," were approved. The plan also included a "25 acre farm and 25 acre wildland area" for science study. The Court rejected various proposals by the State to make "capital improvements necessary to eliminate health and safety hazards and to provide a good learning environment," because these proposals failed to "consider the criteria of suburban comparability." The District Court stated: "This 'patch and repair' approach proposed by the State would not achieve suburban comparability or the visual attractiveness sought by the Court as it would result in floor coverings with unsightly sections of mismatched carpeting and tile, and individual walls possessing different shades of paint." Finding that construction of new schools would result in more "attractive" facilities than renovation of existing ones, the District Court approved new construction at a cost ranging from $61.80 per square foot to $95.70 per square foot as distinct from renovation at $45 per square foot.

By the time of the order at issue here, the District Court's remedies included some "$260 million in capital improvements and a magnet-school plan costing over $200 million." *Missouri* v. *Jenkins* (1989). And the remedial orders grew more expensive as shortfalls in revenue became more severe. As the Eighth Circuit judges dissenting from denial of rehearing in banc put it: "The remedies ordered go far beyond anything previously seen in a school desegregation case. The sheer immensity of the programs encompassed by the district court's order—the large number of magnet schools and the quantity of capital renovations and new construction—are concededly without parallel in any other school district in the country."

The judicial taxation approved by the Eighth Circuit is also without parallel. Other Circuits that have faced funding problems arising from remedial decrees have concluded that, while courts have undoubted power to order that schools operate in compliance with the Constitution, the manner and methods of school financing are beyond federal judicial authority. . . .

Unlike these other courts, the Eighth Circuit has endorsed judicial taxation. . . . The case before us represents the first in which a lower federal court has in fact upheld taxation to fund a remedial decree.

For reasons explained below, I agree with the Court that the Eighth Circuit's judgment affirming the District Court's direct levy of a property tax must be reversed. I cannot agree, however, that we "stand on different ground when we review the modifications to the District Court's order made by the Court of Appeals." At the outset, it must be noted that the Court of Appeals made no "modifications" to the District Court's order. Rather, it affirmed "the actions that the court has taken to this point." It is true that the Court of Appeals went on "to consider the procedures which the district court should use *in the future.*"...

The premise of the Court's analysis, I submit, is infirm. Any purported distinction between direct imposition of a tax by the federal court and an order commanding the school district to impose the tax is but a convenient formalism where the court's action is predicated on elimination of state law limitations on the school district's taxing authority....

Whatever taxing power the KCMSD may exercise outside the boundaries of state law would derive from the federal court. The Court never confronts the judicial authority to issue an order for this purpose. Absent a change in state law, the tax is imposed by federal authority under a federal decree. The question is whether a district court possesses a power to tax under federal law, either directly or through delegation to the KCMSD.

II

Article III of the Constitution states that "[t]he judicial Power of the United States, shall be vested in one supreme Court, and in such inferior Courts as the Congress may from time to time ordain and establish." The description of the judicial power nowhere includes the word "tax" or anything that resembles it. This reflects the Framers' understanding that taxation was not a proper area for judicial involvement....

Our cases throughout the years leave no doubt that taxation is not a judicial function.... The order at issue here ... has the purpose and direct effect of extracting money from persons who have had no presence or representation in the suit. For this reason, the District Court's direct order imposing a tax was more than an abuse of discretion, for any attempt to collect the taxes from the citizens would have been a blatant denial of due process....

A true exercise of judicial power provides due process of another sort. Where money is extracted from parties by a court's judgment, the adjudication itself provides the notice and opportunity to be heard that due process demands before a citizen may be deprived of property.

The order here provides neither of these protections....

... [T]oday's case is not an instance of one branch of the Federal Government invading the province of another. It is instead one that brings the weight of federal authority upon a local government and a State. This does not detract, however, from the fundamental point that the judiciary is not free to exercise all federal power; it may exercise only the judicial power. And the important effects of the taxation order discussed here raise additional federalism concerns that counsel against the Court's analysis.

In perhaps the leading case concerning desegregation remedies, *Milliken* v. *Bradley* (1977), we upheld a prospective remedial plan, not a "money judgment," against a State's claim that principles of federalism had been ignored in the plan's implementation. In so doing the Court emphasized that the District Court had "neither attempted to restructure local governmental entities nor to mandate a particular method or structure of state or local financing." No such assurances emerge from today's decision, which endorses federal court intrusion into these precise matters. . . .

The power of taxation is one that the federal judiciary does not possess. In our system "the legislative department alone has access to the pockets of the people," The Federalist, No. 48, p. 334 (J. Cooke ed. 1961) (J. Madison), for it is the legislature that is accountable to them and represents their will. The authority that would levy the tax at issue here shares none of these qualities. Our federal judiciary, by design, is not representative or responsible to the people in a political sense; it is independent. Federal judges do not depend on the popular will for their office. They may not even share the burden of taxes they attempt to impose, for they may live outside the jurisdiction their orders affect. And federal judges have no fear that the competition for scarce public resources could result in a diminution of their salaries. It is not surprising that imposition of taxes by an authority so insulated from public communication or control can lead to deep feelings of frustration, powerlessness, and anger on the part of taxpaying citizens. . . .

At bottom, today's discussion seems motivated by the fear that failure to endorse judicial taxation power might in some extreme circumstance leave a court unable to remedy a constitutional violation. As I discuss below, I do not think this possibility is in reality a significant one. More important, this possibility is nothing more or less than the necessary consequence of *any* limit on judicial power. If, however, judicial discretion is to provide the sole limit on judicial remedies, that discretion must counsel restraint. Ill-considered entry into the volatile field of taxation is a step that may place at risk the legitimacy that justifies judicial independence.

III

One of the most troubling aspects of the Court's opinion is that discussion of the important constitutional issues of judicial authority to tax need never have been undertaken to decide this case. Even were I willing to accept the Court's proposition that a federal court might in some extreme case authorize taxation, this case is not the one. The suggestion that failure to approve judicial taxation here would leave constitutional rights unvindicated rests on a presumption that the District Court's remedy is the *only* possible cure for the constitutional violations it found. Neither our precedents nor the record support this view. In fact, the taxation power is sought here on behalf of a remedial order unlike any before seen.

It cannot be contended that interdistrict comparability, which was the ultimate goal of the District Court's orders, is itself a constitutional command. We have long since determined that "unequal expenditures between children who happen to reside in different districts" do not violate the Equal Protection Clause. San Antonio Independent School Dist. v. Rodriguez (1973). The District Court in this case found, and the Court of Appeals affirmed, that there was no interdistrict constitutional violation that would support mandatory interdistrict relief. . . . The State's complaint that this suit represents the attempt of a school district that could not obtain public support for increased spending to enlist the District Court to finance its educational policy cannot be dismissed out of hand. . . .

This court has never approved a remedy of the type adopted by the District Court. There are strong arguments against the validity of such a plan. A remedy that uses the quality of education as a lure to attract nonminority students will place the District Court at the center of controversies over educational philosophy that by tradition are left to this Nation's communities. . . .

The prudence we have required in other areas touching on federal court intrusion in local government . . . is missing here. Even on the assumption that a federal court might order taxation in an extreme case, the unique nature of the taxing power would demand that this remedy be used as a last resort. In my view, a taxation order should not even be considered, and this Court need never have addressed the question, unless there has been a finding that without the particular remedy at issue the constitutional violation will go unremedied. By this I do not mean that the remedy is, as we assume this one was, within the broad discretion of the District Court. Rather, as a prerequisite to considering a taxation order, I would require a finding that any remedy less costly than the one at issue would so plainly leave the violation unremedied that its implementation would itself be an abuse of discretion. There is no showing in this record that, faced with the revenue shortfall, the District Court gave due consideration to the possibility that another remedy among the "wide range of possibilities" would have addressed the constitutional violations without giving rise to a funding crisis. . . .

IV

This case is a stark illustration of the ever-present question whether ends justify means. Few ends are more important than enforcing the guarantee of equal educational opportunity for our Nation's children. But rules of taxation that override state political structures not themselves subject to any constitutional infirmity raise serious questions of federal authority, questions compounded by the odd posture of a case in which the Court assumes the validity of a novel conception of desegregation remedies we never before have approved. The historical record of voluntary compliance with the decree of *Brown* v. *Board of Education* is not a proud chapter in our constitutional history, and the judges of the District Courts and Courts of Appeals have been courageous and skillful in implementing its mandate. But courage and skill must be exercised with due regard for the proper and historic role of the courts.

I do not acknowledge the troubling departures in today's majority opinion as either necessary or appropriate to ensure full compliance with the Equal Protection Clause and its mandate to eliminate the cause and effects of racial discrimination in the schools. Indeed, while this case happens to arise in the compelling context of school desegregation, the principles involved are not limited to that context. There is no obvious limit to today's discussion that would prevent judicial taxation in cases involving prisons, hospitals, or other public institutions, or indeed to pay a large damages award levied against a municipality. . . . This assertion of judicial power in one of the most sensitive of policy areas, that involving taxation, begins a process that over time could threaten fundamental alteration of the form of government our Constitution embodies.

James Madison observed: "Justice is the end of government. It is the end of civil society. It ever has been, and ever will be pursued, until it be obtained, or until liberty be lost in the pursuit." The Federalist, No. 51, p. 352 (J. Cooke ed. 1961). In pursuing the demand of justice for racial equality, I fear that the Court today loses sight of other basic political liberties guaranteed by our constitutional system, liberties that can coexist with a proper exercise of judicial remedial powers adequate to correct constitutional violations.

SUPREME COURT ON
CHILD PORNOGRAPHY
April 18, 1990

The Supreme Court ruled April 18 that states could impose criminal penalties for the mere possession of child pornography. The case upheld the constitutionality of an Ohio law that was similar to laws in eighteen other states. The Ohio law had been used to convict Clyde Osborne, in whose home a search by Columbus police turned up four sexually explicit photographs of a fourteen-year-old boy. Although the law was upheld, Osborne's conviction and six-month prison sentence was not. The Court ordered a new trial in Ohio state court on the ground that the jury had been improperly instructed at his trial.

By upholding the Ohio law, the Supreme Court created an exception to its 1969 ruling that the possession of obscene materials in one's home was a constitutionally protected right to privacy. In writing the majority opinion in the case of Osborne v. Ohio, *Justice Byron R. White said entirely different considerations governed the two decisions.*

In the 1969 decision in Stanley v. Georgia, *White said, the Court struck down a Georgia ban on possessing obscene material because the Georgia law "was concerned that obscenity would poison the mind of the viewers." In that decision, the Court held that the Georgia law amounted to an attempt by the state to restrict a "public dissemination of ideas inimical to public morality," and thereby infringed on the First Amendment's freedom of speech guarantee. In contrast, he said, Ohio enacted its law "to protect the victims of child pornography; it hopes to destroy a market for the exploitative use of children."*

White's opinion drew the concurrence of Chief Justice William H. Rehnquist and Justices Harry A. Blackmun, Sandra Day O'Connor,

Antonin Scalia, and Anthony M. Kennedy. Blackmun filed a separate opinion saying that although he endorsed the overall majority view, on a legal technicality he agreed with the dissenting opinion written by Justice William J. Brennan. Justices Thurgood Marshall, who wrote the 1969 decision, and John Paul Stevens joined in the dissent.

"While I share the majority's concerns [about sexual exploitation of children]," Brennan wrote, "I do not believe that it has struck the proper balance between the First Amendment and the state's interests." Brennan quoted a passage from the Stanley *decision that, he said, should apply in* Osborne: *"If the First Amendment means anything, it means that the State has no business telling a man, sitting alone in his own house, what books he may read or what films he may watch."*

Moreover, Brennan argued that the Ohio law was too broadly drawn, even after its focus was narrowed by the Ohio Supreme Court, which upheld Osborne's conviction. The law imposed a criminal penalty for depictions of a "minor who is not the person's child or ward" in "a state of nudity." The Ohio Supreme Court interpreted the law to apply only to "depictions of nudity involving a lewd exhibition or graphic focus on a minor's genitals." Moreover, the state court said that in order to convict under the law, the prosecution had to prove criminal intent. Justice White found those limitations on the Ohio law an adequate constitutional protection; Justice Brennan did not.

Eighteen other states that also outlawed child pornography were listed by the Court: Alabama, Arizona, Colorado, Florida, Georgia, Idaho, Illinois, Kansas, Minnesota, Missouri, Nebraska, Nevada, Oklahoma, South Dakota, Texas, Utah, Washington, and West Virginia.

Following are excerpts from the Supreme Court's majority, concurring, and dissenting opinions issued April 18, 1990, in the case of Osborne v. Ohio, *ruling that states may impose criminal penalties for the possession of child pornography:*

<u>No. 88-5986</u>

Clyde Osborne, Appellant *v.* Ohio	On appeal from the Supreme Court of Ohio

[April 18, 1990]

JUSTICE WHITE delivered the opinion of the Court.

In order to combat child pornography, Ohio enacted Rev. Code Ann. § 2907.323(A)(3) (Supp. 1989), which provides in pertinent part:

"(A) No person shall do any of the following: ...

"(3) Possess or view any material or performance that shows a minor who is not the person's child or ward in a state of nudity, unless one of the following applies:

"(a) The material or performance is sold, disseminated, displayed, possessed, controlled, brought or caused to be brought into this state, or presented for a bona fide artistic, medical, scientific, educational, religious, governmental, judicial, or other proper purpose, by or to a physician, psychologist, sociologist, scientist, teacher, person pursuing bona fide studies or research, librarian, clergyman, prosecutor, judge, or other person having a proper interest in the material or performance.

"(b) The person knows that the parents, guardian, or custodian has consented in writing to the photographing or use of the minor in a state of nudity and to the manner in which the material or performance is used or transferred."

Petitioner, Clyde Osborne, was convicted of violating this statute and sentenced to six months in prison, after the Columbus, Ohio, police, pursuant to a valid search, found four photographs in Osborne's home. Each photograph depicts a nude male adolescent posed in a sexually explicit position.

The Ohio Supreme Court affirmed Osborne's conviction, after an intermediate appellate court did the same. . . .

I

The threshold question in this case is whether Ohio may constitutionally proscribe the possession and viewing of child pornography or whether, as Osborne argues, our decision in *Stanley* v. *Georgia* (1969) compels the contrary result. In *Stanley,* we struck down a Georgia law outlawing the private possession of obscene material. We recognized that the statute impinged upon Stanley's right to receive information in the privacy of his home, and we found Georgia's justifications for its law inadequate.

Stanley should not be read too broadly. . . . But assuming, for the sake of argument, that Osborne has a First Amendment interest in viewing and possessing child pornography, we nonetheless find this case distinct from *Stanley* because the interests underlying child pornography prohibitions far exceed the interests justifying the Georgia law at issue in *Stanley.* . . .

In *Stanley,* Georgia primarily sought to proscribe the private possession of obscenity because it was concerned that obscenity would poison the minds of its viewers. We responded that "[w]hatever the power of the state to control public dissemination of ideas inimical to the public morality, it cannot constitutionally premise legislation on the desirability of controlling a person's private thoughts." The difference here is obvious: the State does not rely on a paternalistic interest in regulating Osborne's mind. Rather, Ohio has enacted § 2907.323(A)(3) in order to protect the victims of child pornography; it hopes to destroy a market for the exploitative use of children.

. . . In [the 1982 case of *New York* v.] *Ferber,* where we upheld a New York statute outlawing the distribution of child pornography, we found a similar argument persuasive: "[t]he advertising and selling of child pornography provide an economic motive for and are thus an integral part of the production of such materials, an activity illegal throughout the Nation." ...

Osborne contends that the State should use other measures, besides penalizing possession, to dry up the child pornography market. Osborne points out that in *Stanley* we rejected Georgia's argument that its prohibition on obscenity possession was a necessary incident to its proscription on obscenity distribution. This holding, however, must be viewed in light of the weak interests asserted by the State in that case. *Stanley* itself emphasized that we did not "mean to express any opinion on statutes making criminal possession of other types of printed, filmed, or recorded materials. ... In such cases, compelling reasons may exist for overriding the right of the individual to possess those materials."

Given the importance of the State's interest in protecting the victims of child pornography, we cannot fault Ohio for attempting to stamp out this vice at all levels in the distribution chain. According to the State, since the time of our decision in *Ferber,* much of the child pornography market has been driven underground; as a result, it is now difficult, if not impossible, to solve the child pornography problem by only attacking production and distribution. Indeed, 19 States have found it necessary to proscribe the possession of this material.

Other interests also support the Ohio law. First, as *Ferber* recognized, the materials produced by child pornographers permanently record the victim's abuse. The pornography's continued existence causes the child victims continuing harm by haunting the children in years to come. The State's ban on possession and viewing encourages the possessors of these materials to destroy them. Second, encouraging the destruction of these materials is also desirable because evidence suggests that pedophiles use child pornography to seduce other children into sexual activity.

Given the gravity of the State's interests in this context, we find that Ohio may constitutionally proscribe the possession and viewing of child pornography.

II

Osborne next argues that even if the State may constitutionally ban the possession of child pornography, his conviction is invalid because § 2907.323(A)(3) is unconstitutionally overbroad in that it criminalizes an intolerable range of constitutionally protected conduct. ...

... [T]he statute, as construed by the Ohio Supreme Court on Osborne's direct appeal, plainly survives overbreadth scrutiny. Under the Ohio Supreme Court reading, the statute prohibits "the possession or viewing of material or performance of a minor who is in a state of nudity, where such nudity constitutes a lewd exhibition or involves a graphic focus on the genitals, and where the person depicted is neither the child nor the ward of the person charged." By limiting the statute's operation in this manner, the Ohio Supreme Court avoided penalizing persons for viewing or possessing innocuous photographs of naked children. We have upheld similar language against overbreadth challenges in the past. In *Ferber,* we affirmed a conviction under a New York statute that made it a crime to promote the " 'lewd exhibition of [a child's] genitals.' " We noted that "[t]he term 'lewd exhibition of the genitals' is not unknown in this area and, indeed, was given in *Miller* [v. *California* (1973)] as an example of a permissible regulation."

The Ohio Supreme Court also concluded that the State had to establish scienter in order to prove a violation of § 2907.323(A)(3) based on the Ohio default statute specifying that recklessness applies when another statutory provision lacks an intent specification. The statute on its face lacks a *mens rea* requirement, but that omission . . . is cured by another law that plainly satisfies the requirement laid down in *Ferber* that prohibitions on child pornography include some element of scienter.

Osborne contends that it was impermissible for the Ohio Supreme Court to apply its construction of § 2907.323(A)(3) to him—*i.e.,* to rely on the narrowed construction of the statute when evaluating his overbreadth claim. Our cases, however, have long held that a statute as construed "may be applied to conduct occurring prior to the construction, provided such application affords fair warning to the defendan[t]."

. . . Osborne had noticed that his conduct was proscribed. It is obvious from the face of § 2907.323(A)(3) that the goal of the statute is to eradicate child pornography. The provision criminalizes the viewing and possessing of material depicting children in a state of nudity for other than "proper purposes." The provision appears in the "Sex Offenses" chapter of the Ohio Code. Section 2907.323 is preceded by § 2907.322, which proscribes "[p]andering sexually oriented matter involving a minor," and followed by § 2907.33, which proscribes "[d]eception to obtain matter harmful to juveniles." That Osborne's photographs of adolescent boys in sexually explicit situations constitute child pornography hardly needs elaboration. Therefore, although § 2907.323(A)(3) as written may have been imprecise at its fringes, someone in Osborne's position would not be surprised to learn that his possession of the four photographs at issue in this case constituted a crime.

Because Osborne had notice that his conduct was criminal, his case differs from three cases upon which he relies: *Bouie* v. *City of Columbia* (1964), *Rabe* v. *Washington* (1972), and *Marks* v. *United States* (1977). In *Bouie,* the petitioners had refused to leave a restaurant after being asked to do so by the restaurant's manager. Although the manager had not objected when the petitioners entered the restaurant, the petitioners were convicted of violating a South Carolina trespass statute proscribing " 'entry upon the lands of another . . . after notice from the owner or tenant prohibiting such entry.' " Affirming the convictions, the South Carolina Supreme Court construed the trespass law as also making it a crime for an individual to remain on another's land after being asked to leave. We reversed the convictions on due process grounds because the South Carolina Supreme Court's expansion of the statute was unforeseeable and therefore the petitioners had no reason to suspect that their conduct was criminal.

suspect that their conduct was criminal.

Likewise, in *Rabe* v. *Washington, supra,* the petitioner had been convicted of violating a Washington obscenity statute that, by its terms, did not proscribe the defendant's conduct. On petitioner's appeal, the Washington Supreme Court nevertheless affirmed the petitioner's conviction, after construing the Washington obscenity statute to reach the petitioner. We overturned the conviction because the Washington Supreme Court's broadening of the statute was unexpected; therefore the petitioner had no warning that his actions were proscribed.

And, in *Marks* v. *United States, supra,* we held that the retroactive application of the obscenity standards announced in *Miller* v. *California* (1973) to the potential detriment of the petitioner violated the Due Process Clause because, at the time that the defendant committed the challenged conduct, our decision in *Memoirs* v. *Massachusetts* (1966), provided the governing law. The defendant could not suspect that his actions would later become criminal when we expanded the range of constitutionally proscribable conduct in *Miller....*

Finally, despite Osborne's contention to the contrary, we do not believe that *Massachusetts* v. *Oakes* [1989] supports his theory of this case. In *Oakes,* the petitioner challenged a Massachusetts pornography statute as overbroad; since the time of the defendant's alleged crime, however, the state had substantially narrowed the statute through a subsequent legislative enactment—an amendment to the statute. In a separation opinion, five Justices agreed that the state legislature could not cure the potential overbreadth problem through the subsequent legislative action; the statute was void as written.

Osborne contends that *Oakes* stands for a similar but distinct proposition that, when faced with a potentially overinclusive statute, a court may not construe the statute to avoid overbreadth problems and then apply the statute, as construed, to past conduct. The implication of this argument is that if a statute is overbroad as written, then the statute is void and incurable. As a result, when reviewing a conviction under a potentially overbroad statute, a court must either affirm or strike down the statute on its face, but the court may not, as the Ohio Supreme Court did in this case, narrow the statute, affirm on the basis of the narrowing construction, and leave the statute in full force. We disagree.

First ... if we accepted this proposition, it would require a radical reworking of our law. Courts routinely construe statutes so as to avoid the statutes' potentially overbroad reach, apply the statute in that case, and leave the statute in place....

III

Having rejected Osborne's *Stanley* and overbreadth arguments, we now reach Osborne's final objection to his conviction: his contention that he was denied due process because it is unclear that his conviction was based on a finding that each of the elements of § 2907.323(A)(3) was present. According to the Ohio Supreme Court, in order to secure a conviction under § 2907.323(A)(3), the State must prove both scienter and that the defendant possessed material depicting a lewd exhibition or a graphic focus on genitals. The jury in this case was not instructed that it could convict Osborne only for conduct that satisfied these requirements.

The State concedes the omissions in the jury instructions, but argues that Osborne waived his right to assert this due process challenge because he failed to object when the instructions were given at his trial. The Ohio Supreme Court so held, citing Ohio law. The question before us now, therefore, is whether we are precluded from reaching Osborne's due process challenge because counsel's failure to comply with the procedural rule constitutes an independent state law ground adequate to support the result below. We have no difficulty agreeing with the State that Osborne's counsel's failure to urge that the court instruct the jury on scienter constitutes an independent and adequate state law ground preventing us from reaching Osborne's due process contention on that point. Ohio law states that proof of scienter is required in instances, like the present one, where a criminal statute does not specify the applicable mental state. . . .

. . . [W]e believe that we may reach Osborne's due process claim because we are convinced that Osborne's attorney pressed the issue of the State's failure of proof on lewdness before the trial court and, under the circumstances, nothing would be gained by requiring Osborne's lawyer to object a second time, specifically to the jury instructions. . . .

IV

To conclude, although we find Osborne's First Amendment arguments unpersuasive, we reverse his conviction and remand for a new trial in order to ensure that Osborne's conviction stemmed from a finding that the State had proved each of the elements of § 2907.323(A)(3).

So ordered.

JUSTICE BLACKMUN, concurring.

I join the Court's opinion. I write separately only to express my agreement with JUSTICE BRENNAN, that this Court's ability to entertain Osborne's due process claim premised on the failure of the trial court to charge the "lewd exhibition" and "graphic focus" elements does not depend upon his objection to this failure at trial.

JUSTICE BRENNAN, with whom JUSTICE MARSHALL and JUSTICE STEVENS join, dissenting.

I agree with the Court that appellant's conviction must be reversed. I do not agree, however, that Ohio is free on remand to retry him under Ohio Rev. Code Ann. § 2907.323(A)(3) (Supp. 1989) as it currently exists. In my view, the state law, even as construed authoritatively by the Ohio Supreme Court, is still fatally overbroad, and our decision in *Stanley* v. *Georgia* [1969] prevents the State from criminalizing appellant's possession of the photographs at issue in this case. I therefore respectfully dissent.

I

A

As written, the Ohio statute is plainly overbroad. Section 2907.323(A)(3) makes it a crime to "[p]ossess or view any material or performance that shows a minor who is not the person's child or ward in a state of nudity." Another section defines "nudity" as

> "the showing, representation, or depiction of human male or female genitals, pubic area, or buttocks with less than a full, opaque covering, or of a female breast with less than a full opaque covering of any portion thereof below the top of the nipple, or of covered male genitals in a discernibly turgid state." Ohio Rev. Code Ann. § 2907.01(H)(Supp. 1989).

In short, §§ 2907.323 and 2907.01(H) use simple nudity, without more, as a way of defining child pornography. But as our prior decisions have made clear, " 'nudity alone' does not place otherwise protected material outside the mantle of the First Amendment." ...

B

Wary of the statute's use of the "nudity" standard, the Ohio Supreme Court construed § 2907.323(A)(3) to apply only "where such nudity constitutes a lewd exhibition or involves a graphic focus on the genitals." The "lewd exhibition" and "graphic focus" tests not only fail to cure the overbreadth of the statute, but they also create a new problem of vagueness.

1

The Court dismisses appellant's overbreadth contention in a single cursory paragraph. Relying exclusively on our previous decision in *New York* v. *Ferber* (1982), the majority reasons that the "lewd exhibition" standard adequately narrows the statute's ambit because "[w]e have upheld similar language against overbreadth challenges in the past." The Court's terse explanation is unsatisfactory, since *Ferber* involved a law that differs in crucial respects from the one here.

The New York law at issue in *Ferber* criminalized the use of a child in a "[s]*exual performance*," defined as " 'any performance or part thereof which includes sexual conduct by a child less than sixteen years of age.' " " ' *Sexual conduct*' ' " was in turn defined as " 'actual or simulated sexual intercourse, deviate sexual intercourse, sexual bestiality, masturbation, sado-masochistic abuse, or lewd exhibition of the genitals.' " Although we acknowledged that "nudity, without more[,] is protected expression," we found that the statute was not overbroad because only "a tiny fraction of materials within the statute's reach" was constitutionally protected. We therefore upheld the conviction of a bookstore proprietor who sold films depicting young boys masturbating.

The Ohio law is distinguishable for several reasons. First, the New York statute did not criminalize materials with a "*graphic focus*" on the genitals, and, as discussed further below, Ohio's "graphic focus" test is impermissibly capacious. Even setting aside the "graphic focus" element, the Ohio Supreme Court's narrowing construction is still overbroad because it focuses on "lewd exhibitions of *nudity*" rather than "lewd exhibitions of *the genitals*" in the context of *sexual conduct*, as in the New York statute at issue in *Ferber*. Ohio law defines "nudity" to include depictions of pubic areas, buttocks, the female breast, and covered male genitals "in a discernibly turgid state," *as well as* depictions of the genitals. On its face, then, the Ohio law is much broader than New York's.

In addition, whereas the Ohio Supreme Court's interpretation uses the "lewd exhibition of nudity" test standing alone, the New York law employed the phrase " 'lewd exhibition of the genitals' " in the context of a longer list of examples of sexual conduct: " 'actual or simulated sexual intercourse, deviate sexual intercourse, sexual bestiality, masturbation, [and] sado-masochistic abuse.' " This syntax was important to our decision in *Ferber*. We recognized the potential for impermissible applications of the New York statute, but in view of the examples of "sexual conduct" provided by the statute, we were willing to assume that the New York courts would not "widen the *possibly invalid* reach of the statute by giving an expansive construction to the proscription on 'lewd exhibition[s] of the genitals.' " In the Ohio statute, of course, there is no analog to the elaborate definition of "sexual conduct" to serve as a similar limit. . . .

Indeed, the broad definition of nudity in the Ohio statutory scheme means that "child pornography" could include any photograph depicting a "lewd exhibition" of even a small portion of a minor's buttocks or any part of the female breast below the nipple. Pictures of topless bathers at a Mediterranean beach, of teenagers in revealing dresses, and even of toddlers romping unclothed, all might be prohibited. Furthermore, the Ohio law forbids not only depictions of nudity *per se*, but also depictions of the buttocks, breast, or pubic area with less than a "full, opaque covering." Thus, pictures of fashion models wearing semitransparent clothing might be illegal, as might a photograph depicting a fully clad male that nevertheless captured his genitals "in a discernibly turgid state." The Ohio statute thus sweeps in many types of materials that are not "child pornography," as we used that term in *Ferber*, but rather that enjoy full First Amendment protection.

. . . Indeed, some might think that *any* nudity, especially that involving a minor, is by definition "lewd," yet this Court has clearly established that nudity is not excluded automatically from the scope of the First Amendment. The Court today is unable even to hazard a guess as to what a "lewd exhibition" might mean; it is forced to rely entirely on an inapposite case—*Ferber*—that simply did not discuss, let alone decide, the central issue here.

The Ohio Supreme Court provided few clues as to the meaning of the phrase "lewd exhibition of nudity." The court distinguished "child pornography" from "obscenity," thereby implying that it did not believe that an exhibition was required to be "obscene" in order to qualify as "lewd." But it supplied no authoritative definition—a disturbing omission in light of the absence of the phrase "lewd exhibition" from the statutory definition section of the Sex Offenses chapter of the Ohio Revised Code. In fact, the word "lewd" does *not* appear in the statutory definition of *any* crime involving obscenity or other sexually oriented materials in the Ohio Revised Code. Thus, when the Ohio Supreme Court grafted the "lewd exhibition" test onto the definition of nudity, it was venturing into uncharted territory. . . .

2

The Ohio Supreme Court also added a "graphic focus" element to the nudity definition. This phrase, a stranger to obscenity regulation, suffers from the same vagueness difficulty as "lewd exhibition." Although the Ohio Supreme Court failed to elaborate what a "graphic focus" might be, the test appears to involve nothing more than a subjective estimation of the centrality or prominence of the genitals in a picture or other representation. Not only is this factor dependent on the perspective and idiosyncrasies of the observer, it also is unconnected to whether the material at issue merits constitutional protection. Simple nudity, no matter how prominent or "graphic," is within the bounds of the First Amendment. Michelangelo's "David" might be said to have a "graphic focus" on the genitals, for it plainly portrays them in a manner unavoidable to even a casual observer. Similarly, a painting of a partially clad girl could be said to involve a "graphic focus," depending on the picture's lighting and emphasis, as could the depictions of nude children on the friezes that adorn our Courtroom. Even a photograph of a child running naked on the beach or playing in the bathtub might run afoul of the law, depending on the focus and camera angle.

In sum, the "lewd exhibition" and "graphic focus" tests are too vague to serve as any workable limit. Because the statute, even as construed authoritatively by the Ohio Supreme Court, is impermissibly overbroad, I would hold that appellant cannot be retried under it.

II

Even if the statute was not overbroad, our decision in *Stanley v. Georgia* forbids the criminalization of appellant's private possession in his home of the materials at issue. "If the First Amendment means anything, it means that the State has no business telling a man, sitting alone in his own house, what books he may read or what films he may watch." Appellant was convicted for possessing four photographs of nude minors, seized from a desk drawer in the bedroom of his house during a search executed pursuant to a warrant. Appellant testified that he had been given the pictures in his home by a friend. There was no evidence that the photographs had been produced commercially or distributed. All were kept in an album that appellant had assembled for his personal use and had possessed privately for several years.

In these circumstances, the Court's focus on *Ferber* rather than *Stanley* is misplaced. *Ferber* held only that child pornography is "a category of material the *production* and *distribution* of which is not entitled to First Amendment protection" (emphasis added); our decision did not extend to private *possession*. The authority of a State to regulate the production and distribution of such materials is not dispositive of its power to penalize possession. . . .

The Court today speculates that Ohio "will decrease the production of child pornography if it penalizes those who possess and view the product, thereby decreasing demand." Criminalizing possession is thought necessary because "since the time of our decision in *Ferber,* much of the child pornography market has been driven underground; as a result, it is now difficult, if not impossible, to solve the child pornography problem by only attacking production and distribution." As support, the Court notes that 19 States have "found it necessary" to prohibit simple possession. Even were I to accept the Court's empirical assumptions, I would find the Court's approach foreclosed by *Stanley,* which rejected precisely the same contention Ohio makes today:

> "[W]e are faced with the argument that prohibition of possession of obscene materials is a necessary incident to statutory schemes prohibiting distribution. That argument is based on alleged difficulties of proving an intent to distribute or in producing evidence of actual distribution. We are not convinced that such difficulties exist, but even if they did we do not think that they would justify infringement of the individual's right to read or observe what he pleases. Because that right is so fundamental to our scheme of individual liberty, its restriction may not be justified by the need to ease the administration of otherwise valid criminal laws."

At bottom, the Court today is so disquieted by the possible exploitation of children in the *production* of the pornography that it is willing to tolerate the imposition of criminal penalties for simple *possession*. While I share the majority's concerns, I do not believe that it has struck the proper balance between the First Amendment and the State's interests, especially in light of the other means available to Ohio to protect children from exploitation and the State's failure to demonstrate a causal link between a ban on possession of child pornography and a decrease in its production.

IV [III omitted]

When speech is eloquent and the ideas expressed lofty, it is easy to find restrictions on them invalid. But were the First Amendment limited to such discourse, our freedom would be sterile indeed. Mr. Osborne's pictures may be distasteful, but the Constitution guarantees both his right to possess them privately and his right to avoid punishment under an overbroad law. I respectfully dissent.

MILKEN'S GUILTY PLEA
April 24, 1990

Michael R. Milken, the junk-bond king who personified Wall Street's highfliers in the 1980s, pleaded guilty in U.S. District Court in New York City, April 24, to six felony charges of securities fraud and conspiracy. The forty-three-year-old entrepreneur had created an enormous market for high-risk, high-return junk bonds that had financed many of the corporate takeovers in that decade. He also received huge compensations—$550 million in 1987 alone.

In a lengthy statement read in the crowded courtroom, Milken said a three-year investigation of his activities had been "extremely painful and difficult" for his family and friends. "I am truly sorry," he said, sobbing. But Milken insisted that his plea was not a "reflection" on the "underlying soundness and integrity" of the junk-bond market. It was a market, he continued, "that enabled hundreds of companies to survive, expand and flourish."

The federal government hailed Milken's plea as a major victory in its long campaign against "insider trading"—divulging inside information about a company to benefit a stock deal—and other financial crimes. But because Milken was not brought to trial, many questions raised in the investigation went unanswered. He remained one of the wealthiest people in the country, with a personal fortune of about $1 billion. He agreed to pay $600 million—$200 million in fines and $400 million for restitution to defrauded investors and clients of his firm, Drexel Burnham Lambert.

However, Milken's plea did not keep him out of prison. Judge Kimba M. Wood sentenced him on November 21 to ten years in prison, followed by three years of probation during which he would perform 5,400 hours of community service. It was the longest sentence handed out to any executive caught up in the Wall Street scandals; however, she later recommended that he be eligible for parole after serving three years.

Following Milken's plea bargain with federal prosecutors, Business Week *magazine commented editorially that he would be remembered as "an important financial innovator." Milken's singular insight was that enormous markets could be built for junk bonds. They were issued by companies that did not qualify for an "investment grade" rating by leading bond-rating agencies. Since junk bonds were considered riskier than investment grade securities, they paid a higher return.*

As the head of the High Yield and Convertible Securities Department at Drexel Burnham Lambert, Milken created markets in junk bonds for the financing of companies that previously had no access to the credit markets. More dramatically and controversially, he also used junk bonds to finance many of the corporate takeovers that were a feature of the high-flying world of Wall Street in the 1980s. Although Drexel Burnham Lambert was a Wall Street investment bank, Milken's office was in Beverly Hills, California—a setting that symbolized the glamour attached to high-risk, big-stakes finance.

Three-Year Investigation

Throughout the investigation by the Securities and Exchange Commission and the U.S. Justice Department, Milken asserted his innocence. However, his firm pleaded guilty to six felony violations of securities law and paid penalties amounting to $650 million. Drexel's securities business collapsed on February 12, 1990, and the firm filed for bankruptcy the next day. Drexel had risen from a third-tier position on Wall Street to great prominence, largely because of Milken's junk-bond operation.

In building a case against Milken, prosecutors had the cooperation of Ivan F. Boesky, a Wall Street arbitrageur who had pleaded guilty to a criminal charge in the largest of the government's Wall Street insider trading prosecutions. Boesky was released from prison in April 1990 after serving two years of a three-year term. It was a case of a big fish, Boesky, leading prosecutors to an even bigger fish, Milken. (Supreme Court on Insider Trading, Historic Documents of 1987, p. 881)

The original charges against Milken did not directly involve his junk-bond operation. The government's case in early stages was largely based on Boesky's information about secret and illegal securities trading between the two men. Later, in return for immunity from prosecution, some of Milken's colleagues at Drexel's junk-bond department provided incriminating information.

Federal investigators have probed the savings and loan (S&L) debacle to determine the impact of Milken's junk-bond operations on the collapse. Seven S&Ls, all under scrutiny by regulators, held $6 billion in junk bonds at the end of 1989. Among them was Columbia Savings and Loan in Beverly Hills, which, according to the Wall Street Journal, *held $4.1 billion in junk bonds as of September 30, 1989. The deterioration of* *the junk-bond market that followed Drexel's collapse escalated losses at a number of "large, troubled thrifts" with major exposure to junk bonds,* the newspaper said. (President Bush's Remarks on Signing S&L Bailout Bill, Historic Documents of 1989, p. 463)

Corporate Takeovers

Milken, his lawyers, and supporters contended that his pioneering use of junk bonds had aided hundreds of small companies and saved thousands of jobs. But about half of the junk bonds in the 1980s were used in financing corporate takeovers. Many economists and other observers believed that the wave of takeovers in the 1980s increased the efficiency of U.S. corporations. Others condemned takeovers for loading formerly solvent companies with mountains of debt and sometimes driving them to bankruptcy. In leveraged buyouts—a widely used form of takeover—investors typically used money raised by issuing junk bonds to buy up a company's stock. The stock's value usually declined drastically. (SEC Report on Corporate Takeovers, Historic Documents of 1988, p. 921)

Such was the case with the vast American retailing operations that had been acquired by the Campeau Corporation of Canada. The retailing empire, including the fashionable Bloomingdale's and Abraham and Straus department stores, had been put together by Canadian real estate operator Robert Campeau, largely on borrowed money and junk bonds. Campeau filed for bankruptcy January 15, 1990.

Milken's Achievement

As Milken's career ended in disgrace, sharp differences of opinion were expressed over the meaning of his work. An editorial in the New York Times *on May 1 said that Milken, besides being a convicted felon, was a financial genius who had transformed junk bonds into a lifeline of credit for hundreds of emerging companies. Snubbed by banks, these businesses would otherwise have shriveled.*

Herbert Stein, chairman of the president's Council of Economic Advisers in the Nixon administration, wrote in the Wall Street Journal *on May 3 that it would not be possible to isolate the effect of Milken's activities until "enough history has passed." Stein also said that "we will never be able to measure the effect of the loss of confidence in financial markets generally that his activities caused."*

Michael Kinsley, writing a guest column in the May 3 Washington Post, *asked, "And how wonderful were junk bonds?" Milken's "main contribution," Kinsley wrote, "was to increase the proportion of unproductive paper in the takeover boom."*

Following is the courtroom statement of Wall Street financier Michael R. Milken, April 24, 1990, from the transcript of his appearance before the U.S. District Court in Manhattan to plead guilty to six felony charges of securities fraud and conspiracy:

... I was the founder and head of the High Yield and Convertible Bond Department at Drexel. In pioneering the creation of new instruments for the financing of companies, most of which did not have access to the capital markets because they did not have investment-grade ratings, and in making markets in such securities, we operated under unique, highly demanding, and intensely competitive conditions. But I do not cite these conditions as an excuse for not conforming to all of the laws that govern our highly regulated business. I am here today because in connection with some transactions, I transgressed certain of the laws and regulations that govern our industry. I was wrong in doing so and knew that at the time, and I am pleading guilty to these offenses.

One of the accounts we did business with was the Boesky Organization, which also did business with many other firms. Drexel did some financings for and trading with the Boesky firm, but Drexel's business with the Boesky Organization never approached 1% of the business of our department. He traded in stocks, and I traded primarily in bonds, or their equivalent. But because he was a major factor in the securities markets, he had the potential to become a more significant account.

We are not social friends, and had little in common. His philosophy of business was different from mine. The relationship started as an arms length and correct one. Unfortunately, however, certain of our transactions involved reciprocal accommodations, some of which violated the law, including those that are referred to in this allocution.

In 1984, our department had purchased some securities of Fischbach, a company in which Victor Posner had an interest. Drexel had provided financing to several other companies which Mr. Posner had an interest in. In early 1984, Mr. Posner publicly announced that he intended to acquire Fischbach. Boesky was familiar with the Fischbach situation and wanted to purchase Fischbach securities. I encouraged him to do so. I do not remember exactly what I told him six years ago, but I indicated to him that he would not lose money.

The Boesky Organization began buying Fischbach securities and eventually bought over 10% of Fischbach including securities that had been owned by Drexel. Over the next months, he called me incessantly to complain that the price of the stock was dropping, that Drexel was responsible for his losses, that my comments to him were guarantees against loss, and that he expected us to make good.

I assured him that Drexel would make good on his losses. These assurances were not recorded on the books of Drexel and I did not expect that they would be reflected in any Schedule 13d's filed by the Boesky Organization [with the Securities and Exchange Commission], and in fact they were not.

Thus, I assisted in the failure to file an accurate 13d. This was wrong and I accept responsibility for it. This is the basis for Count II, and is one of the overt acts in Count I.

As for Count III and the second overt act of the conspiracy count, in the fall of 1984, a client of Drexel, Golden Nugget, wanted to sell a substantial amount of MCA stock. I wanted the shares to hit the market in a way that would not identify our client as a seller and adversely affect the price that it might receive. So I turned to Boesky, whose business it was to buy and sell large amounts of stock, and who I knew had an interest in the entertainment company stocks, including MCA.

I told a Drexel employee to ask him to buy the blocks of MCA shares as they became available from Drexel's client. I did not tell the client how I was disposing of the stock. Drexel crossed the blocks between its client and the Boesky Organization which subsequently resold most of these shares into the marketplace.

When Boesky complained that he had lost money on his initial purchases of MCA, I promised that we would make up any losses the Boesky Organization suffered on its purchases and sales, and thereafter it bought more MCA stock from Drexel acting on behalf of our client. This promise was not recorded on Drexel's books, nor made public, and it was wrong not to do so.

It was my intent that the block sales would enable our client to receive a better price than it might have obtained if I had not agreed that Drexel would make up the Boesky Organization's losses on the MCA stock.

In July 1985, the Boesky Organization asked Drexel to purchase approximately one million shares of stock in Helmerich & Payne. The Boesky Organization agreed that it would repurchase this stock in the future, and promise that it would make up any losses Drexel incurred while holding this stock.

Although I was not involved in the purchase of these securities, I later learned of this understanding. I approved this understanding. I also gave instructions to sell the stock back.

The understanding that the Boesky Organization would make up any losses was an oral one, and the stock, while held by Drexel, was not, therefore, charged to the Boesky Organization's net capital as required by the securities laws and rules. This is the basis for Count IV and the third overt act.

As I stated earlier, there were other accommodations of a similar nature between the Boesky Organization and Drexel, some of which were wrong. After Boesky complained about his losses and insisted that we make them up, I asked a Drexel employee in early 1985 to check the amount of the losses that the Boesky Organization had incurred. In order to make up these losses, I caused Drexel to execute certain bond trades which resulted in profits to the Boesky Organization.

Thereafter, a Drexel employee tried to keep track of how the Boesky Organization stood in terms of profits and losses, on these and certain other transactions, though so far as I know, this score-keeping was never exact.

Counts V and VI and the remaining overt acts relate to transactions between Drexel and David Solomon. Mr. Solomon was a portfolio manager who specialized in high-yield securities. His company, Solomon Asset Management Company, Inc., was a large customer of Drexel, as well as of other firms.

Among the institutions for which Mr. Solomon managed a high-yield portfolio was the Finsbury Fund, an offshore fund that had been underwritten by a Drexel affiliate. Drexel paid an annual 1% commission to its salesmen for selling this fund abroad, and charged this commission to the High-Yield Department because the Finsbury Fund traded in high-yield securities.

Sometime in 1985, I agreed with Solomon and officials of Drexel that the High-Yield Department would recoup the commission for Drexel. To attempt to do so, we charged Solomon a fraction of a point more on certain purchases he made for his clients, or a fraction of a point less on certain sales he made for his clients to help recoup the 1% commission paid to Drexel salesmen.

All adjustments were to be within the bid/ask range for the particular security at the time of the transaction. To the best of my information, this was done on a number of trades and the adjustments totaled several hundred thousand dollars.

These adjustments were not disclosed by Drexel or me to the shareholders of Finsbury or to Solomon's other clients. The confirmations for Solomon's purchase of securities were mailed by Drexel and did not disclose the adjustments or that they were made to reimburse Drexel for the selling expenses of the Finsbury Fund. This failure to disclose was wrong, and is the basis for Count V.

In December 1985, Mr. Solomon asked whether Drexel could engage in securities transactions with him on which he could generate short-term losses for his personal income tax purposes. In light of the customer relationship between Mr. Solomon and Drexel, I assisted him in purchasing from Drexel certain securities, set forth in the Information, which traded at a significant spread between the bid and the ask price.

Drexel thereafter repurchased these securities at a substantially lower price, thus generating a loss for him and a profit for Drexel. I either told him that we would provide him with an investment opportunity or opportunities in the following year to make up his loss to him, or that was implicit in the conversation. In fact, in the following year, we did provide him an investment opportunity which turned out to be profitable and ultimately more than made up for the losses he suffered. I thus assisted Mr. Solomon in taking a tax loss to which he was not entitled, and this is the basis of Count VI, and the fifth overt act.

Because of the tremendous amount of publicity that has surrounded this case, I wish to make clear that my plea is an acceptance of personal responsibility for my own failings and actions, and not a reflection on the underlying soundness and integrity of the segment of the capital markets in which we specialize and which provided capital that enabled hundreds of companies to survive, expand and flourish. Our business was in no way dependent on these practices, nor did they comprise a fundamental part of our business, and I regret them very much.

This investigation and proceeding are now in their fourth year. This long period has been extremely painful and difficult for my family and friends as well as myself. I realize that by my acts I have hurt those who were closest to me. I am truly sorry.

I thank the court for permitting me to add this apology and for its fairness in handling this complex case.

CHAMORRO INAUGURAL
IN NICARAGUA
April 25, 1990

Nicaragua closed a decade of Marxist rule on April 25 with Violeta Barrios de Chamorro's inauguration as president of the strife-torn Central American republic. Chamorro, a sixty-year-old conservative newspaper publisher, defeated Daniel Ortega, the incumbent Sandinista president, in the national election February 25. She upset the findings of pre-election opinion polls that indicated Ortega was way ahead. Chamorro won more than 52 percent of the vote; Ortega received less than 41 percent.

The inaugural ceremony in Managua, the capital, marked the first democratic transfer of power in the turbulent modern history of Nicaragua, as well as the installation of the first popularly elected woman president in the history of the Americas. As the widow of Pedro Joaquin Chamorro, she took up his political cause after his murder in 1978. His slaying triggered the final uprising that brought the Sandinista Movement to power in 1979. But she split with Ortega after he became head of the movement and in her newspaper she gave voice to his political foes.

In an emotion-charged address to an estimated 20,000 persons crowded into Managua's national stadium, Chamorro urged Nicaraguans to pursue peace and rebuild a nation shattered by ten years of civil conflict, oppressive one-party rule, and economic mismanagement. Among the attending dignitaries was Oscar Arias Sanchez, the former president of Costa Rica, principal author of a Central American peace plan that ultimately resulted in the Nicaraguan election. (Agreements on the Future of the Contras, Historic Documents of 1989, p. 161)

Chamorro announced plans to dismantle several major features of the

Sandinista regime. She promised an end to the unpopular military draft, reductions in the size of the army, reallocation of military spending to badly needed health and education programs, amnesty for all political prisoners, and review and possible repeal of laws passed in the closing days of Sandinista rule.

Control of Military a Key

The issue of continued Sandinista control of the Nicaraguan armed forces, the largest in Central America, threatened to split Chamorro's supporters in the days before the inauguration. Ignoring the demands of members of her fourteen-party National Opposition Union, Chamorro announced her intention to retain Humberto Ortega, the brother of the retiring Sandinista president, as chief of the army.

The outcry against her decision was only partly softened when Ortega said he would resign from the nine-member Sandinista directorate, accept civilian authority over the army, and support moves to reduce the size of the armed forces. On June 15, Chamorro, with Ortega's endorsement, announced a cutback from 61,000 troops to 41,000, to be completed by August 3. She ordered the creation of an all-volunteer army and the discharge of all draftees by December 7.

The military reduction was made possible, in part, by the success of Chamorro's government, backed by the United Nations and the Organization of American States, in persuading Nicaragua's anti-Sandinista rebel "contras" to surrender their weapons and disband. The contras originally refused to lay down their American-supplied arms until the Nicaraguan army was fully demobilized. The Sandinistas had insisted that the rebel forces be disarmed before they would agree to reductions in the army.

The stalemate was broken late in May when Chamorro, after days of intense negotiations, agreed to give the rebels a tract of land, about the size of Massachusetts, in the sparsely settled southeastern corner of Nicaragua in exchange for their demobilization. In June she said that 14,000 contras had been demobilized. About 2,000 others still retained their weapons, but rebel leaders promised an end to the conflict.

Economic Problems Abound

Upon taking office, Chamorro inherited an economy shattered by the blunders of the Sandinista government, compounded by a decade of internecine strife and the imposition of harsh economic sanctions by the United States. During the Sandinista rule, the United States ended its aid to Managua and blocked multilateral assistance to Nicaragua. The Reagan administration imposed a trade blockade, cut off Nicaragua's sugar quota in the lucrative U.S. market, froze asset transfers to the country, and withdrew duty-free privileges for Nicaraguan exports under the U.S. Generalized System of Preferences and the Caribbean Basin Initiative.

As a result, Nicaragua's per capita income dropped to $679 a year, the lowest in Central America, according to the Inter-American Development Bank. The value of the country's exports fell from $700 million in 1978 to $200 million in 1989. The bulk of Nicaragua's foreign trade was carried on with Soviet bloc countries and much of it was conducted on barter terms, bringing little foreign exchange to Nicaragua's depleted coffers.

The inflation rate soared to 33,000 percent in 1988, and exceeded 1,700 percent in 1989. Official figures put unemployment at 30 percent of the work force, but rural unemployment and underemployment, especially in impoverished and strife-torn areas, was much higher. The internal and external national debt reached $11 billion, and the Sandinista government fell behind in making scheduled payments to international development banks.

When the February election results were known, and even before Chamorro took office, the United States lifted its trade embargo and reopened air and maritime services between the two countries. Nicaragua's U.S. sugar quota was restored to pre-embargo levels, and the country was declared eligible to apply for duty-free privileges.

After an initial delay caused by domestic U.S. political maneuvering, Congress approved an emergency package of $300 million in aid for Nicaragua. Chamorro earmarked $47 million of the total for resettlement of the contra forces and their reintegration into civilian life. In early June, a group of thirty-four donors pledged an additional $300 million in Nicaraguan assistance. Included in the donor group were the twelve member countries of the European Community, the World Bank, and the International Monetary Fund. The donors further committed $180 million for Nicaragua in 1991.

Challenges Still Ahead

Despite Chamorro's impressive electoral victory and her calls for national unity and reconciliation, Nicaragua remained a sharply divided country. The Sandinistas, now in the opposition, were split between factions willing to cooperate with Chamorro and those who thought too much had been conceded to her. In mid-May, a Sandinista-led strike by government workers brought the country to a halt. Chamorro settled the strike by agreeing to double the wages of government workers and by suspending a decree that gave her government wide powers to dismiss workers. A similar strike in July paralyzed the nation and led to violent clashes between Sandinistas and her supporters. That strike ended only after she agreed to job guarantees, pay raises, and political concessions.

There was division as well within the ranks of Chamorro's ruling coalition. There was particular resentment when she appointed friends and associates to top-level positions, leaving out representatives of the established coalition political parties. And as Chamorro began to take steps to privatize government-owned enterprises and sharply reduce government subsidies, resistance developed among threatened interest groups on both sides.

Her effectiveness depended on whether she could hold together the highly diverse ruling coalition, which included conservative business executives and members of the Nicaraguan Communist party. In addition, she faced the tasks of creating a loyal and competent bureaucracy in a government still dominated by pro-Sandinista civil servants, and bringing about an economic recovery that would require sharp price increases for many essential goods. In a farewell address before surrendering power to Chamorro, retiring president Daniel Ortega warned Chamorro against attempting to roll back social programs and other "revolutionary advances" achieved during the decade of Sandinista rule. While Ortega promised to play a constructive role in opposition to the new government, he also pointedly said that "big brother" would be watching.

Following are excerpts from the inaugural address of Violeta Barrios de Chamorro, president of Nicaragua, delivered April 25, 1990, in Managua, as recorded and translated by the U.S. Foreign Broadcast Information Service:

Dear Dr. Miriam Arguello, president of the National Assembly; friends of the National Assembly, the Supreme Court, and the Supreme Electoral Council; distinguished presidents and heads of state and government; delegations of friendly countries; guests—my friends—at this democratic festivity; my dear friend and esteemed Cardinal Miguel Obando y Bravo; my esteemed Dr. Virgilio Godoy, vice president of the Republic of Nicaragua; dear members of the outgoing and incoming cabinets; Commander Daniel Ortega; compatriots present here and those who are listening to me over the radio and television.

During my electoral campaign, I promised that Nicaragua was going to be a republic again. Today marks the dawn of that republic that was born from the people's vote and that was born not from shouts and bullets, but from the deepest silence of the Nicaraguan soul: from the conscience....

For 100 years, we have wished for this democratic republic where we could all be free and equal before the law. We would win a struggle, but there was always a military ambition that would spoil what had been won. But the republic would rise again as a result of a desire for democracy, a dream. Some died for this dream. Others endured prison and exile for it. My husband, Pedro Joaquin Chamorro Cardenal, gave his life for this Republic.

His blood now flourishes. The people's vote sprouted from his blood and dreams. We have reached the promised land. This is the Nicaragua the poor sought to lift them out of misery. This is the Nicaragua heroes sought when they gave up their lives. This is the Nicaragua that the exiles expelled by the dictatorships are seeking. This is the promised land.

This is the blue and white Nicaragua, without tyrants and without ideologies that destroyed its realities and without lies that concealed our history. This is the blessed Nicaragua that instead of burying children in fratricidal wars will bury arms forever so the voice of cannons will never, never roar again, as our national anthem pleads.

There is no sovereignty without freedom or justice without freedom. There cannot even be any Nicaraguan without freedom because Nicaragua's soul and reason to exist is freedom.

However, freedom also means respect—respect for the rights of others, respect for the law, respect for the property of others, respect for other peoples' feelings and opinions. Freedom will never imply a bored fatherland of puppets who think alike. Freedom is a fatherland of initiatives and pluralism with citizens who respect beliefs and opinions. My government has been blessed with this freedom and respect.

I am here because the majority of the people wanted that: no more killings because of ideological or party beliefs, coexistence among brothers. Choosing me was the plebiscite for fraternity. We can only be free if we are brothers. That is what my maternal instincts tell me.

Saying this brings something to mind; My husband had a boat he used to cross Lake Nicaragua. The boat was called Santa Libertad. I like to think that the name was an omen and that that is the name of the boat on which I will cross my years in government: Santa Libertad. That is why nothing can make me happier than receiving the presidency with a future of peace just over the horizon. The signing of the agreements between the Nicaraguan Resistance, the Sandinist People's Army, and representatives of my government, ensures definitive peace. . . .

I call on everyone to live and coexist with joy within the spirit of those agreements that represent the triumphant return of peace. I believe it is a national duty to honor and deeply thank, on behalf of the people and my government, the highest ranking spiritual authority. His Eminence Miguel Cardinal Obando y Bravo, our Nicaraguan archbishop, an untiring fighter for reconciliation, mediator and witness of the peace agreements. . . .

I address all those who will help me found a republic, those who will be my ministers, deputy ministers, directors of autonomous agencies, diplomats, advisers, officials, employees; all factors in the reconstruction of Nicaragua; to all my people, I ask and demand that you help and support me with solidarity in these four main tasks: First, consolidate democratic liberties; second, promote economic production to a maximum potential; third, reduce social inequality; and fourth, instill in all our actions the spirit of reconciliation.

In the task for the consolidation of democratic liberties, I demand the greatest responsibility from the men who will represent the armed branch and the police. To them and to the judges and magistrates who will impart justice, we demand that they never trample a law or a freedom under my government. I ask my people to be on the lookout to ensure that no abuses are committed. If each person does his job, we will have a government without a stain in which not only a free citizen, but also the citizen who is in jail, will receive the most humane treatment and enjoy every guarantee of the law.

I am going to grant broad and unconditional amnesty for all common political crimes and related crimes committed by Nicaraguan individuals as of this date. This amnesty will include persons arrested, tried, sentenced, or awaiting trial, and those captured and sentenced who have served their sentences, who have now been favored forever with a pardon. Let there be no torture ever again. Human dignity must shine even in the most remote cell during my administration.

We will cause democracy to advance by gradually reducing militarism. Every conflict in Central America must be settled through dialogue, according to the law, and with a fraternal spirit. The new stage in our history demands that we reduce [the size of] the Army and reduce its budget, which is stifling the Nicaraguan people's economy.

. . . I am assuming today the supreme command of the nation's Armed Forces. To fulfill, beginning today, the platform for which the people have voted, the Armed Forces are subordinated to civilian authority. To underscore the civilian authority that the people will exercise over the military, I am also directly assuming the portfolio of Defense Minister to personally direct the demobilization and demilitarization processes and to end the war.

We are ending militarism and warmongering today to establish a definitive, firm, and lasting peace. Loyal to my principles, today I am ordering the definitive suspension of recruitment for obligatory military service and decreeing that youths who are currently mobilized be allowed to shorten their time in service and return to their homes as soon as possible.

While the demobilization of the resistance forces that has been agreed to is being completed, as well as the demobilization of youths in the military service and recovery of weapons in the hands of civilians, I have instructed Army General Humberto Ortega to remain at his post. At the same time, Gen. Ortega must establish an orderly program of reduction of the Armed Forces and must guarantee subordination of the military to civilian authorities with respect for constitutional order.

It is the second task of my government to maximally boost economic production. . . .

To correct the unjust actions that have taken place in the name of the people, I am sending the Legislative Assembly a number of laws that will allow revision of land confiscations and interventions, which in one way or another were carried out to the detriment of many Nicaraguans. I want to guarantee here, however, that properties assigned to cooperatives and peasants as part of the agrarian reform will be respected. Laws will be established to indemnify the former proprietors of these lands because, I am pleased to announce, we are going to maintain a state of rights.

I also want to assure all of you that laws that were recently passed and that go against the nation's interests will be revised because I do not believe we can make arbitrary use of what is part of the nation's capital. On this matter, I again ask all Nicaraguans to keep a close watch on all actions with regard to this matter. Any observed abuse must be reported so that no one takes advantage of his position, so that we all have the same opportunities, and so that our economy is truly democratic.

To further this purpose, we will also eliminate all controls and regulations that hindered and stagnated economic production and creativity. We are going to reconstruct our economy with the largest and most powerful mechanism available to unleash people's creative energy; we are going to use freedom. The farm owner will be able to decide what he is going to produce and to whom he will sell it, and he will be able to negotiate the price for his crops. Workers will be free to organize themselves and work wherever they wish, in whatever type of occupation they prefer, and they will be free to negotiate their wages. Businessmen will be free to choose in which activity they want to invest and what risk they want to take in their businesses. They will be free to win or lose. Youths will be free to study or freely choose their occupation, instead of being obliged to take up the terrible occupation of war.

My government will protect the weakest, most vulnerable sectors— orphans, widows, old people, war cripples—and in a like manner, I am going to appeal to Nicaraguans' patriotism so we may construct a prosperous future for all. In conclusion, I want to announce that my government will promote development and defend our environment. We will form a new organization to watch over, protect, and defend our environment. . . .

The third task of my government is to reduce social inequalities. To achieve this, in addition to the measures I have just explained, I have plans for the wealth we produce to mainly benefit the poorest. Those who have suffered the most are my privileged ones. We will amend the labor laws in a democratic manner, and we will guarantee all Nicaraguans an increasingly fairer salary so that together we will achieve measures of well-being that will bring greater benefits to the worker and his family.

On the other hand, the community spirit that was developing so beautifully in Nicaragua was weakened by the political party spirit and by an ideology that was imposed. The CDS [Sandinist Defense Committees] sought the political control of the people by frightening them with espionage and pressures. We must change this, and we must give new life to the community spirit. We must strengthen the communities where the workers have their natural defenses. We must strengthen the families, labor unions, associations, and municipalities so the people will have power, initiatives, responsibilities, and participation in public affairs.

The fourth task is to have the spirit of reconciliation present in all of our actions. This is the most important task that a divided and impoverished Nicargua demands. The country is filled with disagreements, and we are left with bad memories. We must overcome this sad heritage for the sake of our fatherland and our children. We must be great and generous to reconcile all Nicaraguans once and for all. Those will be our guidelines. We will raise that beautiful flag of peace and humanism.

In the same manner that we were the reason for Central American controversy in the past, we will become in the future a Central American union supporting everything that will reestablish the unity of all Central

Americans, the cultural community, the Central American Common Market, the Central American Parliament. We will also support all joint efforts that will unite this prestigious and great fatherland that proclaimed a united independence as a sign of solidarity and fraternal destiny.

I have chosen the members of my Cabinet with the firm purpose of implementing the government platform I offered the Nicaraguans during my electoral campaign, and of guaranteeing the reconciliation that our country urgently needs.

At this moment I want to pay homage to a great Central American who designed the peace plan, who changed the war situation to a peace situation. I am referring to Costa Rican Oscar Arias Sanchez, who received a well-deserved Nobel Peace Prize.

I hope that his plan continues to attain peace and that once democracy is achieved, the next step will be the complete demilitarization of all Central America. We will then be a model of coexistence and fraternity for the world.

To my recognition of President Arias, I add the other Central American presidents. In like manner, my government's gratitude—without partisan boundaries—to all the countries and foreign institutions that have proved their goodwill toward Nicaragua by giving us all kinds of economic and cultural support with a generosity that moves us. We hope to be worthy, through our government actions, of the democratic support and solidarity we have received from the world.

Upon restoring democracy and liberty, Nicaragua will join the universal ranks that defend man and his rights. We will strive to achieve the goal of national and Central American unity by establishing the priority of giving our children and youths an education for democracy, an education that is the best and most modern in the technical and scientific order, and—simultaneously—the most human in the formation of the Nicaraguan man as the citizen of a republic and a world in which liberty and human rights have again excelled.

I request the support and efforts of all my teachers, our heroic and sacrificing teachers, and all parents to raise our education to its highest levels. We intend to make the education of the Nicaraguan people recognized throughout the world for its scientific and human quality. . . .

Nicaraguans, the eyes of the world are on us. Our road must be the correct one. Our work must be fruitful. I trust my people—my generous, courageous, idealistic, and open-hearted people—and my God, I am proud to be a Nicaraguan; I am strong because I am a Nicaraguan, and I have the solidarity of the Nicaraguans, I am the first woman to receive the Nicaraguan people's mandate to preside over a government.

This is an immense responsibility, but I count on my people and I ask God to help me. He is the God of my people, the God of my parents, the God who is the Lord of our history. I ask him to enlighten me and give me strength to fulfill my duty and fulfill my people's hopes.

Nicaraguans, Nicaraguans, I am your president. I do not want to rule. I want to serve. Thank you, my dear friends! Long live Nicaragua!

FINAL COURT ACTION ON
AMERICA'S CUP RACE

April 26, 1990

A three-year legal battle over the America's Cup, the biggest prize in international yachting, was concluded in a Manhattan courtroom April 26. The New York Court of Appeals decided on a 5-2 vote that the 139-year-old silver trophy would remain with the San Diego Yacht Club. At issue was whether San Diego had violated an 1887 New York legal trust setting forth basic rules of America's Cup racing and had thereby assured victory for its own boat over a challenger from New Zealand. After two New York lower courts issued contradictory rulings in 1989, the case reached the court of appeals, the state's highest.

There the matter ended, with the New Zealand club's acceptance of the ruling, paving the way for San Diego to prepare for the next international competition for the America's Cup in May 1992. San Diego gained possession of the trophy in 1987, when its boat Stars & Stripes '87 defeated Kookaburra III of the defending Royal Perth Yacht Club in a series of races off the Western Australia coast.

In July 1987, five months after San Diego claimed possession of the cup, Michael Fay, a wealthy New Zealander, demanded that the host club prepare to race in ten months, the minimum challenge time permitted by America's Cup rules. Fay served notice that on behalf of the Mercury Bay Boating Club of New Zealand he would enter a yacht ninety feet in length at the water line, the biggest allowed—and far bigger than the twelve-meter-class boats that had been used exclusively in America's Cup racing since the 1950s.

The San Diego Yacht Club had other ideas. It was planning to hold twelve-meter-class races in 1990 or 1991 against competition from several *interested countries—an event that would attract world publicity and possibly tens of millions of dollars in tourism for the city. The club told Fay his terms were unacceptable.*

New Zealand's Court Challenge

Fay promptly responded by requesting that a New York court validate his challenge and, meanwhile, keep San Diego from considering other options. The court held that San Diego's options were to "accept the challenge, forfeit the cup, or negotiate agreeable terms with the challenger."

The two sides were unable to agree to terms and in January 1988 San Diego announced its decision to race against the Mercury Bay's big boat, but with a catamaran—a twin-hull boat, never before entered in America's Cup competition and considered inherently faster than Mercury Bay's monohull entry. Fay said he faced unfair competition and returned to court, claiming the 1887 deed of trust required the defending club to race a vessel "like or similar" to the challenging boat. He was advised to race first and then, if he chose, return to court with a protest.

The catamaran won handily in two races sailed in September 1988 off San Diego, and Fay promptly returned to court asking that the winner be disqualified and the cup awarded to New Zealand by forfeit. Justice Carmen Beauchamp of the New York State Supreme Court so ruled on March 28, 1989, saying that by racing a catamaran the San Diego Yacht Club had "clearly deviated from the intent of the [America's Cup] donor." (America's Cup Rulings, Historic Documents of 1989, p. 183)

Fay filed his lawsuit in New York because its law governed the 1887 trust, which had been executed on behalf of George Schuyler. He was the only survivor of six owners of the America, who had received the silver cup for winning off the southern English coast in 1851. Six years later he donated the cup to the New York Yacht Club, but it was passed back to Schuyler. He again donated the trophy, this time drawing up a "Deed of Gift" saying the cup would be held in trust "upon the condition that it be preserved as a perpetual challenge Cup for the friendly competition between foreign countries." The deed stipulated several rules, which became subject to legal interpretation by the New York courts.

The San Diego club—joined by the Perth club in Australia—appealed Justice Beauchamp's ruling to the New York State Supreme Court's Appellate Division. On September 19, a panel of judges on that court voted 4-1 to overturn Judge Beauchamp's ruling, declaring the catamaran an eligible yacht. From there the case moved up to the court of appeals.

Court of Appeals Decision

Judge Fritz Alexander, writing for the court, said that contrary to Mercury Bay's contention, the original donors of the trophy did not express "an intention to prohibit the use of multihull vessels or to require *the defender ... to race a vessel of the same type ... used by the challenger." The question of whether a particular conduct is "sporting or fair," he said, "is wholly distinct from the question of whether it is legal." Individual sports, Alexander added, must decide their own standards of conduct. Chief Judge Sol Wachtler, in a separate concurring opinion, suggested that the court would open itself to endless challenges if it attempted to adjudicate fairness in sporting events.*

The ruling drew a vigorous dissent from Judge Steward Hancock, who wrote in a thirty-one-page opinion: "It is unthinkable that the donors could ever have intended that the trophy holder ... construe the Deed of Gift in its favor for the express purpose of creating a mismatch to retain the trophy." Hancock said that the San Diego club should schedule a new race with the New Zealand club in similar boats. Judge Vito Titone joined in the dissent.

Fay said he accepted the decision and would send a boat to challenge San Diego in America's Cup races scheduled for May 1992. The America's Cup Organizing Committee announced at that time that fourteen boats from ten countries had challenged the San Diego club. Most of the contestants had signed an agreement to limit the competition to monohulls seventy-five feet in length.

> *Following are excerpts from the majority and dissenting opinions of the ruling by the State of New York Court of Appeals, April 26, 1990, that the San Diego Yacht Club's defense of the America's Cup against New Zealand's Mercury Boating Club in September 1988 was legally valid and that San Diego could therefore retain the cup, the biggest prize in international sailing:*

[I omitted]

II

Mercury Bay asks us to set aside the results of the 1988 America's Cup Match because, in its view, San Diego's defense of the Cup in a catamaran violated the spirit of the Deed of Gift as exemplified both by its terms and various items of extrinsic evidence. It argues that the donors of the Cup never intended to permit such a catamaran defense because a race between a catamaran and a monohull yacht is an inherently unfair "mismatch" which the monohull yacht has no chance of winning. Instead, Mercury Bay contends that the donors intended to restrict the defender's choice of vessel to the type selected by the challenger and to require further that the particular vessel used afford the challenger a chance of winning the match. Mercury Bay also argues that by sailing a catamaran to defend the Cup, San Diego breached its fiduciary duties as trustee under the Deed of Gift.

Although these arguments are clothed in the legal rubric of interpreting the "intent" of the drafters of the trust instrument and determining the fiduciary duties owed by the trustee, the gravamen of Mercury Bay's complaint is that such a race between a multihull catamaran and a monohull yacht is inherently "unfair", whether or not the donors intended to permit it. The measures of "fairness" in this regard, according to Mercury Bay and the dissenters, are standards of sportsmanship as determined by reference to practices which are presently the custom in sporting activities generally and yacht racing in particular.

The question of whether particular conduct is "sporting" or "fair" in the context of a particular sporting event, however, is wholly distinct from the question of whether it is legal. Questions of sportsmanship and "fairness" with respect to sporting contests depend largely upon the rules of the particular sport and the expertise of those knowledgeable in that sport; they are not questions suitable for judicial resolution. As sporting activities evolve in light of changing preferences and technologies, it would be most inappropriate and counterproductive for the courts to attempt to fix the rules and standards of competition of any particular sport. To do so would likely result in many sporting contests being decided, not in the arena of the sport, but in the courts.

Moreover, the Deed of Gift governing the conduct of the America's Cup competitions contemplates that such issues of fairness and sportsmanship be resolved by members of the yachting community rather than by the courts. The deed provides that where the defending and the challenging yacht clubs have not agreed upon the terms of the match, it is to be conducted as specified in the deed and pursuant to the rules and regulations of the defending club, so long as they do not conflict with the deed. As the deed broadly defines the vessels eligible to compete in the match, it is these rules and regulations which the donors intended to govern disputes relating to racing protocol such as the fairness of the vessels to be used in a particular match.

In this case, the dispute over the eligibility of the chosen vessels should have been governed and determined by the rules of yacht racing promulgated by the International Yacht Racing Union (IYRU) and followed by the defending San Diego Yacht Club. Pursuant to these rules, an international jury referees the match and decides all protests jointly submitted to it by the parties. The international jury established to resolve all disputes arising out of the 1988 America's Cup Match was composed of five members, all IYRU-certified racing judges of vast experience and international repute, from countries other than the United States and New Zealand.

Despite Mercury Bay's repeated claims of the unfairness of San Diego's catamaran defense and notwithstanding San Diego's request that a protest be submitted to the international jury, Mercury Bay deliberately chose to keep the issue from these yachting experts, who were of course, best suited to resolve it. Having thus chosen to seek relief in a judicial forum, Mercury Bay is limited to a resolution of only the legal issues presented.

A

The legal issue we must determine is whether the donors of the America's Cup, as the settlors of the trust in which it is held, intended to exclude catamarans or otherwise restrict the defender's choice of vessel by the vessel selected by the challenger. Long settled rules of construction preclude an attempt to divine a settlor's intention by looking first to extrinsic evidence. Rather, the trust instrument is to be construed as written and the settlor's intention determined solely from the unambiguous language of the instrument itself. It is only where the court determines the words of the trust instrument to be ambiguous that it may properly resort to extrinsic evidence.... Therefore, we must examine the plain language of the Deed of Gift at issue here.

Contrary to Mercury Bay's contentions, nowhere in the Deed of Gift have the donors expressed an intention to prohibit the use of multihull vessels or to require the defender of the Cup to race a vessel of the same type as the vessel to be used by the challenger. In fact, the unambiguous language of the deed is to the contrary. The deed accords a foreign yacht club "the right of sailing a match for [the America's] Cup, with a yacht or vessel propelled by sails only and constructed in the country to which the Challenging Club belongs, against *any one yacht or vessel* constructed in the country of the Club holding the Cup" (emphasis added).... [T]he deed expressly permits a defense by any type of yacht or vessel, and restricts the actual vessels to be used only by the length on load waterline restrictions applicable to all "competing vessels", the latter phrase again making clear the donors' intention to leave both the defender's and the challenger's choice of vessel otherwise unrestricted.

Notwithstanding the broad language of the deed, Mercury Bay argues that the donors could not have intended to permit a catamaran defense because the dimensions which the deed requires the challenger to disclose are relevant to monohull but not multihull vessels. This argument misapprehends the role of the dimensions in the competitions contemplated by the deed. Because the deed allows a challenge to be mounted upon ten months' notice, the defender of the Cup is allowed only this short time to construct a defending vessel although the challenger has had unlimited time to mount a challenge and thus may have taken years designing and constructing its challenging vessel. By requiring the challenger to disclose certain dimensions with its ten month notice, the deed provides the defender with notice of the vessel it will be facing and thus removes the competitive advantage which would otherwise inure to the challenger. For the same reason, the deed does not require the defender to disclose any details about its vessel until the start of the race. Thus, the challenger's disclosed dimensions, which may not be exceeded, limit only the challenging vessel, and do not restrict the defending vessel. So understood, the question of whether the dimensions themselves relate to multihull vessels is simply not relevant to the issue of whether the deed precludes a catamaran defense.

In this case, we are not presented with the issue to which Mercury Bay's arguments are relevant—whether the required dimensions preclude the use of a catamaran by a challenger because the dimensions specified do not relate to multihull vessels and therefore do not provide the defender with the disclosure mandated by the deed. While we have no occasion to address this question, we note that the applicability of the required dimensions to multihull vessels is hotly contested by the parties before us, both of whom have submitted expert evidence supporting their respective positions.

We also reject Mercury Bay's contention that the phrase "friendly competition between countries" connotes a requirement that the defender race a vessel which is of the same type or even substantially similar to the challenging vessel described in the ten month notice. Neither the words themselves nor their position in the deed warrant that construction. Although the stated purpose of the Deed of Gift is to foster "the friendly competition between foreign countries," that general phrase does not delineate any of the specific requirements of the matches to be held. Moreover, while each match is a competition, the deed permits the competitors to both construct and race the fastest vessels possible so long as they fall within the broad criteria of the deed. Thus the defender does not become a competitor only when "the warning gun of the race goes off" (Dissent . . .) the deed makes clear that the design and construction of the yachts as well as the races, are part of the competition contemplated. Mercury Bay's suggestion, argued explicitly below and implicit here, that the vessels must be evenly matched is belied by its own assertion that the deed permits a match between a 44 foot monohull and a 90 foot monohull—two vessels which, although within the load waterline length restrictions in the deed and of the same type, cannot be said to be "evenly matched" given the much greater speed potential of the larger boat. Indeed, such a requirement that the vessels be "evenly matched" is antithetical to the consent provisions of the deed. There is no point in permitting a defender to give or withhold its consent on the terms of the matches if by simply making a challenge, the challenger could force the defender to accede to its terms. . . .

In our view, the phrase "friendly competition between countries" more aptly refers to the spirit of cooperation underlying the competitions contemplated by the deed. The matches were to be between yacht clubs of different countries, and the deed contemplated that they would cooperate as to the details of the matches to be held. It was in this spirit of cooperation that the competitors had, since 1958, agreed to race in 44 foot yachts. Indeed, it was Mercury Bay, not San Diego, that departed the agreed-upon conditions of the previous thirty years. San Diego responded to Mercury Bay's competitive strategy by availing itself of the competitive opportunity afforded by the broad specifications in the deed. . . .

B

We also reject Mercury Bay's contention that notwithstanding the plain language of the Deed of Gift, San Diego breached its fiduciary duty as the trustee of the America's Cup. . . . We conclude that in the context of this sporting trust, San Diego fulfilled its fiduciary obligations by reasonably trying to come to an agreement on the terms for Mercury Bay's proposed match, and failing that, by faithfully adhering to the challenge provisions in the deed. . . .

Accordingly, the order of the Appellate Division should be affirmed, with costs.

HANCOCK, JR., J. (dissenting):

The San Diego Yacht Club and Sail America Foundation said they would meet New Zealand on the water in a three-race series for the America's Cup. *But, San Diego officials also said they believe they have the right to set up conditions they think will make it virtually impossible for New Zealand to win* (San Diego Tribune, Dec. 3, 1987 [emphasis added]).

This newspaper comment frames the issue before us: was San Diego faithful to its responsibilities as trustee under the New York State America's Cup charitable trust in contriving a catamaran defense for the express purpose of turning the sailing competition into a mismatch and aborting New Zealand's lawful challenge?

This is not a dispute over whether the contest between the monohull and the catamaran was a fair match. It clearly was *not*. San Diego never intended that it should be. It conceded this point by virtually proclaiming a victory before the start of the races. . . .

From the record, there can be no doubt that San Diego chose the catamaran to race against the monohull for one reason: to be certain that there could be no reasonable possibility of losing. Its purpose was plain—to make sure that it retain the America's Cup so that it could proceed with its plans for the 12-meter competition planned for 1990 or 1991 in San Diego. The question is whether it was *permissible* for San Diego to do this. Could San Diego make this construction of the deed, as allowing a catamaran in order to foreclose any possibility of a New Zealand victory, without violating the terms of its trust. . . . Can it be consistent with the duties of a holder and defender as trustee of the America's Cup to meet a lawful challenge by a monohull with a catamaran for the express purpose of avoiding the very competition which the gift of the cup was intended to promote?

. . .[I]t is unthinkable that the donors could ever have intended that the trophy holder and defender could construe the Deed of Gift in its favor for the express purpose of creating a mismatch to retain the trophy, thereby subverting the very purpose of their gift in trust. We therefore dissent. We would declare the September 1988 races to be nullities but permit San Diego to have a rematch, if it is so minded, in lieu of forfeiting the America's Cup by default. . . .

May

BERNARD LEWIS ON
ISLAM AND THE WEST
May 2, 1990

American attention again was focused on hostages in Lebanon when the annual Jefferson Lecture in Washington was given by the Islamic scholar Bernard Lewis. When he delivered the lecture in Washington on May 2, two American hostages—the first to be released in three and a half years—had recently been set free in Beirut by their Islamic fundamentalist captors.

Lewis spoke of current conflicts between Moslems and Westerners as the continuation of a centuries-old "clash of civilizations." He noted that many factors contributed to contemporary conflicts between Moslem societies and the West and observed that many Moslems remained friendly toward the West. He explained the rising anti-Western passion of Islamic fundamentalists as ultimately a struggle "against two enemies, secularism and modernism."

His lecture, titled "Western Civilization: A View from the East," was the eighteenth in a series that the National Endowment for the Humanities has sponsored annually since 1972. Being chosen to deliver this address is considered the U.S. government's highest honor for intellectual achievement.

Lewis, professor emeritus of Near Eastern studies at Princeton University and the author of several books on Islamic religion and culture, said nothing about the taking or release of hostages. Instead, he saw behind the headlines "the perhaps irrational but surely historic reaction of an ancient rival against our Judeo-Christian heritage, our secular present, and the worldwide expansion of both."

In a May 9 interview, Lewis noted that hostage taking was "not countenanced" by Islamic law or theology or tradition. "One mustn't blame Islam for all the terrible things that some Moslems do, even when they claim to be doing it in the name of Islam," he said.

For several days press and television told of the release April 22 of Robert Pohill, followed April 30 by the release of Frank Herbert Reed. The two men, both in their fifties, had been held hostage thirty-nine and forty-three months, respectively. Both had been seized in Beirut where they lived and worked—Pohill as a professor of accounting at Beirut University and Reed as director of a private school.

Their captors, reportedly at the instigation of the Syrian and Iranian governments, turned the two hostages over to Syrian military authorities in Beirut, who transferred them to Damascus for release to American embassy officials. Six Americans and ten other Westerners remained the hostages of Islamic fundamentalists.

Western Secularism

The secularism of the West, Lewis said, is rooted in a separation of church and state that is peculiar to Western tradition. While this separation found its most explicit legal expression in the American Constitution, it can be traced as far back as Jesus' injunction to "render unto Caesar the things which are Caesar's and unto God the things which are God's."

But Lewis added that the most compelling force driving the West to secularism was "the ferocity of the Christian struggles between Protestants and Catholics" in Europe during the sixteenth and seventeenth centuries. It "finally drove Christians in desperation to evolve a doctrine of the separation of religion from the state."

While the West's unique historical experience has led modern Westerners to see secularism as desirable and even natural, it has never appealed to Moslems, for whom the separation of any part of life from God is both absurd and horrifying. Among Islamic fundamentalists, Lewis observed, "the war against secularism is conscious and explicit." In contrast, Lewis saw the struggle against "modernism" as neither conscious nor explicit.

Islamic fundamentalism, he said, "has given an aim and a form to the otherwise aimless and formless resentment and anger of the Muslim masses at the forces that have disrupted their societies, subverted their institutions, denied or destroyed traditional values and loyalties, aggravated and emphasized their disparities, and, in the final analysis, robbed them of their beliefs, their aspirations, their dignity, and, to an increasing extent, even their livelihood."

As the heir of European civilization and leader of the West, Lewis observed, America has "become the focus on which their pent-up hate and anger converge." It should be clear, he added, "that we are facing a mood and a movement far transcending the level of issues and policies and the governments that pursue them."

Cultural Understanding

Lewis was born in Britain and spent much of his academic career there before he joined the faculty at Princeton in 1974. He became a U.S. citizen in 1982. Lewis had been criticized by some scholars for adhering to a perspective that views the Middle East through the lens of Western experience. While Lewis disputed this view, he did not dismiss the significance of the debate over the interpretation of another culture. He observed in an interview published May 9 in the Chronicle of Higher Education: *"I am not an Arab, and there are things which an Arab . . . will understand which I can never hope to understand if I live to be a thousand." Still, he said, "because I come from another culture and because I have some knowledge of outside history, I can see Arab culture within a different context from that in which the Arab sees it." He added that the study of another culture "is absolutely essential to a better understanding of one's own society."*

> *Following are excerpts from the 1990 Jefferson Lecture, "Western Civilization: A View from the East," delivered May 2, 1990, in Washington, D.C., under the sponsorship of the National Endowment for the Humanities:*

Islam is one of the world's great religions. Let me be explicit on what I mean by that. It has brought comfort and peace of mind to countless millions of men. It has given dignity and meaning to drab and impoverished lives. It has taught men of different races to live in brotherhood and people of different creeds to live side by side in reasonable tolerance. It inspired a great civilization in which others besides Muslims lived creative and useful lives and which, by its achievement, enriched the whole world. But Islam, like other religions, has also known periods when it inspired in some of its followers a mood of hatred and violence. It is our misfortune that we have to confront part—though by no means all or even most—of the Muslim world while it is going through such a period and when much—though again not all—of that hatred is directed against us.

Why? We should not exaggerate the dimensions of the problem. The Muslim world is far from unanimous in its rejection of the West, nor have the Muslim regions of the Third World been the most passionate and the most extreme in their hostility. There are still significant numbers, in some quarters perhaps a majority, of Muslims with whom we share certain basic cultural and moral, social and political beliefs and aspirations; there is still an imposing Western presence—cultural, economic, diplomatic—in Muslim lands, some of which are Western allies. Certainly, nowhere in the Muslim world, neither in the Middle East nor elsewhere, has American policy suffered disasters or encountered problems comparable with those of Southeast Asia or Central America . . . but there is a Libya, an Iran, and a Lebanon, and a surge of hatred that distresses, alarms, and above all baffles Americans.

At times, this hatred goes beyond the level of hostility to specific interests or actions or policies or even countries, and becomes a rejection of Western civilization as such—not only what it does but what it is—and of the principles and values that it practices and professes. These indeed are seen as innately evil, and those who promote or accept them as the "enemies of God."

This phrase, which occurs so frequently in the statements of the Iranian leadership, both in their judicial proceedings and in their political pronouncements, must seem very strange to the modern outsider, whether secular or religious. The idea that God has enemies, and needs human help in order to identify and dispose of them, is a little difficult to assimilate. It is not, however, all that alien. The concept of the enemies of God is familiar in pre-classical and classical antiquity and in both the Old and New Testaments, as well as in the Qur'an [Koran]. . . .

The Qur'an is, of course, strictly monotheistic and recognizes one god, one universal power only. There is a struggle in men's hearts between good and evil, between God's commandments and the tempter, but this is seen as a struggle ordained by God with its outcome preordained by God, serving as a test of mankind, and not, as in some of the old dualist religions, a struggle in which mankind has a crucial part to play in bringing about the victory of good over evil. Despite this monotheism, Islam, like Judaism and Christianity, was at various stages in its development influenced, especially in Iran, by the dualist idea of a cosmic clash of good and evil, light and darkness, order and chaos, truth and falsehood, god and the Adversary, variously known as devil, Iblis, Satan, and other names.

In Islam, the struggle of good and evil acquired, from the start, political and even military dimensions. Muhammad, it will be recalled, was not only a prophet and a teacher, like the founders of other religions; he was also the head of a polity and of a community, a ruler and a soldier. Hence his struggle involved a state and its armed forces. If the fighters in the war for Islam, the holy war "in the path of God," are fighting for God, it follows that their opponents are fighting against God. And since God is in principle the sovereign, the supreme head of the Islamic state, with the Prophet, and after the Prophet the caliphs, as His viceregents, then God as sovereign commands the army. The army is God's army and the enemy is God's enemy. The duty of God's soldiers is to dispatch God's enemies as quickly as possible to the place where God will chastise them, that is to say, in the afterlife.

Clearly related to this is the basic division of mankind as perceived in Islam. Most, probably all, human societies have a way of distinguishing between themselves and others: insider and outsider, in-group and out-group, kinsman or neighbor and foreigner. We all have a definition which not only defines the outsider but also, and perhaps more particularly, helps to define and illustrate our perception of ourselves.

In the classical Islamic view, to which many are again beginning to return, the world and all mankind are divided into two: the House of Islam, where the Muslim law and faith prevail, and the rest, variously known as the House of Unbelief and the House of War, which it is the duty of Muslims ultimately to bring to Islam. But the greater part of the world is still outside Islam, and even inside the Islamic lands, according to the view of the Muslim radicals, the faith of Islam has been undermined, and the law of Islam has been abrogated. The obligation of holy war, therefore, begins at home and continues abroad against the self-same infidel enemy.

[Islamic-Christian Rivalry]

Like every other civilization known to human history, the Muslim world in its heyday saw itself as the center of truth and enlightenment, surrounded on all sides by infidel barbarians whom it would in due course civilize and enlighten. But between these different groups of barbarians there was a crucial difference. The barbarians to the east and the south were polytheists and idolaters, offering no serious threat and no competition at all to Islam. In the north and west, in contrast, Muslims from an early date recognized a genuine rival—a world religion with universalist aspirations, a distinctive civilization inspired by that religion, and an empire which, though much smaller than theirs, was no less ambitious in its claims and aspirations. This was the entity which was known to itself and others as Christendom, and which for long was almost identical with Europe.

The struggle between these two rival systems has now lasted for some 14 centuries. It began with the advent of Islam in the seventh century and has continued virtually to the present day. It has consisted of a long series of attacks and counterattacks, jihads and crusades, conquests and reconquests. For the first thousand years, Islam was advancing, Christendom in retreat and under threat. The new faith conquered the old Christian lands of the Levant and North Africa and invaded Europe, ruling for a while in Sicily, Spain, Portugal, and even parts of France. The attempt by the Crusaders to recover the lost lands of Christendom in the east was held and thrown back, and even the loss of southwest Europe to the Reconquista was amply compensated by the advance into southeast Europe, twice reaching as far as Vienna. For the last 300 years, since the failure of the second Turkish siege of Vienna in 1683 and the rise of the European colonial empires in Asia and Africa, Islam has been on the defensive, and the Christian and post-Christian civilization of Europe and her daughters has brought the whole world, including Islam, within its orbit.

For a long time now there has been a rising tide of rebellion against this Western paramountcy, and a desire to reassert Muslim values and restore Muslim greatness. The Muslim has suffered successive stages of defeat. The first was his loss of domination in the world to the advancing power of Russia and the West. The second was the undermining of his authority in his own country, through the invasion of foreign ideas and laws and ways of life and sometimes even foreign rulers or settlers, and the enfranchisement of native non-Muslim elements. The third—the last straw—was the loss of his mastery in his own house as a result of the abolition of slavery and the emancipation of women. It was too much to endure, and the outbreak of rage was inevitable against these alien, infidel, and incomprehensible forces that had subverted his dominance, disrupted his society, devalued his values, impoverished and subjugated him, and finally violated the sanctuary of his home. It was also natural that this rage should be directed primarily against the millennial enemy and should draw its strength from ancient beliefs and loyalties. . . .

[Perceptions of America]

In the lands of Islam remarkably little was known about America. At first, the voyages of discovery aroused some interest—the only surviving copy of Colombus's own map of America is a Turkish translation and adaptation, still preserved in the Topkapi Palace Museum in Istanbul. A 16th-century Turkish geographer's account of the discovery of the New World, entitled *The History of Western India,* was one of the first books printed in Turkey. But thereafter interest seems to have waned, and not much is said about America in Turkish, Arabic or other Muslim languages until a relatively late date. A Moroccan ambassador who was in Spain at the time wrote what must surely be the first Arabic account of the American Revolution. The sultan of Morocco signed a treaty of friendship with the United States in 1787, and thereafter the new republic had a number of dealings—some friendly, some hostile, mostly commercial— with other Muslim states. These seem to have had little impact on either side. The American Revolution and the American republic to which it gave birth for long remained unnoticed and unknown. Even the small but growing American presence in the 19th century—merchants, consuls, missionaries, and teachers—aroused little or no curiosity and is almost unmentioned in the Muslim literature and the newspapers of the time.

The Second World War, the oil industry, and postwar developments brought many Americans to the Islamic lands; increasing numbers of Muslims also came to America, at first as students, then as teachers, as businessmen or other visitors, eventually as immigrants. Cinema and later television brought the American way of life, or at any rate a certain version of it, before countless millions to whom the very name of America had previously been meaningless or unknown. A wide range of American products, particularly in the immediate postwar years when European competition was virtually eliminated and Japanese competition had not yet arisen, reached into the remotest markets of the Muslim world, winning new customers and, perhaps more important, creating new tastes and ambitions. For some, America represented freedom and justice and opportunity. For many more, it represented wealth and power and success, at a time when these qualities were not regarded as sins or crimes.

And then came the great change, when the leaders of a widespread and widening religious revival sought out and identified their enemies as the enemies of God, and gave them "a local habitation and a name" in the Western Hemisphere. Suddenly, or so it seemed, America had become the archenemy, the incarnation of evil, the diabolic opponent of all that is good, and specifically, for Muslims, of Islam. Why?

Among the components in the mood of anti-Westernism, and more especially of anti-Americanism, were certain intellectual influences coming from Europe. One of these was from Germany, where a negative view of America formed part of a school of thought by no means limited to the Nazis, but including writers as diverse as Rainer Maria Rilke, Oswald Spengler, Ernst Jünger, and Martin Heidegger. In this perception, America was the ultimate example of civilization without culture; rich and comfortable, materially advanced but soulless and artificial; assembled or at best constructed, not grown; mechanical not organic; technologically complex, but without the spirituality and vitality of the rooted, human, national cultures of the Germans and other "authentic" people. German philosophy and particularly the philosophy of education enjoyed a considerable vogue among Arab and some other Muslim intellectuals in the thirties and early forties, and this philosophic anti-Americanism was part of the message.

After the collapse of the Third Reich and the temporary ending of German influence, another philosophy, even more anti-American, took its place—the Soviet version of Marxism, with its denunciation of Western capitalism and of America as its most advanced and dangerous form. And when Soviet influence began to fade, there was yet another to take its place or at least to supplement its working—the influence of the new mystique of Third Worldism, emanating from Western Europe, particularly from France, and later also from the United States, and drawing at times on both these earlier philosophies. This mystique was helped by the universal human tendency to invent a golden age in the past, and the specificially European propensity to locate it elsewhere. A new variant of the old, golden age myth placed it in the Third World, where the innocence of the non-Western Adam and Eve was ruined by the Western serpent. This view took as axiomatic the goodness and purity of the East and the wickedness of the West, expanding in an exponential curve of evil from Western Europe to the United States. These ideas too fell on fertile ground and won widespread support.

[Roots of Anti-Westernism]

But though these imported philosophies helped to provide intellectual expression for anti-Westernism and anti-Americanism, they did not cause it, and certainly they do not explain the widespread anti-Westernism which made so many in the Middle East and elsewhere in the Islamic world receptive to such ideas. . . .

Clearly, something deeper is involved than these specific grievances, numerous and important as they may be, something deeper which turns every disagreement into a problem and makes every problem insoluble.

This revulsion against America, more generally against the West, is by no means limited to the Muslim world, nor have Muslims, with the exception of the Iranian mullahs and their disciples elsewhere, experienced and exhibited its more virulent forms. This mood of disillusionment and hostility has affected many other parts of the world and even reached some elements in the United States. It is from these last, speaking for themselves and claiming to speak for the oppressed people of the Third World, that the most publicized explanations—and justifications—of this rejection of Western civilization and its values have of late been heard.

The accusations are familiar. We of the West are accused of sexism, racism, and imperialism, institutionalized in patriarchy and slavery, tyranny and exploitation. To these charges, and to others as heinous, we have no option but to plead guilty—not as Americans, nor yet as Westerners, but simply as human beings, as members of the human race. In all these sins, we are not the only sinners, and in some of them we are very far from being the worst. . . .

Of all these offenses, the one that is most widely, frequently, and vehemently denounced is undoubtedly imperialism, sometimes just Western, sometimes Eastern (i.e., Soviet) and Western alike. But in the literature of Islamic fundamentalists, the use of this term often suggests that it may not carry quite the same meaning for them as for its Western critics. In many of these writings, the term "imperialist" is given a distinctively religious significance, being used in association, and sometimes interchangeably, with "missionary," and denoting a form of attack which includes the Crusades and the Reconquest of Spain as well as the modern colonial empires. One also sometimes gets the impression that the offense of imperialism is not—as for Western critics—the domination by one people over another, but rather the allocation of roles in this process. What is truly evil and unacceptable is the domination of infidels over true believers. . . . The true faith, based on God's final revelation, must be protected from insult and abuse; other faiths, which may be false or incomplete, have no right to any such protection.

There are ... difficulties in the way of accepting imperialism as an explanation of this hostility, even if we define imperialism, narrowly and specifically, as the invasion and domination of Muslim countries by non-Muslims. If the hostility is directed against imperialism in that sense, why has it been so much stronger against Western Europe, which has relinquished all its Muslim possessions and dependencies, and so much weaker against Russia, which still rules, with no light hand, over many millions of reluctant Muslim subjects and over ancient Muslim cities and countries? And why should it include the United States, which has never ruled any Muslim country?

The last surviving European empire with Muslim subjects, that of Russia, far from being the target of criticism and attack, has been almost exempt. Even the most recent repressions of Muslim revolts in the southern and central Asian republics of the USSR incurred no more than relatively mild words of expostulation, coupled with a disclaimer of any desire to interfere in what are called the "internal affairs" of the USSR and a request for the preservation of order and tranquility on the frontier.

One reason for this somewhat surprising restraint is to be found in the nature of events in Azerbaijan. Islam is obviously an important and potentially a growing element in the Azerbaijani sense of identity, but it is not at present a dominant element, and the Azerbaijani movement has more in common with the liberal patriotism of Europe than with Islamic fundamentalism. Such a movement would not arouse the sympathy of the rulers of the Islamic Republic. It might even alarm them, since a genuinely democratic national state run by the people of Soviet Azerbaijan would exercise a powerful attraction on their kinsmen immediately to the south in the Iranian province of Azerbaijan....

... [T]he relatively minor place assigned to Russia, ... in the demonology of fundamentalism [arises from] ... the great [Western] social and intellectual and economic changes ... which have transformed most of the Islamic world and given rise to such commonly denounced Western evils as consumerism and secularism....

[Western Challenge]

... Soviet secularism, like Soviet consumerism, holds no temptation for the Muslim masses and is losing what appeal it had for Muslim intellectuals. More than ever before, it is Western capitalism and democracy that still provide an authentic and attractive alternative to traditional ways of thought and life. Fundamentalist leaders are not mistaken in seeing in Western civilization the greatest challenge to the way of life that they wish to retain or restore for their people.

The origins of secularism in the West may be found in two circumstances: in early Christian teachings, and still more, experience, which created two institutions, church and state, and in later Christian conflicts, which drove them apart.

Muslims too had their religious disagreements, but there was nothing remotely approaching the ferocity of the Christian struggles between Protestants and Catholics, which devastated Christian Europe in the 16th and 17th centuries and finally drove Christians in desperation to evolve a doctrine of the separation of religion from the state. Only by depriving religious institutions of coercive power, so it seemed at the time, could Christendom restrain the murderous intolerance and persecution which Christians had visited on followers of other religions and, most of all, on those who professed other forms of their own. Muslims experienced no such need and evolved no such doctrine.... Islam was never prepared, either in theory or in practice, to accord full equality to those who held other beliefs and practiced other forms of worship.... It did, however, accord to the holders of partial truth a degree of practical as well as theoretical tolerance rarely paralleled in the Christian world until the adoption of a measure of secularism in the late 17th and 18th centuries.

At first the Muslim response to Western civilization was one of admiration and emulation—an immense respect for the achievements of the West and a desire to imitate and adopt them. This desire arose from a keen and growing awareness of the relative weakness, poverty, and backwardness of the Islamic world as compared with the advancing West. This disparity first became apparent on the battlefield, but soon spread to other areas of human activity. Muslim writers observed and wrote about the wealth and power of the West, its science and technology, its manufactures and its forms of government. For a time, the secret of Western success was seen to lie in two achievements: economic advancement and especially industry; political institutions and especially freedom. Several generations of reformers and modernizers tried to adapt these and introduce them to their own countries, in the hope that thereby they would be able to achieve equality with the West and perhaps restore their lost superiority.

In our own time, this mood of admiration and emulation has given way to one of hostility and rejection. In part this mood is surely due to a feeling of humiliation—a growing awareness, among the heirs of an old, proud, and for long dominant civilization, of having been overtaken, overborne, and overwhelmed by those whom they had long regarded as their inferiors. In part, this change is due to events in the Western world itself. One factor of major importance was certainly the impact of two great suicidal wars in ... which the belligerents conducted an immense propaganda effort in the Islamic world and elsewhere to discredit and undermine each other. The message they brought found many listeners, the more ready to respond, in that their own experience of Western ways was not happy. The introduction of Western commercial, financial, and industrial methods did indeed bring great wealth, but it accrued ... to transplanted Westerners and members of Westernized minorities and to only a few among the main Muslim population.... Even the political institutions that had come from the West were discredited, being judged not by their Western originals but by their local imitators.... For vast numbers of Middle Easterners, Western-style economic methods brought poverty, Western-style political institutions brought tyranny, even Western-style warfare brought defeat. It is hardly surprising that so many were willing to listen to voices telling them that the old Islamic ways were best and that their only salvation was to throw aside the pagan and infidel innovations of the reformers and to return to the True Path which God had prescribed for his people.

[Two Enemies: Secularism and Modernism]

Ultimately the struggle of the fundamentalists is against two enemies, secularism and modernism. The war against secularism is conscious and explicit, and there is by now a whole literature denouncing secularism as an evil, neo-pagan force in the modern world and attributing it variously to the Jews, the West, and the United States. The war against modernity is for the most part neither conscious nor explicit, and is directed against the whole process of change that has taken place in the Islamic world in the last century or more and has transformed the political, economic, social, and even cultural structures of Muslim countries. Islamic fundamentalism has given an aim and a form to the otherwise aimless and formless resentment and anger of the Muslim masses at the forces that have disrupted their societies, subverted their institutions, denied or destroyed traditional values and loyalties, aggravated and emphasized their disparities and in the final analysis, robbed them of their beliefs, their aspirations, their dignity, and to an increasing extent, even their livelihood.

The instinct of the masses is not false in locating the ultimate source of these cataclysmic changes in the West and in attributing the disruption of their old way of life to the impact of Western domination, Western influence, or Western precept and example. And since America is the legitimate heir of European civilization and the recognized and unchallenged leader of the West, it is America that has inherited the resulting grievances and become the focus on which their pent-up hate and anger converge. It should by now be clear that we are facing a mood and a movement far transcending the level of issues and policies and the governments that pursue them. This is no less than a clash of civilizations—the perhaps irrational but surely historic reaction of an ancient rival against our Judeo-Christian heritage, our secular present, and the worldwide expansion of both. It is crucially important that we on our side should study their heritage and understand their present, and that we should not be provoked into an equally historic but also equally irrational reaction against them.

Not all the ideas imported from the West by Western intruders or native Westernizers were rejected. Some were accepted even by the most radical Islamic fundamentalists, usually without acknowledgment of source, and suffering a sea change into something rarely rich but often strange. One such was political freedom, with the associated notions and practices of representation, election, and constitutional government. Even the Islamic Republic of Iran has a written constitution and an elected assembly, as well as a kind of episcopate, for none of which is there any prescription in Islamic teaching or any precedent in the Islamic past. Both are clearly adapted from Western models. . . . From constitutions to Coca-Cola, from tanks and television to T-shirts, the symbols and artifacts, and through them the ideas, of the West have retained—even strengthened—their appeal.

The movement which is nowadays called fundamentalism is not the only Islamic tradition. There are others, more tolerant, more open, which helped to inspire the great achievements of Islamic civilization in the past, and we may hope that these other traditions will in time prevail. But before this issue is decided there will be a hard struggle, in which we of the West can do little to nothing. Even the attempt might do harm, for these are issues which Muslims, and only Muslims, must decide among themselves. And in the meantime, we must take great care, on all sides, to avoid the danger of [a] new era of religious wars, arising from the exacerbation of differences and the revival of ancient, long-forgotten prejudices.

We must then strive to achieve a better appreciation of other religious and political cultures through the study of their history, their literature, and their achievements. At the same time we may hope that they too will try to achieve a better understanding of ours. . . .

SPEECHES MARKING
1970 KENT STATE DEATHS
May 4, 1990

One of the tragedies of the Vietnam War occurred on an American college campus in 1970. Four students at Kent State University in Ohio were killed by the gunfire of National Guard troops during an antiwar demonstration. Nine others were wounded but survived. The incident became a rallying cry of the national antiwar movement, and a landmark event of that turbulent period in American history.

Exactly twenty years later—May 4, 1990—4,000 persons gathered at the university to mourn and dedicate a monument to the slain students. Richard F. Celeste, the governor of Ohio, offered his apology for what had happened. None of his predecessors had done that quite so directly.

Naming each of the four victims—Allison Krause, Jeff Miller, Sandy Sheuer, and Bill Schroeder—the governor said: "I am sorry." For years families and friends of those students bitterly decried the absence of an official expression of remorse for what had occurred.

Some 900 armed guardsmen had been ordered to Kent State after violence and vandalism erupted during a student protest against America's military involvement in Vietnam. State officials and many others, including some students, defended the action of the troops.

Official inquiries determined that twenty-eight of the soldiers had fired into a crowd of protesters and onlookers. Guard officers said that the men felt threatened by stones being hurled by some of the protesters. Eight of the guardsmen were indicted by a federal grand jury on charges of violating the slain students' civil rights, but a trial judge dismissed the charges for lack of evidence.

Keynote Speech by George McGovern

*"Speaking your mind, casting a stone or hurling an obscene comment—
none of those deserve death," Celeste said in remarks, preceding the
keynote speech by former senator George S. McGovern of South Dakota.
McGovern's position against the Vietnam War was the centerpiece of his
unsuccessful Democratic campaign in the 1972 election to unseat President Richard M. Nixon.*

*The 1970 demonstration at Kent State—similar to others taking place
at numerous American campuses—followed Nixon's decision to invade
Cambodia to destroy enemy bases just inside that country's border with
South Vietnam.*

*McGovern expressed hope that the Kent State monument would "help
us come to terms with human tragedy" as had the Vietnam Veterans
Memorial in Washington, D.C. The Kent State monument consists of
four slender pink granite slabs placed at the top of a hill near a parking
lot where the deaths occurred. Blooming on the hillside were many of the
58,175 daffodils that had been planted to represent each of the Americans killed in the Vietnam War.*

"Long Process of Healing"

*"It's been a long process of healing," said Michael Schwartz, president
of the university, at the commemorative ceremony. "This is a day for all
of us to come together, a day for all of us to remember. And having
remembered, we must now move on."*

*Many who attended the dedication walked to four roped-off areas
marking the death sites and picked up lighted candles placed there
during an all-night vigil. In a cold spring rain they carried the flickering
lights to the monument.*

> *Following are excerpts from speeches by Gov. Richard F.
> Celeste of Ohio and former senator George McGovern of
> South Dakota, May 4, 1990, at ceremonies dedicating a
> monument to the four Kent State University students slain
> there during an antiwar demonstration twenty years earlier:*

CELESTE REMARKS

... I'm here today as your governor. I'm here today as an Ohioan. I'm
here today as a parent of a Kent State student.

Two decades ago, I heard the news of the Kent State shootings on the
car radio as I drive myself to one of the crush of events in the closing days
of my first election campaign, the beginning of a journey of public service
that brings me here today, 20 years later, as your governor.

Those campaign events are long since forgotten. The news bulletin is
not. Then in those moments I felt disbelief that we had turned our
weapons on our own children. I felt anger that a distant war in the name of

democracy had invaded so close to home to threaten democracy. I felt pain, especially pain as a parent, for those young people who had died and for their families and for their friends, and yes, for their university.

Surely exercising curiosity on a warm spring day, or even following the crowd, or even speaking your mind or yes, even casting a stone or hurling a curse or making an obscene gesture—none of these youthful deeds deserve death or disability. To Allison Krause, your family and friends, I am sorry. To Jeff Miller, your family and friends, I am sorry. To Sandy Sheuer, your family and friends, I am sorry. To Bill Schroeder, mom and dad here, and your family and friends, I am sorry. To Dean Kahler, and to all of those who were wounded and to all of those who suffered twenty years ago today on this campus, I am sorry.

My prayer this day and for the future is that we turn the undeniable tragedy of Kent State, May 4, 1970, into a calling to be peacemakers right here at this university and in our state more tha[n] at any other place in our nation. We will nurture and we will cultivate skills so that we can face conflict squarely, respecting differences, not rejecting them, embracing differences and learning to resolve conflict constructively.

Anything less would not be a sufficient tribute to those we memorialize today, yet, Allison, flowers are better than bullets. A rose would have gently kissed your forehead. Yes, inquire, learn and reflect but also act as peacemakers. . . .

MCGOVERN SPEECH

I cannot begin today with the traditional greeting: "It is a pleasure to be here."

It is not a pleasure at all; it is a tragedy that brings us here together today.

We meet because of the most disastrous foreign policy blunder in our national history—the American war in Vietnam.

I thought at the time—20 years ago—that this longest war in our history was a military, political, economic and moral disaster. I feel the same way today. And our current policy toward Vietnam is also wrong and self-defeating.

There is nothing good or pleasurable that can be said about the American intervention in Southeast Asia, or our postwar policy since 1975—except to honor those who died and to seek reconciliation with those who survive.

Perhaps as many as 3 million Vietnamese, Laotians and Cambodians died—many of them women, infants and children. The war killed 58,000 American soldiers, plus 2 students at Jackson State [University in Mississippi] and 4 at Kent State.

It crippled and wounded another 300,000 American soldiers and it blasted the emotional health and spirit of countless others—thousands of them having committed suicide and many others living in an emotional hell.

I have nothing but love and compassion for the soldiers and Marines who went to Vietnam. They have had a tougher time than the veterans of other wars. When I came back as a pilot from World War II, I was greeted as a conquering hero. Our Vietnam veterans came back to a country divided, angry and resentful. These young veterans deserve more than we have yet given them. And the war has created other casualties and losses beyond those immediately visible, including the anguish and heartache of those who resisted the war and bravely tried to stop it. They, too, have my love and compassion and admiration for their higher patriotism and moral courage.

How does one count other sacrifices and losses of this endless war, including the loss of credibility of our government under both our major parties in the Johnson-Nixon era?

Vietnam choked off Lyndon Johnson's Great Society—one of the most creative and promising agendas ever devised by an American President— and forced him to give up the presidency four years after he had won a landslide victory promising no wider war.

Vietnam also destroyed the next President of the United States, Richard Nixon, after a landslide victory in 1972. The Watergate scandals grew in considerable part out of the illegal effort to manage the domestic political fall-out of the war in Vietnam. Those illegal, unconstitutional efforts produced the only forced resignation of a President in our history....

... [M]any of the students of America, professors, religious leaders, journalists, and millions of other thoughtful and courageous Americans tried to stop the American involvement in Vietnamese affairs.

They gathered in teach-ins, assembled in antiwar rallies, marched in the streets, went to Canada or to jail, picketed the Pentagon and the White House, worked for the nomination of Gene McCarthy or Robert Kennedy, sang with Martin Luther King "We Shall Overcome," and finally nominated me for President in 1972. Senator McCarthy was denied the nomination, Robert Kennedy and Martin Luther King were shot and killed, and I lost to Richard Nixon in 49 of 50 States.

At Jackson State two black students protesting the war were shot and killed.

At Kent State four white students—two of them walking to class and two of them protesting the war—were shot and killed by the Ohio National Guard. The stupidity and pointlessness of all these killings defies the human imagination. But that is true about nearly everything connected with the American war in Vietnam.

It is argued by some supporters of the American military effort that it failed because of the political opposition in America. I hope there is some truth to that analysis because it is important in our democracy that military operations should be halted if they lack the support of the American people. Any regrets I have about my role in stopping the American war in Vietnam stem from the feeling that I should have done even more, earlier and more vigorously, to end this folly.

One would expect that such loss and tragedy would produce a spirit of humility and tolerance on the part of our leaders. It has not—to judge from their continued stiff-necked policy toward the people and the government of Vietnam and Southeast Asia.

At the end of World War II—notwithstanding that we were brutally attacked and almost destroyed by Japan and Germany in that war—we magnanimously and wisely set out after the war to assist the rebuilding of Germany and Japan and to give them an opportunity for freedom and prosperity. But in Vietnam—after dropping more bombs, napalm and explosives than were used in all of World War II—after killing untold numbers of their people—after poisoning their environment—all of this in a war that we took to them which they never wanted to wage with us, we have turned our backs on them from that day to this. . . .

Is there then any saving grace for Vietnam, for Cambodia, for our surviving veterans, and for Kent State? The answer in part is to face reality and begin the reconciliation of America and Vietnam.

Let us without further delay recognize the Vietnamese government and institute policies of trade, investment and aid. As matters now stand, the war with Vietnam is unfinished. The killing has stopped, but the arrogance and ignorance which produced it survive. So does the agony, the guilt and the separation.

America has not yet come to terms with the tragedy of Vietnam and until we do, we will not be a complete nation or a full member of the human family. Americans need to know the full story of our experience in Vietnam, including the path to war, the mistaken judgments and the lessons to be learned. . . .

Now is the time for both reality and reconciliation.

Our veterans of this war—those who fought and those who protested— should now join hearts and minds—and hands—in volunteering to assist in the restoration of Vietnam. Our biggest Peace Corps units should be in Vietnam. And those units should be sprinkled with American veterans of the war. This is the path of reconciliation and healing and redemption for the suffering veterans of the Vietnam nightmare. . . .

The fact that the Vietnam war is still unfinished was brought home to me after I accepted [Kent State] President Michael Schwartz's invitation to be your speaker today. Several groups wrote to me objecting to this memorial service for a variety of reasons. Some of the correspondents begged me not to come. Others suggested that it would be hazardous for me to write my own speech without their guidance.

But I'm here and you are here and I composed my own speech and you heard it with your own ears.

Sometimes an appropriate memorial can help us come to terms with human tragedy. On November 13, 1982, the veterans of Vietnam dedicated the great Vietnam memorial on the mall in Washington, D.C. One of the most moving monuments ever constructed to honor the dead, this unusual black marble wall with its 58,000 names has helped our veterans and their families and the nation as a whole come to terms with their tragedy and loss.

And we hope that here at Kent State, the memorial we dedicate today will serve to deepen our appreciation and understanding of one of the most tragic episodes of the war.

So now let us join our hearts in reverence to the four young people who died in this place 20 years ago. And let us remember them and their parents and all who grieve for their passing. Let us remember, too, our soldiers who fell because of a policy they didn't shape. Let us remember, too, our suffering veterans, our troubled protesters of the war, and the people of Vietnam who died and those who survive with troubled and difficult futures.

Let us do these things while recalling the Biblical promise: "When a man's ways please the Lord, he maketh even his enemies to be at peace with him."

REPORT ON VOTER PARTICIPATION
May 5, 1990

A report released May 5 by a commission of political experts warned that the U.S. democratic process was threatened by widespread public cynicism, voter ignorance, and low election turnout. The two-year study, undertaken by the Commission on the Media and the Electorate, was sponsored by the John and Mary R. Markle Foundation, a charitable organization devoted to the study of mass communications in democracy. The commission, under the chairmanship of Robert M. O'Neill, president of the University of Virginia, examined the roles of citizens, candidates, and the news media during the 1988 presidential election. They found much to criticize.

Citing "citizen abdication" of the electoral process as its "single most disturbing finding," the commission reported that "American voters do not seem to understand their rightful place in the operation of American democracy" and see themselves as "distant outsiders with little personal consequence at stake in national elections." In contrast to much of the rest of the world, "a dangerous disconnection is widening between the American electorate and its own political process," said Eugene Patterson, editor emeritus of the St. Petersburg Times, *a member of the eight-member commission.*

"We have a very serious problem here and that is half of the public, after more than 200 years of the fight for the right to vote, don't do it," said commission member James David Barber, an author and political science professor at Duke University. Only 50.1 percent of the eligible voters actually voted in 1988, the lowest presidential election turnout in sixty-four years. The commission noted "a clear downward trend since 1960."

Media and Candidates Criticized

The commission also said the news media and political candidates had abandoned or failed to live up to their responsibilities in building an informed and involved electorate. "By any standard higher than self-interest," the report said, "both presidential [George Bush and Michael Dukakis] candidates performed poorly.... [N]either candidate made a serious effort to discuss the state of the nation or the priorities facing the next president." The report pointed to the "emergence of the systematic and pervasive use of negative advertising to discredit an opponent."

The report was highly critical of the media, citing specifically the slowness of news organizations to report candidate distortions, especially those presented in so-called "attack" advertising. "The bulk of media stories about candidate advertising did not scrutinize veracity and emphasized instead the strategic guile" of negative reporting, the commission said. Voters were not equipped to protect themselves against these untruths because they were "not sufficiently well-informed to recognize distortion."

Of some 7,000 stories that the commission analyzed in eighteen news outlets between Labor Day and Election Day, only 20 percent dealt with candidate qualifications and fewer than 10 percent with issues. More than half of the stories dealt with the "horse race," who was presumably winning or losing.

"We have to insist and demand standards and punish and repudiate at the ballot box," said John C. Culver, a former Democratic senator from Iowa, one of the commission's members. "Nothing will correct campaigns quicker."

Voter Education, Other Reforms

The commission called for a number of steps to improve citizens' understanding of the political process. One proposal was to establish a citizens' foundation to create a voter awareness campaign through advertising and education programs in the schools. Another was that the Federal Communications Commission require the broadcast networks to provide free air time to educate the electorate and that candidate participation in four presidential debates be institutionalized, with public campaign funding dependent on whether the candidate participated. In other recommendations, the report called for a simplified voter registration system and the establishment of simultaneous poll hours during a twenty-hour election day, with broadcast projections of winners withheld until polls in all fifty states closed. "None [of the recommendations] are automatic cures," Culver said. "But I hope they provide a means of avoiding some of the low points of the recent past."

Commission members, in addition to O'Neill, Patterson, Barber, and Culver, were: Joan Konner, dean of the graduate school of journalism, Columbia University; Charles McC. Mathias, former U.S. senator from Maryland; and Eddie N. Williams, president of the Joint Center for

Policy Studies, Washington, D.C. Bruce Buchanan, associate professor of government at the University of Texas, Austin, was the commission's executive director.

Following are excerpts from the report, "Electing a President," released May 5, 1990, by the Markle Commission on the Media and the Electorate, examining the role of citizens, candidates, and the media during the 1988 presidential election:

Policy Priorities

...[T]he business of educating the electorate about national priorities during presidential elections has been regarded by media leaders as essentially someone else's responsibility. Some media leaders ... do believe they serve an inchoate educational purpose during presidential campaigns. But most do not regard themselves as ultimately accountable for devising and purveying a conception of the national agenda, nonpartisan or otherwise. Developing a list of national policy priorities has traditionally been a partisan political task that is the special province of political parties. Communicating policy priorities to the voting public and building support for them has heretofore been, and despite recent contrary evidence is still thought to be, the job of presidential candidates and the special focus of presidential campaigns.

But as parties have declined in significance, and as candidates increasingly shy away from substantively specific issue campaigns, responsibility for making sense of issues and clarifying the priorities among them increasingly falls by default on citizens themselves. And since Americans get the vast majority of their political information from the media, they also (unavoidably) take many of their cues about national priorities from the same source. Although news organizations have not sought this responsibility and many news leaders resist accepting it, they increasingly help to shape the agenda that takes root in the public mind....

Since the decline of party kingmakers and the proliferation of primary elections began in 1968, for example, the media's participation in helping to winnow the pack of presidential candidates during primary season has increased to the point of near-dominance. More recently, at least one major network has announced plans to use its control over the airwaves to influence how presidential candidates conduct their campaigns. Disturbed at the manipulation of their campaign coverage by the 1988 presidential candidates, ABC News announced that henceforth candidate "photo opportunities," such as George Bush's infamous visit to a New Jersey flag factory or Michael Dukakis's ride in an Army tank, will not appear on the evening TV news unless the candidate is willing to submit to reporters' questions.

Each of these moves represents a major increase in the media's intermediary role between candidates and voters. In each case, one or more media organizations stepped in to fill a public need no longer being met by traditional political institutions or means. . . .

Campaign Advertising Coverage

. . . [T]he content of the political advertising used in the 1988 presidential campaign represented a sharp downturn in respect for factual accuracy and norms of civility. American political discourse has, of course, descended to nasty levels before. Notable recent examples are found in the criticism of President Roosevelt in the 1930's and in the character assassination common during the McCarthy era. But modern presidential campaigns have not usually featured the kind of distorted advertising and personal attacks seen in 1988.

In its unofficial role as democratic watchdog, vigilant against the abuses and distortions of the powerful, the fourth estate would be expected to complain editorially about the negative tone of the campaign and in news space to beard any misleading ads. Both did happen. Commentators bemoaned the adverse consequences for the political system, and the networks eventually began calling attention to candidate misrepresentations and inconsistencies. But a review of the contents of the advertising coverage . . . shows that while the negativity and distortions were reported, other issues got more attention.

Perhaps the largest number of stories emphasized strategic guile. Coverage of the Democrats, for example, dealt mainly with the political ineffectiveness of their advertising. . . . The Democratic TV spots that featured a group of cynical political advisers discussing how to manipulate public opinion, intended to expose the tawdriness of the Bush campaign style, became particular media targets, roundly dismissed as confusing and therefore politically impotent.

Stories about Republicans advertising, on the other hand, took special note of the manipulative skills of such GOP media masterminds as Stuart Spencer and Roger Ailes, while simultaneously noting the cynicism of the Republican approach to campaigning. Several fall, 1988 news accounts illustrated it with an anecdote from the 1984 presidential campaign. Reagan campaign operative Stuart Spencer, in a tape-recorded 1984 strategy session, was heard saying that the Reagan administration had run out of ideas and programs and that there was "nothing in the pipeline." "But not to worry," he continued, promising that a series of carefully staged photo opportunities dutifully covered by television cameras would be more than enough to restore the luster of vitality and leadership.

By mid-October, as the polls showed increasing public displeasure with the aggressive tenor of the campaign, news stories finally began to take note of the inaccuracies in candidate advertising. But it took a particularly misleading ad to provoke a concerted media response. "Only when the Bush 'tank' ad rumbled into the World Series did its obvious distortion of Dukakis's defense posture prompt ABC, and then the other networks, *The Washington Post* and the other major papers to set the record straight."

Most of the complaining about the unusually negative tone of the campaign appeared in editorials and op ed columns, although some found its way into straight news accounts via quotation of the critics. Unsurprisingly, liberal columnists who blamed the campaign's negative tone on Bush were the most disturbed. John B. Oakes, former editorial page editor of the *New York Times,* exemplifies their outrage: "Have you no sense of decency, sir? . . . (Joseph N. Welch's famous question to Joseph R. McCarthy) "spotlight(s) the level of indecency that has marked the Bush campaign, for which Mr. Bush and his mentor, James Baker are basically responsible" . . . .

More admiring of what they regarded as welcome evidence of Mr. Bush's toughness, conservative columnists like William Safire still acknowledged Bush's authorship of the campaign's tone: "Bush now poses as the great foe of crime and liberalism, embracing the death penalty, and blazing away at gun control, prison furloughs and unpopular defenses of civil liberty. Does this application of his knee to the opposition's political groin trouble him? (He is said to find it distasteful) but experience taught him that Mr. Nice Guy wins no ballgames." . . .

Because it engages so many fundamental issues of electoral propriety and responsibility, the debate over campaign advertising and the press's role in policing it can only intensify in subsequent election years. . . .

REPORT ON AVIATION
SAFETY AND TERRORISM
May 15, 1990

A presidential commission, calling the aviation security system "seriously flawed," concluded that the terrorist bombing of Pan American World Airways Flight 103 "may well have been preventable" by stricter baggage surveillance at Frankfurt and London's Heathrow airports where passengers boarded the New York-bound jetliner. It exploded over Lockerbie, Scotland, December 21, 1988, killing all 259 persons aboard and eleven Scots whose homes were destroyed or damaged by the crash. The commission faulted Pan Am's security procedures at both airports and the Federal Aviation Administration (FAA) for lax enforcement of its safety regulations.

The seven members of the President's Commission on Aviation Security and Terrorism released their report May 15, nearly ten months after President George Bush created the commission at the insistence of families of the victims. The commission, headed by Ann McLaughlin, secretary of labor from 1987 to 1989, was instructed to evaluate practices and policy options in aviation safety "with particular reference" to the Pan Am flight.

British and American authorities who investigated the crash had detected sabotage and said the evidence linked it to Abham Jabril's Popular Front for the Liberation of Palestine, a small terrorist band based in Syria and believed to have been directed by Iran. The bombing was widely believed to have been conducted in response to the downing of an Iranian airliner over the Persian Gulf in 1988 by an American warship protecting oil tankers from Iranian attacks during the Iraq-Iran war. (Report on the Downing of an Iranian Airliner, Historic Documents of

1988, p. 703) *The commission did not identify any individual or country responsible for the bombing.*

It was the worst case of sabotage involving an American airline ever recorded by aviation authorities. Only one other bombing aboard an aircraft had claimed more lives; an explosion on an Air India plane off the coast of Ireland in 1985 was fatal to all 329 persons on board.

Findings of Security Lapses

What the commission found in its examination of "certain civil aviation security requirements, policies and procedures" pertaining to Flight 103 "is a disturbing story," the report said. The original investigation of the crash indicated that the bomb—a small amount of the plastic explosive semtex—was hidden in a radio cassette player inside a suitcase that was loaded into the plane's baggage compartment. The commission said it could not determine exactly how the bomb got onto the plane, but there was abundant evidence that an "extra" unaccompanied bag was put on the plane in Frankfurt.

A key finding was that Pan Am personnel could not account for one piece of luggage that had been checked through from another airline. An X-ray operator's list of parcels delivered from other airlines totaled thirteen, while other records could trace only twelve. The commission reported that in an FAA inspection of Pan Am security operations at Frankfurt in October 1988, the inspector "was troubled by the lack of a tracking system for interline bags transferring from other airlines and the confused state of passenger screening procedures."

Security lapses were also noted in Pan Am operations at Heathrow. Recounting the events immediately preceding the flight's departure from Heathrow, the commission said: "Pan Am baggage handlers were pulling interline bags destined for the London-New York leg of Flight 103 from the conveyor belt. No physical search was made of them, nor was there any control to ascertain that bags were accompanied by passengers who boarded the plane. As in Frankfurt, the bags were X-rayed and loaded into a ... [unattended] baggage container."

FAA regulations required unaccompanied luggage to be physically searched before boarding, but months before Flight 103's fateful departure Pan Am had started X-raying the bags instead. "While the extra bag would have been X-rayed, the explosive semtex cannot be reliably detected by X-ray used at airports," the commission said. Pan Am officials insisted—and the FAA denied—that it had obtained the agency's permission to X-ray rather than physically search unaccompanied luggage. An FAA rule, implemented after the crash, required that every bag carried on a plane belong to someone actually on the plane.

Wrath of Victims' Families

Throughout its 182-page report, the commission found fault with government agencies, from the FAA for inadequate security supervision to the State Department for lack of information and aid to the victims' families. Many of the families banded together to air their grievances against the government and demand a thorough investigation.

They were especially incensed that a warning received by the U.S. Embassy in Helsinki, Finland, on December 5, 1988, had not been made public. The embassy said an anonymous telephone caller said that sometime within the next two weeks a Finnish woman would carry a bomb aboard a Pan Am aircraft flying from Frankfurt to the United States. The FAA issued a security bulletin on the threat, and the State Department distributed the information to its embassies around the world. Finnish police believed that the call was unreliable, and the warning was not distributed further. The commission said there was nothing to suggest that the warning had any connection to Pan Am Flight 103 but that the threat should have been made public or dismissed entirely—not made available only to a select group of people.

"The families' bitterness was compounded by the legal environment," the report added. "U.S. law provides no monetary benefits for private civilian victims of terrorist acts." The Warsaw Pact, a 1974 treaty that governs the liability of air carriers in international travel, "impedes the families in recovering compensation from Pan Am, the American carrier."

After months of opposing the families' request to form a special commission, President Bush signed an executive order August 4, 1989, creating one. Its members, in addition to McLaughlin, were Edward Hidalgo, former secretary of the Navy; Thomas C. Richards, a retired Air Force general; Sens. Alfonso M. D'Amato, R-N.Y., and Frank R. Lautenberg, D-N.J.; and Reps. John Paul Hammerschmidt, R-Ark., and James L. Oberstar, D-Minn.

Reaction to the Report

"The report validates many of the things we have been saying," Bert Ammerman asserted at a Washington news conference as the representative of a New Jersey-based group, The Victims of Pan Am Flight 103. His brother, Tom, was aboard the plane. The day before the report was issued Ammerman and other relatives of the victims met with President Bush at the White House and received a briefing on the report and folded American flags. Paul Hudson of Albany, New York, whose daughter died aboard the plane, expressed satisfaction that the president promised to give the report "urgent study."

Hudson, who heads a separate group, The Families of Pan Am 103 Lockerbie, said it took no position on the commission's most controversial recommendation—that the United States be prepared to take preemptive or retaliatory military action against terrorists. Some of the directors of Victims, the more militant of the two groups, said they supported the idea.

The commission urged the government to adopt a "zero toleration" policy toward terrorist attacks and enforce it with a "heightened emphasis" on making state sponsors of terrorism pay a price for their actions.

An example of the use of U.S. military force in response to terrorism took place in 1986 when President Ronald Reagan ordered air strikes against Libya and its leader, Muammar al-Qaddafi, in retaliation for his sponsorship of several terrorist attacks on Americans. (Air Strike Against Libya, Historic Documents of 1986, p. 347)

James B. Busey, who became FAA administrator after the Pan Am bombing, did not dispute the commission's conclusion that the aviation safety system was "seriously flawed." Six days before the report was released, Busey reassigned the FAA's security chief, Raymond A. Salazar, who had been strongly criticized by families of the victims. Secretary of Transportation Samuel B. Skinner moved even before the commission was appointed to set out new rules to improve the airlines' responses to threats of terrorism. Busey said that members of his staff and Skinner's staff would jointly study the report's recommendations and suggest a course of action.

Pan Am chairman Thomas Plakett was quoted as saying that he disagreed with some of the commission's criticisms, and, although the report strongly criticized the airline for safety flaws, it also acknowledged that its safety operations had since become satisfactory.

Following is the Executive Summary of the report of the President's Commission on Aviation Security and Terrorism, issued May 15, 1990, on its investigation into the in-flight bombing of Pan American Airways Flight 103 over Lockerbie, Scotland, December 21, 1988:

National will and the moral courage to exercise it are the ultimate means for defeating terrorism. The President's Commission on Aviation Security and Terrorism recommends a more vigorous U.S. policy that not only pursues and punishes terrorists but also makes state sponsors of terrorism pay a price for their actions.

With other nations of the free world, the United States must work to isolate politically, diplomatically and militarily the handful of outlaw nations sponsoring terrorism. These more vigorous policies should include planning and training for preemptive or retaliatory military strikes against known terrorist enclaves in nations that harbor them. Where such direct strikes are inappropriate, the Commission recommends a lesser option, including covert operations, to prevent, disrupt or respond to terrorist acts.

Rhetoric is no substitute for strong, effective action.

The Commission's inquiry also finds that the U.S. civil aviation security system is seriously flawed and has failed to provide the proper level of protection for the traveling public. This system needs major reform.

The Commission found the Federal Aviation Administration to be a reactive agency—preoccupied with responses to events to the exclusion of adequate contingency planning in anticipation of future threats. The Commission recommends actions designed to change this focus at the FAA.

Pan Am's apparent security lapses and FAA's failure to enforce its own regulations followed a pattern that existed for months prior to Flight 103, during the day of the tragedy, and—notably—for nine months thereafter.

These are the major findings and conclusions of the Commission, which began its work in mid-November of 1989 and reports to the President on May 15, 1990.

The destruction of Pan American World Airways Flight 103 over Lockerbie, Scotland, on December 21, 1988, was the reference point for the mission of this Commission. Pursuit of the full story of Flight 103 led the Commission also to a series of conclusions on counterterrorism policy in general, as detailed in the section on National Will at the end of the main body of this Report.

The Commission also conducted a thorough examination of certain civil aviation security requirements, policies and procedures surrounding Flight 103. It is a disturbing story.

The destruction of Flight 103 may well have been preventable. Stricter baggage reconciliation procedures could have stopped any unaccompanied checked bags from boarding the flight at Frankfurt. Requiring that all baggage containers be fully secured would have prevented any tampering that may have occurred with baggage left in a partially filled, unguarded baggage container that was later loaded on the flight at Heathrow. Stricter application of passenger screening procedures would have increased the likelihood of intercepting any unknowing "dupe" or saboteur from checking a bomb into the plane at either airport.

The international criminal investigation has not yet determined precisely how the device was loaded onto the plane. Until that occurs and subject to the conclusions reached, the Commission cannot say with certainty that more rigid application of any particular procedure actually would have stopped the sabotage of the flight.

This Report contains more than 60 detailed recommendations designed to improve the civil aviation security system to deter and prevent terrorist attacks. Before new laws are passed and more regulations are promulgated, existing ones must be fully enforced and properly carried out. The Commission emphasizes that no amount of governmental reorganization or technological developments can ever replace the need for well-trained, highly-motivated people to make the security system work.

The Commission salutes the thousands of men and women in the public and private sectors of the U.S. civil aviation security system. The recommendations in this report are designed to help them perform their jobs more effectively. The Commission urges management to face up to the security system failures disclosed by this investigation.

A few facts can be stated with certainty about Pan Am 103. A terrorist element did succeed in having a bomb placed aboard the aircraft. That bomb blew the aircraft apart at 31,000 feet over Lockerbie, killing 259 persons on the airplane and 11 on the ground.

The criminal investigation has indicated that the bomb was placed in a radio cassette player and packed in a suitcase loaded into the plane's baggage hold. The Commission, therefore, was able to concentrate its investigation on security procedures for checked baggage.

Authorities also believe that the bomb was made of a very small quantity of semtex, a plastic explosive, and that it probably was placed aboard at Frankfurt, West Germany, where the flight began.

At the end of an October 1988 inspection of Pan Am's security operations at Frankfurt, the FAA inspector was troubled by the lack of a tracking system for interline bags transferring from other airlines and the confused state of passenger screening procedures. Overall, the inspector wrote, "the system, trying adequately to control approximately 4,500 passengers and 28 flights per day, is being held together only by a very labor intensive operation and the tenuous threads of luck." Even so, the inspector concluded, "it appears the minimum [FAA] requirements can and are being met."

Passenger/baggage reconciliation is the bedrock of any heightened civil air security system. Under current FAA requirements for international flights, implemented since Pan Am 103, every bag carried on an aircraft must belong to someone who is also on that flight.

A key focus of the Commission's inquiry was the FAA written regulation in effect in December 1988 that unaccompanied baggage should be carried only if it was physically searched.

When Pan Am Flight 103 pushed away from the gate at Frankfurt and again at Heathrow, on December 21, 1988, no one knew whether the plane was carrying an "extra" interline bag that had been checked through to Pan Am from another airline. Months before Pan Am stopped reconciling or searching interline baggage and began simply X-raying this luggage.

Records examined by this Commission indicate that Pan Am Flight 103 might have carried one such interline bag that did not belong to a passenger on a flight. While this extra bag would have been X-rayed, the explosive semtex cannot be reliably detected by X-ray used at airports.

Pan Am officials told the Commission that the FAA Director of Aviation Security had given the airline verbal approval to X-ray interline bags rather than searching or reconciling them with passengers. The FAA official denied this.

Passenger screening procedures required by FAA at Frankfurt and Heathrow included questioning to identify for additional screening those fitting a "profile" as most likely—knowingly or unknowingly—to be carrying an explosive in any manner, including checked baggage.

The subsequent FAA investigation of Pan Am 103 found that several interline passengers who boarded at Frankfurt were not even initially screened. Several others identified at the check-in counter for further screening did not receive that additional screening at the gate. A large container holding baggage waiting to be loaded on Flight 103 arriving at Heathrow from Frankfurt was left open and unattended for half an hour. At the time, however, that practice did not violate any FAA regulations.

The FAA investigation of the Pan Am 103 disaster began immediately and concluded on January 31, 1989. While the results were not announced for over three more months, the FAA proposed fines totaling $630,000 against Pan Am for violations of regulations, both on December 21 and during the five-week period thereafter.

The FAA, significantly, did not cite Pan Am for substituting X-ray for interline passenger/baggage reconciliation. The official FAA report made no reference to the fact that the investigation had found that one interline bag loaded on Flight 103 could not be accounted for in any passenger records. The agency also noted in its announcement that none of the violations cited by its investigation had contributed in any way to the bombing.

Both the public and the regulatory spotlight were focused on just those types of security problems throughout early 1989. Congressional hearings were held. The Secretary of Transportation set up a task force expressly to look into the matter. The Commission would have expected the FAA to give top priority to security operations at the two airports that loaded and dispatched Flight 103.

Separate from the Flight 103 probe, the FAA found numerous security discrepancies by Pan Am at Frankfurt and London in January and February of 1989 but took no official action against the airline.

In a major inspection conducted May 8-23, 1989, the FAA found that major security violations still existed in Pan Am's Frankfurt operations.

One FAA inspector wrote in the report dated June 7, 1989, that while the operations of the four other U.S. carriers operating at Frankfurt were "good," Pan Am was "totally unsatisfactory."

Wrote the FAA inspector: "Posture [of Pan Am] considered unsafe, all passengers flying out of Frankfurt on Pan Am are at great risk."

When the FAA Associate Administrator with responsibility for the security division learned of the May inspection results, he called a June 14 meeting with Pan Am officials, who presented a plan for corrective action while contesting some of FAA's allegations.

Still, the security violations and deficiencies at Pan Am's Frankfurt station continued. An unannounced inspection in August of 1989 found that many of the same security problems from the May inspection remained uncorrected, especially unguarded airplanes and failure to search personnel maintaining the aircraft.

Pan Am came to a September 12 meeting with FAA on security at Frankfurt with yet another "action plan." A later gathering, however, included a private session between the FAA Administrator and the chief executive officer of the airline. That same evening, a team of high-level Pan Am managers, accompanied by FAA security inspectors, flew to Frankfurt.

Within one week, personnel changes at the station had been ordered and all security violations and deficiencies corrected. At the next FAA regular inspection, Pan Am at Frankfurt was rated a model station. This corrective action occurred nine months after the Flight 103 bombing.

The bombing of Flight 103 occurred against the background of warnings that trouble was brewing in the European terrorist community. Nine security bulletins that could have been relevant to the tragedy were issued between June 1, 1988 and December 21, 1988. One described a Toshiba radio cassette player, fully rigged as a bomb with a barometric triggering device, found by the West German police in the automobile of a member of the Popular Front for the Liberation of Palestine—General Command (PFLP-GC). The FAA bulletin cautioned that the device "would be very difficult to detect via normal X-ray," and told U.S. carriers that passenger/baggage reconciliation procedures should be "rigorously applied."

On December 5, 1988, an anonymous telephone caller to the U.S. Embassy in Helsinki, Finland, said that sometime within the next two weeks a Finnish woman would carry a bomb aboard a Pan Am aircraft flying from Frankfurt to the United States. The FAA Security Bulletin on the threat was issued December 7 and was redistributed by the State Department to its embassies worldwide December 9.

At the U.S. Embassy in Moscow, the senior staff, with concurrence of the Ambassador, decided that the warning should be made public. Thus the Helsinki threat information was publicly posted at the Embassy on December 14 and was generally made available throughout the 2,000-member community of Americans, including news media and private contractor personnel, in Moscow. For these Americans, Pan Am through Frankfurt was the most accessible and most commonly used route to the United States.

The Commission found no passenger who changed his or her travel plans because of the Helsinki threat except one civilian who was scheduled to fly Pan Am to the United States through Frankfurt on December 16 and switched to a direct flight on December 18. While there were no passengers from Moscow on Flight 103, the connecting Pan Am flight from Moscow was not scheduled to fly on that date.

Any distribution of threat information to one segment of the population, such as the posting of the Helsinki threat in Moscow, creates the perception of a "double standard"—the intentional choice to warn some people but not others. At the same time, the Commission believes that public notification of aviation threat information is appropriate under certain circumstances, described in detail in this Report. Therefore, the Commission recommends that a mechanism be established to consider in individual cases when and how to provide public notification.

As for the Helsinki threat, Finnish police quickly determined that the call was unreliable. All subsequent investigations by other governments have also concluded that the call had no connection to Flight 103. The Commission found no evidence suggesting otherwise.

The Pan Am 103 families registered bitter complaints over the treatment they received from the State Department, and the Commission found that the Department was unprepared to respond effectively and compassionately to the largest aviation terrorist disaster in U.S. history.

The Commission found that the Department failed to obtain a list of passengers, develop a list of next of kin, and notify the families in a timely and compassionate fashion, and failed to staff adequately its consular services effort in Lockerbie.

Although the State Department appears to have begun to recognize the scope of its Pan Am 103 failures, it has only begun to institutionalize mechanisms that will remedy the problems. More must be done, and the Commission's recommendations help point the way.

The Commission firmly believes the U.S. Government owes victims of terrorist acts directed against this country more than just processing the return of remains and personal effects, however important that may be. Accordingly, the Commission recommends that the United States extend financial benefits to these victims and develop appropriate ceremonies to recognize their sacrifice. The outdated Warsaw Convention should be revised to speed increased compensation to passengers' families.

The Commission also finds that the FAA's research and development program should be significantly intensified to keep pace with the changing terrorist threat to civil aviation. Under a contract awarded in 1985 to Science Applications International Corp. (SAIC), the FAA has purchased six thermal neutron analysis (TNA) machines to detect plastic explosives.

These machines, by design specification and by actual performance as observed by the Commission at JFK Airport in New York, will detect plastic explosives in an operational mode only in amounts far greater than the weight of the most sophisticated bombs actually used by terrorists. For example, the bomb that destroyed Pan Am Flight 103 is believed to have weighed half or less than the amount the TNA machine would reliably detect in an operational mode at an international airport.

Despite these limitations, FAA has announced a program to require U.S. airlines operating internationally to purchase 150 TNA machines (or the equivalent, although there is no competing equipment available) and to install them at 40 international airports at an estimated cost of $175,000,000. The Commission recommends that this program be deferred, pending development of more effective TNA machines or an alternative technology.

The Commission's examination of the security program applied by U.S. carriers at foreign airports revealed that much has been done to strengthen them since December 1988, especially at high threat airports. However, foreign governments have not imposed equally stringent requirements on carriers under their jurisdiction, and the U.S. has relied on weak international standards for foreign carrier security. As a result, there are significant imbalances. The Commission recommends steps to improve aviation security internationally and to promote the use of bilateral agreements negotiated by the State Department as the mechanism to achieve a consistently high level of international aviation security.

As part of its mandate, the Commission assessed the coordination and evaluation and dissemination of intelligence information collected. The Commission found that, because of the government's increased intelligence activities targeted at terrorism and the increased resources being devoted to intelligence functions by the FAA, the system is working reasonably well.

The Commission's review showed that no warnings specific to Flight 103 were received by U.S. intelligence agencies from any source at any time. It also showed that no information bearing upon the security of civil aviation in general and flights originating in Frankfurt in particular was received beyond that which was promptly disseminated to the FAA and, in turn, immediately to U.S. air carriers.

Major recommendations of the Commission, as contained in this report, include:

- The United States should pursue a more vigorous counterterrorism policy, particularly with respect to nations sponsoring terrorists.
- Congress should enact legislation to create a position of Assistant Secretary of Transportation for Security and Intelligence, an appointment with tenure to establish a measure of independence.
- The FAA security division should be elevated within the agency to a position that reports directly to the Administrator.
- Through existing FAA resources, the federal government should manage security at domestic airports through a system of federal security managers.
- The State Department should conduct negotiations with foreign governments to permit U.S. carriers operating there to carry out FAA-required screening and other security procedures. Airlines cannot be expected to conduct international negotiations in order to comply with regulations of their own government.
- The FAA and the Federal Bureau of Investigation should proceed with plans to conduct an assessment of the security threat at domestic airports.
- The FAA should launch a top priority research and development program to produce new techniques and equipment that will detect small amounts of plastic explosives, operationally at airports. The program to require U.S. carriers to purchase and deploy the existing TNA machine should be deferred. However, the Commission expects the FAA to continue aggressively its new emphasis on upgrading the aviation security system's human and technical capabilities.
- Public notification of threats to civil aviation should be made under certain circumstances. As a rule, however, such notification must be universal, to avoid any appearance of favored treatment of certain individuals or groups.
- Victims of terrorist actions aimed at the United States Government should qualify for special financial compensation as victims of acts of aggression against their country.
- The State Department must take major steps to ensure that families of victims receive prompt, humane and courteous treatment and service in overseas disasters.

CHIEF JUSTICE REHNQUIST
ON THE DEATH PENALTY
May 15, 1990

As head of the federal judiciary, U.S. Chief Justice William H. Rehnquist on May 15 urged Congress to impose stricter limits on appeals from death sentences. So many appeals can be made by condemned prisoners under the current system that "it verges on the chaotic," the chief justice said. He delivered his remarks at a Washington meeting of the American Law Institute, an organization composed mainly of law professors and leading practitioners. But Rehnquist's request was directed at Congress, where several proposals for changing the system were being considered.

"Today the average length of time between the date on which a trial court imposes a sentence of death, and the date that sentence is carried out—after combined state and federal review of the sentence—is between seven and eight years," Rehnquist said. "Surely," he added, "a judicial system properly designed to consider both the claim of the state to have its laws enforced and the claim of the defendant to the protections guaranteed him by the federal Constitution should be able to reach a final decision in less time than this."

The chief justice asked Congress to adopt the recommendations of the so-called Powell committee. In 1988 Rehnquist appointed Lewis F. Powell, Jr., a retired justice of the Supreme Court, and four lower-court judges to study the appeals question and recommend procedural changes to the Judicial Conference of the United States, the federal court system's chief policy-making body. The committee submitted its conclusions to the conference in September 1989.

Supporters and opponents of the death penalty seized upon one proposal in particular—that death row inmates who have exhausted their appeals at the state level receive only one chance within six months to file challenges in federal courts. Rehnquist pressed the Judicial Conference, of which he is chairman, for immediate approval of the panel's report. Instead, the conference voted 17-7 to defer action until its next scheduled meeting in March 1990.

Apparently unwilling to wait that long, Rehnquist transmitted the report to the Senate Judiciary Committee, a congressional committee that would have to pass on legislation embodying procedural changes in the appeals process. By doing so, according to press accounts, he created ill-will among many of the members of the conference.

Judicial Conference vs. Chief Justice

When the Judicial Conference met again in March, it modified the Powell committee's proposals to make it easier for convicts under death sentences to file repeated appeals. The conference called on Congress to enact legal safeguards for defendants in capital cases and for death-row inmates. It said murder defendants should be assured of competent legal representation, beginning with their trials and extending through their appeals up to, and including, the U.S. Supreme Court. In addition, the conference said that federal judges should be authorized to overturn a death sentence any time they were presented with evidence that would "undermine [their] confidence in the verdict or in the appropriateness" of the penalty.

The Judicial Conference's stand was widely seen as a repudiation of the chief justice's initiative. One of the main arguments in favor of an open-ended appeals process was that many condemned prisoners were indigents and inadequately represented at their trials. Their defenses were typically handled by court-appointed counsels who work for minuscule fees and—critics contend—were likely to be inexperienced, incompetent, or indifferent to the fate of the client. The attorneys, the criticism continued, often neglected to search for mitigating factors that might persuade a jury to impose a sentence less severe than the death penalty.

In 1984 the Supreme Court prescribed a two-pronged test for gauging what constitutes "effective assistance of counsel": (1) Was the defense attorney deficient in his or her trial presentation? If so, (2) was the deficiency prejudicial—would it have made any difference in the outcome? That ruling, in the case of Strickland v. Washington, *seemed to eliminate "ineffective assistance of counsel" as a basis for appeal.*

Most of the thirty-seven states that permitted the death penalty provided for automatic appeal, even if the condemned prisoner objected. Sentences upheld by state appellate courts could be appealed directly to the U.S. Supreme Court, but the case did not necessarily end there. The prisoner could return to the state courts, claiming that some aspect of his trial was in violation of constitutional rights, and win another round of appeals. Finally, a third and final round of appeals could be made through a habeas corpus petition filed in federal district court, again asserting the violation of constitutional rights.

Many governors, state attorneys general, and prosecuting attorneys have contended that defense lawyers abuse habeas appeals to delay executions. In 1983, Chief Justice Warren E. Burger, Rehnquist's predecessor, lashed out at defense lawyers, charging that they were engaged in "calculated efforts to frustrate valid [death penalty] judgments." Rehnquist shared Burger's feelings, as he subsequently made clear in numerous public comments.

Removing Grounds for Appeal

The Senate on July 11 passed an anticrime bill that made the death penalty an option for more than thirty federal crimes and revised the process of habeas corpus appeals but did not restrict the appeals as much as Rehnquist sought. But House objections scuttled those provisions in the anticrime bill that was ultimately passed in October.

Over the past fifteen years, the U.S. Supreme Court has issued several opinions making it more difficult for inmates to have their sentences overturned on appeal. And yet only 132 executions took place between 1976—when the Supreme Court lifted a moratorium on the death penalty—and mid-year 1990. (Court on Cruel and Unusual Punishment, Historic Documents of 1972, p. 499; Court on Death Penalty, Historic Documents of 1976, p. 499) *Moreover, more than two-thirds of those executions occurred in four states—Florida, Georgia, Louisiana, and Texas. The backlog on death row grew larger. When Rehnquist spoke on May 15 he said that some 2,200 prisoners were then awaiting execution— or, possibly, deliverance.*

Despite the relatively small number of executions, public support for the death penalty appeared high. A Gallup Poll taken in the fall of 1988 found that in all sections of the country proponents of the death penalty for murderers outnumber opponents by margins of 4 to 1. It was the highest level of approval in more than fifty years of Gallup polling. Only once, in 1966, were the foes of capital punishment in the majority. Doubts about the death penalty were especially strong when civil rights activists argued in the 1960s that poverty and race played a major role in capital sentencing. For some crimes, statistics showed, blacks stood a far greater chance of getting the death sentence than did whites.

By 1967 there were so many legal challenges to the death penalty that there was in effect an unofficial moratorium on executions. It won official sanction in 1972 when the Supreme Court ruled 5-4 in Furman v. Georgia *that juries handed out death penalties arbitrarily, thus violating the Eighth Amendment's prohibition on cruel and unusual punishment. The ruling voided death penalties in all thirty-two states that then had them. Those states worked quickly to shape new laws that would meet the Court's objections. In the 1976 case of* Gregg v. Georgia, *the Court ruled that "the punishment of death does not violate the Constitution" if "guided direction" is exercised in imposing the death penalty. Gregg became the standard for all subsequent death penalty statutes.*

313

After that the Court began to dismantle a number of legal obstacles that once were commonly used to delay or block executions. For instance, in the 1984 case of Pulley v. Harris, *the Court ruled that death row inmates were not entitled to a special appeals court review to ensure that their sentences were proportionate to sentences given others convicted of similar crimes. In another landmark ruling,* McClesky v. Kemp, *the Court in 1987 upheld the legality of the Georgia system against the challenge of a black man convicted of killing a white police officer.*

The condemned man, Warren McClesky, based his appeal on a study showing sharp racial disparities in the sentencing of white and black killers in Georgia. In separate 1989 decisions, the Court ruled the Constitution did not prohibit the execution of mentally retarded murderers or of juveniles who were sixteen or seventeen years old when they committed homicide.

This narrowing of the scope of relief to condemned prisoners proved insufficient to prevent delays in execution averaging seven to eight years, which, in the view of Chief Justice Rehnquist, was far too long.

Following are excerpts from an address delivered by U.S. Chief Justice William H. Rehnquist to the American Law Institute's meeting in Washington, May 15, 1990, in which he urged Congress to adopt stricter limits on appeals of death sentences:

This morning I want to talk about a serious malfunction in our legal system—the manner in which death sentences imposed by state courts are reviewed in the federal courts. Today the average length of time between the date on which a trial court imposes a sentence of death, and the date that sentence is carried out—after combined state and federal review of the sentence—is between seven and eight years. More than three years of this time are taken up by collateral review alone, with little certainty as to when that review has run its course. Surely a judicial system properly designed to consider both the claim of the state to have its laws enforced and the claim of the defendant to the protections guaranteed him by the federal Constitution should be able to reach a final decision in less time than this.

The essence of the question is not the pros and cons of capital punishment, but the pros and cons of federalism. The Supreme Court has held that capital punishment is lawful if imposed consistently with the requirements of the Eighth Amendment. Whether or not a state should choose to have capital punishment must be up to each state: thirty-seven states have elected to have it, and thirteen states have chosen not to have it. The capital punishment question is one which deeply divides people, and always has. But this question is only tangentially involved when we consider the procedures designed to provide collateral review in the federal courts for federal constitutional claims of defendants who have been sentenced to death. Surely the goal must be to allow the states to carry out a lawful capital sentence, while at the same time assuring the capital defendant meaningful review of the lawfulness of his sentence. . . .

The writ of habeas corpus was originally a creature of the English common law, not designed to challenge judgments of conviction rendered after trial, but to challenge unlawful detention of citizens by the executive. It played much the same role in this country for the first century and a half of our existence. As a result of judicial decisions and congressional ratification of these decisions over the past century, however, it has evolved into something quite different. In civil litigation, as we all know, once the parties have had a trial and whatever appeals are available, the litigation comes to an end and the judgment is final. But in criminal cases a defendant whose conviction has become final on direct review in the state courts may nonetheless raise federal constitutional objections to that conviction and sentence in a federal habeas proceeding. This system is unique to the United States; no such collateral attack is allowed on a criminal conviction in England where the writ of habeas corpus originated.

Reasonable people have questioned whether a criminal defendant ought to have as broad a "second bite at the apple" in the federal courts as he presently does, but that is a question of policy for Congress to decide. So long as we are speaking of non-capital defendants, the present system does not present the sort of practical difficulties in the administration of justice that it presents in the case of capital defendants. This is because someone who is convicted and sentenced to prison for a term of years in state court, and wishes to challenge that conviction and sentence in a federal habeas proceeding, has every incentive to move promptly to make that challenge. He must continue to serve his sentence while his federal claims are being adjudicated in the federal courts. Therefore, the sooner he obtains a decision on these claims, the sooner he will get the benefit of any decision that is favorable to him. This is true even though there is no statute of limitations for bringing the federal habeas proceeding.

But the incentives are quite the other way with a capital defendant. All federal review of his sentence must obviously take place *before* the sentence is carried out; consequently, the capital defendant frequently finds it in his interest to do nothing until a death warrant is actually issued by the state. . . . The upshot is that often no action by the defendant is taken until shortly before the date set for execution. . . . [A] capital defendant, after his first federal habeas petition is decided against him, may file a second petition, and even on occasion a third petition. On each occasion, arguments are pressed that an additional stay of execution is required in order for a court to consider these successive petitions. The result is that at no point until a death sentence is actually carried out can it be said that litigation concerning the sentence has run its course.

The system at present verges on the chaotic. The eight years between conviction in the state court and final decision in the federal courts is consumed not by structured review of the arguments of the parties, but in fits of frantic action followed by periods of inaction. . . . The last-minute nature of so many of the proceedings in both the state courts and the federal courts leaves one with little sense that the legal process has run an orderly course, whether a stay is granted or whether it is denied. . . .

This system cries out for reform. I submit that no one—whether favorable to the prosecution, favorable to the defense, or somewhere in between—would ever have consciously designed it. The question is how the present law can be changed to deal with these problems while still serving the federalism goal which I mentioned previously.

In June 1988 I established an Ad Hoc Committee on Federal Habeas Corpus in Capital Cases under the chairmanship of retired Associate Justice Lewis F. Powell, Jr. . . . The Committee investigated ways of improving both the fairness and efficiency of our system of collateral review in death penalty cases. In September of 1989 it issued its report recommending the coordination of our state and federal legal systems in capital cases and the structuring of collateral review. . . .

Under the Powell Committee proposal, persons convicted of capital crimes and sentenced to death would, after a full set of appeals, have one opportunity to collaterally attack their sentences at the state level and one such opportunity at the federal level. Second and successive petitions for collateral review would be entertained only if the petitioner could cast doubt upon the legitimacy of his conviction of a capital crime. In the absence of underlying doubt concerning guilt or innocence, itself, courts would not entertain repetitive petitions attacking the appropriateness of the death sentence.

In the interests of reliability and fairness, the Powell Committee proposal would permit states to opt into the unified system of collateral review only where they agreed to provide competent counsel in state collateral proceedings. Under current federal law, counsel is provided in federal habeas corpus proceedings, but not in state proceedings. The Powell Committee proposal would also require an automatic stay of execution to permit the prisoner to bring his petition in an orderly fashion and without the pressure of pending execution, and would create a new automatic right of appeal from the federal district court to the federal court of appeals.

I believe that the Powell Committee Report strikes a sound balance between the need for ensuring a careful review in the federal courts of a capital defendant's constitutional claims and the need for the state to carry out the sentence once the federal courts have determined that its imposition was consistent with federal law. The Conference of State Chief Justices at its meeting last February unanimously endorsed the report of the Powell Committee. When that report was presented to the Judicial Conference of the United States in March, five changes were proposed to make it closer to the position taken by the American Bar Association, which would not only enlarge the scope of federal review but make successive habeas petitions more readily available than at present. The Judicial Conference was closely divided on each of these five amendments, and adopted only two of them. . . .

At this moment, there are about twenty-two hundred capital defendants on the various "death rows" in state prisons. There is no doubt that when some of these defendants present their constitutional claims to federal courts, their sentences will be set aside. Others of these defendants will, after full federal review, obtain a determination that the sentences imposed on them were consistent with the federal Constitution. Defendants who will ultimately prevail in their claims should not have to wait eight years for a decision to that effect, and states seeking to carry out the sentence upon defendants whose claims are rejected by federal courts should not have to wait eight years to do that. Fair-minded people, whether they personally oppose or favor the death penalty, should have no difficulty agreeing that the present system is badly in need of reform.

All of the pending Senate bills on this matter are clothed in the garb of "reform," but unfortunately, not all of them are designed to achieve the sort of reform which the system badly needs. The proposal of the Powell Committee, in my view, accomplishes the task while the others do not. Under that proposal the capital defendant is given the necessary tools and the necessary incentives to make all of his constitutional claims in his first federal habeas proceeding, and that proceeding is allowed to run its full course in both the district court and in the court of appeals without any threat of imminent execution. If the result of these proceedings is a determination that the state sentence is consistent with the United States Constitution, that should (with rare exceptions) conclude the federal review, and the state should be able to carry out its sentence. This is a solution to the problem in the best tradition of our federal system. It is a solution which will restore public confidence in the way capital punishment is imposed and carried out in our country.

GAO REPORT CHALLENGING NAVY'S IOWA FINDINGS

May 25, 1990

The General Accounting Office (GAO) gave the Senate Armed Services Committee a report May 25 challenging key findings in the Navy's investigation of an explosion aboard the USS Iowa, *which killed forty-seven sailors. The Navy's findings, released September 17, 1989, concluded that "irrefutable facts" and circumstantial evidence pointed to an act of suicidal sabotage by one of the battleship's gun crewmen, Clayton M. Hartwig. The explosion occurred April 19, 1989, in a gun turret during practice firing of the warship's huge 16-inch guns.* (Navy's Report on the USS Iowa Explosion, Historic Documents of 1989, p. 517)

Energy Department scientists from Sandia National Laboratories in New Mexico, enlisted in the GAO's review of the naval investigation, determined that the explosion could have been set off accidentally by the improper use of a hydraulic ram to load gunpowder into the weapon. Rear Adm. Richard L. Milligan, who supervised the Navy's inquiry, had said that there could be no explanation of an accidental explosion. Acting on that basis, Navy investigators deduced that someone caused the blast, and "most probably" it was Hartwig. He was portrayed as moody, lovelorn, and suicidal in a psychological profile prepared by the FBI at the Navy's request after his death.

The Navy had initially dismissed the Sandia finding as "not relevant" because the scientists' tests had not been performed on 16-inch guns—so-called because their mouths are 16 inches in diameter, the biggest guns afloat. But at the insistence of Sen. Sam Nunn, chairman of the Armed Services Committee, the Navy conducted its own tests at the Naval Surface Weapons Center at Dahlgren, Virginia. His committee had also ordered the GAO review.

The day before the GAO report was released and Sandia witnesses testified before the committee, the Navy said that the testing at Dahlgren demonstrated the possibility of an accidental explosion. Gunpowder bags attached to heavy weights were dropped onto a steel plate to simulate the pressure of an "overram" of a 16-inch gun. On the eighteenth trial, the gunpowder ignited.

Richard L. Schwoebel, a Sandia physicist who supervised the new study, testified before the committee May 25 that the laboratory's experiment "suggests . . . a very simple scenario, in which the explosion could have occurred by accident." It required the presence of two factors, an "overram" creating great pressure on the gunpowder and a certain alignment of the gunpowder pellets, he said.

At Sandia, another of the Navy's key findings was challenged. Sandia tests determined that alleged "foreign matter" found in the gun turret after the blast could be explained by the routine presence of sea water and gun-cleaning fluids—which were commonly found after test firings aboard the Iowa and other battleships. The Navy contended that the minute substances of chlorine and calcium were debris from an incendiary device used in an act of sabotage.

Navy's Investigation Reopened

After the Dahlgren tests, Secretary of the Navy H. Lawrence Garrett III reopened the service's Iowa investigation and suspended all live firings by the four U.S. battleships then on active duty. Senator Nunn said the new findings "eviscerated the Navy's conclusion that the explosion on the Iowa was a wrongful, intentional act" and showed that that conclusion was not supported "by reliable, probative and substantial evidence." The House Armed Services Committee had issued a report March 5 that accused the Navy of using evidence selectively and presenting "an unbalanced view of the facts."

"The Navy's problem was not so much technical as temperamental," The New York Times *commented editorially May 26. "The need to blame someone seems to have skewed the official view of substances found in the gun's powder train."*

The original report had been questioned in Congress, in the press, and by relatives of the deceased Iowa sailors from the time it was issued. The Navy's probe focused almost immediately on Hartwig, a twenty-four-year-old gunner's mate second-class who was the turret's gun captain. The FBI described Hartwig as a troubled man "rehearsing all his life for violence and death." It was suggested in press accounts of the investigation that Hartwig was engaged in a homosexual relationship with a shipmate, Kendall Truitt. Hartwig had named Truitt beneficiary of a $100,000 life insurance policy. Truitt, a married man, denied the allegation.

Truitt, appearing May 25 on the CBS-TV show "This Morning," said the reopening of the Navy's investigation was long overdue. He accused the Naval Investigative Service of making the evidence fit the findings.

"It's like they had their scripts ready and they just wanted to fill in the parts," Truitt said.

Hartwig's sister, Kathleen Kubicina, attended the Senate committee hearing as a spectator and told the press she felt that her brother had been "vindicated" by the GAO report. Mrs. Kubicina, who had campaigned to clear Hartwig's name, said she wanted two things from the Navy: "I want Rear Adm. Milligan to remove my brother's name from the report and I want the Navy to say three little words [about the cause of the explosion]: 'We don't know.' That's it."

Criticism by Iowa's Ex-Skipper

Capt. Fred P. Moosally, skipper of the Iowa, retired from the Navy May 4, 1990, and at a change-of-command ceremony on the deck of the battleship made his first public comments about the investigation. He contended that the investigators relied on "unsubstantiated third-party information, unsubstantiated reports and supposition."

The Navy's report, in addition to holding Hartwig responsible, indirectly criticized Moosally. It said there were deficiencies in the training of the battleship's gun crews. According to the GAO report, the Navy found it difficult to staff battleships with well-trained and experienced seamen. Sailors perceive that battleship duty would deprive them an opportunity to work with the latest electronic equipment and thus slow their advancement in rank, the report said.

The Iowa was one of four World War II battleships recommissioned in the 1980s during President Ronald Reagan's military and naval buildup. To help attain his goal of a 600-ship Navy and provide additional naval firepower, the four battlewagons were outfitted with some new equipment but retained their big guns of an earlier era. The Senate committee asked the GAO, among other things, to "review the battleships' plans and mission."

Assistant Comptroller General Frank C. Conahan, who presented the GAO report to the committee, called the battleships "labor intensive" and costly to operate. He noted that in preliminary plans for cutting defense expenses the Iowa and another of the battleships were slated for deactivation. The two remaining battleships "seem to be top candidates for decommissioning" also, Conahan said.

> Following are excerpts from testimony by Frank C. Conahan, assistant comptroller general, to the Senate Armed Services Committee May 25, 1990, in a report for the committee prepared by the General Accounting Office, titled "Battleships: Issues Arising from the Explosion Aboard the U.S.S. Iowa," and excerpts from the Executive Summary of that report:

CONAHAN'S STATEMENT

I appear before the Committee today to discuss the results of our work concerning several issues pertaining to the April 19, 1989, explosion of the center gun in Turret II aboard the USS *Iowa*. The explosion killed 47 sailors. Since the Navy's September 1989 report on its investigation of the explosion, concern has been expressed on the adequacy of the investigation and the continued safety of battleships.

... We were asked to (1) conduct an independent investigation of the Navy's technical analysis of likely causes of the explosion, (2) review the safety aboard battleships, (3) examine manning and training issues raised by the *Iowa*'s Commanding Officer after the explosion, and (4) review the battleships' employment plans and mission. We engaged the Department of Energy's Sandia National Laboratories to conduct a technical analysis and review the adequacy of the Navy's technical investigation. We addressed the other issues.

Results in Brief

Before discussing in detail our findings in each of the areas reviewed, let me briefly summarize.

Technical Analysis

Sandia's analysis could not corroborate the Navy's technical finding that an improvised chemical device initiated the explosion. Furthermore, Sandia has identified a potential hazard—the impact sensitivity of the gunpowder in combination with an overram at higher than normal speeds which could have caused the explosion. Sandia believes that further testing on this is needed to confirm its finding.

Safety and Serviceability

As discussed in the Navy's report on the explosion and the subsequent Navy Inspector General's report on the gunpowder experimentation that was taking place at the time, safety policies and procedures were not being followed at the time of the explosion. Both Navy reports concluded, however, these violations did not cause the explosion. We examined various equipment, ammunition, and personnel safety records for the four battleships and did not find anything to lead us to believe that the battleships had experienced safety or material problems different than those experienced by other naval ships.

Manning and Training

We found that, as a result of the Navy's assignment process, the *Iowa* and the battleships were assigned a disproportionably low percentage of enlisted supervisory personnel, including gunners mates and fire controlmen, when compared to a selected sample of other ships. Also, we corroborated the *Iowa*'s former Commanding Officer's perception that the quality of manning on the battleships was lower than that for naval ships on average.

We also identified some specific training issues. However, because training records were destroyed in the explosion, we could not reconcile the conflicting statements from the former Commanding Officer that his personnel were adequately trained on the day of the explosion and the Navy's accident investigation report that said they were not.

Battleship Missions

The battleships, with their combination of weapons, provide an imposing array of firepower. They perform a strike mission with their cruise missiles and their 16-inch guns are the best source of naval surface fire support for an amphibious assault. Also, according to Navy officials, the battleships can be a strong deterrent in a third-world scenario. However, other ships with cruise missiles provide excellent strike warfare capability and the changing world security environment brings into question the Navy's need to maintain the battleships to support a large scale amphibious assault.

Moreover, the planned retirement of two battleships, including the *Iowa,* raises questions about the usefulness and supportability of the other two ships in the active fleet. A deployed battleship's presence in overseas theaters will be limited because of the effect of peacetime operating and personnel tempo restrictions on the two remaining battleships. Manning and training problems will also be compounded by a smaller pool of experienced 16-inch gun-related personnel.

It is inevitable that the defense budget will be reduced over the next several years. Given the unanswered safety-related questions, the manning situation, the mission-related questions, and the usefulness and supportability concerns, the two remaining battleships seem to be top candidates for decommissioning as we look for ways to scale back U.S. forces.

Sandia's Review of Navy Technical Findings

When we were asked to obtain technical assistance to review (1) the issue of evidence of foreign material in the rotating band of the projectile lodged in the gun barrel in which the explosion occurred, which the Navy interpreted as being from a detonating device, and (2) the stability of the gunpowder, we counseled with the National Science Foundation and the Office of Technology Assessment. Both stated that the Department of Energy's laboratories, especially Sandia National Laboratories, were capable sources of conducting an independent analysis.

At our request, Sandia performed an analysis concentrating on two areas. First, Sandia explored whether the Navy's finding of foreign material in the rotating band of the projectile lodged in the *Iowa*'s gun and the Navy's analysis of such material indicated that an improvised chemical detonator ignited the powder and caused the explosion. A major constraint to Sandia's analysis was that, after the Navy's and the FBI's analyses, there was no longer any part of the *Iowa*'s rotating band that had not been subjected to an analysis or examination. Furthermore, the Navy could no longer locate a significant piece of evidence—the iron fibers with encrusted material that the Navy said came from a detonating device. However, Sandia was able to build upon the Navy's analysis and to obtain parts of the band to examine. It is confident in its findings, which conclude that the foreign materials that the Navy found were not inconsistent with the nominal levels found throughout gun turrets and were consistent with the maritime environment. For example, calcium and chlorine—two elements in the Navy's postulated detonator—were readily detectable in both Turrets I and II (the turret in which the explosion occurred) on the *Iowa* and in turrets on the battleships *New Jersey* and *Wisconsin*. Therefore, Sandia could not corroborate the Navy's finding that such foreign material was evidence of a detonator.

Second, Sandia explored whether the explosion could have been caused by an accidental ignition of the powder. Sandia agreed with the Navy accident investigation report that the powder was stable and confirmed that a significant overram of the powder charge occurred. However, Sandia has raised a question regarding the Navy's statement that impact and compression of the bag charge were not contributing factors to the *Iowa* incident.

Sandia believes that a possible alternate scenario to the Navy's finding of a deliberate act is that an unintentional high speed overram of the powder bags combined with the impact sensitivity of the powder led to the explosion. Suggestion of an unintentional high speed overram comes from (1) the Navy's accident investigation report which noted that the rammerman was conducting his first live firing and there were reports of an unidentified problem with the center gun immediately before the explosion and (2) Sandia's postulation that the car which brings the powder to the gun room had not returned, which it normally could have during the time of a normal speed ram. Sandia does not consider its study complete, in the sense that a clear and definite cause of the explosion has been identified, and it recommends areas of further investigation by the Navy....

Safety and Serviceability

According to the Navy's investigation report, approved procedures to ensure the safe firing of the 16-inch guns were not followed aboard the *Iowa* on April 19, 1989. Subsequently, the Navy Inspector General also concluded that the experimentation with gunpowder conducted aboard the *Iowa* was "at worst not safe and at best undetermined in its safety." To further investigate the safety and serviceability of battleships we reviewed reports of equipment problems, ammunition mishaps and malfunctions, and personnel-related injury data for all four battleships and compared them to Navy ships in general. This data disclosed no systemic problems with the material condition of the guns or the ammunition components involved in the explosion, or on the battleships, in general, that warrant any corrective action.

Safety Violations

The Navy's investigation of the explosion found that safety policies and procedures were not being followed. For example, although no spark producing items are allowed in the turrets, items such as cigarette lighters, rings and keys were found on the remains of the deceased sailors.

The Navy's investigation at the time of the explosion also believed that *Iowa* personnel had improperly approved and were conducting gunnery experiments. Ship personnel were loading an inappropriate projectile/powder combination when the explosion occurred. This involved 5 bags of an authorized type of powder with a 2,700-pound projectile rather than 6 bags of the authorized type of powder. Improperly authorized combinations were fired on at least two other occasions. The Navy believed that neither the presence of spark producing devices nor the experimental firing caused the explosion.

The Navy Inspector General subsequently investigated the reported experiments with 16-inch projectiles and propellant and concluded that the firings in question on the *Iowa* were, in fact, improperly authorized and contrary to Navy procedures. His report concluded that the safety hazard posed to the *Iowa*'s crew by the experiments was, at best, undetermined.

No Prior Indications of Safety or Serviceability Problems

We reviewed reports of equipment problems, ammunition mishaps and malfunctions, and personnel-related injury data for all four battleships since their reactivation. For example, we examined the equipment failure reports that ships submit for all equipment failures that affect their ability to perform their mission and that cannot be corrected within 48 hours. All of the equipment failure reports the battleships submitted for equipment failures affecting the 16-inch turrets since their reactivation were categorized as having only a minor impact on the ships' primary missions. We also noted no trend or pattern in the reported equipment failures that indicated systemic problems with the guns and other turret equipment.

We also compared the battleships' equipment failure experience to that of other surface ships to determine if the battleships present any undue material or supply support problems. They do not appear to do so. Between 1984 and 1989, for example, the battleships operated without any major equipment failures for a substantially greater percentage of time than did surface combatants as a whole. There were no distinct differences in the percentages of the equipment failure reports submitted because the necessary repair parts were not available on the ships.

Previous Ammunition Mishaps/Malfunctions

We also examined several data sources, including ammunition mishap and malfunction reports and investigations. We found no indications of preexisting problems with the type of propellant involved in the explosion.

However, ammunition problems have been encountered with other 16-inch ammunition components in the past. For example, there were problems with split powder bags. A program is underway to correct that problem. Other problems, which have been addressed, were encountered with earlier versions of the primers used to ignite the powder charges because the primers deteriorated in storage.

Susceptibility to Inadvertent Detonation

Concerns were raised after the explosion over the ammunition's sensitivity to the effects of electromagnetic radiation, frequently referred to as HERO. Communications and radar transmitters can transmit radiation that can cause ammunition components containing electrical circuits to detonate. The primer was the only ammunition component involved on April 19 that contains an electrical circuit and it requires only moderate protection from electromagnetic energy; it cannot be within 56 feet of a transmitting AN/WSC-3 antenna for example. Turret II is about 100 feet from that type of antenna, so HERO should not have been a concern. In their investigations, Sandia and the Navy ruled out the primer as the cause of the explosion. . . .

Personnel Injury Experience

We also reviewed the reports of personal injuries and deaths occurring on board the battleships and compared the results to injury rates on all surface ships to determine if this would reveal any systemic gun or ammunition problems. They did not.

Any accident resulting in a fatality, a lost workday, an electrical shock, a person overboard, or a chemical or toxic exposure must be reported to the Navy Safety Center. We found that the injury rates for the battleships were lower than the rates of other ship types in 1987 and 1988. The battleships' 1989 rate was higher than that for surface ships overall, but it would have been lower if the *Iowa* explosion was excluded from the statistics. . . . Other than the *Iowa*'s turret explosion, none of the reported accidents aboard the battleships involved firing the 16-inch guns. . . .

Manning

We found that battleships, in comparison to other surface ships were not assigned an equal share of authorized enlisted supervisory personnel or personnel in ratings associated with gun turret operations. Additionally, the personnel assigned on battleships rated lower by several measures than those assigned to other ships. . . . The impact of manning for gunners mates aboard the *Iowa* was highlighted at the time of the explosion. In Turret II, two of the three journeymen level gun captain positions, normally E-5s, were filled by E-4 apprentices. The center gun captain was the only journeyman gun captain. All three of the gun captain positions in Turret I were filled by E-4 apprentices and a journeyman was filling the supervisory turret captain's position, which is normally filled by an E-6.

Chief of Naval Personnel officials recently told us that they had difficulties in filling billets on battleships.... The officials also noted that personnel who are assigned to the battleships and who reenlist frequently request duty elsewhere to enhance their promotion opportunities by gaining practical experience in ... weapon systems ... [that] have newer electronic technology.... Sailors aboard the *Iowa* expressed similar views to us.

Battleship Personnel Fare Worse in Advancement Opportunities

As of December 1989, battleship officers had been selected at a lower rate, compared to officers in the sample of other surface warfare ships for leadership positions such as executive officer and commanding officer. Only 23 percent of the commanders serving on battleships were considered qualified for commanding officer compared to 88 percent of the commanders on the sample ships....

Battleship enlisted personnel also fared worse during the March 1989 promotion cycle than did personnel aboard other ships in our sample. Battleship personnel overall scored lower on the promotion tests, a key element in the promotion eligibility process. Gunners mates and fire controlmen failure rates for battleship and Navy-wide personnel were similar. However, the battleship gunners mates and fire controlmen failure rates of 11 and 6 percent, respectively, were significantly higher than the ship sample's failure rates of 0 and 1 percent, respectively....

Higher Rate of Disciplinary Actions

During fiscal year 1989, battleship personnel experienced a higher rate of disciplinary actions, including non-judicial punishments (NJPs), courts-martial, and punitive discharges. For example, the battleships' NJP rate per thousand (195) was approximately 25 percent higher than the ship sample rate (158 per thousand) and 185 percent higher than the Navy-wide rate (69 per thousand). While the *Iowa* had the lowest rate (173 per thousand) among battleships, its NJP rate was still 150 percent higher than the Navy-wide rate. Similar results were noted for the battleships' and the *Iowa*'s courts-martial and punitive discharge rates....

Problems in 16-Inch Training

The adequacy of training on the *Iowa* became an issue because the Navy's accident investigation report on the explosion said that unqualified personnel were manning the turret. However, the former Commanding Officer of the *Iowa* said the crew was trained, just that the records were not up to date. Since the training records for the deceased crew were destroyed in the explosion, never existed, or have not been located, we are unable to reconcile this conflict. We found, however, that oversight inspections, which should have assessed the *Iowa*'s 16-inch Personnel Qualification Standard (PQS) program, failed to do so during the 18 months preceding the explosion.... Additionally, the Navy had not approved a training plan for the battleship class and the advanced training school had limited hands-on training aids for operation and maintenance instruction. . . .

Using reconstructed data, *Iowa* officials attempted to evaluate the qualifications status of the personnel assigned turret positions on April 19. . . . While the information they developed indicated that the personnel assigned in the turret were experienced, we found weaknesses in the analysis. In our opinion, the crew's proficiency cannot be verified because the information merely shows that the crew members were assigned to a position within the turret during the exercises and drills but does not document that they actually performed the responsibilities. . . .

The *Iowa*'s Turret II was authorized five personnel who are required to have completed training at the Navy's formal school for 16-inch gunners. However, on the day of the explosion, only two of the positions were filled with individuals who had attended the school.

Weaknesses exist with the Navy's formal training program for 16-inch gun operations and maintenance. Gunners mates aboard both the *Iowa* and the *New Jersey* were very disappointed with the Navy's formal school for 16-inch gunners because it lacked actual turret equipment and they believed it offered little practical instruction. . . .

Battleship Missions

While the battleships are very capable weapons platforms and have been included in deployment schedules and operational plans, emerging circumstances limit their utility. The battleships were reactivated to alleviate existing force structure shortfalls and to help meet the 600-ship goal. . . . The battleships, with their combination of 9 16-inch guns in 3 turrets, 8 5-inch twin gun mounts, 16 Harpoon antiship cruise missiles, and 32 Tomahawk cruise missiles, provide an imposing array of firepower. The Tomahawk missiles give them a significant capability for attacking land targets and other surface ships. The Harpoon missiles also contribute to the battleships' capability to operate against hostile surface ships. The battleships' 16-inch guns are the best source of naval surface fire support for an amphibious assault and are, in fact, the only guns larger than 5 inches remaining on Navy ships. . . . Because of its imposing size and configuration, the Navy believes a battleship's presence can be a strong deterrent in a third-world scenario.

While the battleships' Tomahawk and Harpoon missile capability is imposing, it is not unique within the Navy. Many other Navy vessels, submarines as well as surface ships, carry those same weapons. Also, the battleships' contribution to future amphibious warfare also may be limited. The current maximum range of just over 23 miles of the battleships' 16-inch guns (their only unique weapon system) impairs the ships' ability to provide effective naval surface fire support within the context of an "over the horizon" amphibious assault—one launched from 25 to 50 miles offshore and extending far inland.

Furthermore, with only two battleships, operating and personnel tempo restrictions will limit future deployments. Current policies, for example, preclude a ship from deploying for an additional 12 months after it returns from a 6-month deployment. Thus, with only two ships in the active force, it is unlikely one would be available on short notice should a crisis erupt. The battleships are also labor intensive, requiring a crew of about 1,500 compared, for example, to a crew of about 360 on an Aegis cruiser. Finally, reducing the number of battleships to two, especially with one homeported on each coast, will compound the manning and training problems discussed earlier and further limit availability....

EXECUTIVE SUMMARY

The essential results of our study are as follows:

- We could neither prove nor disprove the presence of a chemical ignitor proposed by the USN. The interpretation of evidence for a chemical ignitor is complicated by the fact that some chemical constituents of such an ignitor are found throughout 16 in. gun turrets, not only on the USS IOWA, but also the USS WISCONSIN and the USS NEW JERSEY. Forms of these constituents are either commonly used in the turrets or are a part of the maritime environment. Steel wool was another component of the proposed ignitor. We found iron fibers in the rotating band that could be steel wool, but we were unable to clearly identify a source of fibers of their diameter. We believe evidence for the presence of a chemical ignitor is inconclusive.
- Our analyses indicate that the propellant stabilizer was within acceptable limits. We also found only a very remote possibility that this propellant could be initiated in the breech by friction, electrostatic discharge, or electromagnetic radiation. Similarly, we conclude that there is only a very remote possibility the black powder could have been initiated in the breech by any of these mechanisms. Ether/air combustion cannot be achieved because minimum necessary concentrations are precluded. Even if the minimum concentrations are achieved and combustion occurs, our analyses show that the propellant cannot be ignited. These findings are in general agreement with those of the USN.
- We confirmed that the powder bags were overrammed against the projectile and determined that the extent of the overram was approximately 3 in. greater than that established by the USN. Our analyses indicate that the bag charges were under a compressive load of at least 2800 pounds at the time of the explosion. There may have been even higher transient forces due to dynamic loading resulting from a greater than normal ram speed. While the rammer is capable of a speed of 13.9 ft/s, we could only establish that the rammer speed was at least 2 ft/s.
- The cause of the explosion was not conclusively determined. However,

an important factor may have been the increase in impact sensitivity of a powder bag with a reduced number of pellets in its trim layer. (The trim layer is an incomplete layer of pellets lying on their sides in the front of the bag and just behind the black powder pouch on the next bag.) Our half-scale experiments indicate that reducing the number of these pellets lying next to the powder pouch increases impact sensitivity enough that an explosion could have been caused by an overram at a higher than normal speed. Our studies indicate that impact initiation depends on two key factors: the number of pellets in the trim layer, and the speed of the overram. However, these experiments must be extended to actual 16 in. gun conditions to establish the validity of this ignition mechanism. . . .

BUSH-GORBACHEV SUMMIT
REMARKS AND DOCUMENTS
May 31, June 1, 3, and 4, 1990

President George Bush and Soviet leader Mikhail S. Gorbachev met in Washington May 31 for the second time in six months. Their cordiality tended to overshadow some matters left unsettled between the United States and the Soviet Union at the summit's conclusion four days later. "We won't resolve all of the outstanding issues between us," Bush predicted at the White House welcoming ceremony. "But we can and will take significant steps toward a new relationship." His remarks seemed to be borne out during the long hours of discussion, including a full day at Camp David in the Maryland mountains.

The two leaders applauded the fundamental improvement in U.S.-Soviet relations that had occurred in the past year and vowed to continue moving in that direction. Whereas arms control issues once dominated summit agendas, this one dealt largely with the political transformation of the Soviet Union, Eastern Europe, and Germany.

During "presummit" shipboard meetings off the Mediterranean island of Malta in December 1989, Bush and Gorbachev had cleared away much of the ideological debris left over from the Cold War, and both were moved to declare that the era of U.S.-Soviet confrontation had ended. (Bush-Gorbachev on Malta, Historic Documents of 1989, p. 643) *But that meeting, while considered symbolically important, essentially pointed to the Washington summit.*

Conditional Trade Agreement

Bush's apparent willingness to bolster Gorbachev's political standing in the Soviet Union led to Bush's surprise signing of a trade agreement

June 1 even though the Soviet leader had not made concessions on other issues. Before the summit, Bush had linked his willingness to sign the trade agreement normalizing U.S.-Soviet commerce to two actions by Moscow: the passage of legislation guaranteeing the right of Soviet citizens to emigrate and an easing of Moscow's economic pressure on Lithuania over its assertion of independence. (Lithuania Declares Independence, p. 183)

Gorbachev, arguing that the situation in Lithuania was an internal matter, refused to soften his resistance to its bid for independence. Emigration legislation had not been enacted—although in practice more than 60,000 Soviet Jews had been allowed to leave in 1989, and the 1990 figure was expected to be twice as large. Secretary of State James A. Baker III said the trade agreement treaty would not be submitted to Congress for its approval until the Soviet emigration measure had passed.

Apparently in deference to congressional pressure and as an incentive for the Soviets to act on emigration, Bush withheld the critical part of the treaty, the conferring of most-favored-nation trade status on the Soviet Union. Although the Soviet Union still could receive most-favored-nation treatment, Gorbachev seemed miffed that the status had been awarded to China but withheld from his country. The trade pact was announced along with a Soviet agreement to purchase 10 million metric tons of U.S. grain annually. The deal had the strong backing of American farm interests, and Soviet officials had hinted that without a trade agreement they might look to other countries for grain.

German Question and Arms Control

The summit was marked by a disagreement over Germany. Gorbachev refused to consent to a united Germany remaining in the NATO military alliance. However, after the summit, West German chancellor Helmut Kohl persuaded him to change his stand on NATO in return for pledges of German economic assistance to the Soviet Union. That understanding between Moscow and Bonn included West Germany's vow to keep the military strength of a reunited Germany low, and it pushed the Soviets closer to signing a treaty for deep reductions in non-nuclear forces in Western and Eastern Europe. (NATO's Declaration of Peaceful Intent, p. 453)

On arms control, a few unsettled questions blocked the conclusion of a strategic arms reduction treaty (START) that, at Malta, Bush and Gorbachev had said was a goal of the Washington summit. Instead, they signed a statement endorsing the main elements of the pact, including the reduction of their stockpiles of strategic nuclear warheads by nearly one-third. They also signed a pair of treaties to limit the size of underground nuclear test explosions after Soviet negotiators agreed to an addition, or "protocol," to each treaty for tighter verification procedures. They also agreed to reduce stockpiles of chemical munitions.

The chemical warfare treaty would, upon ratification by the U.S. Senate, commit the United States to begin destroying chemical weapons in 1992 and to halve the stockpiles by the year 2000. The Soviet Union would do the same. In the meantime, the two superpowers pledged to press for progress on the negotiations among some forty nations at Geneva for a ban on chemical weapons. Bush had said he wanted the United States to retain a small reserve of chemical weapons until every other nation capable of producing them had signed the Geneva treaty.

In addition, U.S. and Soviet officials signed agreements aimed at (1) increasing airline passenger traffic between the two countries, (2) permitting fuller cooperation in nuclear energy research and oceanic studies, (3) opening additional ports to each other's shipping, (4) setting a goal of 1,500 exchange students yearly by 1995, and (5) settling a boundary dispute over four islands in the East Siberian Sea.

Gorbachev's Problems at Home

Despite Gorbachev's public disclaimers, it seemed clear during the summit that he was worried about a challenge to his political leadership at home. Boris N. Yeltsin, his outspoken rival, recently had been elected president of the Russian Republic, the largest in the Soviet Union. While Gorbachev was in Canada on a stopover visit en route to Washington, Yeltsin told the press in Moscow he expected the republic to declare its sovereignty—in effect assert a large measure of autonomy—as several other Soviet republics had done or were preparing to do.

Bush and his aides lavished praise on the Soviet leader in what some observers regarded as an attempt to strengthen Gorbachev's position in Moscow. "We have moved a long, long way from the depths of the Cold War," Bush said at a joint news conference June 3, which concluded the meetings. "And the more this reform and openness takes place, the more compatible the relationship becomes."

As had occurred in Gorbachev's two previous visits to the United States—for summit meetings with President Ronald Reagan in December 1987 and December 1988—the Soviet leader delighted in making impromptu stops along the routes of his motorcade in Washington and other cities to greet the throngs of cheering bystanders. On this trip, he extended his previous Washington-New York itinerary to include Minneapolis-St. Paul and San Francisco. In those cities, as in Washington, Gorbachev and his wife Raisa drew enthusiastic crowds. In Minneapolis June 3 he spoke to 145 leaders of American industry and in San Francisco the next day—before his flight home—he met with President Roh Tae Woo of South Korea and received a visit from Reagan. Gorbachev also went to nearby Palo Alto, California, to address 1,700 Stanford University students. "The Cold War is now behind us," he told them. "Let us not wrangle over who won it."

Following are remarks of presidents George Bush and Mikhail S. Gorbachev upon the Soviet leader's arrival at the

White House May 31, 1990; a White House fact sheet
summarizing agreements signed June 1 by the two leaders;
excerpts from their joint news conference June 3 at the
White House; and a joint statement June 4 on nuclear
nonproliferation, all issued by the White House (including
Gorbachev's remarks in English translation):

WHITE HOUSE WELCOMING CEREMONY

President Bush. Friends and distinguished guests, welcome to all of
you, especially our guests from the Soviet Union. It is my great honor to
welcome to the White House the President of the Soviet Union, Mikhail
Gorbachev.

Mr. President, just over a year ago I said that the United States wanted
to move beyond containment in its relations with the Soviet Union toward
a new era, an era of enduring cooperation. When we last met in Malta, we
agreed to accelerate our efforts on a full range of issues. Today differences
remain, of course, but in the short 6 months since the Malta summit, we've
made encouraging progress. I want this summit to take us farther still, and
I know that that is your view as well, Mr. President.

We've seen a world of change this past year. Now, on the horizon, we see
what, just 1 short year ago, seemed a distant dream: a continent cruelly
divided, East from West, has begun to heal with the dawn of self-
determination and democracy. In Germany, where the Wall once stood, a
nation moves toward unity, in peace and freedom. And in the other nations
of the most heavily militarized continent on Earth, at last we see the long
era of confrontation giving way to the prospect of enduring cooperation in
a Europe whole and free. Mr. President, you deserve great credit for your
part in these transforming events. I salute you, as well, for the process of
change you've brought to your own country.

As we begin this summit, let me stress that I believe we can work
together at this historic moment to further the process of building a new
Europe, one in which every nation's security is strengthened and no nation
is threatened. Around the world, we need to strengthen our cooperation in
solving regional conflicts and building peace and stability. In Nicaragua,
for example, we've shown that we can work together to promote peaceful
change. In Angola, our support for an early resolution of that country's
tragic conflict—a resolution acceptable to the Angolan people—is now
paying off. So, let us expand this new spirit of cooperation not merely to
resolve disputes between us but to build a solid foundation for peace,
prosperity, and stability around the world.

In that same spirit, Mr. President, let me quote the words of one of your
nation's great minds, one of the world's great men in this or any age,
Andrei Sakharov. Fourteen years ago, he wrote: "I am convinced that
guaranteed political and civil rights for people the world over are also
guarantees of international security, economic and social progress." Sakha-

rov knew that lasting peace and progress are inseparable from freedom, that nations will only be fully safe when all people are fully free.

We in the U.S. applaud the new course the Soviet Union has chosen. We see the spirited debate in the Congress of People's Deputies, in the Soviet press, among the Soviet people. We know about the difficult economic reforms that are necessary to breathe new vigor into the Soviet economy. And as I've said many times before, we want to see *perestroika* succeed. Mr. President, I firmly believe, as you have said, that there is no turning back from the path you have chosen.

Since our meeting in Malta, we've reached agreements in important areas, each one proof that when mutual respect prevails progress is possible. But the agreements we've reached cannot cause us to lose sight of some of the differences that remain. Lithuania is one such issue. We believe that good faith dialog between the Soviet leaders and representatives of the Baltic peoples is the proper approach, and we hope to see that process go forward.

Over the next 4 days, we're not going to solve all of the world's problems. We won't resolve all of the outstanding issues that divide us. But we can and will take significant steps toward a new relationship.

This summit will be a working summit in the strictest sense of the term, one where we mark the real progress we've made by signing new agreements and where we address the differences that divide us in a spirit of candor, in an open and honest search for common ground. In a larger sense, though, the success of this summit depends not on the agreements we will sign but on our efforts to lay the groundwork for overcoming decades of division and discord, to build a world of peace in freedom.

Mr. President, together, your great country and ours bear an enormous and unique responsibility for world peace and regional stability. We must work together to reduce tensions, to make the world a little better for our children and grandchildren. And to this end, I pledge you my all-out effort.

Mr. President, you've brought us a beautiful day, and you've brought back Mrs. Gorbachev—that brings joy to all of our hearts. A hearty welcome to her as well. So, it is my privilege to welcome you to the White House. And may God bless our peoples in their efforts for a better world. Welcome, sir.

President Gorbachev. Mr. President, Mrs. Bush, ladies and gentlemen, comrades, thank you for this welcome. May I also greet all Americans on behalf of the peoples of the Soviet Union.

My present visit to the United States is a confirmation that Soviet-U.S. relations are acquiring greater stability, clarity, and predictability. I am convinced that both the Soviet people and the Americans approve such changes. I think that they are also properly appreciated throughout the world. Therefore, it is the great responsibility of the President and myself to make sure that the capital of trust and cooperation accumulated in recent years is protected and constantly increased.

I remember well my first visit to the United States, and not only because I saw America for the first time them. During those days in December

1987, President Reagan and I signed the treaty on the elimination of INF missiles. That was truly a watershed not only in our relations but in the history of modern times. It was the first step taken together by two powerful countries on the road leading to a safe and sensible world.

Since then, our two great nations have traveled a long way toward each other. Thousands of American and Soviet citizens; dozens of agencies, private companies, and public organizations are involved in political and business contacts, humanitarian exchanges, scientific and technological cooperation.

In the same years, the world around us has also changed beyond recognition. Mr. President, this generation of people on Earth may witness the advent of an irreversible period of peace in the history of civilization. The walls which for years separated the peoples are collapsing. The trenches of the Cold War are disappearing. The fog of prejudice, mistrust, and animosity is vanishing.

I have come to the United States with the impressions still fresh in my mind of how our people celebrated the 45th anniversary of the victory over nazism and of my meetings with war veterans. I recently had many meetings with my countrymen. They all understand the importance of Soviet-U.S. relations. They look upon their improvement with the hope that the tragedies of the 20th century—those horrible wars—will forever remain a thing of the past. I think that this is what the Americans want, too.

Mr. President, living up to these hopes of our two nations is your mission and mine. This meeting is part of it. My colleagues and I have come to do serious work in order to make a decisive step toward an agreement reducing the most dangerous arms, which are increasingly losing their political significance, and to provide further impetus to interaction between our two countries—interaction and, of course, cooperation in solving international problems in trade, scientific, technological, and humanitarian fields; in cultural exchanges; in expanding information about each other; and in people-to-people contacts.

We want progress in relations between the Soviet Union and the United States of America. I am looking forward to meetings with the Americans and, to the extent possible, getting to know better your unique and great country.

On behalf of Mrs. Gorbachev and myself and of all those who have come with me to your Nation's Capital, I thank once again President George Bush and Mrs. Bush and all those present here for this warm welcome.

SOVIET-UNITED STATES BILATERAL AGREEMENTS

Trade Agreement

At Malta, President Bush proposed targeting the June summit for completion of a MFN (most-favored-nation trade status) commercial agreement, provided that the Soviets approve and implement new emigration legislation. New emigration legislation passed the first reading in the Supreme Soviet in November. The Second Supreme Soviet reading, which would codify the law, was set for May 31. No serious opposition has appeared, but the press of other business could delay final passage. We have emphasized to the Soviets at all levels the importance of expeditious passage.

This agreement breaks much new ground in commercial agreements with the Soviets. Specifically, it:

- provides improved market access, for example, by prohibiting adoption of standards which are discriminatory or designed to protect domestic production;
- facilitates business by establishing expedited accreditation procedures for commercial offices, allowing offices to hire directly local and third-country employees on mutually agreed terms, permitting access to all advertising media, and allowing companies to engage and serve as agents and to conduct market studies; and
- offers strong intellectual property rights protections by reaffirming commitments to the Paris Convention and the Universal Copyright Convention, obligating adherence to the Bern Convention for the Protection of Literary and Artistic Works, providing copyright protection for computer programs and data bases and protection for sound recordings; providing product and process patent protection for virtually all areas of technology; and providing comprehensive coverage of trade secrets.

The Soviets have reaffirmed their commitment, once they receive MFN and USG lending restrictions (Stevenson and Byrd amendments) are lifted, to resume lend-lease repayments.

Long-Term Grains Agreement

- The new agreement is to take effect January 1, 1991.
- The Soviets are required to buy a minimum of 10 million metric tons of grain from the United States annually (up from 9 million metric tons), including at least 4 million metric tons of wheat; 4 million metric tons of feed grains (corn, barley, or sorghum); and 2 million additional metric tons of either wheat, feed grains, or soybeans/soymeal, with soy measures counted double for purposes of quantity.
- The Soviets may buy up to 14 million metric tons annually (up from 12 million metric tons) without prior consultation with the Department of Agriculture.

Chemical Weapons Destruction Agreement

The key provisions of the destruction agreement are:

- Destruction of the vast bulk of declared stocks to begin by the end of 1992.

- Destruction of at least 50 percent of declared stocks by the end of 1999.
- Declared stocks are to be reduced to 5,000 agent tons by 2002.
- Both countries will stop producing chemical weapons upon entry into force of this agreement, without waiting for the global chemical weapons ban.
- On-site inspections during and after the destruction process to confirm that destruction has taken place.
- Annual exchanges of data on the stock-pile levels to facilitate monitoring of the declared stockpiles.
- Details of the inspection procedures will be worked out by December 31, 1990.
- Both countries will cooperate in developing and using safe and environmentally sound methods of destruction.
- The United States and U.S.S.R. will take steps to encourage all chemical weapons-capable states to become parties to the multilateral convention.

Both countries took an initial step in this direction by exchanging data on declared chemical weapons stockpiles in December 1989 and by initiating verification experiments to build confidence and gain experience for a chemical weapons ban treaty.

This agreement will be submitted to Congress for its review and approval.

A Global Chemical Weapons Ban

The bilateral U.S.-Soviet agreement was designed to provide new impetus to the conclusion of a comprehensive, verifiable global chemical weapons ban at the earliest possible date. Toward that end:

- Both countries have agreed to accelerate their destruction of chemical weapons under a global chemical weapons convention so that by the eighth year after it enters into force, the United States and U.S.S.R. will have reduced their declared stocks to no more than 500 agent tons.
- The United States and U.S.S.R. will propose that a special conference be convened at the end of the eighth year of a multilateral convention to determine whether participation in the convention is sufficient to complete the elimination of chemical weapons stocks over the following 2 years.

The Nuclear Testing Protocols and Verification Methods

- Two verification protocols being signed at the Washington summit will provide for effective verification of compliance with the treaties.
- Verification methods for Threshold Test Ban Treaty (TTBT) and Peaceful Nuclear Explosions Treaty (PNET) include hydrodynamic

yield measurement, on-site inspection, and some seismic monitoring on the territory of the testing party. The U.S. hydrodynamic method CORRTEX [Continuous Reflectrometry for Radius versus Time Experiments] is the most accurate non-intrusive technique the United States has found. CORRTEX determines the yield by measuring, at the detonating site, the rate at which the supersonic shock wave in the ground crushes coaxial cable buried near the explosive device. On-site inspections permit each side to take core samples and rock fragments from the area of the explosion to confirm geological/geophysical data near the explosion. Seismic monitors measure distant shock waves produced by the explosion (as in measuring earthquakes) in order to arrive at an estimate of the explosive yield.

- National technical means also will be used to monitor all explosions.

How the Protocols Work

- PNET verification: Both sides have the right to hydrodynamic measurement (CORRTEX for the United States) for explosions with planned yields above 50 kilotons; the right to on-site inspections for explosions with planned yields above 35 kilotons; the right to a local seismic network for a group explosion above 150 kilotons.
- TTBT verification: the right to hydrodynamic measurements of nuclear weapons tests with planned yields above 50 kilotons; on-site inspection for tests with planned yields above 35 kilotons; in-country seismic monitoring for tests with planned yields above 50 kilotons, using three designated seismic stations off the test site but within the testing parties' territory; special provisions for monitoring unusual cases; tests with nonstandard geometries, tests with multiple nuclear explosions; in each of the first 5 years of the treaty, if a side does not have at least 2 tests with planned yields above 50 kilotons, the other side may use hydrodynamic measurement that year on up to 2 tests with planned yields below 50 kilotons.
- Required notifications under TTBT (PNET notifications are similar): Each June, the parties will inform each other of the number of explosions with planned yields above 35 kilotons and 50 kilotons for the following calendar year. No later than 200 days prior to the planned date of any explosion, the other side would have the right, under protocol provisions, to monitor; the testing party must provide notification of the planned date, location, and whether the planned yield exceeds 35 or 50 kilotons. Within 20 days of receipt of such notification, the verifying party must inform the testing party whether it plans to carry out verification activities, and, if so, which type.
- Under both treaties, joint commissions will be used to discuss implementation and verification issues.
- Once protocols are signed, the administration will seek Senate advice and consent as to ratification of the TTBT and the PNET and their protocols.

Customs Cooperation Agreement

- The agreement provides for mutual assistance between the customs services of the United States and the U.S.S.R.
- The agreement provides the basis for cooperative activity in deterring and detecting narcotics trafficking.
- The agreement is designed to strengthen cooperative measures which the two services typically undertake.
- The agreement provides a formal basis for cooperation in areas of customs law enforcement assistance, export control, and commercial fraud.

Maritime Boundary Agreement

- The parties agree that the line described as the "western limit" in the 1867 U.S.-Russia convention ceding Alaska is the maritime boundary along its entire length.
- Further, the agreement contains innovative provisions to ensure that all areas within 200 miles of either coast fall under the resource jurisdiction of one or the other party. The U.S.S.R. transfers to the United States jurisdiction in three "special areas" within 200 miles of the Soviet coast, beyond 200 miles of the U.S. coast, and on the U.S. side of the maritime boundary. The United States transfers to the U.S.S.R. jurisdiction in one "special area" within 200 miles of the U.S. coast, beyond 200 miles of the Soviet coast, and on the Soviet side of the maritime boundary.

Cultural Centers Agreement

- The Centers—constituted as non-diplomatic, nonprofit institutions—will be opened in Washington and Moscow.
- The Center Directors and one Deputy Director for each side are to have diplomatic titles and be accredited by their governments to their respective Embassies, with this exception: Center personnel, properties, and papers will not have diplomatic status.
- The Centers will carry out a variety of functions, e.g., operating libraries; sponsoring seminars, films, and performances; and providing student counseling and language instruction.
- The public is guaranteed free, unrestricted access to the Centers.
- The U.S. Center in Moscow has the right to use rubles to cover domestic operating expenses.
- Occupancy and opening dates will be determined by mutual agreement on a basis of reciprocity.
- The agreement is to take effect after an exchange of notes confirming each side has completed the domestic measures required for implementation.

Expansion of Undergraduate Exchanges

- Increase existing exchanges (750 U.S. and 250 Soviet) by 250 students both ways in academic year 1991-1992.
- Increase targeted numbers to 1,500 each way by 1995-1996, subject to availability of funds.
- Mix of private and U.S. Government funding (arrangements to be determined) to cover the costs of the Soviet participants in the United States; the U.S.S.R. is to cover all in-country costs for Americans.
- Participants on both sides are to be chosen on basis of academic excellence and language proficiency.
- Participants would pursue full-time academic work in a variety of disciplines, including agriculture. The preferred length of the students' participation would be 1 year, though shorter periods would be considered.

Memorandum of Understanding to Increase Circulation of America and Soviet Life Magazines

- The memorandum of understanding (MOU) amends the 1989-1991 Program of Cooperation under General Exchanges Agreement.
- The MOU provides for increased circulation of America and Soviet Life magazines up to 250,000 copies in 1991.
- The distribution of both magazines after 1991 is to be governed solely by demand.
- Each side may print commercial advertising and distribute unsold copies of its magazine at official premises, cultural centers, and exhibitions under its sponsorship.

NEWS CONFERENCE

President Bush. Good morning, everybody. Please be seated. Well, when President Gorbachev and I were at Malta, we agreed that we would try to build a fundamentally different U.S.-Soviet relationship, one that would move beyond containment to an era of enduring cooperation. At the time, no one knew the momentous events that would unfold around the world. And our task is, if anything, more urgent, and the case for a new U.S.-Soviet relationship more compelling, because the opportunities before us are so great.

We've not shied away from discussing issues about which we disagree. There were some tough ones before us, particularly the aspiration of the Baltic peoples, a cause which the United States fully supports. I think it's a mark of how far the U.S.-Soviet relationship has come that in all our exchanges, whether about issues on which we agreed or disagreed, the spirit of candor and openness, a desire not just to understand but to build bridges, shone through.

President Gorbachev and I had intensive discussions on the transforming events in Europe, events that have put before us our best chance in four decades to see Europe whole and free. I stressed that the long-held aspirations of the German people should be met without delay. On the matter of Germany's external alliances, I believe, as do Chancellor Kohl and members of the alliance, that the united Germany should be a full member of NATO. President Gorbachev, frankly, does not hold that view. But we are in full agreement that the matter of alliance membership is, in accordance with the Helsinki Final Act, a matter for the Germans to decide.

Over the last 6 months and in Washington this week, we made great progress in our mutual effort toward building a more peaceful and stable world. We signed a very important chemical weapons accord, nuclear testing protocols and gave a political push to others, including negotiations to reduce U.S.-Soviet strategic nuclear forces and conventional military forces in Europe. I'm also hopeful that the good discussion between President Gorbachev and—the one we had about the importance of "open skies"—we'll revive those negotiations. We discussed regional issues and human rights in considerable detail, made progress in the economic sphere, concluding a commercial agreement, a long-term grains agreement.

In closing, let me say how productive I really feel the last few days have been. President Gorbachev and I have agreed to meet on a regular basis, perhaps annually. Both of us would like to think that we can get together more often with less formality because, you see, we're now at a stage in the U.S.-Soviet relationship, and indeed in world history, where we should miss no opportunity to complete the extraordinary tasks before us.

Mr. President, it's been a pleasure having you here, sir.

President Gorbachev. Ladies and gentlemen, comrades, what has happened over these days enables me to characterize this summit meeting as an event of enormous importance, both for our bilateral relations and in the context of world politics. President Bush has listed the results of the work that we have done together here, which enables you to see the scope, the scale, of this work and, I think, confirms the conclusion that I have drawn.

I agree with President Bush fully, who many times emphasized that we took Malta as a point of departure. And it is Malta that added momentum to the process which, of course, given all the difficulties and disagreements which we have and which we do not deny, still leads us to a qualitatively new relationship with the U.S.S.R. and the U.S.A. The atmosphere and the results of this meeting make it possible for us to speak, really, of a new phase of cooperation, which the President has just mentioned.

I believe that this transition is both the result and a factor for further changes that affect all countries. The constructive spirit of these days, the spirit of responsibility in which we discussed all questions, has made our success possible; and that's very important because that has a stabilizing effect on the entire international situation at a time when we are addressing fundamental issues of civilization.

I would not want to now give a listing of all that we discussed, to mention all the agreements, all the important questions and statements that we have made and that have a lot of potential for the future. But let me still mention what is most important: We signed the main provision for a treaty on the reduction of strategic arms. And I would like to emphasize that this is the first time that we're not just limiting but we will be reducing the most devastating means of warfare. And I hope that we will sign the treaty itself this year. We also signed a statement about the future treaty negotiations on nuclear and space arms. We have agreed to make sure that we will complete the Vienna talks this year and sign an agreement on conventional arms at a European summit by the end of this year. Not everything depends on us, but this is our position; we want to achieve that.

We also discussed problems relating to the European process; specifically external aspects of German unification. I cannot say that we have reached agreement, but that does not mean our efforts were futile. Many new arguments emerged as a result of these discussions, and new, possible perspectives. We have clarified our positions, and it is our position that we will continue discussion in order to find a mutually acceptable solution. We could not resolve this issue in Washington with the two of us. There is also the two-plus-four formula and other European countries which are concerned and which want to see a mutually acceptable solution, a solution acceptable to all of us. The position of the Soviet Union is that we have to find solutions that would fit into the overall positive trend of changes in Europe and in the world that would strengthen and not erode security.

I would like, in particular, to emphasize the importance of our dialog at Camp David, where we talked during the day yesterday; and this is a new phase in strengthening mutual understanding and trust between us. We really discussed all world problems. We compared our political perspectives and we did that in an atmosphere of frankness, a constructive atmosphere, an atmosphere of growing trust. We discussed, specifically, such urgent international issues as the situation in the Middle East, Afghanistan, southern Africa, Cambodia, Central America. That is just some of what we have discussed. I would not want to go into detail right now. I think that you will probably seek to get clarification on this. But anyway, I think that the Camp David dialog was very important.

We have agreed to make a special statement on Ethiopia, to support efforts to reestablish peace there and also, with the help of the United Nations, to give humanitarian relief to the Ethiopian people.

Speaking of bilateral relations, we have some important political achievements here. Specifically, there is movement on such important areas as trade agreement, grain trade, agreement on civil aviation cooperation, maritime agreement, peaceful uses of the atomic energy science and technology, and education

While we and the president were working—and our Ministers were also discussing things—there were important contacts and discussions with the various American companies. And some important decisions were made, such as Chevron, that will be participating in the exploration of the Tengiz oil fields. That will mean an investment of about 10 billion rubles. A group of our academicians were here with me, and they had a good discussion which resulted in the signing of a memorandum of intent with IBM, which will participate in the program of using computers for education in the Soviet Union. I think that this economic area and other areas create a good foundation for our political dialog and creates a kind of solid pillar of support for our cooperation.

I would like to express my profound gratification at this work that we have done together with President George Bush. I appreciate very much him as a political leader who is able, in a very human way and in a politically responsible way, to engage in dialog and cooperation. We spent many hours together and were able to come to know each other very well. I don't know whether anyone will be ever able to say that we know each other totally well or completely. I think that would take many, many years. But now we have a good human relationship and, I think, a good human atmosphere between us.

The President has said, and I would like to confirm this, that we have decided to have regular meetings on a working basis in a businesslike manner, and this is really what is necessary. I would like to tell you that I've invited President George Bush, the President of the United States, to visit the Soviet Union, to come for a state visit to our country, in concluding—and that is something that is not within the framework of the official negotiations but was part of our visit.

I would like to say both to the Americans and to the Soviet people that here we—the Soviet delegation—we have felt very good feelings of the American people, feelings of solidarity, and a lot of interest from the Americans toward what we are doing in the Soviet Union for *perestroika*. I have felt that on many occasions in my short exchanges with the Americans and also in various talks. I would like to thank all Americans for that, and they certainly can expect reciprocity from the Soviet Union for that.

And finally, we, the two of us, were discussing things of concern to us, various regions, various problems affecting the lives of other countries; but that does not mean that we were trying to decide anything for others anyway. We remembered always that what we were doing must be useful not only for our countries but for the world—and of course, specifically, for the Third World. . . .

Q. In connection with this meeting, there was a lot of speculation about weak and strong points—somebody speaks from a position of strength, someone from a position of weakness. How would you define what a strong position is, a position of strength? What is the place where a factor of force or strength holds? What are the components of force? What makes politics strong? This is a question that is addressed to both Presidents.

President Gorbachev. Let me begin first in order to let President Bush have a little rest. [*Laughter*] I think there is a certain speculation on this score. Both during the preceding period and in the course of our talks, we have been representing our peoples and countries, well aware of what the dialog is all about. And I think to assume that someone—myself or President Bush—can dictate to each other or to the Soviet Union is absurd. This would be the greatest misconception, on the basis of which no progress could ever be made.

I think that this idea is suggested because at this point in time the Soviet Union is deep into profound change. And since fundamental change is involved, we are walking away from one particular way of life toward different forms of life: we're changing our political system; we're introducing a new model in economy. All these are fundamental things, indeed. Debates are underway. Doubts are being expressed. Views are being compared. And this is very important because what is at stake is our destiny.

Of course, when you look from outside—well, we ourselves can feel the strain of our society; it is very much politicized. But a look from outside, without knowing all the subtleties, without knowing all the depth of sentiments—one could certainly arrive at some erroneous conclusions. Hence, the question of how long will Gorbachev stay in his office and how this whole *perestroika* will end and so on and so forth.

Even this, I think, fits into this process of profound change, and perhaps this is something we cannot do without. But the most important thing is that everything that is happening confirms not only the fact that we're cleaning up our courtyard, we are really revamping our society. We are trying to adapt it to human needs on the basis of freedom and democracy. We want to make it more open toward the outside world. That is the essence, and therein, Soviet people do not differ. And I hope there are no differences on that among the journalistic corps.

Perhaps some part of society thinks otherwise, but the question is how to do all this to avoid losing everything that we should keep and jettison everything that we don't need, that stands in the way. I don't think we have ever tackled tasks like this in the history of our country. I don't know whether anybody else has been able to resolve so many tasks within such a short period of time. So, it is for this particular reason that we appreciate so highly the fact that the whole world understands this correctly.

So, from this particular perspective, I wish to state—and this goes to show the farsightedness of President Bush and his colleagues, to say nothing of the American public, which overall understands what is happening in the Soviet Union today, understands that this is something that we need. Above all, of course, it's up to us to solve all of these problems; but of course, everybody understands full well that this is something that the whole world, all the nations, need. For without such changes, without a stronger, balanced, harmonized world, we will not accomplish our objectives.

So, today the pivotal point of world politics is *perestroika* in the Soviet Union, not because we are there but because this is an objective reality.

President Bush. May I simply add that the United States is not trying to deal from strength or weakness. I tried to say this at the welcoming ceremony for President Gorbachev. We have a unique responsibility to deal with world peace. No other countries have the same degree of responsibility that the Soviet Union and the United States have. So, we're not looking for winners or losers. We salute reforms that make our systems more compatible on the economic side, on the human rights side, the openness side. But we're not looking for trying to achieve advantage. We sat down here, one-on-one, and tried to hammer out agreements and get closer together on vital matters affecting other countries. . . .

Q. Following on President Bush's comment, on a scale that had adversaries at one end and allies at the other, would you now say that each other's country was more of an ally than an adversary?

President Bush. I don't want to get into semantics. "Alliances" have a connotation to some that they might not have for another. "Adversaries" sometimes convey the concept of hostility or enmity. In my view, we've moved a long, long way from the depths of the Cold War. We've moved towards a—I don't quite know how to quantify it for you, but we could never have had the discussions at Camp David yesterday or as we sat in the Oval Office a couple of days before with President Gorbachev 20 years ago. We all know that. So, there's been a dramatic move. And the more this reform and openness takes place, the more compatible the relationship becomes. Neither of us tried to cover over the differences. . . .

JOINT STATEMENT ON NONPROLIFERATION

The United States of America and the Union of Soviet Socialist Republics oppose the proliferation of nuclear weapons, chemical weapons, missiles capable of carrying such weapons, and certain other missiles and missile technologies. The more nations that possess such weapons, the more difficult it will be to realize the desire of people everywhere to achieve effective arms control and disarmament measures and to reduce the threat of war. Weapons proliferation can provoke or intensify insecurity and hostility among nations, and threatens mankind with warfare of unprecedented destructiveness.

Our discussions over the past months point the way to a new era in relations between our two countries. We have taken major steps toward concluding agreements to reduce our own strategic nuclear arsenals, to bring limits on nuclear testing into force, and to reach a global ban on chemical weapons. Together with the nations of Europe, we are taking unprecedented steps to reduce existing conventional weaponry as part of a process of building a lasting structure of European security. The progress we are making and the commitments we have made in these bilateral and multilateral arms control efforts clearly demonstrate that arms reductions can contribute to increased security, even when there have been long-standing and deep-seated differences between countries.

The historic steps we have taken to improve U.S.-Soviet relations and to cooperate in the interests of international stability create the possibility of even closer and more concrete cooperation in the areas of nuclear, chemical, and missile non-proliferation.

With these considerations in mind, the United States and the Soviet Union:

- Declare their commitment to preventing the proliferation of nuclear weapons, chemical weapons, and missiles capable of carrying such weapons and certain other missiles and missile technologies, in particular those subject to the provisions of the Missile Technology Control Regime (MTCR);
- Agree to work closely together and with other members of the international community to develop and to put into action concrete measures against the proliferation of these types of weapons; and
- Call on other nations to join in a renewed commitment to effective nonproliferation measures as a means of securing international peace and stability and as a step toward the effective limitation worldwide of nuclear weapons, chemical weapons, missiles, and missile technology.

The two sides have taken specific actions to advance these commitments.

Nuclear Weapons Non-Proliferation

In order to prevent the proliferation of nuclear weapons, the United States and the Soviet Union:

- Reaffirm their steadfast and long-lasting commitment to prevent the proliferation of nuclear weapons and to strengthen the international nuclear weapons non-proliferation regime;
- Reaffirm their strong support for the Treaty on the Non-Proliferation of Nuclear Weapons (NPT) and agree that it continues to make an invaluable contribution to global and regional security and stability;
- Urge all countries which have not yet done so to adhere to the NPT;
- Urge all NPT parties to implement scrupulously their International Atomic Energy Agency (IAEA) safeguards obligations under the Treaty;
- Affirm their intention to cooperate together and with other Treaty parties to ensure a successful 1990 Review Conference on the Treaty on the Non-Proliferation of Nuclear Weapons which would reaffirm support for the objectives of the Treaty and its importance to international security and stability;
- Support the Treaty for the Prohibition of Nuclear Weapons in Latin America (the Treaty of Tlatelolco) and urge all countries in the region to bring it into force at an early date;
- Reiterate their continuing commitment to strengthening the IAEA, whose unique system of safeguards has contributed to the widespread peaceful use of nuclear energy for social and economic development;
- Support increased international cooperation in the peaceful uses of nuclear energy under IAEA safeguards;

- Call on all non-nuclear-weapons states with unsafeguarded nuclear activities to place these activities under international safeguards;
- Agree on the need for stringent controls over exports of nuclear-related material, equipment and technology, to ensure that they will not be misused for nuclear explosive purposes, and urge all other nations capable of exporting nuclear-related technology to apply similarly strict controls;
- Continue to support efforts to improve and strengthen the international nuclear export control regime;
- Support discussions among states in regions of nuclear proliferation concern for the purpose of achieving concrete steps to reduce the risk of nuclear proliferation, and, in particular, join in calling on the nations of the Middle East, Southern Africa, and South Asia to engage in and pursue such discussions;
- Agree to continue their regular, constructive bilateral consultations on nuclear weapons non-proliferation.

Missile and Missile Technology Non-Proliferation

In order to stem the proliferation of missiles and missile technology, the United States and the Soviet Union:

- Have signed the Treaty between the United States of America and the Union of Soviet Socialist Republics on the Elimination of Their Intermediate-Range and Shorter-Range Missiles, demonstrating that controls on—indeed the elimination of—such missiles can enhance national security;
- Reaffirm their intention that the START Treaty be signed by the end of the year;
- Affirm their support for the objectives of the Missile Technology Control Regime, covering missiles, and certain equipment and technology relating to missiles capable of delivering at least 500 kilograms of payload to a range of at least 300 kilometers and they call on all nations that have not done so to observe the spirit and the guidelines of this regime;
- Are taking measures to restrict missile proliferation on a worldwide basis, including export controls and other internal procedures;
- Have instituted bilateral consultations to exchange information concerning such controls and procedures and identify specific measures to prevent missile proliferation;
- Agree to work to stop missile proliferation, particularly in regions of tension, such as the Middle East;
- To this end, affirm their intent to explore regional initiatives to reduce the threat of missile proliferation, including the possibility of offering their good offices to promote such initiatives;
- Recall that they favor international economic cooperation including cooperation aimed at peaceful space exploration, as long as such cooperation could not contribute to missile proliferation;

- Appeal to all countries—the exporters of missiles and missile technology as well as purchasers—to exercise restraint, and express their willingness to continue their respective dialogues with other countries on the non-proliferation of missiles and missile technology.
- Are resolved, on their part, to continue to work to strengthen such international restraint with respect to missile and missile technology proliferation.

Chemical Weapons Non-Proliferation

In order to stem the use and proliferation of chemical weapons, the United States and the Soviet Union:

- Declare that a multilateral, effectively verifiable chemical weapons convention banning the development, production and use of chemical weapons and eliminating all stocks on a global basis is the best long-term solution to the threat to international security posed by the use and spread of chemical weapons, and that non-proliferation measures are considered a step toward achieving such a convention;
- Will intensify their cooperation to expedite the negotiations in Geneva with the view to resolving outstanding issues as soon as possible and to finalizing the draft convention at the earliest date;
- Have instituted bilateral confidence building measures, including chemical weapons data exchange and reciprocal site visits;
- Have just signed a trailblazing agreement on destruction and non-production of chemical weapons and on measures to facilitate the multilateral convention on chemical weapons;
- Commit themselves, in that agreement to take practical measures to encourage all chemical weapons-capable states to become parties to the multilateral convention;
- Having declared their possession of chemical weapons, urge other states possessing chemical weapons to declare their possession, to commit to their destruction, and to begin immediately to address, through research and cooperation, the need for chemical weapons destruction capability;
- State that they themselves will not proliferate chemical weapons;
- Have instituted export controls to stem the proliferation of chemical weapons. These measures are not intended to hinder or discriminate against legitimate peaceful chemical activities;
- Have agreed to conduct bilateral discussions to improve the effectiveness of their respective export controls to stem the proliferation of chemical weapons;
- Conduct regular bilateral consultations to broaden bilateral cooperation, including the reciprocal exchange of information on the problems of chemical weapons proliferation;
- Confirm their intent to pursue political and diplomatic actions, where specific cases give rise to concerns about the production, use or spread of chemical weapons;

- Join with other nations in multilateral efforts to coordinate export controls, exchange information, and broaden international cooperation to stem the proliferation of chemical weapons;
- Reaffirm their support for the 1925 Geneva Protocol banning the use of chemical weapons in violation of international law;
- Are taking steps to strengthen the 1925 Geneva Protocol by:

— Encouraging states that are not parties to accede;
— Confirming their intention to provide active support to the United Nations Secretary General in conducting investigations of reported violations of the Protocol;
— Affirming their intention to consider the imposition of sanctions against violators of the Protocol, including those under Chapter VII of the United Nations Charter;
— Agreeing to consult promptly in the event of a violation of the Protocol to discuss possible bilateral and multilateral actions against the offender, as well as appropriate assistance to the victims of such violation;

- Agree that the presence and further proliferation of chemical weapons in areas of tension, such as the Middle East, is particularly dangerous. The two countries therefore affirm their intent to explore regional initiatives in the Middle East and other areas, including the possibility of offering their good offices to promote such initiatives as:

— Efforts to broaden awareness of the dangers of chemical weapons proliferation and its negative impact on implementation of the multilateral convention on chemical weapons;
— Bilateral or multilateral efforts to stem chemical weapons proliferation, including the renunciation of the production of chemical weapons;
— Efforts to destroy chemical weapons in advance of the multilateral convention on chemical weapons, as the United States and the Soviet Union are doing.

The United States and the Soviet Union call on all nations of the world that have not already done so to join them in taking comparable, effective measures to stem chemical weapons proliferation.

June

BARBARA BUSH'S SPEECH AT WELLESLEY COMMENCEMENT
June 1, 1990

Barbara Bush delivered the 1990 commencement address at Wellesley College where members of the graduating class had objected that she did not represent the career woman they said the college sought to educate. A petition by about 150 seniors at the women's college in Massachusetts had protested her selection as the graduation speaker. College authorities did not yield to the demand for another speaker, but it touched off responses across the country, often critical of the protesters.

Mrs. Bush had dropped out of Smith, another elite women's college in Massachusetts, to marry George Bush. As his political career propelled him ultimately to the presidency, she received a full measure of attention as a woman who had not pursued her own career but had chosen to be a supportive wife and mother.

At the June 1 graduation exercises, Mrs. Bush gently chided the young women who had questioned the role model she portrayed. "As important as your obligations as a doctor, a lawyer or a business leader may be," the first lady said, "your human connections with spouses, with children, with friends, are the most important investment you will ever make."

Her message was spiced with humor. "Who knows," she said, "out in this audience may even be someone who will one day follow in my footsteps and preside over the White House as the president's spouse." Then she paused and added, "And I wish him well!" At that, the audience of 5,400—graduates, their families, friends, and faculty— erupted in laughter and cheers.

Wellesley president Nan Keohane, recounting some of the controversy that the student protest generated, said it had proved beneficial by providing an opportunity for Americans to ponder what role women should assume. Moreover, she said the 1990 commencement would not be among those "that no one remembers very clearly."

Raisa Gorbachev's Presence

Aside from the controversy and Mrs. Bush's address, the ceremony would be remembered for the presence of Raisa Gorbachev, wife of the Soviet president. Mrs. Gorbachev accompanied Mrs. Bush to Wellesley while their husbands held a U.S.-Soviet summit meeting in Washington, D.C. (Bush-Gorbachev Summit Remarks and Documents, p. 331)

Although Mrs. Gorbachev had nothing to say at Wellesley about the role of women, according to her translators, in her later remarks at the Boston Public Garden she said that striking a balance between careers and family responsibilities was "one of the contradictions of our time. At this juncture, each of us looks for her own solution to the problem." Mrs. Gorbachev, who was a university professor before her husband rose to high position in the Kremlin, held the Soviet equivalent of a doctor of philosophy degree. She declined to identify herself as a "feminist," an unpopular term in the Soviet Union.

Warm Reception and Petition

Both first ladies received warm receptions at Wellesley and in nearby Boston. However, some of the Wellesley petition signers said they still would have preferred a speaker with a record of accomplishment in the workplace. On the other hand, a new student petition was disclosed on commencement day. It stated: "In honoring Barbara Bush as our commencement speaker, we celebrate all the unknown women who have dedicated their lives to the service of others." Some students wore purple armbands, they said, to honor those women.

Purple was the class color, and Wellesley's first choice for commencement speaker was Alice Walker, author of the prize-winning novel The Color Purple. *"Instead you got me—known for the color of my hair!" quipped Mrs. Bush, whose white hair is regarded as her trademark.*

> *Following is the White House text of Barbara Bush's commencement address at Wellesley College, June 1, 1990, in which she advised the women graduates not to shortchange their roles as wives and mothers in pursuit of careers:*

Thank you very much. Thank you President [Nan] Keohane, Mrs. [Raisa] Gorbachev, trustees, faculty, parents, Julie Porter, Christine Bicknell and, of course, the Class of 1990. I am thrilled to be with you today, and very excited, as I know you must all be, that Mrs. Gorbachev could join us. This is an exciting time in Washington, D.C. But I am so glad to be here. I knew coming to Wellesley would be fun, but I never dreamed it would be this much fun.

More than ten years ago when I was invited here to talk about our experiences in the People's Republic of China, I was struck by both the natural beauty of your campus ... and the spirit of this place.

Wellesley, you see, is not just a place ... but an idea ... an experiment in excellence in which diversity is not just tolerated, but is embraced.

The essence of this spirit was captured in a moving speech about tolerance given last year by the student body president of one of your sister colleges. She related the story by Robert Fulghum about a young pastor who, finding himself in charge of some very energetic children, hits upon a game called "Giants, Wizards and Dwarfs." "You have to decide now," the pastor instructed the children, "which you are ... a giant, a wizard or a dwarf?" At that, a small girl tugging at his pants leg, asked, "But where do the mermaids stand?"

The pastor told her there are *no* mermaids, and she says, "Oh yes there are," she said. "I am a mermaid."

Now this little girl knew what she was and she was not about to give up on either her identity *or* the game. She intended to take her place wherever mermaids fit into the scheme of things. Where *do* mermaids stand.... All those who are different, those who do not fit the boxes and the pigeon-holes? "Answer that question," wrote Fulghum, "and you can build a school, a nation, or a whole world."

As that very wise young women said ... "Diversity ... like anything worth having ... requires *effort*." Effort to learn about and respect difference, to be compassionate with one another, to cherish our own identity ... and to accept unconditionally the same in others.

You should all be very proud that this is the Wellesley spirit. Now I know your first choice today was Alice Walker, known for *The Color Purple*. And guess how I know?

Instead you got me—known for ... the color of my hair! Alice Walker's book has a special resonance here. At Wellesley, each class is known by a special color ... for four years the Class of '90 has worn the color purple. Today you meet on Severance Green to say goodbye to all of that ... to begin a new and very personal journey ... to search for your own true colors.

In the world that awaits you beyond the shores of Lake Waban, no one can say what your true colors will be. But this I do know: You have a first class education from a first class school. And so you need not, probably cannot, live a "paint-by-numbers" life. Decisions are not irrevocable. Choices do come back. As you set off from Wellesley, I hope that many of you will consider making three very special choices.

The first is to believe in something larger than yourself.... To get involved in some of the big ideas of your time. I chose literacy because I honestly believe that if more people could read, write and comprehend, we would be that much closer to solving so many of the problems plaguing our society.

Early on I made another choice which I hope you will make as well. Whether you are talking about education, career or service, you are talking about life ... and life must have joy. It's supposed to be fun!

One of the reasons I made the most important decision of my life ... to marry George Bush ... is because he made me laugh. It's true, sometimes we've laughed through our tears ... but that shared laughter has been one of our strongest bonds. Find the joy in life, because as Ferris Bueller said on his day off ... "Life moves pretty fast. Ya don't stop and look around once in a while, ya gonna miss it!"

I won't tell George that you applauded Ferris more than you applauded him!

The third choice that must not be missed is to cherish your human connections: your relationships with friends and family. For several years, you've had impressed upon you the importance to your career of dedication and hard work. This is true, but as important as your obligations as a doctor, lawyer or business leader will be, you are a human being first and those human connections—with spouses, with children, with friends—are the most important investments you will ever make.

At the end of your life, you will never regret not having passed one more test, not winning one more verdict or not closing one more deal. You will regret time not spent with a husband, a friend, a child or a parent.

We are in a transitional period right now ... fascinating and exhilarating times ... learning to adjust to the changes and the choices we ... men and women ... are facing.

As an example, I remember what a friend said, on hearing her husband complain to his buddies that he had to babysit. Quickly setting him straight ... my friend told her husband that when it's your own kids ... it's not called babysitting!

Maybe we should adjust faster, maybe slower. But whatever the era ... whatever the times, one thing will never change: Fathers and mothers, if you have children ... they must come first. You must read to your children, you must hug your children, you must love your children.

Your success as a family ... our success as a society ... depends *not* on what happens at the White House, but on what happens inside your house.

For over 50 years, it was said that the winner of Wellesley's annual hoop race would be the first to get married. Now they say the winner will be the first to become a C.E.O. [chief executive officer]. Both of those stereotypes show too little tolerance for those who want to know where the mermaids stand. So I want to offer you today a new legend: The winner of the hoop race will be the first to realize her dream ... not society's dream ... her own personal dream. Who knows? Somewhere out in this audience may even be someone who will one day follow in my footsteps, and preside over the White House as the president's spouse. I wish him well!

The controversy ends here. But our conversation is only beginning. And worthwhile conversation it has been. So as you leave Wellesley today, take with you deep thanks for the courtesy and the honor you have shared with Mrs. Gorbachev and me. Thank you. God bless you. And may your future be worthy of your dreams.

SUPREME COURT ON
1989 FLAG BURNING LAW
June 11, 1990

The Supreme Court on June 11 rejected a new federal law against desecration of the American flag on the same ground that it struck down a Texas law almost one year earlier. The same 5-4 majority that ruled in the Texas case held that the federal law violated the First Amendment right to freedom of expression. Amid public anger and political opposition to the Court's 1989 ruling, Congress had acted quickly to pass the Flag Protection Act, written with the express intent of meeting the constitutional test. (Court Ruling on Flag Burning, Historic Documents of 1989, p. 343)

In contrast to the Texas law, which referred to the offensive message conveyed by flag-burning protests, the sponsors of the federal legislation tried to overcome the Court's objections by omitting any reference to a flag burner's message or motive. It simply stated: "Whoever knowingly mutilates, defaces, physically defiles, burns, maintains on the floor or ground, or tramples upon any flag of the United States shall be fined . . . or imprisoned for not more than a year, or both."

But Justice William J. Brennan, Jr., writing for the Court, said: "The Act still suffers from the same fundamental flaw: it suppresses expression out of concern for its likely communicative impact." He said that the structure and logic of the federal law made clear that the government's interest was not in the flag's physical protection but in its symbolic meaning.

The Court's decision led immediately to renewed but futile attempts in Congress to take the initial step toward amending the Constitution to outlaw flag burning—that of passing a proposed amendment by both houses and placing it before the states for ratification. The 1989 legislation had been pushed through by the Democratic leadership in Congress to sidetrack mainly Republican efforts to crank up the amendment process.

Court Test of the Flag Law

A court test of the new law was assured in October 1989 by protesters in Washington, D.C., and Seattle, Washington. One group publicly burned American flags on the Capitol steps and another group did so in front of a Seattle post office. The Justice Department brought criminal charges against the protesters, but federal district court judges in Seattle and the District of Columbia dismissed the cases, saying the law was unconstitutional. The government appealed directly to the Supreme Court, which in a rare instance agreed to hear the case before it was reviewed by an intermediate appellate court. The two cases, U.S. v. Eichman *and* U.S. v. Haggerty, *were consolidated for the Court to consider together.*

Both chambers of Congress filed briefs with the Court, as did the legislation's Senate sponsor, Sen. Joseph R. Biden, Jr., D-Del. They argued that the act was narrowly drawn to prohibit conduct, not expression. Solicitor General Kenneth W. Starr told the Court in oral arguments that flag burning was, like "fighting words" and some forms of obscenity, "beyond the pale of free speech."

The briefs and arguments were believed to be directed at persuading Justice Harry A. Blackmun to change his mind. In the Texas flag-burning case, Texas v. Johnson, *Blackmun joined Justices Brennan, Thurgood Marshall, Antonin Scalia, and Anthony M. Kennedy in holding that law unconstitutional. But in a 1974 flag-desecration case Blackmun had said he could support a law that focused exclusively on conduct.*

Blackmun did not change his position, and the same justices who struck down the Texas law also struck down the federal law. The dissenting justices in both cases were John Paul Stevens, Byron R. White, Sandra Day O'Connor, and Chief Justice William H. Rehnquist. Stevens filed the dissenting opinion for all four. The division cut across ideological lines, placing conservatives Scalia and Kennedy on the same side with the Court's liberal wing of Brennan, Marshall, and Blackmun.

Stevens said the case came down to a "a question of judgment" on which "reasonable judges may differ." While saying that he thought the flag's symbolic value had been lessened by the Court's "stamp of approval on the act of flag burning," Stevens added that the "integrity of the symbol" had also been "compromised by those leaders who seem to advocate compulsory worship of the flag even by individuals whom it offends."

Ruling's Aftermath in Congress

Within hours of the Court's decision on June 11, lawmakers were on the Senate and House floors demanding a constitutional amendment. Republicans, well aware of presidential candidate George Bush's success in

*using the flag and patriotism as issues against Democratic opponent
Michael S. Dukakis, in effect dared Democrats facing re-election in 1990
to vote against the amendment. Senate Republican leader Bob Dole of
Kansas, the first senator to speak on the issue, suggested that the
lawmakers who supported such an amendment were on the side of the
armed forces and opponents were on the side of flag burners.*

*The next day, President Bush said flag burning "ought to be outlawed"
and again, as in 1989, lent his support to an amendment. The day after
that, a House Judiciary subcommittee sent an amendment resolution to
the full committee. But what looked like a stampede for an amendment
did not materialize. The Democratic leaders managed to focus the
argument more on a question of amending the Bill of Rights for the first
time in the nation's history than on flag burning. Opinion polls indicated
that while the public strongly opposed flag burning, there was a reluctance to amend the Constitution.*

*When the House vote came on June 21, exactly one year after the Court
had ruled in* Texas v. Johnson, *17 Republicans joined 159 Democrats to
vote "no," leaving the amendment's proponents thirty-four votes short of
the two-thirds majority needed for passage. The House vote doomed the
resolution, which required approval by both chambers. But the Senate in
an essentially meaningless vote June 26 also defeated the measure. The
Senate measure fell nine votes short of the needed two-thirds majority.
Only a few members of Congress ventured to predict that the issue would
return in another legislative session.*

*Following are excerpts from the Supreme Court's majority
and dissenting opinions in the consolidated cases of U.S. v.
Eichman and U.S. v. Haggerty, June 11, 1990, which rulings
declared unconstitutional a federal law enacted in 1989 to
outlaw desecration of the American flag:*

Nos. 89-1433 and 89-1434

United States, Appellant *v.* Shawn D. Eichman, David Gerald Blalock and Scott W. Tyler	On appeal from the United States District Court for the District of Columbia
United States, Appellant *v.* Mark John Haggerty, Carlos Garza, Jennifer Proctor Campbell and Darius Allen Strong	On appeal from the United States District Court for the Western District of Washington

[June 11, 1990]

JUSTICE BRENNAN delivered the opinion of the Court.

In these consolidated appeals, we consider whether appellees' prosecution for burning a United States flag in violation of the Flag Protection Act of 1989 is consistent with the First Amendment. Applying our recent decision in *Texas v. Johnson* (1989), the District Courts held that the Act cannot constitutionally be applied to appellees. We affirm.

I

In No. 89-1433 [*U.S. v. Eichman*], the United States prosecuted certain appellees for violating the Flag Protection Act of 1989 by knowingly setting fire to several United States flags on the steps of the United States Capitol while protesting various aspects of the Government's domestic and foreign policy. In No. 89-1434 [*U.S. v. Haggerty*], the United States prosecuted other appellees for violating the Act by knowingly setting fire to a United States flag while protesting the Act's passage. In each case, the respective appellees moved to dismiss the flag-burning charge on the ground that the Act, both on its face and as applied, violates the First Amendment. Both the United States District Court for the Western District of Washington and the United States District Court for the District of Columbia ... held the Act unconstitutional as applied to appellees and dismissed the charges....

II

Last Term in *Johnson*, we held that a Texas statute criminalizing the desecration of venerated objects, including the United States flag, was unconstitutional as applied to an individual who had set such a flag on fire during a political demonstration. The Texas statute provided that "[a] person commits an offense if he intentionally or knowingly desecrates ... [a] national flag," where "desecrate" meant to "deface, damage, or otherwise physically mistreat in a way that the actor knows will seriously offend one or more persons likely to observe or discover his action." We first held that Johnson's flag-burning was "conduct 'sufficiently imbued with elements of communication' to implicate the First Amendment." We next considered and rejected the State's contention that, under *United States v. O'Brien* (1968), we ought to apply the deferential standard with which we have reviewed Government regulations of conduct containing both speech and nonspeech elements where "the governmental interest is unrelated to the suppression of free expression." We reasoned that the State's asserted interest "in preserving the flag as a symbol of nationhood and national unity," was an interest "related 'to the suppression of free expression' within the meaning of *O'Brien*" because the State's concern with protecting the flag's symbolic meaning is implicated "only when a person's treatment of the flag communicates some message." We therefore subjected the statute to " 'the most exacting scrutiny,' " quoting *Boos v. Barry* (1988), and we concluded that the State's asserted interests could not justify the infringement on the demonstrator's First Amendment rights.

After our decision in *Johnson*, Congress passed the Flag Protection Act of 1989. The Act provides in relevant part:

> "(a)(1) Whoever knowingly mutilates, defaces, physically defiles, burns, maintains on the floor or ground, or tramples upon any flag of the United States shall be fined under this title or imprisoned for not more than one year, or both.
>
> "(2) This subsection does not prohibit any conduct consisting of the disposal of a flag when it has become worn or soiled.
>
> "(b) As used in this section, the term 'flag of the United States' means any flag of the United States or any part thereof, made of any substance, of any size, in a form that is commonly displayed."

The Government concedes in this case, as it must, that appellees' flag-burning constituted expressive conduct, but invites us to reconsider our rejection in *Johnson* of the claim that flag-burning as a mode of expression, like obscenity or "fighting words," does not enjoy the full protection of the First Amendment. *Chaplinsky v. New Hampshire* (1942). This we decline to do. The only remaining question is whether the Flag Protection Act is sufficiently distinct from the Texas statute that it may constitutionally be applied to proscribe appellees' expressive conduct.

The Government contends that the Flag Protection Act is constitutional because, unlike the statute addressed in *Johnson*, the Act does not target expressive conduct on the basis of the content of its message. The Government asserts an interest in "protect[ing] the physical integrity of the flag under all circumstances" in order to safeguard the flag's identity " 'as the unique and unalloyed symbol of the Nation.' " The Act proscribes conduct (other than disposal) that damages or mistreats a flag, without regard to the actor's motive, his intended message, or the likely effects of his conduct on onlookers. By contrast, the Texas statute expressly prohibited only those acts of physical flag desecration "that the actor knows will seriously offend" onlookers, and the former federal statute prohibited only those acts of desecration that "cas[t] contempt upon" the flag.

Although the Flag Protection Act contains no explicit content-based limitation on the scope of prohibited conduct, it is nevertheless clear that the Government's asserted *interest* is "related 'to the suppression of free expression,' " and concerned with the content of such expression. The Government's interest in protecting the "physical integrity" of a privately owned flag rests upon a perceived need to preserve the flag's status as a symbol of our Nation and certain national ideals. But the mere destruction or disfigurement of a particular physical manifestation of the symbol, without more, does not diminish or otherwise affect the symbol itself in any way. For example, the secret destruction of a flag in one's own basement would not threaten the flag's recognized meaning. Rather, the Government's desire to preserve the flag as a symbol for certain national ideals is implicated "only when a person's treatment of the flag communicates [a] message" to others that is inconsistent with those ideals.

Moreover, the precise language of the Act's prohibitions confirms

Congress' interest in the communicative impact of flag destruction. The Act criminalizes the conduct of anyone who "knowingly mutilates, defaces, physically defiles, burns, maintains on the floor or ground, or tramples upon any flag." Each of the specified terms—with the possible exception of "burns"—unmistakably connotes disrespectful treatment of the flag and suggests a focus on those acts likely to damage the flag's symbolic value. And the explicit exemption in § 700(a)(2) for disposal of "worn or soiled" flags protects certain acts traditionally associated with patriotic respect for the flag.

As we explained in *Johnson*: "[I]f we were to hold that a State may forbid flag-burning wherever it is likely to endanger the flag's symbolic role, but allow it wherever burning a flag promotes that role—as where, for example, a person ceremoniously burns a dirty flag—we would be ... permitting a State to 'prescribe what shall be orthodox' by saying that one may burn the flag to convey one's attitude toward it and its referents only if one does not endanger the flag's representation of nationhood and national unity." Although Congress cast the Flag Protection Act in somewhat broader terms than the Texas statute at issue in *Johnson*, the Act still suffers from the same fundamental flaw: it suppresses expression out of concern for its likely communicative impact. . . . The Act therefore must be subjected to "the most exacting scrutiny," *Boos*, and for the reasons stated in *Johnson*, the Government's interest cannot justify its infringement on First Amendment rights. We decline the Government's invitation to reassess this conclusion in light of Congress' recent recognition of a purported "national consensus" favoring a prohibition on flag-burning. Even assuming such a consensus exists, any suggestion that the Government's interest in suppressing speech becomes more weighty as popular opposition to that speech grows is foreign to the First Amendment.

III

... Government may create national symbols, promote them, and encourage their respectful treatment. But the Flag Protection Act goes well beyond this by criminally proscribing expressive conduct because of its likely communicative impact.

We are aware that desecration of the flag is deeply offensive to many. But the same might be said, for example, of virulent ethnic and religious epithets, vulgar repudiations of the draft, and scurrilous caricatures. "If there is a bedrock principle underlying the First Amendment, it is that the Government may not prohibit the expression of an idea simply because society finds the idea itself offensive or disagreeable." *Johnson*. Punishing desecration of the flag dilutes the very freedom that makes this emblem so revered, and worth revering. The judgments are

Affirmed.

JUSTICE STEVENS, with whom THE CHIEF JUSTICE, JUSTICE WHITE and JUSTICE O'CONNOR join, dissenting.

The Court's opinion ends where proper analysis of the issue should begin. Of course "the Government may not prohibit the expression of an idea simply because society finds the idea itself offensive or disagreeable." None of us disagrees with that proposition. But it is equally well settled that certain methods of expression may be prohibited if (a) the prohibition is supported by a legitimate societal interest that is unrelated to suppression of the ideas the speaker desires to express; (b) the prohibition does not entail any interference with the speaker's freedom to express those ideas by other means; and (c) the interest in allowing the speaker complete freedom of choice among alternative methods of expression is less important than the societal interest supporting the prohibition.

Contrary to the position taken by counsel for the flag burners in *Texas* v. *Johnson* (1989), it is now conceded that the Federal Government has a legitimate interest in protecting the symbolic value of the American flag. Obviously that value cannot be measured, or even described, with any precision. It has at least these two components: in times of national crisis, it inspires and motivates the average citizen to make personal sacrifices in order to achieve societal goals of overriding importance; at all times, it serves as a reminder of the paramount importance of pursuing the ideals that characterize our society.

The first question the Court should consider is whether the interest in preserving the value of that symbol in unrelated to suppression of the ideas that flag burners are trying to express. In my judgment the answer depends, at least in part, on what those ideas are. A flag burner might intend various messages. The flag burner may wish simply to convey hatred, contempt, or sheer opposition directed at the United States. This might be the case if the flag were burned by an enemy during time of war. A flag burner may also, or instead, seek to convey the depth of his personal conviction about some issue, by willingly provoking the use of force against himself. In so doing, he says that "my disagreement with certain policies is so strong that I am prepared to risk physical harm (and perhaps imprisonment) in order to call attention to my views." This second possibility apparently describes the expressive conduct of the flag burners in these cases. Like the protesters who dramatized their opposition to our engagement in Vietnam by publicly burning their draft cards—and who were punished for doing so—their expressive conduct is consistent with affection for this country and respect for the ideals that the flag symbolizes. There is at least one further possibility: a flag burner may intend to make an accusation against the integrity of the American people who disagree with him. By burning the embodiment of America's collective commitment to freedom and equality, the flag burner charges that the majority has forsaken that commitment—that continued respect for the flag is nothing more than hypocrisy. Such a charge may be made even if the flag burner loves the country and zealously pursues the ideals that the country claims to honor.

The idea expressed by a particular act of flag burning is necessarily dependent on the temporal and political context in which it occurs. In the 1960's it may have expressed opposition to the country's Vietnam policies, or at least to the compulsory draft. In *Texas* v. *Johnson,* it apparently expressed opposition to the platform of the Republican Party. In these cases, the respondents have explained that it expressed their opposition to racial discrimination, to the failure to care for the homeless, and of course to statutory prohibitions of flag burning. In any of these examples, the protesters may wish both to say that their own position is the only one faithful to liberty and equality, and to accuse their fellow citizens of hypocritical indifference to—or even of a selfish departure from—the ideals which the flag is supposed to symbolize. The ideas expressed by flag burners are thus various and often ambiguous.

The Government's legitimate interest in preserving the symbolic value of the flag is, however, essentially the same regardless of which of many different ideas may have motivated a particular act of flag burning. As I explained in my dissent in *Johnson,* the flag uniquely symbolizes the ideas of liberty, equality, and tolerance—ideas that Americans have passionately defended and debated throughout our history. The flag embodies the spirit of our national commitment to those ideals. The message thereby transmitted does not take a stand upon our disagreements, except to say that those disagreements are best regarded as competing interpretations of shared ideals. It does not judge particular policies, except to say that they command respect when they are enlightened by the spirit of liberty and equality. To the world, the flag is our promise that we will continue to strive for these ideals. To us, the flag is a reminder both that the struggle for liberty and equality is unceasing, and that our obligation of tolerance and respect for all of our fellow citizens encompasses those who disagree with us—indeed, even those whose ideas are disagreeable or offensive.

Thus, the Government may—indeed, it should—protect the symbolic value of the flag without regard to the specific content of the flag burners speech. The prosecution in this case does not depend upon the object of the defendants' protest. It is, moreover, equally clear that the prohibition does not entail any interference with the speaker's freedom to express his or her ideas by other means. It may well be true that other means of expression may be less effective in drawing attention to those ideas....

This case therefore comes down to a question of judgment. Does the admittedly important interest in allowing every speaker to choose the method of expressing his or her ideas that he or she deems most effective and appropriate outweigh the societal interest in preserving the symbolic value of the flag?.... The freedom of expression protected by the First Amendment embraces not only the freedom to communicate particular ideas, but also the right to communicate them effectively. That right, however, is not absolute—the communicative value of a well-placed bomb in the Capitol does not entitle it to the protection of the First Amendment.

Burning a flag is not, of course, equivalent to burning a public building. Assuming that the protester is burning his own flag, it causes no physical harm to other persons or to their property. The impact is purely symbolic, and it is apparent that some thoughtful persons believe that impact, far from depreciating the value of the symbol, will actually enhance its meaning. I most respectfully disagree. Indeed, what makes this case particularly difficult for me is wht I regard as the damage to the symbol that has already occurred as a result of this Court's decision to place its stamp of approval on the act of flag burning. A formerly dramatic expression of protest is now rather commonplace. In today's marketplace of ideas, the public burning of a Vietnam draft card is probably less provocative than lighting a cigarette. Tomorrow flag burning may produce a similar reaction. There is surely a direct relationship between the communicative value of the act of flag burning and the symbolic value of the object being burned.

The symbolic value of the American flag is not the same today as it was yesterday. Events during the last three decades have altered the country's image in the eyes of numerous Americans, and some now have difficulty understanding the message that the flag conveyed to their parents and grandparents—whether born abroad and naturalized or native born. Moreover, the integrity of the symbol has been compromised by those leaders who seem to advocate compulsory worship of the flag even by individuals whom it offends. . . .

Given all these considerations, plus the fact that the Court today is really doing nothing more than reconfirming what it has already decided, it might be appropriate to defer to the judgment of the majority and merely apply the doctrine of *stare decisis* to the case at hand. That action, however, would not honestly reflect my considered judgment concerning the relative importance of the conflicting interests that are at stake. I remain persuaded that the considerations identified in my opinion in *Texas* v. *Johnson* are of controlling importance in this case as well.

Accordingly, I respectfully dissent.

CANADIAN PRIME MINISTER ON MEECH LAKE FAILURE

June 23, 1990

Prime Minister Brian Mulroney, in a televised address from Ottawa on June 23, said that hope for approval of an agreement on Quebec's status in Canada had collapsed. "I do not hide from you my great disappointment at the setback Canadians have suffered today," Mulroney said in announcing that two of the country's ten provinces, Manitoba and New Brunswick, had not ratified the Meech Lake Accord by that day's deadline. The outcome raised the prospect that Quebec, the predominantly French-speaking province, would break away from English-speaking Canada by asserting some measure of political autonomy—possibly outright independence.

The Meech Lake Accord, named for a resort near Ottawa where it was negotiated three years earlier by the prime minister and the provincial premiers, declared Quebec "a distinct society" and yielded the province special rights that it demanded as a condition for accepting a national constitution the other provinces had ratified.

"Today, we must guard against two dangers: first, to despair that anything can be done and, second, to delude ourselves that nothing has happened," Mulroney said during his twelve-minute speech. He pleaded for Canadians to "heal wounds and reach out to fellow Canadians," and he spoke of initiating unidentified programs "to bridge the solitudes in which so many English- and French-speaking Canadians still live." He said, nevertheless, "Today is not the time to launch new constitutional initiatives."

Mulroney thus seemed to leave the next political move up to Robert Bourassa, the premier of Quebec. Bourassa, who pushed for the accords and keeping Quebec within the Canadian confederation, seemed in no hurry to stake out a new position. Political observers said he would be under pressure from Quebec's separatist movement to take steps toward independence.

Generally, the public reaction in Quebec and the rest of Canada was calm. Flags bearing the French fleur-de-lis were prominently displayed in Montreal June 25 in a parade of 150,000 marchers celebrating St. Jean Batiste Day, a religious feast that doubles as Quebec's "national" holiday. An abundance of posters proclaimed "notre vrai pays c'est Quebec" ("Quebec is our true country"). But there were no outbursts of violence or clearly identified political demonstrations. According to news reports, much of English-speaking Canada received the news of the accord's collapse with an air of indifference. Many Canadians, especially on the western prairies and in the Atlantic maritime provinces, said they were pleased it was dead.

Roots of Quebec's Separatism

Ever since an English army seized Quebec from the colonizing French in the eighteenth century, it has been a French-speaking enclave on the North American continent. Quebec became part of the Confederation of Canada created in 1867, but from the beginning it resisted central authority in an effort to preserve its language and culture. Political separatism took hold only in the 1960s. It began early in that decade with a "quiet revolution," which sometimes was compared to the civil rights movement in the United States.

Separatism turned ugly as fringe groups carried out a campaign of terrorist attacks, including kidnappings, bombings, and murder. These events prompted Prime Minister Pierre Trudeau to put Quebec under martial law in October 1970, bringing the terrorist phase to an end.

With the election in 1976 of a separatist government under Premier René Lévesque and his Parti Quebecois, the movement took a new direction. Levesque's quest for "sovereignty-association"—political independence with strong economic ties to Canada—appeared to enjoy widespread support in the province, and Quebec's separation was considered a real possibility. Many English-speaking Quebecers, including business leaders, left and transferred their assets to neighboring Ontario and elsewhere.

Because Quebec's industrial economy was not highly developed at that time, the flight of capital and industry eroded support for the separatist cause. When the question of breaking away from Canada was put to a vote May 20, 1980, Quebecers chose by a 58-42 percent margin to remain in the confederation. Soon after their defeat, the separatists lost control of the provincial government.

For most of the 1980s, separatist agitation gave way to an economic boom. Quebec's economy was strengthened by a U.S. demand for more of its products, especially hydroelectric power, aluminum, and pulp wood *and paper. As a result, Quebec's economic growth began to exceed that of Canada as a whole. No longer was it argued that Quebec would suffer economically if it opted for independence.*

Crisis Over 1982 Constitution

Coinciding with this new economic clout was a constitutional controversy that set the stage for the latest round of Quebec separatism. Canada adopted a Constitution in 1982, replacing a document the British enacted in 1867. Quebec refused to ratify it on the ground it did not grant sufficient authority to the provinces. Quebec also disapproved of the amending formula in the Constitution Act and wanted veto power over changes in certain areas.

Upon becoming Quebec's premier in the December 1985 elections, Bourassa presented the federal government with five conditions he said must be met before the province would accept the Constitution. They were the explicit recognition of Quebec as a "distinct society" and of the right to veto federal measures that adversely affected the province; greater provincial control over immigration; stricter limitations on federal spending authority; and a voice in the nomination of Supreme Court justices.

Those conditions were met in the Meech Lake Accord, drawn up June 3, 1987, by Mulroney and the ten provincial premiers. The drafters of the accord further agreed that the amendments would not take effect until they had been ratified by the federal government and all ten provincial governments by June 23, 1990. The Quebec legislature (called, symbolically, the National Assembly) promptly ratified the accord, as did the Canadian Parliament and seven of the other nine provinces.

But Manitoba and New Brunswick refused to ratify the document unless the "distinct society" clause was deleted. Newfoundland, which ratified Meech Lake, rescinded its approval after the election of a new government, headed by Premier Clyde Wells, who became the most vocal opponent of the clause and rallied opposition throughout Canada.

Opposition to Meech Lake Accords

Some of the foes especially resented a Quebec law, passed in 1977 during Lévesque's premiership, that banned English on commercial signs. Canada's Supreme Court ruled in December 1988 that the ban violated guarantees of freedom of expression in a constitutional Charter of Rights and Freedom, a document akin to the U.S. Bill of Rights. Quebec responded first by liberalizing the law slightly but then by invoking a section of the charter that provided the provinces could pass certain laws "notwithstanding" the constitutional guarantees. The province refused to discard its modified ban despite the court's ruling.

"That really turned off English Canada," commented William Watson, an economics professor at McGill University in Montreal. Soon criticism of the Meech Lake Accord went beyond traditional English-French

antagonisms. Feminists and members of Canada's minority groups complained that the accord was the product of eleven white men working behind closed doors. Other criticisms stemmed from a longstanding theme of Canadian politics, the struggle for power between the provinces and the central government.

Following is the text provided by the Canadian government of Prime Minister Brian Mulroney's televised address to Canada, June 23, 1990, announcing the collapse of the Meech Lake Accord to accommodate Quebec's constitutional demands:

On June 9, here in Ottawa, the 10 provincial premiers and I reached an agreement on making the Meech Lake Accord part of Canada's constitution. All of us agreed to improve Meech Lake in response to concerns that had been expressed over the past three years by women, northerners, minority language groups and aboriginal Canadians.

The Premiers of New Brunswick, Manitoba and Newfoundland agreed to use every possible effort to arrive at a decision on the Meech Lake Accord by June 23. On June 15, the New Brunswick legislature passed the Accord unanimously. And in the two weeks since June 9, Manitoba tried to overcome procedural obstacles and adopt the Accord. The three Manitoba party leaders spoke in favor of the agreement. With more time, there appeared to be every prospect that the Accord would be passed.

However, yesterday evening, the last remaining hope that the Accord would be ratified was dashed when the House of Assembly of Newfoundland and Labrador adjourned without a vote. This action means that the current round of constitutional reform has come to an end.

Today, we must guard against two dangers: first, to despair that anything can be done and, second, to delude ourselves that nothing has happened.

In saying yes to Canada in the 1980 referendum, Quebecers were promised a renewed federalism. But the Constitution Act of 1982 was not accepted by Quebec because it did not respond to the expectations raised in 1980. In particular, it did not reconcile the need to preserve the distinctiveness that Quebec brings to Canada with the need to preserve the equality of all provinces and all Canadians.

The Meech Lake Accord was designed to bridge those realities. I believe sincerely that it was in the interest of all Canadians that it be ratified. But the outcome is clear; we have fallen short of the unanimous consent required and the Accord has not been passed.

It is important that Canadians understand why this has happened. The Accord, which was drafted to achieve unity, became over 3 years a lightning rod for discontent about budgets, interests rates, free trade and taxes. It attracted accusations of favouritism and sentiments of rejection and stimulated regional rivalries and linguistic tensions.

Much of the discontent of Canadians found expression in hostility to the Meech Lake Accord. Its original purpose, as agreed to by the premiers in Edmonton in 1986, was only to bring Quebec back into the constitutional family. But the Accord came to be expected to respond to all the constitutional preoccupations of the country.

That we did not succeed is, at least partly, also the failure of the constitutional amending procedures. Under the 1982 procedures, the Premiers [of Canada's ten provinces] and I were required to re-open negotiations and reproduce unanimity every time a new provincial leader was elected who chose not to honour the undertaking of his predecessor. Or, in the case of Newfoundland, when a new Premier was elected who chose to rescind the approval of the previous legislature.

But, we had created an historic consensus around the Accord and, by persevering, came very close to maintaining it. It was endorsed by 10 provincial premiers representing 4 different political parties. It was approved by eight provincial legislatures representing 94% of the population—and the three political leaders of the 9th province had publicly committed themselves to passing it. It was passed by the House of Commons on two, separate occasions, by overwhelming majorities.

Despite all this effort, we have missed an opportunity to turn the page and to start a new chapter of constitutional development. While the world gears up for the 21st century, we have failed to resolve a debate that predates Confederation itself. That is why I am so deeply disappointed that this attempt at constitutional reform has failed.

To our friends and partners abroad, I urge that this situation be kept in perspective. Canadians have always overcome challenges to our unity and we shall do so again. With a population that totals only 26 million, we have built the eighth most powerful economy in the world, with one of the highest standards of living and one of the best qualities of life. It would be unwise for anyone to underestimate this industrious and resource-rich nation of hard-working and productive people.

Canada's economic prospects continue to be among the most exciting and promising of any country in the world. The government will continue to pursue policies designed to fulfill that promise.

To my fellow Quebecers I want to say how dismayed I am that Quebec has not, at this time, been able to rejoin the constitutional family with "honour and enthusiasm". But Quebec emerged from these negotiations with its dignity and its principles intact. Quebec was never isolated and, in fact, was a member of the majority throughout. Quebec's concerns as eloquently stated by Premier [Robert] Bourassa, were supported time and time again by English-speaking premiers whose sensitivity was always in evidence.

For seven long days, 10 provincial premiers and I struggled to find the basis of reintegrating Quebec into the Canadian constitutional family. However, we were not successful and there are potentially significant implications for Canada—because actions do have consequences.

The debate over the past three years has demonstrated that Canada has changed profoundly—and its outcome signals an era of further change. Today is not the day to launch new constitutional initiatives. It is a time to mend divisions, and heal wounds and reach out to fellow Canadians. There is much to reflect on before we try again to amend the Constitution. One thing is very clear; we simply must find a better way to do it. In the coming months and years, we must find a way to reconcile the need for public participation and open democratic process with the legal requirements now in the Constitution.

I do not hide from you my great disappointment at the setback Canadians have suffered today. But there is not dishonour in having tried to overcome a serious threat to our unity. No achievement is possible without great effort. Such effort always carries with it the risk of failure. But I would rather have failed trying to advance the cause of Canada's unity than to have simply played it safe, done nothing or criticized from the sidelines. To govern is to choose. To lead is to run the risk of failure. We did not succeed but the failure to ratify the Accord was not the failure of Canada.

Canada is not a nation of defeatists—and this is not a government of quitters. We will all be back at work next week. We will implement an agenda of national policy initiatives to respond to the economic and social priorities of Canadians. We will initiate programs to bring Canadians together and bridge the solitudes in which so many English and French-speaking Canadians still live.

There is more to this country than constitutional papers; Canada is more—much more—than dry parchment lying in a drawer in the National Archives. Canada is our inheritance from our parents and our legacy to our children. Canada is admired and respected around the world. I am not prepared to give up on all of that—or any of that.

Despite this setback, despite this great disappointment, the idea of a truly united, generous and tolerant Canada endures. And will, eventually, prevail. Thank you and good afternoon.

SUPREME COURT ON
THE RIGHT TO DIE
June 25, 1990

The Supreme Court on June 25 rendered its first decision in a "right-to-die" case by upholding Missouri's requirement for "clear and convincing" proof of a patient's desire that life-sustaining treatment be withdrawn. The long-awaited decision, refusing a request by parents to let their comatose daughter die, was issued by a divided Court.

In one sense the 5-4 decision was narrowly drawn to apply solely to the question of whether Missouri's proof requirement violated the U.S. Constitution. And yet the decision had immense implications, for the Court enunciated a constitutional right to refuse medical attention, even to save or prolong life.

The case of Cruzan v. Director, Missouri Department of Health *involved Nancy Cruzan, hospitalized in a "persistent vegetative state" since she suffered severe brain damage in an automobile accident in January 1983, when she was twenty-five years old. After medical authorities said that she had virtually no chance of regaining her mental or physical abilities, her parents asked the hospital—the Missouri Rehabilitation Center at Mount Vernon—to remove a tube to her stomach through which she received nutrition and water, thereby letting her die.*

Parents' Legal Quest for Euthanasia

The parents, Lester and Joyce Cruzan of Cartersville, Missouri, who had become their daughter's legal guardians, were told they would have to obtain a court order before the hospital could act. They turned to the American Civil Liberties Union office in Kansas City, and obtained the pro bono services of the city's biggest law firm, Shook, Hardy & Bacon.

With this legal representation, the couple persuaded state Circuit Court judge Charles Teel, Jr., that a person in Nancy Cruzan's condition had a fundamental right under the state and federal constitutions to refuse life-prolonging medical procedures. Teel so ruled July 17, 1988.

Before the hospital could act on Teel's ruling, it was appealed to the Missouri Supreme Court by the state's attorney general, who argued that the Cruzan parents had no constitutional right to decide whether their daughter should be permitted to die, and that the state could not be required to assist in a suicide.

Missouri's Pro-Life "Predisposition"

On a 4-3 vote, the Missouri Supreme Court overturned the judge's ruling. It held that some key testimony was "unreliable for the purposes of determining her [Nancy Cruzan's] intent." A former housemate said Cruzan had expressed thoughts "in somewhat serious conversation" that if sick or injured she would not wish to continue her life "unless she could live at least halfway normally." Moreover, the court pointed out that under Missouri law a guardian was not authorized to order termination of medical treatment. It suggested that such decisions should be relegated to a more neutral party, such as a probate court.

The Missouri high court additionally said the state had a statutory interest in preserving life without regard to its quality. The court cited the preamble to a 1986 Missouri anti-abortion law to show that "Missouri adopts a strong predisposition in favor of preserving life." That law survived a challenge before the U.S. Supreme Court in the famous 1989 Webster case—a case that gave the states more authority to impose restraints on abortion. (Webster Abortion Case, Historic Documents of 1989, p. 365)

In the present case, the Missouri court held that the state's interest in the "sanctity of life" outweighed Nancy Cruzan's right to refuse medical treatment—if indeed she had such a right—because continued treatment caused her no "burden" of pain. The Cruzan family then appealed the case to the U.S. Supreme Court.

The question for the Court, said Chief Justice William H. Rehnquist in writing for the five-member majority, "is simply and starkly whether the United States Constitution prohibits Missouri" from ruling the way it did. He wrote that Missouri's requirement for "clear and convincing evidence" did not violate the Fourteenth Amendment's "due process" clause, which provides that no state shall "deprive any person of life, liberty, or property, without due process of law."

The principle that "a competent person has a constitutionally protected liberty interest in refusing unwanted medical treatment may be inferred from our prior decisions," Rehnquist wrote. But a person's "liberty interests" must be balanced against "the relevant state interests," he added. In his judgment, the state's interests prevailed.

Strong Dissents; Tepid Concurrences

Justice William H. Brennan, Jr., joined by Justices Thurgood Marshall and Harry A. Blackmun, wrote a strongly worded dissenting opinion, and Justice John Paul Stevens wrote a separate dissent. "The Court," Stevens contended, "permits the State's abstract, undifferentiated interest in the preservation of life to overwhelm the best interests of Nancy Beth Cruzan. ..." Similarly, Brennan wrote that her "fundamental right to be free of unwanted artificial nutrition and hydration ... is not outweighed by any interests of the State."

Justice Sandra Day O'Connor, joining with the majority, nevertheless pointedly wrote in a concurring opinion that the decision did not "prevent States from developing other approaches for protecting an incompetent individual's liberty interest in refusing medical treatment." A survey of state court decisions made clear that "no national consensus has yet emerged on the best solution for this difficult and sensitive problem," she wrote. "Today we decide only that one State's practice does not violate the Constitution; the more challenging task of crafting more appropriate procedures ... is entrusted to the ... States."

Justices Anthony M. Kennedy, Antonin Scalia, and Byron R. White rounded out the majority. Scalia also wrote a separate opinion, in which he insisted that the subject was essentially that of suicide and exclusively under state jurisdiction. "While I agree with the Court's analysis today, and therefore join in its opinion," he wrote, "I would have preferred that we announce, clearly and promptly, that the federal courts have no business in this field. ..."

The Supreme Court did not speak the final word in the case. The parents asked Judge Teel on August 30 for another hearing to consider new evidence that their daughter had indicated to three people she would rather die than live in a vegetative state. Missouri, saying it no longer had a "recognizable legal interest," withdrew from the case. A court-appointed guardian for Nancy Cruzan recommended that her feeding tube be removed. Teel so approved December 14, and it was done over the objections of various anti-euthanasia protesters. Nancy Cruzan died December 26.

Case's Competing Interests

No right-to-die case had drawn this much attention since 1976 when the New Jersey Supreme Court permitted a comatose patient, Karen Ann Quinlan, to be removed from a respirator. The U.S. Supreme Court refused to review that ruling. (Right to Die, Historic Documents of 1976, p. 197)

By the time the Supreme Court heard oral arguments in the Cruzan case on December 6, 1989, nearly two dozen organizations had filed friend-of-court briefs—some as advocates but others asking the Court for legal clarification. Organizations in favor of euthanasia filed briefs asking that it be overturned. Kenneth W. Starr, the U.S. soliciter general, received the Court's permission to argue on behalf of Missouri.

Several medical groups and experts on medical ethics expressed dismay at the Supreme Court's decision. John Pickering, an attorney for the American Academy of Neurology, said "the battle must turn" to other states "free to adopt less rigid rules." Representatives of the AMA vowed to push for such laws. The National Right to Life Committee applauded the decision. "I'm sorry to see that ... abortion was just the beginning of the slippery slope of the death ethic," said Dr. John C. Wilke, president of the organization.

In Congress, House and Senate subcommittees prepared legislation that would require federally aided hospitals to inform patients of state laws concerning the acceptance or refusal of medical treatment. The Society for the Right to Die reported unusual interest across the country in the use of "living wills"—written statements by individuals expressing their wishes about their medical care if they become incompetent. Dr. Bernard D. Davis, professor emeritus at Harvard Medical School, wrote in the Wall Street Journal *that the Cruzan case, "confirming the legal force of such a document [legal will], is a real step forward."*

Press reaction to the Court's decision was cautiously favorable, although expressing sympathy for the Cruzans. The Washington Post *observed editorially that Missouri could relax its law and other states could draw up less-restrictive ones. "The Supreme Court's decision to move slowly and encourage the states to act is not unreasonable," it added. The* New York Times *declared that the decision "is bold because it demonstrates a living Constitution at work, giving birth to a newly declared right."*

> *Following are excerpts from the majority, concurring, and dissenting opinions in the Supreme Court's first "right-to-die" case,* Cruzan v. Director, Missouri Department of Health, *issued June 25, 1990, upholding a restrictive Missouri law on euthanasia but at the same time establishing an individual's constitutional right to refuse life-prolonging medical treatment:*

No. 89-1433

Nancy Beth Cruzan, by her parents and co-guardians, Lester L. Cruzan, et ux., Petitioners

v.

Director, Missouri Department of Health, et al.

On writ of certiorari to the Supreme Court of Missouri

[June 25, 1990]

CHIEF JUSTICE REHNQUIST delivered the opinion of the Court.

... In this Court, the question is simply and starkly whether the United States Constitution prohibits Missouri from choosing the rule of decision which it did. This is the first case in which we have been squarely presented with the issue of whether the United States Constitution grants what is in common parlance referred to as a "right to die." We follow the judicious counsel of our decision in *Twin City Bank* v. *Nebeker* (1987), where we said that in deciding "a question of such magnitude and importance ... it is the [better] part of wisdom not to attempt, by any general statement, to cover every possible phase of the subject."

The Fourteenth Amendment provides that no State shall "deprive any person of life, liberty, or property, without due process of law." The principle that a competent person has a constitutionally protected liberty interest in refusing unwanted medical treatment may be inferred from our prior decisions. In *Jacobson* v. *Massachusetts* (1905), for instance, the Court balanced an individual's liberty interest in declining an unwanted smallpox vaccine against the State's interest in preventing disease. ... Just this Term, in the course of holding that a State's procedures for administering antipsychotic medication to prisoners were sufficient to satisfy due process concerns, we recognized that prisoners possess "a significant liberty interest in avoiding the unwanted administration of antipsychotic drugs under the Due Process Clause of the Fourteenth Amendment." *Washington* v. *Harper* (1990). Still other cases support the recognition of a general liberty interest in refusing medical treatment. ...

But determining that a person has a "liberty interest" under the Due Process Clause does not end the inquiry; "whether respondent's constitutional rights have been violated must be determined by balancing his liberty interests against the relevant state interests." *Youngberg* v. *Romeo* (1982).

Petitioners insist that under the general holdings of our cases, the forced administration of life-sustaining medical treatment, and even of artificially-delivered food and water essential to life, would implicate a competent person's liberty interest. Although we think the logic of the cases discussed above would embrace such a liberty interest, the dramatic consequences involved in refusal of such treatment would inform the inquiry as to whether the deprivation of that interest is constitutionally permissible. But for purposes of this case, we assume that the United States Constitution would grant a competent person a constitutionally protected right to refuse life saving hydration and nutrition.

Petitioners go on to assert that an incompetent person should possess the same right in this respect as is possessed by a competent person. They rely primarily on our decisions in *Parham* v. *J.R.*, and *Youngberg* v. *Romeo* (1982). In *Parham*, we held that a mentally disturbed minor child had a liberty interest in "not being confined unnecessarily for medical treatment," but we certainly did not intimate that such a minor child, after commitment, would have a liberty interest in refusing treatment. In *Youngberg*, we held that a seriously retarded adult had a liberty interest in safety and freedom from bodily restraint. *Youngberg,* however, did not deal with decisions to administer or withhold medical treatment.

The difficulty with petitioners' claim is that in a sense it begs the question: an incompetent person is not able to make an informed and voluntary choice to exercise a hypothetical right to refuse treatment or any other right. Such a "right" must be exercised for her, if at all, by some sort of surrogate. Here, Missouri has in effect recognized that under certain circumstances a surrogate may act for the patient in electing to have hydration and nutrition withdrawn in such a way as to cause death, but it has established a procedural safeguard to assure that the action of the surrogate conforms as best it may to the wishes expressed by the patient while competent. Missouri requires that evidence of the incompetent's wishes as to the withdrawal of treatment be proved by clear and convincing evidence. The question, then, is whether the United States Constitution forbids the establishment of this procedural requirement by the State. We hold that it does not.

Whether or not Missouri's clear and convincing evidence requirement comports with the United States Constitution depends in part on what interests the State may properly seek to protect in this situation. Missouri relies on its interest in the protection and preservation of human life, and there can be no gainsaying this interest. As a general matter, the States— indeed, all civilized nations—demonstrate their commitment to life by treating homicide as serious crime. Moreover, the majority of States in this country have laws imposing criminal penalties on one who assists another to commit suicide. We do not think a State is required to remain neutral in the face of an informed and voluntary decision by a physically-able adult to starve to death.

But in the context presented here, a State has more particular interests at stake. The choice between life and death is a deeply personal decision of obvious and overwhelming finality. We believe Missouri may legitimately seek to safeguard the personal element of this choice through the imposition of heightened evidentiary requirements. It cannot be disputed that the Due Process Clause protects an interest in life as well as an interest in refusing life-sustaining medical treatment. Not all incompetent patients will have loved ones available to serve as surrogate decisionmakers. And even where family members are present, "[t]here will, of course, be some unfortunate situations in which family members will not act to protect a patient." *In re Jobes* (1987). A State is entitled to guard against potential abuses in such situations. Similarly, a State is entitled to consider that a judicial proceeding to make a determination regarding an incompetent's wishes may very well not be an adversarial one, with the added guarantee of accurate fact finding that the adversary process brings with it. Finally, we think a State may properly decline to make judgments about the "quality" of life that a particular individual may enjoy, and simply assert an unqualified interest in the preservation of human life to be weighed against the constitutionally protected interests of the individual.

In our view, Missouri has permissibly sought to advance these interests through the adoption of a "clear and convincing" standard of proof to govern such proceedings. . . .

We think it self-evident that the interests at stake in the instant proceedings are more substantial, both on an individual and societal level, than those involved in a run-of-the-mine civil dispute. But not only does the standard of proof reflect the importance of a particular adjudication, it also serves as "a societal judgment about how the risk of error should be distributed between the litigants." *Santosky* [v. *Kramer* (1982).] The more stringent the burden of proof a party must bear, the more that party bears the risk of an erroneous decision. We believe that Missouri may permissibly place an increased risk of an erroneous decision on those seeking to terminate an incompetent individual's life-sustaining treatment. An erroneous decision not to terminate results in a maintenance of the status quo; the possibility of subsequent developments such as advancements in medical science, the discovery of new evidence regarding the patient's intent, changes in the law, or simply the unexpected death of the patient despite the administration of life-sustaining treatment, at least create the potential that a wrong decision will eventually be corrected or its impact mitigated. An erroneous decision to withdraw life-sustaining treatment, however, is not susceptible of correction. . . .

It is also worth nothing that most, if not all, States simply forbid oral testimony entirely in determining the wishes of parties in transactions which, while important, simply do not have the consequences that a decision to terminate a person's life does. At common law and by statute in most States, the parole evidence rule prevents the variations of the terms of a written contract by oral testimony. The statute of frauds makes unenforceable oral contracts to leave property by will, and statutes regulating the making of wills universally require that those instruments be in writing. There is no doubt that statutes requiring wills to be in writing, and statutes of frauds which require that a contract to make a will be in writing, on occasion frustrate the effectuation of the intent of a particular decedent, just as Missouri's requirement of proof in this case may have frustrated the effectuation of the not-fully-expressed desires of Nancy Cruzan. But the Constitution does not require general rules to work faultlessly; no general rule can.

In sum, we conclude that a State may apply a clear and convincing evidence standard in proceedings where a guardian seeks to discontinue nutrition and hydration of a person diagnosed to be in a persistent vegetative state. We note that many courts which have adopted some sort of substituted judgment procedure in situations like this, whether they limit consideration of evidence to the prior expressed wishes of the incompetent individual, or whether they allow more general proof of what the individual's decision would have been, require a clear and convincing standard of proof for such evidence.

The Supreme Court of Missouri held that in this case the testimony adduced at trial did not amount to clear and convincing proof of the patient's desire to have hydration and nutrition withdrawn. In so doing, it reversed a decision of the Missouri trial court which had found that the evidence "suggest[ed]" Nancy Cruzan would not have desired to continue such measures, but which had not adopted the standard of "clear and convincing evidence" enunciated by the Supreme Court. The testimony adduced at trial consisted primarily of Nancy Cruzan's statements made to a housemate about a year before her accident that she would not want to live should she face life as a "vegetable," and other observations to the same effect. The observations did not deal in terms with withdrawal of medical treatment or of hydration and nutrition. We cannot say that the Supreme Court of Missouri committed constitutional error in reaching the conclusion that it did.

Petitioners alternatively contend that Missouri must accept the "substituted judgment" of close family members even in the absence of substantial proof that their views reflect the views of the patient. They rely primarily upon our decisions in *Michael H*. v. *Gerald D*. (1989), and *Parham* v. *J.R.* (1979). But we do not think these cases support their claim. In *Michael H.*, we *upheld* the constitutionality of California's favored treatment of traditional family relationships; such a holding may not be turned around into a constitutional requirement that a State *must* recognize the primacy of those relationships in a situation like this. And in *Parham*, where the patient was a minor, we also *upheld* the constitutionality of a state scheme in which parents made certain decisions for mentally ill minors. Here again petitioners would seek to turn a decision which allowed a State to rely on family decisionmaking into a constitutional requirement that the State recognize such decisionmaking. But constitutional law does not work that way.

No doubt is engendered by anything in this record but that Nancy Cruzan's mother and father are loving and caring parents. If the State were required by the United States Constitution to repose a right of "substituted judgment" with anyone, the Cruzans would surely qualify. But we do not think the Due Process Clause requires the State to repose judgment on these matters with anyone but the patient herself. Close family members may have a strong feeling—a feeling not at all ignoble or unworthy, but not entirely disinterested, either—that they do not wish to witness the continuation of the life of a loved one which they regard as hopeless, meaningless, and even degrading. But there is no automatic assurance that the view of close family members will necessarily be the same as the patient's would have been had she been confronted with the prospect of her situation while competent. All of the reasons previously discussed for allowing Missouri to require clear and convincing evidence of the patient's wishes lead us to conclude that the State may choose to defer only to those wishes, rather than confide the decision to close family members.

The judgment of the Supreme Court of Missouri is affirmed. . . .

JUSTICE O'CONNOR, concurring.

... [T]he Court does not today decide the issue whether a State must also give effect to the decisions of a surrogate decisionmaker. In my view, such a duty may well be constitutionally required to protect the patient's liberty interest in refusing medical treatment. Few individuals provide explicit oral or written instructions regarding their intent to refuse medical treatment should they become incompetent. States which decline to consider any evidence other than such instructions may frequently fail to honor a patient's intent. Such failures might be avoided if the State considered an equally probative source of evidence: the patient's appointment of a proxy to make health care decisions on her behalf. Delegating the authority to make medical decisions to a family member or friend is becoming a common method of planning for the future. Several States have recognized the practical wisdom of such a procedure by enacting durable power of attorney statutes that specifically authorize an individual to appoint a surrogate to make medical treatment decisions. Some state courts have suggested that an agent appointed pursuant to a general durable power of attorney statute would also be empowered to make health care decisions on behalf of the patient. Other states allow an individual to designate a proxy to carry out the intent of a living will. These procedures for surrogate decisionmaking, which appear to be rapidly gaining in acceptance, may be a valuable additional safeguard of the patient's interest in directing his medical care. . . .

Today's decision, holding only that the Constitution permits a State to require clear and convincing evidence of Nancy Cruzan's desire to have artificial hydration and nutrition withdrawn, does not preclude a future determination that the Constitution requires the States to implement the decisions of a patient's duly appointed surrogate. Nor does it prevent States from developing other approaches for protecting an incompetent individual's liberty interest in refusing medical treatment. As is evident from the Court's survey of state court decisions, no national consensus has yet emerged on the best solution for this difficult and sensitive problem. Today we decide only that one State's practice does not violate the Constitution; the more challenging task of crafting appropriate procedures for safeguarding incompetents' liberty interests is entrusted to the "laboratory" of the States. . . .

JUSTICE SCALIA, concurring.

The various opinions in this case portray quite clearly the difficult, indeed agonizing, questions that are presented by the constantly increasing power of science to keep the human body alive for longer than any reasonable person would want to inhabit it. The States have begun to grapple with these problems through legislation. I am concerned, from the tenor of today's opinions, that we are poised to confuse that enterprise as successfully as we have confused the enterprise of legislating concerning abortion—requiring it to be conducted against a background of federal constitutional imperatives that are unknown because they are being newly crafted from Term to Term. That would be a great misfortune.

While I agree with the Court's analysis today, and therefore join in its opinion, I would have preferred that we announce, clearly and promptly, that the federal courts have no business in this field; that American law has always accorded the State the power to prevent, by force if necessary, suicide—including suicide by refusing to take appropriate measures necessary to preserve one's life; that the point at which life becomes "worthless," and the point at which the means necessary to preserve it become "extraordinary" or "inappropriate," are neither set forth in the Constitution nor known to the nine Justices of this Court any better than they are known to nine people picked at random from the Kansas City telephone directory; and hence, that even when it *is* demonstrated by clear and convincing evidence that a patient no longer wishes certain measures to be taken to preserve her life, it is up to the citizens of Missouri to decide, through their elected representatives, whether that wish will be honored. . . .

JUSTICE BRENNAN, with whom JUSTICE MARSHALL and JUSTICE BLACKMUN join, dissenting.

. . . Nancy Cruzan has dwelt in that twilight zone for six years. She is oblivious to her surroundings and will remain so. Her body twitches only reflexively, without consciousness. The areas of her brain that once thought, felt, and experienced sensations have degenerated badly and are continuing to do so. The cavities remaining are filling with cerebrospinal fluid. The " 'cerebral cortical atrophy is irreversible, permanent, progressive and ongoing.' " "Nancy will never interact meaningfully with her environment again. She will remain in a persistent vegetative state until her death." Because she cannot swallow, her nutrition and hydration are delivered through a tube surgically implanted in her stomach.

A grown woman at the time of the accident, Nancy had previously expressed her wish to forgo continuing medical care under circumstances such as these. Her family and her friends are convinced that this is what she would want. A guardian ad litem appointed by the trial court is also convinced that this is what Nancy would want. Yet the Missouri Supreme Court, alone among state courts deciding such a question, has determined that an irreversibly vegetative patient will remain a passive prisoner of medical technology—for Nancy, perhaps for the next 30 years.

Today the Court, while tentatively accepting that there is some degree of constitutionally protected liberty interest in avoiding unwanted medical treatment, including life-sustaining medical treatment such as artificial nutrition and hydration, affirms the decision of the Missouri Supreme Court. The majority opinion, as I read it, would affirm that decision on the ground that a State may require "clear and convincing" evidence of Nancy Cruzan's prior decision to forgo life-sustaining treatment under circumstances such as hers in order to ensure that her actual wishes are honored. Because I believe that Nancy Cruzan has a fundamental right to be free of unwanted artificial nutrition and hydration, which right is not outweighed by any interests of the State, and because I find that the improperly biased procedural obstacles imposed by the Missouri Supreme Court impermissibly burden that right, I respectfully dissent. Nancy Cruzan is entitled to choose to die with dignity.

B [A omitted]

The starting point for our legal analysis must be whether a competent person has a constitutional right to avoid unwanted medical care. Earlier this Term, this Court held that the Due Process Clause of the Fourteenth Amendment confers a significant liberty interest in avoiding unwanted medical treatment. *Washington* v. *Harper* (1990). Today, the Court concedes that our prior decisions "support the recognition of a general liberty interest in refusing medical treatment." The Court, however, avoids discussing either the measure of that liberty interest or its application by assuming, for purposes of this case only, that a competent person has a constitutionally protected liberty interest in being free of unwanted artificial nutrition and hydration. . . .

II

A

The right to be free from unwanted medical attention is a right to evaluate the potential benefit of treatment and its possible consequences according to one's own values and to make a personal decision whether to subject oneself to the intrusion. For a patient like Nancy Cruzan, the sole benefit of medical treatment is being kept metabolically alive. Neither artificial nutrition nor any other form of medical treatment available today can cure or in any way ameliorate her condition. Irreversibly vegetative patients are devoid of thought, emotion and sensation; they are permanently and completely unconscious. As the President's Commission [for the Study of Ethical Problems in Medicine and Biomedical and Behavioral Research, "Deciding to Forego Life Sustaining Treatment" (1983)] concluded in approving the withdrawal of life support equipment from irreversibly vegetative patients:

> "[T]reatment ordinarily aims to benefit a patient through preserving life, relieving pain and suffering, protecting against disability, and returning maximally effective functioning. If a prognosis of permanent unconsciousness is correct, however, continued treatment cannot confer such benefits. Pain and suffering are absent, as are joy, satisfaction, and pleasure. Disability is total and no return to an even minimal level of social or human functioning is possible."

There are also affirmative reasons why someone like Nancy might choose to forgo artificial nutrition and hydration under these circumstances. Dying is personal. And it is profound. For many, the thought of an ignoble end, steeped in decay, is abhorrent. . . .

Such conditions are, for many, humiliating to contemplate, as is visiting a prolonged and anguished vigil on one's parents, spouse, and children. A long, drawn-out death can have a debilitating effect on family members. For some, the idea of being remembered in their persistent vegetative states rather than as they were before their illness or accident may be very disturbing.

B

Although the right to be free of unwanted medical intervention, like other constitutionally protected interests, may not be absolute, no State interest could outweigh the rights of an individual in Nancy Cruzan's position. Whatever a State's possible interests in mandating life-support treatment under other circumstances, there is no good to be obtained here by Missouri's insistence that Nancy Cruzan remain on life-support systems if it is indeed her wish not to do so. Missouri does not claim, nor could it, that society as a whole will be benefited by Nancy's receiving medical treatment. No third party's situation will be improved and no harm to others will be averted.

The only state interest asserted here is a general interest in the preservation of life. But the State has no legitimate general interest in someone's life, completely abstracted from the interest of the person living that life, that could outweigh the person's choice to avoid medical treatment. . . . Thus, the State's general interest in life must accede to Nancy Cruzan's particularized and intense interest in self-determination in her choice of medical treatment. There is simply nothing legitimately within the State's purview to be gained by superseding her decision. . . .

III

This is not to say that the State has no legitimate interests to assert here. As the majority recognizes, Missouri has a *parens patriae* interest in providing Nancy Cruzan, now incompetent, with as accurate as possible a determination of how she would exercise her rights under these circumstances. Second, if and when it is determined that Nancy Cruzan would want to continue treatment, the State may legitimately assert an interest in providing that treatment. But *until* Nancy's wishes have been determined, the only state interest that may be asserted is an interest in safeguarding the accuracy of that determination.

Accuracy, therefore, must be our touchstone. Missouri may constitutionally impose only those procedural requirements that serve to enhance the accuracy of a determination of Nancy Cruzan's wishes or are at least consistent with an accurate determination. The Missouri "safeguard" that the Court upholds today does not meet that standard. The determination needed in this context is whether the incompetent person would choose to live in a persistent vegetative state on life-support or to avoid this medical treatment. Missouri's rule of decision imposes a markedly asymmetrical evidentiary burden. Only evidence of specific statements of treatment choice made by the patient when competent is admissible to support a finding that the patient, now in a persistent vegetative state, would wish to avoid further medical treatment. Moreover, this evidence must be clear and convincing. No proof is required to support a finding that the incompetent person would wish to continue treatment. . . .

B [A omitted]

Even more than its heightened evidentiary standard, the Missouri court's categorical exclusion of relevant evidence dispenses with any semblance of accurate factfinding. The court adverted to no evidence supporting its decision, but held that no clear and convincing, inherently reliable evidence had been presented to show that Nancy would want to avoid further treatment. In doing so, the court failed to consider statements Nancy had made to family members and a close friend. The court also failed to consider testimony from Nancy's mother and sister that they were certain that Nancy would want to discontinue artificial nutrition and hydration, even after the court found that Nancy's family was loving and without malignant motive. The court also failed to consider the conclusions of the guardian ad litem, appointed by the trial court, that there was clear and convincing evidence that Nancy would want to discontinue medical treatment and that this was in her best interests. The court did not specifically define what kind of evidence it would consider clear and convincing, but its general discussion suggests that only a living will or equivalently formal directive from the patient when competent would meet this standard.

Too few people execute living wills or equivalently formal directives for such an evidentiary rule to ensure adequately that the wishes of incompetent persons will be honored. While it might be a wise social policy to encourage people to furnish such instructions, no general conclusion about a patient's choice can be drawn from the absence of formalities. The probability of becoming irreversibly vegetative is so low that many people may not feel an urgency to marshal formal evidence of their preferences. Some may not wish to dwell on their own physical deterioration and mortality. Even someone with a resolute determination to avoid life-support under circumstances such as Nancy's would still need to know that such things as living wills exist and how to execute one. . . .

C

. . . Even if the Court had ruled that Missouri's rule of decision is unconstitutional, as I believe it should have, States would nevertheless remain free to fashion procedural protections to safeguard the interests of incompetents under these circumstances. The Constitution provides merely a framework here: protections must be genuinely aimed at ensuring decisions commensurate with the will of the patient, and must be reliable as instruments to that end. Of the many States which have instituted such protections, Missouri is virtually the only one to have fashioned a rule that lessens the likelihood of accurate determinations. . . .

D

Finally, I cannot agree with the majority that where it is not possible to determine what choice an imcompetent patient would make, a State's role as *parens patriae* permits the State automatically to make that choice itself.... A State's legitimate interest in safeguarding a patient's choice cannot be furthered by simply appropriating it.... A State's inability to discern an incompetent patient's choice still need not mean that a State is rendered powerless to protect that choice. But I would find that the Due Process Clause prohibits a State from doing more than that. A State may ensure that the person who makes the decision on the patient's behalf is the one whom the patient himself would have selected to make that choice for him. And a State may exclude from consideration anyone having improper motives. But a State generally must either repose the choice with the person whom the patient himself would most likely have chosen as proxy or leave the decision to the patient's family....

JUSTICE STEVENS, dissenting.

Our Constitution is born of the proposition that all legitimate governments must secure the equal right of every person to "Life, Liberty, and the pursuit of Happiness." In the ordinary case we quite naturally assume that these three ends are compatible, mutually enhancing, and perhaps even coincident.

The Court would make an exception here. It permits the State's abstract, undifferentiated interest in the preservation of life to overwhelm the best interests of Nancy Beth Cruzan, interests which would, according to an undisputed finding, be served by allowing her guardians to exercise her constitutional right to discontinue medical treatment. Ironically, the Court reaches this conclusion despite endorsing three significant propositions which should save it from any such dilemma. First, a competent individual's decision to refuse life-sustaining medical procedures is an aspect of liberty protected by the Due Process Clause of the Fourteenth Amendment. Second, upon a proper evidentiary showing, a qualified guardian may make that decision on behalf of an incompetent ward. Third, in answering the important question presented by this tragic case, it is wise "not to attempt by any general statement, to cover every possible phase of the subject." Together, these considerations suggest that Nancy Cruzan's liberty to be free from medical treatment must be understood in light of the facts and circumstances particular to her.

I would so hold: in my view the Constitution requires the State to care for Nancy Cruzan's life in a way that gives appropriate respect to her own best interests....

COURT ON PARENTAL CONSENT FOR TEENAGE ABORTIONS

June 25, 1990

The Supreme Court on June 25 said the states could require a woman under eighteen to inform one or both parents before obtaining an abortion as long as she had the alternative of seeking permission from a judge. By a 5-4 vote the Court upheld a Minnesota law requiring that in most cases both parents be notified, and by a 6-3 vote upheld an Ohio law requiring that one parent be informed.

The decisions in Hodgson v. Minnesota *and* Ohio v. Akron Center for Reproductive Health, *handed down on the last day of the 1989-1990 term, gave the states new leeway to regulate abortions. The rulings permitted parental-notification laws to go into effect in Georgia, Illinois, Nevada, and Nebraska, as well as in Minnesota and Ohio. Similar laws were already in effect in Arkansas, Utah, and West Virginia. Abortion foes praised the rulings and looked for more states to enact notification laws. Abortion-rights activists regarded the decisions requiring parental consent or court sanction as a defeat, contending that the laws were aimed more at inhibiting abortion than at promoting family involvement.*

However, the decisions were a rebuff to the Bush administration's effort to use the cases as a vehicle for overturning the 1973 Roe v. Wade *decision that made abortion legal and virtually unrestricted nationwide. Solicitor General Kenneth W. Starr had argued that the Supreme Court should at least find that minors had no fundamental right to abortion without their parents' knowledge. The Court's July 3, 1989, ruling in* Webster v. Reproductive Health Services *weakened but did not discard* Roe's *legal underpinnings. (Supreme Court's Decision on Webster Abortion Case, Historic Documents of 1989, p. 365)* Webster *had the effect of*

387

turning many abortion questions back to the states. After the decision, anti-abortion groups pushed state legislatures for more restrictions and made the issue a troublesome one for both state and national lawmakers, and for state governors who faced political difficulties over abortion legislation. (Veto of Idaho Bill Restricting Abortions, p. 215)

The last time the Supreme Court reviewed the legality of parental notification, in the 1987 case of Hartigan v. Zbaraz, *there was one court vacancy, and the justices split 4-4 on an Illinois statute requiring a minor to notify her parents before a physician performed an abortion. Eight years earlier, in* Bellotti v. Baird, *the Court struck down a Massachusetts parental-consent law and said a minor had to have access to a confidential, expeditious proceeding before a judge. The intent was that the teenager would have an opportunity to persuade the judge that she was mature and well-informed enough to make the abortion decision herself or that the abortion would be in her best interest.*

O'Connor's Position

The Minnesota case marked the first time that Justice Sandra Day O'Connor had voted to find any abortion restriction unconstitutional. She voted with the majority in holding that the state's two-parent requirement was invalid without a judicial bypass. That decision upheld a ruling by the U.S. Court of Appeals for the Eighth District, which includes Minnesota.

However, the Minnesota legislature, in passing the law, had added language stating that in the event it was blocked by a court challenge, another provision would take effect permitting the pregnant woman to seek a court order to proceed with the abortion. That provision resulted in a separate Supreme Court vote on the validity of the law with the judicial bypass provision. On that vote, O'Connor sided with a different majority to find the law constitutional.

Nine separate opinions were issued in the Minnesota and Ohio cases. The majority in the Minnesota case for striking down the two-parent rule without a judicial bypass were Justice John Paul Stevens, who wrote for the Court, Justices O'Connor, William J. Brennan, Jr., Thurgood Marshall, and Harry A. Blackmun. Voting for its constitutionality both with and without the bypass provision were Chief Justice William H. Rehnquist, Justices Byron R. White, Antonin Scalia, and Anthony M. Kennedy. O'Connor joined the dissenters of the first vote to form a majority on the second.

Parent Rights' Question

Stevens, in the Minnesota case, wrote that the Court had considered the constitutionality of statutes providing for parental consent or parental notification in six abortion cases during the past fourteen years but that none had involved two parents. "The requirement of notice to both of the pregnant minor's parents is not reasonably related to legitimate state interests," Stevens added, noting that Minnesota made no excep-

tion for a divorced parent, a non-custodial parent, or a biological parent who never married or lived with the pregnant girl's mother.

Kennedy wrote for the dissenting justices who wanted to uphold the two-parent requirement without a judicial alternative. He cited a "right of each parent to participate in the upbringing of her or his children." Kennedy said that a judicial alternative should not be demanded because a notice requirement, unlike a consent requirement, did not give another person the right to make a decision on behalf of the minor. Kennedy also wrote for the Court's 6-3 majority in the Ohio case that the one-parent notification, plus a forty-eight-hour waiting period, did not impose an undue or unconstitutional burden on a minor seeking an abortion. Stevens, who had often opposed abortion restrictions, voted with the conservative majority of Rehnquist, White, O'Connor, Scalia, and Kennedy to uphold the Ohio law.

Blackmun, in a dissent joined by Brennan and Marshall, assailed the Ohio law as filled with "strident and offensively restrictive provisions" that create a "pattern of obstacles in the path of the pregnant minor seeking to exercise her constitutional right to terminate a pregnancy." Blackmun, author of the 1973 Roe decision and the Court's chief critic of the 1989 Webster ruling, wrote that it seemed as if the Ohio legislature had said: "If the courts of the United States insist on upholding a limited right to abortion, let us make abortion as difficult as possible to obtain. . . . "

Following are excerpts from the Supreme Court's majority and dissenting opinions in the cases of Hodgson v. Minnesota and Ohio v. Akron Center for Reproductive Health Services, in which the Court on June 25, 1990, upheld the right of states to require parental notification by a minor seeking an abortion if she had the option of persuading a judge that she was mature enough to make the decision or that the abortion was in her best interest:

Nos. 88-1125 and 88-1309

Jane Hodgson, et al., Petitioners
v.
Minnesota et al.

} On writs of Certiorari to the United States Court of Appeals for the Eighth Circuit

Minnesota, et al., Petitioners
v.
Jane Hodgson et al.

} On writs of Certiorari to the United States Court of Appeals for the Eighth Circuit

[June 25, 1990]

JUSTICE STEVENS announced the judgment of the Court and delivered the opinion of the Court with respect to Parts I, II, IV, and VII, an opinion with respect to Part III in which JUSTICE BRENNAN joins, an opinion with respect to Parts V and VI in which JUSTICE O'CONNOR joins, and a dissenting opinion with respect to Part VIII.

A Minnesota statute, Minn. Stat. §§ 114.343(2)-(7) (1988), provides, with certain exceptions, that no abortion shall be performed on a woman under 18 years of age until at least 48 hours after both of her parents have been notified. In subdivisions 2-4 of the statute the notice is mandatory unless (1) the attending physician certifies that an immediate abortion is necessary to prevent the woman's death and there is insufficient time to provide the required notice; (2) both of her parents have consented in writing; or (3) the woman declares that she is a victim of parental abuse or neglect, in which event notice of her declaration must be given to the proper authorities. The United States Court of Appeals for the Eighth Circuit, sitting en banc, unanimously held this provision unconstitutional. In No. 88-1309, we granted the State's petition to review that holding. Subdivision 6 of the same statute provides that if a court enjoins the enforcement of subdivision 2, the same notice requirement shall be effective unless the pregnant woman obtains a court order permitting the abortion to proceed. By a vote of 7-3, the Court of Appeals upheld the constitutionality of subdivision 6. In No. 88-1125, we granted the plaintiffs' petition to review that holding.

For reasons that follow, we now conclude that the requirement of notice to both of the pregnant minor's parents is not reasonably related to legitimate state interests and that subdivision 2 is unconstitutional. A different majority of the Court, for reasons stated in separate opinions, concludes that subdivision 6 is constitutional. Accordingly, the judgment of the Court of Appeals in its entirety is affirmed.

I

The parental notice statute was enacted in 1981 as an amendment to the Minors' Consent to Health Services Act. . . .

The 1981 amendment qualified the authority of an "unemancipated minor" to give effective consent to an abortion by requiring that either her physician or an agent notify "the parent" personally or by certified mail at least 48 hours before the procedure is performed. . . .

. . . If the pregnant minor can convince "any judge of a court of competent jurisdiction" that she is "mature and capable of giving informed consent to the proposed abortion," or that an abortion without notice to both parents would be in her best interest, the court can authorize the physician to proceed without notice. The statute provides that the bypass procedure shall be confidential, that it shall be expedited, that the minor has a right to court-appointed counsel, and that she shall be afforded free access to the court "24 hours a day, seven days a week." An order denying an abortion can be appealed on an expedited basis, but an order authorizing an abortion without notification is not subject to appeal.

II

This litigation was commenced on July 30, 1981, two days before the effective date of the parental notification statute. The plaintiffs include two Minnesota doctors who specialize in obstetrics and gynecology, four clinics providing abortion and contraceptive services in metropolitan areas in Minnesota, six pregnant minors representing a class of pregnant minors, and the mother of a pregnant minor. Plaintiffs alleged that the statute violated the Due Process and Equal Protection Clauses of the Fourteenth Amendment and various provisions of the Minnesota Constitution.

Based on the allegations in their verified complaint, the District Court entered a temporary restraining order enjoining the enforcement of subdivision 2 of the statute. After a hearing, the court entered a preliminary injunction which still remains in effect. The District Court refused, however, to rule on the validity of the judicial bypass procedure in advance of trial.

In 1986, after a 5-week trial, the District Court concluded that both the two-parent notification requirement and the 48-hour waiting period were invalid.... The court declared the entire statute unconstitutional and enjoined the defendants from enforcing it.

A three-judge panel of the Court of Appeals affirmed....

The panel opinion was vacated and the Court of Appeals reheard the case en banc. The court unanimously and summarily rejected the State's submission that the two-parent notice requirement was constitutional without any bypass procedure. The majority concluded, however, that subdivision 6 of the statute was valid....

III

...A woman's decision to beget or bear a child is a component of her liberty that is protected by the Due Process Clause of the Fourteenth Amendment to the Constitution.... As we stated in *Planned Parenthood of Central Missouri* v. *Danforth* (1976), the right to make this decision "do[es] not mature and come into being magically only when one attains the state-defined age of majority." Thus, the constitutional protection against unjustified state intrusion into the process of deciding whether or not to bear a child extends to pregnant minors as well as adult women.

In cases involving abortion, as in cases involving the right to travel or the right to marry, the identification of the constitutionally protected interest is merely the beginning of the analysis. State regulation of travel and of marriage is obviously permissible even though a State may not categorically exclude nonresidents from its borders, or deny prisoners the right to marry. But the regulation of constitutionally protected decisions, such as where a person shall reside or whom he or she shall marry, must be predicated on legitimate state concerns other than disagreement with the choice the individual has made. In the abortion area, a State may have no obligation to spend its own money, or use its own facilities, to subsidize nontherapeutic abortions for minors or adults. A State's value judgment favoring childbirth over abortion may provide adequate support for decisions involving such allocation of public funds, but not for simply substituting a state decision for an individual decision that a woman has a right to make for herself. Otherwise, the interest in liberty protected by the Due Process Clause would be a nullity. A state policy favoring childbirth over abortion is not in itself a sufficient justification for overriding the woman's decision or for placing "obstacles—absolute or otherwise—in the pregnant woman's path to an abortion."

In these cases the State of Minnesota does not rest its defense of this statute on any such value judgment. Indeed, it affirmatively disavows that state interest as a basis for upholding this law. Moreover, it is clear that the state judges who have interpreted the statute in over 3,000 decisions implementing its bypass procedures have found no legislative intent to disfavor the decision to terminate a pregnancy. On the contrary, in all but a handful of cases they have approved such decisions. Because the Minnesota statute unquestionably places obstacles in the pregnant minor's path to an abortion, the State has the burden of establishing its constitutionality. Under any analysis, the Minnesota statute cannot be sustained if the obstacles it imposes are not reasonably related to legitimate state interests.

IV

The Court has considered the constitutionality of statutes providing for parental consent or parental notification in six abortion cases decided during the last 14 years. Although the Massachusetts statute reviewed in *Bellotti* v. *Baird* (1976) *(Bellotti I)*, and *Bellotti II* required the consent of both parents, and the Utah statute reviewed in *H. L.* v. *Matheson* (1981), required notice to "the parents," none of the opinions in any of those cases focused on the possible significance of making the consent or the notice requirement applicable to both parents instead of just one. In contrast, the arguments in these cases, as well as the extensive findings of the District Court, are directed primarily at that distinction. It is therefore appropriate to summarize these findings before addressing the constitutionality of the 48-hour waiting period or the two-parent notification requirement, particularly since none of the findings has been challenged in either this Court or the Court of Appeals. . . .

The District Court found—on the basis of extensive testimony at trial— that the two-parent notification requirement had particularly harmful effects on both the minor and the custodial parent when the parents were divorced or separated. Relations between the minor and absent parent were not reestablished as a result of the forced notification thereby often producing disappointment in the minor. . . . Moreover, "[t]he reaction of the custodial parent to the requirement of forced notification is often one of anger, resentment and frustration at the intrusion of the absent parent," and fear that notification will threaten the custody rights of the parent or otherwise promote intrafamily violence. Tragically, those fears were often realized. . . .

The District Court also found that the two-parent notification requirement had adverse effects in families in which the minor lives with both parents. These effects were particularly pronounced in the distressingly large number of cases in which family violence is a serious problem. The court found that many minors in Minnesota "live in fear of violence by family members" and "are, in fact, victims of rape, incest, neglect and violence." The District Court found that few minors can take advantage of the exception for a minor who declares that she is a victim of sexual or physical abuse because of the obligation to report the information to the authorities and the attendant loss of privacy. . . .

Scheduling petitions in the Minnesota court typically required minors to wait only two or three days for hearings. The District Court found, however, that the statutory waiting period of 48 hours was frequently compounded by a number of other factors that "commonly" created a delay of 72 hours, and, "in many cases" a delay of a week or more in effecting a decision to terminate a pregnancy. A delay of that magnitude increased the medical risk associated with the abortion procedure to "a statistically significant degree." . . .

V

Three separate but related interests—the interest in the welfare of the pregnant minor, the interest of the parents, and the interest of the family unit—are relevant to our consideration of the constitutionality of the 48-hour waiting period and the two-parent notification requirement.

The State has a strong and legitimate interest in the welfare of its young citizens, whose immaturity, inexperience, and lack of judgment may sometimes impair their ability to exercise their rights wisely. That interest, which justifies state-imposed requirements that a minor obtain his or her parent's consent before undergoing an operation, marrying, or entering military service, extends also to the minor's decision to terminate her pregnancy. Although the Court has held that parents may not exercise "an absolute, and possibly arbitrary, veto" over that decision, it has never challenged a State's reasonable judgment that the decision should be made after notification to and consultation with a parent. . . .

While the State has a legitimate interest in the creation and dissolution of the marriage contract, the family has a privacy interest in the upbringing and education of children and the intimacies of the marital relationship which is protected by the Constitution against undue state interference. . . . We have long held that there exists a "private realm of family life which the state cannot enter." . . .

VI

We think it is clear that a requirement that a minor wait 48 hours after notifying a single parent of her intention to get an abortion would reasonably further the legitimate state interest in ensuring that the minor's decision is knowing and intelligent. We have held that when a parent or another person has assumed "primary responsibility" for a minor's well-being, the State may properly enact "laws designed to aid discharge of that responsibility." *Ginsberg* v. *New York* (1968). To the extent that subdivision 2 of the Minnesota statute requires notification of only one parent, it does just that. The brief waiting period provides the parent the opportunity to consult with his or her spouse and a family physician, and it permits the parent to inquire into the competency of the doctor performing the abortion, discuss the religious or moral implications of the abortion decision, and provide the daughter needed guidance and counsel in evaluating the impact of the decision on her future. . . .

VII

It is equally clear that the requirement that *both* parents be notified, whether or not both wish to be notified or have assumed responsibility for the upbringing of the child, does not reasonably further any legitimate state interest. The usual justification for a parental consent or notification provision is that it supports the authority of a parent who is presumed to act in the minor's best interest and thereby assures that the minor's decision to terminate her pregnancy is knowing, intelligent, and deliberate. To the extent that such an interest is legitimate, it would be fully served by a requirement that the minor notify one parent who can then seek the counsel of his or her mate or any other party, when such advice and support is deemed necessary to help the child make a difficult decision. In the ideal family setting, of course, notice to either parent would normally constitute notice to both. A statute requiring two-parent notification would not further any state interest in those instances. In many families, however, the parent notified by the child would not notify the other parent. In those cases the State has no legitimate interest in questioning one parent's judgment that notice to the other parent would not assist the minor or in presuming that the parent who has assumed parental duties is incompetent to make decisions regarding the health and welfare of the child.

Not only does two-parent notification fail to serve any state interest with respect to functioning families, it disserves the state interest in protecting and assisting the minor with respect to dysfunctional families. The record reveals that in the thousands of dysfunctional families affected by this statute, the two-parent notice requirement proved positively harmful to the minor and her family. The testimony at trial established that this requirement . . . resulted in major trauma to the child, and often to a parent as well. . . .

VIII

The Court holds that the constitutional objection to the two-parent notice requirement is removed by the judicial bypass option provided in subdivision 6 of the Minnesota statute. I respectfully dissent from that holding. . . .

A judicial bypass that is designed to handle exceptions from a reasonable general rule, and thereby preserve the constitutionality of that rule, is quite different from a requirement that a minor—or a minor and one of her parents—must apply to a court for permission to avoid the application of a rule that is not reasonably related to legitimate state goals. A requirement that a minor acting with the consent of *both* parents apply to a court for permission to effectuate her decision clearly would constitute an unjustified official interference with the privacy of the minor and her family. The requirement that the bypass procedure must be invoked when the minor and one parent agree that the other parent should not be notified represents an equally unjustified governmental intrusion into the family's decisional process. . . .

The judgment of the Court of Appeals in its entirety is affirmed.

It is so ordered.

JUSTICE O'CONNOR, concurring in part and concurring in the judgment in part.

I

I join all but Parts III and VIII of JUSTICE STEVENS' opinion. While I agree with some of the central points made in Part III, I cannot join the broader discussion. I agree that the Court has characterized "[a] woman's decision to beget or to bear a child [as] a component of her liberty that is protected by the Due Process Clause of the Fourteenth Amendment to the Constitution." This Court extended that liberty interest to minors in *Bellotti* v. *Baird* (1979) and *Planned Parenthood of Central Missouri* v. *Danforth* (1976) albeit with some important limitations. . . .

It has been my understanding in this area that "[i]f the particular regulation does not 'unduly burde[n]' the fundamental right, . . . then our evaluation of that regulation is limited to our determination that the regulation rationally relates to a legitimate state purpose." *Akron* v. *Akron Center for Reproductive Health, Inc.* (1983) (O'CONNOR, J., dissenting); see also *Webster* v. *Reproductive Health Services* (1989) (O'CONNOR, J., concurring in part and concurring in judgment). It is with that understanding that I agree with JUSTICE STEVENS' statement that the "statute cannot be sustained if the obstacles it imposes are not reasonably related to legitimate state interests."

I agree with JUSTICE STEVENS that Minnesota has offered no sufficient justification for its interference with the family's decisionmaking processes created by subdivision 2-two-parent notification. Subdivision 2 is the most stringent notification statute in the country. . . .

The Minnesota exception to notification for minors who are victims of neglect or abuse is, in reality, a means of notifying the parents. As JUSTICE STEVENS points out, to avail herself of the neglect or abuse exception, the minor must report the abuse. A report requires the welfare agency to immediately "conduct an assessment." If the agency interviews the victim, it must notify the parent of the fact of the interview; if the parent is the subject of an investigation, he has a right of access to the record of the investigation. . . .

Minnesota's two-parent notice requirement is all the more unreasonable when one considers that only half of the minors in the state of Minnesota reside with both biological parents. . . . Given its broad sweep and its failure to serve the purposes asserted by the State in too many cases, I join the Court's striking of subdivision 2.

II

. . . Subdivision 6 passes constitutional muster because the interference with the internal operation of the family required by subdivision 2 simply does not exist where the minor can avoid notifying one or both parents by use of the bypass procedure.

JUSTICE MARSHALL, with whom JUSTICE BRENNAN and JUSTICE BLACKMUN join, concurring in part, concurring in the judgment in part, and dissenting in part.

I concur in Parts I, II, IV, and VII of JUSTICE STEVENS' opinion for the Court in No. 88-1309. Although I do not believe that the Constitution permits a State to require a minor to notify or consult with a parent before obtaining an abortion, I am in substantial agreement with the remainder of the reasoning in Part V of the Court's opinion. For the reasons stated by JUSTICE STEVENS, Minnesota's two-parent notification requirement is not even reasonably related to a legitimate state interest. Therefore, that requirement surely would not pass the strict scrutiny applicable to restrictions on a woman's fundamental right to have an abortion.

I dissent from the judgment of the Court in No. 88-1125, however, that the judicial bypass option renders the parental notification and 48-hour delay requirements constitutional. The bypass procedure cannot save those requirements because the bypass itself is unconstitutional both on its face and as applied. At the very least, this scheme substantially burdens a woman's right to privacy without advancing a compelling state interest. More significantly, in some instances it usurps a young woman's control over her own body by giving either a parent or a court the power effectively to veto her decision to have an abortion. . . .

II [I omitted]

I strongly disagree with the Court's conclusion that the State may constitutionally force a minor woman either to notify both parents (or in some cases only one parent) and then wait 48 hours before proceeding with an abortion, or disclose her intimate affairs to a judge and ask that he grant her permission to have an abortion. First, the parental notification and delay requirements significantly restrict a young woman's right to reproductive choice. I base my conclusion not on my intuition about the needs and attitudes of young women, but on a sizable and impressive collection of empirical data documenting the effects of parental notification statutes and of delaying an abortion. Second, the burdensome restrictions are not narrowly tailored to serve any compelling state interest. Finally . . . the judicial bypass procedure does not save the notice and delay requirements.

JUSTICE SCALIA, concurring in the judgment in part and dissenting in part.

. . . One will search in vain the document we are supposed to be construing for text that provides the basis for the argument over these distinctions; and will find in our society's tradition regarding abortion no hint that the distinctions are constitutionally relevant, much less any indication how a constitutional argument about them ought to be resolved. The random and unpredictable results of our consequently unchanneled individual views make it increasingly evident, Term after Term, that the tools for this job are not to be found in the lawyer's—and hence not in the judge's—workbox. I continue to dissent from this enterprise of devising an Abortion Code, and from the illusion that we have authority to do so.

JUSTICE KENNEDY, with whom THE CHIEF JUSTICE, JUSTICE WHITE, and JUSTICE SCALIA join, concurring in the judgment in part and dissenting in part.

. . . Today, the Court holds that a statute requiring a minor to notify both parents that she plans to have an abortion is not a permissible means of furthering the interest described with such specificity in *Bellotti II*. This conclusion, which no doubt will come as a surprise to most parents, is incompatible with our constitutional tradition and any acceptable notion of judicial review of legislative enactments. I dissent from the portion of the Court's judgment affirming the Court of Appeals conclusion that Minnesota [sic] two-parent notice statute is unconstitutional. . . .

II [I omitted]

The State identifies two interests served by the law. The first is the State's interest in the welfare of pregnant minors. The second is the State's interest in acknowledging and promoting the role of parents in the care and upbringing of their children. JUSTICE STEVENS, writing for two Members of the Court, acknowledges the legitimacy of the first interest, but decides that the second interest is somehow illegitimate, at least as to whichever parent a minor chooses not to notify. I cannot agree that the Constitution prevents a State from keeping both parents informed of the medical condition or medical treatment of their child under the terms and conditions of this statute. . . .

Protection of the right of each parent to participate in the upbringing of her or his own children is a further discrete interest that the State recognizes by the statute. The common law historically has given recognition to the right of parents, not merely to be notified of their children's actions, but to speak and act on their behalf. . . .

A State pursues a legitimate end under the Constitution when it attempts to foster and preserve the parent-child relation by giving all parents the opportunity to participate in the care and nurture of their children. We have held that parents have a liberty interest, protected by the Constitution, in having a reasonable opportunity to develop close relations with their children. We have recognized, of course, that there are limits to the constitutional right of parents to have custody of or to participate in decisions affecting their children. If a parent has relinquished the opportunity to develop a relation with the child, and his or her only link to the child is biological, the Constitution does not require a State to allow parental participation. But the fact that the Constitution does not protect the parent-child relationship in all circumstances does not mean that the State cannot attempt to foster parental participation where the Constitution does not demand that it do so. . . .

Minnesota has done no more than act upon the common-sense proposition that, in assisting their daughter in deciding whether to have an abortion, parents can best fulfill their roles if they have the same information about their own child's medical condition and medical choices as the child's doctor does; and that to deny parents this knowledge is to risk, or perpetuate, estrangement or alienation from the child when she is in the greatest need of parental guidance and support. The Court does the State, and our constitutional tradition, sad disservice by impugning the legitimacy of these elemental objectives. . . .

No. 88-805

Ohio, Appellant *v.* Akron Center for Reproductive Health et al.	On appeal from the United States Court of Appeals for the Sixth Circuit

[June 25, 1990]

JUSTICE KENNEDY announced the judgment of the Court and delivered the opinion of the Court with respect to Parts I, II, III, and IV, and an opinion with respect to Part V, in which THE CHIEF JUSTICE, JUSTICE WHITE, and JUSTICE SCALIA join.

The Court of Appeals held invalid an Ohio statute that, with certain exceptions, prohibits any person from performing an abortion on an unmarried, unemancipated, minor woman absent notice to one of the woman's parents or a court order of approval. We reverse, for we determine that the statute accords with our precedents on parental notice and consent in the abortion context and does not violate the Fourteenth Amendment.

I

A

The Ohio Legislature, in November 1985, enacted Amended Substitute House Bill 319 (H.B. 319). . . . Section 2919.12(B), the cornerstone of this legislation, makes it a criminal offense, except in four specified circumstances, for a physician or other person to perform an abortion on an unmarried and unemancipated woman under eighteen years of age. . . .

The first and second circumstances in which a physician may perform an abortion relate to parental notice and consent. First, a physician may perform an abortion if he provides "at least twenty-four hours actual notice, in person or by telephone," to one of the women's [sic] parents (or her guardian or custodian) of his intention to perform the abortion. The physician, as an alternative, may notify a minor's adult brother, sister, stepparent, or grandparent, if the minor and the other relative each file an affidavit in the juvenile court stating that the minor fears physical, sexual, or severe emotional abuse from one of her parents. If the physician cannot give the notice "after a reasonable effort," he may perform the abortion after "at least forty-eight hours constructive notice" by both ordinary and certified mail. Second, a physician may perform an abortion on the minor if one of her parents (or her guardian or custodian) has consented to the abortion in writing.

The third and fourth circumstances depend on a judicial procedure that allows a minor to bypass the notice and consent provisions just described. The statute allows a physician to perform an abortion without notifying one of the minor's parents or receiving the parent's consent if a juvenile court issues an order authorizing the minor to consent, or if a juvenile court or court of appeals, by its inaction, provides constructive authorization for the minor to consent.

The bypass procedure requires the minor to file a complaint in the juvenile court, stating (1) that she is pregnant; (2) that she is unmarried, under 18 years of age, and unemancipated; (3) that she desires to have an abortion without notifying one of her parents; (4) that she has sufficient maturity and information to make an intelligent decision whether to have an abortion without such notice, *or* that one of her parents has engaged in a pattern of physical, sexual, or emotional abuse against her, *or* that notice is not in her best interests; and (5) that she has or has not retained an attorney. . . .

The juvenile court must hold a hearing at the earliest possible time, but not later than the fifth business day after the minor files the complaint. The court must render its decision immediately after the conclusion of the hearing. Failure to hold the hearing within this time results in constructive authorization for the minor to consent to the abortion. At the hearing the court must appoint a guardian ad litem and an attorney to represent the minor if she has not retained her own counsel. The minor must prove her allegation of maturity, pattern of abuse, or best interests by clear and convincing evidence, and the juvenile court must conduct the hearing to preserve the anonymity of the complainant, keeping all papers confidential.

The minor has the right to expedited review. The statute provides that, within four days after the minor files a notice of appeal, the clerk of the juvenile court shall deliver the notice of appeal and record to the state court of appeals. The clerk of the court of appeals dockets the appeal upon receipt of these items. The minor must file her brief within four days after the docketing. If she desires an oral argument, the court of appeals must hold one within five days after the docketing and must issue a decision immediately after oral argument. If she waives the right to an oral argument, the court of appeals must issue a decision within five days after the docketing. If the court of appeals does not comply with these time limits, a constructive order results authorizing the minor to consent to the abortion.

B

Appellees in this action include the Akron Center for Reproductive Health, a facility that provides abortions; Max Pierre Gaujean, M.D., a physician who performs abortions at the Akron Center; and Rachel Roe, an unmarried, unemancipated minor woman, who sought an abortion at the facility. In March 1986, days before the effective date of H.B. 319, appellees and others brought a facial challenge to the constitutionality of the statute in the United States District Court for the Northern District of Ohio. The District Court, after various proceedings, issued a preliminary injunction and later a permanent injunction preventing the State of Ohio from enforcing the statute.

The Court of Appeals for the Sixth Circuit affirmed, concluding that H.B. 319 had six constitutional defects. These points, discussed below, related to the sufficiency of the expedited procedures, the guarantee of anonymity, the constructive authorization provisions, the clear and convincing evidence standard, the pleading requirements, and the physician's personal obligation to give notice to one of the minor's parents. The State of Ohio challenges the Court of Appeals' decision in its entirety. Appellees seek affirmance on the grounds adopted by the Court of Appeals and on other grounds as well.

II

We have decided five cases addressing the constitutionality of parental notice or parental consent statutes in the abortion context. See *Planned Parenthood of Central Missouri* v. *Danforth* (1976); *Bellotti* v. *Baird* (1979); *H. L.* v. *Matheson* (1981); *Planned Parenthood Assn. of Kansas City, Mo., Inc.* v. *Ashcroft* (1983); *Akron* v. *Akron Center for Reproductive Health, Inc.* (1983). We do not need to determine whether a statute that does not accord with these cases would violate the Constitution, for we conclude that H. B. 319 is consistent with them.

A

This dispute turns, to a large extent, on the adequacy of H. B. 319's judicial bypass procedure. In analyzing this aspect of the dispute, we note that, although our cases have required bypass procedures for parental consent statutes, we have not decided whether parental notice statutes must contain such procedures. We leave the question open, because, whether or not the Fourteenth Amendment requires notice statutes to contain bypass procedures, H. B. 319's bypass procedure meets the requirements identified for parental consent statutes in *Danforth, Bellotti, Ashcroft,* and *Akron. Danforth* established that, in order to prevent another person from having an absolute veto power over a minor's decision to have an abortion, a State must provide some sort of bypass procedure if it elects to require parental consent. . . .

The plurality opinion in *Bellotti* stated four criteria that a bypass procedure in a consent statute must satisfy. Appellees contend that the bypass procedure does not satisfy these criteria. We disagree. First, the *Bellotti* plurality indicated that the procedure must allow the minor to show that she possesses the maturity and information to make her abortion decision, in consultation with her physician, without regard to her parents' wishes. . . . In the case now before us, we have no difficulty concluding that H. B. 319 allows a minor to show maturity in conformity with the plurality opinion in *Bellotti.* . . .

Second, the *Bellotti* plurality indicated that the procedure must allow the minor to show that, even if she cannot make the abortion decision by herself, "the desired abortion would be in her best interests." We believe that H. B. 319 satisfies the *Bellotti* language as quoted. The statute requires the juvenile court to authorize the minor's consent where the court determines that the abortion is in the minor's best interest and in cases where the minor has shown a pattern of physical, sexual, or emotional abuse.

Third, the *Bellotti* plurality indicated that the procedure must insure the minor's anonymity. Section 2151.85(D) provides that "[t]he [juvenile] court shall not notify the parents, guardian, or custodian of the complainant that she is pregnant or that she wants to have an abortion." Section 2151.85(F) further states:

> "Each hearing under this section shall be conducted in a manner that will preserve the anonymity of the complainant. The complaint and all other papers and records that pertain to an action commenced under this section shall be kept confidential and are not public records."

Section 2505.073(B), in a similar fashion, requires the court of appeals to preserve the minor's anonymity and confidentiality of all papers on appeal. The State, in addition, makes it a criminal offense for an employee to disclose documents not designated as public records. . . .

Fourth, the *Bellotti* plurality indicated that courts must conduct a bypass procedure with expedition to allow the minor an effective opportunity to obtain the abortion. H. B. 319 . . . requires the trial court to make its decision within five "business day[s]" after the minor files her com-plaint, § 2151.85(B)(1); requires the court of appeals to docket an appeal within four "days" after the minor files a notice of appeal, § 2505.073(A); and requires the court of appeals to render a decision within five "days" after docketing the appeal.

The District Court and the Court of Appeals assumed that all of the references to days ... meant business days as opposed to calendar days. They calculated, as a result, that the procedure could take up to 22 calendar days because the minor could file at a time during the year in which the 14 business days needed for the bypass procedure would encompass three Saturdays, three Sundays, and two legal holidays.... Interpreting the term "days" in § 2505.073(A) to mean business days instead of calendar days seems inappropriate and unnecessary because of the express and contrasting use of "business day[s]" in § 2151.85(B)(1)....
The Court of Appeals should not have invalidated the Ohio statute on a facial challenge based upon a worst-case analysis that may never occur....
Moreover, under our precedents, the mere possibility that the procedure may require up to twenty-two days in a rare case is plainly insufficient to invalidate the statute on its face. *Ashcroft,* for example, upheld a Missouri statute that contained a bypass procedure that could require 17 calendar days plus a sufficient time for deliberation and decisionmaking at both the trial and appellate levels....

B

Appellees ... challenge the constructive authorization provisions in H. B. 319, which enable a minor to obtain an abortion without notifying one of her parents if either the juvenile court or the court of appeals fails to act within the prescribed time limits. They speculate that the absence of an affirmative order when a court fails to process the minor's complaint will deter the physician from acting.

We discern no constitutional defect in the statute. Absent a demon-strated pattern of abuse or defiance, a State may expect that its judges will follow mandated procedural requirements. There is no showing that the time limitations imposed by H. B. 319 will be ignored....

III

Appellees contend our inquiry does not end even if we decide that H. B. 319 conforms to *Danforth, Bellotti, Matheson, Ashcroft,* and *Akron.* They maintain that H. B. 319 gives a minor a state law substantive right "to avoid unnecessary or hostile parental involvement" if she can demonstrate that her maturity or best interests favor abortion without notifying one of her parents. They argue that H. B. 319 deprives the minor of this right without due process because the pleading requirements, the alleged lack of expedition and anonymity, and the clear and convincing evidence standard make the bypass procedure unfair. See *Mathews* v. *Eldridge* (1976). We find no merit in this argument.

The confidentiality provisions, the expedited procedures, and the pleading form requirements, on their face, satisfy the dictates of minimal due process. We see little risk of erroneous deprivation under these provisions and no need to require additional procedural safeguards. The clear and convincing evidence standard, for reasons we have described, does not place an unconstitutional burden on the types of proof to be presented. The minor is assisted by an attorney and a guardian ad litem and the proceeding is *ex parte*. The standard ensures that the judge will take special care in deciding whether the minor's consent to an abortion should proceed without parental notification. . . .

IV

Appellees, as a final matter, contend that we should invalidate H. B. 319 in its entirety because the statute requires the parental notice to be given by the physician who is to perform the abortion. In *Akron*, the court found unconstitutional a requirement that the attending physician provide the information and counseling relevant to informed consent. Although the Court did not disapprove of informing a woman of the health risks of an abortion, it explained that "[t]he State's interest is in ensuring that the woman's consent is informed and unpressured; the critical factor is whether she obtains the necessary information and counseling from a qualified person, not the identity of the person from whom she obtains it." Appellees maintain, in a similar fashion, that Ohio has no reason for requiring the minor's physician, rather than some other qualified person, to notify one of the minor's parents.

Appellees, however, have failed to consider our precedent on this matter. We upheld, in *Matheson*, a statute that required a physician to notify the minor's parents. The distinction between notifying a minor's parents and informing a woman of the routine risks of an abortion has ample justification. . . . We continue to believe that a State may require the physician himself or herself to take reasonable steps to notify a minor's parent because the parent often will provide important medical data to the physician. . . .

V

The Ohio statute, in sum, does not impose an undue, or otherwise unconstitutional, burden on a minor seeking an abortion. We believe, in addition, that the legislature acted in a rational matter in enacting H. B. 319. . . . It is both rational and fair for the State to conclude that, in most instances, the family will strive to give a lonely or even terrified minor advice that is both compassionate and mature. The statute in issue here is a rational way to further those ends. It would deny all dignity to the family to say that the State cannot take this reasonable step in regulating its health professions to ensure that, in most cases, a young woman will receive guidance and understanding from a parent. We uphold H. B. 319 on its face and reverse the Court of Appeals.

It is so ordered.

JUSTICE SCALIA, concurring.

I join the opinion of the Court, because I agree that the Ohio statute neither deprives minors of procedural due process nor contradicts our holdings regarding the constitutional right to abortion. I continue to believe, however, as I said in my separate concurrence last Term in *Webster* v. *Reproductive Health Services,* that the Constitution contains no right to abortion. It is not to be found in the longstanding traditions of our society, nor can it be logically deduced from the text of the Constitution.... Leaving this matter to the political process is not only legally correct, it is pragmatically so. That alone—and not lawyerly dissection of federal judicial precedents—can produce compromises satisfying a sufficient mass of the electorate that this deeply felt issue will cease distorting the remainder of our democratic process. The Court should end its disruptive intrusion into this field as soon as possible.

JUSTICE STEVENS, concurring in part and concurring in the judgment.

As the Court emphasizes, appellees have challenged the Ohio statute only on its face. The State may presume that, in most of its applications, the statute will reasonably further its legitimate interest in protecting the welfare of its minor citizens. In some of its applications, however, the one-parent notice requirement will not reasonably further that interest. There will be exceptional situations in which notice will cause a realistic risk of physical harm to the pregnant woman, will cause trauma to an ill parent, or will enable the parent to prevent the abortion for reasons that are unrelated to the best interests of the minor. The Ohio statute recognizes that possibility by providing a judicial bypass. The question in this case is whether that statutory protection for the exceptional case is so obviously inadequate that the entire statute should be invalidated. I am not willing to reach that conclusion before the statute has been implemented and the significance of its restrictions evaluated in the light of its administration. I therefore agree that the Court of Appeals' judgment must be reversed and I join Parts I-IV of the Court's opinion....

JUSTICE BLACKMUN, with whom JUSTICE BRENNAN and JUSTICE MARSHALL join, dissenting.

I

... "Any independent interest the parent may have in the termination of the minor daughter's pregnancy is no more weighty than the right of privacy of the competent minor mature enough to have become pregnant."

"The abortion decision differs in important ways from other decisions that may be made during minority. The need to protect the constitutional right and the unique nature of the abortion decision, especially when made by a minor, require a State to act with *particular sensitivity* when it legislates to foster parental involvement in this matter ... because "there are few situations in which denying a minor the right to make an important decision will have consequences so grave and indelible." ...

The State of Ohio has acted with particular *in*sensitivity in enacting the statute the Court today upholds. Rather than create a judicial-bypass system that reflects the sensitivity necessary when dealing with a minor making this deeply intimate decision, Ohio has created a tortuous maze. Moreover, the State has failed utterly to show that it has any significant state interest in deliberately placing its pattern of obstacles in the path of the pregnant minor seeking to exercise her constitutional right to terminate a pregnancy....

II

... The language of the Ohio statute purports to follow the standards for a bypass procedure that are set forth in *Bellotti II,* but at each stage along the way, the statute deliberately places "substantial state-created obstacles in the pregnant [minor's] path to an abortion," in the legislative hope that she will stumble, perhaps fall, and at least ensuring that she "conquer a multi-faceted obstacle course" before she is able to exercise her constitutional right to an abortion....

A

The obstacle course begins when the minor first enters the courthouse to fill out the complaint forms. The "pleasing trap," as it appropriately was described by the Court of Appeals, requires the minor to choose among three forms. The first alleges *only* maturity; the second alleges *only* that the abortion is in her best interest. Only if the minor chooses the third form, which alleges both, may the minor attempt to prove both maturity *and* best interest as is her right under *Bellotti II.* The majority makes light of what it acknowledges might be "some initial confusion" of the unsophisticated minor who is trying to deal with an unfamiliar and mystifying court system on an intensely intimate matter....

The majority fails to elucidate *any* state interest in setting up this barricade for the young pregnant woman—a barricade that will "serve only to confuse ... her and to heighten her anxiety." The justification the State put forward before the Court of Appeals was the "absurd contention that '[a]ny minor claiming to be mature and well enough informed to independently make such an important decision as an abortion should also be mature enough to file her complaint under [the appropriate subsection].' " This proffered "justification" is even more harsh than the Court of Appeals noted.... Surely, the goal of the court proceeding is to assist, not to entrap, the young pregnant woman....

B

As the pregnant minor attempts to find her way through the labyrinth set up by the State of Ohio, she encounters yet another obstruction.... Far from keeping the identity of the minor anonymous, the statute requires the minor to sign her full name and the name of one of her parents on the complaint form.... Acknowledging that "[c]onfidentiality differs from anonymity," the majority simply asserts that "complete anonymity" is not "critical." That easy conclusion is irreconcilable with *Bellotti*'s anonymity requirement....

As the District Court pointed out, there are no indications of how a clerk's office, large or small, is to ensure that the records of abortion cases will be distinguished from the records of all other cases that are available to the public.... This Court is well aware that, unless special care is taken, court documents of an intimate nature will find their way to the press and public.... I would not permit the State of Ohio to force a minor to forgo her anonymity in order to obtain a waiver of the parental-notification requirement.

C

Because a "pregnant adolescent ... cannot preserve for long the possibility of aborting, which effectively expires in a matter of weeks from the onset of pregnancy," this Court has required that the State "must assure" that the "resolution of the issue, and any appeals that may follow, will be completed with ... sufficient expedition to provide an effective opportunity for an abortion to be obtained." ... Ohio's judicial-bypass procedure can consume up to three weeks of a young woman's pregnancy. I would join the Sixth Circuit, the District Court, and the other federal courts that have held that a time span of this length fails to guarantee a sufficiently expedited procedure....

D

The Ohio statute provides that if the juvenile or appellate courts fail to act within the statutory time frame, an abortion without parental notification is "constructively" authorized. Although Ohio's Legislature may have intended this provision to expedite the bypass procedure, the confusion that will result from the constructive-authorization provision will add further delay to the judicial-bypass proceeding, and is yet one more obstruction in the path of the pregnant minor....

E

If the minor is able to wend her way through the intricate course of preliminaries Ohio has set up for her and at last reaches the court proceeding, the State shackles her even more tightly with still another "extra layer and burden of regulation on the abortion decision." The minor must demonstrate by "clear and convincing evidence" either (1) her maturity; (2) or that one of her parents has engaged in a pattern of physical, sexual, or emotional abuse against her; or (3) that notice to a parent is not in her best interest." ...

By imposing such a stringent standard of proof, this Ohio statute improperly places the risk of an erroneous decision on the minor, the very person whose fundamental right is at stake.... Even if the judge is satisfied that the minor is mature or that an abortion is in her best interest, the court may not authorize the procedure unless it additionally finds that the evidence meets a "clear and convincing" standard of proof....

Although I think the provision is constitutionally infirm for all minors, I am particularly concerned about the effect it will have on sexually or physically abused minors. I agree that parental interest in the welfare of their children is "particularly strong where a *normal* family relationship exists." ...

Sadly, not all children in our country are fortunate enough to be members of loving families. For too many young pregnant women, parental involvement in this most intimate decision threatens harm, rather than promises comfort....

IV [III omitted]

... The underlying nature of the Ohio statute is proclaimed by its strident and offensively restrictive provisions. It is as though the Legislature said: "If the courts of the United States insist on upholding a limited right to an abortion, let us make that abortion as difficult as possible to obtain" because, basically, whether on professed moral or religious grounds or whatever, "we believe that is the way it must be." This often may be the way legislation is enacted, but few are the instances where the injustice is so evident and the impediments so gross as those inflicted by the Ohio Legislature on these vulnerable and powerless young women.

PRESIDENT BUSH'S RETREAT FROM NO-TAXES PLEDGE

June 26, 29, and October 2, 1990

President George Bush retreated June 26 from his 1988 presidential campaign pledge not to raise taxes. The president conceded in a brief written statement that, among other measures, "tax revenue increases" were required to assure a bipartisan agreement for bringing the federal deficit under control. His shift in position took the nation by surprise, and angered some Republicans in Congress who faced mid-term elections. Many of them believed that his no-tax stand gave their party its strongest voter appeal.

Robert S. Walker, R-Pa., a House deputy whip, quickly got more than a hundred Republican representatives to sign a letter to Bush saying that they were "stunned" by his remarks and found a tax increase "unacceptable." Walker himself called Bush's statement "a dumb trial balloon." House Speaker Thomas S. Foley and most of the other Democratic leaders in Congress refrained from gloating, but Rep. Beryl Anthony, Jr., D-Ark., chairman of the Democratic Congressional Campaign Committee, said: "This is an admission that the Republican economic policies of the last ten years were a dismal failure."

At a White House news conference three days later, Bush defended his change of mind as "a necessary step to get budget negotiations moving." Apparently worried about a worsening economy and rising debt projections, he met on May 6 with top congressional leaders to discuss the possibility of budget negotiations between them and key White House staff members. Those "summit" talks began May 15 behind closed doors but got off to a slow start.

Some commentators insisted that the talks had been preordained by the federal budget for fiscal year 1991 that Bush submitted to Congress January 29. It projected revenues falling $64.7 billion short of meeting $1.2 trillion in requested expenditures. Democrats, in control of both houses of Congress, argued that Bush's figures relied on overly optimistic economic projections, and the Congressional Budget Office projected a deficit of $130 billion. Moreover, the Democratic leadership wanted to cut defense spending more, and domestic spending less, than the president requested.

Long Negotiations

The negotiating mood turned optimistic when Bush dropped his no-tax pledge, but not for long. On July 16 the administration released new estimates based on a slowing economy. They forecast a $231.4 billion deficit for fiscal 1991 if agreement could not be reached on far deeper spending cuts. In that event, said Richard G. Darman, director of the Office of Management and Budget (OMB), $100 billion in across-the-board cuts of all government programs might be required on October 1, the start of the new fiscal year, to meet requirements of the Gramm-Rudman deficit-reduction law.

Despite Darman's dire prediction, rank-and-file Republicans in the House defied the White House and their own leadership to approve a nonbinding resolution opposing any new taxes to reduce the deficit. Their revolt forced the president to rely more than ever on congressional Democrats to conclude an agreement. The Democrats used their added leverage during long negotiating sessions through August and September to put a strong Democratic stamp on the budget, including higher taxes on wealthy Americans. Working against a deadline of midnight September 30, the negotiators came up with a budget package that could cut the deficit by nearly $500 billion over five years and by $40.1 billion in fiscal 1991—except for the unknown costs of maintaining a large military force in Saudi Arabia to deter Iraqi aggression. (Iraqi Invasion of Kuwait, p. 533)

At 2 p.m. EDT that day, a Sunday, Bush appeared with several congressional leaders in the White House Rose Garden to announce the agreement. That evening the House and Senate passed a resolution to keep the government running for a few days until they had time to act on the agreement, and meanwhile suspend Gramm-Rudman cuts.

House Rejection

In a televised address to the nation on October 2, the president appealed for support for the budget compromise. George Mitchell of Maine, the Senate majority leader, followed with a speech giving the congressional Democratic leadership's endorsement of the agreement. But three days later the House rejected it by a decisive vote of 247 to 179. The defeat resulted from Democrats who objected to several tax provisions and costlier Medicare benefits aligning themselves with Republican foes of new taxes.

This blow to the White House and congressional leaders of both parties confused all attempts to work out a new agreement. To put pressure on Congress to pass a budget bill, Bush on October 6 vetoed a new continuing resolution, causing the government to close many of its offices and close down nonessential services. He wavered in statements he made on successive days as to whether he would hold out for a long-sought cut in the capital gains tax, which Democrats opposed, and whether he would accede to their plan for raising the top income tax rate on wealthy taxpayers.

Finally, as a new agreement began to take shape, the president on October 19 agreed to sign a resolution for a temporary resumption of government spending. Working almost round the clock, Congress October 27 approved a revised budget package of tax increases and spending cuts totaling $41.4 billion in fiscal 1991 and $492 billion over five years. The House vote of 228 to 200 came shortly before dawn, followed by a Senate vote of 54 to 45 the same day. Congress then recessed, ending the 1990 session only ten days before congressional elections.

In Honolulu President Bush said upon hearing the news of the congressional action, "There were some things in it [the budget bill] I had to gag and digest." But he signed the legislation into law November 5, saying that "the end product is a compromise that merits enactment." Within a month, the Congressional Budget Office estimated that the deficit would keep growing despite the new law.

Tax Stand and the GOP

As for the long, drawn-out process of approving a budget, Lloyd Bentsen, a Texas Democrat and chairman of the Senate Finance Committee, said: "The American people deserved better than that. They're tired of this chaos." Polls and other barometers of opinion indicated that the public blamed both the president and Congress for the confusion. However, political analysts generally concluded that Republicans, and especially Bush, had been harmed more than the Democrats. The president not only reneged on his no-tax pledge but often wavered over accepting higher personal tax rates for the rich in return for a cut in capital gains taxes.

The Democratic party, apparently with some success, sought to portray Bush as a defender of the rich at the expense of the poor. That image may have caused Bush's popularity ratings to drop in all the major polls. In a New York Times-CBS News poll conducted in October, 52 percent of those surveyed disapproved of the president's handling of the economy generally, and 58 percent disapproved of his handling of the federal budget deficit. Comparable figures in August were 44 percent and 51 percent. In some polls, the president's overall job rating slipped below 50 percent for the first time in his presidency.

No issue had defined Bush's candidacy and his presidency so strongly as his no-tax pledge. Probably the most repeated phrase he spoke in the presidential campaign was, "Read my lips: No new taxes." The line was *from a passage in his acceptance speech at the Republican National Convention in Houston, August 18, 1988: "The Congress will push me to raise taxes, and I'll say no, and they'll push again, and I'll say to them: 'Read my lips; No new taxes.'"*

Following are statements issued June 26, 1990, by President George Bush specifying a need for tax increases, by Senate Republican leader Bob Dole of Kansas endorsing that view, and by Rep. Beryl Anthony, Jr., chairman of the Democratic Congressional Campaign Committee, saying that Bush's statement was an admission of Republican economic failure; excerpts from a White House news conference June 29 in which Bush defended his decision; and the text of his televised address October 2 appealing for support for a bipartisan budget agreement that contained tax increases:

BUSH STATEMENT

I met this morning with the bipartisan leadership—the Speaker, the Senate Majority Leader, the Senate Republican Leader, the House Majority Leader and the House Republican Leader—to review the status of the deficit-reduction negotiations.

It is clear to me that both the size of the deficit problem and the need for a package that can be enacted require all of the following: entitlement and mandatory program reform; tax revenue increases; growth incentives; discretionary spending reductions; orderly reductions in defense expenditures; and budget process reform—to assure that any Bipartisan agreement is enforceable and that the deficit problem is brought under responsible control. The Bipartisan leadership agree with me on these points.

The budget negotiations will resume promptly with a view toward reaching substantive agreement as quickly as possible.

DOLE STATEMENT

President Bush today took the next logical step in budget negotiations when he called for a package that contains entitlement reform, growth incentives, discretionary spending reductions, defense cuts, budget reform and yes—tax revenue increases. His remarks are consistent with the original summit ground rules to put everything on the table with no preconditions.

Now comes the really hard part: getting down to specific spending and revenue proposals. If we are going to make any progress on this difficult task, everyone is going to have to work together—Republicans and Democrats, House and Senate, Congress and the Administration.

After this morning's meeting we have a tacit understanding to reach agreement on a budget package by mid-July. We're now on the 20 yard line ... only 80 yards left to go.

ANTHONY STATEMENT

President Bush's statement today that taxes are necessary to solve the budget crisis is an admission, finally, that the Republican economic policies of the last 10 years were a dismal failure. These policies, coupled with the administration's lax enforcement of the S&L industry and HUD and the subsequent expansive scandals, have finally backed the president into a well-deserved corner.

President Bush tried to fool the voters in 1988 about taxes, but he and GOP congressional candidates can no longer demagogue on this issue and try to deceive the American people. The voters are in no mood to hear false promises. This sudden case of honesty by President Bush has already caused problems in his own party. Ed Rollins, head of the GOP House Campaign Committee, has said this admission by Bush will result in election day losses. The politics of deception practiced by the GOP in the 1980s when dealing with taxes has now deeply divided the Republican Party.

NEWS CONFERENCE

President Bush: We now estimate a deficit of over $150 billion in fiscal 1991, not counting the costs of the savings and loan cleanup. And this means that unless Congress acts, there will be a cutoff in October of nearly $100 billion in government services under the sequester provisions of the Gramm-Rudman-Hollings [law].

The potential results? Draconian cuts in defense, student grants and a wide array of other necessary domestic services. And to avoid this, tough decisions must be made. And leadership is needed. And that is exactly what administration officials are seeking to provide and, indeed, I believe, are providing.

The budget negotiations now under way are a make-or-break effort at responsible government. The congressional budgeting process must succeed, and the negotiators are facing tough questions about where to make cuts and where to raise the revenues. And these are not decisions that anyone relishes.

They are decisions that Democrats and Republicans alike have got to face with candor and courage.

And frankly, I believe that ultimately good politics is rooted in good government. And I'm optimistic that we can get a budget agreement legislated which not only tells the world that America puts its fiscal house in order, but also will garner the full support of the American people. . . .

Q: Mr. President, I'd like to ask you about your reversal of "no new taxes." Do you consider that a betrayal of your promise, and what do you say to Republicans who complained that you've robbed them of the same campaign issue that helped get you elected?

P: Well, I don't — I think what I consider it is a necessary step to get stalled budget negotiations moving. And I am very encouraged with the approach taken now by Republicans and Democrats in this—in these important discussions that are going on. I'm not going to discuss details, what I'll accept and what I won't accept, but things are moving, and I think that much more important today is getting this deficit down, continuing economic expansion and employment in this country. So that's the way I'd respond to it.

Q: Mr. President, but do you believe it will hurt your credibility?

P: No, not in the long run.

Q: Why not? What people—

P: Because what people are interested in are jobs, economic growth. People know this deficit is bad. People know that we're going to have to take some action, and that's why I think not.

Q: Well, what will you say to the American people—

P: I'll say I take a look at a new situation, I see an enormous deficit, I see a savings and loan problem out there that has to be resolved, and like Abraham Lincoln said, I'll think anew. I'm not violating or getting away from my fundamental conviction on taxes, anything of that nature. Not in the least. But what I've said is on the table, and let's see where we go. But we've got a different—we've got a very important national problem, and I think the president owes the people his—his judgment at the moment he has to address that problem, and that's exactly what I'm trying to do. And look, I knew I'd catch some flak on this decision, or just those two words, but I've got to do what I think is right and then I'll ask the people for support. But more important than posturing now, or even negotiating, is the result—do we continue to provide jobs for the American people and do we continue to provide economic growth, and do we try to stop saddling the generations on the way up, and the young people, with absolutely unacceptable deficits?

Q: Could you clarify what seems to be a fuzzing up of the issue by some Republicans who are trying to say that your new statement isn't new? Are you telling the American people that this budget outcome is going to be higher taxes?

P: I'm telling the people that there are negotiations going on right now, and there are no preconditions, and everything's on the table. And we will see where we come out, and when we get an agreement that is supported by Democrats and Republicans alike, I will then—and if I think it's a good agreement—I will then tell the American people, clearly, why they need to support it, what's at stake for them in terms of jobs, a continued growth in this economy.

Q: But you're saying—right—you're not saying it. You're not saying: We have to raise taxes. Why aren't you saying that?

P: Oh, I'll tell you—sorry, I missed your point—we agreed with the Democratic leaders that we would not discuss the details of what's going on in these discussions, and we're not going to do that.

So if and when we come up with a program that raises revenues, and our original budget talked about that, and if there are taxes in it, why then, I will go out there and advocate strong bipartisan support for this. But if I get into going into each kind of tax that's discussed, or each kind of political — budget reform, or each kind of spending cut, I will be doing something that I've asked our negotiators and the Congress not to do.

Q: Yes, but when you say in your statement tax revenues are required—

P: Yes.

Q: —is that the same as taxes?

P: And I say budget reforms are required and I say spending cuts are required. And so let's see where we come out on that.

Q: Is it taxes?

P: Is what taxes?

Q: What you're saying? Are you saying taxes—higher taxes are required?

P: Lesley, I've told you what I've said, and I can't help you any more. Nice try.

Q: Mr. President, you've mentioned a couple of times that you're getting arrows from all directions. One newspaper headline declared, "Read my lips: I lied."

Is this kind of criticism justified? Is it fair? Do you deserve it?

P: Well, I expected it. But I don't — I think the deserving of it, the proof of the pudding is going to be in the eating and how it comes out. Because I think the American people recognize that the budget is greater than we had predicted and the Democrats had predicted. The economy has been slower. And so we'll just wait and see how we come out.

But no, I can't say I didn't expect—expect to hear some campaign words played back to me. And it's been fairly intense. But I'll tell you, I've been more relaxed about it than I thought I'd be. I went back into history and took a look at what others have had to go through in this job.

So it hasn't been as—it hasn't been as tense. You know, we had some congressional candidates over there yesterday, people running. And they don't want to see tax increases. And some of them, I could see them, "How are we going to handle this? We don't want to be rude to the president, but we feel strongly."

And so one or two of them, a couple of them, spoke up. And I could totally sympathize—empathize with what they were going through. But I—we didn't have time, because it was about a 45-second handshake. But if we had, I'd have said: "Now look, you got to look at the big picture here. Stay with your position. Advocate what you believe and what you tell your constituents what you'll try to do. And then just stay a little bit open-minded so when we get an agreement, and I hope we will, that is good for the country, that you can say, well, we can accept this."

Because we're going to need support from Republicans and Democrats alike, to say nothing of the American people. But I think the people will support it. I think they want to see jobs and economic growth. And that is what is at stake here. . . .

TELEVISED ADDRESS

. . . This budget agreement is the result of eight months of blood, sweat and fears — fears of the economic chaos that would follow if we fail to reduce the deficit.

Of course, I cannot claim it's the best deficit-reduction plan possible; it's not. Any one of us alone might have written a better plan. But it is the best agreement that can be legislated now.

It is the biggest deficit-reduction agreement ever: half a trillion dollars. It's the toughest deficit-reduction package ever, with new enforcement rules to make sure that what we fix now stays fixed.

And it has the largest spending savings ever, more than $300 billion.

For the first time, a Republican president and leaders of a Democratic Congress have agreed to real cuts that will be enforced by law — not promises. No smoke, no mirrors, no magic act, but real and lasting spending cuts.

This agreement will also raise revenue. I'm not, and I know you're not, a fan of tax increases. But if there have to be tax measures, they should allow the economy to grow. They should not turn us back to higher income tax rates, and they should be fair.

Everyone who can should contribute something, and no one should have to contribute beyond their fair share.

Our bipartisan agreement meets these tests, and through specific new incentives, it will help create more jobs. It's a little-known fact, but America's best job creators and greatest innovators tend to be our smaller companies. So our budget plan will give small and medium-size companies a needed shot in the arm.

Just as important, I am convinced that this agreement will help lower interest rates, and lower interest rates mean savings for consumers, lower mortgage payments for new homeowners, and more investment to produce more jobs. And that's what this agreement will do.

And now let me tell you what this agreement will not do. It will not raise income tax rates, personal or corporate. It will not mess with Social Security in any way. It will not put America's national security at risk, and most of all, it will not let our economy slip out of control.

Clearly, each and every one of us can find fault with something in this agreement. In fact, that is a burden that any truly fair solution must carry.

Any workable solution must be judged as a whole, not piece by piece. Those who dislike one part or another may pick our agreement apart, but if they do, believe me, the political reality is, no one can put a better one back together again.

Everyone will bear a small burden. But if we succeed, every American will have a large burden lifted.

If we fail to enact this agreement, our economy will falter; markets may tumble; and recession will follow. In just a moment, the Democratic majority leader, Senator [George J.] Mitchell [of Maine], will offer what is known as the Democratic response: often, a rebuttal. But not tonight.

Tonight, the Democratic and Republican leadership and I all speak with one voice, in support of this agreement. Tonight we ask you to help us move this agreement forward.

The congressional leadership and I both have a job to do in getting it enacted. And tonight, I ask for your help.

First, I ask you to understand how important, and for some, how difficult this vote is for your congressmen and senators. Many worry about your reaction to one part or another. But I know you know the importance of the whole.

And so second, I ask you to take this initiative, tell your congressmen and senators you support this deficit-reduction agreement. If they are Republicans, urge them to stand with the president. Urge them to do what the bipartisan leadership has done: come together in the spirit of compromise to solve this national problem.

If they're Democrats, urge them to stand with their congressional leaders. Ask them to fight for the future of your kids by supporting this budget agreement.

Now is the time for you, the American people, to have a real impact. Your senators and congressmen need to know that you want this deficit brought down; that the time for politics and posturing is over, and the time to come together is now.

This deficit-reduction agreement is tough, and so are the times. The agreement is fair, and so is the American spirit. The agreement is bipartisan, and so is the vote.

The agreement is real, and so is this crisis.

This is the first time in my presidency that I've made an appeal like this to you, the American people. With your help we can at last put this budget crisis behind us and face the other challenges that lie ahead.

If we do, the long-term result will be a healthier nation. And something more: We will have once again put ourselves on the path of economic growth, and we will have demonstrated that no challenge is greater than the determination of the American people.

SUPREME COURT ON
MINORITY BROADCASTERS

June 27, 1990

In a surprising endorsement of affirmative action, the Supreme Court June 27 ruled that Congress may mandate preferential treatment of minorities to increase their ownership of television and radio stations. The 5-4 decision marked the first time the Court had upheld an affirmative action program that was not devised to remedy past or present discrimination. This program, devised by the Federal Communications Commission (FCC), was aimed at the future. It would promote a greater diversity of voices and viewpoints in broadcasting. The Court said that such "benign race-conscious measures" are constitutional as long as they serve important government objectives.

The decision applied to two cases that had been consolidated for the Court's review. In both, Metro Broadcasting, Inc. v. Federal Communications Commission, *and* Astroline Communications Company v. Shurberg Broadcasting of Hartford, Inc., *the preferential-treatment policies were challenged as unconstitutional. In the first case one federal appellate court upheld the policies, and in the second another appellate court ruled them illegal.*

At issue was a minority set-aside program. One part gave special credit to minorities in proceedings for the award of new broadcast licenses. The other applied to "distress sale" situations, allowing some radio and television stations to be sold only to minority-controlled companies. The National Association of Black-Owned Broadcasters, applauding the Court ruling, said blacks owned 182 radio stations and 17 television stations. It was estimated that all minorities, making up about 20 percent of the population, owned 3.5 percent of the nation's 11,000 broadcast outlets.

During Ronald Reagan's presidency, the FCC tried to dismantle its race-preference system. But beginning in 1987, Congress kept the commission from spending any money to examine or change the minority-ownership policies. Some white-owned broadcasting companies challenged the policies as violating the Constitution's equal protection guarantees. Other opponents, including the Bush administration, contended that the policies were not linked to proof of past discrimination. Solicitor General Kenneth W. Starr filed briefs on behalf of the administration urging the Court to strike down the policies. However, he permitted the FCC to submit its own briefs defending them.

Brennan's Final Victory

The ruling, coming on the last day of the 1989-1990 term, astonished many observers because in the previous term the Court had narrowed the scope of several civil rights laws that dealt with discriminatory practices. (Court on Civil Rights, Historic Documents of 1989, p. 321) For Justice William J. Brennan, Jr., who wrote the decisions for the broadcasting cases, it was a final triumph.

Brennan, the most consistently liberal member, often found himself a minority voice on a Court that had turned increasingly conservative in recent years. On July 21 the eighty-four-year-old justice, after thirty-four years of service, resigned from the Court. (Judge Souter's Testimony to Senate Judiciary Committee, p. 615)

In this decision Brennan drew the backing of Justices Thurgood Marshall, Harry A. Blackmun, Byron R. White, and John Paul Stevens. White had joined Justices Sandra Day O'Connor, Anthony M. Kennedy, and Antonin Scalia in forming the conservative majority in the previous civil rights cases, and Stevens had joined in one of them, Richmond v. J. A. Croson. *Decided in January 1989,* Croson *struck down a plan by the city of Richmond to set aside 30 percent of the city's construction projects for minorities. Similar plans were in effect in thirty-six states and nearly 200 localities.*

In Croson *O'Connor wrote on behalf of the Court that minority set-aside programs could be justified only if they served a "compelling state interest" of redressing "identified discrimination" committed by the government or by private parties. The Richmond plan, she wrote, did not meet that standard. Writing the main dissenting opinion in the broadcasting cases, O'Connor charged that the Court was applying a "lower standard of review" than it had in* Croson.

The Brennan-led decision came as members of Congress were trying to iron out problems in an omnibus bill that would reverse or modify the Court's 1989-1990 civil rights rulings that narrowed the reach and remedies of job-discrimination laws. The Senate gave the legislation final congressional passage October 17 but it was vetoed October 22 by President George Bush, who contended that it set hiring quotas. The Senate sustained his veto two days later.

Deference to Congress

Brennan based his opinion largely on the 1980 Supreme Court case of Fullilove v. Klutznick, *which upheld a federal public works set-aside program and suggested that judgments of Congress in such matters were entitled to special deference under the Constitution.*

He stressed that Congress had long determined what protection was needed for minorities. "It is of overriding significance in these cases that the FCC's minority ownership programs have been specifically approved—indeed, mandated—by Congress," Brennan wrote. He said that the federal government had more authority than state and local governments to set aside contracts for minorities.

"For the past two decades," Brennan added, "Congress has consistently recognized the barriers encountered by minorities in entering the broadcast industry and has expressed emphatic support for the commission's attempts to promote programming diversity by increasing minority ownership." He agreed with the implication from Congress that "the American public will benefit by having access to a wider diversity of information sources." He added that the policies did not place an undue burden on other broadcasters.

O'Connor's "Lenient Standard" Charge

O'Connor, in dissent, said the decision "marks a renewed toleration of racial classifications and a repudiation of our recent affirmation that the Constitution's equal protection guarantees extend equally to all citizens." She claimed that in providing benefits to blacks and other minorities, the FCC was denying benefits to whites based solely on their race.

"Except in the narrowest of circumstances, the Constitution bars such racial classifications as a denial to particular individuals, of any race or ethnicity, of 'the equal protection of the laws,'" O'Connor wrote, quoting a key phrase from the Fourteenth Amendment. She contended that the Court had adopted a more lenient standard of review for the FCC policies than should be applied, and consequently might lead the government to resort more readily to racial distinctions.

Following are excerpts from the Supreme Court's majority, concurring, and dissenting opinions in the consolidated cases of Metro Broadcasting, Inc. v. Federal Communications Commission *and* Astroline Communications Company v. Shurberg Broadcasting of Hartford, Inc., *issued June 27, 1990, affirming the power of Congress to enact programs to favor minorities and upholding government affirmative action programs to increase minority ownership of broadcast outlets:*

<u>Nos. 89-453 and 89-700</u>

Metro Broadcasting, Inc.,
Petitioner
v.
Federal Communications
Commission et al.

Astroline Communications
Company Limited Partnership,
Petitioner
v.
Shurberg Broadcasting of
Hartford, Inc., et al.

On writs of certiorari to the
United States Court of Appeals
for the District of Columbia
Circuit

[June 27, 1990]

JUSTICE BRENNAN delivered the opinion of the Court.

The issue in these cases, consolidated for decision today, is whether certain minority preference policies of the Federal Communications Commission violate the equal protection component of the Fifth Amendment. The policies in question are (1) a program awarding an enhancement for minority ownership in comparative proceedings for new licenses, and (2) the minority "distress sale" program, which permits a limited category of existing radio and television broadcast stations to be transferred only to minority-controlled firms. We hold that these policies do not violate equal protection principles.

I

A

The policies before us today can best be understood by reference to the history of federal efforts to promote minority participation in the broadcasting industry. In the Communications Act of 1934, 48 Stat. 1064, as amended, Congress assigned to the Federal Communications Commission (FCC or Commission) exclusive authority to grant licenses, based on "public convenience, interest, or necessity," to persons wishing to construct and operate radio and television broadcast stations in the United States. Although for the past two decades minorities have constituted at least one-fifth of the United States population, during this time relatively few members of minority groups have held broadcast licenses. In 1971, minorities owned only 10 of the approximately 7,500 radio stations in the country and none of the more than 1,000 television stations; in 1978, minorities owned less than 1 percent of the Nation's radio and television stations; and in 1986, they owned just 2.1 percent of the more than 11,000 radio and television stations in the United States. Moreover, these statistics fail to reflect the fact that, as late entrants who often have been able to obtain only the less valuable stations, many minority broadcasters serve geographically limited markets with relatively small audiences.

The Commission has recognized that the viewing and listening public suffers when minorities are underrepresented among owners of television and radio stations ... [and] has therefore worked to encourage minority participation in the broadcast industry....

... [T]he FCC adopted in May 1978 its *Statement of Policy on Minority Ownership of Broadcasting Facilities.* After recounting its past efforts to expand broadcast diversity, the FCC concluded:

> "[W]e are compelled to observe that the views of racial minorities continue to be inadequately represented in the broadcast media. This situation is detrimental not only to the minority audience but to all of the viewing and listening public. Adequate representation of minority viewpoints in programming serves not only the needs and interests of the minority community but also enriches and educates the non-minority audience. It enhances the diversified programming which is a key objective not only of the Communications Act of 1934 but also of the First Amendment."

Describing its actions as only "first steps," the FCC outlined two elements of a minority ownership policy.

First, the Commission pledged to consider minority ownership as one factor in comparative proceedings for new licenses....

Second, the FCC outlined a plan to increase minority opportunities to receive reassigned and transferred licenses through the so-called "distress sale" policy. As a general rule, a licensee whose qualifications to hold a broadcast license come into question may not assign or transfer that license until the FCC has resolved its doubts in a noncomparative hearing. The distress sale policy is an exception to that practice, allowing a broadcaster whose license has been designated for a revocation hearing, or whose renewal application has been designated for hearing, to assign the license to an FCC-approved minority enterprise....

B

1

In No. 89-453, petitioner Metro Broadcasting, Inc. (Metro) challenges the Commission's policy awarding preferences to minority owners in comparative licensing proceedings. Several applicants, including Metro and Rainbow Broadcasting (Rainbow), were involved in a comparative proceeding to select among three mutually exclusive proposals to construct and operate a new UHF television station in the Orlando, Florida, metropolitan area. After an evidentiary hearing, an Administrative Law Judge (ALJ) granted Metro's application. The ALJ disqualified Rainbow from consideration because of "misrepresentations" in its application. On review of the ALJ's decision, however, the Commission's Review Board disagreed with the ALJ's finding regarding Rainbow's candor and concluded that Rainbow was qualified. The Board proceeded to consider Rainbow's comparative showing and found it superior to Metro's. In so doing, the Review Board awarded Rainbow a substantial enhancement on the ground that it was 90 percent Hispanic-owned, whereas Metro had only one minority partner who owned 19.8 percent of the enterprise. The Review Board found that Rainbow's minority credit outweighed Metro's local residence and civic participation advantage. The Commission denied review of the Board's decision largely without discussion, stating merely that it "agree[d] with the Board's resolution of this case."

Metro sought review of the Commission's order in the United States Court of Appeals for the District of Columbia Circuit, but the appeal's disposition was delayed; at the Commission's request, the court granted a remand of the record for further consideration in light of a separate ongoing inquiry at the Commission regarding the validity of its minority and female ownership policies, including the minority enhancement credit. The Commission determined that the outcome in the licensing proceeding between Rainbow and Metro might depend on whatever the Commission concluded in its general evaluation of minority ownership policies, and accordingly it held the licensing proceeding in abeyance. . . .

Prior to the Commission's completion of its . . . inquiry, however, Congress enacted and the President signed into law the FCC appropriations legislation for fiscal year 1988. The measure prohibited the Commission from spending any appropriated funds to examine or change its minority ownership policies. Complying with this directive, the Commission closed its . . . inquiry. The FCC also reaffirmed its grant of the license in this case to Rainbow Broadcasting.

The case returned to the Court of Appeals and a divided panel affirmed the Commission's order awarding the license to Rainbow. The court concluded that its decision was controlled by prior circuit precedent and noted that the Commission's action was supported by "'highly relevant congressional action that showed clear recognition of the extreme underrepresentation of minorities and their perspectives in the broadcast mass media.'"

2

The dispute in No. 89-700 emerged from a series of attempts by Faith Center, Inc., the licensee of a Hartford, Connecticut television station, to execute a minority distress sale. In December 1980, the FCC designated for a hearing Faith Center's application for renewal of its license. In February 1981, Faith Center filed with the FCC a petition for special relief seeking permission to transfer its license under the distress sale policy. The Commission granted the request, but the proposed sale was not completed, apparently due to the purchaser's inability to obtain adequate financing. In September 1983, the Commission granted a second request by Faith Center to pursue a distress sale to another minority-controlled buyer. The FCC rejected objections to the distress sale raised by Alan Shurberg, who at that time was acting in his individual capacity. This second distress sale also was not consummated, apparently because of similar financial difficulties on the buyer's part.

In December 1983, respondent Shurberg Broadcasting of Hartford, Inc. (Shurberg) applied to the Commission for a permit to build a television station in Hartford. The application was mutually exclusive with Faith Center's renewal application, then still pending. In June 1984, Faith Center again sought the FCC's approval for a distress sale, requesting permission to sell the station to Astroline Communications Company, Limited Partnership (Astroline), a minority applicant. Shurberg opposed the sale to Astroline on a number of grounds, including that the FCC's distress sale program violated Shurberg's right to equal protection. . . . In December 1984, the FCC approved Faith Center's petition for permission to assign its broadcast license to Astroline . . . [and] rejected Shurberg's equal protection challenge to the policy as "without merit."

Shurberg appealed the Commission's order to the United States Court of Appeals for the District of Columbia Circuit, but disposition of the appeal was delayed pending completion of the Commission's . . . inquiry into the minority ownership policies. After Congress enacted and the President signed into law the appropriations legislation . . . the Commission reaffirmed its order granting Faith Center's request to assign its Hartford license to Astroline pursuant to the minority distress sale policy.

A divided Court of Appeals invalidated the Commission's minority distress sale policy. *Shurberg Broadcasting of Hartford, Inc.* v. *FCC* (1989). In a *per curiam* opinion, the panel majority held that the policy "unconstitutionally deprives Alan Shurberg and Shurberg Broadcasting of their equal protection rights under the Fifth Amendment because the program is not narrowly tailored to remedy past discrimination or to promote programming diversity" and that "the program unduly burdens Shurberg, an innocent nonminority, and is not reasonably related to the interests it seeks to vindicate.". . .

II

It is of overriding significance in these cases that the FCC's minority ownership programs have been specifically approved—indeed, mandated—by Congress. In *Fullilove* v. *Klutznick* (1980), Chief Justice [Warren] Burger, writing for himself and two other Justices, observed that although "[a] program that employs racial or ethnic criteria . . . calls for close examination," when a program employing a benign racial classification is adopted by an administrative agency at the explicit direction of Congress, we are "bound to approach our task with appropriate deference to the Congress.". . . We explained that deference was appropriate in light of Congress' institutional competence as the national legislature.

A majority of the Court in *Fullilove* did not apply strict scrutiny to the race-based classification at issue. Three Members inquired "whether the *objectives* of th[e] legislation are within the power of Congress" and "whether the limited use of racial and ethnic criteria . . . is a constitutionally permissible *means* for achieving the congressional objectives." (emphasis in original). Three other Members would have upheld benign racial classifications that "serve important governmental objectives and are substantially related to achievement of those objectives." We apply that standard today. We hold that benign race-conscious measures mandated by Congress—even if those measures are not "remedial" in the sense of being designed to compensate victims of past governmental or societal discrimination—are constitutionally permissible to the extent that they serve important governmental objectives within the power of Congress and are substantially related to achievement of those objectives. . . .

We hold that the FCC minority ownership policies pass muster under the test we announce today. First, we find that they serve the important governmental objective of broadcast diversity. Second, we conclude that they are substantially related to the achievement of that objective.

A

Congress found that the "effects of past inequities stemming from racial and ethnic discrimination have resulted in a severe underrepresentation of minorities in the media of mass communications." H.R. Conf. Rep. No. 97-765, p. 43 (1982). Congress and the Commission do not justify the minority ownership policies strictly as remedies for victims of this discrimination, however. Rather, Congress and the FCC have selected the minority ownership policies primarily to promote programming diversity, and they urge that such diversity is an important governmental objective that can serve as a constitutional basis for the preference policies. We agree.

We have long recognized that "[b]ecause of the scarcity of [electromagnetic] frequencies, the Government is permitted to put restraints on licensees in favor of others whose views should be expressed on this unique medium." *Red Lion Broadcasting* v. *FCC* (1969). The Government's role in distributing the limited number of broadcast licenses . . . may be regulated in light of the rights of the viewing and listening audience and that "the widest possible dissemination of information from diverse and antagonistic sources is essential to the welfare of the public." *Associated Press* v. *United States* (1945). Safeguarding the public's right to receive a diversity of views and information over the airwaves is therefore an integral component of the FCC's mission. . . .

Against this background, we conclude that the interest in enhancing broadcast diversity is, at the very least, an important governmental objective and is therefore a sufficient basis for the Commission's minority ownership policies. . . .

B

We also find that the minority ownership policies are substantially related to the achievement of the Government's interest. One component of this inquiry concerns the relationship between expanded minority ownership and greater broadcast diversity; both the FCC and Congress have determined that such a relationship exists. . . .

C

The judgment that there is a link between expanded minority ownership and broadcast diversity does not rest on impermissible stereotyping. Congressional policy does not assume that in every case minority ownership and management will lead to more minority-oriented programming or to the expression of a discrete "minority viewpoint" on the airwaves. Neither does it pretend that all programming that appeals to minority audiences can be labeled "minority programming" or that programming that might be described as "minority" does not appeal to nonminorities. Rather, both Congress and the FCC maintain simply that expanded minority ownership of broadcast outlets will, in the aggregate, result in greater broadcast diversity. A broadcasting industry with representative minority participation will produce more variation and diversity than will one whose ownership is drawn from a single racially and ethnically homogeneous group. . . .

Our cases demonstrate that the reasoning employed by the Commission and Congress is permissible. We have recognized, for example, that the fair cross-section requirement of the Sixth Amendment forbids the exclusion of groups on the basis of such characteristics as race and gender from a jury venire because "[w]ithout that requirement, the State could draw up jury lists in such manner as to produce a pool of prospective jurors disproportionately ill disposed towards one or all classes of defendants, and thus more likely to yield petit juries with similar disposition." *Holland v. Illinois* (1990). It is a small step from this logic to the conclusion that including minorities in the electromagnetic spectrum will be more likely to produce a "fair cross section" of diverse content. In addition, many of our voting rights cases operate on the assumption that minorities have particular viewpoints and interests worthy of protection. . . .

D

. . . [T]he Commission established minority ownership preferences only after long experience demonstrated that race-neutral means could not produce adequate broadcasting diversity. The FCC did not act precipitately in devising the programs we uphold today; to the contrary, the Commission undertook thorough evaluations of its policies *three* times—in 1960, 1971, and 1978—before adopting the minority ownership programs. In endorsing the minority ownership preferences, Congress agreed with the Commission's assessment that race-neutral alternatives had failed to achieve the necessary programming diversity.

Moreover, the considered nature of the Commission's judgment in selecting the particular minority ownership policies at issue today is illustrated by the fact that the Commission has rejected other types of minority preferences. For example, the Commission has studied but refused to implement the more expansive alternative of setting aside certain frequencies for minority broadcasters. . . .

The minority ownership policies, furthermore, are aimed directly at the

427

barriers that minorities face in entering the broadcasting industry. The Commission's Task Force identified as key factors hampering the growth of minority ownership a lack of adequate financing, paucity of information regarding license availability, and broadcast inexperience. The Commission assigned a preference to minority status in the comparative licensing proceeding, reasoning that such an enhancement might help to compensate for a dearth of broadcasting experience. Most license acquisitions, however, are by necessity purchases of existing stations, because only a limited number of new stations are available, and those are often in less desirable markets or on less profitable portions of spectrum, such as the UHF band. Congress and the FCC therefore found a need for the minority distress sale policy, which helps to overcome the problem of inadequate access to capital by lowering the sale price and the problem of lack of information by providing existing licensees with an incentive to seek out minority buyers. The Commission's choice of minority ownership policies thus addressed the very factors it had isolated as being responsible for minority underrepresentation in the broadcast industry....

... Furthermore, there is provision for administrative and judicial review of all Commission decisions, which guarantees both that the minority ownership policies are applied correctly in individual cases, and that there will be frequent opportunities to revisit the merits of those policies. Congress and the Commission have adopted a policy of minority ownership not as an end in itself, but rather as a means of achieving greater programming diversity. Such a goal carries its own natural limit, for there will be no need for further minority preferences once sufficient diversity has been achieved....

Finally, we do not believe that the minority ownership policies at issue impose impermissible burdens on nonminorities. Although the nonminority challengers in these cases concede that they have not suffered the loss of an already-awarded broadcast license, they claim that they have been handicapped in their ability to obtain one in the first instance. But just as we have determined that "[a]s part of this Nation's dedication to eradicating racial discrimination, innocent persons may be called upon to bear some of the burden of the remedy," *Wygant* v. *Jackson Board of Education* (1986), we similarly find that a congressionally mandated benign race-conscious program that is substantially related to the achievement of an important governmental interest is consistent with equal protection principles so long as it does not impose *undue* burdens on nonminorities....

III

The Commission's minority ownership policies bear the imprimatur of longstanding congressional support and direction and are substantially related to the achievement of the important governmental objective of broadcast diversity. The judgment in No. 89-453 is affirmed, the judgment in No. 89-700 is reversed, and the cases are remanded for proceedings consistent with this opinion.

It is so ordered.

JUSTICE STEVENS, concurring.

Today the Court squarely rejects the proposition that a governmental decision that rests on a racial classification is never permissible except as a remedy for a past wrong. I endorse this focus on the future benefit, rather than the remedial justification, of such decisions.

I remain convinced, of course, that racial or ethnic characteristics provide a relevant basis for disparate treatment only in extremely rare situations and that it is therefore "especially important that the reasons for any such classification be clearly identified and unquestionably legitimate." *Fullilove* v. *Klutznick* (1980) (dissenting opinion). The Court's opinion explains how both elements of that standard are satisfied. . . .

Therefore, I join both the opinion and the judgment of the Court.

JUSTICE O'CONNOR, with whom THE CHIEF JUSTICE, JUSTICE SCALIA, and JUSTICE KENNEDY join, dissenting.

At the heart of the Constitution's guarantee of equal protection lies the simple command that the Government must treat citizens "as *individuals,* not 'as simply components of a racial, religious, sexual or national class.' " *Arizona Governing Committee* v. *Norris* (1983). Social scientists may debate how people's thoughts and behavior reflect their background, but the Constitution provides that the Government may not allocate benefits and burdens among individuals based on the assumption that race or ethnicity determines how they act or think. To uphold the challenged programs, the Court departs from these fundamental principles and from our traditional requirement that racial classifications are permissible only if necessary and narrowly tailored to achieve a compelling interest. This departure marks a renewed toleration of racial classifications and a repudiation of our recent affirmation that the Constitution's equal protection guarantees extend equally to all citizens. The Court's application of a lessened equal protection standard to congressional actions finds no support in our cases or in the Constitution. I respectfully dissent.

I

As we recognized last Term, the Constitution requires that the Court apply a strict standard of scrutiny to evaluate racial classifications such as those contained in the challenged FCC distress sale and comparative licensing policies. "Strict scrutiny" requires that, to be upheld, racial classifications must be determined to be necessary and narrowly tailored to achieve a compelling state interest. The Court abandons this traditional safeguard against discrimination for a lower standard of review, and in practice applies a standard like that applicable to routine legislation. Yet the Government's different treatment of citizens according to race is no routine concern. . . .

In both the challenged policies, the FCC provides benefits to some members of our society and denies benefits to others based on race or ethnicity. Except in the narrowest of circumstances, the Constitution bars such racial classifications as a denial to particular individuals, of any race or ethnicity, of "the equal protection of the laws." . . . Racial classifications, whether providing benefits to or burdening particular racial or ethnic groups, may stigmatize those groups singled out for different treatment and may create considerable tension with the Nation's widely shared commitment to evaluating individuals upon their individual merit. . . .

The Constitution's guarantee of equal protection binds the Federal Government as it does the States, and no lower level of scrutiny applies to the Federal Government's use of race classifications. In *Bolling* v. *Sharpe* [1954], the companion case to *Brown* v. *Board of Education,* the Court held that equal protection principles embedded in the Fifth Amendment's Due Process Clause prohibited the Federal Government from maintaining racially segregated schools in the District of Columbia: "[I]t would be unthinkable that the same Constitution would impose a lesser duty on the Federal Government." Consistent with this view, the Court has repeatedly indicated that "the reach of the equal protection guarantee of the Fifth Amendment is coextensive with that of the Fourteenth." *United States* v. *Paradise* (1987) (plurality opinion).

Nor does the congressional role in prolonging the FCC's policies justify any lower level of scrutiny. As with all instances of judicial review of federal legislation, the Court does not lightly set aside the considered judgment of a coordinate branch. Nonetheless, the respect due a coordinate branch yields neither less vigilance in defense of equal protection principles nor any corresponding diminution of the standard of review. . . .

The Court's reliance on "benign racial classifications," *ante,* at 13, is particularly troubling. " 'Benign' racial classification" is a contradiction in terms. Governmental distinctions among citizens based on race or ethnicity, even in the rare circumstances permitted by our cases, exact costs and carry with them substantial dangers. To the person denied an opportunity or right based on race, the classification is hardly benign. The right to equal protection of the laws is a personal right, securing to *each* individual an immunity from treatment predicated simply on membership in a particular racial or ethnic group. The Court's emphasis on "benign racial classifications" suggests confidence in its ability to distinguish good from harmful governmental uses of racial criteria. History should teach greater humility. Untethered to narrowly confined remedial notions, "benign" carries with it no independent meaning, but reflects only acceptance of the current generation's conclusion that a politically acceptable burden, imposed on particular citizens on the basis of race, is reasonable. The Court provides no basis for determining when a racial classification fails to be "benevolent." By expressly distinguishing "benign" from remedial race-conscious measures, the Court leaves the distinct possibility that any racial measure found to be substantially related to an important governmental objective is also, by definition, "benign.". . .

II

Our history reveals that the most blatant forms of discrimination have been visited upon some members of the racial and ethnic groups identified in the challenged programs. Many have lacked the opportunity to share in the Nation's wealth and to participate in its commercial enterprises. It is undisputed that minority participation in the broadcasting industry falls markedly below the demographic representation of those groups ... and this shortfall may be traced in part to the discrimination and the patterns of exclusion that have widely affected our society. As a Nation we aspire to create a society untouched by that history of exclusion, and to ensure that equality defines all citizens' daily experience and opportunities as well as the protection afforded to them under law.

For these reasons, and despite the harms that may attend the Government's use of racial classifications, we have repeatedly recognized that the Government possesses a compelling interest in remedying the effects of identified race discrimination. We subject even racial classifications claimed to be remedial to strict scrutiny, however, to ensure that the Government in fact employs any race-conscious measures to further this remedial interest and employs them only when, and no more broadly than, the interest demands. The FCC or Congress may yet conclude after suitable examination that narrowly tailored race-conscious measures are required to remedy discrimination that may be identified in the allocation of broadcasting licenses. Such measures are clearly within the Government's power.

Yet it is equally clear that the policies challenged in these cases were not designed as remedial measures and are in no sense narrowly tailored to remedy identified discrimination. The FCC appropriately concedes that its policies embodied no remedial purpose, and has disclaimed the possibility that discrimination infected the allocation of licenses. The congressional action at most simply endorsed a policy designed to further the interest in achieving diverse programming.... The Court refers to the bare suggestion, contained in a report addressing different legislation passed in 1982, that "past inequities" have led to "underrepresentation of minorities in the media of mass communications, as it has adversely affected their participation in other sectors of the economy as well." This statement ... identifies no discrimination in the broadcasting industry.... I agree that the racial classifications cannot be upheld as remedial measures.

III

Under the appropriate standard, strict scrutiny, only a compelling interest may support the Government's use of racial classifications. Modern equal protection doctrine has recognized only one such interest: remedying the effects of racial discrimination. The interest in increasing the diversity of broadcast viewpoints is clearly not a compelling interest. It is simply too amorphous, too insubstantial, and too unrelated to any legitimate basis for employing racial classifications....

... The Court has recognized an interest in obtaining diverse broadcasting viewpoints as a legitimate basis for the FCC, acting pursuant to its "public interest" statutory mandate, to adopt limited measures to increase the number of competing licensees and to encourage licensees to present varied views on issues of public concern. We have also concluded that these measures do not run afoul of the First Amendment's usual prohibition of Government regulation of the marketplace of ideas, in part because First Amendment concerns support limited but inevitable Government regulation of the peculiarly constrained broadcasting spectrum. But the conclusion that measures adopted to further the interest in diversity of broadcasting viewpoints are neither beyond the FCC's statutory authority nor contrary to the First Amendment hardly establishes the interest as important for equal protection purposes.

The FCC's extension of the asserted interest in diversity of views in this case presents, at the very least, an unsettled First Amendment issue. The FCC has concluded that the American broadcasting public receives the incorrect mix of ideas and claims to have adopted the challenged policies to supplement programming content with a particular set of views. Although we have approved limited measures designed to increase information and views generally, the Court has never upheld a broadcasting measure designed to amplify a distinct set of views or the views of a particular class of speakers. Indeed, the Court has suggested that the First Amendment prohibits allocating licenses to further such ends. ... Even if an interest is determined to be legitimate in one context, it does not suddenly become important enough to justify distinctions based on race.

IV

Our traditional equal protection doctrine requires, in addition to a compelling state interest, that the Government's chosen means be necessary to accomplish and narrowly tailored to further the asserted interest. ... The Court instead finds the racial classifications to be "substantially related" to achieving the Government's interest, a far less rigorous fit requirement. The FCC's policies fail even this requirement.

1

... The FCC assumes a particularly strong correlation of race and behavior. The FCC justifies its conclusion that insufficiently diverse viewpoints are broadcast by reference to the percentage of minority owned stations. This assumption is correct only to the extent that minority owned stations provide the desired additional views, and that stations owned by individuals not favored by the preferences cannot, or at least do not, broadcast underrepresented programming. Additionally, the FCC's focus on ownership to improve programming assumes that preferences linked to race are so strong that they will dictate the owner's behavior in operating the station, overcoming the owner's personal inclinations and regard for the market. This strong link between race and behavior, especially when mediated by market forces, is the assumption that Justice Powell rejected in his discussion of health care service in *Bakke*. In that case, the state medical school argued that it could prefer members of minority groups because they were more likely to serve communities particularly needing medical care. Justice Powell rejected this rationale, concluding that the assumption was unsupported and that such individual choices could not be presumed from ethnicity or race.

The majority addresses this point by arguing that the equation of race with distinct views and behavior is not "impermissible" in this particular case. Apart from placing undue faith in the Government and courts' ability to distinguish "good" from "bad" stereotypes, this reasoning repudiates essential equal protection principles that prohibit racial generalizations. The Court embraces the FCC's reasoning that an applicant's race will likely indicate that the applicant possesses a distinct perspective, but notes that the correlation of race to behavior is "not a rigid assumption about how minority owners will behave in every case." The corollary to this notion is plain: individuals of unfavored racial and ethnic backgrounds are unlikely to possess the unique experiences and background that contribute to viewpoint diversity. Both the reasoning and its corollary reveal but disregard what is objectionable about a stereotype: the racial generalization inevitably does not apply to certain individuals, and those persons may legitimately claim that they have been judged according to their race rather than upon a relevant criterion. . . .

2

. . . Moreover, the FCC's programs cannot survive even intermediate scrutiny because race-neutral and untried means of directly accomplishing the governmental interest are readily available. The FCC could directly advance its interest by requiring licensees to provide programming that the FCC believes would add to diversity. The interest the FCC asserts is in programming diversity, yet in adopting the challenged policies, the FCC expressly disclaimed having attempted *any* direct efforts to achieve its asserted goal. The Court suggests that administrative convenience excuses this failure, yet intermediate scrutiny bars the Government from relying upon that excuse to avoid measures that directly further the asserted interest. The FCC and the Court suggest that First Amendment interests in some manner should exempt the FCC from employing this direct, race-neutral means to achieve its asserted interest. They essentially argue that we may bend our equal protection principles to avoid more readily apparent harm to our First Amendment values. But the FCC cannot have it both ways: either the First Amendment bars the FCC from seeking to accomplish indirectly what it may not accomplish directly; or the FCC may pursue the goal, but must do so in a manner that comports with equal protection principles. And if the FCC can direct programming in any fashion, it must employ that direct means before resorting to indirect race-conscious means. . . .

4 [3 omitted]

Finally, the Government cannot employ race classifications that unduly burden individuals who are not members of the favored racial and ethnic groups. The challenged policies fail this independent requirement, as well as the other constitutional requirements. The comparative licensing and distress sale programs provide the eventual licensee with an exceptionally valuable property and with a rare and unique opportunity to serve the local community. The distress sale imposes a particularly significant burden. The FCC has at base created a specialized market reserved exclusively for minority controlled applicants. There is no more rigid quota than a 100% set-aside. This fact is not altered by the observation that the FCC and seller have some discretion over whether stations may be sold through the distress program. For the would-be purchaser or person who seeks to compete for the station, that opportunity depends entirely upon race or ethnicity. The Court's argument that the distress sale allocates only a small percentage of all license sales also misses the mark. This argument readily supports complete preferences and avoids scrutiny of particular programs: it is no response to a person denied admission at one school, or discharged from one job, solely on the basis of race, that other schools or employers do not discriminate. . . .

test that approves of racial classifications that are substantially related to an important governmental objective. Of course, the programs even more clearly fail the strict scrutiny that should be applied. The Court has determined, in essence, that Congress and all federal agencies are exempted, to some ill-defined but significant degree, from the Constitution's equal protection requirements. This break with our precedents greatly undermines equal protection guarantees, and permits distinctions among citizens based on race and ethnicity which the Constitution clearly forbids. I respectfully dissent.

JUSTICE KENNEDY, with whom JUSTICE SCALIA joins, dissenting.

Almost 100 years ago in *Plessy* v. *Ferguson* (1896), this Court upheld a government-sponsored race-conscious measure, a Louisiana law that required "equal but separate accommodations" for "white" and "colored" railroad passengers. The Court asked whether the measures were "reasonable," and it stated that "[i]n determining the question of reasonableness, [the legislature] is at liberty to act with reference to the established usages, customs and traditions of the people, and with a view to the promotion of their comfort." The *Plessy* Court concluded that the "race-conscious measures" it reviewed were reasonable because they served the governmental interest of increasing the riding pleasure of railroad passengers. The fundamental errors in *Plessy,* its standard of review and its validation of rank racial insult by the State, distorted the law for six decades before the Court announced its apparent demise in *Brown* v. *Board of Education*

(1954). *Plessy*'s standard of review and its explication have disturbing parallels to today's majority opinion that should warn us something is amiss here. . . .

Once the Government takes the step, which itself should be forbidden, of enacting into law the stereotypical assumption that the race of owners is linked to broadcast content, it follows a path that becomes even more tortuous. It must decide which races to favor. While the Court repeatedly refers to the preferences as favoring "minorities," and purports to evaluate the burdens imposed on "nonminorities," it must be emphasized that the discriminatory policies upheld today operate to exclude the many racial and ethnic *minorities* that have not made the Commission's list. The enumeration of the races to be protected is borrowed from a remedial statute, but since the remedial rationale must be disavowed in order to sustain the policy, the race classifications bear scant relation to the asserted governmental interest. The Court's reasoning provides little justification for welcoming the return of racial classifications to our Nation's laws.

I cannot agree with the Court that the Constitution permits the Government to discriminate among its citizens on the basis of race in order to serve interests so trivial as "broadcast diversity.". . .

. . . Perhaps the Court can succeed in its assumed role of case-by-case arbiter of when it is desirable and benign for the Government to disfavor some citizens and favor others based on the color of their skin. Perhaps the tolerance and decency to which our people aspire will let the disfavored rise above hostility and the favored escape condescension. But history suggests much peril in this enterprise, and so the Constitution forbids us to undertake it. I regret that after a century of judicial opinions, we interpret the Constitution to do no more than move us from "separate but equal" to "unequal but benign."

July

DOCUMENTS FROM 28TH
COMMUNIST CONGRESS
July 2, 6 and 10, 1990

The Soviet Communist party opened its 28th Congress in Moscow July 2 amid bickering that signaled deep divisions among the 4,610 delegates over President Mikhail S. Gorbachev's pursuit of vast changes in the Soviet Union. The meeting closed ten days later with Gorbachev's populist rival, Boris Yeltsin, leaving the party and predicting its rejection by the people. From beginning to end, the fractious congress—the supreme authority of the 20-million-member party—was occupied by thoughts of the party's weakened ability to retain its political dominance.

This congress stood in contrast to the 27th in 1986, which met only a year after Gorbachev came to power. It hailed his reformist visions and cheered his indictment of former leaders for the country's economic and political stagnation. (Gorbachev's Address to the 27th Soviet Party Congress, Historic Documents of 1986, p. 145) Gorbachev afterward wrought startling changes in Soviet foreign policy, bringing the Cold War to an end and enabling Eastern Europe to move away from Soviet control. At home, he set in motion political reforms that gave the people a far greater voice in their affairs and lifted their fear of speaking out.

Much of the world acclaimed Gorbachev a hero, but at home his popular triumphs were tarnished by a sagging economy that did not respond to half-measures for relaxing the traditional central control. In contrast to his boldness in other matters, he moved toward a Western-style free market only haltingly, incurring the wrath of critics on the radical left and most consumers who encountered higher prices and scarcities of basic goods. Moscow shoppers were shocked during the summer of 1990 when bread disappeared from the stores for days at a time.

In addition to the country's economic discontent, several of the Soviet Union's non-Russian republics demanded more autonomy—even outright independence—and often played up ethnic differences that gave rise to eruptions of civil strife. The Russian majority, in turn, became resentful of the minorities' new assertiveness.

Insults from Demonstrators

Such was the setting of the 28th Congress. Gorbachev's keynote speech at the opening session was delayed nearly two hours by loud arguments on the floor. One delegate seized the microphone and said the party's current leaders should not be allowed to preside. When Gorbachev did speak—for nearly two-and-a-half hours to a generally unresponsive audience—he appealed for party unity between the radical reformists who wanted him to move faster and conservatives who wanted him to move more slowly or not at all. While he spoke inside the ornate Kremlin Palace of Congresses, a large group of demonstrators outside chanted, "Down with the party!"

Similarly, Gorbachev and other top Soviet leaders had been publicly jeered about two months earlier as they reviewed the annual May Day parade outside the Kremlin walls. Marchers shook their fists at the leaders, and chants of "Resign!" and "Shame!" rose above the blaring parade music. Gorbachev's closest ally, Alexander Yakouvlev, denounced the demonstration as insulting, and on May 21 the new Soviet Congress of People's Deputies, in effect the national Parliament, enacted a law making it a crime to insult the president "in an indecent way."

Gorbachev's Power Grip

Although his popularity had waned, Gorbachev retained a strong grip on the levers of party and state control. On February 6 he told the Central Committee—which acts on the party's behalf between congresses—that the Communists should forswear their constitutional monopoly on power and accept the prospect of rival candidates. At his behest, the parliament held a special session in Moscow, March 13-15, and readily approved sweeping constitutional changes, laying the groundwork for a market economy and future multiparty elections.

The parliament also ratified the creation of a powerful executive presidency, and by a vote of 1,497 to 368 named Gorbachev to fill it. Parliament itself had been created by previous constitutional changes. When its members were chosen in March 1989, Gorbachev permitted about half of the seats to be contested; that election was considered the freest in the Soviet Union in seventy years. (Remarks on Soviet Election and Perestroika, Historic Documents of 1989, p. 173)

Gorbachev assumed the new office with its broader legal authority March 15, saying it was a "powerful step on the road to democracy." Political commentators saw the new office as providing Gorbachev a way of freeing himself from party power struggles and possibly distancing himself somewhat from an increasingly unpopular party. Upon the completion of his presidential term in 1995, the officeholder would be determined by a vote of the Soviet people rather than by a vote of Parliament.

But at the 28th Party Congress, Gorbachev showed no inclination to relinquish control. He retained the position of general secretary and won a leadership fight to enlarge the Politburo by adding the party leaders of the fifteen Soviet republics—thus preventing conservatives from stacking that rule-making body with his critics. And he succeeded in turning back a bold challenge from Yegor K. Ligachev, an orthodox Marxist, for the new post of deputy party leader. Had Ligachev won, the job of running the party on a day-to-day basis would have fallen to someone who had just denounced Gorbachev's "blind radicalism" in a rousing speech to the congress. The post went instead to the president of the Ukrainian republic, Vladimir A. Ivashko, a centrist.

Yeltsin's Challenge

Gorbachev had little time to savor his intraparty victories. Just when it appeared that he had held the divided Communist party together, Yeltsin and several fellow radicals told the delegates that their loyalties were with the people and not to a party they considered incapable of taking the drastic steps necessary to reinvigorate the Soviet economy or save itself politically.

In an address July 6, Yeltsin admonished the delegates to look at the demise of Eastern Europe's Communist parties once the people were allowed to express their will. He urged the party to drop the word "communist" from its name and give up control of the armed forces, the KGB secret police, and many other institutions. Gorbachev refused to take any of those steps.

Yeltsin, arguably the most popular public figure in the Soviet Union, was Gorbachev's severest critic on the left. Ousted from the Politburo in 1987, he staged an astonishing political comeback two years later by winning nearly 90 percent of the vote for a seat in the new parliament. Yeltsin completed the triumph in May by defeating Gorbachev's candidate for the presidency of the Russian republic. With 147 million people, about half of the Soviet Union's total, it was by far the biggest and most powerful of all the republics. Under his direction, the Russian republic's Communist party held its own congress in June and sent many of its active participants to the Soviet party congress.

Later, Yeltsin struck the semblance of an alliance with Gorbachev for action on the economic crisis. On September 11, as the Soviet parliament was angrily debating a national economic reform plan, the Yeltsin-controlled Russian parliament met in another part of Moscow and quickly adopted it for the republic on a vote of 251 to 1. The vote had the effect of forcing a hesitant Gorbachev to commit himself to the plan. Afterward, the two leaders pledged to work together to put it into effect, moving the state-controlled Soviet economy to a free enterprise system within 500 days.

*Following are excerpts from a report by Soviet president
Mikhail S. Gorbachev to the 28th Soviet Communist Party
Congress in Moscow, July 2, 1990, urging the party to adopt
his reforms; from a speech July 6 to the congress by Boris
Yeltsin, arguing for a revamped party that would no longer
bear the communist name; and from a speech by Gorbachev
to the congress July 10 defending his policies, as recorded
and translated by the Federal Broadcast Information Service, a U.S. government agency:*

GORBACHEV REPORT

[I and II omitted]

III. The Party and Perestroyka

Comrade delegates, the main feature of our 28th congress consists
precisely of the fact that we have come together at, as I have already said,
the crucial stage of perestroyka, of radical change in our society within the
framework of the socialist choice. Everyone is concerned by the questions
as to where revolutionary transformations will lead, to what extent they
correspond to the interests of the working people, and whether they will
strengthen social justice, democracy, and freedom. Naturally, a great many
viewpoints arise in such a situation. All this was taken into account when
drawing up the draft program statement which you have in your hands. In
it the party, proceeding from its responsibility to the people, proposes a
program and policies for the immediate future. During the precongress
discussions, the party's theoretical activity was the subject of intense
interest. The view is even voiced that the party leadership has allegedly
dragged the country into a "global experiment" without theoretical studies
or concepts of reform. Moreover, this has begun to be repeated with such
frequency that a sort of anti-perestroyka stereotype has formed. Let's get
to the bottom of this.

First of all, I have to repeat what I have said more than once, that the
concept of perestroyka did not suddenly dawn on a certain group of
people. Starting from the 20th CPSU Congress [in 1956] the search was on
in the party and society. Unfortunately, it was not supported and in the
majority of cases was suppressed. During the years of stagnation when
attempts were made to rehabilitate the Stalinist model of socialism, theory
was allotted the role of providing apologies for official policies. It is with
complete justification that we say that we have gained perestroyka literally
through suffering; and the concept that lies at its basis absorbed all the
best that had long been ripening in the depths of society, the party,
science, and culture. The April plenum of 1985 gave a powerful boost to
theoretical searching and opened up the possibility of freely discussing
painful problems in the life of society.

It is of fundamental importance that the party and its Central Committee headed this creative work, exceptionally needed by the country, and created favorable political conditions for it. Even in its first stage we realized that society was in need of fundamental renewal. It was in this way that the basic idea of perestroyka came into being, profound democratization and humanization of society within the framework of the socialist choice, of making it free and creating conditions of life that were worthy of mankind.

In the course of the implementation of that plan, the ideas of radical economic reform and of radical transformations in the political system, in the federation, and in the formation of a law-governed state were being developed. The foundations of the new political thinking have been elaborated, at the core of which lies the priority of common human values. The theory of perestroyka would have been impossible without an understanding of all the enormous changes with which the world has approached the end of the 20th century. Step by step, we have been deepening our understanding of the goal and of the methods of the revolutionary transformation. As a matter of fact, that required, in Lenin's words, a reconsideration of the whole of our view of socialism. As a result, we have arrived at an understanding of perestroyka as a new revolution and as a logical continuation of the cause, the beginning of which was laid by the Great October [Revolution].

I am far from the intention to present the theory of perestroyka as something completed in every respect, as some finished system, as an ultimate truth. We have had enough of such pretentions and ambitions. Our experience has taught us to be ready for self-critical assessments, for introducing necessary corrections into theory and policy which must respond to real processes in the country and in the world. So, when they say to us: Give us a new completed theory of socialism, we reply: Only life, only free labor, self-administration and the wellbeing of the people can fill the concept of socialism with new content.

If this does not happen, if this concept only keeps roaming through reports and front page articles, the authors of which are trying out model concepts, the socialist idea will be hopelessly devalued. Tell us, first, what you intend to do for your country and for your people, and then it will become clear what you indeed want and what you mean by socialism. We say that socialism is a real movement and it is the vital creativity of the masses, and I am convinced that the CPSU has correctly defined the goal of the movement as humane democratic socialism. Our views on the subject have been formulated in the draft program statement of the 28th CPSU Congress. How do they relate to Marxism? That is a fundamental issue for our party. Everyone knows that the content of the social theory created by Marx, Engels, and Lenin was shaped on the basis of an analysis of the realities of the 19th century. And Lenin's social sphere theory was based in addition on the first decades of the 20th century. Since then, the world has radically changed under the influence, among other things, of Marxist thought itself, of the October Revolution, and of the international revolutionary and democratic movement.

We, for our part, have tried for decades to find the answers to all the incidents which crop up in life, in quotations from the classics, forgetting that the classic writers themselves demanded we bear in mind that all theory is conditioned by history. They scoffed at those who tried to turn Marxism into some kind of holy scripture. Life itself has forced us to remember this and to make a proper assessment of the significance of the fundamental laws of Marxist dialectics, above all the demand for a concrete analysis of concrete situations, and to base conclusions for policy solely on this.

The concept of perestroyka is, I repeat, in motion and is self-developing, and must enrich itself with new ideas and conclusions as we make advances. The CPSU resolutely opposes dogmatism, quotation-mongering, and favors a consistent, creative approach toward the theory and practice of socialism, the interpretation of 20th century experience, and the heritage of Marx, Engels, and Lenin, and other luminaries of revolutionary and progressive thought.

The work on improving our concept of perestroyka is continuing. Therefore, it would evidently be correct, having adopted a program statement, to recognize that the currently operating program of the CPSU has lost its force, to proceed toward a new party program, and for this purpose to form an appropriate commission at the congress.

Comrades, communists and all society are expecting from the congress answers to the most crucial questions on the party itself.

A natural yet difficult process is now under way whereby it is reinterpreting its own role in society and the principles, the structure, and the methods of activity that have taken shape over decades. The earlier depiction of the CPSU is in need of critical assessment and serious changes.

Recently the party has been subject to serious criticism—both just and unjust. We do not spare ourselves, and people do not spare us. This is what I would like to talk about here. For many decades the CPSU was adapted to serve the authoritarian-bureaucratic system and that has led to serious deformations in relations inside the party, in the selection of cadres, and effectively to millions of communists having been kept out of decisionmaking—something which has effectively created an atmosphere of indifference, apathy, and passivity in party organizations. That is why when criticism is being made of the deformations in the country, and for which the party leadership, of course, bears responsibility, this does not at all mean that every communist is to blame....

How do we see the renewed CPSU? As a party of socialist choice and of a communist future: a voluntary union of like-minded people whose policy expresses the interests of the working class, the peasantry, and the intelligentsia; a party which adheres to common human and humanist ideals, which is sensitive to national traditions and ambitions, and which is at the same time uncompromising with regard to chauvinism, nationalism, racism, and any "manifestations" or "developments" of a reactionary ideology and obscurantism; a party which is free of ideological blinkers and dogmatism and which strives to play an initiating role in political and ideological processes using methods of persuasion, and of propaganda of its policy and developing relations of dialogue, discussion, cooperation, and partnership with all progressive, social, and political forces of the country; a party which constructs relations among its members solely upon the basis of party comradeship, of respect for others' opinions, and of the recognition of the rights of a minority to have their own position, upon the basis of full freedom of discussion and of the decision adopted by the majority being compulsory for everyone; a party which asserts in its internal life principles of selfgovernment, a freedom of action in party organizations, the independence of the Communist Parties of the Union republics united by the unity of their program goals and statutory provisions; a party open to contacts and interaction with communists, social democrats, socialists of various countries and of varying orientation and with representatives of many other tendencies of modern political and scientific thought. . . .

Various documents, including the draft keynote statement of the 28th congress, talk of the need to return to the Leninist understanding of the party as the vanguard of society. But will it not transpire, is it not transpiring—and people are asking such questions—that we are once again laying claim to some kind of exceptional position, merely changing the term 'leading role' to 'vanguard'? There must be clarity on this: We believe that one cannot foist a vanguard role on society, it can only be won by an active struggle for the interests of the working people, by practical deeds, and by our whole political and moral image. The party will pursue its policy and fight to maintain its mandate as the ruling party within the framework of the democratic process and elections to the central and local legislative bodies. In this respect it is acting as a parliamentary party.

The most difficult task for the party now is to make its influence commensurate with the new political and organizational opportunities. We must proceed from the premise that the party does not meddle with the functions of the local soviet organs. This means it does not carry responsibility for the decisions which are made without it being consulted and that it reserves the right to criticize them publicly. The primary party organizations do not consider it possible and, in practice, no longer have the right to implement control over administrative activity at enterprises, in organizations, or over the work of the apparatus of ministries and departments and of local soviet and economic institutions. But the party organizations cannot be detached observers of the processes taking place in labor collectives or in the regions. They must learn to influence the solution of various tasks through new political and organizational methods, through communists and primarily, through communist leaders.

The new role of the party organization consists in working out positions collectively, at meetings, congresses, conferences, plenums, on the most important issues of the life of society, to bring these to the attention of the appropriate state and economic bodies, to explain these positions in public discussions, to orientate communists toward defending them in their practical deeds. The scale of the CPSU's influence will be determined primarily by the strength of the ideas proclaimed by the party and by their attractiveness to the working people.

On relations with other political parties and public movements: I think that our party congress will come definitely in favor of extensive cooperation with all parties and movements of a progressive orientation and in favor of consolidation, in the interests of perestroyka and in the interests of the people. Within the framework of such cooperation, it is possible to discuss any problems that are worrying the public and to seek paths toward accord and joint action. . . .

The party's relations with trade unions, with other working organizations will be based on partnership and comradeship. Not in the least interfering in trade unions' internal affairs, party committees must use all their authority to support their [trade unions'] well-grounded demands and initiatives.

Among other mass public organizations, the Komsomol [All-Union Leninist Communist Youth League] has to be mentioned in particular. It is the organization closest to the party, related to it, if you will, in ideological and political respect. Our comrades in the Komsomol are experiencing difficult times, which was possible to observe at the congress of the Komsomol, which took place recently. The issues of whether the Komsomol should exist at all have been the subject of heated discussions there. And if it should exist, then what kind of Komsomol should it be? . . .

The party's attitude toward women needs radical restructuring. We have to recognize that the question of women is among the most acute for us. Contrary to all the slogans, of which more than enough have been pronounced, starting, if we are to talk about our period of perestroyka, with the 27th CPSU Congress, even today comrades, women's living and working conditions need considerable attention and radical improvement. This is one of the most important issues, a fundamental issue. And it is particularly intolerable, comrades, that there is an extremely insignificant presence of women in political life. I think that we should all be simply ashamed when we see that in many countries at the moment, women take an active part in high politics. But let's glance around this hall; how many women delegates are there here? We will wait for the report of the chairman of the Credentials Commission for complete clarity to be brought to this issue. And how many of them are there in the government? We have left this in such neglect, and the efforts of recent times have done very little to change things, very little. Perhaps we, at this congress, should take real steps, such that both in the Central Committee, in the Politburo, and in the Secretariat—everywhere—in all these bodies, women are really represented. . . .

On the Communist Parties of the Union Republics: I think the congress delegates will agree that this is an issue of the greatest current relevance. And it is not just an organizational question, since it touches on the very nature of our party as an internationalist organization. As such it was created by Lenin, and as such it has for many decades fulfilled its role as the binding force of our multinational state. It is of fundamental importance that it should retain precisely this character, otherwise both the country, the state, and the party itself will suffer great and possibly irretrievable losses. Probably no one has any doubts about the principled approach to solving the problems which have arisen.

Our premise is that the integrity of the CPSU [Communist Party of the Soviet Union] is entirely compatible with the maximum independence of the Communist Parties of the Union republics and autonomous entities, and in no way limits their scope for taking account of their national, historical, local, and other special characteristics, and deciding at their own discretion the cadres, financial, and other questions with which they are concerned. But insofar as these questions are interwoven with the process of the reform of our Union, there are various tendencies here, down to the federalization of the party and separation from it.

You know the situation in the Baltic republics. In spite of all the measures taken by the Central Committee, we have not succeeded in averting the split into parties which still adhere to the CPSU platform and others which have withdrawn from it. As a result, the communist movement in the republics has been dramatically weakened and other political forces have come to power there. . . .

There is another issue being raised at the moment, and pungently at that: The issue of depoliticizing the bodies of state administration, the courts, procuracy, other law-and-order bodies, in addition to the Army. Our stance on this is determined by the fact that the right to association is an inalienable political freedom. Nobody can prohibit party members from setting up their cells in enterprises, establishments, and so on. It is hard to imagine depoliticized state bodies acting to maintain morale and to educate soldiers, officers, and so on. But we do not lay claim to exclusiveness here either: This is the natural right of all parties which will be registered in our country on a legal basis. That is our approach. . . .

An important step has been taken in the democratic development of the party, but it would be wrong to close our eyes to the fact that the election struggle turned out to be far from favorable for the workers, peasants, women, and young communists. Evidently we need to give all of our attention to fully grasping the proposal on introducing direct representation of primary and other party organizations in higher party bodies. Let's discuss this question, comrades.

The structure of the party's central bodies is a special issue. The proposals on this set forth in the draft program statement and rules have not met with great objections, although these do exist. There is a view that the new aspects of party building connected with the autonomy of Union republic communist parties have been ill considered and the Central Committee Presidium appears not to be a sufficiently effective organ. This matter was discussed in some detail by the council of delegations' representatives on the eve of the congress, and I can tell you, on their behalf, that the comrades believe that the majority of communists are not in favor of creating a Presidium and introducing the posts of party chairman and his deputies, but are in favor of keeping the Politburo and the post of general secretary, elected by the congress, and of the election of a Central Committee deputy general secretary as number two in the party leadership. I think I am reporting accurately the opinion of the council of delegations. We need to discuss and decide these questions which are important for the party.

The party Central Committee in the period between congresses. The present congress and the CPSU Central Committee, comrades, have had to tackle the tasks of perestroyka in conditions where the course of events has forced us constantly to seek new approaches, to reassess what seemed to be interpreted and clear. When today you read the material of the 27th party congress, you see that life has far outstripped the very boldest ideas which you and I were capable of in those days. . . .

I'm finishing my report. We are faced with very difficult tasks, comrades, and the party believes they can only be performed and a way out of the crisis situation can only be found in looking ahead, and only along the route of the further democratization and intensification of perestroyka.

YELTSIN ADDRESS

. . . The last years have shown that it has not proved possible to neutralize the activity of the party's conservative forces. On the contrary. We have spoken too much about us all being in the same boat, on the same side of the barricades, that we are fighting shoulder to shoulder with identical thinking. This position has discredited those communists who are sincere and consistent supporters of change. This position has created a regime of security for the conservative forces in the CPSU [Communist Party of the Soviet Union] and has strengthened their conviction that it is possible to gain revenge. . . .

. . . [D]uring discussions at the congress, the main issue has not been perestroyka in the country and ways for it to develop. The question is being tackled by the people outside this building and it is being tackled in the soviets of people's deputies. The question facing this congress is primarily that of the fate of the CPSU itself. To be more precise, the only question being tackled here is the fate of the apparatus of the party upper echelons.

The question is an extremely acute one: Will the apparatus of the CPSU find within itself the strength to make up its mind on changes? Will it make use of that last chance which the congress is giving it? It is either yes or no. Either the party apparatus makes up its mind on the radical restructuring of the party, under the pressure of the political reality, or it will clutch to doomed forms and remain in opposition to the people, in opposition to perestroyka.

In that case the representatives of the apparatus will inevitably be squeezed out of all bodies of legitimate authority. Such a party will not hold out in either a vanguard role or even in the role of a party which has representation in the soviets. Let us bury the illusions of those who think that once all the dissidents have left the party who do not wish to be cogs and screws in the party apparatus, it will retain all the property of the CPSU and the power connected with it. This is not so. . . .

Is everything so gloomy? Is there another way out? Yes, there is. True, there is little chance of this being victorious at this congress. That can be seen quite clearly. But all of us who have devoted decades of our lives to the party considered it our duty to come here in order to try to say that there is a way out for the CPSU. It is a hard and difficult one, but it does exist.

In a democratic state the changeover to a multi-party system is inevitable. In our country, various political parties are gradually being formed. At the same time, a radical renewal of the CPSU is inevitable. What process of modernizing the party is the most painless for the people and the most civilized?

First, it is essential to give organizational form to the various platforms which exist within the CPSU, and to give each communist time to determine his political position. I am convinced that the majority of rank-and-file communists will link the future of the party with its democratic wing. Second, it is essential to change the name of the party. It should be the Party of Democratic Socialism. Third, it is too early to discuss platforms and rules at the congress. Only a general declaration on the transformation of the CPSU should be adopted. Next, it is necessary to elect a new leadership capable of preparing a new congress in about six months' or a year's time.

Fourth, the party should free itself from any state functions. Primary party organizations should be abolished in the Army, in the state security system, and in state establishments. In the production sector, the fate of primary party organizations should be determined by the labor collectives themselves, and by the party members themselves. Members should pay only a minimum of dues to the new party or to the alliance it forms part of.

In this way a parliamentary-type party will arise. In conditions of the powerful renewal of society, only a party of this sort will be able to assume the leading role and to be victorious in elections in the person of one or other of its factions. . . .

GORBACHEV SPEECH

. . . In taking in the criticism, with all its harshness against the initiators of perestroyka and those who led its advance, and in spite of everything that has been written just recently about the congress and the report, I want to state: The report was evaluated very critically here in the hall, particularly in the press, let's say, particularly in the left-wing press. I do not go back on anything that I said in the report. I stand firmly on what I stated. For that reason [pauses] everything that was said to you there was thought out and weighed.

The main overall positive aspect of what has been achieved—and I want to stress this, and we need to go on continuing the process of deepening recognition—is, after all, freedom. Society has received freedom. This has unleashed the energy of the people. It has given a way out to ideas and concerns about the fate of the country, about the fate of socialism that were squeezed in the pincers of dogmas and old programs. It has made it possible to bring millions of people into politics, and to start the transformations that had become vitally urgent. Were there no freedom, there would not be this congress either, nor would it be of this nature or have the atmosphere it is being held in.

Not everything that had accumulated in the stifling, repressive atmosphere of Stalinism and stagnation, and that has now burst onto the surface, has turned out to be pleasant and constructive, but we have to reckon that. This is what the revolution is for. Its first function is always to give the people freedom. And perestroyka, with its democratization and glasnost, has fulfilled this its primary task. Spiritual rebirth is as essential to society as oxygen. It is taking place before our very eyes for all the costs of this process. And it has already had a huge influence on the whole state of society. A huge influence. Society has become different, and all of us have become different.

It is a different matter that neither the party, nor the country as a whole, nor the old nor the newly formed organizations and movements, nor our new power—all of us, comrades—have yet learned to use the freedom of society that we have gained. For that reason the most urgent task is to learn this faster and better.

We have advanced political reform quite far. We have set up structures from top to bottom on the basis of the democratic expression of the people's will and the improvement of these structures continues by virtue of the old ones breaking up and new ones arising. . . .

Communists and party organizations have taken part, and are taking part, in all of this, and yet one can feel in places a certain gulf, I would say a coolness, between the soviets and the party. Here we, comrades, and all communists, have to be very careful, and primarily we have to look at ourselves, you always have to start with yourself. Isn't this alienation connected with the fact that we are quite unable to renounce the former methods of communicating with the soviets, inherited from the command and administrative system?

The new organs of power, for their part, are also ignoring such complaints to an unhealthy degree, perhaps even to an excessively unhealthy degree. . . . I would urge the deputies of all soviets to work constructively, within the framework of the Constitution and the law. I am appealing here, primarily, as president of the country, because, I'll be blunt, a confrontation position is taking shape on the part of the new organs, a certain section of deputies. This does not bode well. It is bad if communists do not understand what renewed soviets are today, and that they have to play their part for the normalization of the whole situation. . . .

I will say plainly that this party crisis that we talk of, and there has been much said about it here, I have to say that this crisis has its very roots in fact in the inability, and in a number of cases the reluctance to understand fully that we are living and working in a new society now, an unprecedented politicized one, a society of broad and virtually unlimited glasnost, a society of a freedom unseen throughout history. But many party organizations and communists continue to act according to their habitual methods, inherited from the past, which are pulling us back by our coattails. And if any of the delegates—and judging from the speeches that came up during the meetings, there are some of these among us—has come to the congress in the hope of returning the party to the previous conditions, comfortable or uncomfortable is beside the point, but to the previous conditions of commands and orders, then I have to say, comrades, they are deliberately and profoundly misleading themselves. . . .

It is essential to overcome the alienation of the people that is rooted in the times long past. This must be done, first and foremost, through the primary party organizations and through renewing their activities, through renewing cadres and enhancing their prestige in practical work. I especially wanted to mention this. In general, I am deeply worried by our current situation and I think that a great deal of misunderstanding arises here between us.

Comrades, if we fail to comprehend that everything that had taken place in the past has already and to a significant degree become obsolete and is unacceptable, we will not move forward, nor will we be able either to strengthen the party's position or to lead further, offering effective policies to our society, thereby giving it new impetus along the path of perestroyka.

The point is that, both as far as the atmosphere of the congress is concerned and as far as many speeches are concerned and as far as the conduct of the delegates is concerned, along with their way of conversing and discussing things, I heard, felt it, as it were, simply in my bones, sensed it and saw that far from everyone understood the fact that the party is already living and working in the new conditions; that it is in a different society and that a different, renewed party with a different style of conduct and work is what is needed.

We do not change our line, we do not change our choice, we adhere to the socialist values, but, do believe me that the party's success depends on the party understanding that society is already different. Otherwise the party will be squeezed out by other forces and we will lose our positions.

Whereas at the moment we have enormous potential. Whenever they form and whatever the others do, we have vast opportunities if we understand the main thing: Without renewal, without democratization, without strengthening our living bond with the people and conducting vigorous work among the masses, we will not advance very far.

I have had a great many personal conversations in the last few days with the most varied comrades, and I have to say that I could sense a greater understanding of the unusualness, the novelty of the situation in which the party finds itself on the part of rank-and-file comrades, as it is customary to call them, although this is an outmoded expression of former times and I have used it perhaps to no purpose, but there you are. I mean by this the worker, peasant, and intelligentsia delegates and secretaries of primary party organizations. . . .

The next lesson I have drawn from the discussions that we have held is on how to act in future in the main directions of perestroyka. The party—and indeed the state—leadership has been criticized mercilessly for the economic situation, the state of the market and of goods supplies to the population. The key tasks here are active involvement in tackling the issue of food. I put that to the fore. . . .

Then comes the transition to a regulated market and the housing issue and in this connection I am not going to conceal the fact that I was very disturbed when the congress decided, by three-fourths of the votes, to alter the name of the economic reform commission, leaving out the word "market". So, there remains a lack of understanding of the sharp about-turn to making radical changes to the situation in the national economy, which society has been offered. Has our entire history really failed, comrades, to demonstrate the futility of attempts to get away from the plight in which the state and citizens found themselves by means of darning and patching the command management system? I think we are united on that nowadays. We have already borne huge losses by stubbornly hanging on to it for decades and even now people continue to hand on and thereby to hold up renewal and our arrival at new forms of economic life within the country.

And if we proceed like this further, then, I will say directly, we will lead the country to bankruptcy. I am voicing my point of view quite definitely. The advantages of the market economy have been proven on a world-wide scale. . . .

. . . From this platform I repeat once again, for the congress, for the party, for the whole country—our position consists of what is needed: Firstly, to give total freedom to all kinds of farms in the countryside on the basis of total freedom of choice. Second, to establish a sensible exchange between the town and the countryside, industry and agriculture, that would promote the revival of the countryside in the shortest possible time. Third, the state has to promote to the maximum degree the resolution of the urgent problems of the rural sector, primarily the creation of decent living conditions for our peasantry. It is on these three foundations that the countryside can be regenerated, and the country be supplied with food. And not a single element can be removed from this triad, otherwise the system will collapse. . . .

We inherit from Marx, Engels, and Lenin a high class of methodology in thinking, a dialectical form of ideas, which we will continue to depend on both in theory and in politics. But we will not allow everything created by the classics to be turned into another short course, something that evidently some people regret, judging from speeches. This will not happen. It would mean ruin for perestroyka and for society. . . .

What is the lesson of the congress here? Comrades have expressed their acute concern that the party is losing its prestige and is weakening its positions. It is being squeezed by other political forces and in some places communists have been forced to go into opposition. The blame for this is being laid on the leadership of the CPSU and particularly on some of its members. I will say right away that this criticism is justified in many respects, comrades. [applause] Justified in essence. I am only against the forms and against the fact . . . [pauses] There should not be two extremes here at the congress, there should be no talking down to anyone nor loutishness. That's all. But all the rest must be said. . . .

Comrades, I do not see any other path than the continuation, resolute and purposeful, of all that we have been doing to restructure the economy and the social sphere, and further to intensify the political reform and to implement the profound transformation of our multinational state. Let us get to work. We have begun the most crucial phase of perestroyka. Major reforms await us. [applause]

NATO'S DECLARATION
OF PEACEFUL INTENT

July 6, 1990

*The North Atlantic Treaty Organization (NATO), declaring July 6
that it "must and will adapt" to a new, warmer era in East-West
relations, extended "the hand of friendship" to the Soviet Union with
proposals for cooperation and joint military cutbacks. Leaders of NATO's
sixteen member nations approved the formal declaration in London,
forty-one years after the military alliance was created to defend Western
Europe against the threat of Soviet expansionism.*

*Moscow responded enthusiastically to the twenty-two point document,
and ten days later Soviet president Mikhail S. Gorbachev dropped his
opposition to NATO membership for a reunified Germany. His approval
removed the last major obstacle to German reunification.* (Reunification
of East and West Germany, p. 681)

*President George Bush and other leaders of the Atlantic alliance
purposely used the document to assure Moscow that a peaceful Soviet
Union had nothing to fear from NATO. That assurance was seen as
strengthening Gorbachev's ability to resist his foreign policy critics
within the Kremlin and to undermine the views of Soviet generals who
regarded a reunited Germany within NATO as a potential threat to their
country.*

*West Germany entered NATO in 1954, and the next year East
Germany became a founding member of the communist counterpart
Warsaw Treaty Organization. It linked Soviet forces with those of its
satellite states in Eastern Europe. As those states wrested free of
Moscow's control in 1989, the Warsaw pact group became virtually
defunct, weakening Soviet military strength in Europe.*

Helping Gorbachev at Home

Only a day before the declaration was issued, Maj. Gen. Ivan Mikulin, a military delegate to the Twenty-Eighth Soviet Communist Party Congress then meeting in Moscow, accused Soviet diplomats of "seeing the world through rose-colored glasses" and of rushing recklessly to withdraw troops from Eastern Europe. (Documents from 28th Communist Congress, p. 439) Gennadi I. Gerasimov, a spokesman for the Soviet Foreign Ministry, was quoted as saying that the London Declaration made it possible for Gorbachev to rebut the hard-liners who opposed concessions to the West.

Telling the Warsaw pact members that "we are no longer adversaries," NATO pledged "never in any circumstance" to be the first to use force and, in the event of a defensive action, to use nuclear weapons only as a "truly ... last resort." Moreover, it added, "our alliance will do its share to overcome the legacy of decades of suspicion [between East and West]." Echoing an oft-repeated Gorbachev proposal, the declaration said that the Conference on Security and Cooperation in Europe (CSCE), a thirty-five member forum including neutral nations as well as those of the Warsaw and NATO groupings, "should become more prominent in Europe's future."

The Western leaders invited Gorbachev to address the North Atlantic Council, NATO's diplomatic arm, at the Brussels headquarters. They also invited the Soviet Union, Czechoslovakia, Hungary, Poland, Bulgaria, and Romania—the Warsaw pact nations—to establish "regular diplomatic liaison" with the alliance. Gorbachev received Manfred Wörner, secretary general of NATO, in Moscow July 14 and accepted the speaking invitation for a date to be set later.

Soviet-U.S. Reaction

At the time the declaration was issued, Soviet foreign minister Eduard A. Shevardnadze said the measure approved in the London meeting would "pave the way to a safe future for the entire European continent." He stressed the "potentially important" offer by NATO to revise its military doctrine of "flexible response," which reserved the right to make first use of nuclear weapons.

President Bush was equally enthusiastic. At a news conference after the London meeting, he said: "For more than 40 years we've looked for this day—a day when we've already moved beyond containment [of communism], with unity on this continent overcoming division. And now that day is here, and all peoples from the Atlantic to the Urals, from the Baltic to the Adriatic, can share in its promise."

He was asked, "How do you expect that Mr. Gorbachev can be helped in his present problems in the Soviet Union with this London Declaration?" The president answered: "I think he will say, look, NATO has indeed changed in response to the changes that have taken place in Eastern Europe. ... I would think he would view this as a very positive step forward and one that vindicates some of the moves that he's made over the past year or two."

R. W. Apple, Jr., reporting from London for the New York Times, *commented: "Having lost an enemy, NATO is seeking a new role, and it has not yet found it. The search is complicated by the wish to do three things at once: reassure the Russians, avoid sounding so friendly that calls for slashes in military budgets become irresistible, and find a rational underpinning for continued American involvement, both political and military, in Europe." Left untouched by the London Declaration, he added, was the question of whether NATO would ultimately be supplanted by the CSCE, or whether it would survive as a unit within the larger group.*

Following are the London Declaration issued July 6, 1990, by heads of state and government of the sixteen member nations of the North Atlantic Treaty Organization proposing a cooperative role with its former Soviet adversaries, and excerpts from a news conference President George Bush held in London immediately after the NATO meeting:

LONDON DECLARATION

1. Europe has entered a new, promising era. Central and Eastern Europe is liberating itself. The Soviet Union has embarked on the long journey toward a free society. The walls that once confined people and ideas are collapsing. Europeans are determining their own destiny. They are choosing freedom. They are choosing economic liberty. They are choosing peace. They are choosing a Europe whole and free. As a consequence, this Alliance must and will adapt.

2. The North Atlantic Alliance has been the most successful defensive alliance in history. As our Alliance enters its fifth decade and looks ahead to a new century, it must continue to provide for the common defence. This Alliance has done much to bring about the new Europe. No one, however, can be certain of the future. We need to keep standing together, to extend the long peace we have enjoyed these past four decades. Yet our Alliance must be even more an agent of change. It can help build the structures of a more united continent, supporting security and stability with the strength of our shared faith in democracy, the rights of the individual, and the peaceful resolution of disputes. We reaffirm that security and stability do not lie solely in the military dimension, and we intend to enhance the political component of our Alliance as provided for by Article 2 of our Treaty.

3. The unification of Germany means that the division of Europe is also being overcome. A united Germany in the Atlantic Alliance of free democracies and part of the growing political and economic integration of the European Community will be an indispensable factor of stability,

which is needed in the heart of Europe. The move within the European Community towards political union, including the development of a European identity in the domain of security, will also contribute to Atlantic solidarity and to the establishment of a just and lasting order of peace throughout the whole of Europe.

4. We recognise that, in the new Europe, the security of every state is inseparably linked to the security of its neighbours. NATO must become an institution where Europeans, Canadians and Americans work together not only for the common defence, but to build new partnerships with all the nations of Europe. The Atlantic Community must reach out to the countries of the East which were our adversaries in the Cold War, and extend to them the hand of friendship.

5. We will remain a defensive alliance and will continue to defend all the territory of all of our members. We have no aggressive intentions and we commit ourselves to the peaceful resolution of all disputes. We will never in any circumstance be the first to use force.

6. The member states of the North Atlantic Alliance propose to the member states of the Warsaw Treaty Organization a joint declaration in which we solemnly state that we are no longer adversaries and reaffirm our intention to refrain from the threat or use of force against the territorial integrity or political independence of any state, or from acting in any other manner inconsistent with the purposes and principles of the United Nations Charter and with the CSCE [Conference on Security and Cooperation in Europe] Final Act. We invite all other CSCE member states to join us in this commitment to non-aggression.

7. In that spirit, and to reflect the changing political role of the Alliance, we today invite President Gorbachev on behalf of the Soviet Union, and representatives of the other Central and Eastern European countries to come to Brussels and address the North Atlantic Council. We today also invite the governments of the Union of Soviet Socialist Republics, the Czech and Slovak Federal Republic, the Hungarian Republic, the Republic of Poland, the People's Republic of Bulgaria and Romania to come to NATO, not just to visit, but to establish regular diplomatic liaison with NATO. This will make it possible for us to share with them our thinking and deliberations in this historic period of change.

8. Our Alliance will do its share to overcome the legacy of decades of suspicion. We are ready to intensify military contacts, including those of NATO Military Commanders, with Moscow and other Central and Eastern European capitals.

9. We welcome the invitation to NATO Secretary General Manfred Wörner to visit Moscow and meet with Soviet leaders.

10. Military leaders from throughout Europe gathered earlier this year in Vienna to talk about their forces and doctrine. NATO proposes another such meeting this Autumn to promote common understanding. We intend to establish an entirely different quality of openness in Europe, including an agreement on "Open Skies".

11. The significant presence of North American conventional and U.S.

nuclear forces in Europe demonstrates the underlying political compact that binds North America's fate to Europe's democracies. But, as Europe changes, we must profoundly alter the way we think about defence.

12. To reduce our military requirements, sound arms control agreements are essential. That is why we put the highest priority on completing this year the first treaty to reduce and limit conventional armed forces in Europe (CFE) along with the completion of a meaningful CSBM [Confidence- and Security-Building Measures] package. These talks should remain in continuous session until the work is done. Yet we hope to go further. We propose that, once a CFE [Conventional Forces in Europe] Treaty is signed, follow-on talks should begin with the same membership and mandate, with the goal of building on the current agreement with additional measures, including measures to limit manpower in Europe. With this goal in mind, a commitment will be given at the time of signature of the CFE Treaty concerning the manpower levels of a unified Germany.

13. Our objective will be to conclude the negotiations on the follow-on to CFE and CSBMs as soon as possible and looking to the follow-up meeting of the CSCE to be held in Helsinki in 1992. We will seek through new conventional arms control negotiations, within the CSCE framework, further far-reaching measures in the 1990s to limit the offensive capability of conventional armed forces in Europe, so as to prevent any nation from maintaining disproportionate military power on the continent. NATO's High Level Task Force will formulate a detailed position for these follow-on conventional arms control talks. We will make provisions as needed for different regions to redress disparities and to ensure that no one's security is harmed at any stage. Furthermore, we will continue to explore broader arms control and confidence-building opportunities. This is an ambitious agenda, but it matches our goal: enduring peace in Europe.

14. As Soviet troops leave Eastern Europe and a treaty limiting conventional armed forces is implemented, the Alliance's integrated force structure and its strategy will change fundamentally to include the following elements:

- NATO will field smaller and restructured active forces. These forces will be highly mobile and versatile so that Allied leaders will have maximum flexibility in deciding how to respond to a crisis. It will rely increasingly on multinational corps made up of national units.
- NATO will scale back the readiness of its active units, reducing training requirements and the number of exercises.
- NATO will rely more heavily on the ability to build up larger forces if and when they might be needed.

15. To keep the peace, the Alliance must maintain for the foreseeable future an appropriate mix of nuclear and conventional forces, based in Europe, and kept up to date where necessary. But, as a defensive Alliance, NATO has always stressed that none of its weapons will ever be used except in self-defence and that we seek the lowest and most stable level of

nuclear forces needed to secure the prevention of war.

16. The political and military changes in Europe, and the prospects of further changes, now allow the Allies concerned to go further. They will thus modify the size and adapt the tasks of their nuclear deterrent forces. They have concluded that, as a result of the new political and military conditions in Europe, there will be a significantly reduced role for sub-strategic nuclear systems of the shortest range. They have decided specifically that, once negotiations begin on short-range nuclear forces, the Alliance will propose, in return for reciprocal action by the Soviet Union, the elimination of all its nuclear artillery shells from Europe.

17. New negotiations between the United States and the Soviet Union on the reduction of short-range nuclear forces should begin shortly after a CFE agreement is signed. The Allies concerned will develop an arms control framework for these negotiations which take into account our requirements for far fewer nuclear weapons, and the diminished need for sub-strategic nuclear systems of the shortest range.

18. Finally, with the total withdrawal of Soviet stationed forces and the implementation of a CFE agreement, the Allies concerned can reduce their reliance on nuclear weapons. These will continue to fulfil an essential role in the overall strategy of the Alliance to prevent war by ensuring that there are no circumstances in which nuclear retaliation in response to military action might be discounted. However, in the transformed Europe, they will be able to adopt a new NATO strategy making nuclear forces truly weapons of last resort.

19. We approve the mandate given in Turnberry to the North Atlantic Council in Permanent Session to oversee the ongoing work on the adaptation of the Alliance to the new circumstances. It should report its conclusions as soon as possible.

20. In the context of these revised plans for defence and arms control, and with the advice of NATO Military Authorities and all member states concerned, NATO will prepare a new Allied military strategy moving away from "forward defence," where appropriate, towards a reduced forward presence and modifying "flexible response" to reflect a reduced reliance on nuclear weapons. In that connection, NATO will elaborate new force plans consistent with the revolutionary changes in Europe. NATO will also provide a forum for Allied consultation on the upcoming negotiations on short-range nuclear forces.

21. The Conference on Security and Cooperation in Europe (CSCE) should become more prominent in Europe's future, bringing together the countries of Europe and North America. We support a CSCE Summit later this year in Paris which would include the signature of a CFE agreement and would set new standards for the establishment, and preservation, of free societies. It should endorse, inter alia:

- CSCE principles on the right to free and fair elections;
- CSCE commitments to respect and uphold the rule of law;
- CSCE guidelines for enhancing economic cooperation, based on the

development of free and competitive market economies; and
- CSCE cooperation on environmental protection.

22. We further propose that the CSCE Summit in Paris decide how the CSCE can be institutionalised to provide a forum for wider poliical dialogue in a more united Europe. We recommend that CSCE governments establish:

- a programme for regular consultations among member governments at the Heads of State and Government or Ministerial level, at least once each year, with other periodic meetings of officials to prepare for and follow up on these consultations.
- a schedule of CSCE review conferences once every two years to assess progress toward a Europe whole and free;
- a small CSCE secretariat to coordinate these meetings and conferences;
- a CSCE mechanism to monitor elections in all the CSCE countries, on the basis of the Copenhagen Document;
- a CSCE Centre for the Prevention of Conflict that might serve as a forum for exchanges of military information, discussion of unusual military activities, and the conciliation of disputes involving CSCE member states; and
- a CSCE parliamentary body, the Assembly of Europe, to be based on the existing parliamentary assembly of the Council of Europe, in Strasbourg, and include representatives of all CSCE member states.

The sites of these new institutions should reflect the fact that the newly democratic countries of Central and Eastern Europe form part of the political structures of the new Europe.

23. Today, our Alliance begins a major transformation. Working with all the countries of Europe, we are determined to create enduring peace on this continent.

BUSH'S NEWS CONFERENCE

... I'm pleased to announce that my colleagues and I have begun a major transformation of the North Atlantic alliance, and we view it as a historic turning point. NATO has set a new path for peace. It's kept the peace for 40 years and today charted a new course for stability and cooperation in Europe.

We, as you know, are issuing a document, the London Declaration; and it makes specific proposals and establishes directions for the future in four key areas.

First, the London Declaration transforms our relationship with old adversaries. To those Governments who confronted us in the Cold War, our alliance extends the hand of friendship. We reaffirm that we shall never be the first to use force against other states in Europe. And we propose a joint declaration between members of the alliance and member states of the Warsaw Pact which other CSCE [Conference on Security and Cooperation in Europe] states could join in, making a solemn commitment to nonaggression. We say to President Gorbachev: Come to NATO. We say to all the member states of the Warsaw Pact: Come to NATO and establish regular diplomatic liaison with the alliance.

And second, the London Declaration transforms the character of NATO's conventional defenses. We can start, and must start, by finishing the current CFE [conventional forces in Europe] talks this year. Once CFE is signed, we would begin follow-on negotiations to adopt additional measures, including measures to limit manpower in Europe. With this goal in mind, a commitment will be given when the CFE treaty is signed concerning the manpower levels of the armed forces of a united Germany. We will also seek in the nineties to achieve further far-reaching measures to limit the offensive capability of conventional armed forces. We'll change our strategy for a conventional defense. We agreed to move away from NATO's current strategy of forward defense to a reduced forward presence. We agreed, in addition, to make the principle of collective defense even more evident by organizing NATO troops into multinational corps.

And third, the London Declaration transforms NATO's nuclear strategy. For 23 years we've had a nuclear strategy called flexible response, developed to meet a danger of sudden overwhelming conventional attack. As that danger recedes, we've agreed to modify flexible response.

Nuclear deterrence has given us an unprecedented period of peace, and it will remain fundamental to our strategy. But by reducing its reliance on nuclear weapons, NATO in the new Europe will adopt a new strategy making its nuclear forces truly weapons of last resort.

This new strategy will require different forces. We've decided that once negotiations begin on short-range nuclear forces we are prepared to eliminate all NATO nuclear artillery shells from Europe in return for reciprocal action by the Soviet Union. We agreed that this review should report its conclusions as soon as possible.

And fourth, the London Declaration transforms the alliance's vision for the CSCE and the structure for building a Europe whole and free. We know the CSCE process—bringing together North America and all of Europe—can provide a structure for Europe's continued political development; and that means new standards for free elections, the rule of law, economic liberty, and environmental cooperation. And we agreed today on six initiatives to give life to CSCE's principles and realize its potential.

As you can see, the London Declaration will bring fundamental change to every aspect of the alliance's work. This is indeed a day of renewal for the Atlantic community. For more than 40 years, we've looked for this day—a day when we have already moved beyond containment, with unity on this continent overcoming division. And now that day is here, and all peoples from the Atlantic to the Urals, from the Baltic to the Adriatic, can share in its promise. . . .

U.S. Armed Forces in Europe

Q. Mr. President, with the threat receding, in the way your communique describes, do you think it's inevitable that at some point in the next few years the Europeans will decide it's better that American troops just go home? And what do you say to American taxpayers to convince them that it's worth continuing to pay the bill to have them in Europe?

THE PRESIDENT. I don't think the American troops will stay against the will of the host country. I don't want to see American forces deployed where American forces are not wanted. I don't want to see Soviet forces deployed where Soviet forces are not wanted. And I expect the same would be true of other nationalities' forces as well. But I don't foresee that day because I think the alliance has spoken rather eloquently about the need for a common defense. And all the members of the alliance are united in their view that a U.S. force presence in Europe is stabilizing and very, very important. So, I don't see that day looming up on the horizon.

Q. But do you fear that American taxpayers' support for that continuation might be eroding?

THE PRESIDENT. I see some attacks on this, and I think this NATO declaration should help in that regard. But I view it as my responsibility to make clear to the American taxpayer why it is in our interest to help keep the peace. And that's exactly what these forces are engaged in. . . .

Eastern European Membership in NATO

Q. Mr. President. . . . You're inviting the Warsaw Pact countries to come to NATO as observers. What if they want to become members of NATO—Hungary, for instance, or even Poland? Are you saying by inviting them to just be observers that you do not look favorably on them becoming full members?

THE PRESIDENT. I'm saying NATO views this as an open invitation, and who knows what will happen in terms of membership down the line? That's not in the cards right this minute. We're just coming out of an adversarial environment of varying—I think there's varying degrees of enthusiasm for what you're talking about amongst the members of the Warsaw Pact at this juncture, so I'd say it's premature.

Q. Would you oppose any country—for instance, Hungary—becoming a member of NATO?

THE PRESIDENT. Not forever. But at this juncture, I support the NATO doctrine.

Modernization of Strategic Nuclear Weapons

Q. Mr. President, in your communique you talk about nuclear weapons becoming truly weapons of last resort. You say the fundamental strategy of the alliance is being transformed here. As part of this review, are you considering going back home and taking another look at some of the strategic nuclear modernization programs that you have supported—looking at some of the very expensive weapons programs that some say

463

should be a bonus, a part of the "peace dividend?"

THE PRESIDENT. Not as a result of anything that's transpired here in NATO, no. We are interested in strategic arms agreements with the Soviets. The Soviets, as we all know, have indeed modernized their forces. We're on the horns of a dilemma in that question, you might say, because we have not to the degree they have. But that was not a consideration here at NATO, nor has anything transpired here that will make me go home with a different approach to strategic arms.

Q. If I may follow up: So, you'll proceed across the board with strategic modernization? Your commitment to that --

THE PRESIDENT. Yes. I will proceed in negotiating with the Soviets to achieve a strategic arms agreement.

NATO Policy

Q. Mr. President, how much did threats to *perestroika* and reforms in the Soviet Union play in changes you've announced today at NATO?

THE PRESIDENT. You mean, what's going on at the Congress [28th Communist Party Congress of the Soviet Union]? None, in my view. I mean, I think what's contributed to the changes in our approach—NATO—are the changes that have taken place, particularly since our last meeting, in terms of Eastern Europe and in terms of the Soviets' willingness to withdraw forces, hopefully, through a CFE agreement. So, I don't think anything was short—that there was short-term thinking as a result of the debates that are going on in Moscow this very day.

Q. Well, if I can follow up then: What kind of messages do the changes announced today send to Gorbachev?

THE PRESIDENT. They send to him that here's an alliance that you should view, Mr. Gorbachev, as defensive and not threatening. And, please, convince your military and others in the Soviet Union of this fact.

You see, from my discussions with Mr. Gorbachev and others, I've had the feeling that they have viewed NATO as much more threatening to them than the way in which I've looked at NATO. But now, as a result of the actions that we've taken here, I think it should be clear to the Soviet military, to Mr. Gorbachev, to his adversaries, and to his friends inside the Soviet Union that NATO is changing. And to the degree they had seen it as a threat to their shores or to their borders, they should look at it as not a threat to their borders or to their people.

Anytime you sit down with people from the Soviet Union, they tell you of the fact that they lost from 20 million to 27 million lives. It's ingrained in them. They do it not as a defensive mechanism but they do it because they feel very strongly about that. I hope that they will look at the changes that NATO has taken and say, Well, if NATO had been a threat to us, it no longer is a threat to us. And then I hope we can go forward to further document that spirit by mutual agreements on arms control.

Q. How are you going to communicate what's in this document to Mr. Gorbachev and the people there? Are you going to talk with him personally? Did the NATO leaders decide on some other method of communication with him to let him know what it means, what the communique means?

THE PRESIDENT. The NATO leaders have decided that the Secretary General will be going there, and that will be a very good face-to-face chance to discuss these matters. I believe our Secretary of State [James A. Baker III] is meeting soon with Mr. Shevardnadze [Soviet Foreign Minister], and you can be sure the matters will be discussed then. And then, in all likelihood, I will discuss it personally by telephone with Mr. Gorbachev. . . .

Soviet Response to NATO Policies

Q. Mr. President, what kind of tangible response would you like to see from President Gorbachev now to this? And I'm thinking particularly of the issue of Germany and NATO.

THE PRESIDENT. . . . I would like to see the tangible response be an acceptance of the concept that a unified Germany in NATO is not only good but that it certainly is no threat to them. And we've had long talks with Mr. Gorbachev about that. And perhaps this declaration will be a document that he can use to convince others that a unified Germany in NATO is in the interest of stability and world peace. . . .

President Gorbachev's NATO Address

Q. Mr. President, Mikhail Gorbachev is already under fire from conservatives for essentially giving away Eastern Europe. Are you at all concerned, sir, that by inviting him to speak to NATO you're further undermining him?

THE PRESIDENT. No, not only do I think we're not undermining him but I would think that would send a signal that NATO has no hostile intentions to the Soviet Union. . . .

East-West Relations and
Political and Economic Change

Q. Having attended quite a number of these things, these NATO conferences, I'd like to ask a question, Mr. President, that I asked— [*inaudible*]—is this to some extent a celebration of the victory of NATO in the Cold War—the Cold War is over and NATO has won? Or don't you believe it's the idea that NATO has won the Cold War?

THE PRESIDENT. Excuse me, back up, now. I've tried to avoid code words, and the Cold War being over is something that I'd rather not comment on. I don't think we're dealing in terms of victory and defeat. We're dealing in terms of how do we stabilize and guarantee the peace and security of Europe. So, to the degree a chief of state or head of government dwells on the kinds of rhetoric that you understandably ask about, I think it is counterproductive. Does that answer it?

Q. Would you say that NATO has to a great extent caused Gorbachev to be—that the whole changes in Eastern Europe have to some extent been caused by what's been going on in Western Europe for the last 40 years?

THE PRESIDENT. I would say to some degree that the changes in Eastern Europe and in the Soviet Union have been because they have seen the success of market economies. They've seen a craving for freedom and democracy on the parts of people. And to the degree NATO countries contributed to that proper perception, so be it. I'd like to think that—I'm convinced that NATO's solidarity during the last 40 years has guaranteed the peace for Europe. And when you look back at history, it is a long peace, given some of the conflagrations on this continent. So, I think NATO deserves a lot of credit....

Changes in the Soviet Union

Q. Mr. President, how do you square your concern over stability in Europe, which is the new purpose of NATO, with increasing signs of instability in the Soviet Union, particularly on the political and economic front? And what can you do to put those two pieces of the puzzle together?

THE PRESIDENT: A very good and very difficult question because, frankly, one thing we do is stay out of the internal affairs of the Soviet Union. I realize that some think that I'm not staying out of the internal affairs of the Soviet Union when I speak pleasantly about Mr. Gorbachev.

But I think they have to sort it out now. They have to decide what they want, how much of their gross national product ought to go into arms, whether the threat is much less than they have historically perceived. And once they take that decision, then we in the West will stand ready to work very cooperatively with them....

Q. How do you expect that Mr. Gorbachev can be helped in his present problems in the Soviet Union with this London Declaration?

THE PRESIDENT. I think he will say, Look, NATO has indeed changed in response to the changes that have taken place in Eastern Europe....

I would think that he would view this as a very positive step forward and one that vindicates some of the moves that he's made over the past year or two....

HOUSTON ECONOMIC
SUMMIT CONFERENCE
July 11, 1990

Leaders of the Group of Seven economic powers—the United States, Japan, West Germany, Britain, France, Italy, and Canada—and the European Economic Community (EEC) met July 9-11 in Houston, Texas, for their sixteenth annual summit conference. But in the welcoming words of President George Bush, it was the first economic summit of the "post-postwar era."

No longer did cold war questions haunt the conference; during the past year, various leaders had declared that the old East-West antagonisms had been replaced by a spirit of cooperation. Instead, the major question was how best to provide the Soviet Union with economic aid.

West German chancellor Helmut Kohl favored a $15 billion international aid package for the Soviets. He apparently considered the aid especially important to calming Moscow's fears about the coming reunification of East Germany and West Germany. Bush preferred giving technical assistance to help Soviet president Mikhail S. Gorbachev bring about needed economic reforms. The U.S. president insisted that any other kinds of aid should be made conditional on Soviet progress toward a free-market economy.

Kohl's plan drew backing from French president François Mitterrand and EEC president Jacques Delors, whereas Bush received support from Japanese premier Toshiki Kaifu, British prime minister Margaret Thatcher, and Canadian prime minister Brian Mulroney. Italian premier Giulio Andreotti did not identify with either side. In the end, the leaders decided each country would be free to give whatever level of aid it wished. They would, meanwhile, await the outcome of a study of the Soviet economy by the International Monetary Fund to determine what collective steps should be taken.

To some summit observers, Kohl had gained added stature from his success in engineering German unification and winning Gorbachev's acceptance of it. As expressed in a New York Times *news analysis from Houston on the conference's final day, it had been "a coming-out party" for Kohl. "Mr. Kohl emerged here, even more than at the North Atlantic Treaty Organization meeting in London last week, as a dominant figure in these international deliberations ..."* (NATO's Declaration of Peaceful Intent, p. 455)

At the summit's conclusion, a reporter asked Bush, "Now that we're seeing key allies going their own way on aid to the Soviet Union, aren't we seeing at least a subtle change in the way the United States has led the alliance? Aren't you having to give a little more leeway to the allies now that the Cold War is over?" The president responded, "We're dealing in entirely different times.... [I]f your question is, Is it bad or does it alter the U.S. role if Chancellor Kohl, for very special reasons, goes forward, I would argue that it does not."

Global Warming Differences

The Bush administration appeared to achieve a victory on the ticklish issue of global warming. The White House long had resisted efforts by European nations to take speedier action to reduce carbon dioxide emissions, which many scientists contended were causing a "greenhouse" effect in the atmosphere and a consequent warming of the Earth. John H. Sununu, the White House chief of staff, had contended that emission reductions would harm the U.S. economy and that the scientific evidence of global warming was not conclusive.

The summit statements deemphasized environmental issues, and the seven nations postponed until 1992 the question of making a definite commitment to cut back carbon dioxide emissions. However, the economic communique implicitly rebuffed the White House view by saying that a lack of complete certainty was no excuse to postpone actions "which are justified in their own right." Before the summit, Kohl had sent the other leaders letters saying that "the threat of climate change ... [was] a threat to all mankind" and that "the world expects the seven summit countries to come up with specific proposals." West Germany already had pledged a 25 percent cutback over the next fifteen years.

The Group of Seven pledged to help Brazil preserve its tropical rain forests and to develop strategies for worldwide reforestation. At his July 11 conference, Bush defended his stand against mandatory emission cuts. "We cannot govern by listening to the loudest voice on the extreme of an environmental movement," he said.

The United States reluctantly had joined ninety-two other nations in signing an agreement in London June 29 to banish by the year 2000 the production of chemicals that destroy the Earth's ozone layer, which forms a protection against the sun's harmful ultra-violet rays. The nations also agreed to establish a global fund to help less-developed countries phase out the use of the chemicals. The agreement was adopted unanimously after the United States changed its position under international pressure. On June 15 the White House announced U.S. support for the fund. Previously it had opposed helping those countries.

The London agreement amended a 1987 treaty, the Montreal Protocol, that had called for a lesser cut of 50 percent in the production of chlorofluorocarbons (CFCs), the chlorine-based gases used in electronics, refrigerants, fire extinguishers, and aerosols. The gases combine with elements in the atmosphere to deplete the ozone layer.

Farm Subsidy Problems

On the thorny subjects of farm subsidies and protectionism in agricultural trade, the United States won less than it wanted from its summit partners. Instead of pledging to phase out agricultural trade barriers and domestic subsidies to farmers, the parties signed agreements with the understanding that such policies would take into account "differences in the social and economic conditions of farming" in individual countries.

Bush had lobbied energetically for commitments from the other nations to open their agricultural markets to lower-priced farm products grown in the United States and Third World countries. The problem of agricultural subsidies was blocking progress at the Uruguay Round of international trade talks scheduled for completion by the end of 1990. The protection of Europe's farmers against foreign competition was a highly sensitive issue in France and West Germany.

Following are excerpts from the Houston economic summit conference's "Economic Declaration," issued July 11, 1990, and from President George Bush's news conference held the same day.

ECONOMIC DECLARATION

1. We, the Heads of State and Government of the seven major industrial democracies and the President of the Commission of the European Communities, meeting in Houston for our annual Economic Summit, celebrate the renaissance of democracy throughout much of the world. We welcome unreservedly the spread of multiparty democracy, the practice of free elections, the freedom of expression and assembly, the increased respect for human rights, the rule of law, and the increasing recognition of the principles of the open and competitive economy. These events proclaim loudly man's inalienable rights: When people are free to choose, they choose freedom.

2. The profound changes taking place in Europe, and progress toward democracy elsewhere, give us great hope for a world in which individuals have increasing opportunities to achieve their economic and political aspirations, free of tyranny and oppression.

3. We are mindful that freedom and economic prosperity are closely linked and mutually reinforcing. Sustainable economic prosperity depends upon the stimulus of competition and the encouragement of enterprise— on incentives for individual initiative and innovation, on a skilled and motivated labor force whose fundamental rights are protected, on sound monetary systems, on an open system of international trade and payments, and on an environment safeguarded for future generations.

4. Around the world, we are determined to assist other peoples to achieve and sustain economic prosperity and political freedom. We will support their efforts with our experience, resources, and good will.

The International Economic Situation

5. In recent years, substantial progress has been achieved in promoting a stronger world economy through sound macroeconomic policies and greater economic efficiency. The economic expansion in our countries, now in its eighth year, has supported notable income growth and job creation in the context of rapid growth of international trade. However, unemployment remains high in a number of countries. Inflation, although considerably lower than in the early 1980s, is a matter of serious concern in some countries and requires continued vigilance. . . .

6. In the developing world, the experience of the late 1980s varied widely. Some economies, particularly in East Asia, continued to experience impressive domestic growth rates. The economies of a number of other developing countries have been stagnant or declined. Nonetheless, serious efforts—in some cases by new leadership—to implement economic adjustment and market-oriented policies have begun to yield positive results and should be continued. . . .

[7-12 omitted]

International Monetary Developments and Policy Coordination

13. Within the European Community, the European Monetary System is leading to a high degree of economic convergence and stability. We note the European Community's decision to launch the Intergovernmental Conference on Economic and Monetary Union and the beginning of the first stage of that union. During this first stage, closer surveillance and coordination of economic and monetary policies will contribute toward non-inflationary growth and a more robust international economic system.

14. We welcome the prospect of a unified, democratic Germany which enjoys full sovereignty without discriminatory constraints. German economic, monetary, and social union will contribute to improved non-inflationary global growth and to a reduction of external imbalances. This

process will promote positive economic developments in Central and Eastern Europe.

15. We call on the member countries of the International Monetary Fund (IMF) to implement the agreement by the IMF to increase quotas by 50 percent under the Ninth General Review of Quotas and to strengthen the IMF arrears strategy.

Measures Aimed at Economic Efficiency

16. Considerable progress has been made over the past few years in supplementing macroeconomic policies with reforms to increase economic efficiency. We welcome the progress in the realization of the internal market in the European Community and the continuing efforts to reduce structural rigidities in North America and Japan....

17. We welcome the major contributions of the Organization for Economic Cooperation and Development (OECD) in identifying structural policy challenges and options. We encourage the OECD to strengthen its surveillance and review procedures, and to find ways of making its work operationally more effective.

The International Trading System

18. The open world trading system is vital to economic prosperity. A strengthened General Agreement on Tariffs and Trade (GATT) is essential to provide a stable framework for the expansion of trade and the fuller integration of Central and Eastern Europe and developing countries into the global economy. We reject protectionism in all its forms.

19. The successful outcome of the Uruguay Round [of trade talks] has the highest priority on the international economic agenda. Consequently, we stress our determination to take the difficult political decisions necessary to achieve far-reaching, substantial results in all areas of the Uruguay Round by the end of this year. We instruct our negotiators to make progress and in particular to agree on the complete profile of the final package by the July meeting of the Trade Negotiations Committee.

20. We confirm our strong support for the essential broad objectives of the negotiations: reform of agricultural policies; a substantial and balanced package of measures to improve market access; strengthened multilateral rules and disciplines; the incorporation of new issues of services, trade-related investment measures, and intellectual property protection within the GATT framework; and integration of developing countries into the international trading system.

21. As regards agriculture, achieving the long-term objective of the reform of agricultural policies is critical to permit the greater liberalization of trade in agricultural products. Experience has shown the high cost of agricultural policies which tend to create surpluses. The outcome of the GATT negotiations on agriculture should lead to a better balance between supply and demand and ensure that agricultural policies do not impede the effective functioning of international markets. We therefore reaffirm

our commitment to the long-term objective of the reform, i.e., to allow market signals to influence agriculture production and to establish a fair and market-oriented agricultural trading system.

22. The achievement of this objective requires each of us to make substantial, progressive reductions in support and protection of agriculture—covering internal regimes, market access, and export subsidies—and develop rules governing sanitary and phytosanitary measures. Variations among countries in the mechanisms of agricultural support reflect differences in the social and economic conditions of farming. The negotiations on agriculture should therefore be conducted in a framework that includes a common instrument of measurement, provides for commitments to be made in an equitable way among all countries, and takes into account concerns about food security. The framework should contain specific assurances that, by appropriate use of the common measure as well as other ways, participants would reduce not only internal support but also export subsidies and import protection in a related way.

23. Agreement on such a framework by the time of the July meeting of the Trade Negotiations Committee is critical to the successful completion of the Uruguay Round as a whole. Accordingly, we commend to our negotiators the text submitted by the Chairman of the Agricultural Negotiating Group as a means to intensify the negotiations. We intend to maintain a high level of personal involvement and to exercise the political leadership necessary to ensure the successful outcome of these negotiations.

24. Negotiations on market access should achieve agreement on a substantial and balanced package of measures. As regards textiles, the objective is to liberalize the textile and clothing sector through progressive dismantling of trade barriers and its integration, under a precise timetable, into GATT on the basis of strengthened GATT rules and disciplines.

25. Negotiations on multilateral rules and disciplines should strengthen GATT rules in areas such as safeguards, balance of payments, rules of origin, and updated disciplines for dumping and antidumping measures. Concerning subsidies, rules are needed which will effectively discipline domestic subsidies so as to avoid trade distortions, competitive subsidization, and trade conflicts. Improved disciplines must also cover countervailing measures so that they do not become barriers to trade.

26. As regards the new areas, the aim is to develop new rules and procedures within the GATT framework, including: a framework of contractually enforceable rules to liberalize services trade, with no sector excluded *a priori*; an agreement to reduce trade distorting effects of trade-related investment measures; and an agreement to provide for standards and effective enforcement of all intellectual property rights.

27. A successful Uruguay Round is essential for industrialized and developing countries alike. We seek the widest possible participation of developing countries in the Round and their further integration into the multilateral trading system. To achieve this objective, developed countries are prepared to accept greater multilateral disciplines in all areas and to

offer improved market access in areas of interest to developing countries such as textiles and clothing, tropical products, and agriculture.

28. For their part, developing countries should substantially reduce their tariffs and increase the percentage of tariffs that are bound; subscribe to balanced and effective restraints on all forms of exceptions, including measures imposed for balance-of-payments difficulties; and participate meaningfully in agreements covering the new areas. The end result should be a single set of multilateral rules applicable to all GATT contracting parties, although some developing countries, especially the least developed, may need longer transitional periods or other transitional arrangements on a case by case basis.

29. The wide range of substantive results which we seek in all these areas will call for a commitment to strengthen further the institutional framework of the multilateral trading system. In that context, the concept of an international trade organization should be addressed at the conclusion of the Uruguay Round. We also need to improve the dispute settlement process in order to implement the results of the negotiations effectively. This should lead to a commitment to operate only under the multilateral rules. . . .

[30-32 omitted]

Reform in Central and Eastern Europe

33. We welcome the political and economic reforms taking place in Central and Eastern Europe. At the recent Conference on Security and Cooperation in Europe (CSCE) in Bonn and by the agreement to establish the European Bank for Reconstruction and Development (EBRD), the participating countries of the region accepted the key principles underpinning market economies. However, the degree of implementation of economic and political reform varies widely by country. Several countries have taken courageous and difficult measures to stabilize their economies and shorten the transition to a market economy.

34. We and other countries should assist Central and Eastern European nations that are firmly committed to economic and political reform. Those providing help should favor countries that implement such reforms.

35. Foreign private investment will be vital in the development of Central and Eastern Europe. Capital will flow to countries with open markets and hospitable investment climates. Improved access for their exports will also be important for those Central and Eastern European countries that are opening up their economies. Western Governments can support this process by various means, including trade and investment agreements. The recent decision by the Coordinating Committee for Multilateral Export Controls (COCOM) to liberalize export controls is a positive step.

36. We commend the work done by the Commission of the European Communities on the coordination by the Group of 24 (G-24) of assistance to Poland and Hungary. . . . We welcome the decision of the G-24 to

enlarge the coordination of assistance to other emerging democracies in Central and Eastern Europe, including Yugoslavia. . . .

[37-41 omitted]

The Soviet Union

42. We discussed the situation in the Soviet Union, and exchanged views regarding the message that Soviet President Gorbachev sent us several days ago on his economic plans. We welcome the efforts underway in the Soviet Union to liberalize and to create a more open, democratic, and pluralistic Soviet society, and to move toward a market-oriented economy. These measures deserve our support. The success of perestroika depends upon the determined pursuit and development of these reform efforts. In particular, we welcome President Gorbachev's suggestion for a sustained economic dialogue.

43. We have all begun, individually and collectively, to assist these reform efforts. We all believe that technical assistance should be provided now to help the Soviet Union move to a market-oriented economy and to mobilize its own resources. Some countries are already in a position to extend large scale financial credits.

44. We also agreed that further Soviet decisions to introduce more radical steps toward a market-oriented economy, to shift resources substantially away from the military sector and to cut support to nations promoting regional conflict will all improve the prospect for meaningful and sustained economic assistance.

45. . . .We have agreed to ask the IMF, the World Bank, the OECD and the designated president of the EBRD to undertake, in close consultation with the Commission of the European Communities, a detailed study of the Soviet economy, to make recommendations for its reform and to establish the criteria under which Western economic assistance could effectively support these reforms. This work should be completed by year's end and be convened by the IMF.

46. We took note of the importance to the Government of Japan of the peaceful resolution of its dispute with the Soviet Union over the Northern Territories.

47. The host Government will convey to the Soviet Union the results of the Houston Summit.

The Developing Nations

48. We reiterate that our commitment to the developing world will not be weakened by the support for reforming countries in Central and Eastern Europe. The poorest of the developing nations must remain the focus of special attention. The International Development Association replenishment of SDR [special drawing rights] 11.6 billion, agreed to last December, will provide needed resources for these countries, and marks the incorporation of environmental concerns into development lending. It is our intention to take a constructive part in the Paris Conference on the

least developed countries in September.

49. The advanced industrial economies can make a number of major contributions to the long-run development of the developing countries. By sustaining economic growth and price stability, we can offer stable, growing markets and sources of capital for the developing world. By providing financial and technical support to developing countries undertaking genuine political and economic reform, we can reinforce their ongoing liberalization. . . .

[50-54 omitted]

Third World Debt

55. Significant progress has been made during the past year under the strengthened debt strategy, which has renewed the resolve in a number of debtor countries to continue economic reforms essential to future growth. In particular, the recent commercial bank agreements with Chile, Costa Rica, Mexico, Morocco, the Philippines, and Venezuela involve significant debt and debt-service reduction. Important financial support for debt and debt-service reduction is being provided by the IMF and the World Bank, as well as by Japan. The Paris Club has agreed, in order to support medium term IMF-supported reform and financing programs, to provide adequate restructuring agreements, notably through multiyear reschedulings and through lengthening of the repayment period. The combination of debtor reform efforts and commercial bank debt reduction has had a notable impact on confidence in debtor economies, as clearly demonstrated through flows of both new investment and the return of flight capital to Mexico, in particular.

56. These measures represent major innovations in the case by case debt strategy and are potentially available to all debtor nations with serious debt-servicing problems which are implementing economic adjustment policies.

57. The adoption by debtor nations of strong economic reform programs with the IMF and World Bank remains at the heart of the debt strategy, and a prerequisite for debt and debt service reduction within commercial bank financing packages. It is vital that debtor countries adopt measures to mobilize savings and to encourage new investment flows and the repatriation of flight capital to help sustain their recovery. In this connection, the recent U.S. Enterprise for the Americas initiative to support investment reform and the environment in Latin America needs to be given careful consideration by Finance Ministers.

58. For countries implementing courageous reforms, commercial banks should take realistic and constructive approaches in their negotiations to conclude promptly agreements on financial packages including debt reduction, debt-service reduction and new money. . . .

[59-61 omitted]

The Environment

62. One of our most important responsibilities is to pass on to future generations an environment whose health, beauty, and economic potential are not threatened. Environmental challenges such as climate change, ozone depletion, deforestation, marine pollution, and loss of biological diversity require closer and more effective international cooperation and concrete action. We as industrialized countries have an obligation to be leaders in meeting these challenges. We agree that, in the face of threats of irreversible environmental damage, lack of full scientific certainty is no excuse to postpone actions which are justified in their own right. We recognize that strong, growing market-oriented economies provide the best means for successful environmental protection.

63. Climate change is of key importance. We are committed to undertake common efforts to limit emissions of greenhouse gases, such as carbon dioxide. We strongly support the work of the Intergovernmental Panel on Climate Change (IPCC) and look forward to the release of its full report in August. The Second World Climate Conference provides the opportunity for all countries to consider the adoption of strategies and measures for limiting or stabilizing greenhouse gas emissions, and to discuss an effective international response. We reiterate our support for the negotiation of a framework convention on climate change, under the auspices of the United Nations Environment Program (UNEP) and the World Meteorological Organization (WMO). The convention should be completed by 1992. Work on appropriate implementing protocols should be undertaken as expeditiously as possible and should consider all sources and sinks.

64. We welcome the amendment of the Montreal Protocol to phase out the use of chlorofluorocarbons (CFCs) by the year 2000 and to extend coverage of the Protocol to other ozone depleting substances. The establishment of a financial mechanism to assist developing countries to tackle ozone depletion marks a new and positive step in cooperation between the developed and developing worlds. . . .

65. . . . We recognize the importance of working together to develop new technologies and methods over the coming decades to complement energy conservation and other measures to reduce carbon dioxide and other greenhouse emissions. We support accelerated scientific and economic research and analysis on the dynamics and potential impact of climate change, and on potential responses of developed and developing countries.

66. We are determined to take action to increase forests, while protecting existing ones and recognizing the sovereign rights of all countries to make use of their natural resources. The destruction of tropical forests has reached alarming proportions. We welcome the commitment of the new Government of Brazil to help arrest this destruction and to provide sustainable forest management. We actively support this process, and we are ready for a new dialogue with developing countries on ways and means to support their efforts. We are ready to cooperate with the Government of Brazil on a comprehensive pilot program to counteract the threat to

tropical rain forests in that country. We ask the World Bank to prepare such a proposal, in close cooperation with the Commission of the European Communities, which should be presented at the latest at the next Economic Summit. . . .

67. We are ready to begin negotiations, in the appropriate fora, as expeditiously as possible on a global forest convention or agreement, which is needed to curb deforestation, protect biodiversity, stimulate positive forestry actions, and address threats to the world's forests. The convention or agreement should be completed as soon as possible, but no later than 1992. The work of the IPCC and others should be taken into account.

68. The destruction of ecologically sensitive areas around the world continues at an alarming pace. Loss of temperate and tropical forests, developmental pressures on estuaries, wetlands and coral reefs, and destruction of biological diversity are symptomatic. . . .

69. Efforts to protect the environment do not stop at the water's edge. Serious problems are caused by marine pollution, both in the oceans and in coastal areas. A comprehensive strategy should be developed to address land-based sources of pollution; we are committed to helping in this regard. We will continue our efforts to avoid oil spills, urge the early entry into force of the existing International Maritime Organization (IMO) Convention, and welcome the work of that organization in developing an international oil spills convention. . . .

70. To cope with energy-related environmental damage, priority must be given to improvements in energy efficiency and to the development of alternative energy sources. For the countries that make such a choice, nuclear energy will continue to be an important contributor to our energy supply and can play a significant role in reducing the growth of greenhouse gas emissions. Countries should continue efforts to ensure highest world-wide performance standards for nuclear and other energy in order to protect health and the environment, and to ensure the highest safety.

71. Cooperation between developed and developing countries is essential to the resolution of global environmental problems. In this regard, the 1992 UN Conference on Environment and Development will be an important opportunity to develop widespread agreement on common action and coordinated plans. We note with interest the conclusions of the Siena Forum on International Law of the Environment and suggest that these should be considered by the 1992 UN Conference on Environment and Development. . . .

[72-74 omitted]

Narcotics

75. We urge all nations to accede to and complete ratification of the UN Convention Against Illicit Traffic in Narcotic Drugs and Psychotropic Substances (the Vienna Convention), and to apply provisionally terms of the Convention.

76. We welcome the conclusion of the UN Special Session on Drugs and

urge the implementation of the measures contained in the Program of Action it has adopted.

77. We support the declaration adopted at the ministerial meeting on drugs convened by the United Kingdom that drug demand reduction should be accorded the same importance in policy and action as the reduction of illicit supply. Developed countries should adopt stronger prevention efforts and assist demand reduction initiatives in other countries. . . .

[78-79 omitted]

80. We support a strategy for attacking the cocaine trade as outlined in particular in the Cartagena Declaration. We recognize the importance of supporting all countries strongly engaged in the fight against drug trafficking, especially Colombia, Peru, and Bolivia, with economic, law enforcement, and other assistance and advice, recognizing the need to make contributions within the framework of actions against drug trafficking carried out by the producer countries.

81. The heroin problem is still the most serious threat in many countries, both developed and developing. All countries should take vigorous measures to combat the scourge of heroin.

82. We should support an informal narcotics consultative arrangement with developed countries active in international narcotics control. Such a group could strengthen efforts to reduce supply and demand, and improve international cooperation.

83. We welcome the current review of UN drug abuse control agencies and urge that it result in a more efficient structure.

Next Economic Summit

84. We have accepted the invitation of Prime Minister Thatcher to meet next July in London.

BUSH NEWS CONFERENCE

Summit Accomplishments

. . . This, the first economic summit of the postwar period, celebrates the resurgence of democracy and free markets around the world. Over the past 3 days, we've had full discussions on the key issues of our times: advancing political and economic freedom; promoting sustained economic growth, both in developed and in developing countries; assisting the transition to market economies in central and eastern Europe and, indeed, in the Soviet Union; and protecting the environment. We are united in a common goal to extend to those who seek political and economic freedom a helping hand with our resources, talents, and experience. As our declaration states, when people are free to choose, they choose freedom.

We identified the successful completion of the Uruguay round of global trade talks as one of the highest economic priorities. We recognize that agreement on fundamental reform of agriculture is critical to achieving this goal. We commended the report by the chairman of the GATT agricultural group, the De Zeuuw report, to our negotiators as a vehicle to move these talks forward; and we also committed to maintain our personal involvement and to exercise political leadership at every step along the way as we move toward the final ministerial meeting in December.

On the Soviet Union, we discussed our common efforts to assist the Soviet reform effort, the success of which is in our common interest. In addition to offering the Soviets technical assistance, we've asked the IMF [International Monetary Fund] to coordinate a major study of the Soviet economy and make recommendations for its reform. In keeping with the agreements reached here, I will be conveying to President Gorbachev the results of our deliberations.

We achieved major progress on the environment, particularly on climate change and forests. We committed to finish the negotiations on a framework climate change convention by 1992. In a first, we agreed that implementing protocols should consider all sources and sinks of greenhouse gases, consistent with the comprehensive approach that we recommend. We agreed to launch a special effort to address the deforestation in the rain forests, a concern that was very forcefully raised by Chancellor [Helmut] Kohl [of the Federal Republic of Germany]. I found a very receptive audience for my proposal that a freestanding global forest convention be negotiated without delay, and we agreed to move ahead on this rapidly.

In short, this was a summit that addressed itself to a rapidly changing world. We agreed to welcome, respond to, and manage the changes on behalf of free markets, free political systems, and a better life for people everywhere. It is no small achievement that we came to a positive and unanimous conclusion on so many important and difficult issues, and I would stress those two words: positive and unanimous. . . .

Economic Assistance for the Soviet Union

Q. Mr. President, I'd like to ask you about Soviet aid. Is this 6-month study of Soviet needs a way of delaying the political decision on aid, or at the end of that, will the United States make a commitment to send some cash to Moscow?

THE PRESIDENT. It's not an effort to delay anything. It is, as we said in the report, a step towards assisting the reforms. And I'll make clear to President Gorbachev that he ought to view this outcome of this summit very positively. You may remember that in London only a few days ago I gave my views on the U.S. lending money at this time. So, it's not an effort to forestall anything; it's an effort to move forward, encourage forward motion, and be helpful to the Soviet Union in terms of reform. They need much, much more reform, and they're the ones that say this. And in Gorbachev's letter, he asked for assistance in many areas—personnel management and how they change their systems. And we've already started bilaterally, as have other countries, in trying to assist. So, it's really a coordinated effort to help the Soviet Union.

Q. Well, in 6 months, then, can Mr. Gorbachev expect that the United States would be sending some financial assistance to meet these needs?

THE PRESIDENT. Not particularly. Not necessarily. But what he can expect is that we will have been helpful to him in the reforms that he knows that he has to undertake, and maybe this could lead to support. . . .

Q. Mr. President, for 40 years we've spent untold billions to fight the Soviet Union. Is it conceivable, as you and Secretary Baker have portrayed, that the American taxpayer would not be willing to spend a dime to help them now?

THE PRESIDENT. We are trying to help them now; and I think we're going to send the kind of help that, in the long run, will be most beneficial to them. . . . But we have some problems. I'm not particularly enthusiastic about the intercontinental ballistic missiles aimed at U.S. cities. I find it a little contradictory to think that they will continue to spend $5 billion a year for Cuba, a totalitarian system whose leader is swimming against this tide of democracy and freedom that is lifting up most hopes in the Soviet Union. So, certain things have to happen before I, as President, will make recommendations for direct financial aid. So, what we're trying to do is carry our part of the load in helping the reforms.

Q. In your discussions, why did Germany and other countries think it's necessary now?

THE PRESIDENT. Well, Germany has some very special interest that we understand. . . . [W]e're not urging everybody to march in lockstep. . . .

Agricultural Subsidies

Q. Mr. President, the Final Communique here reflecting your views in no small part on agriculture subsidies calls upon each nation to "make substantial progressive reductions in support and protection of agriculture." Does this mean, sir, that you're prepared to ask Congress to abolish some of the more notorious forms of support and subsidy that are part of our farm program?

THE PRESIDENT. Absolutely! And we have to do it, and it's a two-way street. And I expect there would be some political opposition because like many of these countries, we protect. But I am convinced, and I believe Congress would support the concept, that if we all do this and we all reduce barriers and we all make a freer trading system, that the United States can compete. . . .

Environmental Policies

Q. Mr. President, on the question of the environment, you, in the past, and your Chief of Staff [John H. Sununu], to say at least two, have always said that there has not been enough information—you needed to study more. Now you're prepared to move, particularly on the global warming question. Who twisted your arm? What changed your mind, sir?

THE PRESIDENT. I think we're moving forward because we recognize there is a problem. I thought we called for more data in here. Clearly, we need more....

But the steps that we've recommended here in this communique we can enthusiastically endorse. So, I think we came out with a reasoned position, not a radical position that's going to throw a lot of American men and women out of jobs. And yet we've done an awful lot—and I think others at the summit recognized it—in terms of cleaning up the air....

Economic Assistance for the Soviet Union

Q. I understand that it would take some time for the Soviet economy to reform. But are you suggesting, when you link Soviet aid to arms control, that you could never imagine any direct aid so long as there are any Soviet weapons aimed at the West?

THE PRESIDENT. No, I didn't say that. But I would really prefer to stand on what I've simply said. The world is changing very fast. But they know that we've got some big difficulties on the regional questions and on the fact that a lot of missiles are aimed at the United States. A good way to start in doing something about that is to have a successful conclusion on the START [strategic arms reduction] treaty.... If you'd have asked me last year at this time if I could have predicted the rapidity of change, the changes that have taken place, I couldn't have predicted them. So, I don't know exactly where we will be, but I do know that this proposal we've made is sound....

Q. On aid to the Soviets, you keep saying that the American people simply aren't ready to give cash to Gorbachev. Now, if the IMF comes back with a report, Gorbachev accepts some of those recommendations, they cut way back on aid to Cuba—largely which consists of oil shipments, after all, not money—he does these things you want, are you ready before the 1992 presidential campaign to go out there and tell the American people you would send American cash or supply credits to Gorbachev?

THE PRESIDENT. Your question is too hypothetical. I can't go into a hypothesis like that. And we will wait and see....

Economic Summit

Q. Let me ask you this. You got some sort of a delay on aid to the Soviets because of this study, which will not be completed until December. A lot of people are painting this summit as they did the NATO summit: as a victory for George Bush across the board, whether it's cutting agricultural subsidies for Europeans or whether it's the environment. What didn't you get at this summit that you wanted? What did you lose here?

THE PRESIDENT. In the first place, I don't—I'm glad to hear that— but really, honestly, we don't look at it as a victory for one side and a defeat for another. That's the good thing about this G-7 group. And so, there weren't any winners or losers in it, but there was compromise along the way. But again, I'm not going to reopen the hard work that went into this agreement by saying what we would like to have had that was different. But it did work out in a way that I can strongly support....

Chancellor Kohl of the
Federal Republic of Germany

Q. Mr. President, at the NATO summit and then again here, it seems as though you have developed a special working relationship with Chancellor Kohl. I wondered—one of the German delegation also said that after you had supported him on Soviet aid he couldn't come back and not support you on the environment. Can you describe that relationship, and would you say that's a fair assessment?

THE PRESIDENT. It's not a fair assessment because he's a bulldog when it comes to the environment. He's a fighter for what he believes in. And I think he felt satisfied with what he got. . . .

But the relationship is—it's hard to explain. I do think that the Germans appreciate the fact that we have stood at their side on this question of German reunification. I think that's an element. But there isn't any quid pro quo. . . .

Q. Would you say, however, that you find more common ground or common interest with Chancellor Kohl now than you would perhaps with [Prime Minister of the United Kingdom] Margaret Thatcher?

THE PRESIDENT. No, I wouldn't say that at all. But I find plenty of common ground with both. Nice try. [Laughter] You're going to get me in trouble; they haven't even left town here. . . .

Changes in the Western Alliance

Q. . . . In the past, the United States did call the tune on allied relations with the Soviet Union. Now that we're seeing key allies going their own way on aid to the Soviet Union, aren't we seeing at least a subtle change in the way the United States has to lead the alliance? Aren't you having to give a little more leeway to the allies now that the Cold War is over?

THE PRESIDENT. We're dealing in entirely different times. . . . For the United States side, I think we have very good understanding inside the G-7 about the Soviet Union. But if your question is, Is it bad or does it alter the U.S. role if Chancellor Kohl, for very special reasons, goes forward, I would argue that it does not. . . .

ROSE'S SENTENCING
AND STEINBRENNER'S REMOVAL
July 19 and July 30, 1990

The mid-summer news of major league baseball was dominated by two off-the-field events: the sentencing of former superstar Pete Rose to five months in prison for filing false tax returns and the removal of owner George M. Steinbrenner III from operating control of the New York Yankees for the good of baseball. Rose's sentencing on July 19 came nearly eleven months after he was banished from baseball by its commissioner, the late A. Bartlett Giamatti, for allegedly betting on baseball games, including those involving the team he managed, the Cincinnati Reds. (Statements on Banning Pete Rose from Baseball, Historic Documents of 1989, p. 477)

Professional baseball's fear of being tainted by gambling also underlay Steinbrenner's trouble. An inquiry ordered by Fay Vincent, Giamatti's successor, disclosed that in January the Yankees' owner paid $40,000 to Howard Spira, a self-described gambler, for information to discredit Dave Winfield, a disgruntled outfielder who was traded to another team. Vincent announced July 30 that Steinbrenner had agreed to give up his control of the team and within twelve months to reduce his majority ownership to less than 50 percent. For five years he would be barred from participating in the ownership decisions.

Rose and Steinbrenner, two of the biggest names in baseball, had made their mark on the sport in entirely different ways. Rose had achieved almost legendary status for a long list of records and achievements, and for his zest for the game over twenty-four seasons as a player before becoming a full-time manager in 1986. He was considered a shoo-in for membership in baseball's Hall of Fame before his gambling and tax problems arose. Steinbrenner repeatedly made sports page headlines for his antics and controversies. He often scorned his star players, and he changed managers eighteen times in seventeen and a half years.

Rose's Remorse

Rose's sentence, handed down by Judge S. Arthur Spiegel of the U.S. District Court in Cincinnati, included a fine of $50,000. The judge also required that after Rose served his five months at the Federal Correctional Institute Camp at Ashland, Kentucky, he spend three months at a community treatment center and continue to receive psychiatric help to overcome a gambling addiction. After Rose's time in the community center, he would be required to work at least twenty hours a week assisting community service projects in Cincinnati for a total of 1,000 hours. Rose could have been sentenced to as much as three years and fined $250,000 on each of the two tax-evasion counts.

"I accept my punishment," Rose said in a statement released after the sentencing. "I will serve my sentence, pay my debt to society and get on with my life." Standing before the judge in the crowded courtroom, the forty-nine-year-old defendant was asked if he had anything to say before being sentenced. In a quavering voice, Rose said: "I would like to say that I am very sorry. I am very shameful to be here in front of you." He added that he had lost his dignity, self-respect, a lot of fans, and almost lost some very dear friends.

The judge, explaining his reasoning for the sentence, said, "I do not think society needs to be protected from Mr. Rose, but he must serve some time in a prison setting for his crime in order to maintain respect for the law and as a deterrent to others who might consider cheating on their taxes."

Rose had pleaded guilty April 20 to the two tax-evasion counts in a plea-bargaining agreement with federal prosecutors. Their investigation determined that he failed to pay $126,703 in taxes on unreported income of $345,967 he derived from baseball-card shows, personal appearances, and sale of memorabilia from 1984 to 1987. Interest and penalties raised his tax debt to $366,043, which he paid as part of the plea agreement. He was never charged with illegal drug activity, as were some of his acquaintances who were also investigated.

Steinbrenner's Case

Steinbrenner, a shipbuilder and horse racer, headed a group of buyers that acquired the New York Yankees from CBS, Inc., in 1973. In November 1974 he was suspended from baseball for fifteen months after pleading guilty and being fined in federal court for violation of election laws on campaign contributions. During his tenure, Steinbrenner drew an additional suspension (for one week) and five fines amounting to $335,000 for tampering with players on other teams and making disparaging remarks about umpires and another owner.

As he had promised baseball commissioner Vincent, Steinbrenner resigned August 20 as general partner among the Yankee owners. He held

55 percent of the stock and the rest was spread among eighteen limited partners. They named one partner, Robert Nederlander, to fill the general partner's role. His selection was subsequently ratified by the other major league clubs. Steinbrenner initially sought to place his son Hank in that position. Commissioner Vincent said the son would be permitted to take over only if he remained free of his father's influence in supervising the ball club. The son later said he did not want the job.

"I made the baseball deal [with Vincent] to protect my Olympic deal," Steinbrenner told news reporters in Colorado Springs at a meeting August 23 of the United States Olympics Committee, which he served as vice president. (The committee is in charge of America's planning for the 1992 Olympic Games.) He noted that his agreement did not mention words such as "banned," "suspended," or "probation." "Those are the things that would have kept me from going on with the Olympics," he said. However, after deliberations among the Olympics Committee, he was asked—and agreed—to become inactive in his position.

Past Action Against Others

Previous baseball commissioners had taken similar action against four other major league owners during the past half-century. In 1941 Charles Adams had to give up his racing stables in order to keep his stock in the Boston Braves. Kenesaw Mountain Landis, the commissioner who forced Adams's choice, two years later suspended William D. Cox of the Philadelphia Phillies for life for betting on games. Another commissioner, Ford Frick, in 1953 forced Fred Saigh, Jr., of the St. Louis Cardinals to turn the club's operations over to a committee of trustees after Saigh pleaded no contest to federal charges of tax evasion. And in 1976 Commissioner Bowie Kuhn suspended Ted Turner of the Atlanta Braves for one year for tampering with the contract of San Francisco outfielder Gary Matthews.

Rose was believed to be the first manager—but not the first big league player—ever sentenced to prison. Over the past two decades, at least eight players or former players have served time in prison. Four of them—Dennis McLain, Vida Blue, Lamar Hoyt, and Ferguson Jenkins— were winners of the coveted Cy Young Award, given yearly to the outstanding pitcher in the majors. The other four players were Orlando Cepeda, Willie Wilson, Willie Aikens, and Jerry Martin.

> *Following are excerpts from Judge S. Arthur Spiegel's remarks in U.S. District Court in Cincinnati at his sentencing, July 19, 1990, of baseball star Pete Rose to five months imprisonment for filing false income-tax returns; baseball commissioner Fay Vincent's announcement in New York July 30 that owner George M. Steinbrenner III had agreed to relinquish his control over the New York Yankees and the text of that agreement:*

JUDGE SPIEGEL ON PETE ROSE SENTENCING

I have a number of comments to make before imposing sentence.

... Foremost, we must recognize that there are two people here: Pete Rose, the living legend, the all-time hit leader, and, the idol of millions; and, Pete Rose, the individual who appears today convicted of two counts of cheating on his taxes.

Today, we are *NOT* dealing with the legend. History and the tincture of time will decide his place among the all-time greats of baseball. With regard to Pete Rose, the individual, he has broken the law, admitted his guilt, and stands ready to pay the penalty. Under our system of law and sense of fairness, when he has completed his sentence, he will have paid his debt to society and should be accepted by society as rehabilitated. Only time will tell whether he is to be restored to his position of honor for his accomplishments on the ball fields of America.

Neither, are we here to consider whether Pete Rose was treated fairly by the Baseball Commissioner, whether the Dowd Report was an objective and balanced report of his activities, whether Pete Rose gambled on baseball, or whether he should have been banished from baseball.

We are here today to impose sentence on a man whose life has been an inspiration for millions of people because of his exploits on the ball diamond and his determination to succeed in his chosen profession. We hope that he understands that the sentence we impose is fair and necessary under the circumstances, and that he will make the most of the opportunities presented to him while confined and under supervision so that he can regain confidence in himself, continue his rehabilitation, help others, and therefore return to society with a clean slate having paid his debt....

In determining the appropriate punishment for a criminal offender, a judge must consider the need for respect for the law, deterrence, the protection of society, rehabilitation, retribution and fairness.... After carefully considering all of these factors, I have concluded that Mr. Rose must serve some time in a prison setting for his crime in order to maintain respect for the law and as a deterrent to others who might consider cheating on their taxes. Although I do not think that society needs to be protected from Mr. Rose, since he is on the road to rehabilitating himself, our law requires that when one commits a crime he must be punished and that the punishment must be fair. Recognizing that Mr. Rose is a well-known figure, it might be a temptation to make an example of him by imposing a heavy sentence. On the other hand, because he has suffered much in this past year, in his career and financially, there might be a temptation to go light. I have attempted to weigh all of these considerations in determining Mr. Rose's sentence in an effort to be fair to the defendant and to fulfill the Court's responsibility to society.

Mr. Rose's sentence will include incarceration at a Federal Correctional Institution and a halfway house, supervised release and community service, and a fine to cover the cost of prosecution, confinement, and supervision. We are also fashioning his sentence to recognize the fact that during his career he has been unselfish, helping others, particularly children, both on and off the ball field. Hopefully, Mr. Rose will help the adult prisoners where he will be confined. The sentence will also require Mr. Rose to return to his roots in the inner city during his supervised release in order to help children there make something of themselves and to encourage them to work to succeed in their goals with the same determination and dedication that he did in his own life. We particularly want him to show these children that in spite of the mistakes he has made he can learn and profit from them and become a more humble and better person from the experience. Mr. Rose's lawyers have pointed out that his hard work led him to "unprecedented heights" and "even his mistakes can serve as an example that no one is immune from personal problems nor above the law." We believe his enormous desire to succeed can be harnessed to help children in the inner city. The children with whom Mr. Rose will be working need a role model with whom they can identify in order to make the most of their chances in life. Pete Rose can provide the necessary inspiration, if he is the person I think he is. . . .

BASEBALL COMMISSIONER'S STATEMENT

This morning I met with Mr. George M. Steinbrenner, III, in my office. He was accompanied by his lawyer, Stephen Kaufman. I advised Mr. Steinbrenner of my decision in the proceeding which focused on his dealings with Howard Spira and provided them with copies of my opinion and judgment in the matter. Copies of the final opinion and judgment are being released at this time.

Mr. Steinbrenner has agreed to and accepted the following arrangement which disposes finally of this matter:

1. Mr. Steinbrenner has accepted the opinion and the findings contained in my decision to the effect that his conduct violated Rule 21 (f) of the Major League Agreement and constituted conduct "not in the best interests of Baseball" within the meaning of that Rule.
2. Mr. Steinbrenner has agreed to resign on or before August 20, 1990 as the general partner of the New York Yankees. From thereon, Mr. Steinbrenner will have no further involvement in the management of the New York Yankees or in the day-to-day operations of that club.
3. A new general partner will be appointed pursuant to the New York Yankees' Partnership Agreement on or before August 20, 1990; such new general partner will be subject to my approval and to approval by the Major League Clubs in accordance with standard practice.
4. For all purposes, Mr. Steinbrenner agrees that he is to be treated as if he had been placed on the permanent ineligible list, subject to the following exceptions:
   i. With my approval, he may consult upon and participate in major

financial and business decisions of the New York Yankees solely in his capacity as a limited partner.

ii. Commencing in the Spring 1991, he may seek my approval in writing to attend a limited number of games in the Major Leagues on such terms and conditions as I may impose.

5. By accepting these sanctions, Mr. Steinbrenner has agreed he will not litigate or challenge the decision or these sanctions and that he will not institute litigation as a result of any decision I might make arising out of this agreement or these sanctions.

6. All officers of the Yankees and any member of Mr. Steinbrenner's family who may become involved in the operation of the Yankees will be bound by the terms of the supplemental order governing conduct of New York Yankees officials and restricting the involvement of Mr. Steinbrenner in New York Yankees management.

7. Violation of this agreement or of the supplemental order may result in additional discipline up to and including permanent ineligibility.

This sad episode is now over. My decision in this case and the result will serve, I trust, to vindicate once again the important responsibility of the Commissioner to preserve and protect our noble Game. . . .

STEINBRENNER AGREEMENT

On March 20, 1990, the Commissioner of Baseball instituted an investigation of George M. Steinbrenner, III, the principal owner and general partner of the New York Yankees Baseball Club, concerning allegations that Mr. Steinbrenner engaged in conduct not in the best interests of Baseball in violation of Major League Rule 21.

The Commissioner engaged a Special Counsel to conduct a full, fair and confidential inquiry of the allegations against Mr. Steinbrenner. Mr. Steinbrenner was given notice of the allegations and he and his counsel were generally apprised of the nature and progress of the investigation.

On June 4, 1990, the Commissioner wrote to Mr. Steinbrenner to advise him of the various issues that, in his judgment, had been raised by the investigation. The Commissioner conducted a hearing into this matter on July 5 and 6, 1990.

The Commissioner, recognizing the benefits to Baseball from a resolution of this matter, orders and directs that Mr. Steinbrenner be subject to the following sanctions, and Mr. Steinbrenner, recognizing the sole and exclusive authority of the Commissioner and recognizing the benefits to Baseball from a resolution of this matter without further proceedings, agrees to accept the following sanctions imposed by the Commissioner:

1. Mr. Steinbrenner recognizes, agrees and submits to the sole and exclusive jurisdiction of the Commissioner pursuant to the Major League Agreement, including but not limited to Articles I and VII.

2. Mr. Steinbrenner acknowledges and accepts the findings of the Decision to which this Agreement is attached and, specifically, that his conduct as described in the Decision was not in the best interests of Baseball. Mr. Steinbrenner further accepts the sanctions imposed on him by the Commissioner and agrees not to challenge the sanctions in court or otherwise. He also agrees he will not institute any legal proceedings of any nature against the Commissioner or any of his representatives, either Major League or any Major League Club relating to this matter.

3. On or before August 30, 1990, Mr. Steinbrenner will resign as General Partner of the New York Yankees; within twelve months after that date, he will reduce his ownership interest to less than 50% by transfer through sale, gift or otherwise, subject to all necessary approvals by the Commissioner, the American League and the National League. The Commissioner will approve any transfer to any member of the Steinbrenner family.

4. On or before August 20, 1990, consistent with the terms of the New York Yankees Partnership Limited Partnership Agreement and subject to the subsequent approval of the Major League clubs, a new General Partner will be appointed for the New York Yankees. The Commissioner will approve the appointment of either of Mr. Steinbrenner's sons as general partner.

5. Any of Mr. Steinbrenner's family members who become involved in the operations of the New York Yankees or become a General Partner of the New York Yankees shall be bound by the terms of the Supplemental Order governing the conduct of New York Yankees officials, which is attached hereto and incorporated herein by reference.

6. Effective August 20, 1990, Mr. Steinbrenner will be treated, for all purposes, as if he were on the Ineligible List (although he will not actually be placed on the Ineligible List). Accordingly, until further notice from the Commissioner, Mr. Steinbrenner shall not (a) visit or be physically present in the clubhouse, offices, owners box, or press box at Yankee Stadium or the Yankees' spring training facility, or any other area not generally open to the public at either location, without the prior approval of the Commissioner, or the clubhouse, offices or press box at any other Major League Club; or (b) associate or communicate with any Major League Club (including the New York Yankees) or its personnel or any person having business or financial dealings with the New York Yankees, in connection with any matter involving the New York Yankees or Baseball.

7. The prohibitions enumerated in paragraph 6, above, shall not be revoked or amended without the prior written approval of the Commissioner.

8. Notwithstanding the provisions of paragraph 6, it is recognized that circumstances may arise involving material and extraordinary finan-

cial or business affairs of the New York Yankees in which Mr. Steinbrenner may feel his participation is necessary. On these occasions, a written request may be submitted to the Commissioner seeking permission for Mr. Steinbrenner to attend business meetings or otherwise communicate regarding financial or business matters affecting the Club. Unless and until such permission is granted by the Commissioner, Mr. Steinbrenner shall not attend such a meeting or otherwise become involved in such matters. It is contemplated that such requests will be made infrequently and that they will not involve (a) day-to-day operations of the Yankees, (b) the routine transmittal of information to or from financial institutions, members of the New York Yankees Partnership or other persons involved in the operations of the Club, (c) matters that can be performed adequately by other persons or (d) matters customarily handled by limited partners.

With respect to any request pursuant to the preceding paragraph, if the matter involved falls within any of the four categories enumerated below, then the Commissioner shall approve such request:

    (i) negotiations or disputes concerning television or radio contracts;

    (ii) negotiations or disputes concerning concession agreements;

    (iii) governmental negotiations or agreements, including lease agreements; or

    (iv) banking relationships, including financial arrangements.

9. It is clearly understood by Mr. Steinbrenner and all Yankees officials that it is the intention of the Commissioner to monitor closely their behavior to insure full compliance with this Agreement. Any noncompliance with this Agreement by Mr. Steinbrenner shall be deemed conduct not in the best interests of Baseball and shall subject Mr. Steinbrenner to further discipline, up to and including permanent placement on the Ineligible List. Accordingly, copies of this Agreement will be directed to all present partners of the New York Yankees Partnership and appropriate officials of the New York Yankees organization.

10. The Commissioner and Mr. Steinbrenner may make any public statement so long as any such public statement is consistent with the attached Decision in this matter and the terms of this Agreement and Resolution.

This Agreement represents the entire understanding between the parties hereto with respect to the subject matter of this Agreement and supersedes all previous representations, understandings, or agreements, oral or written, between the parties. This Agreement may not be amended except in a writing signed by both parties.

APPEALS COURT RULING
ON NORTH CONVICTION
July 20, 1990

All three of Oliver L. North's convictions of wrongdoing in the Iran-contra scandal were set aside July 20 by the U.S. Court of Appeals for the District of Columbia. A three-judge panel reversed one conviction outright and ordered the trial court to conduct an elaborate inquiry to determine if the other two guilty verdicts had been tainted by testimony North gave Congress during nationally televised hearings in July 1987. North, a former Marine Corps lieutenant colonel who served on the National Security Council staff, was implicated in an alleged White House cover-up of selling U.S. arms to Iran to win the release of American hostages in Lebanon and illegally funneling profits from those sales to guerrilla fighters (contras) in Nicaragua. (Tower Commission Report, Historic Documents of 1987, p. 205)

North was convicted in Washington, D.C., May 4, 1989, by a U.S. District Court jury of three felonies: deceiving Congress about the arms sales, illegally accepting a home security system as a gift, and altering and destroying government documents. The trial judge, Gerhard A. Gesell, fined North $150,000 and ordered him to perform 1,200 hours of community service in lieu of a jail sentence. (Sentencing of Oliver North, Historic Documents of 1989, p. 391) *The appellate panel, splitting 2-1 in its rulings, vacated the first two convictions and struck down the third one.*

North said he was "very pleased." He added: "It has been, for my family and me, three and a half years and a bitter legal ordeal.... I certainly hope that the special prosecutor ends it now." North could be retried on the charges of deceiving Congress and receiving an illegal gift, or they could be dismissed by the trial court. Instead of having the case retried, independent counsel Lawrence E. Walsh, who led the special prosecuting team, said later that "in all probability" he would petition the Supreme Court to overturn the panel's rulings "because of the importance of the questions involved." He had until late March 1991 to file the appeal.

If the panel's decision stood, it would threaten to undo not only the North case but also the April 7 conviction of John M. Poindexter on five felony charges stemming from the Iran-contra affair. Poindexter, an admiral who was North's boss as national security adviser, drew a six-month prison sentence June 11.

Judges David B. Sentelle and Laurence H. Silberman, two appointees of former president Ronald Reagan on the appellate court, supported North's legal arguments over the strong dissent of Chief Judge Patricia M. Wald, an appointee of former president Jimmy Carter. All three wrote lengthy legal opinions, taking up 216 printed pages. In overturning North's conviction for destroying documents, the two-member majority held that Gesell had instructed the jurors improperly by failing to specify that they had to agree unanimously as to whether North "destroyed" the documents, "altered" them, or illegally "removed" them from his office.

As for North's other two convictions, the majority ruled that the trial judge failed to ensure that witnesses had not made use of the defendant's prior congressional testimony to refresh their memories or otherwise influence their testimony. In contrast to that view, Wald declared that North "received all of the constitutional protections to which he was entitled" and found no errors in the conduct of the trial substantial enough to warrant a reversal of the district court's verdict.

Congressional Immunity Question

Congress, in its Iran-contra investigations, granted more than twenty witnesses—including North—partial immunity from prosecution to obtain their testimony. Nothing they said before Congress could be used against them in court. Walsh and his prosecution team had to draw their evidence against North from other sources. For three days before the trial, Gesell heard arguments on whether North's congressional testimony had influenced prosecutors and witnesses. Such judicial hearings had been held since 1972 when the Supreme Court, ruling in Kastigar v. United States, *required prosecutors to show that immunized testimony was not being used in a criminal trial.*

The appeals court appeared to stiffen the level of scrutiny required to comply with the Kastigar *decision, particularly as to how trial witnesses should be reviewed. The appeals court said Gesell's hearing was not thorough enough—that it should not have focused on what the prosecutors may have learned from that testimony, but on what all witnesses might have learned from the televised congressional hearings.*

"A central problem in this case," said the appeals court, "is that many grand jury and trial witnesses were thoroughly soaked in North's immunized testimony . . . . Papers filed under seal indicate that officials

and attorneys from the Department of Justice, the Central Intelligence Agency, the White House and the Department of State gathered, studied and summarized North's immunized testimony in order to prepare themselves or their superiors and colleagues for their testimony before the investigating committees and the grand jury."

The judges gave several examples, including the trial testimony of Robert C. McFarlane, Poindexter's predecessor as national security adviser and a key prosecution witness at North's trial. McFarlane had pleaded guilty in 1988 to four misdemeanor counts of withholding information from Congress about Iran-contra matters. The appeals panel said McFarlane "testified before the [congressional] investigating committees prior to North's immunized testimony, but then specifically requested and was granted a second appearance to respond to North's testimony." At North's trial, the judges added, "No effort was made to determine what use, if any, this government witness made of North's testimony."

Some members of Congress expressed second thoughts about the use of immunity for witnesses. And Louis Fisher, a senior specialist in separation of executive, legislative, and judicial powers for the Congressional Research Service, said the decision "should be troubling for future investigations." However, Sen. Warren B. Rudman, R-N.H., a former state attorney general who was vice chairman of the Senate's special Iran-contra committee, defended the committee's grant of immunity to North. "We were looking at a possible [presidential] impeachment," he said, adding that a matter of such importance "would have had to wait more than three years" until North was tried in court.

Absence of Reagan's Testimony

Judge Silberman was especially critical of the fact that Reagan was not compelled to testify in court, as North sought. North's legal staff tried to subpoena Reagan, but Gesell quashed the subpoena at the urging of Attorney General Dick Thornburgh. "The instructions and actions of North's superiors ... were critical to his main defense that he did not believe that he was acting unlawfully when he destroyed the relevant documents," Silberman wrote in his legal opinion.

"Of his superiors," Silberman added, "only McFarlane testified at the trial, and he testified against North pursuant to a plea agreement with the government. North was not permitted to call Mr. Reagan, [ex-CIA director William] Casey was deceased, and Poindexter was unavailable because of his Fifth Amendment privilege [against self-incrimination]. Under those circumstances, it is hard to overemphasize the importance that corroborative testimony from Mr. Reagan may have had on the knowledge of [the] unlawfulness question."

Following are excerpts from the majority, concurring, and dissenting opinions in the decision July 20, 1990, by a three-judge panel of the U.S. Court of Appeals for the District of

Columbia dismissing one conviction of Oliver L. North and setting aside two other convictions for further trial-court consideration:

<u>No. 89-3118</u>

Oliver L. North, Appellant	On appeal from the United States
v.	District Court for the District of
United States of America	Columbia

[July 20, 1990]

Summary

Because of the length and complexity of our disposition of North's appeal, we summarize our holdings.

(1) The District Court erred in failing to hold a full hearing as required by *Kastigar v. United States* (1972), to ensure that the IC [Independent Counsel] made no use of North's immunized congressional testimony. North's convictions on all three counts are therefore vacated and remanded to the District Court for a *Kastigar* proceeding consistent with this opinion.

(2) The District Court's jury instructions on Count 9 were erroneous in that they allowed the jury to convict without unanimously concluding that North committed any one of the criminal acts charged in Count 9. The instructions therefore violated *United States v. Mangieri,* 694 F.2d 1270 (D.C. Cir. 1982). This error mandates reversal of North's conviction on Count 9.

(3) The District Court did not err in refusing to instruct the jury on the defense of authorization purportedly recognized in *United States v. Barker,* 546 F.2d 940 (D.C. Cir. 1976). The District Court did err, however, in limiting the jury's consideration of authorization evidence as that evidence was relevant to the issue of intent in Count 9. North's conviction on Court 9 is therefore reversed.

(4) The District Court did not err in quashing North's subpoena of former President Reagan, and the quashal did not violate North's Sixth Amendment rights.

(5) The District Court erred by instructing the jury that, as a matter of law, a congressional inquiry was "pending," a necessary element of 18 U.S.C. § 1505 that must be found by the jury in order to convict. We conclude, however, that this error was harmless.

(6) Although the prosecution made highly improper remarks during closing argument, the District Court did not err in refusing to grant a new trial on that basis.

(7) The District Court's rulings with regard to the Classified Informa-

tion Procedures Act ("CIPA") did not violate the Due Process Clause and were not otherwise erroneous.

(8) The credit given by the District Court to a juror's denial of bias, even though the juror made false statements on the juror questionnaire, was not erroneous and in no way prevented North from exercising his peremptory challenges.

(9) The District Court did not err in declining to allow into evidence an edited videotape of the congressional testimony of Admiral John Poindexter, North's former superior at the NSC.

(10) The District Court did not violate the Jury Selection and Service Act ("JSSA").

(11) Although the District Court may have been better advised to use a different verdict form, the District Court did not improperly foreclose a general verdict of guilty or not guilty on Counts 6 and 9.

(12) Other than with respect to the element of intent in Count 9, the District Court committed no reversible error in its jury instructions concerning the critical elements of each offense.

(13) Venue in the District of Columbia was proper for Count 10.

(14) The District Court committed no error in allowing North to be tried as an aider and abettor on Count 6.

Therefore, North's convictions on Counts 6, 9 and 10 are vacated and remanded for a *Kastigar* hearing. His conviction on Count 9 is reversed. Chief Judge Wald dissents from our holdings numbered (1) and (2). She also dissents from our holding numbered (3) insofar as we reverse North's conviction on Count 9. Judge Silberman dissents from our holdings numbered (4), (5) and (7), and concurs *dubitante* in our holding number (6). He also dissents from our holding number (3) insofar as we do not reverse North's conviction on Count 6.

I. Use of Immunized Testimony

A. Introduction

... North argues that his Fifth Amendment right against self-incrimination was violated, asserting that the District Court failed to require the IC to establish independent sources for the testimony of witnesses before the grand jury and at trial and to demonstrate that witnesses did not in any way use North's compelled testimony. North further argues that his Fifth Amendment right was violated by the District Court's failure to determine whether or not the IC made "nonevidentiary" use of the immunized testimony.

North's argument depends on the long-recognized principle that a predicate to liberal constitutional government is the freedom of a citizen from government compulsion to testify against himself. . . .

The prohibition against compelled testimony is not absolute, however. Under the rule of *Kastigar v. United States*, a grant of the use immunity enables the government to compel a witness's self-incriminating testimony. This is so because the statute prohibits the government both from using the immunized testimony itself and also from using any evidence derived directly or indirectly therefrom. . . .

When the government proceeds to prosecute a previously immunized witness, it has the "heavy burden of proving that all of the evidence it proposes to use was derived from legitimate independent sources." . . . A trial court must normally hold a hearing (a "*Kastigar* hearing") for the purpose of allowing the government to demonstrate that it obtained all of the evidence it proposes to use from sources independent of the compelled testimony. . . .

B. District Court Proceedings

Before North's trial, the District Court held a "preliminary" *Kastigar* inquiry and issued an order based thereon which it subsequently adopted as final (with certain changes) without benefit of further proceedings or hearings. . . .

After reviewing the relevant factual and statutory background, the District Court made four findings concerning the government's alleged use of immunized testimony before the grand jury. First, "[d]efendants' immunized testimony was not submitted to the grand jury in any form." Second, "[t]he grand jurors were effectively warned not to read about or look at or listen to this immunized testimony and it played no part in the grand jury's unanimous decision to indict." Third, "[t]he grand jury transcript and exhibits reflect solid proof and ample probable cause to indict on each and every count." Fourth, "[n]one of the testimony or exhibits presented to the grand jury became known to the prosecuting attorneys on Independent Counsel's staff or to him personally either from the immunized testimony itself or from leads derived from the testimony, directly or indirectly."

In reaching these conclusions, the District Court noted that the "Independent counsel's legitimate independent leads to every significant witness were carefully documented"; that the grand jury heard many witnesses before the immunity order issued; that North's testimony was undertaken and concluded while the grand jury was in recess; and that the "grand jurors were specifically, repeatedly and effectively instructed to avoid exposure to any immunized testimony". . . .

Addressing what it referred to as nonevidentiary problems, the District Court noted that "[w]itnesses, probably a considerable number of them, have had their memories refreshed by the immunized testimony," but because of its belief that "there is no way of determining, except possibly by a trial before the trial, whether or not any defendant was placed in a substantially worse position by the possible refreshment of a witness' memory through such exposure," the District Court concluded that "[i]f testimony remains truthful the refreshment itself is not an evidentiary use."

C. Analysis

North's primary *Kastigar* complaint is that the District Court failed to require the IC to demonstrate an independent source for each item of evidence or testimony presented to the grand jury and the petit jury, and that the District Court erred in focusing almost wholly on the IC's leads to witnesses, rather than on the content of the witnesses' testimony. North also claims that the IC made an improper nonevidentiary use of the immunized testimony (as by employing it for purposes of trial strategy), or at least that the District Court failed to make a sufficient inquiry into the question. North also protests that his immunized testimony was improperly used to refresh the recollection of witnesses before the grand jury and at trial, that this refreshment caused them to alter their testimony, and that the District Court failed to give this question the careful examination it deserved. . . .

Assuming without deciding that a prosecutor cannot make nonevidentiary use of immunized testimony, we conclude that the IC here did not do so and that the District Court's inquiry and findings on this issue are not clearly erroneous. Thus, we do not decide the question of the permissibility or impermissibility of nonevidentiary use. However, contrary to the District Court, we conclude that the use of immunized testimony by witnesses to refresh their memories, or otherwise to focus their thoughts, organize their testimony, or alter their prior or contemporaneous statements, constitutes evidentiary use rather than nonevidentiary use. The District Court on remand is to hold the searching type of *Kastigar* hearings described in detail below, concerning North's allegations of refreshment. Finally, because the District Court apparently interpreted *Kastigar* as prohibiting the government only from using immunized testimony *as a lead* rather than *using it at all*, we hold that the District Court's truncated *Kastigar* inquiry was insufficient to protect North's Fifth Amendment right to avoid self-incrimination. . . .

II. Jury Unanimity Instruction

North alleges error as to Count 9 in the trial court's refusal to give a specific unanimity instruction. The Court gave a general unanimity instruction:

> The verdict must represent the considered judgment of each juror. In order to return a verdict on any aspect of this case it is necessary that each juror agree to the verdict. Your verdict must be unanimous.

In addition to this instruction, North contends that he was entitled to further instruction directing the jury that it must be unanimous as to the specific act (or acts), method, mode or manner by which North violated the statute as charged in Count 9. Upon review of the facts of this case and the appropriate authorities, we conclude that the District Court committed reversible error as to Count 9 in its refusal to include a specific unanimity requirement in its instructions to the jury. . . .

...Count 9 charged that North, having custody of NSC documents, "willfully and knowingly did conceal, remove, mutilate, obliterate, falsify and destroy and did cause to be concealed, removed, mutilated, obliterated, falsified and destroyed records, papers and documents filed and deposited in a public office...." In his jury instruction on Count 9, the trial judge summarized the indictment as charging North with destroying, altering, and removing documents from mid- to late November 1986. In effect, then, the jury had three alternative theories of destroying, altering, or removing on which it might have convicted North....

Where several factual predicates support a guilty verdict, a defendant is entitled to unanimous agreement among the jury as to which of these "alternative factual predicates" provided a basis for conviction. As a general rule, when an indictment charges several "distinct conceptual groupings" of activities in an individual count, as opposed to "a single conceptual grouping of related facts," the jury must agree unanimously as to which of these distinct groupings the defendant is guilty.... When a statute criminalizes false statements, for example, each false statement charged in a single count is properly treated as a distinct conceptual grouping; to convict, the jury must unanimously agree upon which one of those statements the defendant made....

In North's case, the factual predicates on which the indictment was based are, in our view, distinct enough to necessitate specific unanimity. North testified that he destroyed documents beginning in late October 1986 and that he continued to do so until he was fired in November 1986.... North also testified that, on [National Security Adviser Robert C.] McFarlane's instructions, he altered five official documents—apparently System IV NSC documents—relating to the Iranian arms sales.... Finally, North testified that after he was fired, he removed documents from his NSC office on the advice of [Air Force Maj. Gen. Richard V.] Secord's counsel. He returned the documents a few days later on the advice of his present counsel, whom he had retained in the intervening period.

Thus, ... circumstances of his destruction, alteration, and removal of documents were distinct; any of those activities could serve as an underlying criminal act. Furthermore, the evidence bearing on North's knowledge of the lawfulness of his actions—and, in effect, on the criminality of his intent—varied from instance to instance. Each of the possible predicates for a conviction on Count 9 therefore, required distinct, individuated proof. As a result, we conclude that the jury had to agree unanimously as to which, if any, of these combinations of *actus reus* and *mens rea* actually occurred, and the trial court should have so instructed....

III. Authorization

North argues that his convictions on Counts 6 and 9 must be reversed because the jury was improperly instructed concerning North's claimed authorization from his superiors to do the acts underlying those counts. He raises two arguments that at least appear to be conceptually distinct. First, North asserts that under our decision in *United States v. Barker,* 546 F.2d 940 (D.C. Cir. 1976), the jury should have been instructed to return a verdict of not guilty if it found the necessary elements of a so-called "authorization defense." That is, he claims that he was entitled to an instruction that reasonable reliance on the apparent authority of one's superiors is an absolute defense. We hold that the District Court did not err in refusing to give an authorization defense instruction. Second, North claims that the District Judge erred when he instructed the jury to ignore all evidence of authorization in deciding whether North had the requisite intent in either count unless "the defendant was specifically ordered and directed by a superior to act contrary to the law, and if no alternative was available to him to comply with the order by other lawful means ... [and if] he reasonably believed the order was legally proper." We hold that the District Court erred in limiting the jury's consideration of the evidence of authorization with reference to Count 9 but not as to Count 6....

In *Barker,* we reversed the convictions of Bernard Barker and Eugenio Martinez, who participated in the burglary of Dr. Lewis Fielding's office at the behest of E. Howard Hunt. Hunt, who was known to Barker and Martinez as a long-time CIA agent, worked under the supervision of John Ehrlichman in the White House and was attempting to obtain information about Daniel Ellsberg, the source of the Pentagon Papers leak. Dr. Fielding was Ellsberg's psychiatrist, and Hunt hired Barker and Martinez to break into Fielding's office for the purpose of photographing Ellsberg's file. That break-in led to charges against Barker and Martinez, among others, for conspiring to violate Dr. Fielding's Fourth Amendment rights. The defendants claimed that they lacked the *mens rea* [criminal intent] necessary for conviction because they had reasonably relied on Hunt's authority to engage them in carrying out the burglary, and that the district court had erred by refusing to instruct the jury accordingly and by excluding evidence that would tend to establish their theory of the case.

All three judges issued separate opinions, two of which supported reversal on grounds that the defendants were entitled to put on evidence and have the jury instructed on the defense of good faith reasonable reliance on the apparent authority of Hunt. Judge [Malcolm R.] Wilkey thought the case presented an exception to the usual rule that a mistake of law is no defense to a criminal charge.... Judge Wilkey thought there was evidence to support the conclusion that the defendants "honestly and reasonably believed they were engaged in a top-secret national security operation lawfully authorized by a government intelligence agency...."

Sitting by designation, Judge [Robert R.] Merhige of the Eastern District of Virginia also thought the case fit into an exception to the "mistake of law is not an excuse" rule and analogized the case to situations in which a defendant acted on the basis of erroneous government advice, thereby making a criminal conviction unduly harsh. The quintessential examples mentioned by Judge Merhige were individuals acting in reliance on a statute later held to be unconstitutional or on a court decision that a statute is unconstitutiional that is subsequently overruled. In order to avoid convictions in those situations, Judge Merhige thought a defense should be available to a defendant who

> (1) reasonably, on the basis of an objective standard, (2) relies on a (3) conclusion or statement of law (4) issued by an official charged with interpretation, administration, and/or enforcement responsibilities in the relevant legal field....

North cannot even approach the showing that Judge Merhige's formulation of the defense requires. North does not even claim that he relied on *any* "conclusion or statement of *law*," let alone one issued by an official charged with interpretation, administration, and/or enforcement responsibilities in the relevant legal field." On the other hand, neither did Barker or Martinez, yet Judge Merhige voted that their convictions had to be reversed. Despite all that was recounted above, Judge Merhige concluded:

> Barker and Martinez assert that they relied on Hunt's authority as delegated from an intelligence super-structure controlled by the White House.... The Executive Branch ... is vested with substantive responsibilities in the field of national security, and decisions of its officials on the extent of their legal authority deserves some deference from the public. A jury may well find that John Ehrlichman ... expressed or implied that the break-in of Dr. Fielding's office was legal ... and that Hunt ... passed the position on to the defendants, which they, acting as reasonable men, relied upon in performing the break-in.

We suppose we could simply ignore the reasoning of Judge Merhige's opinion and merely infer the contours of an authorization defense from the facts in *Barker* that he thought warranted an authorization instruction. But the very premise of appellate review is that reasoning matters. Indeed, that is one of the crucial reasons why we are bound only by prior *published opinions* of this Circuit and not by other means of deciding cases. We do not think that any coherent principle can be gleaned from the *Barker* case because the reasoning of Judge Merhige's opinion does not mesh with its outcome. In such a situation, we could not fault a district court solely for a failure to "follow" *Barker*.

North's suggested instruction ... goes so far as to conjure up the notion of a "Nuremberg" defense, a notion from which our criminal justice system, one based on individual accountability and responsibility, has historically recoiled. In the absence of clear and comprehensible Circuit authority that we must do so, we refuse to hold that following orders, without more, can transform an illegal act into a legal one....

B. Evidence of Authorization [A omitted]

1. Count 6

... North's evidence ... does not support a mistake-of-law defense. In effect, he is arguing that the jury should have been instructed or permitted to consider the authorization evidence not as it bore on his intent to commit the acts charged or the nature of the acts, but rather on his motive in committing the acts. This argument invites us to establish a rule that in determining whether a defendant charged with violating section 1505 acted corruptly, the trial judge should instruct the jury that in order to find the defendant guilty, it must find that he acted from a "corrupt motive." We have seen no authority to this effect, and we cannot agree. . . .

The implications of a contrary view are stunning. Could a jury sympathetic to the official's individual notion of morality exculpate a self-styled Robin Hood bureaucrat who concealed, altered, or destroyed documents that he knew Congress needed for its oversight of budgetary disbursements? Could a bigoted jury excuse a white supremacist official who altered documents eventually slated for Congress's review of misuse of government set-asides by minority businesses? To hold that North was entitled to have the jury consider the authorization of his superiors because it bore on his motive for committing the acts in question does little more than restate the purported *Barker* defense which we have already rejected. . . .

2. Count 9

In Count 9, North was charged with violating 18 U.S.C. § 2071(b), which makes it a crime for anyone who has custody of "any record, proceeding, map, book, paper, document, or other thing, filed or deposited with any clerk or officer of any court of the United States, or in any public office, or with any judicial or public officer of the United States," to "*willfully and unlawfully* conceal[], remove[], mutilate[], obliterate[], falsify[], or destroy[] the same. . . ." (emphasis supplied). North was alleged to have violated this section by concealing, removing, and destroying a number of NSC documents concerning both the provision of aid and assistance to the Contras and the sale of arms to Iran, acting with the knowledge that doing so contravened an internal NSC regulation governing the proper means of handling documents. As both parties agree, a conviction under section 2071(b) requires that the government prove that North acted with knowledge that his conduct was unlawful.

With regard to the relevance of authorization to the jury's deliberations about North's state of mind on this (and other) counts, the District Court instructed:

> If the defendant was *specifically ordered and directed* by a superior to act contrary to the law, and if *no alternative was available to him to comply with the order by other lawful means,* you may weigh this authorization along with other facts in determining his specific intent, provided under the facts and circumstances he *reasonably believed the order was legally proper.*
>
> However, authorization requires *clear, direct instructions to act at a given time in a given way.* It must be specific, not simply a general admonition or vague expression of preference. . . . A person's general impression that a type of conduct was expected, that it was proper because others were doing the same, or that the challenged act would help someone or avoid political consequences, does not satisfy the defense of authorization.
>
> Finally, if an authorization can be satisfied by two different courses of action, *one clearly legal and one illegal or of dubious legality,* and a person

chooses the illegal or dubious course when other, legal action would comply, authorization *cannot be viewed as affecting intent....*

It may well have been acceptable if the District Court had said nothing at all about authorization when instructing the jury about intent and merely told them to consider all of the surrounding circumstances when deciding if North knew his actions were unlawful. Instead, the District Judge decided that the jury could not *consider* at all the instructions, statements, and behavior of North's colleagues, whether superiors or not, unless the evidence sufficed to warrant an "authorization defense" instruction to the jury. But whatever might have once been thought to constitute an "authorization defense" it was error to preclude the jury from considering whatever evidence of authorization exists in the record as it bears on the jury's determination of whether North had subjective knowledge of unlawfulness. As we have made clear above, authorization from one's superiors cannot convert illegal activity into legal, yet it surely can affect a defendant's *belief* that his conduct was lawful—particularly when we are dealing in an area of international security concerns, and when the authorization is thought to come from the President himself.... Because the District Court's instruction on authorization precluded the jury from fully considering whether North's claim of authorization rebutted the prosecution's burden of showing North's knowledge that his behavior was unlawful, and because it is impossible to say that the error was harmless— authorization being the core defense—North's conviction on Count 9 must be reversed.

IV. The Reagan Subpoena

North contends that his convictions on Counts 6 and 9 should be reversed because the District Court erroneously quashed his subpoena to former President Ronald Reagan. Finding that Mr. Reagan's testimony would not have added anything material to North's defense to Counts 6 and 9, we decline to reverse North's convictions on this ground....

V. Pending Inquiry Instruction

North's conviction on Count 6 for aiding and abetting the obstruction of a congressional inquiry required the IC to prove that an "inquiry or investigation is *being had* by either House, or any committee of either House or any joint committee of the Congress...." North contends that his Fifth Amendment right to due process and his Sixth Amendment right to a jury verdict were violated when the District Judge instructed the jury

as a matter of law that congressional inquiries were pending and that Congress was authorized to inquire into arms sales [to Iran] and Contra assistance, both of which were relevant and material issues. [Paragraph] You need only deliberate regarding the other three elements....

North's counsel objected to the finding "that as a matter of law" congressional inquiries were underway in November 1986 on the grounds that "what this permits the jury to do is to find there was an obstruction of an investigation concerning a matter that was in fact not pending at that time."...

We agree that the District Court erred by removing this element of the offense from the jury's province. Indeed, in their proposed jury instructions both North and the IC requested that the jury decide whether the inquiry was pending. We do not, however, believe that the judge's charge deprived North of a fair trial....

VI. Closing Argument

North contends that certain comments made by the IC to the jury during closing arguments were improper and mandate reversal of his convictions. In particular, North complains about the IC's comparison of his conduct to Adolf Hitler's, and about the IC's statement that Richard Secord and Albert Hakim made a "killing" from arms sales to Iran and the Contras, despite the absence of any evidence in the record concerning the amount of their profits. Although both of the prosecutor's remarks were clearly improper, we find that neither was sufficiently prejudicial to North as to warrant the reversal of any or all of his convictions....

North does not make out any of the components of substantial prejudice resulting from the prosecutor's closing argument. The District Court found that the reference to Hitler plainly was not prejudicial, and we have no reason to disagree. Furthermore, while a verdict of not guilty on Count 10 would not have been irrational, in light of North's own testimony about the scope of Secord's and Hakim's arms dealings, it appears virtually certain that the jury would have convicted North on this Count in the absence of the prosecutor's reference to the size of their profits. Finally, the prosecutor's misconduct was at most marginal, limited to a few lines in a closing statement; and the trial judge offered clear curative instructions.

VII. CIPA Claims

North argues that the District Court's application of the Classified Information Procedures Act ("CIPA") violated his right to due process by compelling him to reveal to the IC before trial a 162-page summary of anticipated classified defense testimony, and by not imposing a reciprocal burden on the IC. Although the District Judge did not hew precisely to CIPA's procedural outline, we believe that his balancing of the obligations imposed by CIPA on both parties does not warrant reversal of North's conviction....

VIII. Juror Dishonesty

North contends that he was denied his Sixth Amendment right to an impartial jury because a trial juror lied under oath, on both a pretrial jury questionnaire and a post-trial hearing, about her immediate family's involvement in judicial proceedings. We are not persuaded by North's argument.

A. Background

Before trial, jurors were asked several questions, including whether they or any member of their immediate family had "ever been involved as a party to or appeared as a witness in any court proceeding (civil or criminal) or in any investigation by a federal or state authority or by an official legislative body or agency." Tara King, who was eventually selected as a trial juror, checked the box marked "No" even though several of her brothers had been charged with criminal conduct, one was sent to prison, and King herself had testified before the grand jury investigating a robbery allegedly committed by one of her brothers. After trial, upon obtaining evidence that King had improperly completed her pretrial questionnaire, North moved for an *in camera* hearing concerning King's qualifications and for a mistrial.

At the hearing, King testified that she had "forgotten" about one of her brothers' guilty plea, conviction, and time in jail. Although the District Judge did not "credit" King's testimony of forgetfulness, he denied North's motion for a mistrial because North had not demonstrated any resultant bias against him "by fact or implication."

B. Analysis

At issue is whether deliberate concealment of information at *voir dire* is sufficient to require a mistrial, absent a showing of actual bias. The Supreme Court has laid down the following standard for overturning a conviction when a juror withholds critical information on *voir dire:*

> [A] party must first demonstrate that a juror failed to answer honestly a material question on *voir dire,* and then further show that a correct response would have provided a valid basis for a challenge for cause. The motives for concealing information may vary, but only those reasons that affect a juror's impartiality can truly be said to affect the fairness of a trial....

In sum, the District Court applied the correct legal standard in addressing North's claim of juror misconduct. Seeing no evidence that the District Judge's factual findings concerning King's lack of bias were clearly erroneous, we affirm his denial of North's motion for a mistrial.

IX. Videotape

After the prosecution had rested its case and on the eve of the presentation of defense evidence, North, by motion, sought leave of the District Court to introduce a three-to-four-hour excerpted version of John Poindexter's thirty hours of immunized testimony before the congressional committees investigating the Iran/Contra affair. The District Court denied the motion.... North now contends that the District Court erred in not admitting the videotape.... We disagree. The District Court acted well within its broad discretion over evidentiary matters....

WALD, CHIEF JUDGE, dissenting as to Parts I, II, and III(B)(2):
Oliver North's was a case of epic proportions, massively publicized, for

many weeks engaging the rapt attention and emotions of the nation. The panel today reverses his convictions on three separate grounds, including a remand for an "item-by-item, line-by-line" hearing on whether any bit of evidence, as yet unidentified, may have reflected exposure to North's immunized testimony before Congress.

After studying for months the thousands of pages of transcripts and hundreds of documents produced for the grand jury and trial, I, on the other hand, am satisfied that North received a fair trial—not a perfect one, but a competently managed and a fair one. As in all trials of this magnitude, a few errors were made, but in analyzing and researching North's claims, including the three grounds on which the Per Curiam reverses, I do not find, singly or cumulatively, that any of them rose to the status of reversible error. I am convinced that the essentials of a fair trial were accorded North, and that his conviction on the three Counts of which the jury found him guilty should be affirmed....

SILBERMAN, Circuit Judge, concurring dubitante as to Part VI, and dissenting as to Parts III(B)(1), IV, V, and VII.

I. Closing Argument

Unlike my colleagues, I find the issue whether the IC's improper statement at closing argument that Secord and Hakim were making a "killing" and "millions" requires reversal of Count 10 quite troubling and therefore choose this unorthodox form—concurring dubitante—to register my opinion....

I consider the improper comments in the IC's closing argument to be egregious prosecutorial misconduct because they were deliberate rather than inadvertent. The Majority raises the possibility that the IC's statements were "slips of the tongue in the heat of oral argument," but I have no doubt that these improper statements were intentional. The notion that the IC's counsel somehow *forgot* about the colloquy at the bench in which he promised not to introduce evidence of the amount of profits, or that he did not grasp the difference between the existence of profits and the size of profits is too fanciful for serious consideration. Indeed, the IC's brief does not assert the benign motive that the Majority raises as a possibility. Surely the IC knew perfectly well that North's defense, that he took the fence solely to protect his wife and children, would tug powerfully at the jurors' hearts and therefore the IC wished, even to the extent of violating the agreed upon "rules of engagement" of the trial, to impugn North's motives....

II. CIPA

I believe that the District Judge committed reversible error in the way he decided, or more accurately, refused to decide, the CIPA issue. Buried within the Majority's exhaustive and, frankly, impenetrable discussion of the "Statutory Framework" and "Course of Events" is the following simple and discrete issue. Prior to trial, North was forced to disclose to the IC a 162-page "narrative summary" of all the classified evidence he expected to reveal at trial, pursuant to the CIPA statute. As might be expected, whenever a defendant is compelled to disclose aspects of his case prior to trial, the statute directs the District Court to "order the United States to provide the defendant with the information it expects to use to rebut the classified information," "unless the interests of fairness do not so require." Even though North filed a motion praying for the reciprocal discovery guaranteed him by the statute, the District Court *ignored* the motion and the IC never had to reveal the information it used to rebut the evidence disclosed in North's 162-page narrative summary. . . .

III. Authorization and Intent

I disagree with my colleagues on the question whether the District Judge's instructions were also erroneous regarding the relevance of North's evidence of his superior's instructions or communications as to Count 6. I do not see the sharp distinction the court does between how those instructions bear on Count 6 and 9; I think on *both* Counts the District Judge was in error. . . .

"I was only following orders" resonates powerfully (and horrifyingly) in the world's collective memory—but to so describe North's defense is, in my view, an unfair characterization of it. His appeal on this count is that the District Court did not permit the jury to consider whether North thought he was acting corruptly, thus illegally. . . .

IV. Reagan Subpoena

Appellant seeks reversal of his convictions on Counts 6 and 9 on the added ground that the District Court erroneously quashed his subpoena to former President Ronald Reagan. On the basis of the record as it appears before us, I believe it was serious error to have quashed the subpoena, and therefore I dissent from the Majority opinion on this ground also. . . .

I can think of no more powerful corroboration for North's claim that he believed McFarlane's, Casey's and Poindexter's efforts to conceal the Iran and Contra initiatives were authorized by the President than testimony from Mr. Reagan himself that he had indeed authorized them, either explicitly or implicitly. . . . The instructions and actions of North's superiors—as well as their accounts to him of their direct meetings with the President—were critical to his main defense that he did not believe he was acting unlawfully when he destroyed the relevant documents. But on this issue, North was forced to rely at trial on his own testimony alone. Of his superiors, only McFarlane testified at trial, and he testified against North pursuant to a plea agreement with the government. North was not permitted to call Mr. Reagan, Casey was deceased, and Poindexter was unavailable because of his Fifth Amendment privilege. Under those circumstances, it is hard to overemphasize the importance that corroborative testimony from Mr. Reagan may have had on the knowledge of unlawfulness question. . . .

Presidents, even ex-Presidents, may not be called to testify capriciously or needlessly but this is not such a case. North worked in the White House, only one step removed from the President himself, with what appears to have been enormous responsibility.... [North's] defense is that he was *lawfully* doing the President's bidding....

V. Pending Inquiry

... North contends that his Fifth Amendment right to due process and his Sixth Amendment right to a jury verdict were violated when the District Judge instructed the jury, over North's explicit objection. I agree....

I believe that under relevant Supreme Court decisions reversal is automatically required when the judge, as here, directs a verdict on an essential element of a crime, no matter how overwhelming—or even uncontested—the evidence is on that issue. Indeed, the IC neither argues that a harmless error test could be applied here, nor that this error was harmless in any event. Nevertheless, the Majority reaches both conclusions, in my view misreading the Supreme Court's instructions on this issue and directly contradicting the holdings of three of our sister circuits that have faced this very same issue....

VI. Conclusion

There is a great temptation in a case such as this to focus on the institutional interests at stake. The Presidency, the Congress, even the District Judge, faced, as he was, with a daunting task. But I think that is the wrong angle from which to view the appellant's arguments. The District Judge was not on trial nor was the Congress or the president; North was.

The Chief Judge believes that although the District Judge made "a few" errors, they were *all* harmless. Of course we see only the issues appealed, but it seems to me there were quite a few errors among them and they were serious indeed—some even constitutional in nature....

LOUISIANA GOVERNOR'S VETO OF "TRASH LYRICS" BILL

July 25, 1990

Louisiana governor Buddy Roemer vetoed a bill that required warning labels on recordings of songs whose lyrics extolled drugs, violence, and deviant sex. The bill also would have set jail terms and fines for retailers who sold the recordings to youngsters under age seventeen, and for manufacturers and distributors of the records who did not heed the labeling requirement.

Roemer, acting July 25 after weeks of indecision, said that he supported the bill's aim of identifying "trash lyrics" for the benefit of parents. But he thought the legislation infringed on constitutionally protected free speech, and that its purpose could be achieved "through voluntary compliance with industry standards."

In an explanatory statement, the governor said that the veto would avoid both a constitutional test, "which the majority of experts believe we would lose," and "the negative economic and publicity consequences in the short term to our great state." However, he insisted at a news conference in Baton Rouge, the state capital, that music industry protests—including threats of canceled performances and conventions in Louisiana—did not sway him to cast his veto.

The governor was joined at the news conference by Jay Berman, president of the Recording Industry Association of America; Mike Greene, president of the National Association of Recordings Arts and Sciences; Pat Moreland, president of the National Association of Retail Merchandisers; and Tipper Gore, wife of Sen. Albert Gore, D-Tenn., and president of Parents' Music Resource Center (PMRC), an organization critical of offensive recordings.

Berman praised Roemer's "courageous vote for freedom of expression in America" and said artistic freedom could co-exist with voluntary labeling. Gore said: "We all recognize the concern to protect children from violent and explicit messages. But we don't want the government to legislate that concern." The national Parent-Teacher Associations and PMRC opposed the bill, apparently in the belief that it would not be upheld by the courts.

The governor's veto message implicitly threatened mandatory laws if voluntary compliance by the record industry was not adequate. He noted that in the 1991 legislative session, Louisiana lawmakers could "review the status of voluntary compliance and act accordingly."

Record Industry's Own Labeling

In November 1985 PMRC and the Recording Industry Association of America, a trade group representing 85 percent of the record companies, including all major labels, negotiated an agreement whereby the member companies would choose between two options when they released records with potentially offensive lyrics involving sex, violence, or drugs. One was to print a parental-advice warning on the record package, and the other was to print the relevant lyrics on the album cover.

PMRC's follow-up monitoring of the agreement suggested that it had an impact. Of the 7,500 albums released between January 1986, when the agreement went into effect, and August 1989, the organization deemed 121 to have offensive lyrics. Forty-nine of those albums bore warning labels or lyric sheets. However, that did not deter lawmakers in a score of state legislatures from proposing mandatory labeling and penalties for noncompliance. Louisiana's bill was the first to reach a governor's desk for signing.

Obscenity Cases Elsewhere

In Broward County, Florida, Charlie Freeman, a record store owner, was convicted in October by a Fort Lauderdale jury of violating the state's obscenity laws for selling an album, "As Nasty as They Wanna Be," recorded by the 2 Live Crew rock group. Paradoxically, Luther Campbell, the leader of the rock group, and two of its other members, were tried in the same courtroom later that month and acquitted of obscenity charges that arose from a nightclub performance in which they used the same lyrics.

Obscenity was at issue in another celebrated case decided the same month in Cincinnati, Ohio. A state Superior Court jury found the Contemporary Arts Gallery and its director, Dennis Barrie, not guilty of charges that they pandered to obscenity by displaying an exhibit of photographs by the late Robert Mapplethorpe. Some of the photos depicted homosexual and sadomasochistic activities. Barrie and the gallery were indicted by a grand jury on April 1, the day the exhibit opened.

The Mapplethorpe photos had set off a furor the previous year when *the Corcoran Gallery of Art in Washington, D.C., canceled the exhibit amid a political battle led by Sen. Jesse Helms, R-N.C., over the financing of the exhibit by the National Endowment for the Arts. It was subsequently shown without incident elsewhere in Washington, and in Philadelphia, Berkeley, Hartford, and Boston. But in Cincinnati, a city with strict obscenity laws and headquarters of the National Coalition Against Pornography, it caused trouble. A leader of the effort to ban the exhibit was Rev. Donald E. Wilmon, who headed the American Family Association in Tupelo, Mississippi.*

> *Following is a statement issued by Gov. Buddy Roemer of Louisiana, July 25, 1990, explaining his veto of the Louisiana legislature's bill to require warning labels on records with offensive lyrics:*

I agree with the authors of this bill concerning the need to inform parents of the content of records purchased by youngsters. Trash lyrics explicitly referencing suicide, sex, drugs, rape and incest are potentially harmful to impressionable youth. We parents need to know.

In a free America where speech is constitutionally protected the best method of informing the public—and under broad parameters the only legal way—is through voluntary compliance within industry standards, similar to what the movie industry has done with success.

Voluntary labeling, therefore, honors our Constitution (and our freedom) and informs our parents and represents the way to go.

Finally, the record industry, after years of promising, is moving to implement voluntary labeling.

How best to ensure voluntary compliance of labeling is the question.

Unfortunately this bill at this time is not the best way. The National PTA [Parent-Teacher Associations] and the parents' association headed by Tipper Gore (the Parents' Music Resource Center) feel this bill should be vetoed. A veto would avoid a constitutional test which a majority of experts believe we would lose and thereby take away the momentum for voluntary compliance. A veto would also avoid the negative economic and publicity consequences in the short term to our great state.

Since the bill doesn't go into effect until January 1, 1992, a veto would allow us ample time in the next regular session of the Legislature to review the status of voluntary compliance and act accordingly within the time frame outlined in the bill.

In short, with a veto we maintain all our options, lose no time, allow maximum pressure on the industry to respond to our legitimate concerns, avoid a messy, doubtful, expensive constitutional test, promote voluntary labeling, and maintain Louisiana's strong musical heritage.

REPORT ON *EXXON*
VALDEZ OIL SPILL
July 31, 1990

The National Transportation Safety Board (NTSB) concluded its investigation of the 1989 Alaskan oil spill with a report on July 31. It portrayed Capt. Joseph J. Hazelwood, master of the Exxon Valdez, as alcohol-impaired when he left a fatigued and inexperienced third mate in charge of manuevering the tanker through a treacherous passage in Prince William Sound. The ship hit a reef and ruptured, dumping more than 10 million gallons of crude oil into the icy waters.

That March 24, 1989, accident caused the worst oil spill in American waters. It resulted in widespread damage to marine life and waterfowl and spawned several investigations and dozens of lawsuits. The cleanup effort, the costliest ever recorded in an industrial accident, passed the $2 billion mark in 1990. (Congressional Hearing on Alaskan Oil Spill, Historic Documents of 1989, p. 225)

The NTSB is an independent federal agency responsible for determining the probable cause of major accidents in transportation and making safety recommendations. In this investigation, it also found fault with the Coast Guard for deficiencies in its surveillance of shipping traffic in and out of Valdez, Alaska, which the tanker had just left; the Exxon Shipping Company, the ship's owner, for failure "to provide a fit master and a rested and sufficient crew"; and the harbor's pilot services for not escorting outbound ships beyond Bligh's Reef, where the Exxon Valdez ran aground.

Additionally, the board made recommendations to the Department of Transportation for better detection of alcohol and drug usage by sea-going officers and crews, and to the Environmental Protection Agency, the state of Alaska, and the Alyeska Pipeline Service Company for better procedures and coordination in dealing with oil spills.

Alyeska is a consortium of oil companies (including Exxon Corporation, parent of Exxon Shipping Company) that operates the Trans-Alaska pipeline. The pipeline brings oil from fields on Alaska's North Slope across hundreds of miles of wilderness to the port of Valdez. The 1972 Clean Water Act gave the Coast Guard responsibility for developing and monitoring plans to contain an oil spill in Prince William Sound, but the Coast Guard ceded authority to Alyeska.

Finding of Cleanup Confusion

After the ship hit the reef, fourteen hours elapsed before the first cleanup equipment reached the site. High winds and strong currents impeded cleanup efforts. By then, oil had spread miles from the ship. It eventually fouled hundreds of miles of shoreline, causing extensive damage to marine life, birds, and the local fishing industry.

Following an initial round of confusion and recriminations between Exxon and the federal government, the state stepped in to direct the cleanup. Exxon eventually assumed cleanup responsibility, undertaking a project that continued until the onset of cold weather and resumed in May 1990. In addition to the cleanup costs, Exxon faced litigation expenses. It was named defendant in lawsuits filed by fishermen and wildlife groups. Moreover, the state sued it and Alyeska for damages. In 1981 Alyeska had disbanded its twenty-member round-the-clock oil-spill response team, over the protests of the Alaska Department of Environmental Conservation. Exxon, in turn, sued the state, contending that its refusal to permit the use of oil-dispersing chemicals drove up the cleanup costs.

Charges Against Hazelwood

The state filed criminal charges against Hazelwood, who also had been named defendant in several civil suits. He was tried in March on the criminal charges, but an Anchorage jury acquitted him on all but one count—negligence of his duties aboard the ship. That count was a misdemeanor for which he was sentenced to 1,000 hours of community service cleaning the oily beaches and ordered to pay $50,000 restitution to the state.

Hazelwood appealed the sentence, arguing that he was protected against any criminal prosecution by an immunity clause in Alaskan oil-spill legislation. The jury had found him not guilty of more serious charges that he was drunk and reckless in command of the Exxon Valdez.

Hazelwood's blood was not tested for alcohol until ten hours after the accident, and the prosecution was unable to persuade the jury that he was drunk at the time it occurred. The defense successfully argued that it was neither mandatory nor customary for the captain of an oil tanker to remain on the bridge while the ship moved through Prince William Sound.

The NTSB came to different conclusions. The board brushed aside claims by Hazelwood's attorneys that blood samples had been mishandled and did not provide proof that he was drunk on the night of the accident. The NTSB's chief staff investigator, William Woody, said an analysis of alcohol tests and eyewitness accounts indicated Hazelwood drank before boarding the ship.

Other evidence, including certain actions and a voice analysis of his recorded commands aboard the ship, indicated alcoholic impairment, the board concluded in its report. The board criticized Exxon for failing to learn or simply ignoring that Hazelwood had previously encountered drinking problems. As to the question of whether he should have been on the bridge, the board said the situation "demanded" his presence there.

Exxon dismissed Hazelwood from his job after the accident, and on July 25, six days before the NTSB released its report, his license to operate a ship was suspended for nine months. The suspension was ordered by a federal administrative law judge, Harry J. Gardner, who acted on Coast Guard allegations that the captain violated regulations by drinking less than four hours before sailing. The Coast Guard had dropped other allegations, including drunkenness.

Following are excerpts from the National Transportation Safety Board's investigative report on the Exxon Valdez *oil spill, issued July 31, 1990:*

Executive Summary

About 0009, on March 24, 1989, the U.S. tankship *Exxon Valdez,* loaded with about 1,263,000 barrels of crude oil, grounded on Bligh Reef in Prince William Sound, near Valdez, Alaska. At the time of the grounding, the vessel was under the navigational control of the third mate. There were no injuries, but about 258,000 barrels of cargo were spilled when eight cargo tanks ruptured, resulting in catastrophic damage to the environment. Damage to the vessel was estimated at $25 million, the cost of the lost cargo was estimated at $3.4 million, and the cost of the cleanup of the spilled oil during 1989 was about $1.85 billion. . . .

Probable Cause

The National Transportation Safety Board determines that the probable cause of the grounding of the *Exxon Valdez* was the failure of the third mate to properly maneuver the vessel because of fatigue and excessive workload; the failure of the master to provide a proper navigation watch because of impairment from alcohol; the failure of Exxon Shipping Company to provide a fit master and a rested and sufficient crew for the *Exxon Valdez;* the lack of an effective Vessel Traffic Service because of inadequate equipment and manning levels, inadequate personnel training, and deficient management oversight; and the lack of effective pilotage services.

Analysis

The Accident

... The Safety Board concludes that the waterway that the *Exxon Valdez* was navigating, which was bordered by heavy ice on one side and a dangerous reef on the other, demanded the master's [Joseph J. Hazelwood's] presence on the bridge.

There are great demands on a master's time, among them the pressing requirements of administrative duties, such as compiling records and reports and sending messages by radio to shoreside company management. Occasionally, such reports should be submitted as soon as possible. However, no matter how urgent such administrative duties may seem, they must not prevent the master from attending to those things that are important to the safety of the vessel. The master's primary responsibility is to ensure the safety of his vessel, its cargo, and its crew. When his vessel is proceeding in confined or congested waters, the master must place the safe navigation of his vessel above all other considerations. He must identify the parts of the transit that present the greatest danger, the possible consequences of an error in navigation, what constitutes an adequate navigation watch, and, above all, when he should be on the bridge supervising the navigation watch.

In this case, the master knew that his vessel would be passing close to Bligh Reef and that the grounding on this reef could result in grave danger to his vessel, crew, and cargo. Hence, it was critically important that the vessel be navigated with great care and with adequate manning of the navigation watch until it was safely past the reef. Once the vessel had passed Bligh Reef, the master could expect that most of the ice floe would be astern of the vessel and that the vessel would be in relatively open water, where a minor error in navigation or shiphandling would be unlikely to cause grave consequences. The master was familiar with the area, and he could easily have determined that the vessel would be past the reef in about 20 minutes. Also, he was familiar with the watch officer [Gregory T. Cousins], whom he regarded as a competent third mate, and knew that the third mate had had only about a year of experience as a deck officer. He was also aware of the number of extra hours that his officers had worked to load the vessel and should have recognized that the third mate might be very tired and, by virtue of his limited conning experience and possible fatigue, might not be competent to navigate the vessel between the ice and the reef by himself. The Safety Board concludes that these are very compelling factors that the master should have considered before deciding to leave the bridge.

Moreover, there were clear directives that required the master to be on the bridge in this particular situation. The *Exxon Bridge Organization Manual* directed that under conditions, such as those existing in Price

William Sound on March 23, the master or the chief mate was to be on the bridge with the watch officer. As usual, the chief mate had been up during most of the deballasting and loading of the vessel and needed rest. Thus, the master was the officer obligated by the *Bridge Organization Manual* to be on the bridge. Furthermore, the vessel was navigating in pilotage waters, and Federal regulations required that a Federal pilot be in charge of the vessel's navigation. Although rescinding the regulation had been proposed, the regulation was still in effect. Because the master was the only officer on board who possessed the required Federal pilotage endorsement, he was required by Federal law and regulations to be on the bridge. Finally, under the conditions confronting the *Exxon Valdez,* it was normal practice for the master to be on the bridge. The Safety Board concludes that the situation was complex and dangerous and hence warranted the master's presence on the bridge in active supervision of the vessel's navigation. . . .

The third mate stated that he did not believe that his attention was distracted from his duties by fatigue. However, a fatigued person might not realize that there were longer lapses of time between events or that his duties, such as navigating, were requiring more than the normal time to execute. . . .

Regardless of what caused the critical delay in starting the turn until well beyond Busby Island Light, very little of the testimony provided by the third mate helps to resolve the matter. The Safety Board concludes, however, that the delay was most likely owing to inexperience in shiphandling and piloting, fatigue, or both. . . .

By allowing the vessel to be turned slowly with an average of 4° to 5° of rudder through nearly 67° of heading change during a period of approximately 6 minutes, the third mate demonstrated that he did not know the location of Bligh Reef in relation to his vessel. If he had had more experience or possibly more training in navigation, he probably would have know how important it was to plot the vessel's position on the chart and then to plot his next course, making allowance for the advance and transfer that the vessel would make during the turn. Instead, the third mate relied too much on the radar, possibly because he was mistakenly more concerned about the danger of colliding with the ice than the danger of being grounded on Bligh Reef. This accident demonstrates that an inexperienced officer, who was probably fatigued, simply became confused.

Performance of the Master

. . . The Safety Board investigation did not identify any well-founded reason for the master's decision to leave the bridge. According to the third mate, the master departed to send messages before the ship left the Sound. However, the vessel had more than 2 hours of transit ahead before reaching Cape Hinchinbrook. In order for the master to have completed the maneuver himself or to have monitored the third mate's conduct of the transit, he would have had to remain on the bridge only about 20 minutes longer. Thus, there would have been ample time to send messages after the vessel transited Valdez Arm. His departure again shows that his judgment was unsound since he relegated vessel safety to a secondary priority at a critical time.

When the master left the navigation watch to the supervision of the third mate, he exposed the *Exxon Valdez* to considerable risk. Several uncertainties associated with the maneuver around the ice floe made his departure from the bridge particularly ill advised. When he left, the course of 180° headed the vessel directly toward shoal water. The master should have realized that both careful timing and judgment were required to extricate the vessel from its location outside the traffic lanes between the reef and the ice floe. He should also have known that frequent fixing of the vessel's position was necessary. He should have been concerned that the third mate might be tired and that the helmsman might require greater than normal supervision. Thus, he was giving his responsibility for the vessel's safety to crewmembers whose capabilities were diminished at the very time that navigation was becoming complex and demanding and also at the very time that a failure to navigate correctly and precisely could result in very grave consequences. Also, putting the vessel on automatic pilot in confined waters and not telling the third mate that he had done so was extremely inconsistent with normally accepted practice.

Although the master had recently had marital problems and had been described by the radio electronics officer as depressed, nothing indicated that his personal problems were sufficient to have altered his ability to execute command responsibilities with his usual competency. He was also reportedly in good health.

The master did not inform the Safety Board of the reasons for his actions. As a result, the rationale and priorities that entered into his decisions remain undetermined at the time of this report.

Impairment of the Master

One explanation for the master's decision to allow the third mate to supervise the navigation watch under such critical circumstances is that the master was impaired by alcohol. There was evidence that he had been drinking with the radio electronics officer and chief engineer for several hours during the day in Valdez. They returned to the vessel without incident, and no witnesses, including security guards at the terminal and their cab driver for the return trip to the terminal, described anyone's behavior as impaired.

The master probably consumed additional alcohol after he boarded the vessel. Additional drinking could explain why, according to witnesses, his condition appeared normal when he returned from Valdez about 2030 [8:30 p.m.] but that his speech was unusual by about 2325 [10:35 p.m.]. The master had a history of alcohol abuse that included alcohol-related traffic violations, and he had undergone a rehabilitation treatment program. It would not be uncommon for a person for whom a treatment program had been unsuccessful to continue drinking alone after consuming several social drinks with companions. Also, one witness stated that the master on at least one occasion had consumed alcohol on board the vessel. His absence from the bridge for about 1½ hours while the State pilot was aboard gave him an opportunity to resume drinking.

Toxicological analysis of blood and urine samples taken from the master about 1050 on the morning of the grounding showed that his BAC [blood alcohol content] was 0.06 percent (urine 0.09 percent). His expected BAC at the time of the grounding can be calculated from the blood value measured at 1050 [a.m.], assuming that (1) he did not drink between the grounding and the sample collection, (2) he was in the elimination phase of alcohol metabolism (approximately 1 hour after the last drink) during the period of back calculation, and (3) he metabolizes alcohol at an accepted average rate (for a light alcohol user it is about 0.015 percent per hour and for a heavy user it may be as high as 0.018 percent per hour). Based on these assumptions, on an elimination rate of 0.015 percent per hour (a conservative value for the master), and on a 10-hour period for the back calculation, his BAC at the time of the grounding would have been about 0.2 percent. If the master did not ingest alcohol after returning to the vessel, his BAC at the time of boarding the vessel (2030), using the same assumptions, would have been about 0.27 percent. A BAC of 0.2 percent is close to the master's BAC value of 0.19 percent during his most recent DWI, when he was stopped for speeding but not for driving erratically. It is unlikely that the master could have had a BAC of 0.27 percent when he returned to the vessel and not have been observed as intoxicated; therefore, he probably consumed additional alcohol after he returned to the vessel. He most likely had an opportunity when he left the bridge after the vessel got underway while the pilot was piloting the vessel out of port. He had another opportunity after he left the bridge about 2352, leaving the third mate in charge of the navigation.

The Safety Board concludes that the master was impaired by alcohol when he returned to the bridge to prepare for disembarking the pilot. Although his decision to navigate around the ice floe was reasonable, his execution of the maneuver demonstrated impaired judgment, as was evidenced by placing the vessel on automatic pilot and then leaving the third mate to continue the maneuver. In addition to toxicological findings, the master's speech at 2325 was uncharacteristically slower and less fluent than it had been about 2130, when the ship's agent spoke with him on the VHF/FM radio. Slower and less fluent speech has been identified as an indication of alcohol impairment. . . .

The Safety Board's interpretation of the toxicological analysis presumes that the master did not ingest alcohol after the accident. The investigation established that he was told that the onboard computer results showed that the grounded vessel was not meeting required stability standards and that stresses on the vessel's hull were exceeding established limits. He took the precaution of having all crewmembers awakened and notified of the casualty. He explained to the chief mate that he did not want to use the general alarm because it might cause panic. Furthermore, he could anticipate that his vessel soon would be boarded by Coast Guard and other official personnel whom he would have to meet and work with....

The master's attempts to maneuver the vessel from its grounded position until about 0145 also demonstrate that he was trying to improve the situation. However, the Safety Board concludes that it was not wise of him to continue using the main engine to free the vessel because there was no way to assess the seriousness of the damage. However, the Safety Board could not determine whether there were any detrimental consequences from these actions after the grounding.

New Investigative Techniques

Speech Analysis

The Safety Board examined speech analysis as a new investigative technique and found it provided information useful to the investigation in an area in which scientific information has not been previously available.

No single aspect of speech provides conclusive evidence by itself, but a collection of difficulties was found in the master's speech that constitute a trend. The master displayed slow speech, speech errors, misarticulation characteristic of alcohol impairment, and degraded speech quality in the time period around the accident. Two sets of researchers—from the Addiction Research Foundation and the Indiana University Speech Research Laboratory—concluded independently that the speech changes shown by the master were consistent with those produced by alcohol impairment. The evidence suggests that speech changes of the sort produced by substantial alcohol consumption occurred just before the accident, and this conclusion is consistent with the extrapolated blood alcohol estimation determined from toxicological results.

This information based on speech analysis may contradict information provided by eyewitnesses, who reported unanimously that the master did not appear impaired on the evening of the accident, although several witnesses stated that the master smelled of alcohol. Two considerations seem relevant to the possible contradiction. First, eyewitnesses might have difficulty recognizing impairment because of the master's ability at masking it. The master had a history of alcohol abuse, including possible use of alcohol aboard the vessel, and had probably developed a considerable tolerance for alcohol. Individuals with such a history are commonly adept at masking the effects of alcohol on their performance of routine and familiar tasks.

A second consideration concerns eyewitness credibility and the possibility that some witnesses were unwilling to acknowledge officially an alcohol situation with which they may have been well acquainted. The many possible motivations for such reluctance include protecting the master, protecting themselves from legal exposure, and protecting their employment. Issues of eyewitness credibility have surfaced in previous Safety Board investigations concerning the issue of alcohol impairment. Eyewitness credibility issues also surfaced in the current investigation in several areas, most notably the contradictory statements from the radio electronics officer and the third mate concerning a previous incident in which the master allegedly drank alcohol aboard the vessel with several other crewmembers.

The recordings suggest that the master was impaired to such a degree that he was unable to mask speech difficulties before the accident, and it seems likely that everyone on the bridge would have been aware of this situation.

During the outbound voyage, the master made a series of questionable decisions—he left the bridge during the passage through Valdez Narrows, he ordered the autopilot engaged when departing the traffic lanes, he failed to tell the third mate that the autopilot was engaged, and he left the third mate as the sole officer on the bridge as the vessel approached a critical course change to maneuver around the ice. While there might be justification for individual aspects of the master's actions, taken together, the actions provide a picture of impaired judgment that is consistent with the toxicological and speech evidence.

The Safety Board concludes that the master of the *Exxon Valdez* was impaired by alcohol at the time the vessel grounded on Bligh Reef and that impairment of his judgment owing to alcohol consumption caused him to leave the bridge at a critical time.

By conducting an examination of the National Driver Register (NDR) and driving records, the Safety Board was able to determine that the master of the *Exxon Valdez* had an alcohol abuse problem. A similar periodic, routine review of the NDR could be made to ascertain if any licensed merchant marine officers are involved in drug or alcohol abuse that is affecting their driving record. Furthermore, each time a person applies for a license or license renewal, in addition to checking the NDR, a review of the applicant's driving record could be made to determine if there are any offenses related to drug or alcohol abuse. Accordingly, the Safety Board believes that the Coast Guard should have access to the NDR and other driving records and make use of such information to prevent persons with a drug or alcohol problem from holding a merchant marine license.

Exxon Management Oversight of the Master

The Exxon alcohol policy directive in effect during 1985 when the master underwent treatment instructs supervisors to refer to the medical department employees whose job performance is unsatisfactory owing to the perceived use of alcohol. In this case, the master's supervisor was apparently unaware that the master had an alcohol dependency problem prior to his hospitalization. Upon learning of his dependency problem, his supervisor, according to Exxon procedures, was supposed to have referred his case to the medical department. The personnel documents provided by Exxon showed that a followup treatment program was recommended by the attending physician at the hospital. While it is documented that the master was given a 90-day leave of absence, no documents were provided to establish that this recommended outpatient treatment program was followed or that his progress was monitored by management. Nor does the Exxon medical department appear to have contacted the hospital where he received in-patient treatment. The lack of records suggests that no guidance, advice, or information was provided by Exxon management or the Exxon medical department to the master's supervisor.... It must be surmised from the absence of information that the Exxon management and the medical department were unprepared or unwilling to deal with an alcoholic master.... Considering the investment Exxon had made in the master, the potential cost of a marine accident in terms of human loss or environmental damage as a result of having an alcohol-impaired master, and the lack of oversight documentation, it can be concluded that the Exxon corporate management demonstrated inadequate knowledge of and concern about the seriousness of having an alcohol-impaired master. The Safety Board concludes that Exxon should have removed the master from seagoing employment until there was ample proof that he had his alcohol problem under control....

Third Mate's Qualifications and Workload

Although the third mate was a relatively new officer, he was an experienced seaman who had served many years as an AB [able seaman]. The third mate was properly licensed and experienced for his position on the *Exxon Valdez*, and he could be expected to conduct routine navigation tasks properly during a normal at-sea watch.

The third mate testified that two officers normally served on the navigation watch of Exxon vessels when maneuvering in confined or congested waters. One officer usually conned the vessel, and the other conducted the navigation. Without the assistance of a fellow deck officer on the night of the grounding, the third mate's workload included both tasks. This workload might have been manageable for an alert, experienced officer even though it became progressively intensive as the *Exxon Valdez* approached the location from the turn back to the traffic lanes. Notwithstanding the intensity of the workload, the third mate's failure to plot positions of the *Exxon Valdez* on the navigation chart was a crucial compromise between the requirements of conning and navigating the vessel. He reduced his work by relying extensively on radar so that he could monitor the waterway and navigate at the same time. However, the perimeters of the submerged reef were not displayed by radar. If he had practiced conventional navigation techniques of plotting frequent fixes on the chart, he could have methodically incorporated the perimeters and location of the reef into his judgment for a trackline around the ice.

Impairment of the Third Mate

The third mate had probably had very little sleep the night before the grounding and had worked a stressful, physically demanding day.... The Safety Board concludes that the third mate could have had as little as 4 hours sleep before beginning the workday on March 23 and only a 1- to 2-hour nap in the afternoon. Thus, at the time of the grounding, he could have had as little as 5 or 6 hours of sleep in the previous 24 hours. Regardless, he had had a physically demanding and stressful day, and he was working beyond his normal watch period. . . .

Both performance deterioration relating to attention at times of maximum capacity and memory impairment from sleep loss have been documented in human factors literature. . . .

Giving the chief mate responsibility for the loading and discharging of the cargo and/or ballast and having him on duty during all critical stages of these operations is widely practiced. The result is many hours of work for the chief mate and, in most cases, the assumption of his in-port watches by the other two mates. Thus, on three-mate vessels, the other two mates are essentially or in fact standing 6 hours on watch and 6 hours off, a schedule that seldom enables any officer to acquire adequate rest until the vessel returns to sea and can resume a three-watch system. Consequently, the first part of the voyage, the transit through the port and other confined or congested waters, is likely to be conducted by navigation watch officers who are in varying stages of fatigue. This problem is recognized by some masters, who assume the navigation watch until one of their watch officers has obtained sufficient rest to assume the watch, but this is not the practice on all three-mate vessels. The Safety Board believes that vessel operators should be held accountable for ensuring that a rested officer, in addition to the master, is available to stand the navigation watch when the vessel departs for sea. This could be achieved by the costly, but simple, procedure of keeping the vessel in port long enough after loading the cargo to enable an officer to acquire the needed rest. Also, a fourth deck officer could be assigned to the vessel, as was the practice in the past on many tankships, including those of the Exxon Shipping Company, or a qualified tankship officer could be temporarily assigned to assume the chief mate's watch in port. Furthermore, having an overworked, fatigued chief mate in charge of cargo transfer operations could result in a catastrophic accidental release of the cargo while the vessel is in port. The Safety Board also believes that the Coast Guard should monitor working conditions on tankships, both domestic and foreign, in U.S. ports to ensure that enough officers are available in port to load the vessel so that at least one rested deck officer is available, besides the master, to take the vessel to sea. . . .

Drug and Alcohol Testing of the *Exxon Valdez* Crew

Specimen collection from the master and the crew of the *Exxon Valdez* for drug and alcohol testing was delayed about 10 hours after the grounding occurred. Some of this delay could be attributed to the serious nature of the grounding and the need to assess the extent of the damage and the stability of the vessel. The greater part of the long delay, however, was owing to the failure of the Coast Guard to have a collection procedure in place to enforce the alcohol and drug regulation. Such a plan should have included procedures to be followed and provisions for ready availability of the necessary equipment for specimen collection in the event of a marine casualty. Two Coast Guard officers boarded the vessel at approximately 0335, about 3 hours after the grounding, and shortly thereafter noted the strong smell of "stale" alcohol on the master's breath. Although the vessel had equipment on board for taking toxicological specimens, Coast Guard officials did not have this information until at least 7 hours after the grounding. . . .

The Safety Board, therefore, believes that the Coast Guard should develop procedures to facilitate the timely collection of toxicology specimens following every marine accident. . . .

Manning on the *Exxon Valdez*

The *Exxon Valdez* was operated with a reduced crew complement. Evidence indicated that watchkeeping safeguards on the *Exxon Valdez* had been compromised because of the manning level. The number of unlicensed crewmembers in the deck department was not sufficient to provide uninterrupted lookout capability when other routine deck-department duties arose. When one AB was required to serve as helmsman, the remaining ABs on duty had to cover all work and lookout responsibilities unless an AB from another watch was "turned to" on overtime. Moreover, when a lookout was required for long transits through congested waterways, no other qualified persons on duty were available to relieve that crewmember for breaks. As a result, on the *Exxon Valdez,* the lookout position routinely went unattended when the AB was called for other tasks or took a break. . . .

The mates on the *Exxon Valdez* were usually fatigued after cargo handling operations in Valdez, and the vessel usually put to sea with a fatigued crew. Although the *Exxon Valdez* had cargo handling automation, the equipment did not eliminate the need for deck officers to spend many hours on cargo watches. The Safety Board is concerned that the manning and working conditions producing fatigue on the *Exxon Valdez* are likely to exist on other U.S. tankships that carry three mates and/or have reduced manning.

Compliance with the Exxon Shipping Company procedures that require two officers on the bridge during maneuvering may have provided sufficient sharing of the workload to prevent the grounding of the *Exxon Valdez*. However, the Safety Board is reluctant to endorse the routine use of two officers, who may not have had adequate rest, as a means of obtaining a sufficient number of personnel for a navigation watch. The Safety Board contends that manning levels aboard ships should incorporate realistic expectations for human endurance and fallibilities so that the amount of work required for peak periods, such as cargo handling in port and tank cleaning at sea, can be accomplished without debilitating fatigue.

Reduced Crews

Coast Guard Manning Practices

. . . The Safety Board believes that the Coast Guard must promptly implement manning safeguards that directly address crew working conditions in port, as well as at sea. If additional authority is needed, the Coast Guard should seek such authority. These safeguards should incorporate verifiable man-hour requirements for cargo handling in port and for all vessel operations, including tank cleaning, at sea. The safeguards should directly address risk factors associated with fatigue, low morale, and other consequences of longer work hours. The safeguards must also address the consequences of the social isolation that results from lower manning levels and longer- tours of sea duty. The Safety Board believes that human capacities and limitations require no less attention in the manning process than the shipboard equipment criterion. . . .

Exxon Shipping Company Practices

The Safety Board identified several general operating practices of the Exxon Shipping Company pertaining to reduced crews that prompted concern. First, no evidence indicated that the company had policies or procedures intended to compensate for the risks involved in having smaller crews on its vessels. For example, Exxon had no program to ensure that mates complied with the requirement in U.S.C. 8401(a) that they have 6 hours of off-duty time in 12 hours before taking charge of the navigation watch. Aside from one introductory reduced-crew manning conference, officers received no specific supervisory training in recognizing fatigue in subordinates or in understanding the debilitating effects of fatigue on themselves or on their subordinates.

Finally, Exxon Shipping Company policy was to manipulate overtime records relevant to crew workload for vessels assigned to at least one "ship group coordinator" in order to support periodic unmanned status for enginerooms and thus to permit reducing crew size. Payment of overtime for officers on all Exxon vessels had been discontinued several years earlier, and during the investigation, no company method was identified that was designed to monitor officers' work in excess of 8 hours daily. Aside from concern about the morale problem created by the loss of direct compensation for time worked, the Safety Board is concerned that unrecorded overtime was not reflected in the work load data used by Coast Guard personnel who evaluated reduced-manning requests. Also, this investigation uncovered evidence that deck officers were used to do maintenance and other work previously done by unlicensed crew who had since been eliminated from service on the vessels.

Because of the Exxon Shipping Company memoranda that directed officers to minimize reports of equipment maintenance and overtime, the minimum manning requirements on Exxon Shipping Company vessels may have been based upon incomplete and inaccurate information. Assuming that the recipients of the memoranda complied with the directive, their maintenance and overtime records would not be representative of actual crew work loads. In addition, the Coast Guard had probably agreed to minimum manning reductions using the same deficient information for its evaluations and consequently may have underestimated crew workloads on all reduced-crew Exxon Shipping Company vessels.

Exxon submitted graphs to the Safety Board that showed a favorable comparison between lower manning levels and casualty and personal injury statistics. The Safety Board does not consider these comparisons useful evidence of safe vessel operation. Gross measurements, such as the number of oil spills per vessel or injuries per million man-hours over a 15-year interval, do not provide sufficient information for causal inferences about any safeguards on these vessels. The evaluations did not provide information on safety programs in effect, composition of crew complements, crew overtime, length of crewmember tours, equipment installed on the vessels, or other variables from which the effects of lower manning on safety may be methodically deduced.

The Safety Board is also concerned that Exxon has continued to increase crew work load in its fleet even after the grounding of the *Exxon Valdez*. A recent company directive, issued after the grounding, required manning of periodically unmanned machinery spaces while vessels are in inland waterways. . . .

Evidence also indicated that the Exxon Shipping Company planned to further reduce the crew size and to lower crew qualifications for most vessels in its operating fleet. . . . The Safety Board considers the reduced manning practices of the Exxon Shipping Company generally incautious and without apparent justification from the standpoint of safety. The financial advantage derived from eliminating officers and crew from each vessel does not seem to justify incurring the foreseeable risks of serious accidents. . . .

Recommendations

As a result of its investigation, the National Transportation Safety Board made the following recommendations.

- to the Exxon Shipping Company and all shipping companies operating in Prince William Sound:

    Eliminate personnel policies, including performance appraisal criteria, that encourage marine employees to work long hours without concern for debilitating fatigue and commensurate reduction in safety of vessel operations.

    Implement manning policies that prevent excessively long working hours for crewmembers during cargo handling operations.

    Institute a written policy forbidding deck officers to share navigation and cargo watch duties on a 6-hours-on, 6-hours-off basis, except in emergencies. (Class II, Priority Action)

    Require that two licensed watch officers be present to conn and navigate vessels in Prince William Sound. (Class II, Priority Action)

    Implement an alcohol/drug program for seagoing employees that prevents such personnel from returning to sea until their alcohol/drug dependency problem is under control. (Class II, Priority Action)

Train persons who monitor the alcohol/drug rehabilitation program in the recognition of recidivism after treatment, in the utilization of appropriate professional referrals, and in the interpersonal skills necessary for competent rehabilitation supervision.

- to the Coast Guard:

Develop a means for rigorous enforcement of 46 U.S.C. 8104(a) to ensure that officers on watch during departures from ports have had at least 6 hours of off-duty time in the previous 12 hours.

Expedite the study programs to establish manning levels and safeguards based on human factors, as well as on shipboard hardware and equipment, and incorporate the findings into the manning review process.

Establish manning standards to ensure that crew complements reflect all expected shipboard operating situations and that procedures are in place for dealing with unusually high workloads at sea, such as tank cleaning, and with cargo handling operations in port.

Seek authority for access to the National Driver Register and other driving records and make use of the information from these sources to prevent any person with a drug and/or alcohol problem from holding a merchant marine license.

Adopt a permanent policy to plot all vessels participating in the Valdez Vessel Traffic System between the pilot station south of Bligh Reef, or as near the pilot station as possible, and their berths in Port Valdez.

Increase the manning level at the Marine Safety Office, Valdez, Alaska, to provide the following: enough watchstanders to plot all participating vessels between the pilot station south of Bligh Reef and their berths in Port Valdez; an officer-in-charge of the Vessel Traffic System who will have time to manage and supervise the system effectively; and sufficient additional officers to staff a duty officer watch with officers capable of monitoring and supervising vessel traffic watchstanders outside normal working hours.

Install an additional radar site as close to Bligh Reef as feasible to enable the Vessel Traffic Center to accurately monitor and plot all participating vessels and ice in the area of Valdez Arm from Busby Island to the pilot station south of Bligh Reef.

Initiate procedures to collect information on ice conditions in Valdez Arm so that all participating vessels receive accurate and timely ice reports before departing port and so that all supervisory personnel associated with the Valdez Traffic System are cognizant of ice conditions in Valdez Arm.

Improve the communications system operated by the Marine Safety Office in Valdez, Alaska.

Improve the microwave system operated by the Marine Safety Office in Valdez, Alaska.

Limit any proposed reduction in Federal pilotage to that part of Prince William Sound from the entrance outside Cape Hinchinbrook to the current pilot station at latitude 69°49' N, longitude 174°01' W, which is south of Bligh Reef, thus ensuring that Federal pilots will be required between the entrance to Valdez Arm south of Bligh Reef and the berths in Port Valdez.

Incorporate into the Vessel Traffic Service regulations for all vessels the provisions of former COTP Order 1-80 (except the requirement for daylight transit), including the requirements about vessel condition, crews, navigation equipment, and publications, as well as the requirement that a licensed officer in addition to the licensed officer on watch be available to plot the vessel's position.

- to the Environmental Protection Agency:

Develop guidance in the National Contingency Plan for Regional Response Teams and On-Scene Coordinators about dispersant use.

Develop guidance for Regional Response Teams and On-Scene Coordinators about in-situ burning of oil and include the guidance in the National Contingency Plan. (Class II, Priority Action)

Develop procedures that would eliminate the need for the On-Scene Coordinator to obtain burn permits from a State after the Regional Response Team has agreed that the spilled oil can be burned in situ.

Develop guidance for Regional Response Teams that enables them to establish the minimum amount of cleanup equipment that must be immediately available to initiate a cleanup response.

- to the Alaska Regional Response Team:

Develop clearer guidance for dispersant use in order to eliminate the need for a dispersant test before dispersants are used on an oil spill and include that information in the Alaska Regional Contingency Plan.

Develop guidelines and procedures for in-situ burning of oil, identify the range of wind and sea conditions for which in-situ burning of oil can be used effectively, and incorporate that information into the Alaska Regional Contingency Plan.

- to the State of Alaska:

Require that the oil spill contingency barge or barges at the Alyeska Pipeline Service Company Terminal at Valdez be loaded at all times with the response equipment specified in the plan. If a barge is unloaded and unavailable for immediate deployment, require that a replacement barge be provided and loaded with the equipment specified in the plan. (Class II, Priority Action)

Require that the companies loading oil at the Alyeska Pipeline Service Company Terminal in Valdez provide a plan for assuming cleanup responsibility from Alyeska Pipeline Service Company in the event of a major oil spill or potential major oil spill of more than 100,000 gallons.

Develop and require minimum levels of mechanical oil spill cleanup equipment, fire- or burn-proof boom, air-deployable dispersant system packs, and other dispersant application equipment to be stockpiled and immediately available at the Alyeska Pipeline Service Company's Valdez Terminal.

- to Alyeska Pipeline Service Company:

Provide at its Valdez terminal two or more oil spill contingency barges that are loaded with pollution-response cleanup equipment, lightering equipment, and fire- or burn-proof booms that are maintained and ready for immediate deployment, thus facilitating an effective response to different spill conditions.

Identify the range of wind and sea conditions for which dispersants can be used effectively and incorporate that information into company contingency plans. (Class II, Priority Action)

In conjunction with each of the companies that load oil at its terminal in Valdez, develop a plan or procedures for relieving Alyeska Pipeline Service Company of primary cleanup responsibility in the event of a major oil spill or potential major oil spill of more than 100,000 gallons and include the procedures in its contingency plan after they have been approved by the State of Alaska. (Class II, Priority Action)

In its company contingency plans, list also the companies that do not have a plan for relieving Alyeska Pipeline Service Company of cleanup responsibility. (Class II, Priority Action)

Store air-deployable dispersant system packs and other dispersant application equipment at its Valdez Terminal, as agreed upon with the State of Alaska, for use with fixed wing aircraft, or helicopters, or vessels. (Class II, Priority Action)

Store fire- or burn-proof booms at its Valdez Terminal, as agreed upon with the State of Alaska, and include procedures for their use in the company's oil spill contingency plan.

- to the U.S. Geological Survey:

Intensify efforts to monitor the state of the Columbia Glacier, particularly to identify the amount of ice calving from the glacier and any changes in the rate that might affect the number and size of icebergs emanating from the glacier, and make this information available to agencies, such as the U.S. Coast Guard, tasked with assuring the safety of shipping into and out of Valdez Harbor. . . .

• to the U.S. Coast Guard:

Seek legislation to require all pilots of commercial vessels on the navigable waters of the United States to have a Federal pilot's license which would be legally superior to all State-issued documents, licenses or commissions that a State may continue to employ to accredit those pilots that it desires to pilot vessels engaged in foreign commerce.

By the National Transportation Safety Board

James L. Kolstad
  Chairman
Susan Coughlin
  Vice Chairman
John K. Lauber
  Member
Jim Burnett
  Member

July 31, 1990

JIM BURNETT, Member, filed the following concurring and dissenting statement:

I concur with the probable cause as adopted but would have added that "contributing to the severity of the environmental damage was: (1) the lack of a double bottom on the *Exxon Valdez* and (2) the failure to initiate early in-situ burning of released crude oil due to lack of an appropriate boom." I would also favor the adoption of a recommendation to require that all U.S. tank vessels over 20,000 deadweight tons, and foreign-flag tank vessels entering U.S. waters over 20,000 deadweight tons, have double hulls.

August

IRAQI INVASION OF KUWAIT
August 2, 3 and 8, 1990

Iraq invaded its smaller Persian Gulf neighbor Kuwait August 2, sending shock waves around the world. Iraqi tank and troop columns sped across the border during the predawn hours, quickly seizing Kuwait's rich oil fields and its capital, Kuwait City. In only a few days virtually all armed resistance had ceased. But the invasion encountered a different kind of resistance abroad. President George Bush angrily told White House reporters on the day of the invasion that it was "naked aggression," and he called for "the immediate and unconditional withdrawal of all Iraqi forces."

The president promptly issued executive orders freezing the American assets of Iraq and Kuwait to keep them out of Iraqi hands. The next day he declared a national emergency, calling the invasion "an unusual and extraordinary threat to the national security, foreign policy, and economy of the United States." At his urging and organizing, and with the Soviet Union's consent, the United Nations Security Council condemned the invasion. Soon afterward it devised and approved an economic embargo against Iraq that included a shipping blockade to be enforced mostly by American warships. (UN Action Against Iraq With U.S.-Soviet Cooperation, p. 545)

Bush left open the prospect of military action if economic sanctions did not force Iraqi president Saddam Hussein to withdraw his army from Kuwait. Saudi Arabia, fearful that Hussein also coveted its immense oil fields, appealed to the United States for help in defending its country. Some of the biggest Saudi fields and Riyadh, the capital, lay less than 300 miles south of occupied Kuwait, within range of Iraqi surface-to-

surface missiles. Bush responded August 7 by ordering American air and ground forces to Saudi Arabia.

Protecting "Vital Interests"

"The sovereign independence of Saudi Arabia is of vital interest to the United States," Bush said in a televised address the next morning, wherein he explained his decision to commit American troops to a potential battle zone.

The first ground troops to arrive were a brigade of about 4,000 paratroopers from the 82nd Airborne Division, flown in by chartered jetliners. Other units quickly followed, resulting in the biggest deployment of U.S. forces to a foreign country since the Vietnam War.

Within two months, more than 200,000 military personnel with their armor, equipment, and supporting aircraft, had been flown or shipped to Saudi Arabia. Egypt, Syria, Britain, France, and a score of other countries pledged or provided military, naval, or air support. But the biggest assistance, by far, came from the United States.

In an August 8 address, Bush said that the decision to dispatch military units to Saudi Arabia grew out of "the longstanding friendship and security relationship" between the two countries. Afterward, at a news conference, the president said: "My military objective is to see Saudi Arabia defended.... Our overall objective is to see Saddam Hussein get out [of Kuwait] and go back [to Iraq] and have the rightful regime of Kuwait back in place." Otherwise, Bush did not define the U.S. "vital interest." On other occasions, he spoke of the importance of Saudi Arabian oil but did not explicitly state it as a governing reason for the commitment of American troops.

The Oil Factor

Saudi Arabia, with a quarter of the world's crude oil reserves, is America's premier foreign supplier. It provided about 15 percent of all U.S. oil imports—or 7-8 percent of the total that Americans used in recent years. Oil from Iraq and Kuwait furnished an additional 9 percent of America's imports. By seizing and annexing Kuwait—an annexation declared "null and void" by the United Nations Security Council—Hussein doubled his control over the world's crude oil reserves to nearly 20 percent.

The impact on the world oil market was dramatic. Prices soared from $18 a barrel just before the invasion to beyond $30 within a month, even though the supply remained plentiful. The loss of oil from Iraq and Kuwait, some 4 million barrels a day, was soon offset by increased output from Saudi Arabia and other members of the Organization of Petroleum Exporting Countries (OPEC). However, the fear that war might break out and cut off Middle Eastern oil exports kept prices high. American motorists saw the price of gasoline rise thirty cents a gallon by autumn.

If the president was cautious of defining America's vital interest in terms of ensuring the United States an ample supply of Middle Eastern oil, others were not. Rep. Les Aspin, D-Wis., chairman of the House Armed Services Committee, wrote in the Washington Post *August 8 that the invasion had done more "to change strategic realities than any other military action in the postwar era." The reason, he said, "is simple. . . . It's oil. . . . Figuratively, he [Hussein] has placed a knife at our jugular."*

Plight of Hussein's Hostages

At the time of the invasion, hundreds of thousands of foreigners, including about 3,600 Americans, were working or traveling in Iraq and Kuwait. Hussein would not allow most of the Americans and Europeans—especially Britons—to leave. At first the White House declined to apply the word "hostages" to those being detained for fear of worsening their plight. But as Hussein's intent to hold them became unmistakable, his hostage taking was bitterly denounced. On August 20 he offered to free the foreigners—his "guests"—in return for a U.S. military and political withdrawal from the Persian Gulf region.

Hussein left no doubt that the hostages would be used as shields against potential American bombing. He said "their presence . . . at vital targets may prevent military aggression." Bush said repeatedly that the presence of the hostages would not deter him from attacking Iraq militarily if he deemed it necessary.

Following are excerpts from President George Bush's remarks to White House reporters, August 2, 1990, condemning Iraq's invasion of Kuwait; his message to Congress the next day declaring a national emergency; his address to the nation August 8 explaining his decision to send troops into Saudi Arabia; and excerpts from a White House news conference later the same day:

REMARKS TO WHITE HOUSE REPORTERS

Let me make a brief statement here about recent events. The United States strongly condemns the Iraqi military invasion of Kuwait. We call for the immediate and unconditional withdrawal of all the Iraqi forces. There is no place for this sort of naked aggression in today's world, and I've taken a number of steps to indicate the deep concern that I feel over the events that have taken place.

Last night I instructed our Ambassador at the United Nations, Tom Pickering, to work with Kuwait in convening an emergency meeting of the Security Council. It was convened, and I am grateful for that quick, overwhelming vote condemning the Iraqi action and calling for immediate and unconditional withdrawal. Tom Pickering will be here in a bit, and we are contemplating with him further United Nations action.

Second, consistent with my authority under the International Emergency Economic Powers Act, I've signed an Executive order early this morning freezing Iraqi assets in this country and prohibiting transactions with Iraq. I've also signed an Executive order freezing Kuwaiti assets. That's to ensure that those assets are not interfered with by the illegitimate authority that is now occupying Kuwait. We call upon other governments to take similar action.

Third, the Department of State has been in touch with governments around the world urging that they, too, condemn the Iraqi aggression and consult to determine what measures should be taken to bring an end to this totally unjustified act. It is important that the international community act together to ensure that Iraqi forces depart Kuwait immediately.

Needless to say, we view the situation with the utmost gravity. We remain committed to take whatever steps are necessary to defend our longstanding, vital interests in the Gulf, and I'm meeting this morning with my senior advisers here to consider all possible options available to us. I've talked to Secretary [of State] Baker just now; General Scowcroft [Assistant to the President for National Security Affairs] and I were on the phone with him. And after this meeting, I will proceed to deliver a longstanding speech. I will have consultations—short ones—there in Aspen [Colorado] with Prime Minister Thatcher [of the United Kingdom], and I will be returning home this evening, and I'll be here in Washington tomorrow. . . .

MESSAGE TO THE CONGRESS ON NATIONAL EMERGENCY

To the Congress of the United States:

Pursuant to section 204(b) of the International Emergency Economic Powers Act, 50 U.S.C. section 1703(b), and section 201 of the National Emergencies Act, 50 U.S.C. section 1621, I hereby report that I have exercised my statutory authority to declare a national emergency and to issue two Executive orders that:

- prohibit exports and imports of goods and services between the United States and Iraq and the purchase of Iraqi goods by U.S. persons for sale in third countries;
- prohibit transactions related to travel to or from Iraq, except for transactions necessary for journalistic travel or prompt departure from Iraq;
- prohibit transactions related to transportation to or from Iraq, or the use of vessels or aircraft registered in Iraq by U.S. persons;

- prohibit the performance of any contract in support of Government of Iraq projects;
- ban all extensions of credit and loans by U.S. persons to the Government of Iraq;
- block all property of the Government of Iraq now or hereafter located in the United States or in the possession or control of U.S. persons, including their foreign branches; and
- prohibit all transfers or other transactions involving assets belonging to the Government of Kuwait now or hereafter located in the United States or in the possession or control of U.S. persons, including their foreign branches.

The Secretary of the Treasury is authorized to issue regulations implementing these prohibitions. These two orders were effective 5:00 a.m. e.d.t., August 2, 1990.

I am enclosing a copy of each Executive order that I have issued making these declarations and exercising these authorities.

I have authorized these measures in response to the Iraqi invasion of Kuwait, which clearly constitutes an act of aggression and a flagrant violation of international law. This action is in clear violation of the national sovereignty and independence of Kuwait and the charter of the United Nations. It threatens the entire structure of peaceful relations among nations in this critical region. It constitutes an unusual and extraordinary threat to the national security, foreign policy, and economy of the United States.

The measures we are taking to block Iraqi assets will have the effect of expressing our outrage at Iraq's actions, and will prevent that government from drawing on monies and properties within U.S. control to support its campaign of military aggression against a neighboring state. Our ban on exports to Iraq will prevent the Iraqi government from profiting from the receipt of U.S. goods and technology. Our ban on imports, while not preventing sales of Iraqi oil to third countries, denies Iraq access to the lucrative U.S. market for its most important product.

At the same time, in order to protect the property of the legitimate Government of Kuwait from possible seizure, diversion, or misuse by Iraq, and with the approval of the Kuwaiti government, we are blocking Kuwaiti assets within the jurisdiction of the United States or in the possession or control of U.S. persons.

We are calling upon our friends and allies, and all members of the world community who share our interest in the peaceful resolution of international disputes, to join us in similar actions against Iraq and for the protection of Kuwait.

ADDRESS TO THE NATION

In the life of a nation, we're called upon to define who we are and what we believe. Sometimes these choices are not easy. But today as President, I ask for your support in a decision I've made to stand up for what's right and condemn what's wrong, all in the cause of peace.

At my direction, elements of the 82nd Airborne Division as well as key units of the United States Air Force are arriving today to take up defensive positions in Saudi Arabia. I took this action to assist the Saudi Arabian Government in the defense of its homeland. No one commits America's Armed Forces to a dangerous mission lightly, but after perhaps unparalleled international consultation and exhausting every alternative, it became necessary to take this action. Let me tell you why.

Less than a week ago, in the early morning hours of August 2d, Iraqi Armed forces, without provocation or warning, invaded a peaceful Kuwait. Facing negligible resistance from its much smaller neighbor, Iraq's tanks stormed in blitzkrieg fashion through Kuwait in a few short hours. With more than 100,000 troops, along with tanks, artillery, and surface-to-surface missiles, Iraq now occupies Kuwait. This aggression came just hours after Saddam Hussein [President of Iraq] specifically assured numerous countries in the area that there would be no invasion. There is no justification whatsoever for this outrageous and brutal act of aggression.

A puppet regime imposed from the outside is unacceptable. The acquisition of territory by force is unacceptable. No one, friend or foe, should doubt our desire for peace; and no one should underestimate our determination to confront aggression.

Four simple principles guide our policy. First, we seek the immediate, unconditional, and complete withdrawal of all Iraqi forces from Kuwait. Second, Kuwait's legitimate government must be restored to replace the puppet regime. And third, my administration, as has been the case with every President from President Roosevelt to President Reagan, is committed to the security and stability of the Persian Gulf. And fourth, I am determined to protect the lives of American citizens abroad.

Immediately after the Iraqi invasion, I ordered an embargo of all trade with Iraq and, together with many other nations, announced sanctions that both freeze all Iraqi assets in this country and protect Kuwait's assets. The stakes are high. Iraq is already a rich and powerful country that possesses the world's second largest reserves of oil and over a million men under arms. It's the fourth largest military in the world. Our country now imports nearly half the oil it consumes and could face a major threat to its economic independence. Much of the world is even more dependent upon imported oil and is even more vulnerable to Iraqi threats.

We succeeded in the struggle for freedom in Europe because we and our allies remained stalwart. Keeping the peace in the Middle East will require no less. We're beginning a new era. This new era can be full of promise, an age of freedom, a time of peace for all peoples. But if history teaches us anything, it is that we must resist aggression or it will destroy our freedoms. Appeasement does not work. As was the case in the 1930's, we see in Saddam Hussein an aggressive dictator threatening his neighbors. Only 14 days ago, Saddam Hussein promised his friends he would not invade Kuwait. And 4 days ago, he promised the world he would withdraw. And twice we have seen what his promises mean: His promises mean nothing.

In the last few days, I've spoken with political leaders from the Middle East, Europe, Asia, and the Americas; and I've met with Prime Minister Thatcher [of the United Kingdom], Prime Minister Mulroney [of Canada], and NATO Secretary General Woerner. And all agree that Iraq cannot be allowed to benefit from its invasion of Kuwait.

We agree that this is not an American problem or a European problem or a Middle East problem: it is the world's problem. And that's why, soon after the Iraqi invasion, the United Nations Security Council, without dissent, condemned Iraq, calling for the immediate and unconditional withdrawal of its troops from Kuwait. The Arab world, through both the Arab League and the Gulf Cooperation Council, courageously announced its opposition to Iraqi aggression. Japan, the United Kingdom, and France, and other governments around the world have imposed severe sanctions. The Soviet Union and China ended all arms sales to Iraq.

And this past Monday, the United Nations Security Council approved for the first time in 23 years mandatory sanctions under chapter VII of the United Nations Charter. These sanctions, now enshrined in international law, have the potential to deny Iraq the fruits of aggression while sharply limiting its ability to either import or export anything of value, especially oil.

I pledge here today that the United States will do its part to see that these sanctions are effective and to induce Iraq to withdraw without delay from Kuwait.

But we must recognize that Iraq may not stop using force to advance its ambitions. Iraq has massed an enormous war machine on the Saudi border capable of initiating hostilities with little or no additional preparation. Given the Iraqi government's history of aggression against its own citizens as well as its neighbors, to assume Iraq will not attack again would be unwise and unrealistic.

And therefore, after consulting with King Fahd [of Saudi Arabia], I sent Secretary of Defense Dick Cheney to discuss cooperative measures we could take. Following those meetings, the Saudi Government requested our help, and I responded to that request by ordering U.S. air and ground forces to deploy to the kingdom of Saudi Arabia.

Let me be clear: The sovereign independence of Saudi Arabia is of vital interest to the United States. This decision, which I shared with the congressional leadership, grows out of the longstanding friendship and security relationship between the United States and Saudi Arabia. U.S. forces will work together with those of Saudi Arabia and other nations to preserve the integrity of Saudi Arabia and to deter further Iraqi aggression. Through their presence, as well as through training and exercises, these multinational forces will enhance the overall capability of Saudi Armed Forces to defend the kingdom.

I want to be clear about what we are doing and why. America does not seek conflict, nor do we seek to chart the destiny of other nations. But America will stand by her friends. The mission of our troops is wholly defensive. Hopefully, they will not be needed long. They will not initiate hostilities, but they will defend themselves, the Kingdom of Saudi Arabia, and other friends in the Persian Gulf.

We are working around the clock to deter Iraqi aggression and to enforce U.N. sanctions. I'm continuing my conversations with world leaders. Secretary of Defense Cheney has just returned from valuable consultations with President Mubarak of Egypt and King Hassan of Morocco. Secretary of State Baker has consulted with his counterparts in many nations, including the Soviet Union, and today he heads for Europe to consult with President Ozal of Turkey, a staunch friend of the United States. And he'll then consult with NATO Foreign Ministers.

I will ask oil-producing nations to do what they can to increase production in order to minimize any impact that oil flow reductions will have on the world economy. And I will explore whether we and our allies should draw down our strategic petroleum reserves. Conservation measures can also help; Americans everywhere must do their part. And one more thing: I'm asking the oil companies to do their fair share. They should show restraint and not abuse today's uncertainties to raise prices.

Standing up for our principles will not come easy. It may take time and possibly cost a great deal. But we are asking no more of anyone than of the brave young men and women of our Armed Forces and their families. And I ask that in the churches around the country, prayers be said for those who are committed to protect and defend America's interests.

Standing up for our principle is an American tradition. As it has so many times before, it may take time and tremendous effort, but most of all, it will take unity of purpose. As I've witnessed throughout my life in both war and peace, America has never wavered when her purpose is driven by principle. And on this August day, at home and abroad, I know she will do no less.

Thank you, and God bless the United States of America.

BUSH NEWS CONFERENCE

Q: Mr. President, are we in a war? And what other nations have agreed to join our forces in defending Saudi Arabia? And I take it you also have included other Gulf nations in that umbrella.

The President: We're not in a war. We have sent forces to defend Saudi Arabia. I will leave announcements about what other nations will be participating to the Saudis. But I believe Margaret Thatcher, after talking to King Fahd [of Saudi Arabia], has announced that forces will be going in; and then I think you'll see other such actions. . . .

Q: Mr. President, there are several dozen Americans in Baghdad apparently not able to leave at this point, and perhaps hundreds more in Kuwait—perhaps elsewhere in Iraq as well. In view of the extreme political sensitivity of Americans toward this whole question of hostages, why should not Saddam Hussein feel that he holds very high cards now in dealing with the United States?

The President: I've been encouraged that there have been actually announcements, I believe, saying people were free to leave. So, I'm not going to speculate or hypothecate beyond that. I want to see them out of there, obviously. But what he does—that's a bit unpredictable. But I'm not going to try to heighten tensions in this regard by responding to hypothetical questions that might go beyond your questions. . . .

Q: Mr. President, was there any one single thing that tipped your hand into deciding to send U.S. troops and aircraft into Saudi Arabia? And secondly, how supportive have the Soviets been of your decision?

The President: There was no one single thing that I can think of, but when King Fahd requested such support, we were prompt to respond. But I can't think of an individual, specific thing. If there was one, it would perhaps be the Saudis moving south when they said they were withdrawing.

Q: You mean the Iraqis, sir?

The President: I mean the Iraqis. Thank you very much. It's been a long night. The Iraqis moving down to the Kuwait-Saudi border when, indeed, they had given their word that they were withdrawing. That heightened our concern.

Q: How supportive have the Soviets been of your decision, sir?

The President: The Soviets have been very responsible, in my view. They have joined the United Nations on that resolution [to employ economic sanctions against Iraq] and [Secretary of State] Jim Baker, as recently as yesterday afternoon or evening, was in touch with [Soviet Foreign Minister] Shevardnadze again. And you know, I can't ask for a more favorable response than he received. . . .

Q: Mr. President, is it your intention to let economic pressure alone provide the force that drives Iraq out of Kuwait? And are you prepared to wait several months, which is how long it might take for the economic sanctions to really bite?

The President: Well, we've taken this first significant step to defend Saudi Arabia. The economic sanctions should begin to bite pretty soon. There will be further steps taken to ensure that they are fully effective. And then we'll wait and see where we go from there. But I have no—we're not—I'm not beyond that in my thinking. There obviously is a lot of contingency planning that always goes on and, prudently, should go on. . . .

Q: Mr. President, you said in your speech this morning that the puppet regime in Kuwait was unacceptable, and so was the acquisition of territory. At the same time, though, you said that the deployments are wholly defensive. The question is: How do you actually expect to force Hussein to withdraw from Kuwait?

The President: Economic sanctions, in this instance, if fully enforced, can be very, very effective. It's a rich country in terms of oil resources. They're a poor country, in a sense, because he squandered much of the resource on military might. And there are some indications that he's already beginning to feel the pinch, and nobody can stand up forever to total economic deprivation. . . .

Q: Mr. President, could you share with us the precise military objective of this mission? Will the American troops remain there only until Saddam Hussein removes his troops from the Saudi border?

The President: I can't answer that because we have a major objective with those troops, which is the defense of the Soviet Union, so I think it's beyond—

Q: Saudi Arabia. *[Laughter]*

The President: A defense of Saudi Arabia. So, I think it's beyond just the question of the tanks along the border.

Q: Are you prepared for a prolonged ground war?

The President: They have a lot of air power, for example.

Q: Are you prepared for a prolonged ground war in the Persian Gulf?

The President: I'm not preparing for a long ground war in the Persian Gulf. There's not a war going on there right now.

Q: But I'm just saying, could you just tell the American people what your specific military objective is?

The President: My military objective is to see Saudi Arabia defended. That's the military objective. Our overall objective is to see Saddam Hussein get out and go back and to have the rightful regime of Kuwait back in place.

President Saddam Hussein of Iraq

Mr. President, can you tell us what U.S. and Saudi forces will be up against? You mentioned surface-to-surface missiles. You've spoken previously of the chemical warfare capability of the Saudis. What are they up against? And the second part of the question is: Did we misread Saddam Hussein? A couple of months ago the administration was up on the Hill [in Congress] deflecting a move to put sanctions on Iraq.

The President: . . . [W]e've tried very hard to see if there wasn't a way to have somewhat improved relations. There's no question about that. And I have no regret about having tried to have discussions that might have led to a better relationship. But that had to stop the minute you have this kind of aggression. But I think, having tried tentatively to have a little better relationship with the person over the last couple of years, we've still been very, very wary all along of his intentions.

U.S. Intelligence Capability in the Persian Gulf

Q: Did our intelligence let us down, or did you know that what has happened—when did you get an indication it would be, as far as moving into Kuwait and that sort of thing?

The President: No, I don't feel let down by the intelligence at all. When you plan a blitzkrieg-like attack that is launched at 2 o'clock in the morning, it's pretty hard to stop, particularly when you have just been given the word of the people involved that there wouldn't be any such attack. And I think the intelligence community deserves certain credit for picking up what was a substantial buildup and then reporting it to us....

Q: Mr. President, you said this morning that our troops would also defend our other friends in the Gulf. Do we view the American troops there as peacekeepers throughout the Gulf?

The President: We view them there to defend Saudi Arabia, and hopefully, their presence will deter adventurism against any of the other Gulf countries.

Q: What other countries, sir, are we prepared to defend in the Gulf region?

The President: I'm not going to give you a list, but we're certainly interested in the freedom and the independence of all those countries in the GCC [Gulf Cooperation Council], just for openers....

Q: Mr. President, national security analysts say that this crisis demonstrates once again the constant vulnerability of the oil fields in the Middle East. Doesn't this suggest that this force that you've sent over there may be there for some time or at least fragments of it will be there to make sure that there is a steady flow?

The President: You might interpret it that way. I'm not prepared to say that I think that's what the outcome will be because I think if there is this pullback that the world is calling for, and if the sanctions are effective, I think you would reduce the risk of future adventurism....

Q: Assuming that you achieve your withdrawal of Iraqi forces out of Kuwait, Saddam Hussein is still going to be sitting there on top of a million-man army that he's shown an inclination to use. What happens in the long run after that? And can you contain that, short of removing Saddam Hussein from power?

The President: I would think that if this international lesson is taught well that Saddam Hussein would behave differently in the future. And that's what has been so very important about this concerted United Nations effort—unprecedented, you might say, or certainly not enacted since 19—what was it—23 years ago, 23 years ago. So, I don't think we can see that clearly down the road. But a line has been drawn in the sand. The United States has taken a firm position. And I might say we're getting strong support from around the world for what we've done....

UN ACTION AGAINST IRAQ
WITH U.S.-SOVIET COOPERATION
August 2, 6, 25, and September 9, 11, 1990

The Iraqi invasion of Kuwait brought a succession of strong responses from the United Nations in which the United States and the Soviet Union acted in tandem. This superpower harmony, which the world community began to witness only in the late 1980s, enabled the Security Council not only to deplore aggression but also to take action against the aggressor.

On August 3, the day after Iraq's armed forces entered Kuwait, the Security Council passed a resolution condemning the invasion and demanding an immediate withdrawal of Iraqi forces. On August 6, for only the third time in the UN's forty-five years of existence, the council invoked economic sanctions against a nation that refused to obey its directives. They were applied to Rhodesia in 1967, banning exports and imports, and to South Africa in 1977, banning arms sales.

On this occasion the Security Council called on all nations to stop trading with Iraq and Iraqi-occupied Kuwait. It followed on August 25 by authorizing a naval blockade to enforce the trade ban. Never before had the Security Council sanctioned military force without linking it to a UN command. This time the force was primarily an American fleet, augmented by a few warships of other cooperating nations.

Before the end of August the council passed two more resolutions—bringing the total to five, officially numbered 660, 661, 662, 664, and 665—declaring Iraq's annexation of Kuwait illegal and demanding that the Baghdad government free the thousands of foreigners it held in both countries as hostages. None of the resolutions drew a negative vote from Security Council members, although Cuba abstained twice and

Yemen, the only Arab member, three times. Cuba and Yemen were among the council's ten rotating members, which also included Canada, Colombia, Ethiopia, Finland, Ivory Coast, Malaysia, Romania, and Zaire. But the real power rested with the five permanent members: Britain, China, France, and—especially—the Soviet Union and the United States.

U.S.-Soviet Cooperation

With the easing of East-West tensions, the two powers began to act together at the United Nations on some long-unsettled issues. This new cooperation enabled the UN to devise a Soviet withdrawal from Afghanistan in 1988 and 1989, to conclude the 1980-1988 war between Iraq and Iran, and to bring about a peace settlement in Southwest Africa that led to an independent Namibia in March 1990. (Agreements on Afghanistan, Historic Documents of 1988, p. 257; Dignitaries Welcome Namibia's Independence, p. 199)

Even judged by the standards of cooperation during the past two years, the Soviet Union's stand against Iraq in August 1990 was striking. For a decade or more, Iraq was considered a Soviet "client" state in the Middle East—backed by the Kremlin in the long war with Iran. Armed largely with Soviet weapons, Iraq also was aided by several Arab nations and even the United States, which feared that an Iranian victory would loose a fiery brand of Islamic fundamentalism throughout the Middle East.

John Newhouse, reporting for the New Yorker, *wrote that the first four Security Council resolutions against Iraq were approved with ease, but the fifth required an unusually close working relationship between Secretary of State James Baker III and Foreign Minister Eduard Shevardnadze to overcome Moscow's reluctance to endorse the use of force to enforce the trade ban. Once the United States accepted the Soviet suggestion for replacing an explicit reference to the use of "minimum force" with the words "measures commensurate to the specific circumstances." Newhouse quoted an unidentified "involved ambassador" as saying: "Day and night, the U.S.-Soviet alliance flourished, with only occasional small differences on tactics." The diplomatic maneuvering produced a 13-0 vote of approval by the Security Council on August 25.*

U.S.-Soviet cooperation moved to a higher level in September when Gorbachev met with President George Bush in Helsinki, and, in a joint statement September 9, proclaimed themselves to be "united in the belief that Iraq's aggression must not be tolerated."

Discarding a longstanding U.S. policy of trying to limit Soviet participation in Middle Eastern affairs, President Bush invited Moscow to play a greater diplomatic role there. He also opened the door to the kind of regional peace conference that Moscow advocated—one that could link the gulf crisis to the "Palestine issue"—the Palestinians' demand that Israel lift its occupation of the West Bank and other territories it captured in the 1967 Six-Day War. While giving the United States full diplomatic backing in the gulf crisis, Gorbachev reportedly made no commitment to use Soviet military power in the Middle East.

Upon his return from Helsinki, Bush reported in an address September 11 to a joint session of Congress that his meeting with Gorbachev was "very productive." He told the lawmakers and a national television audience: "Clearly, no longer can a dictator count on East-West confrontation to stymie concerted United Nations action against aggression."

Following are UN Security Council Resolution 660 of August 2, 1990, condemning the Iraqi invasion of Kuwait; Resolution 661 of August 6, invoking economic sanctions against Iraq; Resolution 665 of August 25, authorizing their enforcement; the statement issued by Presidents Bush and Gorbachev on September 9; and excerpts from Bush's address to Congress September 11.

RESOLUTION 660

The Security Council,

Alarmed by the invasion of Kuwait on 2 August 1990 by the military forces of Iraq,

Determining that there exists a breach of international peace and security as regards the Iraqi invasion of Kuwait,

Acting under Articles 39 and 40 of the Charter of the United Nations,

1. *Condemns* the Iraqi invasion of Kuwait;
2. *Demands* that Iraq withdraw immediately and unconditionally all its forces to the positions in which they were located on 1 August 1990;
3. *Calls upon* Iraq and Kuwait to begin immediately intensive negotiations for the resolution of their differences and supports all efforts in this regard, and especially those of the League of Arab States;
4. *Decides* to meet again as necessary to consider further steps to ensure compliance with the present resolution.

UN RESOLUTION 661

The Security Council,

Reaffirming its resolution 660 (1990) of 2 August 1990,

Deeply concerned that the resolution has not been implemented and that the invasion by Iraq of Kuwait continues with further loss of human life and material destruction,

Determined to bring the invasion and occupation of Kuwait by Iraq to an end and to restore the sovereignty, independence and territorial integrity of Kuwait,

Noting that the legitimate Government of Kuwait has expressed its readiness to comply with resolution 660 (1990),

Mindful of its responsibilities under the Charter of the United Nations for the maintenance of international peace and security,

Affirming the inherent right of individual or collective self-defence, in response to the armed attack by Iraq against Kuwait, in accordance with Article 51 of the Charter,

Acting under Chapter VII of the Charter of the United Nations,

1. *Determines* that Iraq so far has failed to comply with paragraph 2 of resolution 660 (1990) and has usurped the authority of the legitimate Government of Kuwait;

2. *Decides,* as a consequence, to take the following measures to secure compliance of Iraq with paragraph 2 of resolution 660 (1990) and to restore the authority of the legitimate Government of Kuwait;

3. *Decides* that all States shall prevent:

   (a) The import into their territories of all commodities and products originating in Iraq or Kuwait exported therefrom after the date of the present resolution;

   (b) Any activities by their nationals or in their territories which would promote or are calculated to promote the export or trans-shipment of any commodities or products from Iraq or Kuwait; and any dealings by their nationals or their flag vessels or in their territories in any commodities or products originating in Iraq or Kuwait and exported therefrom after the date of the present resolution, including in particular any transfer of funds to Iraq or Kuwait for the purposes of such activities or dealings;

   (c) The sale or supply by their nationals or from their territories or using their flag vessels of any commodities or products, including weapons or any other military equipment, whether or not originating in their territories but not including supplies intended strictly for medical purposes, and, in humanitarian circumstances, foodstuffs, to any person or body in Iraq or Kuwait or to any person or body for the purposes of any business carried on in or operated from Iraq or Kuwait, and any activities by their nationals or in their territories which promote or are calculated to promote such sale or supply of such commodities or products;

4. *Decides* that all States shall not make available to the Government of Iraq or to any commercial, industrial or public utility undertaking in Iraq or Kuwait, any funds or any other financial or economic resources and shall prevent their nationals and any persons within their territories from removing from their territories or otherwise making available to that Government or to any such undertaking any such funds or resources and from remitting any other funds to

persons or bodies within Iraq or Kuwait, except payments exclusively for strictly medical or humanitarian purposes and, in humanitarian circumstances, foodstuffs;

5. *Calls upon* all States, including States non-members of the United Nations, to act strictly in accordance with the provisions of the present resolution notwithstanding any contract entered into or license granted before the date of the present resolution;

6. *Decides* to establish, in accordance with rule 28 of the provisional rules of procedure of the Security Council, a Committee of the Security Council consisting of all the members of the Council, to undertake the following tasks and to report on its work to the Council with its observations and recommendations:

   (a) To examine the reports on the progress of the implementation of the present resolution which will be submitted by the Secretary-General;

   (b) To seek from all States further information regarding the action taken by them concerning the effective implementation of the provisions laid down in the present resolution;

7. *Calls upon* all States to co-operate fully with the Committee in the fulfillment of its task, including supplying such information as may be sought by the Committee in pursuance of the present resolution;

8. *Requests* the Secretary-General to provide all necessary assistance to the Committee and to make the necessary arrangements in the Secretariat for the purpose;

9. *Decides* that, notwithstanding paragraphs 4 through 8 above, nothing in the present resolution shall prohibit assistance to the legitimate Government of Kuwait, and *calls upon* all States;

   (a) To take appropriate measures to protect assets of the legitimate Government of Kuwait and its agencies;

   (b) Not to recognize any regime set up by the occupying Power;

10. *Requests* the Secretary-General to report to the Council on the progress of the implementation of the present resolution, the first report to be submitted within thirty days;

11. *Decides* to keep this item on its agenda and to continue its efforts to put an early end to the invasion by Iraq.

U.N. RESOLUTION 665

The Security Council,

Recalling its Resolutions 660 (1990), 661 (1990), 662 (1990) and 664 (1990) and demanding their full and immediate implementation;

Having decided to impose sanctions in accordance with Chapter VII of the Charter of the United Nations;

Determined to bring an end to the occupation of Kuwait by Iraq, which imperils the existence of a member state, and to restore the legitimate authority and the sovereignty, independence and territorial integrity of Kuwait, which requires the speedy implementation of the above resolutions;

Deploring the loss of innocent life stemming from the Iraqi invasion of Kuwait and determined to prevent further such losses:

Gravely alarmed that Iraq continues to refuse to comply with Resolutions 660 (1990), 661 (1990), 662 (1990) and 664 (1990) and in particular at the conduct of the Government of Iraq in using Iraqi flag vessels to export oil;

1. *Calls upon* those member states cooperating with the Government of Kuwait which are deploying maritime forces to the area to use such measures commensurate to the specific circumstances as may be necessary under the authority of the Security Council to halt all inward and outward maritime shipping in order to inspect and verify their cargoes and destinations and to ensure strict implementation of the provisions related to such shipping laid down in Resolution 661 (1990);

2. *Invites* member states accordingly to cooperate as may be necessary to ensure compliance with the provisions of Resolution 661 (1990) with maximum use of political and diplomatic measures, in accordance with paragraph 1 above;

3. *Requests* all states to provide in accordance with the Charter such assistance as may be required by the states referred to in paragraph 1 of this resolution.

4. *Further requests* the states concerned to coordinate their actions in pursuit of the above paragraphs of this resolution using as appropriate mechanisms of the Military Staff Committee and after consultation with the Secretary General to submit reports to the Security Council and its committee established under Resolution 661 (1990) to facilitate the monitoring of the implementation of this resolution.

5. *Decides* to remain actively seized of the matter.

BUSH-GORBACHEV STATEMENT

With regard to Iraq's invasion and continued military occupation of Kuwait, President Bush and President Gorbachev issue the following joint statement:

We are united in the belief that Iraq's aggression must not be tolerated. No peaceful international order is possible if larger states can devour their smaller neighbors.

We reaffirm the joint statement of our Foreign Ministers of August 3,

1990 and our support for United Nations Security Council Resolutions 660, 661, 662, 664 and 665. Today, we once again call upon the Government of Iraq to withdraw unconditionally from Kuwait, to allow the restoration of Kuwait's legitimate government, and to free all hostages now held in Iraq and Kuwait.

Nothing short of the complete implementation of the United Nations Security Council Resolutions is acceptable.

Nothing short of a return to the pre-August 2 status of Kuwait can end Iraq's isolation.

We call upon the entire world community to adhere to the sanctions mandated by the United Nations, and we pledge to work, individually and in concert, to ensure full compliance with the sanctions. At the same time, the United States and the Soviet Union recognize that UN Security Council Resolution 661 permits, in humanitarian circumstances, the importation into Iraq and Kuwait of food. The Sanctions Committee will make recommendations to the Security Council on what would constitute humanitarian circumstances. The United States and the Soviet Union further agree that any such imports must be strictly monitored by the appropriate international agencies to ensure that food reaches only those for whom it is intended, with special priority being given to meeting the needs of children.

Our preference is to resolve the crisis peacefully, and we will be united against Iraq's aggression as long as the crisis exists. However, we are determined to see this aggression end, and if the current steps fail to end it, we are prepared to consider additional ones consistent with the UN Charter. We must demonstrate beyond any doubt that aggression cannot and will not pay.

As soon as the objectives mandated by the UN Security Council resolutions mentioned above have been achieved, and we have demonstrated that aggression does not pay, the Presidents direct their Foreign Ministers to work with countries in the region and outside it to develop regional security structures and measures to promote peace and stability. It is essential to work actively to resolve all remaining conflicts in the Middle East and Persian Gulf. Both sides will continue to consult each other and initiate measures to pursue these broader objectives at the proper time.

ADDRESS TO CONGRESS

PRESIDENT BUSH: Mr. President, Mr. Speaker, members of the Congress, distinguished guests, fellow Americans, thank you very much for that warm welcome.

We gather tonight witness to events in the Persian Gulf as significant as they are tragic. In the early morning hours of Aug. 2, following negotiations and promises by Iraq's dictator Saddam Hussein not to use force, a powerful Iraqi army invaded its trusting and much weaker neighbor, Kuwait. Within three days, 120,000 Iraqi troops with 850 tanks had poured into Kuwait and moved south to threaten Saudi Arabia. It was then I decided to act to check that aggression.

At this moment, our brave servicemen and women stand watch in that distant desert and on distant seas, side by side with the forces of more than 20 other nations. They are some of the finest men and women of the United States of America, and they're doing one terrific job.

These valiant Americans were ready at a moment's notice to leave their spouses, their children, to serve on the front line halfway around the world. And they remind us who keeps America strong—they do.

In the trying circumstances of the gulf, the morale of our servicemen and women is excellent. In the face of danger, they are brave, they're well-trained and dedicated.

A soldier, Pfc. Wade Merritt of Knoxville, Tenn., now stationed in Saudi Arabia, wrote his parents of his worries, his love of family, and his hopes for peace. But Wade also wrote: "I am proud of my country and its firm stand against inhumane aggression. I am proud of my army and its men. I am proud to serve my country."

Well, let me just say, Wade, America is proud of you and is grateful to every soldier, sailor, marine, and airman serving the cause of peace in the Persian Gulf.

I also want to thank the chairman of the Joint Chiefs of Staff, Gen. [Colin L.] Powell [Jr.], the chiefs here tonight, our commander in the Persian Gulf, Gen. [H. Norman] Schwarzkopf, and the men and women of the Department of Defense.

What a magnificent job you all are doing, and thank you very, very much from a grateful country.

I wish I could say that their work is done, but we all know it is not.

So if ever there was a time to put country before self and patriotism before party, the time is now. And let me thank all Americans, especially those here in this chamber tonight, for your support for our armed forces and their mission. That support will be even more important in the days to come.

So tonight, I want to talk to you about what's at stake, what we must do together to defend civilized values around the world and maintain our economic strength at home. Our objectives in the Persian Gulf are clear, our goals defined and familiar:

Iraq must withdraw from Kuwait completely, immediately and without condition.

Kuwait's legitimate government must be restored. The security and stability of the Persian Gulf must be assured, and American citizens abroad must be protected.

These goals are not ours alone. They've been endorsed by the United Nations Security Council five times in as many weeks. Most countries share our concern for principle. And many have a stake in the stability of the Persian Gulf. This is not, as Saddam Hussein would have it, the United States against Iraq. It is Iraq against the world.

As you know, I've just returned from a very productive meeting with Soviet President [Mikhail S.] Gorbachev. And I am pleased that we are working together to build a new relationship. In Helsinki, [Finland,] our joint statement affirmed to the world our shared resolve to counter Iraq's threat to peace. Let me quote: "We are united in the belief that Iraq's aggression must not be tolerated. No peaceful international order is possible if larger states can devour their smaller neighbors. Clearly, no longer can a dictator count on East-West confrontation to stymie concerted United Nations action against aggression."

A new partnership of nations has begun, and we stand today at a unique and extraordinary moment. The crisis in the Persian Gulf, as grave as it is, also offers a rare opportunity to move toward an historic period of cooperation. Out of these troubled times, our fifth objective—a new world order—can emerge: a new era—freer from the threat of terror, stronger in the pursuit of justice, and more secure in the quest for peace, an era in which the nations of the world, East and West, North and South, can prosper and live in harmony.

A hundred generations have searched for this elusive path to peace, while a thousand wars raged across the span of human endeavor. And today that new world is struggling to be born, a world quite different from the one we've known, a world where the rule of law supplants the rule of the jungle, a world in which nations recognize the shared responsibility for freedom and justice, a world where the strong respect the rights of the weak. This is the vision I shared with President Gorbachev in Helsinki. He, and other leaders from Europe, the gulf and around the world, understand that how we manage this crisis today could shape the future for generations to come.

The test we face is great and so are the stakes. This is the first assault on the new world that we seek, the first test of our mettle. Had we not responded to this first provocation with clarity of purpose, if we do not continue to demonstrate our determination, it would be a signal to actual and potential despots around the world.

America and the world must defend common vital interests, and we will.

America and the world must support the rule of law, and we will.

America and the world must stand up to aggression. And we will.

And one thing more—in the pursuit of these goals—America will not be intimidated.

Vital issues of principle are at stake. Saddam Hussein is literally trying to wipe a country off the face of the Earth. We do not exaggerate. Nor do we exaggerate when we say Saddam Hussein will fail.

Vital economic interests are at risk as well. Iraq itself controls some 10 percent of the world's proven oil reserves. Iraq plus Kuwait controls twice that.

An Iraq permitted to swallow Kuwait would have the economic and military power, as well as the arrogance, to intimidate and coerce its neighbors, neighbors who control the lion's share of the world's remaining oil reserves. We cannot permit a resource so vital to be dominated by one so ruthless—and we won't.

Recent events have surely proven that there is no substitute for American leadership. In the face of tyranny, let no one doubt American credibility and reliability.

Let no one doubt our staying power. We will stand by our friends. One way or another, the leader of Iraq must learn this fundamental truth.

From the outset, acting hand in hand with others, we've sought to fashion the broadest possible international response to Iraq's aggression. The level of world cooperation and condemnation of Iraq is unprecedented. Armed forces from countries spanning four continents are there at the request of King Fahd of Saudi Arabia to deter and, if need be, to defend against attack. Muslims and non-Muslims, Arabs and non-Arabs, soldiers from many nations stand shoulder to shoulder, resolute against Saddam Hussein's ambitions.

And we can now point to five United Nations Security Council resolutions that condemn Iraq's aggression. They call for Iraq's immediate and unconditional withdrawal, the restoration of Kuwait's legitimate government, and categorically reject Iraq's cynical and self-serving attempt to annex Kuwait.

Finally, the United Nations has demanded the release of all foreign nationals held hostage against their will and in contravention of international law. It is a mockery of human decency to call these people "guests." They are hostages, and the whole world knows it.

[British] Prime Minister Margaret Thatcher, our dependable ally, said it all: "We do not bargain over hostages. We will not stoop to the level of using human beings as bargaining chips—ever."

Of course—of course our hearts go out to the hostages and their families. But our policy cannot change. And it will not change. America and the world will not be blackmailed by this ruthless policy.

We're now in sight of a United Nations that performs as envisioned by its founders. We owe much to the outstanding leadership of Secretary General Javier Pérez de Cuéllar. The United Nations is backing up its words with action. The Security Council has imposed mandatory economic sanctions on Iraq, designed to force Iraq to relinquish the spoils of its illegal conquest. The Security Council has also taken the decisive step of authorizing the use of all means necessary to ensure compliance with these sanctions.

Together with our friends and allies, ships of the United States Navy are today patrolling Mideast waters, and they've already intercepted more than 700 ships to enforce the sanctions.

Three regional leaders I spoke with just yesterday told me that these sanctions are working. Iraq is feeling the heat. We continue to hope that Iraq's leaders will recalculate just what their aggression has cost them.

They are cut off from world trade, unable to sell their oil, and only a tiny fraction of goods gets through.

The communiqué with President Gorbachev made mention of what happens when the embargo is so effective that children of Iraq literally need milk or the sick truly need medicine. Then, under strict international supervision that guarantees the proper destination, then food will be permitted.

At home, the material cost of our leadership can be steep. And that's why Secretary of State [James A.] Baker [III] and Treasury Secretary [Nicholas F.] Brady have met with many world leaders to underscore that the burden of this collective effort must be shared.

We are prepared to do our share and more to help carry the load; we insist others do their share as well.

The response of most of our friends and allies has been good. To help defray costs, the leaders of Saudi Arabia, Kuwait and the UAE, the United Arab Emirates, have pledged to provide our deployed troops with all the food and fuel they need. And generous assistance will also be provided to stalwart front-line nations, such as Turkey and Egypt.

And I'm also heartened to report that this international response extends to the neediest victims of this conflict—those refugees. For our part, we have contributed $28 million for relief efforts. And this is but a portion of what is needed. I commend, in particular, Saudi Arabia, Japan, and several European nations who have joined us in this purely humanitarian effort.

There's an energy-related cost to be borne as well. Oil-producing nations are already replacing lost Iraqi and Kuwaiti output. More than half of what was lost has been made up, and we're getting superb cooperation.

If producers, including the United States, continue steps to expand oil and gas production, we can stabilize prices and guarantee against hardship. Additionally, we and several of our allies always have the option to extract oil from our Strategic Petroleum Reserves, if conditions warrant. As I've pointed out before, conservation efforts are essential to keep our energy needs as low as possible.

And we must then take advantage of our energy sources across the board: coal, natural gas, hydro and nuclear. Our failure to do these things has made us more dependent on foreign oil than ever before.

And finally, let no one even contemplate profiteering from this crisis. We will not have it.

And I cannot predict just how long it will take to convince Iraq to withdraw from Kuwait. Sanctions will take time to have their full intended effect. We will continue to review all options with our allies, but let it be clear: We will not let this aggression stand. Our interest—

Our interest, our involvement in the gulf, is not transitory. It predated Saddam Hussein's aggression and will survive it. Long after all our troops come home—and we all hope it's soon, very soon—there will be a lasting role for the United States in assisting the nations of the Persian Gulf. Our role then, is to deter future aggression. Our role is to help our friends in their own self-defense and something else: to curb the proliferation of chemical, biological, ballistic missiles and, above all, nuclear technologies.

And let me also make clear that the United States has no quarrel with the Iraqi people. Our quarrel is with Iraq's dictator and with his aggression. Iraq will not be permitted to annex Kuwait. And that's not a threat, it's not a boast—it's just the way it's going to be. . . .

KING FAHD ON
U.S. TROOP ARRIVAL
August 9, 1990

King Fahd Bin Abdel Aziz of Saudi Arabia broke a week-long public silence August 9 to tell his people that Iraq was guilty of aggression against Kuwait and had "massed huge forces on the borders of the Kingdom of Saudi Arabia." In his broadcast to the nation one week after the invasion of Kuwait, the Saudi monarch seemed almost hesitant in mentioning that foreign troops were coming to his assistance. He emphasized that they would be in Saudi Arabia solely for defensive purposes, to engage in training exercises with Saudi forces, and would leave "immediately at the request of the Kingdom."

His cautious choice of words indicated that Saudi leaders, although making a bold choice to resist Iraq, wanted to remove any notion that Saudi Arabia—backed by United Nations decrees and the American military—might attack Iraq, its bigger and better-armed neighbor. Iraq, with 17 million people, had nearly 1 million in uniform, including reserves and second-line units. Saudi Arabia, with 12 million people, had only 65,000 under arms. Although the country had lavished money on foreign manufacturers for modern warplanes and other sophisticated military equipment, the monarchy deliberately had restricted the size of the armed forces to ensure their loyalty and to achieve a tribal and geographical balance among the segments of the population.

Only after the invasion of Kuwait did the Saudi government appeal for volunteers. A government directive also retreated from some restrictions on women's employment. Few other countries restrict women's activities as much as Saudi Arabia, where a puritanical enforcement of Islamic law is observed. Women were now permitted to seek more jobs in the workplace to free men for military service. However, few new careers were opened to them.

Until the Saudi leaders agreed to seek foreign military help, it was unclear whether they would take a stand against Iraq or continue with their traditional diplomacy—trying to placate potential enemies with money. The Saudi government, fearful of Iran's brand of Islamic fundamentalism, had given Iraqi president Saddam Hussein strong financial backing in his eight-year war with Iran.

Arab League Vote

The invasion and the Saudi decision to stand firm removed any remaining pretense of Arab unity. Egypt, in cooperation with the United States, attempted to enlist help from other Arab nations for Saudi Arabia. After failing once, Egyptian president Hosni Mubarak convened a meeting of the Arab League in Cairo to condemn the invasion. When the Arab leaders met August 10, twelve of the twenty-one league members voted to send military forces to assist Saudi Arabia. Only Iraq, Libya, and the Palestine Liberation Organization (PLO) rejected the proposal outright. Mauritania, Jordan, and Sudan expressed reservations; Algeria and Yemen abstained; and Tunisia was absent.

The Arab League vote elicited pro-Iraq protest demonstrations in several Arab capitals. That same day Hussein appealed to "Arab and Muslim masses" to engage in a holy war against American Zionists to "save Mecca and the Tomb of the Prophet [Mohammad, in Medina] from occupation." He accused the Saudi rulers of putting the holy places "under the spear of the foreigner." The Saudi monarch's title includes the words "Custodian of the Two Holy Mosques," and the country's leadership appeared sensitive to disturbing the Moslem faithful—especially the Saudis—by letting in non-Arab soldiers. American commanders attempted to keep their troops apart from Saudi civilians, especially Saudi women, in an effort to avert violations of moral or religious taboos and consequent offense to Islamic fundamentalists. Since alcohol is proscribed in Islam, American GI's were not permitted alcoholic drinks even in their encampments.

Despite the protests it aroused, the Arab League vote was considered a triumph for Egyptian, Saudi, and American diplomacy. Much of the credit was attributed to President George Bush and Secretary of Defense Dick Cheney, whom Bush had sent on a fast-paced trip throughout the Middle East to bolster support in friendly Arab capitals. Egypt and Morocco were the first to send troops. President Hafez al-Assad of Syria, an Arab hard-liner who often had incurred American wrath, also sent troops to Saudi Arabia. Foreign affairs analysts surmised that Assad's rivalry with the Iraqi president was greater than his presumed distaste for Mubarak and the United States.

King Hussein of Jordan (unrelated to the Iraqi leader), traditionally an Arab "moderate" of the Mubarak stripe, broke ranks with his usual allies, including the United States, on this issue. His small kingdom is next door to Iraq and filled with Palestinians, many of them refugees from Israeli-occupied territory, who expressed strong admiration for the Iraqi president.

Portraying himself as a peacemaker, the king failed in his attempt to persuade Iraqi and Saudi leaders to negotiate a political settlement. He drew harsh words from Bush administration officials, who regarded his activities as undercutting their efforts to isolate the Iraqi president in the Arab world. The Jordanian monarch complained that his efforts had been misunderstood in Washington and that his country was suffering economically from the UN economic embargo of Iraq. A sizable portion of Iraq's commerce was funneled through the Jordanian port of Aqaba. In contrast to King Hussein, Mubarak enhanced his prestige in Washington. A grateful Bush persuaded Congress to forgive Egypt's $7 billion debt to the United States. Until the gulf crisis, Syria was somewhat isolated politically in the Arab world—an enemy of Iraq and not on the best of terms with the Egypt-led moderate nations. But it was expected to enhance its standing among those nations that backed Saudi Arabia.

Following is King Fahd Bin Abdel Aziz's address to his country on the Iraqi threat, August 9, 1990, as translated by the Saudi Arabian government:

In the name of God, the Merciful, the Compassionate. Thanks be to God, Master of the Universe and Prayers of Peace be upon the last of Prophets Mohamad and all his kinfolk and companions.

Dear brother citizens, May God's peace and mercy be upon you.

You realize, no doubt, through following up the course of the regrettable events in the Arab Gulf region during the last few days the gravity of the situation the Arab Nation faces in the current circumstances. You undoubtedly know that the government of the Kingdom of Saudi Arabia has exerted all possible efforts with the governments of the Iraqi Republic and the State of Kuwait to contain the dispute between the two countries.

In this context, I made numerous telephone calls and held fraternal talks with the brothers. As a result, a bilateral meeting was held between the Iraqi and Kuwaiti delegations in Saudi Arabia with the aim of bridging the gap and narrowing differences to avert any further escalation.

A number of brotherly Arab kings and presidents contributed, thankfully, in these efforts based on their belief in the unity of the Arab Nation and the cohesion of its solidarity and cooperation to achieve success in serving its fateful causes.

However, regrettably enough, events took an adverse course, to our endeavors and the aspirations of the Peoples of the Islamic and Arab nation, as well as all peace-loving countries.

Nevertheless, these painful and regrettable events started in the pre-dawn hours of Thursday 11 Muharram 1411H., corresponding to 2nd August A.D. 1990. They took the whole world by surprise when the Iraqi forces stormed the brotherly state of Kuwait in the most sinister aggression witnessed by the Arab nation in its modern history. Such an invasion inflicted painful suffering on the Kuwaitis and rendered them homeless.

While expressing its deep displeasure at this aggression on the brotherly neighbor Kuwait, the Kingdom of Saudi Arabia declares its categorical rejection of all ensuing measures and declarations that followed that aggression, which were rejected by all the statements issued by Arab leaderships, the Arab League, the Islamic Conference Organization, and the Gulf Cooperation Council, as well as all Arab and international bodies and organizations.

The Kingdom of Saudi Arabia reaffirms its demand to restore the situation in the brotherly state of Kuwait to its original status before the Iraqi storming as well as the return of the ruling family headed by H.H. [His Highness] Sheik Jaber al-Ahmed al-Sabah, the Emir of Kuwait and his government.

We hope that the emergency Arab summit called by H.E. [His Excellency] President Mohamad Hosni Mubarak of sisterly Egypt will lead to the achievement of the results that realize the aspirations of the Arab nation and bolster its march towards solidarity and unity of opinion.

In the aftermath of this regrettable event, Iraq massed huge forces on the borders of the Kingdom of Saudi Arabia. In view of these bitter realities and out of the eagerness of the Kingdom to safeguard its territory and protect its vital and economic potentials, and its wish to bolster its defensive capabilities and to raise the level of training of its armed forces—in addition to the keenness of the government of the Kingdom to resort to peace and non-recourse to force to solve disputes—the Kingdom of Saudi Arabia expressed its wish for the participation of fraternal Arab forces and other friendly forces.

Thus, the governments of the United States, Britain and other nations took the initiative, based on the friendly relations that link the Kingdom of Saudi Arabia and these countries, to dispatch air and land forces to sustain the Saudi armed forces in performing their duty to defend the homeland and the citizens against any aggression with the full emphasis that this measure is not addressed to anybody. It is merely and purely for defensive purposes, imposed by the current circumstances faced by the Kingdom of Saudi Arabia.

It is worth mentioning in this context that the forces which will participate in the joint training exercises with the Saudi armed forces are of a temporary nature. They will leave the Saudi territory immediately at the request of the Kingdom.

We pray to Almighty God to culminate our steps towards everything in which lie the good of our religion and safety of our homeland, and to guide us on the right path.

May God's peace and blessing be upon you.

UN PEACE PLAN FOR CAMBODIA
August 28, 1990

After twenty years of warfare and strife in Cambodia, the five perma-
nent members of the United Nations Security Council announced an
agreement August 28 on the main features of a proposed political
settlement in that troubled land. The agreement, accepted in principle
the next month by the four main contending factions in Cambodia, would
place the country's affairs largely under UN administrators and a
peacekeeping force until national elections could be held and an orderly
transfer of authority assured.

A new spirit of global cooperation between the United States and the
Soviet Union in the glasnost era enabled them to lay aside their
differences over Cambodia and agree to a peace plan. This agreement
followed others that Moscow and Washington entered into during Au-
gust. They made common cause for the first time not only in Cambodia
but also in the Middle East, signing a series of U.S.-sponsored Security
Council resolutions demanding the withdrawal of Iraqi invasion forces
from Kuwait. (Iraqi Invasion of Kuwait, p. 533)

The Soviet Union had backed a puppet government that Vietnam
installed after its invasion of Cambodia in 1978. The United States
supported a fragile coalition of three opposition groups, which included
the notorious Khmer Rouge, until Secretary of State James A. Baker III
abruptly announced a shift in policy. Immediately after meeting with
Soviet Foreign Minister Eduard A. Shevardnadze in Paris July 18, Baker
told reporters that the United States was withdrawing its diplomatic
recognition of the guerrilla coalition.

That move was necessary, Baker said, because the existing U.S. policy
increased the prospect of the Khmer Rouge returning to power. In its
brief rule between seizing power in 1975 and being deposed by the

Vietnamese invasion, the Khmer Rouge's zealous efforts to "purify" society with a fanatical brand of communism resulted in the deaths of approximately 1 million Cambodians. Most of the inhabitants of cities— including Phnom Penh, the capital—were forced into the countryside to do hard labor with scant food, shelter, and medical care. According to reports by eyewitnesses and findings of international human rights organizations, many Cambodians were murdered outright, and great numbers died from starvation, disease, and beatings.

Big Power Involvement

China, one of the Security Council's other permanent members (along with Britain and France), backed the Khmer Rouge against the regime that was installed by Vietnam and backed by the Soviet Union. After the United States pulled out of the Vietnam War in 1975, it tried to isolate Vietnam both economically and politically. Washington would not recognize the Phnom Penh government, but balked at directly supporting the Khmer Rouge, which had been driven out of the cities but continued as a guerrilla force.

Instead, the United States aided the Khmer Rouge indirectly, as part of a UN-recognized coalition that included two non-Communist guerrilla groups. The weaker of the two was led—at least nominally—by Prince Norodom Sihanouk. He had ruled Cambodia for nearly three decades, until 1970. He was ousted that year in a coup carried out by Lon Nol, a pro-U.S. premier, who vainly demanded that Hanoi remove its troops that had infiltrated into Cambodia to carry out attacks on U.S. and South Vietnamese positions in South Vietnam. The United States, in turn, heavily bombed those infiltrated areas. The deposed Sihanouk set up a government in exile in Peking.

Despite U.S. economic and military assistance to Lon Nol's government, it fell to Khmer Rouge insurgents in 1975. They were driven back into hiding by Vietnam's 1978 invasion, but began to reassert themselves after Vietnam withdrew most of its troops from Cambodia in September 1989—in an apparent attempt to restore diplomatic relations with the United States and restructure its economy along capitalist lines. The Khmer Rouge's success in regaining control of sizable areas of the countryside fueled a new effort by outside powers to bring about peace in Cambodia.

UN Settlement "Framework"

The first sign of movement in a long stalemate was glimpsed at a Paris conference in January, attended by representatives of the four Cambodian factions and the Security Council. Some observers reported that the factions could no longer count on rigid backing by their principal supporters—China, Vietnam, the Soviet Union, and the United States. At a previous conference in the French capital in August 1989, Cambodian prime minister Hun Sen rejected a UN role. But in January, he and leaders of the other factions seemed to accept it. After eight months of *negotiations among the parties, the Security Council could announce August 28 a "framework" for a political settlement in Cambodia. It might involve as many as 10,000 UN peacekeeping troops and possibly as many civilian personnel to administer the country and supervise the election of a permanent government—a project that by some estimates might cost $5 billion. The sources of that money had not been identified.*

In the interim, the document called for the four parties to form a Supreme National Council to represent Cambodia, but the UN plan was vague as to how the council should be formed. The four parties met in Jakarta, Indonesia, September 10, and, in what they called a "historic" joint statement, announced the formation of a twelve-member council of which six members would be designated by the Phnom Penh government and two each by the three opposition groups.

The council would have the option of naming a thirteenth member as chairman, and Prince Sihanouk was reported to be the likely choice. However, his acceptance of the role was uncertain, for he had declined to attend the Jakarta meeting. The next step, after the council became fully organized, was to reconvene the Paris conference and flesh out the UN "framework" with necessary details.

Following are excerpts from the UN text of a "Framework for a Comprehensive Political Settlement of the Cambodian Conflict," on which the Security Council's five permanent members announced their agreement, August 28, 1990:

Transitional Arrangements Regarding the Administration of Cambodia During the Pre-Electoral Period

1. In order to restore and maintain peace in Cambodia, prevent the continuation of the conflict, promote national reconciliation and ensure the realization of national self-determination through free and fair general elections, it is essential to establish a unique legitimate body and source of authority in which, throughout the transitional period, national sovereignty and unity would be enshrined.

2. In the light of their discussions during their first five meetings and taking account of the wishes of parties concerned, the Five believe it is appropriate to establish at an early date a Supreme National Council (SNC) of Cambodia.

3. The composition of the SNC, including the selection and number of its members, should be decided by the Cambodian parties through consultations. No party should be dominant in this process.

4. The SNC should be composed of representative individuals with authority among the Cambodian people. They should be acceptable to each other. They may include representative individuals of all shades of opinion among the people of Cambodia. The members of the SNC should be committed to the holding of free and fair elections as the basis for forming a new and legitimate government.

5. Should Prince Norodom SIHANOUK be elected by the SNC as its President, the Five would welcome this decision.

6. All countries should respect an agreement on this matter reached among the Cambodian parties.

7. The SNC should be the embodiment of the independence, sovereignty and unity of Cambodia. It should represent Cambodia externally and occupy the seat of Cambodia at the United Nations, in the UN specialised agencies, and in other international institutions and international conferences.

8. Being the unique legitimate body and source of authority in Cambodia during the transitional period, the SNC, at the time the comprehensive political settlement is signed, will delegate to the United Nations Transitional Authority in Cambodia (UNTAC) all powers necessary to ensure the implementation of the comprehensive agreement, including those relating to the conduct of free and fair elections and the relevant aspects of the administration of Cambodia.

9. The SNC should offer advice to the UNTAC which will comply with this advice provided there is a consensus among the members of the SNC, and provided this advice is consistent with the objectives of the comprehensive political settlement. The Special Representative of the UN Secretary-General will determine whether such advice is consistent with the comprehensive political settlement. He should attend the meetings of the SNC and give its members all necessary information on the decisions taken by UNTAC.

10. In order to ensure a neutral political environment conducive to free and fair general elections, administrative agencies, bodies and offices which could directly influence the outcome of elections should be placed under direct UN supervision or control. In that context special attention will be given to foreign affairs, national defence, finance, public security and information. To reflect the importance of these subjects, UNTAC needs to exercise such control as is necessary to ensure the strict neutrality of the bodies responsible for them. The UN in consultation with the SNC would identify which agencies, bodies and offices could continue to operate in order to ensure normal day-to-day life in the country.

11. Adequate provision must be made within the terms of the comprehensive political settlement for the exercise of routine law enforcement functions under UNTAC supervision.

12. The Special Representative of the Secretary-General should investigate complaints and allegations regarding actions by the existing administrative structures in Cambodia that are inconsistent with or work against the objectives of a comprehensive political settlement.

Military Arrangements During the Transitional Period

13. The enhanced United Nations role requires the establishment of a United Nations Transitional Authority in Cambodia (UNTAC) with a military as well as a civilian component.

14. The function of the military component should be to carry out the

peacekeeping aspects of the comprehensive political settlement.

15. Once a ceasefire takes effect, UNTAC will supervise, monitor and verify the ceasefire and related measures, including:

a. Verification of the withdrawal from Cambodia of all categories of foreign forces, advisers and military personnel and their weapons, ammunition and equipment, and their non-return to the country.

b. Liaison with neighbouring governments over any developments in or near their territory which could endanger the implementation of the comprehensive political settlement.

c. Monitoring the cessation of outside military assistance to all Cambodian parties.

d. Locating and confiscating cases of weapons and military supplies throughout the country.

e. Undertaking training programs in mine clearance and a mine awareness program among the Cambodian people.

16. The military component should be composed of a certain number of contingents provided by member States at the request of the UN Secretary General. These contingents will be chosen in consultation with parties concerned and with the approval of the Security Council.

17. The Five consider that a ceasefire is an indispensible element of a comprehensive agreement. As a first step, they call on all parties to the conflict to exercise maximum self restraint. To facilitate the UN deployment necessary for the agreement to come into effect, a peaceful situation should prevail in Cambodia. At the time of the signing of the agreement, all forces should immediately disengage and refrain from any deployment, movement or action which would extend the territory they control or which might lead to the resumption of fighting. The formal ceasefire envisaged should enter into force at the time the comprehensive political settlement agreement takes effect.

18. In accordance with an operational timetable to be agreed upon, all forces will begin regrouping and relocating to specifically designated cantonment areas under the supervision of UNTAC. While the forces are in the cantonments, their arms will be stored on site under UNTAC supervision.

19. UNTAC will then initiate a phased process of arms control and reduction in such a way as to stabilize the security situation and build confidence among the parties to the conflict. The ultimate disposition of the factional forces and their weapons will be dealt with so as to reinforce the objectives of a comprehensive political settlement and minimize the risks of a return to warfare.

Elections Under United Nations Auspices

20. The United Nations should be responsible for the organization and conduct of free and fair elections on the basis of genuine and verified voter registration lists of Cambodian citizens. Eligibility to vote, including provisions regarding the conditions of residence in Cambodia, will be established in the electoral regulations. Principles covering voting and

candidate eligibility criteria will also be set out within the comprehensive political settlement. Special electoral arrangements should be agreed to guarantee the right to vote of Cambodian refugees and displaced persons.

21. The electoral process should be guided by the following principles:

a. The system and procedures adopted should be, and be seen to be, absolutely impartial while the arrangements should be as administratively simple and efficient as possible;

b. All Cambodian participants in the elections should have the same rights, freedoms and opportunities to take part in the election process;

c. All parties should commit themselves to honouring the results.

22. The provisions for the holding of free and fair elections under United Nations auspices, as part of a comprehensive political settlement, must include inter alia;

a. The establishment of a system of laws, procedures and administrative measures necessary for free and fair elections required by the electoral process;

b. The design and implementation of a voter education program (ballot secrecy, voting procedures, etc.) to support the election process and a voter registration process to guard against fraud and to ensure that eligible voters have the opportunity to register;

c. Measures to monitor and facilitate the participation of Cambodians in the elections, the political campaign, and the balloting procedures;

d. Coordinated arrangements by the United Nations in consultation with the Supreme National Council to facilitate the presence of foreign observers wishing to observe the campaign and voting;

e. Identification and investigation of complaints of electoral irregularities and appropriate corrective action;

f. Fair access to the media, including press, TV and radio, for all candidates;

g. Overall direction of polling and the vote count;

h. Certification by the United Nations whether or not the elections were free and fair and the list of persons duly elected;

i. Adoption of a Code of Conduct regulating participation in the elections in a manner consistent with respect for human rights, including the prohibition of coercion or financial inducement in order to influence voter preference.

23. A comprehensive political settlement must include a specified period within which elections will take place. The duration of the electoral process should be consistent with the above and as short as possible. It should lead to a single election of a constituent assembly which would draft and approve a Constitution and transform itself into a legislative assembly, which will create the new Government. . . .

Human Rights Protection

24. Cambodia's tragic recent history requires special measures to assure protection of human rights. Therefore, the comprehensive political settle-

ment should commit Cambodia to comply with the obligations of the relevant international human rights instruments as well as with relevant resolutions of the UN General Assembly. Necessary measures should be taken in order to observe human rights and ensure the non-return to the policies and practices of the past.

25. Articles 55 and 56 of the UN Charter pledge all member States to take joint and separate action to promote universal respect for, and observance of, human rights and fundamental freedoms for all without distinction as to race, sex, language or religion.

26. All Cambodian people and others in Cambodia and all Cambodian refugees and displaced persons should enjoy the rights enshrined in the Universal Declaration of Human Rights and other relevant international human rights instruments. Fundamental rights and freedoms should form part of the constitutional principles within the comprehensive political settlement.

27. In recognition of the need to promote respect for human rights in Cambodia and for all Cambodians, the comprehensive political settlement should include provisions under UN auspices to guarantee the following during the transitional period:

a. Development and implementation of a program of human rights education to promote respect for and understanding of human rights;

b. General human rights oversight of all aspects of the transitional administration, and

c. Investigation of human rights complaints, and, where appropriate, corrective action.

28. Following the elections, the UN Human Rights Commission should continue to monitor closely the human rights situation in Cambodia, including if necessary by the appointment of a Special Rapporteur who would report his findings annually to the Commission and to the General Assembly.

29. As part of the comprehensive political settlement the other participating States should undertake to promote and encourage respect for and observance of human rights and fundamental freedoms in Cambodia as embodied in relevant international instruments so as to prevent the recurrence of human rights abuses.

30. In the event of future serious violations of human rights in Cambodia, other States should, consistent with the provisions of the section on international guarantees, call upon the competent organs of the UN to take appropriate action in accordance with relevant international instruments.

International Guarantees

31. The aim of the provisions of this section should be to: safeguard the independent and neutral status of Cambodia; prevent foreign aggression against Cambodia or interference in the affairs of that country; safeguard human rights in Cambodia and prevent a return to the policies and practices of the past; facilitate a comprehensive and durable political

settlement based on self-determination of the Cambodian people, and ensure that the settlement agreed upon is implemented in its entirety.

32. Cambodia will solemnly undertake to maintain, preserve and defend its independence, sovereignty, territorial integrity and inviolability, and national unity, with perpetual neutrality proclaimed and enshrined in the Cambodian Constitution to be adopted after free and fair elections.

33. As part of a comprehensive political settlement, the states participating in the Paris Conference will conclude a multilateral agreement to recognize and respect the independence, sovereignty, territorial integrity and inviolability, neutrality, and national unity of Cambodia. This agreement will be open to adherence by all member States of the United Nations.

34. The details of the respective obligations of Cambodia and the other participating States will be based upon the consensus achieved in the Second Committee of the Paris Conference on Cambodia, including in particular undertakings with respect to:

a. Refraining from entering into military alliances or other military agreements between Cambodia and other States that would be inconsistent with Cambodia's neutrality without prejudice to its right to receive or acquire the necessary military equipment, arms, munitions and assistance to enable it to exercise its legitimate right of self-defence and to maintain law and order;

b. Refraining from interference in any form in the internal affairs of Cambodia;

c. Terminating the treaties and agreements which are incompatible with Cambodia's independence, sovereignty, territorial integrity and inviolability, neutrality and national unity;

d. Settling all disputes between Cambodia and other States through peaceful means;

e. Consistent with the United Nations Charter, refraining from the use or threat of use of force, or the use of their territories or the territories of other States to impair the independence, sovereignty, territorial integrity and inviolability, neutrality and national unity of Cambodia;

f. Refraining from the use of Cambodian territory to impair the independence, sovereignty and territorial integrity of other States;

g. Refraining from the introduction or stationing of foreign forces or the establishment of foreign military bases or facilities in Cambodia, except pursuant to the United Nations authorisation for the implementation of the comprehensive political settlement;

h. Respect for human rights in Cambodia, including observance of relevant international instruments.

35. The participating States will call upon all other States to recognize and respect in every way the independence, sovereignty, territorial integrity and inviolability, neutrality and national unity of Cambodia and to refrain from any action inconsistent with these principles.

36. In the event of a violation or threat of violation of the independence, sovereignty, territorial integrity, neutrality and national unity of Cambodia, or of any of the other commitments herein, including those relating to

human rights, the participating States will immediately undertake appropriate consultations with a view to adopting all appropriate measures to ensure respect for these commitments. Such measures may include, inter alia, reference to the Security Council of the United Nations or recourse to the means for the peaceful settlement of disputes referred to in Article 33 of the Charter of the United Nations. The participating States may also seek the good offices of the co-chairmen of the Paris conference on Cambodia.

September

REPORT ON CARE OF
THE MENTALLY ILL
September 11, 1990

American services for people with serious mental illnesses "are a disaster by any measure used," said the authors of a state-by-state study of mental health care. "Not since the 1820's," they reported, "have so many mentally ill individuals lived untreated in public shelters, on the streets and in the jails." Noting that the presence of many mentally ill persons in the nation's poorhouses during the 1820s and 1830s led to the creation of mental hospitals as more "humane" alternatives, the authors observed in the report: "We have, in essence, returned to where we were 170 years ago."

Dr. E. Fuller Torry, a psychiatrist and writer noted for outspoken criticism of his profession and the state of mental health care, was one of the authors. The others were Dr. Sidney M. Wolfe, a medical internist and director of the Public Citizen Health Research Group in Washington, D.C.; Laurie M. Flynn, executive director of the National Alliance for the Mentally Ill, based in Arlington, Virginia; and Karen Erdman, project director of a survey of state services for the alliance.

The study was conducted by the two private, nonprofit advocacy and research organizations. The 200-page report, "Care of the Seriously Mentally Ill: A Rating of State Programs," was issued September 11 in Washington. Its findings were based on surveys of mental care professionals and the families of patients, and on an examination of records in fifty states and the District of Columbia. The two organizations had published similar but less comprehensive reports in 1986 and 1988, which also ranked the efforts of individual states to provide mental health care.

Community Care Failure

Within the past four decades, the focus on providing for the mentally ill has shifted from state mental hospitals to the communities. Aided by mood-altering drugs, the hospitals virtually emptied their once-crowded wards. Hundreds of thousands of patients were released to what was supposed to be community care. "Whenever one surveys the current scene, it is clear that whatever was supposed to happen did not happen and that deinstitutionalization was a disaster," the authors contended. Services for people with serious mental illnesses "are the shame of the nation," they said, despite about $20 billion spent annually on the services, plus federal funding of $3 billion to create community health centers and $2 million to train health professionals to deal with the mentally ill. Some of the study's strongest criticism was directed at psychiatrists, whom it accused of abandoning the seriously mentally ill in the public sector "for the monetary rewards of private practice." Overall, it concluded, "such an enormous expenditure has not produced a system of services that is even minimally acceptable."

"Excellent models for providing the necessary community support were developed as long as 25 years ago," the study commented. "One would think, then, that the quality of life of the now two million people with serious mental illness in the United States would have improved dramatically from the days of the hospital 'snake pits.'" Instead, the study found community services generally inadequate or nonexistent. Community mental health centers, in particular, drew the authors' scorn. They were depicted as typically serving the "worried well" rather than the truly mentally ill, often failing to provide needed services, and sometimes profiting illegally on government contracts. Only 30 of 575 that received construction funds "are operating as Congress originally intended." Most of them, the study added, "have been abysmal failures."

Without community support, many of the patients walked out of the mental hospitals only to become "street people," swelling the ranks of America's homeless. Typically, those who were sent back to mental hospitals were promptly released — time and again.

Prisons and jails often became de facto mental hospitals. The largest of these, the study said, was the Los Angeles County Jail, which on an average day housed 3,600 persons with serious mental illnessness — some 700 more than the nation's largest mental institution. The study drew on estimates that nationwide as many as 150,000 persons suffering from schizophrenia and manic depressive psychosis were in jails — usually on misdemeanor charges and often because the authorities had nowhere else to place them. In all, it was reported that less than half that number, some 68,000, were in the 268 state and county psychiatric hospitals.

Inadequate State Support

"Despite the fact that mental illness services have been the responsibility of state government for more than 200 years, they are usually

*neglected when state governments are being evaluated," the authors said.
To encourage such accountability, they added, the study attempted to
answer the question: "If I or a family member had a serious mental
illness, in what state would that person be most likely to receive good
public services?"*

*Vermont scored highest in the study's rankings. It was accorded
seventeen points out of twenty five on which the state programs were
judged. Rhode Island, the leader in 1988, slipped to second place in a tie
with New Hampshire. Connecticut and Ohio tied for the next-highest
rankings. Colorado, New York, North Carolina, Wisconsin, and Utah
rounded out the top ten. At the bottom of the list was Hawaii, just below
Idaho and Wyoming.*

*The study recommended that public mental health centers be required
to give priority to the care of the seriously mentally ill; those with lesser
problems would receive assistance as it became available. Other proposals
were to require professionals in mental health care to donate one hour of
their services each week to public programs; in the absence of psychiatrists, give psychologists, physician assistants, and nurse practitioners
special training to prescribe psychiatric medication; overhaul the "chaotic" funding of public services; and require administrators of public
mental health programs to spend one-half day each week working
directly with the mentally ill.*

Varied Reactions

*Among health care professionals, the study was pronounced "laudable"
in most of its conclusions. But Dr. Melvin Sabshin, its medical director,
objected to "scapegoating statements that psychiatrists have abandoned
the public sector." He said 7,000 of the association's 36,000 members
worked in federal and state clinics.*

*Harry Schnibbe, executive director of the National Association of State
Mental Health Directors, said, "We have to swallow this one, but they are
right." James K. Finley, director of governmental relations for the
National Council of Community Health Centers, said he agreed that
there were "very serious unmet needs" but portrayed the centers as
"doing a lot of good in a virtually impossible situation."*

> *Following are excerpts from the study, "Care of the Seri-
> ously Mentally Ill: A Rating of State Programs," sponsored
> by the Public Citizen Health Research Group and the
> National Alliance for the Mentally Ill, issued September 11,
> 1990, in Washington, D.C.:*

Eight Current Crises

The modern era in public services for people with serious mental
illnesses began immediately following World War II with the realization

that such illnesses were common and that state mental hospitals were on the best of days remarkably untherapeutic and on the worst of days snake pits. The response of the federal government was to create a National Institute of Mental Health, to which it gave a responsibility for research on mental illnesses and for the training of increased numbers of psychiatrists, psychologists, psychiatric social workers, and psychiatric nurses.

But services for people with serious mental illnesses remained the exclusive responsibility of state government until 1963, when Congress passed President John F. Kennedy's Community Mental Health Centers (CMHC) Act. In describing what the legislation would accomplish, the President said that "reliance on the cold mercy of custodial isolation will be supplanted by the open warmth of community concern and capability." Following passage of the CMHC Act, people with serious mental illnesses were made eligible for several other federal programs including Supplemental Security Income (SSI), Social Security Disability Income (SSDI), Medicaid and Medicare. Prior to 1963, then, states had almost total fiscal responsibility for serving their mentally ill residents; after 1963, an increasing proportion of this fiscal burden shifted from the states to the federal government. Today, the federal share of the approximately $20 billion annual public cost of services to people with mental illnesses is 40 percent, or approximately $8 billion.

The CMHC Act and subsequent efforts of federal and state governments to improve services seemed reasonable at the time and clearly were motivated by the best of intentions. These efforts coincided with the introduction of antipsychotic medication, which became widely available by the late 1950s, making deinstitutionalization of people with mental illnesses feasible. In the 30-year period from 1955 to 1984, the number of patients in public mental hospitals dropped from 552,150 to 118,647, a reduction of just under 80 percent. Hundreds of thousands of mentally ill individuals who previously had been held in custodial state mental hospitals were discharged to what was supposed to be community care. The federally funded CMHCs, income assistance programs such as SSI and SSDI, and increased numbers of mental health professionals were all going to work with state governments to provide care for these individuals. That was the way it was supposed to happen.

When one surveys the current scene, it is clear that whatever was supposed to happen did not happen and that deinstitutionalization was a disaster. Despite the approximately $20 billion per year in public funds spent on services, despite almost $3 billion in federal funds spent to create community mental health centers, despite over $2 billion in federal funds and uncounted additional billions in state funds spent to train more mental health professionals, services for people with serious mental illnesses in the United States in 1990 are the shame of the nation. The road to hell truly is lined with good intentions; the gateposts on this road are painfully evident.

1. There are more than twice as many people with schizophre-

nia and manic-depressive psychosis living in public shelters and on the streets than there are in public mental hospitals.

Estimates of the total number of homeless individuals in the United States have ranged from 300,000 to 3 million. In probably the best study done to date, the Urban Institute in Washington, D.C. in 1988 estimated that the total number was between 567,000 and 600,000. In March 1990, the United States Bureau of the Census undertook an exhaustive count of the homeless population but that count is not yet available.

There are many causes of homelessness. Most surveys have found that between 30 and 40 percent of single homeless people are alcoholics or drug addicts; some of these people have lost their housing because of their addictions (some are also mentally ill). Another important cause of homelessness is the reduced availability of low-income housing as inner cities have become gentrified and as federal support for such housing has eroded drastically (particularly in the 1980s). There are also some homeless people who have no job skills and no family support and use shelters as places to try and get their lives together.

The most controversial segment of the homeless population is the group with serious mental illnesses such as schizophrenia and manic-depressive psychosis. The question of what percentage of homeless people this group constitutes has unfortunately become a political football, with liberals arguing that it is a small percentage (and that cuts in social programs and housing are the cause of most homelessness) while conservatives contend that mentally ill people make up a large percentage (and thus that state mental health authorities, not the failure of social programs and housing, are to blame). Many of the studies done on this question have been tainted by such political preconceptions, with widely varying results.

Increasingly, however, there is a consensus that approximately 25 to 30 percent of single homeless adults living in shelters are seriously mentally ill. Studies done in the mid-1980s in Boston, Philadelphia, and Washington, D.C. reported that between 36 and 39 percent of adult shelter residents had schizophrenia. With the influx of large numbers of crack users into city shelters in many urban areas the percentage of homeless persons with schizophrenia has probably decreased. A 1988 study in Los Angeles found that 28 percent of homeless people in shelters had schizophrenia, manic-depressive psychosis, or major depression; this survey, however, failed to include the 15 percent of shelter residents who refused to cooperate, among whom there were certainly many with paranoid schizophrenia. Another 1988 California study of three counties reported that 30 percent of homeless people in shelters had a severe mental disorder. A 1989 study of homeless people in Baltimore shelters found that 31 percent of men and 41 percent of women had schizophrenia, manic-depressive psychosis, or major depression, while another 1989 study in New York reported that 17 percent of shelter residents had "a definite or probable history of psychosis" and another 8 percent "a possible history of psychosis."

For homeless individuals not living in shelters but rather in parks, alleys, abandoned buildings, doorways, subway tunnels, etc., the percentage with serious mental illness appears to be even higher than 25 to 30 percent. A study of individuals living on heating grates and on the streets of New York City estimated "that 60 percent exhibit evidence of schizophrenia as manifested by disorganized behaviour and chronic delusional thinking." In Los Angeles, a 1988 study of homeless persons (two-thirds of whom slept in places other than shelters) found that 40 percent of them had psychotic symptoms. By contrast, a study of homeless individuals living on grates and sleeping in doorways in Washington, D.C. found that only 29 percent had a history of psychiatric hospitalization as reported by the individual.

Taking all available data into consideration, it would appear that approximately 30 percent of single adult homeless individuals living either in shelters or on the streets are seriously mentally ill, mostly with schizophrenia and manic-depressive psychosis. If the total number of homeless adults is conservatively estimated to be only 500,000, then the number of seriously mentally ill homeless would be approximately 150,000 individuals. By comparison, the most recent data available on patients in the nation's 286 state and county psychiatric hospitals reveals that there are just over 68,000 patients with schizophrenia and manic-depressive psychosis. *There are, then, more than twice as many people with schizophrenia and manic-depressive psychosis living in public shelters and on the streets as there are in public mental hospitals.*

Common sense says that many of the homeless people with serious mental illnesses must be the same people who were discharged from state mental hospitals, and several studies have shown that this is so. A study carried out at the Central Ohio Psychiatric Hospital in 1985 followed 132 patients for six months after their discharge and found that within that period 36 percent of the discharged patients had become homeless. The truly alarming aspect of this study however, is that these 132 patients were not the sickest people being discharged from that hospital; another 61 discharged patients "were not medically cleared by hospital staff to participate in the study because of the severity of their psychotic behavior," and it seems likely that an even higher proportion of this group became homeless. In Massachusetts, a 1983 study of 187 patients discharged from a public psychiatric hospital found that 27 percent had been homeless at least occasionally within the previous six months. And in Los Angeles, a 1988 study of 53 homeless mentally ill individuals living on the streets, on beaches, or in parks reported that 79 percent of them had been previously hospitalized in state mental hospitals or on the psychiatric ward of general hospitals.

Having approximately 150,000 seriously mentally ill individuals living in public shelters and on the streets in 1990 in the United States, the wealthiest nation in the world, is quite an extraordinary and unacceptable state of affairs. It was, in fact, the existence of large numbers of seriously mentally ill individuals in the nation's poorhouses in the 1820s and 1830s which led to the building of state mental hospitals as a "humane" alternative. We have, in essence, returned to where we began 170 years ago; at no time in the intervening years have there been as many seriously mentally ill individuals, most receiving no treatment, living in the community.

Staying alive on the streets or in public shelters when one's mind is working normally is extremely difficult. When the mind cannot think clearly because of schizophrenia or manic-depressive psychosis, it is a living hell.

- "I know one woman who has been raped 17 times," says an official of the Central City Hospitality House in San Francisco. Infectious diseases, tuberculosis, and other untreated medical problems are endemic.
- In New York City "a homeless man, attacked by seven teenagers, was thrown over a wall and dropped about 50 feet into Riverside Park early yesterday leaving him with a fractured leg and back injuries."
- In Massachusetts, a homeless man and woman were savagely beaten to death. Such vulnerable people, editorialized a newspaper, "are the natural prey of anyone looking for some loose change, a pack of cigarettes, a bottle. They are rabbits forced to live in company with dogs." ...

There have been a few tentative steps toward solving the problem of homelessness among people with mental illness. The federal McKinney Act funds included $35 million in 1989 for mental health services for the homeless. The National Institute of Mental Health elevated the problem to "priority" status in 1989 and allocated $4.5 million for research and demonstration grants. But most care for people who are homeless and mentally ill continues to come largely on a voluntary basis from the private sector, especially the community groups, churches and synagogues that operate 90 percent of public shelters and soup kitchens. These are President Bush's 1,000 points of light, individuals who are doing their best to fill the holes left by the breakdown in public psychiatric services and by the failures of American psychiatry, psychology, and social work. The crisis of homelessness among people with mental illnesses will continue until such time as public psychiatric services are significantly improved. The private sector is doing more than its share; as *U.S. News and World Report* recently noted, "it is difficult to see ... how the thousand points of light can put out much more wattage."

2. There are more people with schizophrenia and manic-depressive psychosis in prisons and jails than in public mental hospitals.

According to the United States Department of Justice, on any given day in 1989 there were 1,042,136 individuals in the nation's prisons and jails (56,500 in federal prisons, 644,000 in state prisons, and 341,636 in local jails). Studies to ascertain how many of the prisoners have serious mental illnesses have shown varying results; a 1989 review of these studies concluded that "10 to 15 percent of prison populations ... need the services usually associated with severe or chronic mental illness." This review defined chronic mental illness as including "schizophrenia, unipolar and bipolar depression, or organic syndromes with psychotic features."

On the lower end of the scale, a study in Chicago's main jail found that only 6.4 percent of prisoners had schizophrenia, mania or major depression. A study of a prison in Maryland reported that 9.5 percent of the inmates met diagnostic criteria for schizophrenia and another 3.1 percent had a major depressive disorder.... The Los Angeles County Jail presently holds 24,000 inmates on any given day and, according to professionals who have worked there, approximately 15 percent of them have serious mental illnesses. That means that there are approximately 3,600 seriously mentally ill individuals in that jail, which is 700 more than the largest mental hospital in the United States. The Los Angeles County Jail is, *de facto*, the largest mental hospital in this country.

Given all the data it seems reasonable to conclude that approximately 10 percent of inmates in prisons and jails, or approximately 100,000 individuals, suffer from schizophrenia or manic-depressive psychosis. For comparison, there are approximately 68,000 patients with schizophrenia and manic-depressive psychosis in the nation's public mental hospitals. *Thus, there appear to be approximately 100,000 individuals with schizophrenia and manic-depressive psychosis in prisons and jails compared with approximately 68,000 in public mental hospitals....*

Prisons and jails were not created to be mental hospitals. And yet, because of the failure of public psychiatric services, prisons and jails have become *de facto* shelters of last resort for psychiatrically ill individuals. In Buffalo, when police took mentally ill individuals to the emergency unit of the local mental health center, psychiatrists refused to admit the persons 43 percent of the time. The police then charged such persons with misdemeanors and put them in jail just to get them off the streets, often for their own safety. In Oregon, a study of seriously mentally ill individuals in prisons and jails found that "in about half the cases a failed attempt at commitment had preceded the arrest." The person's family had sought help for them by trying to get them admitted to a psychiatric hospital but was turned down, often because no beds were available or because the person did not meet stringent state laws for dangerousness to self or others. The person then commits a minor crime such as trespassing, shoplifting, or disorderly conduct and ends up in jail rather than in a psychiatric hospital. In many communities public officials representing mental health and corrections spend much time and effort shuttling mentally ill individuals back and forth between the two systems. As a recent reviewer summarized the situation: "With both agencies exhibiting a 'he's yours' posture, the mentally ill offender falls through a crack, if not a gaping hole, in the system of care for the mentally ill.".

The quality of care mentally ill inmates receive in prisons and jails varies greatly. There are a few programs that provide good psychiatric care and that have been cited as models for the rest of the country; the Contra Costa County Jail in Martinez, California, the Boulder County Jail in Boulder, Colorado and the Multnomah County Jail in Portland, Oregon are examples of such programs. Much more common, however, are prisons and jails where mentally ill inmates are neglected or abused. In Arizona's maximum security prison for example, mentally ill prisoners may be "chained naked to bed posts and left there 20 hours a day for up to three days at a time," according to a 1989 report in the *Arizona Republic*. "Prison officials said the procedure is part of standard mental-health practice to keep 'self-abusive and suicidal' inmates from hurting themselves."

A major problem in providing care for the mentally ill inmates of prisons and jails is the inability of psychiatrists to give them medication because of stringent laws designed to protect prisoners from involuntary medication. Such laws do indeed protect non-mentally ill prisoners from the abuse of a "Clockwork Orange" system of chemical mind control. But the laws also make it difficult or impossible to medicate blatantly psychotic inmates who, because of their brain disease, have no insight into their illnesses or need for medication. In Kentucky, for example, the *Lexington Herald-Leader* described an inmate with paranoid schizophrenia who had refused to come out of his cell "for years." "He refuses to take psychotropic drugs, which probably could reduce his delusions, possible even eliminate them. But courts almost never allow prisons or mental hospitals to force medication."

3. Increasing episodes of violence by seriously mentally ill individuals are a consequence of not receiving treatment.

Mentally ill individuals are inherently no more violent than non-mentally ill persons. When they are treated, in fact, studies suggest that their arrest rate is *lower* than that of the average citizen. The wards of a well-run mental hospital are much safer on any given day than the streets of most cities.

When individuals with serious mental illnesses such as schizophrenia and manic-depressive psychosis are *not* treated, however, some of them will occasionally commit acts of violence. These acts may be in direct response to imagined threats (e.g. a belief that another person is going to kill him so he strikes first), delusional thinking (e.g. that another person is really the Devil in disguise), or auditory hallucinations (e.g. voices commanding the person to hurt another). The violent acts, in short, are usually part and parcel of the person's illness.

The mass exodus of people with serious mental illnesses from public mental hospitals in the last three decades has placed literally hundreds of thousands into the community. Many receive little or no treatment once they leave the hospital. As noted above, approximately 150,000 mentally ill individuals are living in public shelters or on the streets; another 100,000 are in prisons and jails, most of them charged with misdemeanors. Another several hundred thousand—nobody knows the precise number—are living with their families or by themselves. *The majority of these are receiving little or no psychiatric treatment because most public psychiatric services have broken down completely.* Occasional episodes of violence then become inevitable.

It is clear that episodes of violence by individuals with untreated serious mental illnesses are on the increase. One only has to listen to daily news reports to become aware of frequent stories about acts of violence committed by individuals identified as former mental patients. Since 1965 there have been eight separate studies documenting the rise in violent acts by untreated psychiatric patients. In one of the studies, for example, psychiatric patients in a New York City hospital in 1975 were compared with those in 1982; the latter group had significantly more encounters with the criminal justice system and almost twice as many episodes of violence toward persons.

Most such episodes need not happen if the public system of psychiatric care is operating as it should. Men like Juan Gonzalez do not arrive from outer space; most such individuals have been treated in psychiatric hospitals on multiple occasions but then released with no aftercare or follow-up. Jorge Delgado, who walked naked into St. Patrick's Cathedral in New York in 1988 and killed an elderly man, had been hospitalized psychiatrically seven times; in the six months preceding his act of violence he had been evaluated twice by psychiatrists who found no reason to commit him involuntarily for treatment....

While it is not possible to predict dangerousness with a high degree of accuracy, it *is* possible to pick out those untreated mentally ill individuals who are most likely to become violent. Recent studies have shown that the four most important predictors of dangerousness in mentally ill individuals are: (1) neurological abnormalities; (2) paranoid symptoms; (3) refusal to take medications; and (4) a history of violent behavior. The last factor is by far the most accurate predictor for future violence and yet *most mentally ill individuals with histories of violence are released to the community without aftercare or follow-up.*

This fact was frighteningly well-illustrated in a 1983 study carried out by Dr. Richard Lamb in Los Angeles. He followed up 85 mentally ill men who had been arrested and found incompetent to stand trial. Of the 85 men, 92 percent had been arrested on felony charges (murder, attempted murder, rape, armed robbery, assault with a deadly weapon), 68 percent had previous felony records, and 86 percent had previous psychiatric hospitalizations. Despite this record of psychiatric illness and felonies, two years after their arrest 54 of the 85 men had been released and, for 34 of them (40 percent), *no plan whatsoever had been made for aftercare or follow-up.*

Such situations are deplorable, needlessly endangering both the individual who is mentally ill, the person's family members who are frequent victims, and the community at large. It is further evidence of the breakdown in public psychiatric services; when the public fully recognizes the needless dangers that this breakdown in services entails, it will demand that services for people with mental illnesses be improved.

4. Mental health professionals have abandoned the public sector and patients with serious mental illnesses.

In 1945, during Congressional hearings that led to the creation of the National Institute of Mental Health (NIMH), it was said that there were only about 3,000 psychiatrists in the United States and that many of them were not fully trained. Although half of the 3,000 were employed in the public sector—mostly in state mental hospitals caring for individuals with serious mental illnesses—it was said to be very difficult to recruit psychiatrists for rural state hospitals such as Montana State Hospital or Wyoming State Hospital, each of which had only two psychiatrists on staff. The answer, everyone agreed, was to train more psychiatrists, and the fiscal responsibility for doing so was given to NIMH.

Federally funded training for mental health professionals began in 1948 with a $1.4 million program. The money was given directly to university departments of psychiatry, psychology, and psychiatric social work to support faculty salaries and pay stipends to some students. A small program was also implemented to support psychiatric nursing. By 1969 the NIMH training funds had reached $118.7 million per year and by the early 1980s, when the program was phased down, they had totalled over $2 billion. Most states supplemented the federal training funds. Virtually every mental health professional trained in the United States since 1948 has had the majority of his or her training costs subsidized by public—federal and state—funds.

From the point of view of numbers alone, the subsidized training of mental health professionals has been a huge success. In the past 45 years, psychiatrists have increased from 3,000 to 40,000, psychologists from 4,200 to 70,000, and psychiatric social workers from 2,000 to approximately 80,000. The total increase in these three professions has been more than twentyfold, during a period in which the population of the United States increased less than twofold.

From the point of view of individuals with serious mental illnesses, however, the publicly subsidized training of mental health professionals has been an abysmal failure. The reason, quite simply, is that once psychiatrists, psychologists, and psychiatric social workers were trained, almost all of them abandoned the public sector for the monetary rewards of private practice. No payback obligation was included with the subsidized training, despite assurances from federal officials during the original 1945 Congressional hearings that a payback would be built into the program; specifically, Dr. Robert Felix, who would become the first director of NIMH, testified that "I would think that a reasonable requirement of these men [sic] would be that they would spend at least one year in public service for every year they spent in training at public or state expense." However, this payback obligation was not implemented until 35 years later when federal training funds had been almost phased out.

What kinds of patients do psychiatrists, psychologists, and psychiatric social workers see in their private practices? This question was answered by a 1980 survey of mental health professionals in private practice, which found that only six percent of patients seen by psychiatrists and three percent of patients seen by psychologists had ever been hospitalized for mental illness. The authors of another survey summarized it as follows: "The [psychiatrists, psychologists, and psychiatric social workers] appeared to spend much of their time treating conditions that many people would consider minor."

And what has happened to individuals with serious mental illnesses who must rely on the public sector? Increasingly such individuals are seen by no psychiatrist at all. At the Wyoming State Hospital, for example, in 1987 *for almost a year there was no regular psychiatrist on the hospital staff at all.* In 1947, when there were 3,000 psychiatrists in the United States, the hospital had two full-time psychiatrists, but in 1987, with 40,000 psychiatrists in the nation (and 15 in the state of Wyoming), it had none. The Montana State Hospital, which had two full-time psychiatrists in the late 1940s, still had only two full-time psychiatrists in the late 1980s despite the fact that there were 37 elsewhere in the state. Both hospitals had to resort to private firms that hire out psychiatrists for exorbitant sums—the current rate is approximately $180,000 per year—and that are popularly referred to as "rent-a-shrink" companies. The director of one such firm noted in 1988: "Business is booming. We're getting requests all the time from rural areas." Under such programs it is common for a new psychiatrist to take over the wards of a state hospital as frequently as every two weeks; the consequences for continuity and quality of patient care are obvious.

It should be noted that many of these jobs for mental health professionals in the public sector pay decent salaries. A perusal of advertisements placed in 1990 in the newspaper of the American Psychiatric Association revealed annual salaries for public-sector psychiatrists ranging from $100,000 to $120,000, with liberal leave policy (up to six weeks vacation) and fringe benefits. A few, such as Wyoming State Hospital, even offer free housing. Despite this, most mental health professionals opt for the private sector where monetary rewards are greater and the patients are easier to treat.

In addition to using "rent-a-shrink" companies, public sector psychiatric facilities have filled psychiatric vacancies in the United States by hiring foreign-trained physicians. This practice became widespread in the 1970s, and it is currently estimated that approximately two-thirds of the psychiatrists in public psychiatric hospitals and clinics in the United States are foreign medical graduates. Some of these are as competent as any American medical graduate, but there is evidence from licensing examination results that many others are not. The overreliance on foreign medical graduates in public mental health facilities also raises moral issues; one of the world's wealthiest nations is hiring psychiatrists from poorer countries to fill public-sector jobs that American-trained psychiatrists have abandoned. By 1986, in fact, there were more than twice as many Indian, Pakistani, and Egyptian psychiatrists in the United States as there were in India, Pakistan, and Egypt. We should be grateful to foreign medical graduates for keeping American public psychiatric services from collapsing entirely, but we should also remember that they are needed because of the refusal of most American psychiatrists to work in the public sector.

The worst news of all, however, is that finding mental health professionals to treat patients with serious mental illnesses in public facilities is becoming increasing difficult. The primary reason for this is the explosive growth in the 1980s of for-profit psychiatric hospitals, which hire away at higher salaries the few professionals remaining in the public system. These hospitals, the majority of which are owned by the Hospital Corporation of America, National Medical Enterprises, Community Psychiatric Centers, and Charter Medical Corporation, have proliferated rapidly, especially in those states that have abandoned "certificate-of-need" laws which limit the building of new hospitals.

The profit margin of these for-profit psychiatric hospitals is very high. A major reason for this is that they accept few seriously mentally ill patients. Instead, they fill their beds with substance abusers (especially alcoholics) and teenagers who are unhappy for one reason or another. In fact, these for-profit hospitals have invented a new disease—teenagism—which coincidentally lasts only as long as the family's medical insurance benefits. Through aggressive advertising these hospitals convince parents that teenage problems are best treated by psychiatric hospitalization. "If you have a child who is out of control," the advertisement reads, "send him to us." Some of these for-profit hospitals are even starting to specialize in specific teenage problems, such as Hartgrove Hospital in Chicago, which recently set up "one of the nation's first treatment programs to wean teenagers from Satanism." John E. Halasz, M.D., Medical Director of Chicago's Institute for Juvenile Research, called the rapidly rising hospitalization of teenagers "a racket." But it is a profitable racket and in 1989 the *Wall Street Journal* said that the four major hospital chains "plan to build at least 45 more psychiatric hospitals in the next three years." The staff for these hospitals, like those built in recent years, will be drawn heavily from among the psychiatrists, psychologists, psychiatric social workers, and psychiatric nurses remaining in public-sector positions.

5. Most community mental health centers have been abysmal failures.

In 1963, Congress passed legislation setting up community mental health centers (CMHCs) with federal construction and staffing grants. The purpose of CMHCs was clearly outlined by Boisfeuillet Jones, special assistant to then Department of Health, Education and Welfare Secretary Celebrezze: "The basic purpose of the 'President's' program is to redirect the focus of treatment of the mentally ill from state mental hospitals into community mental health centers."

Since 1967 a total of 575 CMHCs have received federal construction grants ($294.7 million), and 697 CMHCs received staffing and operations grants ($2,364.6 million); the total CMHC program has thus cost $2.7 billion. CMHCs that received construction grants legally obligated themselves to provide five basic services for 20 years.

Using the federal Freedom of Information Act, the Health Research Group obtained from the National Institute of Mental Health data on CMHCs including site visit reports carried out on contract by Continuing Medical Education, Inc. A report issued in March 1990 by the Health Research Group and the National Alliance for the Mentally Ill documents the magnitude of the CMHC failure:

- Some CMHC's took federal funds but "never materialized," i.e., never even began delivering services. Others simply disappeared or went out of business. Still others are being used for completely different purposes (e.g. offices for physical therapists in private practice).
- Some CMHCs were used as private hospitals or are being run illegally by for-profit corporations such as the Hospital Corporation of America.
- Some CMHCs built swimming pools and tennis courts with the construction funds, and hired lifeguards, swimming instructors, and gardens with the staffing grants. One CMHC used federal construction funds to build both a swimming pool and a chapel, the latter presumably constructed so that seriously mentally ill individuals who were not receiving services could at least pray.
- Some CMHCs, once in operation, requested and received NIMH permission to reduce their public psychiatric beds at the same time as state and local authorities said more beds were needed.
- Many CMHCs have failed to provide "a reasonable volume of services to persons unable to pay therefor" as specified by law.
- Overall, it is estimated that approximately 140 of the 575 CMHCs, or 25 percent, are seriously out of compliance and subject to recovery of federal funds. The amount to be recovered is estimated at $50 to $100 million. Approximately another 140 CMHCs are technically out of compliance.
- Only approximately 30 CMHCs of the 575 that received construction funds (5 percent) are operating as Congress originally intended: "to redirect the focus of treatment of the mentally ill from state mental hospitals into community mental health centers."

It is important to note that a small number of federally funded CMHCs developed into excellent programs and provide quality services to individuals with serious mental illnesses. These programs further accentuate the contrast with the vast majority of CMHCs that did not develop along such lines. Among the best CMHCs identified by our survey are the following:

Aroostook MHC-Fort Fairfield, ME

Solomon MHC-Lowell, MA
Corrigan MHC-Fall River, MA
Kent County MHC-Warwick, RI
Northern Rhode Island CMHC-Woonsocket, RI
Rockland County CMHC-Pomona, NY
Shawnee Hills CMHC-Charleston, WV
Range MHC-Virginia, MN
Red Rock Comprehensive MHC-Oklahoma City, OK
Salt Lake Valley MHC-Salt Lake City, UT
San Mateo County MHC-San Mateo, CA
Spokane CMHC-Spokane, WA

Defenders of CMHCs argue that most centers are seeing large numbers of individuals with serious mental illnesses. They point to a 1988 survey carried out by the National Council of Community Mental Health Centers, the Washington lobbying office for CMHCs, which claimed that "the proportion of clients on a typical community mental health agency caseload who are seriously mentally ill averages 45 percent." What they fail to point out is that in this survey "serious mental illness" was defined as including everything under the sun, such as "passive-aggressive personality disorders" which, according to the American Psychiatric Association, is a diagnosis applied to individuals who procrastinate and dawdle and are stubborn, forgetful, and intentionally inefficient. This, says the National Council of CMHCs, is "serious mental illness." A much more accurate analysis of the patients seen in CMHCs, published by the National Institute of Mental Health in 1988, showed that *only 9 percent of individuals being treated by CMHCs had either "schizophrenia" or "other psychotic disorders."* By contrast, 20 percent were diagnosed as having "social maladjustment" or "no mental disorder."...

6. Funding of public services for individuals with serious mental illness is chaotic.

One need only visit an emergency room in any large city hospital to witness the disaster of public psychiatric services for people with serious mental illnesses. In one emergency room in New York City, individuals with schizophrenia and manic-depressive psychosis "were handcuffed to the armrests of wheelchairs Friday morning as they waited for beds ... Sometimes patients have to sleep in shifts [in the waiting area] because there is not enough room." Mental health administrators in the city blame state authorities for the lack of public psychiatric beds, while the state maintains that it is the city's responsibility. What neither says publicly is that they are playing a game of shift-the-fiscal-burden; the losers in this game are inevitably the individuals with serious mental illnesses.

The funding of public services for people with mental illnesses in the United States is an incredible pastiche of federal, state, and local sources with no overall coordination and with individual pieces that are often at odds with each other. Federal dollars, comprising approximately 40 percent of the total, include Medicaid, Medicare, Supplemental Security

Income (SSI), Social Security Disability Insurance (SSDI), block grants, and housing programs of various kinds. State and local funds for people with serious mental illnesses come from a variety of departments including mental health, social services, housing, vocational rehabilitation, and corrections. To run a department of mental health at the state or local level one needs to be primarily an accountant to keep track of the many sources of funds and what they can be used for. This chaotic funding system has grown piecemeal over the 25 years since Medicaid and Medicare were enacted; new programs have been added incrementally, with virtually no attempt made to fit the funding pieces together into a coherent whole. The system of funding public services for people with mental illnesses in the United States is, in short, more thought-disordered than most of the individuals the system is intended to serve.

At the federal level, funding programs strongly favor hospitalization for people with mental illnesses despite an official policy of deinstitutionalization. Dr. Rohn S. Friedman has called this contradiction a "psychiatric chimera—an official policy of deinstitutionalization grafted onto an everyday practice of hospitalization. Medicaid and Medicare will pay for the institutionalization of a mentally ill individual on the psychiatric ward of a general hospital or in a nursing home, but will usually not pay for maintaining the same individual in a state mental hospital. For this reason states shut down wards of state hospitals, even when the beds are clearly needed, to try to force psychiatric admissions into general hospitals or nursing homes where the federal government will cover most costs.

States publicly rationalize their action as promoting community living and a less restrictive environment for patients, but these rationalizations are often a thin veneer covering an underlying economic imperative. This was clearly demonstrated by economist William Gronfein, who published an analysis of data on deinstitutionalization from 1973 to 1975 and concluded that "Medicaid payments are very strongly associated with the amount of deinstitutionalization in the early 1970s." While the states, cities, and federal governments are playing this fiscal tug-of-war, mentally ill individuals needing hospitalization get caught in the middle, handcuffed to an emergency room wheelchair while the search for a bed continues. . . .

Another aspect of the chaotic funding of services for people with serious mental illnesses is the failure to implement and use service models that have proved effective. An example is the Louisville Homecare Project, carried out between 1961 and 1964, which showed that 77 percent of psychiatric admissions could be averted by using public health nurses to give medication in clients' homes. The use of crisis homes in Southwest Denver was another experimental program demonstrating that hospitalization rates could be reduced dramatically. Both of these programs were allowed to die because the effective mechanisms of providing service—public health nurses and crisis homes—were not reimbursable by federal Medicaid. The same is true for many model rehabilitation programs that have proven to be effective for mentally ill individuals, but which are rarely replicated because they do not fit existing federal reimbursement schemes; an example is the Fairweather Lodge, a group of mentally ill individuals who live together and operate a community business.

In all of these cases states are reluctant to use a service delivery system, no matter how effective it is, if federal programs such as Medicaid will not reimburse them for it. . . .

7. An undetermined portion of public funds for services to people with serious mental illnesses is literally being stolen.

Public programs serving people with serious mental illnesses are not generally thought of as likely venues for theft or other criminal activity. And yet such programs spend approximately $20 billion each year, much of it in government contracts with non-profit corporations, with remarkably little auditing or oversight of these expenditures. It is a situation ready-made for theft, which is usually not labeled as such; rather, among mental health professionals, as in other white-collar circles, it is euphemistically called "misappropriation of public funds."

There are many forms of theft from publicly funded programs for people with mental illness. Petty theft of personal property from mentally ill patients occurs commonly in psychiatric hospitals, facilitated by the fact that other patients can be blamed and the victims themselves are often so confused that they cannot assist in pinpointing when the property was taken. Another common form of petty theft in programs for people with mental illnesses is some mental health professionals' practice of seeing private patients during the same time as they are being paid to see public patients; this has become widespread and implicitly condoned as it has become increasingly difficult to recruit mental health professionals to public-sector jobs. This is in essence the theft of time, the cost of which adds up very quickly since such professionals are comparatively well paid.

We can only guess how frequently larger "misappropriation of public funds" occurs in the delivery system for public psychiatric services. In the few instances when it has been looked for, it has often been found, sometimes glaringly obvious and undetected for years by officials who were performing virtually no oversight function. . . .

8. Guidelines for serving people with mental illnesses are often made at both the federal and state level by administrators who have had no experience in this field.

The actual care of people with mental illnesses in the United States takes place in hundreds of hospitals and thousands of outpatient clinics and rehabilitation programs. Decisions about how such care should be provided, however, is often determined by guidelines established by federal and state administrators in such programs as Supplemental Security Income (SSI), Social Security Disability Income (SSDI), Medicaid, Medicare, the Community Support Program (CSP), Department of Housing and Urban Development (HUD) programs, and special grant programs such as the Stewart B. McKinney Homeless Assistance Act.

These guidelines determine which services will be funded or reimbursed by the federal or state government and which will not; since federal and state funds comprise approximately 90 percent of the funds supporting public mental illness services, the guidelines in effect determine both what care will be given and how it will be given.

One of the biggest frustrations for professionals working hands-on with mentally ill people in hospitals and clinics is trying to tailor their treatment decisions to meet federal and state guidelines. For example, for a senior citizen with schizophrenia who needs an injection every three weeks, a home visit by a nurse to give the injection is not reimbursable by Medicare, but a visit to a clinic for the injection is reimbursable. In a rural area with no public transportation, the difference between these services often is critical. Most professionals who provide direct service to mentally ill individuals have long suspected that many administrators who set the guidelines for federal and state reimbursement have had no personal experience providing direct services to people with mental illnesses and do not know what they are talking about. In most cases this turns out to be precisely the case.

At the federal level, for example, crucial decisions regarding Medicaid reimbursement for services to people with mental illnesses are made in the sprawling headquarters of the Social Security Administration in Baltimore. Since Medicaid is the single largest source of public funds for mental illness services in the United States, it might be expected that the government's theoretical think-tank on such matters, the National Institute of Mental Health (NIMH), would have expertise to contribute and input into Medicaid decisions. In fact, NIMH has virtually no input to the Medicaid funding decisions made by the Social Security Administration.

NIMH itself is virtually devoid of professionals who have had practical, hands-on experience working with seriously mentally ill individuals in the public sector beyond the brief and in some cases ephemeral exposure during their professional training, which often took place a decade or two ago. Despite having administered the $3 billion community mental health center (CMHC) program for more than 22 years, as well as the multimillion dollar Community Support Program for the past 13 years, NIMH has almost no professional staff who can speak from experience in treating individuals with serious mental illnesses in the public sector....

The situation at the state level is only modestly better than at the federal level. In each state, the most important official in determining policies for state programs serving people with mental illnesses is the director of the state department of mental health. As of May 1990, only about 20 percent of such directors had ever had any clinical experience in treating people with mental illness. With respect to professional background, the current group of state mental health directors includes two psychiatrists, 13 psychologists, eight social workers, two lawyers, one person with a degree in education, two people with degrees in public administration, and 23 people without advanced degrees but with administrative experience in state government. Only a handful of them have extensive experience working with people with mental illnesses. . . .

In probably no other area of federal or state government—including education, corrections, social services, and transportation—has the primary responsibility for programs been turned over to administrators who have so little academic training or practical experience in the relevant field. Public programs for people with serious mental illnesses are unique in the degree to which responsibility for them has been assigned to individuals who do not know what they are talking about. Good intentions are not a sufficient qualification for important positions in this field.

Six Proposals to Improve Services

. . . Given the dimensions of the current disaster, it is clear that mere tinkerings with the status quo will not produce significant improvement. The time for exhortations, admonitions, and white-haired commissions to study the problem is past. The time has come for action that will directly address the problems and lead to measurable improvements. The following are recommendations for such action.

1. Public mental health programs must serve people with serious mental illness as a priority; if less than 75 percent of a program's resources are going to this group, its state and federal subsidies should be terminated.

The abysmal failure of most public mental health programs to serve individuals with serious mental illness is a major reason why so many such individuals are in shelters and on the streets, in prisons and jails, and involved in episodic incidents of violence. Mental health programs cannot solve all the personal and social problems in the world although many of them aspire to do so. When mental health programs spend the majority of their resources on counseling individuals who do not have serious mental illnesses, providing stress management courses, and related activities, it is individuals with serious mental illnesses who are left without services.

The elements of good services for individuals with serious mental illnesses are well known but rarely put into practice. There must be a system of coordinated care between hospitals and outpatient units with unified administrative and fiscal management. There must be assertive case management with continuity of cases such as is found in Wisconsin's PACT model and in continuous treatment teams. Hospital admissions and readmissions must be coordinated through a single community entity, and crisis beds and other alternatives to hospitalization must be available. For individuals who have little insight into their illnesses and need medication to remain well, outpatient commitment or guardianship must be available. Housing, rehabilitation and vocational opportunities must all be integral parts of the system.

State legislatures can easily ensure treatment for people with serious mental illnesses, including those homeless and in jails, by decreeing that they must have priority for services in all state-supported mental health programs. If such programs fail to allocate and expend a minimum of 75 percent of their resources to serve such patients, state funds should be automatically terminated. States should conduct independent financial and performance audits to ensure that these standards are met. The federal government can do random audits of federal block grant funds that still go to many mental health centers, but these constitute a much smaller proportion of mental health center funds than do state monies, so federal pressure would be less effective than state pressure. For the 575 CMHC's that received federal construction funds, the National Institute of Mental Health must follow through on the site visits and follow-up that are underway and recover funds that have been misallocated by many of the CMHC's.

2. All psychiatrists, psychologists, and psychiatric social workers should be required to donate, pro bono, one hour a week of work to public programs. Federal and state-supported training programs for such professionals should include an automatic payback obligation.

The current deluge of untreated seriously mentally ill individuals on the nation's streets is an emergency situation just as surely as is the flooding of a river. As such, it calls for emergency measures. One such measure available to all states is to require each psychiatrist, psychologist and psychiatric social worker to donate one hour each week *pro bono* to public services for people with serious mental illnesses. The requirement could be instituted easily as a stipulation for continued state licensure to practice; that is, professionals would not be allowed to practice their profession in the state unless they did. Many professionals should be assigned to shelters and jails for their *pro bono* work. For those who have lost their skills in treating such patients, the state should offer refresher courses.

The major argument against such a *pro bono* work requirement for mental health professionals is that it is coercive and therefore violates individual liberty. Yet the legal profession has had a tradition of voluntary *pro bono* work that continues to be effective. The medical profession also once had such a tradition, but it has weakened considerably in recent years; Dr. James E. Davis, 1989 president of the American Medical Association, urged all physicians to donate four hours of work *pro bono* each week, arguing that since taxpayers subsidized their medical education the physicians had "a basic responsibility to see that they take care of the poor and needy of their community."

The mental health professions, however, have never had such a tradition. One reason for this undoubtedly was Sigmund Freud's admonition that unless the patient is paying for psychotherapy it will not be effective; this has provided a reliable rationalization for not seeing patients who cannot pay. A laudable attempt by the Mental Health Association of Colorado to get mental health professionals to work *pro bono* with homeless mentally ill individuals in Denver's shelters has been largely a failure; despite intensive recruitment efforts, at the end of three years there were only 18 professionals contributing any time (three psychiatrists, six psychologists, five social workers, and four nurses). Those who argue that such *pro bono* work is an infringement on professionals' liberties should weigh this against the disease-caused infringement of liberties that untreated mentally ill individuals must live with each day.

There should also be an automatic payback obligation built into all state and federally supported training programs for mental health professionals. That there is not such an obligation in most programs, given the shortage of professionals in public-sector jobs, is incomprehensible. With an automatic payback built into such training programs, state legislatures would be more likely to support their funding.

3. Since psychiatrists have abandoned the public sector, psychologists, physician assistants and nurse practitioners should be given special training and allowed to prescribe psychiatric medication. This program should initially be piloted in three to five states.

The abandonment of public clinics and state hospitals by psychiatrists has been one of the most striking developments in American psychiatry in the past three decades. As we stated in Chapter 1, it is virtually impossible to hire psychiatrists for most public positions despite salaries that are often above $100,000 per year with liberal fringe benefits. The lack of well-trained psychiatrists has had a devastating impact on services for mentally ill individuals, both those in hospitals and those being served by outpatient clinics. Many patients are overmedicated or improperly medicated, kept on the same medications for years even though it is not effective, or not properly monitored for signs of tardive dyskinesia.

When applicants do appear for public-sector jobs serving people with mental illness, they are sometimes professionals who have problems such as alcohol or drug addiction or who have lost their licenses to practice in other states because of unethical behavior. Even more disturbing is the fact that the situation is likely to worsen as for-profit psychiatric hospitals continue to proliferate and hire away the few competent professionals remaining in the public sector.

One solution to this crisis is to use specially trained psychologists, physician assistants and nurse practitioners to fill vital psychiatric jobs in the public sector. All three of these groups have had some medical training, which could be supplemented by additional training programs. Individuals selected for such programs should already have had at least three years of experience working with individuals with serious mental illnesses. After completing a training program and fulfilling special certification requirements, psychologists, physician assistants and nurse practitioners could diagnose and prescribe from a limited formulary of commonly used medications (e.g. four antipsychotics, two antidepressants, lithium and carbamazepine). The few psychiatrists still in the public sector could provide supervision and treat people with treatment-resistant or more complicated illnesses. Annual recertification and training of these practitioners should be required. Such individuals could presumably be hired at salaries considerably less than the $100,000+ now required for psychiatrists, so more professionals could be hired for the same amount of money. A proposal to allow psychologists to prescribe medication in Department of Defense facilities has already been put forth by Senator Daniel K. Inouye of Hawaii and also introduced in the Hawaii state legislature, so such ideas are not entirely new. The current crisis in care demands that we at least try this strategy as a pilot program in a few states.

4. The chaotic funding of public services for individuals with serious mental illnesses needs a total overhaul.

Public services for individuals with serious mental illnesses are shaped by the availability of federal funds, especially Medicaid, to reimburse states for specific services. The system is a massive game of shift-the-fiscal burden played between states and the federal government, states and county governments, states and city governments, and different agencies within state governments. It is a game that nobody is winning and which individuals with serious mental illnesses most definitely are losing.

After 35 years of deinstitutionalization, one of the largest social experiments in American history, it is time to go back to the drawing board and re-evaluate the economics of the system. What is the proper mix of federal, state and local funding? How can levels of government and different departments be encouraged to cooperate toward the common goal of better services? Innovative funding strategies should be strongly encouraged and closely evaluated. These might include prepaid and HMO financing schemes, other forms of capitation funding, and plans that reimburse more for better outcomes. Especially interesting are proposals to consolidate federal and state funds under a single authority in each state, which could then decide which services to fund based on the clinical needs of seriously mentally ill individuals, not merely based on how the fiscal burden can be shifted to another level of government. In the past 35 years we have learned much about what works and what does not work, yet we persist in doing the latter. If mentally ill people persisted in behavior as self-defeating as that of the current public psychiatric system, we would accept it as evidence of continuing illness. Until we address the economic aspects of the present system of care of individuals with serious mental illnesses, things are not likely to improve significantly.

5. Budgets of public mental illness programs should be examined for possible theft.

There is no way to estimate how much money allocated for public mental illness programs is currently being stolen. The instances that have come to light suggest strongly that such theft is relative easy to accomplish and that federal, state and local authorities are engaging in virtually no oversight to detect it.

We recommend that public programs for people with mental illnesses be scrutinized much more closely than has heretofore been the case for possible theft of funds. Each dollar diverted for personal use is a dollar not available for badly needed services. States with a tradition of corruption in state and local government, including New York, Illinois, Florida, Hawaii, Louisiana, West Virginia, and the District of Columbia, should be examined especially vigorously. An excellent model for such investigations is the New York State Commission on Quality of Care for the Mentally Disabled, an independent state watchdog agency set up in 1977, which describes itself as "an overseer of New York's mental hygiene system and as an advocate for people with disabilities." For information write to the Commission on Quality of Care for the Mentally Disabled, 99 Washington Avenue, Albany, New York 12210.

6. All administrators of public programs for people with mental illness should spend at least one-half day each week working with mentally ill people.

A major failing of virtually all administrators of programs for people with serious mental illness is that they have lost touch with the consumers of their services. Departments of mental health become increasingly insulated from the real world of services, rehabilitation, and housing with ever more bureaucratic encrustations added over time like barnacles on a sunken ship. All of this can be remedied simply and at no additional expense by requiring that all employees of local, state, and federal agencies responsible for mental illness programs spend one-half day each week in the community, in clinics, or on hospital wards delivering services.

Administrators who have not been trained as mental health professionals can be assigned to companionship programs like Compeer, in which they would do things like go shopping or to the movies with a mentally ill person, teach him or her how to ride the bus, or help him or her to apply for a job or a driver's license. No administrator—including state mental health commissioners, the director of the National Institute of Mental Health, and the state and federal directors of Medicaid—should be exempt from this requirement. The time lost from bureaucratic activities would be more than paid for by the time spent and experience gained in service delivery. More importantly, the remaining four and one-half days a week of administrative duties would be carried out much more effectively because of the enrichment provided by the administrator's clinical duties. This is one of the simplest, least expensive and most important steps that could be taken to improve services for people with serious mental illness.

[Chapters 3 and 4 omitted]

Ratings of States

Overall Ratings

Vermont, with 17 out of a possible 25 points, is the leading state in providing public care to people with serious mental illnesses. Although far from ideal, especially in its inpatient services, Vermont sets a standard for

1990 Ratings of States

Total points (of 25)	1990 Rank:	State	Total points (of 25)	1990 Rank:	State
17	1:	Vermont	8	26:	Arkansas
16	2:	New Hampshire			Georgia
		Rhode Island			Michigan
15	4:	Connecticut			North Dakota
		Ohio			South Carolina
			7	31:	California
14	6:	Colorado			District of
12	7:	New York			Columbia
		North Carolina			Illinois
		Wisconsin			Indiana
11	10:	Utah			Kansas
10	11:	Delaware			Oklahoma
		Maine			Tennessee
		Oregon	6	38:	Arizona
		Pennsylvania			Florida
		Virginia			Iowa
9	16:	Alabama			Louisiana
		Alaska			New Mexico
		Kentucky			South Dakota
		Maryland			West Virginia
		Massachusetts	5	45:	Nevada
		Minnesota			Texas
		Missouri	4	47:	Mississippi
		Nebraska			Montana
		New Jersey	3	49:	Idaho
		Washington			Wyoming
			2	51:	Hawaii

modest respectability that makes reasonably good care for the majority of its citizens with serious mental illnesses a real possibility. However, even Vermont's score of 17 was only 68 percent of the 25 possible points it could have achieved. Rhode Island, the leader in the 1988 state survey, tied for second place with New Hampshire, with 16 points; both Rhode Island and New Hampshire scored very low (1 point) for services to seriously emotionally disturbed children, providing Vermont (which got 3 points for children's services) with its margin of victory.

Connecticut and Ohio tied for fourth place, each with 15 points, and Colorado followed in sixth position with 14 points. It should be noted that all six of these states received 4 out of 5 points for at least one of the five services being rated; as a group they accounted for 13 of the 15 "4's" received by all 50 states and the District of Columbia.

Since the possible total score was 25, these six states (Vermont, Rhode Island, New Hampshire, Connecticut, Ohio, Colorado) were the only ones in the country to achieve a score of more than 50 percent (more than 12.5 points) of the possible 25. In other words, all other states (44 plus the District of Columbia) failed to get even one-half of the total possible points, clearly pointing out the failure of most states' services for people with serious mental illness. The average state score—8.6 points—represents only 24.4 percent of the possible 25 points.

At the other end of the ratings, Hawaii finished last, as it did in the state surveys of both 1986 and 1988, achieving only 2 (eight percent) out of a possible 25 points. Idaho and Wyoming tied for 49th with 3 points each, Montana and Mississippi tied for 47th with 4 points each, and Texas and Nevada tied for 45th with 5 points each. As might be expected in states with such low total scores, these seven lowest states each scored 0 points for at least one of the five services, and in fact, Wyoming and Hawaii each scored 0 for three services, a disgraceful record. As a group, these seven states accounted for 12 of the 15 "0's" given to all states. . . .

Just as there are a few states at the top that do reasonably well, there are a few others at the bottom that offer truly dreadful public services to individuals with serious mental illnesses. More than half of the states, however, are bunched together with between 6 and 9 points out of a possible 25 points in what may be described as pack mediocrity. Because of this phenomenon, a state (e.g. Kentucky or Massachusetts) can be rated as tied for 16th with as few as 9 points while Vermont, in first place, has almost twice as many points. Thus, all 10 states that tied for 16th position with 9 points are actually closer to Hawaii (2 points) at the bottom than they are to Vermont (17 points) at the top.

Another problem in interpreting the results is that the population of the state must be taken into consideration. The logistics of organizing services in California or New York are very different from the logistics in Rhode Island or North Dakota. . . . In the small states, care for individuals with serious mental illnesses was either good (Vermont, New Hampshire, and Rhode Island—the top three states) or below average. With the exception of #11 Delaware (10 points) and the above three states, all small states had fewer than 9 points, ranking 26th through 51st. Centralized organization of services, for better or worse, is more possible in smaller states. This is true to a lesser degree in the medium-sized states. Combining small and medium-sized states, six of the 10 top-ranked states were in this size category as were six of the seven bottom-ranked states.

Conversely, in larger states, it appears to be more difficult to organize a top-rated program (#4 Ohio notwithstanding) or to get away with a bottom-ranked program (#45 Texas notwithstanding). This argues strongly for decentralization, in an accountable way, of the mental health authority in larger states.

How should the results be interpreted? It should be emphasized that although states like Vermont, New Hampshire and Rhode Island achieve respectable public services for residents with serious mental illnesses, such services are still far from excellent. Most states provide such poor services, in fact, that it is possible for a state to rank near the top and still be doing only modestly by any meaningful standard. . . .

TREATY ON GERMAN REUNIFICATION
September 12, 1990

The Big Four victors of World War II signed away their occupational rights to Germany on September 12, clearing the way for East Germany and West Germany formally to reunite as a single nation on October 3. (Reunification of East and West Germany, p. 681) The treaty-signing ceremony came forty-five years after a defeated Germany was divided into spheres of occupation by American, British, French, and Soviet forces. The Federal Republic (West Germany) later emerged in the western zones and the People's Republic (East Germany) in the eastern, Soviet-controlled, zone. Berlin, although lying within the Soviet zone, was divided between East and West.

Foreign ministers of the four Allied powers and the two Germanys took turns signing the document at the Oktyabrskaya Hotel in Moscow, as Soviet President Mikhail S. Gorbachev looked on with approval. His acquiescence in East Germany's complete break from Soviet control averted the possibility of bloodshed, thereby paving the way for reunification.

German authorities insisted that the "Treaty on the Final Settlement With Respect to Germany," its formal title, was not a peace treaty. This united Germany had been achieved peacefully, they noted, unlike the first united Germany that Otto von Bismarck proclaimed in 1871. West German chancellor Helmut Kohl said it was "the first unification of a country in modern history achieved without war, pain or strife."

Opening a New Era

Not only did the treaty remove the last legal vestiges of the 1945 Potsdam Treaty by which Germany was divided into occupational zones;

599

it was viewed as the end of one era of European history and the beginning of another. "We have drawn a line under World War II and we have started keeping the time of a new age," said Foreign Minister Eduard A. Shevardnadze after signing the treaty for the Soviet Union. As expressed by a New York Times *analyst, "[T]he European powers were laying the groundwork for a new European order, with a potent, wealthy Germany at its heart. Perhaps more clearly than any previous event, the treaty demonstrated the retreat of Communism from Europe."*

"The new Germany is here," said Secretary of State James A. Baker III, upon signing for the United States. "Let our legacy be that after forty-five years, we finally got the political arithmetic right. Two plus four adds up to one Germany in a Europe whole and free." Baker referred to "two-plus-four" negotiations, first between the two Germanys and then among the four occupying powers, whose foreign ministers had met in February in Ottawa, Canada, and announced a negotiating framework. Their action coincided with Moscow's acceptance of a proposal by President George Bush for Soviet and American troop reductions in Europe.

The Ottawa meeting tacitly recognized that reunification had seemed inevitable since the previous November. At that time East Germany ceased trying to stop an outflow of its people into West Germany through neighboring countries and opened the Berlin Wall, which for twenty-eight years had been a visible symbol of a divided Germany and the Cold War. (Statements on the Berlin Wall and German Reunification, Historic Documents of 1989, p. 625)

Prelude to a Treaty

The Communist government collapsed and East Germans voted March 18 in their first free election since 1933. They strongly supported candidates who called for prompt unification. The voting quickened the reunification process, resulting in the beginning of a formal economic union on July 1. Among other measures, East Germans gave up their weak currency in exchange for the strong West German mark. On August 31, the two governments signed a lengthy treaty that spelled out in detail a merger of their legal systems.

Outside of Germany, the key missing pieces in the unification drive were Soviet approval of a united Germany remaining in the North Atlantic Treaty Organization (NATO) and a German renunciation of any claims to the territory east of the Oder and Neisse Rivers, which marked the East German-Polish border. At a summit meeting of NATO leaders in Brussels in July, the alliance declared it had no aggressive intention toward the Soviet Union and extended a hand of friendship.

That declaration cleared the way for Gorbachev, in a subsequent meeting with Kohl, to drop his objection to Germany's membership in NATO. The West German chancellor, destined to lead the united German government, agreed to reduce German troop strength to 375,000 by 1994 and to give Moscow until then to withdraw the last of its 380,000 troops from eastern Germany.

During that time all NATO forces, German or foreign, would be excluded from eastern Germany. Afterward, German but not foreign NATO-affiliated troops could be stationed there, but all nuclear weapons would be prohibited. Kohl further agreed for Germany to pay the Soviet Union $7.5 billion to house and resettle its returning soldiers. Hans-Dietrich Genscher, the West German foreign minister, said that was "the price of unity."

Soviet-German Friendship Treaty

Germany and the Soviet Union initialed a friendship treaty on September 13 pledging the two countries not to use force against each other and to "honor without reservation the territory of all European states in their current borders." A German government spokesman said the signing and ratification of the treaty would await the conclusion of similar nonaggression treaties among all the member nations of NATO and the Warsaw Pact later in the year. The initialing ceremony was held one day after the signing of the treaty on occupational rights. Shevardnadze initialed the pact for the Soviet Union and Foreign Minister Hans-Dietrich Genscher for Germany. It was signed by Gorbachev and Kohl in Bonn on November 9.

This treaty was more comprehensive than the 1970 treaty obtained by West German chancellor Willy Brandt. The 1990 treaty specified, for instance, that if one side was attacked by a third nation, the other would not aid the aggressor and would seek a settlement of the conflict through the United Nations or some other collective security arrangement. Furthermore, the German and Soviet foreign ministers would meet twice a year to seek "binding, effective and verifiable agreements for significant reductions in armed forces and armaments, to attain a stable balance at low levels, especially in Europe, suitable for defense but not for attack."

Soviet, Polish Security Guarantees

As for Poland, domestic German politics long had caused Kohl to hesitate in making an outright renunciation of land claims. But at last on July 17, at a meeting of the two-plus-four foreign ministers in Paris, both East German and West German authorities pledged to guarantee the existing border. These pledges were stated in a treaty that Genscher signed in Warsaw November 14 on behalf of a newly reunited German state.

Many of the provisions in the German settlement treaty with Moscow aimed to satisfy the security concerns of the Soviet Union, which lost 20 million people during the struggle with Germany in World War II. "It is no secret that the German 'issue, for well-known reasons, has been sensitive for the Soviet people and the people of Europe," Shevardnadze said after the treaty signing. "There are widespread concerns that the new country will do damage to Soviet security and the security of Europe.

We took that into account, and I believe we have received all the necessary safeguards and guarantees."

Foreign Minister Genscher said: "In this hour, we remember the victims of the war and totalitarian domination—not only the people represented here in Moscow. We are particularly thinking of the Jewish people. We would not want their agony to ever be repeated." Appended to the treaty, at Moscow's insistence, was a letter signed by Genscher and Prime Minister Lothar de Maizière of East Germany committing a united Germany to a ban on Nazi political parties and protection of Soviet war memorials.

Following is the "Treaty on the Final Settlement With Respect to Germany," ceding full sovereignty to a united Germany; an agreed minute to that treaty; a letter from the foreign ministers of the two Germanys; and the Soviet-German treaty; all from September 12, 1990:

TREATY ON THE FINAL SETTLEMENT WITH RESPECT TO GERMANY

The Federal Republic of Germany, the German Democratic Republic, the French Republic, the Union of Soviet Socialist Republics, the United Kingdom of Great Britain and Northern Ireland and the United States of America,

Conscious of the fact that their peoples have been living together in peace since 1945;

Mindful of the recent historic changes in Europe which make it possible to overcome the division of the continent;

Having regarded to the rights and responsibilities of the Four Powers relating to Berlin and to Germany as a whole, and the corresponding wartime and post-war agreements and decisions of the Four Powers;

Resolved in accordance with their obligations under the Charter of the United Nations to develop friendly relations among nations based on respect for the principle of equal rights and self-determination of peoples, and to take other appropriate measures to strengthen universal peace;

Recalling the principles of the Final Act of the Conference on Security and Cooperation in Europe, signed in Helsinki;

Recognizing that those principles have laid firm foundations for the establishment of a just and lasting peaceful order in Europe;

Determined to take account of everyone's security interests;

Convinced of the need finally to overcome antagonism and to develop cooperation in Europe;

Confirming their readiness to reinforce security, in particular by adopting effective arms control, disarmament and confidence-building measures; their willingness not to regard each other as adversaries but to work for a relationship of trust and cooperation; and accordingly their readiness to consider positively setting up appropriate institutional arrangements within the framework of the Conference on Security and Cooperation in Europe;

Welcoming the fact that the German people, freely exercising their right of self-determination, have expressed their will to bring about the unity of Germany as a state so that they will be able to serve the peace of the world as an equal and sovereign partner in a united Europe;

Convinced that the unification of Germany as a state with definitive borders is a significant contribution to peace and stability in Europe;

Intending to conclude the final settlement with respect to Germany;

Recognizing that thereby, and with the unification of Germany as a democratic and peaceful state, the rights and responsibilities of the Four Powers relating to Berlin and to Germany as a whole lose their function;

Represented by their Ministers for Foreign Affairs who, in accordance with the Ottawa Declaration of February 13, 1990, met in Bonn on May 5, 1990, in Berlin on June 22, 1990, in Paris on July 17, 1990 with the participation of the Minister for Foreign Affairs of the Republic of Poland, and in Moscow on September 12, 1990;

Have agreed as follows:

Article 1

1. The united Germany shall comprise the territory of the Federal Republic of Germany, the German Democratic Republic and the whole of Berlin. Its external borders shall be the borders of the Federal Republic of Germany and the German Democratic Republic and shall be definitive from the date on which the present Treaty comes into force. The confirmation of the definitive nature of the borders of the united Germany is an essential element of the peaceful order in Europe.
2. The united Germany and the Republic of Poland shall confirm the existing border between them in a treaty that is binding under international law.
3. The united Germany has no territorial claims whatsoever against other states and shall not assert any in the future.
4. The Governments of the Federal Republic of Germany and the German Democratic Republic shall ensure that the constitution of the united Germany does not contain any provision incompatible with these principles. This applies accordingly to the provisions laid down in the preamble, the second sentence of Article 23, and Article 146 of the Basic Law for the Federal Republic of Germany.
5. The Governments of the French Republic, the Union of Soviet Socialist Republics, the United Kingdom of Great Britain and Northern Ireland and the United States of America take formal note of the corresponding commitments and declarations by the Governments of the Federal Republic of Germany and the German Democratic Republic and declare that their implementation will confirm the definitive nature of the united Germany's borders.

Article 2

The governments of the Federal Republic of Germany and the German Democratic Republic reaffirm their declarations that only peace will emanate from German soil. According to the constitution of the united Germany, acts tending to and undertaken with the intent to disturb the peaceful relations between nations, especially to prepare for aggressive war, are unconstitutional and a punishable offense. The governments of the Federal Republic of Germany and the German Democratic Republic declare that the united Germany will never employ any of its weapons except in accordance with its constitution and the Charter of the United Nations.

Article 3

1. The Governments of the Federal Republic of Germany and the German Democratic Republic reaffirm their renunciation of the manufacture and possession of and control over nuclear, biological and chemical weapons. They declare that the united Germany, too, will abide by these commitments. In particular, rights and obligations arising from the Treaty on the Non-Proliferation of Nuclear Weapons of July 1, 1968 will continue to apply to the united Germany.

2. The government of the Federal Republic of Germany, acting in full agreement with the Government of the German Democratic Republic, made the following statement on August 30, 1990 in Vienna at the Negotiations on Conventional Armed Forces in Europe:

   "The Government of the Federal Republic of Germany undertakes to reduce the personnel strength of the armed forces of the united Germany to 370,000 (ground, air and naval forces) within three to four years. This reduction will commence on the entry into force of the first CFE agreement. Within the scope of this overall ceiling no more than 345,000 will belong to the ground and air forces which, pursuant to the agreed mandate, alone are the subject of the Negotiations on Conventional Armed Forces in Europe. The federal government regards its commitment to reduce ground and air forces as a significant German contribution to the reduction of conventional armed forces in Europe. It assumes that in follow-on negotiations the other participants in the negotiations, too, will render their contribution to enhancing security and stability in Europe, including measures to limit personnel strengths."

   The government of the German Democratic Republic has expressly associated itself with this statement.

3. The governments of the French Republic, the Union of Soviet Socialist Republics, the United Kingdom of Great Britain and Northern Ireland and the United States of America take note of these statements by the [two German] governments....

Article 4

1. The governments of the Federal Republic of Germany, the German Democratic Republic and the Union of Soviet Socialist Republics

state that the united Germany and the Union of Soviet Socialist Republics will settle by treaty the conditions for and the duration of the presence of Soviet armed forces on the territory of the present German Democratic Republic and of Berlin, as well as the conduct of the withdrawal of these armed forces which will be completed by the end of 1994, in connection with the implementation of the undertaking of the Federal Republic of Germany and the German Democratic Republic referred to in paragraph 2 of Article 3 of the present treaty.

2. The governments of the French Republic, the United Kingdom of Great Britain and Northern Ireland and the United States of America take note of this statement.

Article 5

1. Until the completion of the withdrawal of the Soviet armed forces from the territory of the present German Democratic Republic and of Berlin in accordance with Article 4 of the present treaty, only German territorial defense units which are not integrated into the alliance structures to which German armed forces in the rest of German territory are assigned will be stationed in the territory as armed forces of the united Germany. During that period and subject to the provisions of paragraph 2 of this Article, armed forces of other states will not be stationed in that territory or carry out any other military activity there.

2. For the duration of the presence of Soviet armed forces in the territory of the present German Democratic Republic and of Berlin, armed forces of the French Republic, the United Kingdom of Great Britain and Northern Ireland and the United States of America will, upon German request, remain stationed in Berlin by agreement to this effect between the government of the united Germany and the governments of the states concerned. The number of troops and the amount of equipment of all non-German armed forces stationed in Berlin will not be greater than at the time of signature of the present treaty. New categories of weapons will not be introduced there by non-German armed forces. The government of the united Germany will conclude with the governments of those states which have armed forces stationed in Berlin treaties with conditions which are fair taking account of the relations existing with the states concerned.

3. Following the completion of the withdrawal of the Soviet armed forces from the territory of the present German Democratic Republic and of Berlin, units of German armed forces assigned to military alliance structures in the same way as those in the rest of German territory may also be stationed in that part of Germany, but without nuclear weapon carriers. This does not apply to conventional weapon systems which may have other capabilities in addition to conventional ones but which in that part of Germany are equipped for a conventional role and designated only for such. Foreign armed forces

605

and nuclear weapons or their carriers will not be stationed in that part of Germany or deployed there.

Article 6

The right of the united Germany to belong to alliances, with all the rights and responsibilities arising therefrom, shall not be affected by the present treaty.

Article 7

1. The French Republic, the Union of Soviet Socialist Republics, the United Kingdom of Great Britain and Northern Ireland and the United States of America hereby terminate their rights and responsibilities relating to Berlin and to Germany as a whole. As a result, the corresponding, related quadripartite agreements, decisions and practices are terminated and all related Four Power institutions are dissolved.
2. The united Germany shall have accordingly full sovereignty over its internal and external affairs.

Article 8

1. The present treaty is subject to ratification or acceptance as soon as possible. On the German side it will be ratified by the united Germany. The treaty will therefore apply to the united Germany.
2. The instruments of ratification or acceptance shall be deposited with the government of the united Germany. That government shall inform the governments of the other contracting parties of the deposit of each instrument of ratification or acceptance.

Article 9

The present Treaty shall enter into force for the united Germany, the French Republic, the Union of Soviet Socialist Republics, the United Kingdom of Great Britain and Northern Ireland and the United States of America on the date of deposit of the last instrument of ratification or acceptance by these states.

Article 10

The original of the present treaty, of which the English, French, German and Russian texts are equally authentic, shall be deposited with the government of the Federal Republic of Germany, which shall transmit certified true copies to the governments of the other contracting parties.

AGREED MINUTE TO THE TREATY

Any questions with respect to the application of the word "deployed" as used in the last sentence of paragraph 3 of Article 5 will be decided by the government of the united Germany in a reasonable and responsible way taking into account the security interests of each contracting party as set forth in the preamble.

For the Federal Republic of Germany
Hans-Dietrich Genscher

For the German Democratic Republic
Lothar de Maizière

For the French Republic
Roland Dumas

For the Union of Soviet Socialist Republics
Eduard Shevardnadze

For the United Kingdom of Great Britain and Northern Ireland
Douglas Hurd

For the United States of America
James W. Baker III

GENSCHER AND MAIZIERE LETTER

[to the foreign ministers of the United States, France, Great Britain and the Soviet Union]

Mr. Foreign Minister,

In connection with the signing today of the Treaty on the Final Settlement with Respect to Germany, we would like to inform you that the governments of the Federal Republic of Germany and the German Democratic Republic declared the following in the negotiations.

1. The Joint Declaration of June 15, 1990, by the governments of the Federal Republic of Germany and the German Democratic Republic on the settlement of outstanding property matters contains, inter alia, the following observations:

    The expropriations effected on the basis of occupation law or sovereignty (between 1945 and 1949) are irreversible. The governments of the Soviet Union and the German Democratic Republic do not see any means of revising the measures taken then. The government of the Federal Republic of Germany takes note of this in the light of the historical development. It is of the opinion that a final decision on any public compensation must be reserved for a future all-German parliament.
    According to Article 41(1) of the treaty of August 31, 1990, between the Federal Republic of Germany and the German Democratic Republic establishing German unity (Unification Treaty), the aforementioned Joint Declaration forms an integral part of the Treaty. Pursuant to Article 41(3) of the

Unification Treaty, the Federal Republic of Germany will not enact any legislation contradicting the part of the Joint Declaration quoted above.

2. The monuments dedicated to the victims of war and tyranny which have been erected on German soil will be respected and will enjoy the protection of German law. The same applies to the war graves, which will be maintained and looked after.

3. In the united Germany, too, the free democratic basic order will be protected by the Constitution. It provides the basis for ensuring that parties which, by reason of their aims or the behavior of their adherents, seek to impair or abolish the free democratic basic order as well as associations which are directed against the constitutional order or the concept of international understanding, can be prohibited. This also applies to parties and associations with National Socialist aims.

4. On the treaties of the German Democratic Republic, the following has been agreed in Article 12(1) and (2) of the treaty of August 31, 1990, between the Federal Republic of Germany and the German Democratic Republic establishing German unity:

> "The contracting parties agree that, as part of the process of establishing German unity, the international treaties concluded by the German Democratic Republic shall be discussed with the contracting parties in terms of the protection of bona fide rights, the interests of the states concerned and the treaty obligations of the Federal Republic of Germany as well as in the light of the principles of a free democratic basic order founded on the rule of law and taking into account the responsibilities of the European Communities in order to regulate or ascertain the continuance, adjustment or termination of such treaties.
>
> The united Germany shall lay down its position on the continuance of international treaties of the German Democratic Republic after consultations with the respective contracting parties and with the European Communities insofar as their responsibilities are affected."

Accept, Mr. Foreign Minister, the assurances of our high consideration.

SOVIET-GERMAN TREATY

The Federal Republic of Germany and the Union of Soviet Socialist Republics,

Conscious of their responsibility for the preservation of peace in Europe and in the world,

Desiring to set the final seal on the past and, through understanding and reconciliation, render a major contribution towards ending the division of Europe,

Convinced of the need to build a new, united Europe on the basis of common values and to create a just and lasting peaceful order in Europe including stable security structures,

Convinced that great importance attaches to human rights and fundamental freedoms as part of the heritage of the whole of Europe and that respect for them is a major prerequisite for progress in developing that peaceful order,

Reaffirming their commitment to the aims and principles enshrined in the United Nations Charter and to the provisions of the Final Act of Helsinki of 1 August 1975 and of subsequent documents adopted by the Conference on Security and Cooperation in Europe,

Resolved to continue the good traditions of their centuries-long history, to make good-neighbourliness, partnership and cooperation the basis of their relations, and to meet the historic challenges that present themselves on the threshold of the third millennium,

Having regard to the foundations established in recent years through the development of cooperation between the Union of Soviet Socialist Republics and the Federal Republic of Germany as well as the German Democratic Republic,

Moved by the desire to further develop and intensify the fruitful and mutually beneficial cooperation between the two States in all fields and to give their mutual relationship a new quality in the interests of their peoples and of peace in Europe,

Taking account of the signing of the Treaty of 12 September 1990 on the Final Settlement with respect to Germany regulating the external aspects of German unity,

Have agreed as follows.

Article 1

The Federal Republic of Germany and the Union of Soviet Socialist Republics will, in developing their relations, be guided by the following principles:

They will respect each other's sovereign equality, territorial integrity and political independence.

They will make the dignity and rights of the individual, concern for the survival of mankind, and preservation of the natural environment the focal point of their policy.

They reaffirm the right of all nations and States to determine their own fate freely and without interference from outside and to proceed with their political, economic, social and cultural development as they see fit.

They uphold the principle that any war, whether nuclear or conventional, must be effectively prevented and peace preserved and developed.

They guarantee the precedence of the universal rules of international law in their domestic and international relations and confirm their resolve to honour their contractual obligations.

They pledge themselves to make use of the creative potential of the individual and modern society with a view to safeguarding peace and enhancing the prosperity of all nations.

Article 2

The Federal Republic of Germany and the Union of Soviet Socialist Republics undertake to respect without qualification the territorial integrity of all States in Europe within their present frontiers.

They declare that they have no territorial claims whatsoever against any State and will not raise any in the future.

They regard and will continue to regard as inviolable the frontiers of all States in Europe as they exist on the day of signature of the present Treaty.

Article 3

The Federal Republic of Germany and the Union of Soviet Socialist Republics reaffirm that they will refrain from any threat or use of force which is directed against the territorial integrity or political independence of the other side or is in any other way incompatible with the aims and principles of the United Nations Charter or with the CSCE Final Act.

They will settle their disputes exclusively by peaceful means and never resort to any of their weapons except for the purpose of individual or collective self-defence. They will never and under no circumstances be the first to employ armed forces against one another or against third States. They call upon all other States to join in this non-aggression commitment.

Should either side become the object of an attack the other side will not afford any military support or other assistance to the aggressor and resort to all measures to settle the conflict in conformity with the principles and procedures of the United Nations and other institutions of collective security.

Article 4

The Federal Republic of Germany and the Union of Soviet Socialist Republics will seek to ensure that armed forces and armaments are substantially reduced by means of binding, effectively verifiable agreements in order to achieve, in conjunction with unilateral measures, a stable balance at a lower level, especially in Europe, which will suffice for defence but not for attack.

The same applies to the multilateral and bilateral enhancement of confidence-building and stabilizing measures.

Article 5

Both sides will support to the best of their ability the process of security and cooperation in Europe on the basis of the Final Act of Helsinki adopted on 1 August 1975 and, with the cooperation of all participating States, develop and intensify that cooperation further still, notably by creating permanent institutions and bodies. The aim of these efforts is the consolidation of peace, stability and security and the coalescence of Europe to form a single area of law, democracy and cooperation in the fields of economy, culture and information.

Article 6

The Federal Republic of Germany and the Union of Soviet Socialist Republics have agreed to hold regular consultations with a view to further developing and intensifying their bilateral relations and coordinating their positions on international issues.

Consultations at the highest political level shall be held as necessary but at least once a year.

The Foreign Ministers will meet at least twice a year.

The Defence Ministers will meet at regular intervals.

Other ministers will meet as necessary to discuss matters of mutual interest.

The existing mixed commissions will consider ways and means of intensifying their work. New mixed commissions will be appointed as necessary by mutual agreement.

Article 7

Should a situation arise which in the opinion of either side constitutes a threat to or violation of peace or may lead to dangerous international complications, both sides will immediately make contact with a view to coordinating their positions and agreeing on measures to improve or resolve the situation.

Article 8

The Federal Republic of Germany and the Union of Soviet Socialist Republics have agreed to substantially expand and intensify their bilateral cooperation, especially in the economic, industrial and scientific-technological fields and in the field of environmental protection, with a view to developing their mutual relations on a stable and long-term basis and deepening the trust between the two States and people. They will to this end conclude a comprehensive agreement on the development of cooperation in the economic, industrial and scientific-technological fields and, where necessary, separate arrangements on specific matters.

Both sides attach great importance to cooperation in the training of specialists and executive personnel from industry for the development of bilateral relations and are prepared to considerably expand and intensify that cooperation.

Article 9

The Federal Republic of Germany and the Union of Soviet Socialist Republics will further develop and intensify their economic cooperation for their mutual benefit. They will create, as far as their domestic legislation and their obligations under international treaties allow, the most favourable general conditions for entrepreneurial and other economic activity by citizens, enterprises and governmental as well as non-governmental institutions of the other side.

This applies in particular to the treatment of capital investment and investors.

Both sides will encourage the initiatives necessary for economic cooperation by those directly concerned, especially with the aim of fully exploiting the possibilities afforded by the existing treaties and programs.

Article 10

Both sides will, on the basis of the Agreement of 22 July 1986 concerning Economic and Technological Cooperation, further develop exchanges in this field and implement joint projects. They propose to draw on the achievements of modern science and technology for the sake of the people, their health, and their prosperity. They will promote and support parallel initiatives by researchers and research establishments in this sphere.

Article 11

Convinced that the preservation of the natural sources of life is indispensable for prosperous economic and social development, both sides reaffirm their determination to continue and intensify their cooperation in the field of environmental protection on the basis of the agreement of 25 October 1988.

They propose to solve major problems of environmental protection together, to study harmful effects on the environment, and to develop measures for their prevention. They will participate in the development of coordinated strategies and concepts for a transborder environmental policy within the international, and especially the European, framework.

Article 12

Both sides will seek to extend transport communications (air, rail, sea, inland waterway and road links) between the Federal Republic of Germany and the Union of Soviet Socialist Republics through the use of state-of-the-art technology.

Article 13

Both sides will strive to simplify to a considerable extent, on the basis of reciprocity, the procedure for the issue of visas to citizens of both countries wishing to travel, primarily for business, economic and cultural reasons and for purposes of scientific and technological cooperation.

Article 14

Both sides support comprehensive contacts among people from both countries and the development of cooperation among parties, trade unions, foundations, schools, universities, sports organizations, churches and social institutions, women's associations, environmental protection and other social organizations and associations.

Special attention will be given to the deepening of contacts between the parliaments of the two States.

They welcome cooperation based on partnership between municipalities and regions and between Federal States and Republics of the Union.

An important role falls to the German-Soviet Discussion Forum and cooperation among the media.

Both sides will facilitate the participation of all young people and their organizations in exchanges and other contacts and joint projects.

Article 15

The Federal Republic of Germany and the Union of Soviet Socialist Republics, conscious of the mutual enrichment of the cultures of their peoples over the centuries and of their unmistakable contribution to Europe's common cultural heritage, as well as of the importance of cultural exchange for international understanding, will considerably extend their cultural cooperation.

Both sides will give substance to and fully exploit the agreement on the establishment and work of cultural centres.

Both sides reaffirm their willingness to give all interested persons comprehensive access to the languages and cultures of the other side and will encourage public and private initiatives.

Both sides strongly advocate the creation of wider possibilities for learning the language of the other country in schools, universities, and other educational institutions and will for this purpose assist the other side in the training of teachers and make available teaching aids, including the use of television, radio, audio-visual and computer technology. They will support initiatives for the establishment of bilingual schools.

Soviet citizens of German nationality as well as citizens from the Union of Soviet Socialist Republics who have their permanent abode in the Federal Republic of Germany and wish to preserve their language, culture or traditions will be enabled to develop their national, linguistic and cultural identity. Accordingly, both sides will make possible and facilitate promotional measures for the benefit of such persons or their organizations within the framework of their respective laws.

Article 16

The Federal Republic of Germany and the Union of Soviet Socialist Republics will advocate the preservation of cultural treasures of the other side in their territory.

They agree that lost or unlawfully transferred art treasures which are located in their territory will be returned to their owners or their successors.

Article 17

Both sides stress the special importance of humanitarian cooperation in their bilateral relations. They will intensify this cooperation with the assistance of the charitable organizations of both sides.

Article 18

The Government of the Federal Republic of Germany declares that the monuments to Soviet victims of the war and totalitarian rule erected on German soil will be respected and be under the protection of German law.

The same applies to Soviet war graves; they will be preserved and tended.

The Government of the Union of Soviet Socialist Republics will guarantee access to the graves of Germans on Soviet territory, their preservation and upkeep.

The responsible organizations of both sides will intensify their cooperation on these matters.

Article 19

The Federal Republic of Germany and the Union of Soviet Socialist Republics will intensify their mutual assistance in civil and family matters on the basis of the Hague Convention relating to Civil Procedure to which they are signatories. Both sides will further develop their mutual assistance in criminal matters, taking into account their legal systems and proceeding in harmony with international law.

The responsible authorities in the Federal Republic of Germany and the Union of Soviet Socialist Republics will cooperate in combating organized crime, terrorism, drug trafficking, illicit interference with civil aviation and maritime shipping, the manufacture or dissemination of counterfeit money, and smuggling, including the illicit transborder movement of works of art. The procedure and conditions for mutual cooperation will be the subject of a separate arrangement.

Article 20

The two Governments will intensify their cooperation within the scope of international organizations, taking into account their mutual interests and each side's cooperation with other countries. They will assist one another in developing cooperation with international, especially European, organizations and institutions of which either side is a member, should the other side express an interest in such cooperation.

Article 21

The present Treaty will not affect the rights and obligations arising from existing bilateral and multilateral agreements which the two sides have concluded with other States. The present Treaty is directed against no one; both sides regard their cooperation as an integral part and dynamic element of the further development of the CSCE process.

Article 22

The present Treaty is subject to ratification; the instruments of ratification will be exchanged as soon as possible in [blank].

The present Treaty will enter into force on the date of exchange of instruments of ratification.

The present Treaty will remain in force for twenty years. Thereafter it will be tacitly extended for successive periods of five years unless either Contracting Party denounces the Treaty in writing subject to one year's notice prior of its expiry.

JUDGE SOUTER'S TESTIMONY TO SENATE JUDICIARY COMMITTEE

September 13, 1990

After thirty-four years on the Supreme Court, Justice William J. Brennan, Jr., age eighty-four, resigned July 20, citing health reasons. President George Bush moved quickly to fill the vacancy. Making his first appointment to the Court, Bush on July 23 selected David H. Souter, a little-known jurist from New Hampshire. From then until the Senate confirmed Souter's nomination October 2, his views and background were closely examined by legal scholars, interest groups, the news media, and especially the Senate Judiciary Committee.

During several lengthy appearances before the committee, beginning September 13, Souter skillfully deflected questions on controversial legal issues, particularly abortion, and seemed to dispel much of the concern by potential detractors that politically he might be a hidebound conservative and socially out of touch with modern norms of behavior.

Souter, a fifty-year-old bachelor, had lived most of his life in or near Concord, New Hampshire. He was identified with two conservative Republican governors: Meldrim Thompson, who appointed Souter attorney general of New Hampshire in 1976, and John H. Sununu, who in 1983 placed Souter on the state's Supreme Court. As Bush's White House chief of staff, Sununu told the press July 24 that he endorsed Souter for the U.S. Supreme Court when Attorney General Dick Thornburgh and White House counsel C. Boyden Gray "brought David's name out of the pack" of twenty candidates, or more.

At a White House news conference, Bush said he was certain Souter "will interpret the Constitution" and "not legislate from the federal bench." That phrase echoed Ronald Reagan's oft-expressed preference for "strict constitutionists"—justices who read the Constitution narrowly to limit federal involvement in many social issues. As president, Reagan had created a conservative majority on the Court with his appointments of Sandra Day O'Connor, Antonin Scalia, and Anthony M. Kennedy.

Praise for Justice Brennan

Bush also praised Brennan, who for years had led the Court's liberal wing. Bush spoke of Brennan's "powerful intellect, his winning personality, and importantly, his commitment to civil discourse on emotional issues that at times tempt uncivil voices." All of that, the president added, had made the retiring justice "one of the greatest figures of our age."

Brennan had kept alive some of the Warren Court's activism for two decades after Chief Justice Earl Warren retired in 1969. The Warren Court took on social issues that previously had been left to legislators. Its 1954 Brown v. Board of Education decision, outlawing racial segregation in public schools, was a catalyst for the civil rights revolution. Brennan particularly rejected the notion that the Constitution should be construed strictly in terms of the eighteenth-century framers' understanding. He read it in the context of modern times.

Brennan wrote the Court's opinions in many significant cases, including Baker v. Carr (1962), ushering in an era of federal court involvement in reapportionment and congressional redistricting, and Sullivan v. New York Times (1964), extending the press First Amendment protection in political commentary. Court scholars said he helped shape the 1973 Roe v. Wade decision recognizing a right to privacy in the Fourteenth Amendment that provided a woman the right to an abortion.

Attempt to Avert a "Bork Battle"

With Souter's nomination, Bush apparently sought to avoid a bruising political fight like the one that culminated in the Senate's rejection of Reagan nominee Robert H. Bork in 1987. Bork's voluminous writings and frank testimony, detailing his conservative judicial approach, aided his foes in their rejection battle. Souter, in contrast, had written little on major constitutional questions, and his ideology was difficult to define. He was quiet-spoken, almost reticent. Sen. Howell Heflin, D-Ala., a member of the Judiciary Committee, spoke of him as a "stealth nominee."

Along that line of thinking, the Wall Street Journal commented July 25 on Bush's "artful selection" of a "judicial conservative with virtually no record on the abortion issue." Few issues were as controversial. In 1989 a conservative Court placed new restrictions on abortion and left open the possibility of rejecting it outright in some future decision. That threat mobilized abortion-rights backers to political activism, including a lobby against Bork. (Supreme Court's Decision in Webster Abortion Case, Historic Documents of 1989, p. 365)

When asked about Souter's position on abortion, Bush told reporters:

"My selection process was not geared simply to any legal issue. It is not appropriate, in choosing a Supreme Court justice, to use any litmus test." The president went on to praise Souter "as a remarkable judge of keen intellect and highest ability, one whose scholarly commitment to the law and whose wealth of experience mark him of the first rank." Souter was a graduate of Harvard and its law school, and was a Rhodes scholar at Oxford. He went into private law practice in Concord in 1966 and two years later joined the staff of state attorney general Warren B. Rudman, a moderate Republican, and came to be considered his political protege.

Rudman, elected to the U.S. Senate in 1980 and 1986, was considered Souter's chief sponsor in two of his nominations to come before the Senate. Souter assumed a judgeship on the U.S. Circuit Court of Appeals for the First District (New England) less than three months before being named to the Supreme Court. The Senate confirmed Souter for the federal judgeship April 27 without objection. Few questions had been raised in his brief appearance before the Senate Judiciary Committee April 5.

Souter's Judiciary Committee Testimony

But things were different the second time around. The Wall Street Journal *quipped October 3 that Souter had "completed the toughest job interview in America." It reported on the months of study that brought about his "transformation from a solitary New England scholar to the 105th associate justice of the U.S. Supreme Court." In preparation for the committee hearings, the newspaper said, Souter "plowed through 26 books of briefing materials, watched videotapes of previous confirmation hearings, benefited from the research of 10 Justice Department and White House lawyers."*

In his testimony, Souter sidestepped several of the contentious issues. He endorsed a fundamental right to privacy in the Constitution—but declined to say whether the right to privacy extended to abortion. He implicitly separated himself from the Supreme Court's conservative justices in interpreting the Free Exercise Clause of the First Amendment; Souter said a state should be required to demonstrate a "compelling interest" to justify outlawing a practice associated with religious activity.

Souter took a middle-of-the-road approach to constitutional interpretation by saying he would look at the "principles" behind the words of the eighteenth century framers and not merely "original intent." He defended his civil rights record; as attorney general in 1976 he had submitted a brief to the U.S. Supreme Court defending New Hampshire's failure to comply with a federal equal-employment law that required employers to file statistics on racial composition in the workplace. He told the committee that discrimination was a great national tragedy but was sketchy on the extent of government authority to remedy it.

Some committee members appeared frustrated by his answers, but only one, Sen. Edward M. Kennedy, D-Mass., declined to recommend Senate confirmation. Souter was approved September 2 by a vote of 90 to 9 after four hours of speeches but relatively little debate. Sen. Joseph R. Biden, Jr., D-Del., chairman of the Judiciary Committee, told his colleagues that "Judge Souter falls within the sphere of candidates acceptable to the Senate." He was sworn into office October 9.

> *Following are excerpts from the Senate Judiciary Committee's opening hearing, September 13, 1990, on the nomination of David H. Souter to the U.S. Supreme Court:*

Today, we, the members of the Judiciary Committee and the Senate as a whole, embark on a solemn task that Article II of the Constitution commits to this body: the Senate's responsibility to offer its "advice and consent" to the president's nomination.

As these hearings begin, I believe this committee's role in that process is threefold.

First, and foremost in my view, we must conduct a fair and thorough hearing that will provide you with a full opportunity to present your constitutional philosophy to the Senate and, I might add, to the nation;

Second, we must explore those views with you, to try to identify the meaning you would give to our Constitution, if you become "Justice Souter"; and

Third, we must decide—each senator, bound by his own conscience—whether that constitutional vision is the one that this nation should have.

These have been our obligations for many years now, obligations that the Constitution makes it our duty to complete. And to fulfill our constitutional duties, Judge Souter, we will need your help.

You come before us without an extensive record that details your views on important constitutional questions of our time. And I say that not critically. I say that as an observation. You are an extremely bright man with an extremely admirable record. But the past responsibilities you have had have not required you to enunciate your views in any detail on major constitutional issues and questions. As a result, we need your help for us to be able to understand your constitutional philosophy, the philosophy that you would bring to the nation's highest court. We need you to join us in a meaningful and important dialogue about the Constitution. . . .

And let me be clear on one point, Judge. We—I speak for myself. I should say I, as chairman of this committee, am not asking you for any commitments as to how you would vote on any specific case, nor am I trying to pry nor am I attempting to pry into your personal views on publicly debated issues.

Rather, we want to know what principles you would apply, what philosophies you would employ as you exercise the awesome—and I emphasize awesome—the awesome power you will hold if you are confirmed as a justice, an associate justice to the Supreme Court of the United States.

Judge, I sincerely hope—and expect, quite frankly—that you will join me in a dialogue on the Constitution, a dialogue in which you respond with specific answers to specific questions, specific questions about the Due Process Clause and its protection of our right to private and individual liberty; the Equal Protection Clause and its guarantees of racial equality and equal rights for women; the First Amendment and its protection of freedom of speech and freedom of religion; and other important constitutional issues of our day.

At this fateful moment in our history, Judge, we have a right to know, a duty to discover, precisely what you, Judge David Hackett Souter, think about the great constitutional issues of our time.

I believe we can engage in a real discussion on these issues while respecting your judicial independence. We value impartiality in our judicial officers, and it is not a function of these hearings to trespass upon any boundaries that are set by or need to be maintained to guarantee that independence. . . .

Sen. Strom Thurmond, S.C., the ranking Republican on the committee: Our magnificent Constitution confers tremendous responsibility on both the House and the Senate to declare war, maintain the armed forces, borrow money, regulate commerce, mint currency and make all laws necessary for the operation of government. However, the Senate alone holds exclusive to "advise and consent" on all judicial nominations, without a doubt one of the most important responsibilities undertaken by the Senate. It is a responsibility that takes on greater significance when a nomination is made to the highest court in the land. The Senate has assigned the task of holding hearings and reviewing judicial nominees to the Judiciary Committee. It is our duty to make the recommendation to the full Senate. This critical role in the judicial process must be equitable, thorough and diligent. It is this committee that will be called upon to cast the first vote which will in all likelihood determine the fate of this nomination. I am not aware of any nominee to the Supreme Court in this country who has failed to attain a majority of the votes of the members of this committee and then been confirmed by the full Senate. This track record clearly underscores the importance of our responsibility. . . .

Mr. Chairman, our critical role in the selection process of a Supreme Court justice requires us to carefully examine and review the intellectual capacity, moral character and background of a nominee. However, it does not convey the right to question a nominee about how he or she would decide a particular case. It is inappropriate to ask a nominee how he would rule, for several reasons. A nominee cannot, and should not be expected to, indicate how he would rule until there has been an opportunity to fully examine precedent and relevant law, to study briefs, and to listen to oral argument. Only after a complete review of all the facts and relevant law, and after sufficient time for calm, rational deliberation, should an individual be called upon to render a decision.

Direct questioning about sensitive issues that may come before the court could impinge on the concept of an impartial, independent judiciary. We must take all precautions to ensure that the judiciary is shielded from the political pressures that are imposed on the legislative and executive branches. For these reasons, I urge all members of this committee to be diligent, thorough, and thought-provoking in questioning this nominee, but not to exceed the appropriateness to the purpose for which these questions are intended.

Mr. Chairman, a member of the Supreme Court must consider hundreds, even thousands of issues during his or her tenure. No one issue should be the sole criteria by which a nominee is judged fit to serve. While any one issue may now be more prominent than others, as times change so will the issues before the court. A Supreme Court member is confirmed for life, not put in place to make short-term decisions to satisfy any political constituency. A member of the Supreme Court makes decisions in a vast array of areas which affect all the people of this nation and not just one individual or a particular group. To expect otherwise would diminish this august institution. . . .

Judge David H. Souter: . . . I would like to take a minute before we begin our dialogue together to say something to you about how I feel about the beginnings that I have come from and about the experiences that I have had that bear on the kind of judge that I am and the kind of judge that I can be expected to be.

I think you know that I spent most of my boyhood in a small town in New Hampshire — Weare, New Hampshire. It was a town large in geography, small in population.

The physical space, the open space between people, however, was not matched by the interspace between them because, as everybody knows who has lived in a small town, there is a closeness of people in a small town which is unattainable anywhere else.

There was in that town no section or place or neighborhood that was determined by anybody's occupation or by anybody's bank balance. Everybody knew everybody else's business, or at least thought they did.

And we were, in a very true sense, intimately aware of other lives. We were aware of lives that were easy, and we were aware of lives that were very hard.

Another thing that we were aware of in that place was the responsibility of people to govern themselves. It was a responsibility that they owed to themselves, and it was a responsibility that they owed and owe to their neighbors. I first learned about that or I first learned the practicalities of that when I used to go over to the town hall in Weare, New Hampshire, on Town Meeting Day. I would sit in the benches in the back of the town hall after school, and that is where I began my lessons in practical government.

As I think you know, I went to high school in Concord, New Hampshire, which is a bigger place, and I went on from there to college and to study law in Cambridge, Massachusetts, and Oxford, England, which are bigger places still. And after I had finished law school, I came back to New Hampshire, and I began the practice of law. And I think probably it is fair to say that I resumed the study of practical government.

I went to work for a law firm in Concord, New Hampshire, and I practiced there for several years. I then became, as I think you know, an assistant attorney general in the criminal division of that office. I was then lucky to be deputy attorney general to Warren Rudman, and I succeeded him as attorney general in 1976.

The experience of government, though, did not wait until the day came that I entered public as opposed to private law practice; because although in those years of private practice I served the private clients of the firm, I also did something in those days which was very common then.

Perhaps it is less common today — I know it is — but it was an accepted part of private practice in those days to take on a fair share of representation of clients who did not have the money to pay.

I remember very well the first day that I ever spent by myself in a courtroom. I spent [that day] representing a woman whose personal life had become such a shambles that she had lost the custody of her children, and she was trying to get them back. She was not the last of such clients. I represented clients with domestic relations problems who lived sometimes, it seemed to me, in appalling circumstances. I can remember representing a client who was trying to pull her life together after being evicted because she couldn't pay the rent.

Although cases like that were not the cases upon which the firm paid the rent, those were not remarkable cases for lawyers in private practice in those days before governmentally funded legal services. And they were the cases that we took at that time because taking them was the only way to make good on the supposedly open door of our courts to the people who needed to get inside and to get what courts had to offer through the justice system.

I think it is fair to say—I am glad it is fair to say—that even today, with so much governmentally funded legal service, there are lawyers in private practice in our profession who are doing the same thing.

As you know, I did go on to public legal service, and in the course of doing that, I met not only legislators and the administrators that one finds in the government, but I began to become familiar with the criminal justice system in my state and in our nation. I met victims and sometimes I met the survivors of victims. I met defendants. I met that train of witnesses from the clergy to con artists who passed through our system and find themselves, either willingly or unwillingly, part of a search for truth and part of a search for those results that we try to sum up with the words of justice.

As you also know, after those years I became a trial judge, and my experience with the working of government and the judicial system broadened there because I was a trial judge of general jurisdiction, and I saw every sort and condition of the people of my state that a trial court of general jurisdiction is exposed to. I saw litigants in international commercial litigation for millions, and I saw children who were the unwitting victims of domestic disputes and custody fights which somehow seemed to defy any reasonable solution, however hard we worked at it.

I saw, once again, the denizens of the criminal justice system, and I saw domestic litigants. I saw appellants from the juvenile justice system who were appealing their findings of delinquency.

And, in fact, I had maybe one of the great experiences of my entire life in seeing week in and week out the members of the trial juries of our states who are rightly called the consciences of our communities. And I worked with them, and I learned from them, and I will never forget my days with them.

When those days on the trial court were over, there were two experiences that I took away with me or two lessons that I had learned, and the lessons remain with me today.

The first lesson, simple as it is, is that whatever court we are in, whatever we are doing, whether we are on a trial court or an appellate court, at the end of our task some human being is going to be affected. Some human life is going to be changed in some way by what we do, whether we do it as trial judges or whether we do it as appellate judges, as far removed from the trial arena as it is possible to be.

The second lesson that I learned in that time is that if, indeed, we are going to be trial judges, whose rulings will affect the lives of other people and who are going to change their lives by what we do, we had better use every power of our minds and our hearts and our beings to get those rulings right.

I am conscious of those two lessons, as I have been for all of the years that I was on an appellate [court]. I am conscious of them as I sit here today, suddenly finding myself the nominee of the president of the United States to undertake the greatest responsibility that any judge in our republic can undertake: The responsibility to join with eight other people, to make the promises of the Constitution a reality for our time, and to preserve that Constitution for the generations that will follow us after we are gone from here.

I am mindful of those two lessons when I tell you this: That if you believe and the Senate of the United States believes that it is right to confirm my nomination, then I will accept those responsibilities as obligations to all of the people in the United States whose lives will be affected by my stewardship of the Constitution.

Biden: Judge, before I begin my questioning, I want to make it clear to you that under precedents — we can debate and argue, which we will up here, about how long they have existed — but under precedents dating back, as one of my colleagues said, at least to the 1950s, and arguably much earlier, each member of the committee can decide whatever questions he deems proper to ask you. We have never imposed a gag rule on any committee member.

But, Judge, while we may ask any questions we deem proper, you are free to refuse to answer any questions you deem to be improper. No one is going to try to force you to answer any question you think in good conscience you cannot appropriately address. . . . .

Now, Judge, let me begin. . . . A close friend of yours, and I consider him, quite frankly, a close friend of mine, my colleague Warren Rudman, has . . . indicated that one of the Supreme Court justices you most admire was the second Justice [John M.] Harlan, who served on the Supreme Court between 1955 and 1971 and who was widely regarded, is widely regarded as one of the great conservative justices ever to serve on the court.

Now, Justice Harlan concurred in the court's landmark decision of *Griswold*. That is the Connecticut case that said that the state of Connecticut, the legislature and the governor couldn't pass a law that constitutionally—could not pass constitutional muster when they passed a law that said that married couples could not use birth control devices to determine whether or not they wished to procreate or not.

Justice Harlan indicated that that Connecticut law violated the Due Process Clause of the 14th Amendment, which says that no state can deprive any person of life, liberty or property without process of law.

Now, my question is this, Judge: Do you agree with Justice Harlan's opinion in *Griswold* that the Due Process Clause of the 14th Amendment protects a right of a married couple to use birth control to decide whether or not to have a child?

Souter: I believe that the Due Process Clause of the 14th Amendment does recognize and does protect an unenumerated right of privacy. . . .

The only reservation I have is a purely formal reservation in response to your question, and that simply is: No two judges, I am sure, will ever write an opinion the same way, even if they share the same principles.

And I would not go so far as to say every word in Justice Harlan's opinion is something that I would adopt.

And I think for reasons that we all appreciate, I would not think that it was appropriate to express a specific opinion on the exact result in *Griswold*, for the simple reason that as clearly as I will try to describe my views on the right of privacy, we know that the reasoning of the court in *Griswold*, including opinions beyond those of Justice Harlan, are taken as obviously a predicate toward the one case which has been on everyone's mind and on everyone's lips since the moment of my nomination—*Roe v. Wade* [the 1973 case in which the Supreme Court struck down state laws prohibiting abortion], upon which the wisdom or the appropriate future of which it would be inappropriate for me to comment.

But I understand from your question, and I think it is unmistakable, that what you were concerned about is the principal basis for deriving a right of privacy, and specifically the kind of reasoning that I would go through to do so. And in response to that question, yes, I would group myself in Justice Harlan's category.

Biden: Justice [Lewis F.] Powell [Jr.] said, freedom of personal choice in matters of marriage and family life is one of the liberties protected by the Due Process Clause of the 14th Amendment.

Now, my question, Judge, is do you believe that that assertion by Justice Powell is accurate?

Souter: I think that assertion by Justice Powell represents a legitimate judgment in these kinds of problems. . . . I am going to ask you to excuse me from specifically endorsing the particular result, because I recognize the implications from any challenge that may come from the other privacy case that is on everyone's mind.

But the one thing that I want to make very clear is that my concept of an enforceable marital right of privacy would give it fundamental importance. What the courts are doing in all of these cases is saying—although we speak of tiers of scrutiny—what the courts are saying, it seems to me in a basically straightforward way—is that there is no way to escape a valuation of the significance of the particular manifestation to privacy that we are concerned with, and having given it a value we, indeed, have to hold the state to an equally appropriate or commensurate reason before it interferes with that value.

Biden: That is exactly what I am trying to find out in your answering. So the valuation applied to a definition of family is fundamental. The valuation applied to whether a married couple can use contraception is fundamental. The valuation applied to whether or not an unmarried couple can use contraception is fundamental.

Now, I would like to ask you . . . that when it comes to personal freedom of choice, as Justice Powell put it, in family and in marriage, one basic aspect of that freedom is the right to procreate. Now, early in the '40s, in the *Skinner* case, the Supreme Court said that criminals could not be sterilized. The court made it very clear and it said, "Marriage and procreation are fundamental" and that sterilization affected "one of the basic civil rights of man."

. . . Do you agree that procreation is a fundamental right?

Souter: I would assume that if we are going to have any core concept of marital privacy, that would certainly have to rank at its fundamental heart.

Biden: Now, the reason I am pursuing this is not merely for the reason you think, I suspect. It is because you have been categorized as—I believe you have described yourself as an interpretivist.

Souter: I did and I have, yes.

Biden: . . . Now, you have just told us that the right to use birth control, to decide whether or not to become pregnant is one of those fundamental rights—the value placed on it is fundamental.

Now, let us say that a woman and/or her mate uses such a birth control device and it fails. Does she still have a constitutional right to choose not to become pregnant?

Souter: Senator, that is the point at which I will have to exercise the prerogative which you were good to speak of explicitly. I think for me to start answering that question, in effect, is for me to start discussing the concept of *Roe v. Wade*. I would be glad — I do not think I have to do so for you — but I would be glad to explain in some detail my reasons for believing that I cannot do so, but of course, they focus on the fact that ultimately the question which you are posing is a question which is implicated by any possibility of the examination of *Roe v. Wade*. That, as we all know, is not only a possibility but a likelihood that the court may be asked to do it.

Biden: Judge, let me respectfully suggest the following to you: That to ask you what principles you would employ does not, in any way, tell me how you would rule on a specific fact situation.

For example, all eight justices, whom you will be joining, all eight of them have found there to be a liberty interest that a woman retains after being pregnant. That goes all the way from Justice [William J.] Brennan [Jr.] — who is no longer on the court — who reached one conclusion from having found that liberty interest, to Justice [Antonin] Scalia, who finds a liberty interest and yet, nonetheless says, explicitly he would like to see *Roe v. Wade,* he thinks *Roe v. Wade* should be overruled.

So the mere fact that you answer the question whether or not a woman's liberty interest, a woman's right to terminate pregnancy exists or does not exist, in no way tells me or anyone else within our earshot how you would possibly rule on *Roe v. Wade.*

Souter: I think to explain my position, I think it is important to bear in mind there are really two things that judges may or may not be meaning when they say there is a liberty interest to do thus and so, whatever it may be.

They may mean simply that in the whole range of human interests and activities the particular action that you are referring to is one which falls within a broad concept of liberty. If liberty means what it is, we can do [it] if we want to do it. Then obviously in that sense of your question, the answer is, yes.

Sen. Howard M. Metzenbaum, D-Ohio: Judge Souter, I want to focus on your view of really what is at stake in the abortion debate. Now, we write the laws in Congress, the Court interprets the laws, but we all must be aware that the laws affect the personal lives and the hopes and the dreams of the people who must live with the laws we make.

I want to start to talk with you on a personal level, not as a constitutional scholar nor as a lawyer. This year, I held hearings on legislation that would codify the principles of *Roe v. Wade.* I heard stories from two women who had had illegal abortions prior to 1973. They were women about your age. They told horrifying stories. . . .

My real question to you is not how you would rule on *Roe v. Wade* or any other particular case coming before the Court. But what does a woman face, when she has an unwanted pregnancy, a pregnancy that may be the result of rape or incest or failed contraceptives or ignorance of basic health information, and I would just like to get your own view and your own thoughts of that woman's position under those circumstances.

Souter: Senator, your question comes as a surprise to me. I was not expecting that kind of question, and you have made me think of something that I have not thought of for 24 years.

When I was in law school, I was on the board of freshmen advisors at Harvard College. I was a proctor in a dormitory at Harvard College. One afternoon, one of the freshmen who was assigned to me, I was his adviser, came to me and he was in pretty rough emotional shape, and we shut the door and sat down, and he told me that his girlfriend was pregnant, and he said she is about to try to have a self-abortion and she does not know how to do it. He said she is afraid to tell her parents what has happened, and she is afraid to go to the health services, and he said will you talk to her, and I did.

I know you will respect the privacy of the people involved, and I will not try to say what I told her. But I spent two hours in a small dormitory bedroom that afternoon, in that room because that was the most private place we could get so that no one in the next suite of rooms could hear, listening to her and trying to counsel her to approach her problem in a way different from what she was doing, and your question has brought that back to me. I think the only thing I can add to that is I know what you were trying to tell me, because I remember that afternoon.

Metzenbaum: Well, I appreciate your response. I think it indicates that you have empathy for the problem. In your writings, as a matter of fact, you reveal real empathy for those who are morally opposed to abortion.

For instance, in 1986, as a state Supreme Court justice, you wrote a special concurrence in a wrongful-birth case called *Smith v. Cody*, outlining, in your words, how a physician with conscientious scruples against abortion — this is a quote — "how a physician with conscientious scruples against abortion and the testing and counseling that may inform an abortion decision can discharge his professional obligation, without engaging in procedures that his religious or moral principles condemn."

As a matter of fact, that was sort of dictum. That was dictum in the case, it was not necessary. . . .

Now, you obviously indicated a concern for the doctor with conscientious scruples against abortion, you indicated your concern about feelings of individuals and groups, both public and privately. My concern is, do you have the same degree of empathy for the woman who must make a difficult decision when faced with an unwanted pregnancy? That is really the thrust of my concern, and I think the thrust of the concern, frankly, Judge Souter, of millions of American women, not really wanting to know how you will vote on a particular case but wanting to know whether you can empathize with their problem.

Souter: If they were to ask me whether I could, I would ask them to imagine what it was like to be in that room that fall afternoon that I described to you. That is an experience which has not been on my mind, because it has not had to be, but I learned that afternoon what was at stake.

I hope I have learned since that afternoon what is at stake on both sides of this controversy. You mentioned my opinion in the *Smith v. Cody* case. I do not know whether that was dictum or not. I did not think it was at the time. What I thought I was addressing at the time was a moral dilemma which had been created not unnecessarily, but which had necessarily been raised by the majority opinion of my court.

If I were to generalize from that concurrence in *Smith v. Cody*, it would be that I believe I indeed can empathize with the moral force of the people whom I addressed, and I can with equal empathy appreciate the moral force of people on the other side of that controversy.

Sen. Dennis DeConcini, D-Ariz.: Over the last few terms of the Supreme Court, almost 50 percent of the Supreme Court cases involve issues of statutory interpretation. Your judicial experience has been in a state court, so you have not had much exposure to cases of federal statutory interpretation, and that is why I would like to ask a few questions.

I did notice in the committee's questionnaire, you stated, and I quote: "The foundation of judicial responsibility in statutory interpretation is respect for the enacted text and for the legislative purpose that may explain a text that is unclear."

Based on that response, to what extent do you believe the legislative history should be taken into consideration, if you were sitting on the Supreme Court interpreting a statute passed by the Congress?

Souter: Senator, I am very much aware, in answering or in approaching an answer to that question, about the great spectrum of evidence that gets grouped under the umbrella of legislative history. It seems to me that the one general rule — and it is a truism to state it, but the one general rule that I can state is, when we look to legislative history in cases where the text is unclear, we at least have got to look to reliable legislative history.

When we are looking to legislative history on an issue of statutory construction, what we are doing is gathering evidence, and the object of gathering evidence for statutory interpretation is ultimately not in any way different from the object of gathering evidence of extraneous fact in a courtroom.

We are trying to establish some kind of standard of reliability, in this case to know exactly what was intended. And what we want to know is, to the extent we can find it out, is whether, aside from the terms of the statute itself, there really is a reliable guide to an institutional intent, not just a spectrum of subjective intent. I suppose a vague statute can get voted on by five different senators for five different reasons, so that if we are going to look to pure subjectivity, we are going to be in trouble.

What we are looking for is an intent which can be attributed to the institution itself, and, therefore, what we are looking for is some index of intended meaning, perhaps signaled by adoption or by, at the very least, an informed acquiescence that we can genuinely point to and say this represents not merely the statement of one committee member or committee staffer or one person on the floor, but in fact to an institution or to a sufficiently large enough number of the members of that institution, so that we can say they probably really do stand as surrogates for all those who voted for it.

DeConcini: So, in looking at legislative history, I take it from that, the amount, the intensity of it, those that are associated with the subject matter are of importance in a judge's interpretation?

Souter: Yes, indeed.

DeConcini: What other sources should a judge rely on in a statutory construction case outside the statutes and legislative history?

Souter: Well, there is a kind of, I suppose, broad principle of coherence that we look to. The fact is we so frequently speak of interpreting sections of statutes. What we are really obligated to do is to interpret whole statutes. We should not be interpreting a statutory section, without looking at the entire statute that we are interpreting.

One of the things that I have found . . . and that is when I get a statutory interpretation issue in front of me, I read the brief, I listen to the argument. But if I am going to write that opinion, I sit down, I tell my law clerks to sit down, but I do it myself before I am done, and I just sit there, and I read the whole statute. Fortunately, I do not have to construe the Internal Revenue Code, in which case I would be in serious trouble with that methodology. But within reason, I try to read the whole statute, and I am amazed at the number of times when I do that, I will find a clear clue in some other section that nobody has bothered to cite to me in a brief.

We are trying to come up with statutory coherence, not with just a bunch of pinpoints in individual sections. So, the first thing to do, in a very practical way, is to read the whole statute.

SOVIET AND AMERICAN PRAISE
FOR THE UNITED NATIONS
September 19, 25, October 1, 3

In a rare congratulatory mood, the United Nations General Assembly opened its forty-fifth session in September. Even the prospect of war in the Persian Gulf could not dispel the euphoria that arose from recent UN successes in dealing with various global trouble spots. Among the ministers and heads of government who went to New York to address the General Assembly soon after its September 18 opening, none had greater praise for the United Nations than did U.S. president George Bush and Soviet foreign minister Eduard Shevardnadze.

The past year was not "just a calendar year, but a light year in the history of the world," Shevardnadze said in his address September 25. "The cold war . . . is no longer a part of our lives," he declared. "Gone is the strain of daily confrontation, propaganda, bickering and reciprocal threats." From the same podium on October 1, Bush said that during the past year "we've come closer than ever" to realizing the hope for world peace that underlay the UN's founding in 1945. On October 3, the U.S. and Soviet governments issued a joint statement pledging to continue working together. The statement approvingly said that the United Nations "is fast becoming a real center for agreed common actions." Shevardnadze and Bush both noted that their governments had acted together in the UN Security Council to condemn Iraq's seizure of Kuwait and invoke sanctions against the aggressor. (UN Action Against Iraq With U.S.-Soviet Cooperation, p. 545) *While "today is no time for rejoicing," the Soviet foreign minister observed, "one cannot help being satisfied at the unprecedented unity of the Security Council and the clear attitude of international public opinion in the face of Iraq's behavior. This gives us confidence in the ability of the United Nations to deal with this grave international crisis."*

The president, for his part, said that when the Soviet Union "agreed with so many of us here to condemn the aggression of Iraq, there could be no doubt ... that we had, indeed, put four decades of history behind us."

In congressional testimony September 19, John R. Bolton, assistant secretary of state for international organizations, called August 1990 "the most significant and eventful month" in the forty-five-year history of the United Nations. He told a House Foreign Affairs subcommittee that the Iraqi invasion of Kuwait on August 2 could have destroyed the United Nations had it not responded as firmly as it did.

"As the Cold War wound down," Bolton testified, "the United Nations provided an invaluable forum where the United States and the Soviet Union could find common cause in reducing tensions arising from regional conflicts. The UN's key role in forging an agreement for the withdrawal of Soviet occupying forces from Afghanistan, in a cease-fire between Iran and Iraq, in monitoring the election process in Namibia and Nicaragua ... are unmistakable signs that the UN has emerged as the organization in which countries of the world actually can unite to confront challenges to international peace and stability."

Previous U.S.-Soviet Dealings

Bolton referred to the UN-sponsored Geneva Accords in 1988 that provided for the withdrawal of Soviet troops from Afghanistan, which they occupied in December 1979; the UN's 1988 role in ending eight years of fighting that had cost Iran and Iraq possibly a million battlefield deaths; UN-mediated agreements in December 1988 that were the blueprint for Namibia's independence (from South Africa) in March 1990; and UN assistance to the Organization of American States in overseeing elections in 1990 in Nicaragua, concluding a long civil war and the country's rule by the Sandinista regime. (Agreements on Afghanistan, Historic Documents of 1988, p. 257; Iraq-Iran Truce, Historic Documents of 1988, p. 529; Dignitaries Welcome Namibia's Independence, p. 199; Chamorro Inaugural in Nicaragua, p. 259)

Previous U.S.-Soviet dealings were marked by mistrust rather than cooperation. In those dealings, Moscow and Washington tended to bypass the United Nations. As permanent members of the Security Council, each tended to veto whatever resolutions the other might push, effectively deadlocking action. Until the final phase of the Reagan presidency, Washington was openly critical of the UN, viewing it as an ineffectual forum for anti-American rhetoric.

Slowly, though, Washington accepted Soviet president Mikhail S. Gorbachev's foreign policy changes. When Bush, a former U.S. ambassador to the UN, succeeded Ronald Reagan as president in January 1989, he signaled a stronger commitment by inviting Secretary General Javier Perez de Cuellar to the White House ahead of a host of foreign leaders.

The president also asked Congress to restore UN funding that Reagan had cut.

> *Following are excerpts from Assistant Secretary of State John R. Bolton's statement to the House Foreign Affairs Subcommittee on Human Rights, September 19, 1990; UN General Assembly addresses by Soviet foreign minister Eduard Shevardnadze on September 25 and by President George Bush on October 1, except for introductory remarks; and the U.S.-Soviet statement, "Responsibility for Peace and Security in the Changing World," issued jointly by the two governments at the United Nations October 3:*

BOLTON STATEMENT

The events of the past month and a half have presented the United Nations with a clear and unequivocal challenge to the principles and values contained in its charter. As the Cold War wound down, the United Nations provided an invaluable forum where the United States and the Soviet Union could find common cause in reducing tensions arising from regional conflicts. The UN's key role in forging an agreement for the withdrawal of Soviet occupying forces from Afghanistan, in a cease-fire between Iraq and Iran, in monitoring the electoral process in Namibia and Nicaragua—thereby providing for the people of those two countries the opportunity to exercise genuine self-determination—and the UN's response to the momentous events of the past several weeks, are unmistakable signs that the UN has emerged as the organization in which countries of the world actually can unite to confront challenges to international peace and stability.

New Challenges, New Threats

The events in the Persian Gulf over the past month and a half serve as a stark reminder, however, that even as peaceful change sweeps through regions long regarded as global "hot spots" new challenges and threats are posed. Saddam Hussein, at the beginning of last August, cynically gambled—in invading, looting, and purporting to annex Kuwait—that the international community would look the other way while he committed this act of wanton aggression. The invasion of Kuwait now poses a new and critical challenge to the United Nations as we move into the post-Cold War era. So far it has met that challenge superbly, but it is up to all of us to work together to ensure that the international community's forceful response to Saddam Hussein is sustained, and that his gamble does not pay off.

One of the consequences of his aggression which Saddam obviously did not anticipate, is the opportunity it has provided for a joint US-Soviet response to this grave threat to an orderly post-Cold War world. Having accompanied the President to Helsinki for his summit with President

631

Gorbachev, I am happy to say that the Soviets are standing shoulder to shoulder with us in the United Nations in helping to ensure that there is truly a united front against Iraq's invasion. In Helsinki, the Soviets demonstrated how, under their new thinking, they now calculate their interests. It was clear that while in the middle levels of their foreign policy bureaucracy there remains considerable sentiment in favor of maintaining their ties to one of their longest standing clients in the Middle East, the highest levels of the Soviet leadership understand that for the new relationship with the United States to move forward in a mutually beneficial manner, the Soviets must stand squarely behind the UN Charter.

As a prelude to the Helsinki summit, Secretary Baker had maintained almost daily contact with Foreign Minister [Eduard] Shevardnadze. It was this constant contact that reassured the Soviets that we looked to them not as token players who could present obstacles to US plans, but as partners who as permanent members of the Security Council had a crucial role in maintaining international solidarity against Iraq's actions. The understanding that has developed between Secretary Baker and the Soviet foreign minister provided a high-level channel that could be utilized as the need arose, and it proved in fact an invaluable channel as negotiations on certain Security Council resolutions—particularly 665 on the use of force—came to a head.

Humanitarian Assistance

Shortly after we returned from Helsinki, I traveled to Geneva to consult with the newly appointed personal representative of the Secretary General for humanitarian assistance to those affected by the Iraqi invasion, Prince Sadruddin Aga Khan. In Geneva I had the opportunity to discuss with Sadruddin, as well as the heads of many of the UN agencies involved in the effort to extend relief to the thousands of third-country nationals trapped in Iraq and Kuwait or stranded in Jordan, about the high priority the President and the Secretary accord to resolving the problems caused by Iraq's inhumane policies. Although the UN effort has been slow in becoming organized, there has been an outpouring of pledges of assistance from the international community. I am proud to say that the United States has been in the forefront of those countries in acting swiftly to see that our pledges are turned into reality, both cash and in kind, for the UN effort. We have the highest confidence that Sadruddin will be able to effectively coordinate this effort so that the untold human suffering can be swiftly ameliorated.

Security Council Sanctions Committee

August 1990 is the most significant and eventful month in the 45-year history of the United Nations. It was as if Iraq's invasion administered shock therapy that could either destroy the United Nations or revitalize it. Following the condemnation of the invasion and a demand for the immediate withdrawal of Iraq's forces, the Security Council moved with breathtaking speed to impose sweeping economic sanctions under Article VII of the charter. The following week the Security Council unanimously condemned Iraq's action against embassies accredited to the legitimate Kuwaiti government, as well as its actions in holding innocent third-country nationals hostage, and finally authorized the use of force to uphold the mandatory economic sanctions it had earlier imposed. At the same time, a hopeful agreement on a potential UN role in Cambodia was forged by the permanent members of the Security Council.

I believe that what we are seeing in the UN today is a return to the principles contained in the UN's charter and to the intentions of its founders, who believed that a world body should not just rely upon lofty international legal formulations, but should have the capacity to act to enforce the charter's cardinal rule: use of force in the settlement of international disputes is illegitimate and represents a threat to the vital interests of all UN member states.

Unfortunately, the millions of persons who have perished in conflicts since the founding of the United Nations are a grim testimony to the failure of the international community in living up to this principle. Instead of a united body of nations determined to counter aggression from any quarter, the world was divided first between ideologies, then between newly independent states and the traditional powers, and then between rich countries and poor. The United Nations could not function effectively within the divisions of the bi-polar international system created by the stand-off and conflict between the United States and the Soviet Union.

I believe that the continuing efforts spearheaded by the government of the United States and others to reform the United Nations, testify to our steadfast adherence to the original intent of the framers of the UN Charter. Instead of walking away from an organization which cost us all a great deal of money, which was ineffectual at best, and at worst was monopolized by countries attacking the very values upon which the charter is based, we stayed and worked to restore the United Nations to its original purpose. First, through a series of budgetary and management reforms which had a dramatic effect in restoring the confidence of major contributors that their funds were not being squandered, and then through a renewed political commitment to multilateral cooperation in confronting serious international or transnational problems such as drug trafficking and abuse, environmental degradation, and most important, regional conflicts, we have rededicated ourselves to utilizing the United Nations in the manner its founders foresaw. In fact we are now reading articles of the charter which have been gathering dust for 45 years.

Security Council Unity

Current US policy in the United Nations is focused on four goals. These are to strengthen UN peacekeeping efforts, especially making use of the good offices of the secretary general; to restore a sense of responsibility on the part of the UN's membership and avoid the sterile politicization and rigid posturing which has, for much of the UN's history, prevented the

attainment of practical measures that would promote international cooperation; to pursue the concept of a unitary UN in which better coordination
would avoid much of the budget inefficiencies and overlapping duplication
of programs and activities among the various UN bodies and specialized
and technical agencies; and finally to meet fully our financial obligations so
that the United Nations has the resources necessary to perform the tasks
we expect of it.

President Gorbachev's reform of Soviet foreign policy—"new thinking"—is a second major factor which has contributed to the birth of the
real UN. The effect of new thinking has been to re-align Soviet foreign
policy with the idea of collective action to preserve international peace and
security. The Soviets have expressed interest in the concept of the unitary
UN, and I have been engaged for over a year in a dialogue with Deputy
Foreign Minister Petrovsky seeking to elaborate this concept in a mutually
acceptable form. Of course, in the current crisis, we have enjoyed a level of
support from the Soviet Union unprecedented in the post-World War II
era. This cooperation is a hopeful harbinger of a close US-Soviet working
relationship in the United Nations in areas where we have mutual and
coincident interests.

The Chinese, too, have been active in promoting the use of the UN
Security Council to settle regional conflicts. Traditionally wary of unilateral use of force by other superpowers, the Chinese find a strengthened
international peacekeeping function within the UN to be generally harmonious with other foreign policy goals. We have seen this in the ongoing
discussions on Cambodia among the five permanent members of the
Security Council in which the Chinese have strongly supported a UN role
in the transition between the Phnom Penh regime and a government which
truly represents the will of the Cambodian people.

We are pleased by developments during the last month which improve
substantially prospects for a peaceful resolution to the Cambodian conflict. At a pivotal meeting in Jakarta, the four Cambodian factions last
week accepted the permanent five framework for peace and committed
themselves to negotiate a comprehensive political settlement. Parties to
the conflict further agreed to establish a supreme national council, which
will represent Cambodia externally and occupy the Cambodian seat at the
United Nations. We look forward to the Cambodians working with the
United Nations, the permanent five, and the Paris Conference on Cambodia to work out details of a settlement process leading to free and fair
elections organized and conducted by the United Nations.

The Chinese position on Resolution 665, which authorized the use of
measures necessary to enforce the mandatory sanctions against Iraq
contained in Resolution 661, was also revealing. At first they were
extremely reluctant to have the Security Council give such unprecedented
authorization. As Iraqi attempts to breach the sanctions became apparent
and as Iraqi violations of international law and expressions of contempt for
the international community mounted, I think the Chinese realized that
the fullest pressure had to be exerted on Saddam Hussein's regime by the

Security Council. Their assent probably influenced the votes of at least some of the non-aligned members of the council.

Although we will have differences with the Soviets and the Chinese, as well as other nations, on the particulars of our policy, I think there is a developing international consensus that will make it possible to utilize more fully the UN's peacekeeping machinery. Of course, this greatly depends on the effectiveness of the present economic sanctions and whether they are adhered to by every member of the United Nations. The stakes are high—every member has a strong interest in seeing that no one benefits from such a naked act of aggression as has been committed by Iraq against Kuwait. And it will be this unanimity of interest which will sustain our efforts to reverse this act. The enormity of Saddam Hussein's miscalculation is in part measured by the degree to which he is now isolated. We must all work to ensure that that isolation is not diminished until Security Council Resolutions 660, 661, 662, 664, 665, 666, and 667 have been implemented by the government of Iraq.

As I mentioned earlier, we are utilizing parts of the charter that haven't been read for 45 years. For instance, resolution 661 mandates the establishment of a sanctions committee consisting of the members of the Security Council. The sanctions committee is charged with overseeing implementation of the economic sanctions against Iraq and occupied Kuwait. As part of its functions, this committee has grappled with the issues of providing relief and assistance for the immediate humanitarian problems caused by displaced third-country nationals in Iraq, Kuwait, and neighboring countries such as Jordan, of defining a procedure of providing for the shipment of foods and medicine as an exception to the economic embargo on a humanitarian basis, and of providing relief to third countries adversely affected by the embargo....

SHEVARDNADZE SPEECH

... [F]rom the exceptional vantage point of this 45th session of the United Nations General Assembly, one might look back in amazement at how strikingly different is the terrain we have covered in just one year from the familiar landscape of the more than 4 decades which had preceded it.

Politically, this was not just a calendar year, but a light year in the history of the world. The cold war, which is—with its accompanying stress, psychoses and anticipation of disaster is no longer—no longer a part of our life. Gone is the strain of daily confrontation, propaganda, bickering and reciprocal threats.

This has been a year during which pieces of the Berlin Wall were a popular souvenir. And now an end has been put to the division of Europe, and a final line has been drawn unto the Second World War. The unification of the two German states has been completed. The German question; this great and classical problem of world politics, which only yesterday seemed intractable, has been resolved calmly and to mutual satisfaction. On behalf of the Soviet people, I wish to offer sincere and heartfelt congratulations to the German people, the German nation, on this tremendous event in the history of that state, their people, and in the history of Europe.

Almost unnoticed, the military alliances have lost their enemies. They are beginning to build their relations on a new basis, moving away from confrontation, which is being eroded by disarmament, by lower defense spending, more wide-ranging confidence-building measures, and the emergence of collective and cooperative security structures.

Unprecedented progress has been made in the peaceful resolution of regional conflicts by political means. In Southern Africa, the United Nations plan for the independence of Namibia has been implemented. The situation around Nicaragua has been settled, and a dynamic search for peace is under way in Cambodia, Afghanistan, and other hot spots of the globe.

We haven't forgotten Angola, Ethiopia, Cyprus, the Korean Peninsula, Western Sahara; and all of this has been done with the most active participation of the United Nations.

These positive changes in the world, we can safely say, have been propelled by a new relationship between the Soviet Union and the United States, which is evolving from cooperation to partnership in a direction. The meetings of the presidents of the superpowers in Malta, Camp David and Helsinki have been major events in world politics. The political environment is clearly being defined by the global recognition of the supremacy of universal human values.

Democratic forums are becoming established and running the affairs of states, and in the conduct of international affairs. The United Nations, too, is being reborn. We are pleased to note that President Mikhail Gorbachev's ideas concerning the role of the organization in a changing world, have been seen to reflect majority opinion and the real needs of the international community.

The central concepts of today's politics are cooperation, interaction, and partnership in facing the global challenges of combating severe problems, such as economic backwardness, poverty, and social inequality, and protecting the environment.

Had this session taken place before last August, we would have had every reason to say that mankind had cleared a narrow and dangerous passage, that had a wide—that had wide and glowing horizons ahead of it. But now, our field of vision has been obscured by the dark cloud of aggression against Kuwait.

On that black Thursday, Iraq flagrantly violated the United Nations charter, the principles of international law, the universally recognized norms of morality, and the standards of civilized behavior. Iraq committed an unprovoked aggression, and next the neighboring sovereign states seized thousands of hostages and resorted to unprecedented blackmail, threatening to use weapons of mass destruction.

[Iraq's 'Affront to Mankind']

There is also another dimension to Iraq's action. It has dealt a blow to all that mankind has recently achieved, all that we have been able to accomplish together by adopting the new political thinking, as our guide to the future.

An act of terrorism—I think one can call it that without exaggeration—has been perpetrated against the emerging new world order. This is a major affront to mankind. Unless we find a way to respond to it and cope with the situation, civilization will be thrown back by half a century.

Iraq's actions are having, and will have, the gravest consequences for the people of Iraq, and for millions of men, women and children in many countries of the world; and for their hopes and their future. War, a great war, may break out in the Persian Gulf region any day, at any moment.

From this rostrum, we should like to appeal once again to the leaders of Iraq. We are making this appeal as their old friends, and as a country which has found the courage to condemn its own wrongdoings against certain states in the past.

We call upon them to heed reason and to obey the demands of law, and also of plain common sense, and to take a responsible and humane attitude, above all, vis-a-vis the Iraqi people who surely yearn for peace, tranquility and good relations with their neighbors.

We also hope that at this time of grave trial the Arab states will live up to the expectations of mankind and help find a way out of the Persian Gulf crisis. This would make it possible to deal with other hotbeds of conflict in the Middle East, and at last to find an equitable solution to the Palestinian problem.

If the world has survived to this day, it is because at tragic moments in its history the forces of evil were always opposed by the forces of good; arbitrary power by the rule of law; treachery and meanness by honour and decency; and violence by the strength of the spirit and belief in justice.

But today is no time for rejoicing. But one cannot help being satisfied at the unprecedented unity of the Security Council and the clear attitude of international public opinion in the face of Iraq's behavior. This gives us confidence in the ability of the United Nations to deal with this grave international crisis.

The positions taken by members of this organization give the Security Council the mandate to go as far as the interests of world peace require. I do not doubt that today's meeting, on which agreement has already been reached, will yet again demonstrate the determination and unity of our collective organ, the Council—the Security Council in this critical situation.

Some may find that Iraq is being judged by a different, higher standard than that applied to other countries, even in the quite recent past. My answer is this; it's good that we've reached this point. It's a good thing that we have adopted a universal, human yardstick of good and evil; that we are calling aggression by its proper name; and consider it necessary to condemn and punish its perpetrator, and to help the victims of injustice.

These days are a trying time, a test for organization. If it passes this test it will immeasurably enhance its prestige, gain new experience and new capabilities. There is no doubt that it will use them to restore peace and justice in other conflict situations, and to ensure the implementation of its resolutions bearing on all regional problems, to which reference was made by previous speakers.

An approach based on mankind's common interest does not permit any other kind of behavior. From now on the world community intends to act by a common set of standards. International relations are being freed from the vestiges of the cold war, which for many years had a negative effect on the international legal order. We are again becoming the United Nations and we're returning to our own global constitution; the United Nations Charter, and to those of its provisions that were forgotten for a while but have been proven to be indispensable for the most important and vitally necessary of our tasks; the maintenance of international peace and security.

The establishment of the principles of new thinking in world politics has enabled us to start implementing the effective measures of persuasion and enforcement provided for in the Charter. In the context of recent events I should remind those who regard aggression as an acceptable form of behavior that the United Nations has the power to suppress acts of aggression. There is already ample evidence that this right can be exercised.

Of course, before—I reiterate—before this, all political, peaceful, non-military forms of pressure must be applied to the aggressor; obviously in combination with economic and other enforcement measures.

In a way the Gulf crisis is not just a tragedy and an extremely dangerous threat to peace; it is also a serious challenge for all of us to review the ways and means of maintaining security in our world; methods of protecting law and order on our planet; the mechanisms for controlling the processes which affect the state of human civilization in the broadest meaning of this term; and the role of the United Nations in all of this.

It cannot be otherwise in today's world. Only in this way can we make the period of peace lasting and irreversible, and follow up on our initial success in bringing about a healthier climate in international relations.

Life poses new challenges; what will be needed in the first place is, in our view, a theoretical and conceptual reassessment of the political, technological, economic, environmental, humanitarian and cultural realities of the modern world and of its human dimension.

[Partnership Replacing Rivalry]

The world is consolidating on the basis of universal human values. Partnership is replacing rivalry. It is becoming the basis for relations between many countries that used to regard each other as adversaries and rivals. Partnership is not just a fashionable term. It became evident that during the latest crisis—or it came in evidence during the latest crisis and underlied the close and constructive interaction among the permanent members of the Security Council.

But the decline of East-West rivalry as a real or perceived factor in international relations may bring to the arena of world politics new figures and new phenomena. One such phenomenon we will probably have to deal with is claims to regional hegemony. Among the issues assuming a critical importance for the future of mankind are the non-proliferation of nuclear, chemical, bacteriological and missile technologies; and more generally, the disproportionate growth of the military sector in some economies and societies.

Even in the past the doctrines of the balance of terror and nuclear deterrence were questionable means of maintaining peace and security. In the new conditions they have simply become irrelevant.

We need to define the criteria of defense sufficiency. The Iraqi aggression would seem to make it difficult even to discuss this. After all, what can be sufficient in the face of the irrational? On the other hand, this aggression has once again underscored the validity of the argument that no nation should have the exclusive prerogative or absolute freedom to determine its own level of armament. Any other approach would result in an unbridled arms race and all out militarization. We must look towards different principles, towards an accommodation of reciprocal concerns and a balance of armaments at the lowest possible levels.

We in the Soviet Union have the unfortunate experience of having built up a redundant defense capability, and we all know what that costs. This was due more to an erroneous assessment of the situation and a desire to protect the country against any eventuality than to any evil intent or aggressiveness. At the time, we and our adversaries took an overly arithmetical approach to military parity. Of course, parity is needed for global stability, but it should not go beyond the limits of reasonable defense sufficiency. We have drawn and continued to draw appropriate conclusions for ourselves. It is now common knowledge that militarization is wasteful for any country and can be ruinous when taken to extremes.

In the longer-term the world community will need to monitor the military power of states, arm supplies and transfers of military technology. Such an approach will be in everyone's interests and will strengthen stability and trust. Otherwise, we will continue to be confronted with armed conflicts and attempts to intimidate and blackmail.

Above all, it will be necessary to keep a close watch on those countries that are making determined efforts to build up the offensive capabilities of their armed forces. Moreover, not just to watch what they do, but to have them explain why this is being done. Of course, the United Nations itself will have to play the primary role in this. But the organization will need effective support from regional security structures which are already becoming a reality in Europe and which we hope will emerge in Asia and the Pacific, in the Middle East, in Central America and elsewhere in the world.

[World Arms Registration]

We might consider the idea of introducing, on a global and regional level, the international registration of certain types of armaments that are produced or required. And there is unquestionably a need for transferrency in this area.

We need to agree on principles governing the sale and supply of arms. Such attempts were made in the past, but unfortunately they were not carried through to their logical conclusion. In our view we must urgently request the Geneva Conference on Disarmament to address this issue and to submit recommendations to the next session of the General Assembly.

Two years ago the Soviet delegation raised the issue of reactivating the work of the Security Council's Military Staff Committee. Recent developments have convinced us of the need to return to the original idea conceived by the founders of this organization and of its Charter. We know why the Military Staff Committee has never become a functioning body. During the Cold War, the Committee could not and did not have a role to play. Now, however, we see that without substantive recommendations from this body, the Security Council is unable to carry out its functions under the Charter.

The architects of our organization proceeded from the harsh realities of the Second World War and were right in assuming that for the organization to be effective in keeping the peace and preventing war, it must have the means to enforce its decisions, and if necessary to suppress aggression. And also to have a mechanism for preparing and coordinating such actions.

The Soviet delegation believes that the Security Council must take the necessary organizational steps to be able to act in strict conformity with the provisions of the Charter. It should begin by initiating steps to reactivate the work of the Military Staff Committee, and to study the practical aspects of assigning national military contingents to serve under the authority of the council.

The Soviet Union is prepared to conclude an appropriate agreement with the Security Council. We are sure that the other permanent members of the Council, and states that might be approached by it, will do the same. If the Military Staff Committee had worked properly, if appropriate agreements had been concluded between the Council and its permanent members, and if other organizational aspects of countering threats to peace had been worked out, there would now be no need for individual states to act unilaterally; after all, however justified they might be, such actions provoke a mixed response and create problems for those same states and may not be acceptable to all.

By contrast, there is no reason to object to steps taken by legitimate international law enforcement bodies. The Security Council and its military staff—

We also should not underestimate even the psychological effect of the Security Council acquiring structures and forces to counter aggression. I should like to emphasize that the use of force is only possible as a last resort. We must rely on nonmilitary political means and pursue our objectives in a peaceful manner. Today, more than ever before, it is these methods that are becoming effective. The latest crisis has dramatically illustrated the importance of preventing the spread of weapons of mass destruction.

[Nuclear Arms Peril]

To be frank, the situation is beginning to cause alarm. Let's face it— cracks have appeared in the Nuclear Non-proliferation regime. The International Atomic Energy Agency is having difficulty expanding the zone of application of its safeguards. It is time to trigger the emergency systems in order to save the situation.

And as a matter of the utmost urgency, nuclear tests have to be stopped. If testing is stopped, we have a chance to survive. Otherwise, the world will perish. I am in no doubt about this. We need to tell people about this, frankly, without taking refuge in all sorts of specious arguments. Perhaps we should invite the parliaments of all countries to express their attitude to nuclear explosions, to nuclear tests. We should organize a worldwide parliamentary referendum.

What else has to happen in order to set in motion the elimination of chemical weapons? And to complete this process by the completion of a convention. The Soviet Union and the United States are setting an example by doing so on a bilateral basis, but what about the others? It is really odd that while there is no person, no politician who would publicly call for retaining toxic agents, things are, in fact, at a standstill. And we still have no convention.

Perhaps we should—we should ask for a roll call vote right here in this United Nations hall to see who votes against. If everyone is in favor, let's just work out a binding schedule for completing work on the convention and set a time frame for the destruction of chemical weapons.

Similar problems—mostly concerning verification—arise with regard to biological weapons. Swift action is needed on all these issues. Yet, the debate at the Geneva Conference on Disarmament, quite honestly, let's admit, proceeds in a quiet and leisurely manner. Can we stand for this?

Even as dangerous developments are gaining critical momentum in the world, the negotiations there continue at a pace which was set at the time of the Cold War. I think the negotiators at the Palais des Nations in Geneva should roll up the blinds. Let them see what's going on outside. And let people know what those disarmament pundits are reflecting upon. I don't want to offend anyone. I know that eminent people work there, but what's to be done? The time has come to cry out. The time has come to act decisively and firmly.

I cannot fail to mention yet another aspect of security. The world community should also consider the possibility of various unconventional situations rising from the mass taking of hostages and cases of blackmail involving particularly dangerous and destructive weapons.

These problems will have to be addressed at two levels—technical and legal. We could start out by setting up a group of experts for contingency planning under the Security Council. This group could include experts on combatting terrorism, psychologists, nuclear physicists, chemists, physicians, disaster relief workers, experts on the physical protection of facilities, and so on.

Recommendations concerning the management of unconventional situations should be made known to a limited number of people. The Security Council may find it necessary, upon the recommendation of the military staff committee, to recommend—oh, sorry—to establish a rapid response force to be formed upon a contract basis from units specially designated by different countries, including the five permanent members of the Security Council.

This idea also deserves discussion. But technical methods alone are not enough to deal with such things. In our view there is an urgent need to institute a new known in international law which would declare a threat by any individual for purposes of blackmail, of using weapons of mass destruction, hostage taking or mass terror, to be a crime against mankind. Such work is currently under way somewhere in the labyrinths of this organization, but so far inconclusively.

What we need, however, is to create as soon as possible a moral and legal environment in which anyone guilty of grave crimes against mankind, or participating in atrocities, in taking hostages, acts of terrorism or torture, or those guilty of particular cruelty in the use of force could not escape punishment and would not be absolved from personal responsibility even if they acted under orders. The principle of suppressing aggression and threats to peace should, in our view, be complemented with the principle of individual responsibility and commensurate punishment.

[Economic Effect of Gulf Crisis]

The Gulf crisis is causing a major dislocation in the entire system of the world economy, as other speakers have pointed out. Its true magnitude is even difficult to assess at present. It is clear that the consequences will be severe for the economies of the developing countries, particularly the poorest of them.

Merely stating this is not enough. Action must be taken without delay. It is necessary to establish, as soon as possible, an international machinery, maybe a temporary one for the time being. For example, under the auspices of the International Monetary Fund, or the World Bank to mitigate the negative consequences of this crisis for countries which are in a particularly vulnerable position.

We are of the view that sounding out the economic repercussions of the crisis should be primarily the function of the United Nations. The organization should be the center of action in situations affecting the interests of many countries. History, particularly modern history, teaches all kinds of lessons. They should not be ignored or underestimated.

One of them is that security can hardly be lasting unless it is supported by economic growth combined with spiritual health, and by traditional, cultural values combined with new technologies, and a concern for the environment. Hence, the need for cooperation in the '90s to be geared to the resolution of the entire state of global economic and environmental problems.

A new poverty curtain, this time between North and South, must not be allowed to fall. If it does, a division of the world that will follow may prove fatal to our civilization. We have no time to lose. A global strategy for development and for solving universal problems is needed now, and the report of the secretary general on the work of the organization rightly makes this point. The United Nations, supported by its specialized agencies and by outside intellectual resources, should take the lead in formulating such a strategy.

An interdependent world calls for a new level of multinational economic partnership. Cooperation on a bilateral basis, and in selected areas, is no longer enough. It's precisely global cooperation that's needed.

The special session of the General Assembly on International Economic Cooperation has clearly shown that everybody would gain if each group of countries were to adjust its approaches and show willingness to forsake individual or group self-interest in economic cooperation, setting as its highest priority the interests of the common good—a global self-interest, if you will, which would no longer be as selfish. We welcome those provisions—the provisions of the declaration of the special session which support the integration of the Soviet Union and East European countries into the world economy. We hope that the United Nations will give a concrete expression to its support for this process.

The Soviet contribution to these efforts will certainly be growing as we move ahead with perestroika at home and deepen our economic reform and switch over to a market economy.

We have firmly opted for a closer association with GATT [General Agreement on Tariffs and Trade], the International Monetary Fund, the World Bank, and the Organization for Economic Cooperation and Development with a view to joining them as soon as the necessary internal and external conditions are in place. It's true that we're rather late, but nonetheless, we have come to a stand on this very important question.

We also see a unique contribution that we can make to the development in international cooperation. For geographical and other reasons, we are in a better position than others to serve as a link between Europe and Asia and to contribute to the establishment of a single Eurasian space in the economic, scientific, technological, environmental and other areas. This could be facilitated, for instance, by Soviet communication lines and equipment, including space communication systems. Scientific and technological progress has become a major factor shaping the world's future. The global nature of its implications places in a new perspective the need to coordinate national policies in this new area.

The United Nations and its system of organizations can and must, in our view, assume a leading role in these efforts. This is an area in which trust among states is of special importance. Without trust, barriers to international scientific and technological cooperation cannot be dismantled. We think that the international community should take a stand against monopolism in the field of science and technology. Without that, it will be difficult to deal effectively with underdevelopment and with the numerous problems of the developing world.

If we succeeded in really focusing the global development strategy on scientific and technological progress, we could substantially mitigate such alarming trends as the brain drain, the growing professional migration and the rising cost and narrowing scope of the search.

The United Nations would do well to take the lead in organizing a wide-ranging discussion on the role of thought, science and technology in addressing the problems of today's world. The Soviet Union is prepared to take the initiative of holding such a major international forum in our country.

Much has been said lately on environmental issues. We even run the risk of talking away our future. For, until now, at a global level—I emphasize at the global level—very little has been done while the destruction of the environment is outstripping our preparation to deal with the ecological threat. I hope that, even as we continue to prepare for the 1992 Conference on the Environment and Development in Brazil, we shall be able to start implementing specific environmental projects.

[UN Environmental Assistance]

In our view, one of the priority measures would be to establish a United Nations Center for Emergency Environmental Assistance. We have submitted to the Secretary General a list of Soviet scientists and specialists who, upon the center's request, we will be ready to send at our expense as part of an international expert team, to areas of environmental disasters. We are well aware that a healthy environment requires considerable investment, both on the national and global level.

As we see it, the way to go is to reduce military expenditures and to promote conversion in the defense production sector. There is no alternative. The figures are well known: $800 billion must be spent before the end of the century to avert environmental degradation. That sum is almost equal to what the world spends on the military each year.

The Chernobyl tragedy has highlighted the urgency of environmental protection programs. We are grateful to the governments and the various agencies which are joining in the hard work of dealing with the consequences of the disaster. On behalf of the Soviet people, I also wish to express our gratitude to all international, governmental and public organizations and private citizens who have offered help to the victims. A special thanks goes to UNESCO and to those countries and organizations that have reached out so movingly to Chernobyl's children, inviting them to come for Western medical treatment and sharing with them the warmth of their hearts. The Secretary General's decision to designate a special representative for Chernobyl disaster relief has been received with warm approval in our country.

The multi-dimensional approach to security, supported by our organization, brings into focus the interrelationship between the security of states and the well-being and freedom of the individual. The human being is coming to the fore, and the human dimension is becoming a universal yardstick for any international initiative. For us and for the United Nations, the security of the individual, of every citizen, and the protection of fundamental human rights are inseparable from the national security of states and international security as a whole.

I think the time has also come to look at regional conflicts from the standpoint of human rights. Those rights include the right to life and personal safety, as well as the right to enjoy fundamental freedoms and to participate in the democratic process of government. The main task for the international community is to create conditions in which people would be able to make a free choice. Disputes must be settled through the ballot box, not in the trenches of war, both in regions and individual countries.

Speaking about the future, we should also like to respond to those who have been following, with understandable concern, developments in our country. It is true that our domestic situation is not at all simple, and it's still far from stable. We will understand that concern. The stability of the Soviet Union, obviously, has a great influence on the stability of the world. But whatever the complexity of our situation, one has to see that it is evolving against the background of the emancipation and active political involvement and reaffirmation of the national identities by all of our country's nations. They are opening themselves to the world, and the world is discovering them.

That this process is accompanied by certain difficulties, and even losses, should be no reason for excessive alarm, because the Soviet people and the democratic forces that are assuming responsibility for the future of our union are aware of the Soviet Union's place in the world, and of its responsibility for the maintenance of global stability. This awareness is shared by all the nations of our multinational country, and they will all act responsibly, realizing that stability in the world will also mean peace in their own home.

In working for the renewal of our society, we have seen how important it is to defend democratic principles at all levels, domestically and internationally. If attempts to embark on the part of democracy were it to end [in] failure, or worse still in defeat, it would have grave consequences for the world's future, not to mention the risk of chaos and new dictatorship. To prevent that should be in everyone's interest.

As we meet for the organization's 45th General Assembly, we are speaking not so much of the organization's maturity, but of the beginning of its rebirth, its restoration according to the blueprints of 1945, and wiping off the grime left by Cold War we see a work of collective wisdom. The United Nations devised it—the organization as an instrument of action, and we must see to it that from now on all of us gear our words, to joint actions. This is what our time is about.

The philosophy of today is precisely a philosophy of action, distinguished delegates. This is the sixth time that I have spoken from this rostrum, and the sixth time I have attended a session of the General Assembly. It has certainly been a great school, a first-rate school. Where else can one become so closely involved with the entire gamut of human problems and encounter such a constellation of personalities, intellectuals, professionals, and scholars whose brilliant qualities are epitomized by the Secretary General of our organization, Mr. Perez de Cuellar.

I consider myself very fortunate to have met and worked here with real political leaders and great men during the years when the United Nations returned to what it was meant to be, a center for harmonizing the activities of the nations.

I thank you, my friends.

BUSH SPEECH

... Forty-five years ago, while the fires of an epic war still raged across two oceans and two continents, a small group of men and women began a search for hope amid the ruins. They gathered in San Francisco, stepping back from the haze and horror, to try to shape a new structure that might support an ancient dream.

Intensely idealistic, and yet tempered by war, they sought to build a new kind of bridge, a bridge between nations, a bridge that might help carry humankind from its darkest hour to its brightest day.

The founding of the United Nations embodied our deepest hopes for a peaceful world. And during the past year, we've come closer than ever before to realizing those hopes. We've seen a century sundered by barbed threats and barbed wire give way to a new era of peace and competition and freedom.

[1989's Revolutionary Breeze of Freedom]

The revolution of 1989 swept the world almost with a life of its own, carried by a new breeze of freedom. It transformed the political climate from Central Europe to Central America and touched almost every corner of the globe.

That breeze has been sustained by a now almost universal recognition of a simple, fundamental truth: The human spirit cannot be locked up forever. The truth is, people everywhere are motivated in much the same ways. People everywhere want much the same things: the chance to live a life of purpose; the chance to choose a life in which they and their children can learn, and grow healthy, worship freely, and prosper through the work of their hands and their hearts and their minds.

We're not talking about the power of nations but the power of individuals—the power to choose, the power to risk, the power to succeed.

This is a new and different world. Not since 1945 have we seen the real possibility of using the United Nations as it was designed—as a center for international collective security.

The changes in the Soviet Union have been critical to the emergence of a stronger United Nations. The US-Soviet relationship is finally beyond containment and confrontation, and now we seek to fulfill the promise of mutually shared understanding.

The long twilight struggle that for 45 years has divided Europe, our two nations, and much of the world, has come to an end. Much has changed over the last 2 years. The Soviet Union has taken many dramatic and important steps to participate fully in the community of nations.

And when the Soviet Union agreed with so many of us here in the United Nations to condemn the aggression of Iraq, there could be no doubt—no doubt then—that we had, indeed, put four decades of history behind us.

We are hopeful that the machinery of the United Nations will no longer be frozen by the divisions that plagued us during the Cold War, that at last—long last—we can build new bridges and tear down old walls, that at long last we will be able to build a new world based on an event for which we have all hoped—an end to the Cold War.

Two days from now, the world will be watching when the Cold War is formally buried in Berlin. And in this time of testing, a fundamental question must be asked, a question not for any one nation but for the United Nations. The question is this: Can we work together in a new partnership of nations? Can the collective strength of the world community, expressed by the United Nations, unite to deter and defeat aggression? Because the Cold War's battle of ideas is not the last epic battle of this century.

[Iraqi Aggression]

Two months ago, in the waning weeks of one of history's most hopeful summers, the vast, still beauty of the peaceful Kuwaiti desert was fouled by the stench of diesel and the roar of steel tanks. Once again the sound of distant thunder echoed across a cloudless sky, and once again the world awoke to face the guns of August.

But this time, the world was ready. The United Nation's Security Council's resolute response to Iraq's unprovoked aggression has been without precedent. Since the invasion on August 2d, the council has passed eight major resolutions setting the terms for a solution to the crisis.

The Iraqi regime has yet to face the facts. But as I said last month, the annexation of Kuwait will not be permitted to stand. And this is not simply the view of the United States. It is the view of every Kuwaiti, the Arab League, the United Nations. Iraq's leaders should listen: It is Iraq against the world.

Let me take this opportunity to make the policy of my government clear. The United States supports the use of sanctions to compel Iraq's leaders to withdraw immediately and without condition from Kuwait. We also support the provision of medicine and food for humanitarian purposes, so long as distribution can be properly monitored. Our quarrel is not with the people of Iraq. We do not wish for them to suffer. The world's quarrel is with the dictator who ordered that invasion.

Along with others, we have dispatched military forces to the region to enforce sanctions, to deter and, if need be, defend against further aggression. And we seek no advantage for ourselves; nor do we seek to maintain our military forces in Saudi Arabia for 1 day longer than is necessary. US forces were sent at the request of the Saudi government. The American people, and this President, want every single American soldier brought home as soon as this mission is completed.

Let me also emphasize that all of us here at the United Nations hope that military force will never be used. We seek a peaceful outcome—a diplomatic outcome. And one more thing: In the aftermath of Iraq's unconditional departure from Kuwait, I truly believe there may be opportunities—for Iraq and Kuwait to settle their differences permanently, for the states of the gulf themselves to build new arrangements for stability, and for all the states and the peoples of the region to settle the conflicts that divide the Arabs from Israel. But the world's key task—now, first, and always—must be to demonstrate that aggression will not be tolerated or rewarded.

Through the UN Security Council, Iraq has been judged—fairly judged by a jury of its peers, the very nations of the Earth. Today, the regime stands isolated and out of step with the times, separated from the civilized world, not by space but by centuries.

Iraq's unprovoked aggression is a throwback to another era, a dark relic from a dark time. It has plundered Kuwait; it has terrorized innocent civilians; it has held even diplomats hostage. Iraq and its leaders must be held liable for these crimes of abuse and destruction. But this outrageous disregard for basic human rights does not come as a total surprise. Thousands of Iraqis have been executed on political and religious grounds and even more through a genocidal, poison-gas war waged against Iraq's own Kurdish villagers.

[Elimination of Chemical Weapons]

As a world community, we must act—not only to deter the use of inhumane weapons like mustard and nerve gas but to eliminate the weapons entirely. And that is why, 1 year ago, I came to the General Assembly with new proposals to banish these terrible weapons from the face of the Earth.

I promised that the United States would destroy over 98% of its stockpile in the first 8 years of a chemical weapons ban treaty, and 100%—all of them—in 10 years, if all nations with chemical weapons capabilities—chemical weapons—signed the treaty.

We've stood by those promises. In June, the United States and the Soviet Union signed a landmark agreement to halt production and to destroy the vast majority of our stockpiles. Today, US chemical weapons are being destroyed.

But time is running out. This isn't merely a bilateral concern. The gulf crisis proves how important it is to act together—and to act now—to conclude an absolute, worldwide ban on these weapons. We must also redouble our efforts to stem the spread of nuclear weapons, biological weapons, and the ballistic missiles that can rain destruction upon distant peoples.

The United Nations can help bring about a new day, a day when these kinds of terrible weapons, and the terrible despots who would use them, are both a thing of the past. It is in our hands to leave these dark machines behind, in the Dark Ages where they belong, and to press forward to cap a historic movement toward a new world order and a long era of peace.

[A New Partnership of Nations]

We have a vision of a new partnership of nations that transcends the Cold War. A partnership based on consultation, cooperation, and collective action, especially through international and regional organizations. A partnership united by principle and the rule of law and supported by an equitable sharing of both cost and commitment. A partnership whose goals are to increase democracy, increase prosperity, increase the peace, and reduce arms.

And as we look to the future, the calendar offers up a convenient milestone, a signpost by which to measure our progress as a community of nations.

The year 2000 marks a turning point, beginning not only the turn of the decade, not only the turn of the century, but also the turn of the millennium.

And 10 years from now, as the 55th session of the General Assembly begins, you will again find many of us in this hall, hair a bit more gray perhaps, maybe a little less spring in our walk. But you will not find us with any less hope or idealism or any less confidence in the ultimate triumph of mankind.

I see a world of open borders, open trade, and, most importantly, open minds. A world that celebrates the common heritage that belongs to all the world's people taking pride not just in hometown or homeland but in humanity itself.

I see a world touched by a spirit like that of the Olympics—based not on competition that's driven by fear but sought out of joy and exhilaration and a true quest for excellence.

I see a world where democracy continues to win new friends and convert old foes and where the Americas—North, Central, and South—can provide a model for the future of all humankind; the world's first completely democratic hemisphere.

And I see a world building on the emerging new model of European unity—not just Europe but the whole world whole and free.

This is precisely why the present aggression in the gulf is a menace not only to one region's security but to the entire world's vision of our future. It threatens to turn the dream of a new international order into a grim nightmare of anarchy in which the law of the jungle supplants the law of nations.

That's why the United Nations reacted with such historic unity and resolve. And that's why this challenge is a test that we cannot afford to fail. I am confident we will prevail. Success, too, will have lasting consequences—reinforcing civilized standards of international conduct, setting a new precedent in international cooperation, brightening the prospects for our vision of the future.

There are 10 more years until this century is out—10 more years to put the struggles of the 20th century permanently behind us, 10 more years to help launch a new partnership of nations. And throughout those 10 years, and beginning now, the United Nations has a new and vital role in building toward that partnership. Last year's General Assembly showed how we can make greater progress toward a more pragmatic and successful United Nations. And, for the first time, the UN Security Council is beginning to work as it was designed to work.

Now is the time to set aside old and counterproductive debates and procedures and controversies and resolutions. It's time to replace polemic attacks with pragmatic action.

We've shown that the UN can count on the collective strength of the international community. We've shown that the UN can rise to the challenge of aggression just as its founders hoped that it would. And now is the time of testing. We must also show that the United Nations is the place to build international support and consensus for meeting the other challenges we face.

The world remains a dangerous place, and our security and well-being often depend, in part, on events occurring far away. We need serious international cooperative efforts to make headway on the threats to the environment, on terrorism, on managing the debt burden, on fighting the scourge of international drug trafficking, and on refugees and peacekeeping efforts around the world.

But the world also remains a hopeful place. Calls for democracy and human rights are being reborn everywhere. And these calls are an expression of support for the values enshrined in the UN Charter. They encourage our hopes for a more stable, more peaceful, more prosperous world.

Free Elections and UN Membership

Free elections are the foundation of democratic government and can produce dramatic successes, as we have seen in Namibia and Nicaragua. The time has come to structure the UN role in such efforts more formally. And so today, I propose that the UN establish a special coordinator for electoral assistance, to be assisted by a UN electoral commission comprised of distinguished experts from around the world.

As with free elections, we also believe that universal UN membership for all states is central to the future of this organization and to this new partnership we've discussed. In support of this principle, and in conjunction with UN efforts to reduce regional tensions, the United States fully supports UN membership for the Republic of Korea. We do so without prejudice to the ultimate objective of reunification of the Korean Peninsula and without opposition to simultaneous membership for the Democratic People's Republic of Korea.

Bringing the UN into the 21st Century

Building on these and other initiatives, we must join together in a new compact—all of us—to bring the United Nations into the 21st century. I call today for a major long-term effort to do so. We should build on the success—the admirable success—of our distinguished Secretary General, my longtime friend and yours—my longtime colleague, I might also say— Javier Perez de Cuellar. We should strive for greater effectiveness and efficiency of the United Nations.

The United States is committed to playing its part—helping to maintain global security, promoting democracy and prosperity. And my administration is fully committed to supporting the United Nations and to paying what we are obliged to pay by our commitment to the Charter. International peace and security—and international freedom and prosperity— require no less.

The world must know and understand: From this hour, from this day, from this hall, we step forth with a new sense of purpose, a new sense of possibilities. We stand together, prepared to swim upstream, to march uphill, to tackle the tough challenges as they come—not only as the United Nations, but as the nations of the world united.

And so let it be said of the final decade of the 20th century: This was a time when humankind came into its own, when we emerged from the grit and the smoke of the industrial age to bring about a revolution of the spirit and the mind and began a journey into a new day, a new age, and a new partnership of nations.

The United Nations is now fulfilling its promise as the world's parliament of peace. I congratulate you. I support you. And I wish you Godspeed in the challenges ahead.

U.S.-SOVIET STATEMENT

The 45th session of the United Nations General Assembly is taking place amidst the most profound changes in international affairs that have occurred since the Second World War. The confrontational nature of relations between East and West is giving way to a cooperative relationship and partnership. The UN is fast becoming a real center for agreed common actions and the Security Council is reestablishing its crucial role in the maintenance of international security, peaceful settlement of disputes, and prevention of conflicts. Yet there remain many challenges to meet and problems to solve on the way to a peaceful and prosperous future.

Reaffirming the resolution presented last year by the United States and Soviet Union and unanimously adopted by the UN General Assembly, our two countries will attach special importance in the United Nations and its specialized agencies and programs to promoting practical, multifaceted solutions to the issues of international peace and security, political, economic, social, cultural and humanitarian problems.

To accomplish this we will pursue cooperation with all member-states in attainment of the following:

- Strengthen the UN's efforts to promote international peace and security in all its aspects by working to improve UN peacekeeping, peacemaking and crisis prevention functions, by encouraging more active use of the Secretary General's good offices and, at the request of individual countries, electoral assistance;
- Establish a new sense of responsibility at the UN by encouraging the trend away from rhetorical excess toward efforts to deal pragmatically with the major issues of the 1990's, including transnational issues like narcotics, the environment, development, terrorism, and human rights;
- Promote a new way of conducting diplomatic efforts within the UN system to eliminate duplicative programs and activities and ensure that the UN system is utilized in the most efficient manner possible— we call this a "unitary UN";
- Ensure the availability of sufficient resources to the UN for it to function effectively and efficiently by timely payment of financial obligations to the UN.

Promoting Peace and Security in All Its Aspects

Joint efforts have contributed significantly to the easing of tensions in southern Africa and Central America, and are part of efforts to prepare a peaceful settlement in Cambodia. But serious problems still remain. Our search continues for workable solutions to conflict and instability in the Persian Gulf, the Middle East, Afghanistan, and El Salvador.

In the Persian Gulf, we face a most serious threat to the integrity of the emerging international system. The United States and the Soviet Union are working together with other members of the Security Council to fashion a concerted response, unprecedented in UN history, to this crisis. The swift reaction of the international community to Iraq's dangerous and unwarranted aggression serves as a sobering reminder to any future aggressor; the international community will not tolerate the kind of wanton aggression which Iraq has committed. We call upon all United Nations members to continue to support the sanctions invoked by Security Council Resolutions 661 and 670 until Iraq abides by the call of the Security Council to withdraw its forces from Kuwait immediately, totally and unconditionally. We call also for the restoration of the legitimate government of Kuwait.

The rapidly changing structure of international relations requires a United Nations that, while remaining faithful to its original purposes, can also respond flexibly and effectively to new challenges as they occur, like drugs, the environment, and the need to ensure the protection of human rights.

Tangible examples of the UN movement away from divisive rhetoric and political excess were last December's special session of the General Assembly on apartheid and the resumed session last month, where the world community underscored its resolute opposition to apartheid while agreeing, by consensus, on a positive approach based on dialogue among all South African parties. We will work for equally positive results at the General Assembly this year.

The UN Special Session on International Economic Cooperation in April 1990 also reflected the growing convergence of views worldwide on the need for more effective approaches to national economic development, in the context of a supportive international economic environment. Our two countries will continue working together to promote further convergence in this direction. We will also support efforts to ensure careful and pragmatic preparation for the 1992 Conference on Environment and Development. We want to see the Conference fashion a realistic action plan to set the UN's course in the coming decades.

Another area in which the UN is actively promoting peaceful change is in facilitation of free and fair elections. UN assistance in Namibia and Nicaragua was dramatically successful, and there are many other situations where the UN's services are being requested. Our two countries will work with other UN members and the Secretary General to structure a UN electoral assistance process to enable the organization, at the request of countries concerned, to carry out effectively this important new effort.

Promoting a Unitary UN and Assuring Needed Financial Resources

An important area of our bilateral and multilateral cooperation has been the administration and management of the United Nations, particularly its budget. As major contributors to the United Nations, we believe it is essential that all views on the budget are taken into account, and that the agreement of all major contributors is required in order to approve the budget.

For there to be consensus, the UN system must improve the setting of priorities and improve coordination among various UN programs. The aim should be to eliminate duplicative programs and activities and ensure that the various components of the United Nations are utilized in the most efficient manner possible. For priority setting and coordination to be effective, members will need clearer and more comprehensive data on what the UN and the specialized agencies are doing with assessed and voluntary contributions.

Our two countries provide an important element of UN resources. As such, we recognize our responsibility to pay assessments promptly so that the United Nations has the resources required to perform the tasks as expeditiously as possible, keeping in mind the necessity of strengthening the administrative and budgetary reforms that have taken place in recent years.

We intend to work for further enhancing the efficiency of the executive machinery of the organization.

Establish a New Sense of Responsibility for Peace

The challenges before the international community and the UN are great. So, too, are the opportunities for more and better multilateral cooperation to confront and master the problems of our time.

In all spheres of UN activities the renunciation of sterile and rigid positions dictated by ideology rather than by practicality constitutes an essential prerequisite for creating an atmosphere of confidence within the United Nations among all United Nations members.

The United Nations can play a leading role on issues of global concern. We will actively support efforts, throughout the UN system, to implement and strengthen the principles and the system of international peace, security and international cooperation laid down in the Charter.

KUWAITI EMIR'S APPEAL
TO THE UNITED NATIONS
September 27, 1990

The emir of Kuwait went before the United Nations General Assembly on September 27 to urge that it keep pressure on Iraq to withdraw from his kingdom, which its army invaded August 2 and quickly seized. The emir, Sheik Jaber al-Ahmed al-Sabah, fled his palace in the Kuwaiti capital only minutes ahead of the invaders and reached safety across the border in Saudi Arabia. He and other Kuwaiti leaders who also escaped—most of them his kinsmen—set up a government in exile in the Saudi resort city of Taif. (Iraqi Invasion of Kuwait, p. 533)

"I came here to tell you of the horrors and suffering we are enduring both inside and outside our occupied homeland, and to put before you our just cause," said the sixty-four-year-old Kuwaiti leader, speaking softly in Arabic. In flowing robes, he entered the packed assembly hall to a standing ovation just as the Iraqi delegation walked out in protest. He again drew heavy applause after he finished speaking.

Sheik Jaber expressed gratitude for the "multitude of resolutions" the UN Security Council had adopted condemning the invasion. The council's member nations—including the United States and the Soviet Union—had worked in rare harmony to declare Iraq a transgressor and its annexation of Kuwait illegal. At Washington's insistence and with Moscow's cooperation, the Security Council also imposed economic sanctions—consisting principally of an American-directed naval blockade—in an attempt to force Iraq's withdrawal from Kuwait.

The Security Council later authorized the use of force against Iraq if it did not withdraw by January 15, 1991. (UN Action Against Iraq With U.S.-Soviet Cooperation, p. 545) *The United States had been sending combat troops to Saudi Arabia since August in response to that kingdom's fear of Iraq, and by autumn they formed the biggest buildup of American forces on foreign soil since the Vietnam War.*

"There is no doubt that the key role played by the Security Council is indeed a propitious one ... [and] it is our earnest hope that this role will continue to grow," Sheik Jaber said. He cast the issue as "not an ordinary conflict between two states over a piece of land" but a test of the international rule of law.

In an apparent attempt to offset Iraq's portrayal of Kuwait as an oil-rich fiefdom unsympathetic to needy Arabs, the emir pointed to Kuwait's past assistance to poor countries and recalled that, at the same forum two years earlier, he had made a plea for their debt relief. This time, he announced that interest on all loans the Kuwaiti government had made to those countries would be forgiven. Although the government had gone into exile, its London-based Kuwaiti Investment Office still managed an estimated $100 billion in overseas assets.

Prince Bandar bin Sultan Abdul Aziz, Saudi Arabia's ambassador in Washington, praised the speech as speaking "to the conscience of the world." The ambassador added that by making an offer of debt forgiveness, the Kuwaiti leader showed his generosity. The speech also won praise from Farouk al-Sharaa, the foreign minister of Syria, whose country joined with Saudi Arabia, Egypt, and several other Arab states in opposition to Iraqi president Saddam Hussein.

Having delivered his speech in New York, the emir went to Washington to meet with President Bush the next day. After their meeting at the White House, the Kuwaiti leader spoke—in translation from the Arabic—of "our stand together in the face of treachery and aggression" and expressed his country's "deep feelings of friendship" for the president and the American people.

> *Following are excerpts from the speech Sheik Jaber al-Ahmad al-Sabah delivered to the UN General Assembly in New York, September 27, 1990, as provided in English translation by the Kuwaiti government in exile:*

. . . I speak from this rostrum today as my peaceful country is passing through extremely harsh circumstances that have given rise to an unprecedented crisis in the history of the United Nations, which, since its inception, has sought to uphold justice on the basis of international law. Indeed, the Security Council has demonstrated that role by recently adopting a series of firm resolutions in the face of naked and brutal aggression against the State of Kuwait.

There is no doubt that the key role played by the Security Council is indeed a propitious one under the prevailing grave circumstances in Kuwait, and, in fact, in the world at large. It is our earnest hope that this role will continue to grow without waning and gain momentum without setbacks, in order to consolidate the rule of international law.

Today, I bring to you the message of a peace-loving nation. A nation that has consistently worked for peace; a nation that reached out with a helping hand to all those who truly needed help; a nation that sought mediation and reconciliation among adversaries. It is this very nation whose security and stability have been trampled upon as a result of its abiding belief in lofty principles inspired by our true Moslem faith and echoed in universal charters, pacts and codes of morality.

Today, I plead before you the cause of a people whose land, until so recently, was a beacon for peaceful co-existence and genuine brotherhood among the family of nations. A people whose national territory was a gathering place for individuals from various peaceful nations who sought a decent and dignified life through constructive work. Some of these people have now been made homeless, wanderers living only on hope in their banishment, while others have become prisoners or fighters refusing, even at the risk of their own lives, to surrender or yield to occupation with all its violence and brutality. . . .

[World Stability Jeopardized]

The crisis of Kuwait is a manifold tragedy, whose dire consequences affect not only Kuwaitis but other peoples as well. In fact, it has jeopardized stability in the world, especially in the Gulf region.

And so, I come to this forum, which is the focal point of international collective action, in order to acknowledge the overwhelming global solidarity that has been shown to us in a multitude of Security Council resolutions that have been passed in an unprecedented fashion. This demonstrates rock-solid international rejection of the assassination of the norms of international law, rules of good neighbourly relations and established customs and practices at the hands of armed military invaders whose tanks rolled over and crushed all those concepts. Indeed, this is what makes the Iraqi aggression against the State of Kuwait quite a peculiar case. For we have never seen in contemporary post World War Two history a country that overran a sovereign independent state, a member of the United Nations, and then sought not only to annex it by brutal force but also to erase its name and entire entity from the world political map and wipe out the parameters of its national identity as defined by its institutions and its political, economic and social structures. All of this, Mr. President, has taken place as we approach the end of the twentieth century!

I came here to tell you of the horrors and suffering we are enduring both inside and outside our occupied homeland, and to put before you our just case. Now, the fate of a people, of a nation, is in your hands. . . .

The aggression by the Iraqi regime against the State of Kuwait which resulted in occupation of the Iraqi vicious attempts to annex Kuwait in flagrant violation of all charters, norms of conduct and treaties, including those legal instruments concluded between the two countries and deposited right here with the United Nations, is not an ordinary conflict between two states over a piece of land. Rather, the Iraqi aggression was the culmination of a pre-meditated scheme to occupy and seize the entire state by force of arms. This aggression, alas, was perpetrated by a country with which we have several internationally recognized treaties and agreements within the League of Arab States, the Organization of the Islamic Conference, the United Nations and other international organizations.

[Iraq's Unfounded Claims]

This Iraqi regime has invented false pretexts and untenable claims against my peaceful and peace-loving country. In response to them, and despite our firm conviction that those claims were totally unfounded, we proposed the constitution of a mutually acceptable, neutral Arab arbitration panel to which both parties would submit their differences. However, Iraq turned down that offer out of hand. Our last attempt at a peaceful resolution of our problems with Iraq was the bilateral round of talks in Jiddah, Kingdom of Saudi Arabia, in the course of which Kuwait stressed the need to resolve its outstanding problems with Iraq within an Arab context. But Iraq's plans were not anchored in any legal framework or based on any formal legal instruments. In fact, Iraq was bent on sweeping through the entire territory of Kuwait, violating its sovereignty and violating the sanctity of Kuwaiti citizens' lives and property. As a consequence, rape, destruction, terror and torture are now the rule of the day in the once peaceful and tranquil land of Kuwait. Hundreds of thousands of Kuwaiti citizens along with nationals of various other countries who were our guests have been made homeless and many of them have had their life savings robbed. Hundreds have lost their lives. Others have been held hostage. Indeed, at this very moment, an intense campaign of terror, torture and humiliation continues unabated in that dear land. We receive daily reports of massacres and continuing systematic armed looting and destruction of state assets and individual property.

This has prompted the forces of rightness, justice and peace in the world to try to acquaint themselves with the calamity of those innocents. In accordance with its responsibilities derived from the Fourth Geneva Convention of 1949 on the protection of civilians in times of war, the International Committee of the Red Cross has attempted to dispatch a team that would have reported on their conditions. But the aggressor, persisting in his inhumane conduct, declined to allow this international committee to send representatives to Kuwait in order to carry out their tasks. He also refused to let envoys of the United Nations Secretary-General visit Kuwait to stand on the conditions of its population.

Such conduct constitutes yet another violation by the aggressor of international and humanitarian covenants, thus demanding a resolute stand against it.

Against all these odds, an enormous source of solace to us has been the position taken by virtually all countries of the world in support of Kuwait's rights. Hence, the League of Arab States, the Conference of the Foreign

Ministers of the Islamic Countries and the United Nations Security Council all took appropriate decisions condemning the Iraqi aggression and calling for the annulment of the Annexation Act and the immediate and unconditional withdrawal of the invading Iraqi forces to the border that existed prior to the aggression. Thus, the legitimate government of Kuwait would be able to exercise its functions and responsibilities as it used to before the invasion. . . .

[Forgives Foreign Debts]

Two years have now elapsed since I made an initiative from this rostrum calling for the cancellation of foreign debts under the burden of which numerous countries suffer enormously. In point of fact, these countries have fallen victim to a host of factors that not only thwarted any prospect for their economic prosperity but also generated mounting pressure on them. Though some measure of progress has indeed been made in this area, the magnitude and scope of the problem continue to pose a grave threat to the lives of millions of human beings, a threat that in all likelihood may undermine world peace and stability. The long standing academic argument that economic stability and political stability are closely interlinked is perhaps as valid and timely now as it has ever been. Along these lines, it would be advisable for us all to review the conclusions of the United Nations-sponsored Conference on the Problems of the Least Developed Countries, held in Paris earlier this month, in order to appreciate better the weight of the problem and the urgency it has assumed with a view to making tangible headway towards an effective remedy in the interest of all mankind. In this spirit, Kuwait, for its part, has decided, in line with our previous proposal regarding this issue, to write off all interests on its loans. In addition, Kuwait will consider with the poorest nations arrangements regarding the principal of its loans with a view to easing the burden of their debts. . . .

From the early years of independence, my country has been privileged to be in the forefront of states that gave development aid to other countries. Kuwait's contributions represent the highest rate in the world in terms of gross national product, amounting to 8.3% of its GNP. This highlights Kuwait's genuine desire to contribute towards raising the standard of living in the developing nations. It also proves that Kuwait has been a leader in the efforts to improve the economic infrastructure of other countries. . . .

In closing, may I take this opportunity, Mr. President, to address a few words to my people, my kinsfolk, the loyal sons and daughters of Kuwait, from this august forum, a forum for justice and fairness, a forum for guidance and hope, to assure each and every one of you that Allah, the Almighty, will ultimately secure triumph for us, thanks to your struggle and resolve, thanks to the gracious role of the United Nations, thanks to the support lent to us by our brethren and friends along with all people of good conscience throughout the world. The withdrawal of the invaders is,

God willing, undoubtedly imminent. We shall return to our Kuwait, the oasis of safety and peace, which embraces all Kuwaitis and foreigners living in our midst as brothers. Together, we will join hands in concert and harmony to secure our development and progress. This will be a fulfillment of God's promise as rendered in the following verse:

"O ye who believe,
If you will aid (the cause of)
Allah, He will aid you,
And plant your feet firmly."

(Surah 47, *Mohammad,* Verse 7.)

And whose word can be truer than Allah's?

Thank you and may Allah, our Lord, bring you all peace and grace.

October

WAR POWERS DEBATE

October 2, 1990

President George Bush created a dilemma for Congress when he sent American military forces to the Persian Gulf in an effort to stop Iraqi aggression. Congress repeatedly and indecisively pondered whether and how boldly to assert its war power prerogatives without undermining the president's strategy for dealing with Iraq's August 2 takeover of Kuwait. (Iraqi Invasion of Kuwait, p. 533)

At the heart of the dilemma was the constitutional question of how far an American president, as commander in chief, can go to commit the nation to war. The Constitution explicitly confers on Congress the power to declare war, but, since the nineteenth century, American presidents often have sent the armed forces into battle without consulting Congress, much less asking for a declaration of war.

In some 125 major and minor conflicts involving U.S. forces since the country's founding, only 5 were preceded by a declaration of war. And only once, in the War of 1812, did Congress conduct a full debate on the merits of taking the nation into war. In the war with Mexico, and in the first and second world wars, Congress merely ratified the president's decision. In 1898 an expansionist-minded Congress forced a declaration of war (with Spain) on President William McKinley.

When American troops entered combat in Korea and in Vietnam, Congress did not press the president to seek its approval, and in neither war did the chief executive acknowledge that a formal declaration of war was warranted or required. In Korea U.S. troops were sent into battle under the auspices of the United Nations; in Vietnam, Congress approved the so-called Gulf of Tonkin resolution, which President Lyndon

B. Johnson insisted was equivalent to a declaration of war. The resolution easily passed Congress after Johnson reported that North Vietnam had attacked U.S. ships.

As the Vietnam War dragged on, Congress attempted to reassert its war powers, most notably by passing the War Powers Act in 1973 in reaction to President Richard Nixon's decision to bomb Cambodia. The resolution required the president "in every possible instance" to consult Congress before committing U.S. forces to existing or imminent hostilities. Once troops were committed, the president was required to report the action to Congress within forty-eight hours and to withdraw troops within sixty (extendable to ninety) days unless Congress authorized the operation to continue.

Bush's Persian Gulf Action

This background framed the discussion—at times debate—in Congress over its proper role in the gulf crisis. Because Congress was in recess when Bush first ordered U.S. forces into the region, the president had added leeway to act on his own. Like all recent presidents, he refused to recognize the legality of the War Powers Act, contending that Congress could not curtail or modify a president's power as commander in chief to take actions necessary to protect national security or the lives of Americans.

Maintaining that he did not feel compelled to report his military plans to Congress, Bush nevertheless sent congressional leaders a statement of intent on August 10. As he had announced in a speech two days earlier, Bush said he was sending U.S. forces to Saudi Arabia at its request. The Saudis feared that Iraq might also invade their country. Although the U.S. forces "are equipped for combat," the presidential statement asserted, "their mission is defensive." It added that "this deployment will facilitate a peaceful resolution of the crisis."

The statement did not use the specific language of the War Powers Act and presumably did not trigger a sixty-day timetable. But some individual lawmakers contended congressional approval would be needed if the U.S. military buildup in the gulf continued. "We're going to have to be in some form of ratifying mode if this thing goes over sixty days," said Dan Glickman, D-Kan., a member of the House Intelligence Committee.

About 170 lawmakers interrupted their recess to return to Washington August 28 for a briefing on the Persian Gulf situation by Bush and other administration officials. Those who attended reported wide support for the president's policy, but Democrats were quick to note that there were no guarantees that this support would last indefinitely. "Approval for past actions isn't approval for all future actions," said Senate Majority Leader George J. Mitchell of Maine.

Congressional Support Resolutions

Early in October, both houses of Congress passed carefully worded resolutions supporting Operation Desert Shield—the military's code name for its gulf operations—but without expressly authorizing the use of force. "We fashioned a resolution that went through essentially without debate," said Rep. Dante B. Fascell, D-Fla., chairman of the House Foreign Affairs Committee, who was the principal author of the House resolution. It was approved October 1 by a 380-29 vote. The Senate passed a similar resolution the next day 96-3.

The lopsided votes, however, did not reveal the misgivings and doubts many members expressed during consideration of the resolutions. The Senate debate demonstrated how Congress was trying to walk a fine line between showing national unity in a crisis while refusing to yield the executive branch full control in a matter of grave national importance.

For instance, Sen. John Kerry, D-Mass., said he believed in sending "an unequivocal signal" to Iraqi president Saddam Hussein that he was "in total agreement with the President and the international community in actions taken thus far to force the Iraqi withdrawal from Kuwait." But, Kerry added, "it should be pointed out that this resolution is not a Gulf of Tonkin resolution on the Persian Gulf." The Gulf of Tonkin resolution was discredited when, years later, it was disclosed that the purported attacks may not have occurred. Congress rescinded the resolution in 1970 but retained a bitter memory of it.

Baker Defends Presidential Direction

The congressional action on October 1 and 2 was only an interlude in the war powers debate. On October 17 Secretary of State James A. Baker III testified before the Senate Foreign Relations Committee that he had reservations about a "formal mechanism" for presidential consultation with Congress on Persian Gulf matters. Baker was more emphatic in rejecting requests for advance congressional authorization for military action. He said the administration would have no difficulty with Congress voting a formal declaration of war, but only if Iraq were to launch an all-out attack on U.S. forces.

Congress recessed October 28 but President Bush's announcement November 8 of an additional buildup of U.S. forces in the Persian Gulf triggered a call for a special session. Senate Minority Leader Robert Dole, R-Kan., and Sen. Richard G. Lugar, R-Ind., suggested that the members return to Washington long enough to provide the president with standing authorization for military action.

Bush quelled the demands for a special session by calling congressional leaders to the White House November 14 and assuring them that "no Rubicon was crossed" in the movement toward war. He invited House and Senate leaders to join him on a trip to Saudi Arabia, where they spent Thanksgiving Day with American troops.

Although Congress was out of session, several major committees continued to hold hearings in December on the Persian Gulf situation.

Secretary of Defense Dick Cheney, testifying December 3 before the Senate Armed Services Committee, said the president had all the authority he needed to order offensive military action. The next day, fifty-four Democrats in Congress sought a federal court injunction to bar President Bush from ordering American troops to take offensive action in the Persian Gulf without a formal declaration of war. U.S. District Court judge Harold R. Greene declined December 13 to decide the issue, but he left open the door for future consideration if "action by the courts would appear to be the only available means to break the deadlock."

Democratic leaders made plans for the new Congress that convened January 3, 1991, to remain on call rather than recessing until January 13, as was originally scheduled. "The Senate will and should debate the issue," Mitchell said December 13, as he and seven Democratic colleagues left Washington for an information-gathering trip to the Middle East. The Senate and House both conducted three days of debate, January 11-13, and approved a resolution authorizing the president to commit the nation to war against Iraq.

Following are excerpts from the Senate debate October 2, 1990, on a resolution on American involvement in the Persian Gulf and the text of the resolution:

SENATE DEBATE

SENATE MAJORITY LEADER ROBERT DOLE. Mr. President, I am pleased to join the majority leader in offering this resolution. I would also like to affirm that the administration supports the resolution.

The resolution is important for what it says—and equally important for what it does not say.

It does express the strong, bipartisan support in the Senate for the President's leadership, policies and actions in the Persian Gulf crisis.

In doing that, it will send another strong and important message to Saddam Hussein: The United States is united in its determination to achieve the goals of the President's policies. Saddam Hussein is not going to get what he wants, period; and he surely is not going to get what he wants because of indecision or dissent in the U.S. Senate.

The resolution also includes a strong call to all nations in the world, to keep up the pressure on Saddam; and, at the same time, to respond to the needs of those adversely affected by the enforcement of the sanctions....

Most importantly, while properly reaffirming the constitutional processes by which our foreign policy is developed and implemented, the resolution does not plunge us into a pointless and damaging confrontation over war powers.

There is a time and a place for everything. And one of these days, we must confront this war powers issue, and get it resolved in a manner that is consistent with the Constitution, preserves the legitimate role of the Congress, and serves the national interest.

But debates here on the floor of the Senate can be misunderstood, when translated into headlines, or soundbites in the media around the country, and around the world.

A debate right now, which could be misunderstood or misreported as evidence of an erosion of support for the President's stance, would serve no one's interest—except Saddam Hussein's.

So this is a good resolution. I commend the administration, which urged us to pursue this resolution, and the majority leader, who has been very involved in working out this draft.

It was a bipartisan process, which has resulted in a bipartisan product. That is the way we ought to deal with these serious foreign policy issues.

I urge all Senators to vote for this resolution. . . .

SEN. HERBERT KOHL, D-WIS. Mr. President, I firmly believe that the President's response to the invasion of Kuwait by Iraq has been fundamentally sound. Iraq's behavior has been unjustified and unacceptable. The President's ability to forge an international response to this aggression has been both skillful and effective. The actions he has taken so far have my support and deserve the thanks of the civilized world.

Having said that, Mr. President, I must also say that I am less than pleased with the resolution now before us. To begin with, I believe that the President should have sought congressional approval for the actions he has taken—approval which he would have gotten—as required by the War Powers Resolution. The President may not like the War Powers Resolution but it is the law of the land and one of the issues at stake in the Persian Gulf is respect for the rule of law. The law requires congressional approval of deployment of American forces in situations in which hostilities are imminent. Hostilities are, unfortunately, imminent in the gulf. And that means that the President is required to seek congressional authorization for his actions.

Second, I believe that the President should have been—and should be—working more closely with the Congress in developing our Nation's ongoing response to events in the Persian Gulf. So far, I am afraid, the executive branch is working with the other nations of the world but not with the Congress of our own country. I understand the realities of the modern world: Secrecy is often essential, events take place quickly, responses have to be almost instantaneous. But planning is going on now. And the Congress, perhaps represented by a leadership group, ought to be aware of what options are developed, and involved in the process of evaluating those choices.

Third, I am concerned about the specific language of the resolution because some may read it as giving the President a blank check for future action. That is simply not the case with this Senator. I do support the actions the President has taken so far. But I cannot signal my support for future actions unless I know what strategy will guide them and what operational details will control them. Of course I support "continued action to deter Iraqi aggression and to protect American lives and vital interests in the region." But what does continued action mean? Military action? Diplomatic action? Capitulation to Iraq? The resolution does not define its terms—and that disturbs me deeply and offends greatly. Military action may be essential at some point. But I do not want to see us take any military action until that point is reached. By committing us to "support continued action by the President" some may see the resolution as a grant of authority to the President. Perhaps it is wishful thinking, but I read the language of the resolution more restrictively; after all, there is at least the requirement that such action be in accordance with the decisions of the United Nations and our own domestic legal processes. That, I hope, is enough to suggest that additional authorization or approval would be required before our actions move in a new direction or shift their current emphasis.

Finally, while I recognize the value of this resolution, I also recognize its limitations. This resolution doesn't really endorse or encompass or create a comprehensive policy in the Persian Gulf; at best it simply speaks to the current crisis. And that is precisely what is wrong with the resolution and with our policy: It only addresses the immediate crisis. Look at some selective recent history: 2 years ago we tilted toward Iraq because they were fighting Iran—now Iraq has tilted against us and who knows where Iran is; 2 months ago Syria was branded a terrorist state—now we invite them to lunch; today we are all frightened by the proliferation of weapons and military might in the region—so we propose to sell an additional $21 billion in arms to Saudi Arabia. Mr. President, over the past few years we have bounced from one policy extreme to another: We have shifted goals, altered alliances, modified the means we are willing to use. It is really time for us to figure out what our policy in the region is going to be. This resolution, as important as it may be, simply does not help us do that.

Despite these concerns, Mr. President, when all is said and done, I will vote for this resolution. I will do so because I agree with what the President has done so far and because I want to send a clear signal of American unity to Iraq and to all other nations. But I also want to send a clear signal to the President of the United States that increased consultation and involvement is necessary if that support is to be sustained and that unity is to be maintained. The American people have a right to fully understand what we are doing; the Congress has an obligation—a legal, constitutional and moral obligation—to be involved in, and give approval to, American action in the gulf. And our nation has a need to develop a comprehensive and consistent policy in the Middle East.

SEN. ROBERT KERRY, D-NEB. Mr. President, I support this resolution which I believe sends an unequivocal signal to Saddam Hussein that the Senate is in total agreement with the President and the international community in actions taken thus far to force the Iraqi withdrawal from Kuwait.

In so doing, it should be pointed out that this resolution is not a Gulf of Tonkin resolution on the Persian Gulf. Quite the contrary, this resolution reflects the near unanimity of the global community in condemning this aggressive act by a brutal dictator.

Unlike our experience in Vietnam, the United States is not acting unilaterally in the Persian Gulf. We are not acting in the absence of an international consensus in support of our presence in the region. The emphasis that the President is placing on the role of the United Nations is a critical element of our policy in dealing with this crisis. The President has done a superb job in mobilizing the international consensus, as manifested by the eight resolutions passed by the U.N. Security Council in response to the Iraqi invasion.

The success of U.S. policy will be largely contingent upon the maintenance of this international solidarity. It is imperative that the United States continue to operate under the auspices of the United Nations.

While the resolution is not statutorily binding upon the President, I would like to differ with its characterization offered by our distinguished colleague from Oregon [Sen. Mark O. Hatfield]. Subsection (b) of the resolved clause expresses support for the President's actions, or continued action, in "accordance with the decisions of the United Nations Security Council and in accordance with United States constitutional and statutory processes, including the authorization and appropriations of funds by the Congress."

Mr. President, I believe this phrase appropriately defines the limit of our support. We are telling the administration that Congress will support continued action so long as this action is in accordance with the decisions of the U.N. Security Council, in accordance with the U.S. constitutional and statutory processes. I would submit that since the War Powers Resolution is part of our statutory process, this resolution is covered in the legislation we are considering today.

And quite frankly, if the Congress is so predisposed to correcting a perceived policy miscalculation, the ultimate weapon we have is the power of the purse. As one who fought and bled for my country, the failure of the Congress to cut off funding for the Vietnam war for so many years represented the ultimate derogation of the responsibilities of this institution.

I am a strong supporter and advocate of the War Powers Resolution. But the War Powers Resolution, and its invocation, should not be used as an excuse for not exercising the most effective tool we have to decide these issues—the power of the purse.

Mr. President. I am supporting this resolution because it is my belief that it does not authorize the President to operate unilaterally either apart from the U.N. framework, or without specific authorization from the Congress. The success of the President's policy, thus far, has been the international consensus behind our efforts and those of our allies—a consensus which has contributed to, and strengthened, the broad base of support among the American people.

I would caution anyone in the administration who would be inclined to engage in a twisted or convoluted interpretation of this resolution that we are not giving the President carte blanche to wage offensive military action unilaterally. All our actions must be predicated upon support from the

Congress, the American people, and under the continued sanction of the United Nations.

I am concerned that the Iraqi invasion of Kuwait may be an ominous omen of the potential dangers facing the global community in the post-cold war era.

The global community has emerged from 45 years of superpower competition, during which the threat of nuclear confrontation was never far from our consciousness. Fortunately, the cold war did not bring our worst fears to fruition.

The end of the cold war era, however, does not mean the world is safe from global catastrophe. The greatest danger to international security and stability can come from traditional regional hot spots which, if left unattended, could be the spark that could turn local confrontations into more widespread conflagration.

Today, we are confronted by a regional power, Iraq, which has attacked a weaker state, Kuwait, for both territorial gain and control of an important resource. The crisis is even more threatening by virtue of the fact that Iraq has developed a chemical weapons capability, and is pursuing a nuclear weapons development program. And Saddam Hussein has demonstrated a willingness to use such weapons of mass destruction in the past, whether in his war against Iran or against his own Kurdish population. . . .

The fundamental issue associated with the Iraqi invasion of Kuwait, in my estimation, has nothing to do with oil prices or who controls how much of the world's petroleum reserves. The fundamental issue has nothing to do with our rushing in to support, or prop up, so-called feudal monarchies in the Persian Gulf.

Even the question of energy independence, or the failure to develop a national energy policy, is peripheral to what should concern us, our Western allies, and our new-found allies in the region.

If local or regional aggressions are allowed to go unchallenged, then the entire global community could open itself up to nuclear and/or chemical weapons blackmail, particularly if a despot's appetite has been whetted by local or regional successes. . . .

If there is one lesson, among many, to be learned from this crisis, it is the fact that the West, and the United States as the leader of the West, has to realize that unilateral action will threaten seriously our own long-term security. In the coming decades, we could find ourselves in a world at least as dangerous and unfriendly as that of the cold war. Only by promoting a truly international security system based on the rule of international law and the United Nations can our Nation hope to promote both our own and wider global security.

The fact that the President has been sensitive to the need for responding to this crisis under the United Nations auspices and framework, has been a very important consideration in my support for his policy. He has been skillful in working with the United Nations to establish an international partnership to respond to this aggression. In the process, I believe the

United States is making an important contribution in the long overdue requirement for strengthening multilateral responses to present and future crises which do and will face this global community of ours.

SEN. JOSEPH BIDEN, D-DEL. Mr. President, 8 weeks have passed since American troops were sent to the Arabian peninsula to deter further aggression by the nation of Iraq.

We have seen the largest buildup of American forces since the Vietnam war—in a fraction of the time that it took to make a similar commitment in Indochina, with a fraction of the debate.

It is now October 1, nearly 2 months since the first United States soldiers arrived in Saudi Arabia, and 3 weeks since Congress reconvened after the August recess.

In these 2 months, the U.N. Security Council has approved no less than eight resolutions regarding the gulf crisis.

Yet the Senate has remained, as an institution, largely silent.

A New American Doctrine

The debate on this policy is long overdue. For the deployment of United States Forces in the Persian Gulf is not just, to use the President's words, "a line drawn in the sand."

It is a new American doctrine to justify massive United States intervention in the Middle East.

Ten years ago, in response to the Soviet invasion of Afghanistan, President Carter articulated a doctrine that now bears his name. He said:

> An attempt by any outside force to gain control of the Persian Gulf region will be regarded as an assault on the vital interests of the United States.

The American people understood that we could not accept an alien hand—at the time, a Soviet hand—grabbing control of this essential resource.

But President Bush has responded to a new threat—not from an outside power—but from an Arab aggressor seeking to control Arab oil.

This is a dramatic shift in American foreign policy—a Bush corollary to the Carter doctrine.

We have declared to the world that we will not permit an unfriendly Arab nation to control gulf oil.

A commitment potentially limitless in its scope that at a minimum, could well mean a long-term presence of U.S. Forces—at least Naval Forces—in the Persian Gulf Region.

Congress must play a role in helping to more clearly define this long-term commitment, just as Congress must play a role in the current deployment of U.S. Forces.

To date, Congress has been simply an observer, heartily congratulating the President for his brilliant diplomatic skills and praising American soldiers for their service to the country.

Such praise has not been undeserved.

The President has done a tremendous job thus far in uniting the world in opposition to Iraq's aggression.

And American forces have been heroic in their rapid deployment to the Middle East and in their commitment to duty under harsh conditions.

But to continue in this sideline role would be not merely an evasion of responsibility, but an abdication of congressional power.

Congress and the War-Making Power

That Congress has the power to declare war is unambiguous in our Constitution.

But students of the doctrine of original intent would perhaps be surprised to learn that the framers did not intend for congressional involvement in the use of force to end there.

Indeed, an early draft of the Constitution reserved exclusively for Congress the power to make war.

Later this was changed to declare war. But the reason for this change is instructive.

At the Constitutional Convention, James Madison and Elbridge Gerry argued for the amendment for one reason—to allow the President "the power to repel sudden attacks."

In fact, the framers had no interest in the ceremonial aspects of declaring war—which has only been used five times in our history as a nation.

Even then, as Alexander Hamilton noted, "the ceremony of a formal denunciation of war" has "of late fallen into disuse." (Federalist 25).

The real issue was authorization of war, which the framers did not intend to give to the President.

Even so staunch an advocate of Presidential authority as Hamilton emphasized that the President's power as Commander in Chief would be "much inferior" to that of the British King.

Amounting to "nothing more than the supreme command and direction of the military and naval forces" (Federalist 69).

The framers of the Constitution wanted Congress involved, on an equal basis, in any decision on the use of force—the most fundamental decision a nation can make—for two important reasons:

First, to balance power within our Government; and

Second, because congressional support is a sound barometer of a policy's wisdom and a prerequisite of a policy's sustainability.

Supporting the Current Policy

Congress must have a role to play in authorizing the current deployment of troops in the Middle East, as well as any further action.

It cannot be merely reduced to providing the funds to continue the military operation, "which as a practical matter is guaranteed, since Congress rarely uses the power of the purse to cut off support when American soldiers are on the brink of war."

The question then becomes: By what form does Congress add its voice to the policy?

I believe the best approach would be to provide a statutory authorization, rather than the hortatory resolution before us today.

In truth, I do have concerns about the resolution now before us.

The best that can be said about it is that it is only a concurrent resolution, and thus has no force of law.

I would be happier if we set down some guidelines for U.S. policy, in order to clarify our objectives in the gulf, and to provide signposts for future actions.

The resolution's ambiguity leaves open the possibility that the President will interpret this resolution very broadly and consider it as the first and last word of Congress on this matter.

It mentions neither future actions by Congress, nor the need to seek a declaration of war if hostilities occur.

It merely "supports continued action by the President."

Now we must make declarative statements about the intent of Congress in approving this resolution.

But we must remember that Presidents have not hesitated to ignore legislative history when it suited them.

We need only to recall the Vietnam experience, where the Johnson administration cited the Gulf of Tonkin resolution—enacted in response to alleged North Vietnamese attacks on the U.S.S. *Maddox* and the U.S.S. *Turner Joy*—as an authorization to escalate the war.

Despite the fact the resolution said nothing about authorizing anyone to do anything.

We know these resolutions are subject to selective interpretation—and abuse.

The words of Nicholas Katzenbach are instructive. While serving as Johnson's Attorney General, Katzenbach acknowledged in an internal memorandum that there was some legislative history to indicate that in passing the Gulf of Tonkin resolution, Congress did not intend to approve a large-scale land war in Asia.

But later, as Under Secretary of State, Katzenbach testified to Congress that the Gulf of Tonkin resolution constituted the "functional equivalent" of a declaration of war.

A similarly clever administration official might use this resolution as justification for military action. . . .

Despite my reservations and concerns about this resolution, I intend to vote for it, but only on the assumption that the language does not constitute congressional support in advance for a Presidential decision to use force in the gulf—in the absence of prior authorization by Congress or a decision by the U.N. Security Council under article 42 to undertake a collective action designed to remove Iraqi forces from Kuwait.

In other words, congressional support for "continued actions" does not mean that the President can take any action that does not contradict existing Security Council decisions or that he can use force to implement existing Security Council decisions without seeking authority from Congress.

SEN. TOM HARKIN, D-IOWA. Mr. President, I rise to cast my vote in support of Senate Concurrent Resolution 147, but do with the explicit understanding that this resolution will not serve as a blanket authorization for the President to go to war in the Persian Gulf or as approval of the President circumventing the War Powers Act. Specifically, this resolution does not give the President the authority to conduct military operations against Iraq without additional authorization from Congress. It does endorse the deployment of United States forces for defensive purposes, to deter Iraqi aggression against Saudi Arabia. It does endorse the use of economic sanctions and diplomatic means to pressure Iraq into withdrawing from Kuwait. And it does embrace the United Nations and the five Security Council resolutions which condemn Iraq's aggression in the Persian Gulf. . . .

I had hoped that this resolution would advocate the option of putting U.S. forces, along with the troops of other countries now stationed in the gulf, under the command of the United Nations.

In addition, the meaning and intent of paragraph (b) of the resolution needs to be clarified so that the President does not interpret it as a blank check for future military action in the Persian Gulf. Specifically, that provision expresses the support of Congress for continued action by the President in accordance with the decisions of the United Nations Security Council and in accordance with U.S. constitutional and statutory processes. . . .

No resolution, no matter how loosely drafted, can absolve Congress of its constitutional and legal mandates. Simply put, we have an obligation to approve sending U.S. forces into combat, if that unfortunate situation were to occur.

The American people deserve no less from their elected representatives. After all, we are asking nearly 200,000 of our young men and women to risk their lives in defense of our national interest in the Persian Gulf. The least that Congress can do is fulfill its legal and constitutional responsibilities. . . .

SEN. SAM NUNN, D-GA. Mr. President, I rise today as one of the original sponsors of this bipartisan concurrent resolution. I want to emphasize at the outset that this is not legislation, which would be in the form of a joint resolution that would have to be signed by the President or enacted over his veto if he chose to veto it. It is a concurrent resolution. Nevertheless, it is an important measure for a number of reasons.

First, it is important because it expresses the strong approval of the Congress for the leadership of the President in working with the U.S. Security Council. The Security Council has to date passed eight separate resolutions dealing with Iraq's aggression and its violations of the U.N. charter and fundamental principles of international law.

It is also important because it expresses congressional approval of the President's actions in achieving and supporting the Security Council's resolutions and in involving friendly governments.

Finally, and most importantly, the concurrent resolution expresses congressional support for the President's continued action in accordance with the decisions of the Security Council and in accordance with U.S. constitutional and statutory processes, including the authorization and appropriation of funds by the Congress, to deter Iraqi aggression, and to protect American lives and vital interests in the region.

It is this last point that I would like to discuss briefly this afternoon. The concurrent resolution doesn't express congressional support for every future action by the President. Rather it limits congressional support for the President's actions that are in accordance with the Security Council's decisions and with U.S. constitutional and statutory processes. The Constitution grants to the Congress the power to declare war; to raise and support armies; and to provide and maintain a navy. Additionally, the Constitution provides that "no money shall be drawn from the Treasury, but in consequence of appropriations made by law." Without wanting to get into a prolonged discussion concerning the strengths or weaknesses of the War Powers Resolution, I believe it is worth emphasizing that in the final analysis the Congress can most appropriately and most effectively play its proper role in matters such as this through the power of the purse. For after all is said and done, no President can use the Armed Forces of the United States unless the Congress authorizes and appropriates funds to support and sustain such action. . . .

SEN. ERNEST F. HOLLINGS, D-S.C. Mr. President, I will vote for Senate Concurrent Resolution 147 supporting the President's actions in rallying the United Nations and the international community to oppose Iraqi aggression. In a time of crisis, such as we now face in the Persian Gulf, we Americans have only one President, and we must give him the benefit of the doubt. But while I give President Bush the benefit of the doubt, nonetheless the doubt remains. Indeed, let me be very blunt in saying that I vote for this resolution with the gravest of reservations about the wisdom of our evolving policy in the Persian Gulf.

Let's go right to the point of these U.N. Security Council resolutions. Taken in isolation, each one of the eight resolutions is correct and unobjectionable. Of course we demand that Iraq withdraw its forces from Kuwait. Of course we support the international embargo of Iraq. Of course we are outraged by Iraq's violation of foreign embassies and by its abduction of foreign nationals, including thousands of Americans.

But, as history amply demonstrates, Security Council resolutions, in and of themselves, are impotent and innocuous. What deeply concerns me is that the administration has used these Security Council resolutions as sugar coating for what remains, in essence, a unilateral U.S. response in taking on Saddam Hussein. We have willy-nilly committed an extraordinary U.S. expeditionary force, including an air and sea armada not seen since the Vietnam war, to back up President's Bush's assertion that Saddam's aggression "will not stand."

Let me be very clear on the following point. I supported the initial United States deployment for the express and limited purpose of defending Saudi Arabia from the clear and present danger of attack by Iraq.

There was a fire raging out of control on Saudi Arabia's border, and the United States had the only available fire brigade. We did what we had to do. But we have now moved beyond that limited purpose. The administration has stated that it is United States policy to compel Iraq to leave Kuwait, and to restore the Kuwaiti emir to his throne and riches. I do not believe—and prior to August 2 the United States Government did not believe—that preservation of Kuwait's territorial integrity and the emir's regime is a vital interest of the United States justifying the expenditure of American blood.

Almost as an afterthought to U.S. deployment in early August, the administration cajoled other nations to send troops and treasure to back up the U.S. commitment in the gulf. But, nonetheless, it remains overwhelmingly a U.S. initiative. I am also troubled by the fact that, in order to retain the U.N. imprimatur, we are going to have to yield control of U.S. forces to questionable U.N. policymaking and to questionable U.N. military command.

If there is war in the Persian Gulf, as it now stands it will clearly be a war between Iraq and the United States, not between Iraq and the United Nations. Whether or not we win such a war, it would have catastrophic consequences for future U.S. relations vis-a-vis the Persian Gulf and the nations of the Arab masses. In the wake of a United States offensive against Arab Iraq, so great would be the tidal wave of anti-U.S. reaction that even those Arab governments now favorably disposed toward us would be compelled by public opinion to break with the United States. We would win the war but lose the peace.

In early August, we were the only fire brigade available, but that situation has now changed. We need to recall two lessons from the Vietnam war. The first lesson is that there will be no Gulf of Tonkin resolution this time around. Senate Concurrent Resolution 147 is limited in its scope, and neither explicitly nor implicitly gives license to the President to wage an unprovoked offensive against Iraq. The second lesson from Vietnam is that, this time around, we need to do the "-ization" before hostilities break out. President Nixon came up with his Vietnamization policy only after tens of thousands of American boys had been killed. We must Arabize this present conflict, and we must do so before American GI's are sacrificed by the thousands. Our imperative is to Arabize the forces and voices opposing Saddam Hussein.

Bear in mind that Saddam is not primarily our problem. He is the Arab world's problem. Accordingly, it is up to the Arabs, in concert with the Iranians, to deal with him. If they lack the political and military will to contain him, then our own sacrifices would be for nought. An American-Iraq war would be as futile as it would be disastrous for our country. . . .

The PRESIDING OFFICER. Under the previous order, the hour of 2:15 p.m. having arrived, the Senate will now proceed to vote on Senate Concurrent Resolution 147, which the clerk will report.

The bill clerk read as follows:

A concurrent resolution (S. Con. Res. 147) supporting the actions taken by the President with respect to Iraqi aggression against Kuwait.

The **PRESIDING OFFICER.** The question is on agreeing to the concurrent resolution. The yeas and nays have been ordered. The clerk will call the roll.

The assistant legislative clerk called the roll.

MR. SIMPSON. I announce that the Senator from California [Mr. Wilson], is necessarily absent.

The **PRESIDING OFFICER.** Are there any other Senators in the Chamber desiring to vote?

The result was announced—yeas 96, nays 3, as follows:

[Roll call Vote No. 256 Leg.]

YEAS-96

Adams	Fowler	Mitchell
Akaka	Garn	Moynihan
Armstrong	Glenn	Murkowski
Baucus	Gore	Nickles
Bentsen	Gorton	Nunn
Biden	Graham	Packwood
Bingaman	Gramm	Pell
Bond	Grassley	Pressler
Boren	Harkin	Pryor
Boschwitz	Hatch	Reid
Bradley	Heflin	Riegle
Breaux	Heinz	Robb
Bryan	Helms	Rockefeller
Bumpers	Hollings	Roth
Burdick	Humphrey	Rudman
Burns	Inouye	Sanford
Byrd	Jeffords	Sarbanes
Chafee	Johnston	Sasser
Coats	Kassebaum	Shelby
Cochran	Kasten	Simon
Cohen	Kerry	Simpson
Conrad	Kohl	Specter
Cranston	Lautenberg	Stevens
D'Amato	Leahy	Symms
Danforth	Levin	Thurmond
Daschle	Lieberman	Wallop
DeConcini	Lott	Warner
Dixon	Lugar	Wirth
Dodd	Mack	NAYS-3
Dole	McCain	Hatfield
Domenici	McClure	Kennedy
Durenberger	McConnell	Kerrey
Exon	Metzenbaum	NOT VOTING-1
Ford	Mikulski	Wilson

So the concurrent resolution (S. Con. Res. 147) was agreed to.

The preamble was agreed to.

The concurrent resolution, with its preamble, reads as follows:

S. Con. Res. 147

Whereas on August 2, 1990, the armed forces of Iraq invaded and occupied the State of Kuwait, took large numbers of innocent hostages, and disregarded the rights of diplomats, all in clear violation of the United Nations Charter and fundamental principles of international law;

Whereas the President condemned Iraq's aggression, imposed comprehensive United States economic sanctions upon Iraq, and froze Iraqi assets in the United States;

Whereas the United Nations Security Council, in a series of five unanimously approved resolutions, condemned Iraq's actions as unlawful, imposed mandatory economic sanctions designed to compel Iraq to withdraw from Kuwait, called on all states to take appropriate measures to ensure the enforcement of sanctions, called for the immediate release of all hostages, and reaffirmed the right of individual and collective self-defense; and

Whereas, in response to requests from governments in the region exercising the right of collective self-defense as provided in Article 51 of the United Nations Charter, the President deployed United States Armed Forces in the Persian Gulf region as part of a multilateral effort; Now, therefore, be it.

Resolved by the Senate (the House of Representatives concurring). That (a) the Congress strongly approves the leadership of the President in successfully pursuing the passage of United Nations Security Council Resolutions 660, 661, 662, 665, 667, and 670, which call for—

1. the immediate, complete, and unconditional withdrawal of all Iraqi forces from Kuwait;
2. the restoration of Kuwait's sovereignty, independence, and territorial integrity;
3. the release and safe passage of foreign nationals held hostage by Iraq;
4. the imposition of economic sanctions, including the cessation of airline transport, against Iraq; and
5. the maintenance of international peace and security in the Persian Gulf region.

   (b) The Congress approves the actions taken by the President in support of these goals, including the involvement of the United Nations and of the friendly governments. The Congress supports continued action by the President in accordance with the decisions of the United Nations Security Council and in accordance with United States constitutional and statutory processes, including the authorization and appropriation of funds by the Congress, to deter Iraqi aggression and to protect American lives and vital interests in the region.

(c) The Congress calls on all nations to strengthen the enforcement United Nations imposed sanctions against Iraq, to provide assistance for those adversely affected by enforcement of the sanctions, and to provide assistance to refugees fleeing Kuwait and Iraq.

SEC. 2. The Secretary of the Senate shall transmit a copy of this concurrent resolution to the President.

REUNIFICATION OF
EAST AND WEST GERMANY
October 3, 1990

Germany proclaimed itself a united and sovereign state October 3, 1990, forty-five years after it was divided in defeat and disgrace at the close of World War II. At the stroke of midnight, bells pealed and the red, black, and gold national banner was raised over the rebuilt Reichstag building in Berlin. At that moment West Germany and East Germany officially ceased to exist as separate political entities. Some 16 million East Germans were formally joined with 62 million West Germans to form the most populous nation in Europe.

Within sight of the place where the infamous Berlin Wall once stood, a cheering crowd of about 1 million people greeted the ceremonial event. It was the city's biggest celebration since the joyous frenzy that occurred when the wall was abruptly opened—then torn down—in November 1989, removing a barrier that for twenty-eight years had divided the city and symbolized the division of Germany and Europe. From that time forward, Germans regarded unification not as merely possible but as inevitable. Less than thirteen months later it was achieved. (Statements on the Berlin Wall and German Reunification, Historic Documents of 1989, p. 625)

Celebrations took place all over German cities October 3. At a state ceremony in Berlin's Philharmonie concert hall, President Richard von Weizsacker spoke of the day of unity as "a day of fundamental significance" for Germany and its neighbors. He said that German unity was dedicated to a new peaceful order in Europe and that Germans would never forget that it was Hitler's war that led to the division of Germany. In 1945 at the end of World War II, the victorious allies divided Germany into four zones of occupation. The American, British, and French zones became West Germany, and the Soviet zone East Germany.

The path toward unification was cleared of its last big obstacle when the four occupiers gave up their rights in a treaty they signed with East and West German governments September 12. (Treaty on German Reunification, p. 599)

Speaking October 4 before the Bundestag, the lower and dominant house of Parliament, Chancellor Helmut Kohl called for "solidarity" among Germans to overcome problems that remained in fully integrating the formerly Communist-controlled East Germans into a united nation dominated by Western democratic thought and a free-market economy. "German unity is not completed; it is only beginning," said Oskar Lafontaine, leader of the Social Democrats, the main opposition party to Kohl's ruling Christian Democratic Union.

New Nation's Western Dominance

The political structure of the new nation was essentially an adaptation of West Germany's. The name Federal Republic remained the same. Kohl and von Weizsacker, chancellor and president of West Germany, remained in those positions. The new nation retained West Germany's constitution (albeit amended), flag, and anthem—with the opening words "Unity and justice and freedom for the German fatherland" in place of the forbidden pre-1945 words "Germany, Germany over all" (Deutschland, Deutschland über Alles).

West Germans not only outnumbered East Germans in the new nation but also possessed 70 percent of its territory, some 137,854 square miles in all, an area slightly larger than Missouri and Iowa. In economic terms, the disparity was even greater. East Germany's state-controlled economy never attained West Germany's status as a world economic power. And East Germans never shared in the West Germans' postwar prosperity. On a per person basis in 1989, the gross domestic income of West Germans was about $19,300, roughly four times higher than for East Germans.

East Germans traded in their virtually worthless currency for the West German mark on July 1, and their government agreed to transform some 8,000 state-owned businesses into private companies. The transition did not come without costs, however. As unprofitable factories were closed in East Germany, unemployment shot up despite new investments by West German enterprises and billions in assistance by the West German government.

Negotiating a Merger

After months of negotiations and intense debate on how the two states should be merged, the East German legislature—the Volkskammer— voted August 23 to accept West Germany's Basic Law of 1949 (constitution) rather than insist on a new one. On August 30 East and West Germany signed a treaty laying the legal and social framework for German unification. In a thousand printed pages, the treaty regulated the merging of countless aspects of life. In some matters on which the two sides could not agree, the treaty stipulated a transitional period in which two conflicting laws would exist side by side until the new Federal Republic determined which would prevail.

Another sticking point in the negotiations concerned the storage and evaluation of 6 million files of the now-disbanded Stasi, East Germany's security police. West Germany wanted the files transferred to the Federal Archives in Koblenz and access to them strictly limited. However, the Volkskammer passed a law saying the files had to stay in East Germany and each citizen would have unlimited access. The treaty reflected a compromise, in that it allowed the files to remain in East Germany until an all-German Parliament agreed on their final storage and access.

All-German Elections

The unification treaty created in East Germany the new states of Brandenburg, Mecklenburg-Vorpommern, Saxony, Saxony-Anhalt, and Thuringia, which elected new governments October 14. In all the states but Brandenburg, Kohl's center-right Christian Democratic Union was the clear winner. As the ruling West German party, its strong stand for unification won favor among East Germans.

In a national election December 2—the first free election across Germany since before Hitler came to power in 1933—Christian Democrats outpolled their rivals from four other major parties. "If there is a general significance to the result," said Johannes Gross, a prominent German political commentator, "it is that unity is now being ratified by the people."

The new Bundestag of 662 deputies included 17 Communists, representing the last vestiges of East Germany's generally disowned political past. The legislative body met December 20 in Berlin's old Reichstag, rebuilt from wartime ruins, but delayed a vote on whether to move the government permanently from Bonn to Berlin, which the unification treaty designated the capital.

Following are excerpts from the unity day speech delivered by German president Richard von Weizsacker at a state ceremony in Berlin's Philaharmonie concert hall, October 3, 1990:

I.

The preamble to our constitution, which is now valid for all Germans, expresses the quintessence of what is uppermost in our minds today: We have achieved the unity and freedom of Germany in free self-determination. We are resolved to serve world peace in a united Europe. In pursuing this aim we are conscious of our responsibility to God and man.

Our hearts are filled with gratitude and joy, and at the same time we are aware of the magnitude and seriousness of our commitment. History in Europe and Germany now offers us a chance we have never had before. We are going through one of those rare phases in history when something really can be changed for the better. Let us not for one moment forget what this means to us.

Massive problems confront us at home and abroad. We do not ignore them. We take the reservations expressed by our neighbors seriously. We also realize how difficult it will be to fulfill the expectations placed in us by all sides. But we will be guided by confidence, not fear and doubt. Decisive for us is our firm determination to see our responsibilities clearly and to face up to them together. That determination gives us the strength to see our day-to-day problems in the perspective of our history and future in Europe.

For the first time we Germans are not a source of dispute in Europe. Our unity was not forced upon anyone but agreed peacefully. It is part of a historical process embracing the whole of Europe aimed at securing freedom for the nations and establishing a new peaceful order in our continent. We Germans wish to serve this aim. Our unity is directed to its achievement.

We now have a state which we ourselves no longer regard as provisional and whose identity and integrity are no longer disputed by our neighbors. On this day the German nation finds its acknowledged place in Europe.

What this means is obvious from the significance of frontiers. No European country has as many neighbors as we. For centuries frontiers have been a source of violence and terrible bloodshed. Now all our neighbors and we ourselves live within secure borders. These borders are protected not only by the renunciation of force but by the clear awareness of their changed function. Those who were forced to leave their homeland suffered immeasurably. But there is no point in any new dispute over national boundaries. All the greater is our desire to remove their divisive character. We want all Germany's frontiers to be bridges to our neighbors.

II.

The ideals of the French Revolution, together with the constitutional evolution in the United States and the United Kingdom, laid the foundations for Western democracy. A perception of freedom based on humanity and the rule of law emerged which has increasingly become the standard. It cannot be applied everywhere right away, but wherever the urge for political freedom, or a system marked by efficiency, social justice and respect for human rights breaks through—even into the heart of Peking— the values and rules of the Western democracies are everyone's yardstick.

We Germans participated in the democratic evolution at a very early stage but we applied its ideals and principles only half-heartedly. The rule of law in our country had grown from our own traditions. In the Prussian reforms of the Napoleonic era local self-government became the source of democratic convictions. The people sought unity, right and freedom as personified by the St. Paul's Church parliament. They definitely wanted to be united, and this aim was finally achieved in 1871, but they had no say in the matter. Time and again the Germans went on a romantic search for a third road to their country's internal order and its place in Europe. But that was an illusion. The Weimar Republic, too, failed to establish a viable democracy.

When the Federal Republic of Germany [West Germany] was founded there was deep concern at first that its integration with the West might perpetuate the division of Germany. This time, however, the path did not lead to a dead end. Initially only one part of Germany was allowed to follow that path, but from today we can together make a new beginning. The unification of Germany is more than the mere enlargement of the Federal Republic. The day has come when, for the first time in history, Germany as a whole can take its permanent place among the western democracies.

To us and to all our neighbors this is a process of fundamental importance. It will change the center of Europe. We shall play a major part in the process, jointly with our western partners with whom we are closely linked by virtue of our common values and objectives.

III.

Amidst our European neighbors we were destined to remain divided for over forty years. For the one part of the country this proved to be a boon, for the other a burden, but it was, and remains, our common German fate. A fate which embraces the past and the responsibility for its consequences. The SED [Socialist Unity Party] in East Germany tried to decree the country's division. It thought it sufficient to proclaim the socialist society of the future in order to free itself from the burden of history.

But in the German Democratic Republic [East Germany] the people saw, and felt, it differently. They had to carry a far greater part of the burden of the war than their countrymen in the West and they have always felt that recalling the past with a sense of responsibility would give them the indispensable strength to free themselves for the future. Hardly had the imposed ideological parlance gone when they faced up squarely to history's outstanding questions. The world has noted with great respect how sincerely the free forces, and especially young people, in eastern Germany considered it their responsibility to make up for the old regime's failure to bear its share of the responsibility for the past. The recent visit to Israel by the presidents of both freely-elected parliaments to commemorate the holocaust, the most heinous of all crimes, left a deep impression in that country. It symbolizes the common identity of the Germans precisely as regards their historical responsibility. Nazi tyranny and the war it unleashed brought untold suffering and injustice on nearly the whole of Europe and our own country. We will always remember the victims, and we are grateful for the growing signs of reconciliation between people and nations.

IV.

At no time in the post-war era did the Germans, particularly the Berliners, cease to hope that freedom would return and that the division of Europe would be overcome. And yet no one had the imagination to predict the course of events. So what is happening today is to us a gift. This time history was well-disposed towards us Germans. But this is all the more reason for conscientious reflection.

After the Second World War the division of Germany epitomized the division of Europe. It was not the result of the joint will of the victors but rather of their disagreement. The growing East-West confrontation cemented that division. But we will not use that as an excuse. No one in our country will forget that there would have been no division if the war started by Hitler had not happened.

Against the background of the Cold War and under the protective shield of the nuclear stalemate, the social systems in East and West competed with one another for over forty years. That phase is now drawing to a close.

The Soviet leadership under President [Mikhail S.] Gorbachev has realized that reforms leading to democracy and a market economy have become inevitable. But without freedom such reforms would be doomed to failure. As a result, courageous decisions were taken. The Soviet Union ceased dominating its allies and respected their right to decide their own political future. This led to the unprecedented peaceful revolutions in Central, Eastern and South-Eastern Europe. It led to the acceptance of the German people's free decision in favor of national unity.

The success of the reform course pursued by the Soviet leadership is still in considerable jeopardy, but it has already gone down in history as a worthy endeavor. And many people, including we Germans, have reason to be grateful.

We are grateful to the civil rights movements and peoples in Hungary, Poland and Czechoslovakia. The citizens of Warsaw, Budapest and Prague have set examples. They saw the path leading to freedom in the German Democratic Republic as part of a common historical process and gave it their encouragement.

Nor will we forget the help they gave to refugees, which was a very direct contribution toward overcoming the wall and the barbed wire. In [the] future the united Germany will seek an open, a close neighborly relationship with them.

The defense of freedom and human rights is fundamental to the commitment of our Western allies and friends, above all the Americans, the French and the British. Their protection, their resolve and cooperation, have been of crucial assistance to us. Most important of all, they place their confidence in us. For this we are deeply grateful.

How important our partners' understanding was for German unification is apparent from the unequivocal and constructive position taken by the European Community. I take great pleasure in welcoming among us today the President of the European Commission, Jacques Delors, and his colleagues and wish to express our respect and thanks for their far-sightedness.

Our thanks today go out in particular to those Germans in the German Democratic Republic who summoned the courage to rise up against oppression and despotism. For over ten years meetings and prayers for peace in the churches developed and spread the ideas which ultimately sparked the peaceful revolution. But the power of the state security services remained omnipresent. The use of force was imminent well into the autumn of 1989. It would have been quite understandable if the people had backed down and retreated. But it was no longer possible to suppress the hope lodged in their hearts.

"We are the people." With these four simple and magnificent words a whole system was shattered. Those words expressed the desire of the people to take the country, the res publica, into their own hands. Thus the peaceful revolution in Germany became truly republican. The fact that it happened after almost 60 years of bitter oppression makes it all the more amazing and credible. Democrats had joined forces in the cause of freedom and solidarity, both forming one mission for us all.

But on this occasion we must also thank the people in the West. If they had not trusted us Germans we would not have been able to unite. That trust has grown with the development of the Federal Republic over a period of forty years. Our people have established themselves in a free and democratic system and in the European consciousness.

The Germans have become predictable, reliable and respected partners. This was a crucial factor which won our neighbors and the whole world's approval for the country's unification.

V.

Now those four words have developed into many thousands. In an almost incredible effort, agreements and treaties have been completed which made it possible for us to set the seal today on both the internal and the external aspects of our unity. The subject-matter was often very complex and there was no lack of controversy. The pressure of time was constantly mounting. All concerned worked day and night—something we can do, of course, when it matters.

In future there will be more than one doubt to clear up, more than one dispute to settle. But all in all we can only admire what has been achieved.

I wish to thank the political leaders on both sides, their parliaments, and not least the many excellent staff of the public authorities for the work they have done. Their devotion to the cause was exemplary. Their accomplishment is reward in itself.

The form of unity has been determined. Now we must give it substance. Parliaments, governments and parties must help in this task, but only the sovereign nation, the minds and hearts of the people themselves, can translate it into practice. Everyone is aware how much still has to be done. It would be neither sincere nor helpful if at this hour we sought to conceal how much still separates us.

The external constraints of division were devised to estrange us. This they failed to do. Inhumane as the Wall and barbed wire were, they only served to strengthen the people's will to come together. We felt this above all in Berlin, that city which was and will remain of crucial significance to the nation. The sight of the Wall day by day never let us stop believing in, hoping for, the other side. Now the Wall has gone, and that's what matters.

But now that we have our freedom we must prove ourselves worthy of it. Today we have a clearer picture of the consequences of our different courses of development. The gap in our material standards is what strikes us most. Although the people in the German Democratic Republic had to cope with shortages day in, day out, they made the best of their situation and worked hard—this we will not forget—the magnitude of their problems and the gulf between them and the West became fully clear only during recent months. If we are to close that gap soon we shall not only have to help but also, and above all, to respect one another.

To the Germans in the former German Democratic Republic, unification is a transformation process which affects them directly in their daily lives, touches their very existence. This often confronts them with demands beyond their human capacity. A woman wrote to me that the people in East Germany were sincerely grateful for their freedom but had not realized how nerve-racking changes would be which required them to take leave of themselves, as it were. After all, they yearned for nothing more than to rid themselves of their regime. But replacing nearly all elements of one's life with something new, something unknown, overnight is beyond human measure.

The people in the West were overjoyed when the Wall came down, but many fail to realize or consider it most unwelcome that unification has something to do with their personal lives. This must not remain so. We shall first have to learn to understand one another better. Not until we really appreciate that both sides have gained valuable experience and acquired important qualities which are worth keeping in unity will we be on the right road.

First, let us look at the West. There is one development here which deserves special emphasis. Over the years the people have developed an affection for their state which is free from ungenuine feelings and nationalistic pathos. True, in the forty-year history of the Federal Republic there have been many serious conflicts between the generations and between the different social and political groups. They were often bitter struggles but without a destructive tendency as during the Weimar Republic. The revolt by young people in the late sixties, notwithstanding all the offense it caused, ultimately helped strengthen the people's commitment to democracy.

As we learned how to settle conflicts we developed a mutual confidence in the constitution. The internal uncertainty has gone. We are no longer constantly comparing ourselves with other nations. Conditions in other countries must not be altogether bad to make ours look good. Conversely, favorable conditions are not only to be found beyond our borders. We have become more self-assured in our judgment, in our awareness of life.

Some in the West are only now really discovering the merits of their own country. Some of the severest critics of conditions in the Federal Republic are worried today that our open-mindedness, our federalism, our integration with Europe, might suffer in the united Germany. I do not share their anxiety.

But I will say this: It is gratifying when especially young people identify themselves with their state in the West and appreciate that the Bonn republic has earned a good reputation. They have grown into an international and liberal society. They don't want to lose their cosmopolitan outlook. And why should they?

And now let us consider the German Democratic Republic. From its viewpoint, hardship on the one side and prosperity on the other meet on the day of unity. But it would be both foolish and inhumane were we to perceive this as those who have failed and those who have succeeded—or worse still the bad and the good coming together between East and West. It is the systems that differ in their degree of success, not the people. And that will surely become very clear when the Germans in what used to be the German Democratic Republic at long last receive the same opportunities which the people in the West have enjoyed.

Every life has its meaning and its innate dignity. No period in life is in vain, especially if it is marked by hardship. In human terms, the people in the German Democratic Republic achieved something very substantial under the most difficult conditions and we can only hope that it will be part of the substance of the united Germany.

If we overlooked this we would be thoroughly taken in one last time by the system now gone. Its aim was to control the people's thoughts and aims by means of absolute rules—indeed to create a new, uniform socialist being. If it had succeeded then the people, too, would have had to stand down together with their system. But communism foundered on the futility of that attempt. The freedom of the human spirit prevailed over the presumptuousness of the state, the individual over the collective.

The seeds of liberation took root under the dictatorship. It is precisely political bondage which makes people more aware of the limits of legitimate policy, and that a human freedom exists outside the public domain. Bondage teaches freedom—the people in the German Republic know this from personal experience.

True, the state did take care of its citizens within the system's meaning. But it did not perceive man's needs and his dignity. Thus in many cases people could only survive in silent, mutual support. Necessity united people. Solidarity did not remain an abstract word in theoretical programs but became a reality in people's lives. It required courage and self-denial to work for the Church and its charitable organizations. But it was fruitful. It gave inner strength. Disabled people neglected by the state were looked after. Respect for human life was thus translated into practice.

The regime tried particularly hard to make art and culture serve its aims. Now the conduct of artists and the quality of their work are a source of much dispute. Nothing is omitted, and that is a good thing. But a subsequent ethical rigor is only convincing and helpful if it is used for self-examination. To a large extent art in the German Democratic Republic did not have any impact as a political force, but certainly as a force able to change and intensify life. Isn't this also proved by the music we heard last night and this morning?

The regime caused a spiritual drought. Art has often been nourishment for the soul. It has in its own way helped to achieve something which was largely the task of the religious communities: to widen the capacity for inner freedom. This gradually led to the liberation from the compulsory lie, the deadliest poison of recent decades, which undermined confidence in the state and society, between neighbors, and ultimately in oneself. Thus freedom to stick to the truth became the most precious asset which the people acquired through the uprising which was sparked by their own courage.

We in the West have been spared such a test. We can only express our respect and we should demonstrate it in the process of unification.

Since the autumn of 1989 the human substance of the German Democratic Republic has, under incredibly difficult circumstances, become visible in a new way, in the civil rights movements, at the Round Table, and in the renaissance of communal activity.

In the Volkskammer [East German Parliament] people who were totally unprepared assumed responsibility which could not have been greater. They were sometimes referred to as amateurs. Was that intended as a reproach? They devoted themselves to the solution of the most difficult problems without cultivating the ritual of party confrontation. . . .

VI.

Now we are in the midst of our work. A particularly heavy and depressing burden is the legacy of distrust left behind by the [East German] State Security Service. The system's power has been shattered, but the trauma is still there. This cannot be digested from the outside. In this matter there is no external Solomonic authority. Those who were exposed to the poison are the ones most capable of carrying out the detoxification.

It is not the state's political concept as such that was evil but its equation with absolute truth. The state believed it possessed that truth and presumptuously forced everyone to accept it. And the State Security Service was its instrument. This rendered the moral claims of the leadership deeply immoral. Using methods that were as banal as they were ruthless, the security service spied upon, blackmailed and corrupted people and encouraged denunciation. The most insidious method of all was to make victims accomplices.

It would be unreasonable, from a human point of view, and intolerable in a country based on the rule of law to throw a cloak of oblivion over the Stasi [State Security Service] oppression. Justice and the law must take their course. In dealing with the Stasi's files, the need to protect personal data must not serve to protect the culprits. But nobody will deny that the means of clearing up these cases are dubious. In a system which can not exist without lies, files too can lie. There is a political-ethical responsibility which cannot be prosecuted. Guilt extends further than punishability. In any case, what now appears to be guilt was in reality at times something quite different. It was often the result of conscientious self-examination under heavy external pressure.

Emotional wounds will heal but slowly. The expunging of mistrust will take time. But it is vital. It would fail if we tried to prosecute every single incident. This would only bring ourselves close to being dangerous moralists. Our aim is justice, not in the sense of reprisal, but of reconciliation and inner peace.

VII.

Priority must now be given to economic and social problems. The old system failed not least because of the critical economic situation. This makes it all the more important to ensure that the people in the former German Democratic Republic do not experience their newly-won freedom as another period of severe hardship.

They have opted for the social market economy which has proved successful in the West. The monetary union paved the way for the free movement of people and private enterprise. We have pushed the task of creating the legal basis for the development of competition and social security.

But this framework will not of itself translate into economic output. That is the work of people. Social market economy does not come alive in the statute books but in the minds and actions of the people. By the same token, freedom cannot be secured without making demands on the people, just as an economic upswing will not come overnight. Those affected know this best of all. To many the cut is deep and severe: learning afresh, changing attitudes, moving from one place to another, looking for new opportunities, starting all over again. But experience teaches us that individual initiative is always worthwhile.

No less decisive is our cooperation in the united country. We must now act in solidarity—in our most fundamental interest. Now we share responsibility for economic recovery in the new federal states. The success of our efforts is in our mutual interest, for failures hence-forth will in the long term be a burden on the Germans in the West as in the East. The mandate given us by our constitution is to secure comparable living conditions and opportunities for all Germans. At the same time we must be open-minded and fair towards foreigners in our country. . . .

No theory, however wise, and no calculation, however elaborate, can replace the fundamental experience of all cultures and religions that people do not really care for their fellow creatures until they share with them. We will not be truly united until we are prepared to show such care and concern. We can do so, and many, most people I think, want to do so.

VIII.

The nation-state has not ceased to exist, but anyone who believes we can cope with the future with the nation-state alone is living in a bygone era. No nation in the world can solve the world's major problems by itself. Modern systems do not think and function nationally. This applies to security and the environment, to industry and energy, to transport and telecommunications. In our age sovereignty means playing our part within the community of states.

The European Community has created a convincing model for such cooperation. It has fused national powers—and precisely those which are crucial for peaceful neighborly relations—into a supernational framework. In the contest between the systems of East and West it has been the source of powerful impulses for reform in Eastern Europe.

The Cold War is over. Freedom and democracy have prevailed in nearly every country. Not through coercion by the countries that dominated them but of their own free will they can now intensify and institutionalize their relations in order to create, for the first time, a common peaceful order. This marks the beginning of a completely new chapter in the history of the nations of Europe. The goal is pan-European unification.

It is an ambitious goal. We can achieve it, but we can also fall short. There is no time to lose. We face the clear alternative of uniting Europe or relapsing into the sorrowful nationalistic confrontations of the past.

Tangible prospects for the economic and social development of the countries of Central, Eastern and South-Eastern Europe must now be given priority. The newly acquired freedom must take root. It must not be allowed to wither for lack of nourishment. The European Community can provide crucial assistance. It will above all depend on the Community how the situation in the whole of Europe develops.

We Germans have a key role to play. We speak out in support of a common, constructive Eastern policy by the West as a whole. Now that all Germans have become direct neighbors of the Poles, who are so important to us, it is our duty to urge that the Community concludes an association agreement with them, not in the distant future but very soon. The same applies to Czechoslovakia and Hungary.

The Soviet Union, to mention another extremely important example, needs close European cooperation on its incomparably difficult course. The Soviet Union wishes to close the traditional gap between itself and the rest of Europe. It has realized that German unification is not an obstacle but rather a condition for that step. This is the principal message of the highly significant Two-plus-Four conference. As we all know Europe's future stability depends to a large extent on Moscow's contribution. The Soviet Union's western frontier must not become Europe's eastern frontier....

We will on no account jeopardize our Atlantic and European partnership....

We Germans can best look after our interests and dispel our partners' doubts by not allowing ourselves to be outdone in our efforts to strengthen the Community, and by continuing without any hesitation along the road to economic and monetary union leading to political union, as we have promised....

The faster we Europeans settle our own conflicts, the better will we be able to met our global responsibilities. During the Cold War Europeans time and again exported tension and weapons to the southern hemisphere. Our duty now is to promote the CSCE [Conference on Security and Cooperation in Europe] process, to reduce armaments and to boost assistance for the South....

IX.

We share responsibility especially for the environment.... This is in the truest sense a global undertaking. It places an obligation on every country, every community, and every individual in the world. It is a universal and thus the most political issue we face. As our nation embarks on its new beginning it must find a clear normative answer....

X

Today, fellow countrymen, we have founded our common state. What we make of unity in human terms will not be decided by any government treaty, constitution, or law. It depends on the attitude adopted by each one of us, on our own openness and our care for one another....

I am confident we shall succeed in filling existing and newly emerging gulfs. We can fuse the constitutional patriotism of the one side with human solidarity experienced by the other into a powerful whole. We share the will to carry out our great responsibilities as expected by our neighbors.

We realize how much harder life is for other nations at present. History has given us a chance. We must seize it, with confidence and trust.

And joy—we heard it last night—the joy we feel, is a divine spark.

VIOLENCE ON THE TEMPLE MOUNT
October 12, 24, and 26

A deadly riot erupted October 8 on Jerusalem's Temple Mount, a site holy to Jews and Moslems, creating an international furor. About twenty Palestinians were killed—the exact number was uncertain—and about 150 persons, Palestinians and Israelis, were injured. It was the worst outbreak of violence in Jerusalem since the Six Day War of June 1967. At that time Israeli forces captured the eastern (Arab) section and brought the entire city under their control.

The United States, breaking with past practice, joined October 12 with the fourteen other members of the United Nations Security Council in approving a resolution condemning Israel for its handling of the riot. American diplomacy managed to soften the resolution—and two similar ones that would follow by the year's end—but the new U.S. position nevertheless won favor among Arab members allied with Washington against Iraqi president Saddam Hussein. The U.S. vote was credited with holding together the alliance and sidetracking Hussein's effort to divert Arab attention from his invasion of Kuwait. He tried to link the UN resolution to Palestinian demands for the removal of Israeli control in the West Bank and Gaza Strip. (Iraqi Invasion of Kuwait, p. 533)

Until the October 12 vote on Security Council Resolution 672, Israel could consistently depend on the United States not to side with its detractors in the United Nations. Foreign affairs analysts spoke of new strains on U.S.-Israeli relations, and some regarded the vote as a move by the Bush administration to distance itself somewhat from Israeli prime minister Yitzhak Shamir, who had repeatedly balked at U.S. attempts to bring about Israeli negotiations with the Palestinians. However, after

Shamir visited President George Bush in December, Israeli officials indicated that relations with Washington had improved.

America's UN representative, Thomas R. Pickering, in explaining his vote for Resolution 672, said the "tragic event" in Jerusalem "never should have happened." The resolution condemned "the acts of violence committed by the Israeli security forces"—the police and Border Patrol—and requested a fact-finding report from Secretary General Javier Perez de Cuellar. The Israeli government, declaring the security forces blameless, accused the Palestine Liberation Organization (PLO) of fomenting the violence.

Israel reasserted its sovereignty over all of Jerusalem—which the United Nations does not accept—and said it would refuse to cooperate with any fact-finders the secretary general might send. Only an internal police inquiry was planned originally, but on October 10 Shamir appointed a three-member investigative commission headed by Zvi Zamir, a reserve major general and former director of the Mossad intelligence agency. The prime minister said he would consider but not be bound by the commission's conclusions. His office insisted that U.S. support of the then-pending resolution had no bearing on his decision to open an investigation.

The Zamir commission issued its report October 26, two days after the Security Council unanimously passed another resolution, this one urging the Israeli government to reconsider its refusal to admit UN investigators. The report, labeled a "whitewash" by Palestinian leaders, generally backed the government's version of what had occurred on the Temple Mount. It held Palestinian agitators responsible for the violence and concluded that the authorities had not used excessive force. The use of live ammunition by policemen was justified "under the prevailing conditions," the report said, because they "were afraid for their lives."

However, the commission criticized two senior police officials, Aryeh Bibi and Rahavam Comfort, for failing to prepare adequately for the probability of violence. It suggested some administrative changes for better coordination between Jerusalem police and the Israeli Border Patrol, which also has jurisdiction on the Temple Mount, but it made no recommendation for disciplinary action. Shamir said a copy of the report would be sent to the United Nations to demonstrate that Israel, alone among the nations of that region, was willing to investigate itself.

Sacredness of the Site

The riot occurred on the Jewish holiday of Sukkot, a day on which tens of thousands of Jews gather for worship at the Western (or Wailing) Wall, the holiest site in Judaism. It is the only identifiable portion of the so-called Second Temple, which was razed by a Roman army in the year 70. The wall forms the western side of the Temple Mount, known to Arabs as Haram al-Sharif. It rises, platform-like, above the adjoining Old City of Jerusalem and is the site of two historic mosques, the Dome of the Rock and Al-Aqsa. The Dome of the Rock was Islam's first major sanctuary, built in the seventh century after the Moslem conquest of Jerusalem. From that site, according to Moslem tradition, the prophet Mohammed ascended to heaven.

In Jewish tradition, the Temple Mount has been considered holy for some 3,000 years, since the time of King David, who decreed Jerusalem the central worship site for his united kingdom of ancient Israel and Judah. Upon gaining control of Temple Mount in 1967, the Israeli government left Moslem clerics in charge of its mosques but gave Israeli civilian authorities responsibility for its security. Some Jewish religious groups in Jerusalem periodically demand that Jewish worship replace Moslem worship on the Temple Mount. One such group, the Temple Mount Faithful, requested but was denied permission to lay a symbolic cornerstone for a Third Temple.

Israeli Commission Findings

According to the Zamir commission report, Moslem clerics became alarmed at the possibility of Jewish encroachment and called on Palestinian youth to come to the Temple Mount and physically prevent Jews from laying the cornerstone. Some 2,000 to 3,000 Palestinians gathered there the morning of October 8. Police officers met with them and appealed for calm, the report said, but they were "incited by preachers on loudspeakers." About twenty members of the Temple Mount Faithful appeared briefly at the wall under police guard. The assembled Palestinians began throwing stones at Jewish worshipers below, and then pelted the police who attempted to stop them.

A central question in the inquiry was when and why the police resorted to live ammunition. The commission determined that the Jewish worshipers had retreated from the range of the rock throwers by the time the police began to use live ammunition. But the commission said, as had Israeli police authorities in contradiction of Palestinian claims, that the police acted in self-defense. "Masked assailants stormed the policemen and, since they were not halted by rubber bullets, live ammunition was fired, first in the air, and subsequently toward the rioters," the report said.

Compromise on UN Inspector

Secretary General Perez de Cuellar, frustrated by Israel's refusal to permit a UN investigation, recommended in early November that the 1949 Geneva Convention on treatment of civilians under military occupation be reconvened to examine the protection of Palestinians living under Israeli occupation. The Israeli government rejected his recommendation but one week later, November 11, offered to accept a single UN investigator.

The offer appeared to be part of a compromise agreement engineered by the United States to keep the Security Council from calling for such an international conference—which Washington feared would divert

Arab attention from the Persian Gulf crisis and possibly split the anti-Iraq alliance.

Ultimately, the United States prevailed in obtaining the passage of a Security Council resolution that deplored Israel's deportation of Palestinians and asked the secretary general to monitor more closely the treatment of Palestinians under Israeli occupation. A separate statement issued in the name of the Security Council president added that the council members "agree that an international conference, at an appropriate time, should facilitate efforts" to settle the Arab-Israeli conflict. But the statement said that the issue "must be addressed independently."

Following are UN Security Council resolutions 672 and 673, of October 12 and 24, 1990, calling on Israel to permit a United Nations investigation of the October 8 violence in Jerusalem; and excerpts from the Israeli government's summary of a report on the violence:

RESOLUTION 672

The Security Council,

Recalling its resolutions 476 (1980) and 478 (1980),

Reaffirming that a just and lasting solution to the Arab-Israeli conflict must be based on its resolutions 242 (1967) and 338 (1973) through an active negotiating process which takes into account the right to security for all States in the region, including Israel, as well as the legitimate political rights of the Palestinian people.

Taking into consideration the statement of the Secretary-General relative to the purpose of the mission he is sending to the region and conveyed to the Council by the President on 12 October 1990.

1. *Expresses* alarm at the violence which took place on 8 October at the Al Haram Al Shareef and other Holy Places of Jerusalem resulting in over 20 Palestinian deaths and the injury of more than one hundred and fifty people, including Palestinian civilians and innocent worshippers;

2. *Condemns* especially the acts of violence committed by the Israeli security forces resulting in injuries and loss of human life;

3. *Calls* upon Israel, the occupying Power, to abide scrupulously by its legal obligations and responsibilities under the Fourth Geneva Convention, which is applicable to all the territories occupied by Israel since 1967;

4. *Requests,* in connection with the decision of the Secretary-General to send a mission to the region, which the Council welcomes, that he submit a report to it before the end of October 1990 containing his findings and conclusions and that he use as appropriate all of the resources of the United Nations in the region in carrying out the mission.

RESOLUTION 673

The Security Council,

Reaffirming the obligations of Member States under the United Nations Charter,

Reaffirming also its resolution 672 (1990),

Having been briefed by the Secretary-General on 19 October 1990,

Expressing alarm at the rejection of Security Council resolution 672 (1990) by the Israeli Government, and its refusal to accept the mission of the Secretary-General,

Taking into consideration the statement of the Secretary-General relative to the purpose of the mission he is sending to the region and conveyed to the Council by the President on 12 October 1990,

Gravely concerned at the continued deterioration of the situation in the occupied territories,

1. *Deplores* the refusal of the Israeli Government to receive the mission of the Secretary-General to the region;

2. *Urges* the Israeli Government to reconsider its decision and insists that it comply fully with resolution 672 (1990) and to permit the mission of the Secretary-General to proceed in keeping with its purpose;

3. *Requests* the Secretary-General to submit to the Council the report requested in resolution 672 (1990);

4. *Affirms* its determination to give full and expeditious consideration to the report.

ISRAELI REPORT SUMMARY

Chapter 1: Introduction

1. The Commission [of Investigation] expresses its deep sorrow over the loss of life on the Temple Mount, and conveys its sorrow to the families that lost loved ones. The Commission also expresses its sorrow over the injuries caused to civilians and police at the Western Wall Plaza and its vicinity and wishes a full recovery to the injured.

2. The Commission recommends that its conclusions be revealed in their entirety to the public and, therefore, has omitted from the report the evidence and the sources of its decisions and conclusions.

3. Despite its being a "commission of investigation" and not a "commission of inquiry," the Commission was authorized by the minister of justice to "receive statements in writing and to warn the witnesses to tell the truth. . . ." The Commission also operated according to section 14 of the Inquiry Commission Law of 5729 [1968] and has decided that all testimony and material received will not serve as evidence in a legal proceeding, except for a criminal trial.

4. The Commission heard 124 witnesses, among them: the minister of

police, the mayor of Jerusalem, the police commissioner, the head of the GSS [Israeli intelligence agency], police and Border Patrol commanders, and also police officers and Border Patrol police. The Commission also heard a number of detainees, among them Faisal Husseini and Sheikh Muhammad Said Al-Jamal Al-Rifa'i.

5. The Commission visited Mukased Hospital and heard reports from doctors and the wounded, and also visited the Temple Mount and its vicinity a number of times.

6. The Commission was not requested to draw personal conclusions in the realm of civil, criminal or disciplinary responsibility of any of those involved in the events—and it is the opinion of the Commission that it has no authority to do so in accordance with the law. The objective of the Commission was to examine that which was demanded of it in its letter of appointment—it is not the purview of the Commission of Investigation to deal with or to recommend the drawing of personal conclusions by any one of those involved in the events. The conclusions of the Commission do not make reference to the actions or the malfeasance of a given individual. All resultant decisions and inferences—if any are made at all—to the Commission's conclusions with respect to individuals involved in the Temple Mount events of 8 October 1990, will be determined by the competent authorities.

7. The Commission received written material from different sources including "Betzelem," but the witnesses whose statements were attached to the "Betzelem" report refused to appear for questioning before the Commission. Appeals by the Commission to the High Muslim Council and the Waqf administration to meet with the Commission were refused.

8. The opinion of a medical expert, submitted to the Commission, regarding seven of the wounded admitted to Mukased Hospital in Jerusalem, determined that not a single one of them was struck from behind.

9. The Commission calls on the National Insurance Institute to clarify, as soon as possible, who among the wounded—who did not take an active part in the disturbances of public order on the Temple Mount—is eligible for benefits under the Victims of Hostile Action (Pensions) Law—5730 [1970].

Chapter 2: Conclusions and Inferences

Causes of the Incident

... The Muslim gathering on the Temple Mount exceeded the intended purpose of the site and the norms which a holy site oblige. The members of the Waqf [Moslem leadership] knew that the High Court refused the "Temple Mount Faithful" petition to lay the cornerstone of the Third Temple, and did not respond to requests by Israel Police officers on the morning of the incident to calm the crowd. This, even after the fact that the police informed the Waqf that they would also prevent the "Temple Mount Faithful," and anyone else, from visiting the area, though such visits are allowed by law.

The incident itself began when, suddenly, violent and threatening calls were sounded on the speakers ("Allah Akbar," "Jihad," "Itbakh Al-Yahud" [Slaughter the Jews]). Immediately afterwards, enormous amounts of rocks, construction materials and metal objects were thrown at Israeli policemen who were present at the site. Many in the incited, rioting mob threw stones and metal objects from a very short range, and some even wielded knives in their hands. The actions of the rioters, and certainly the incitors, constituted a threat to the lives of the police, the thousands of worshipers at the Western Wall and to themselves. This was a serious criminal offense committed by masses who were incited by preachers on loudspeakers, and this is what led to the tragic chain of events.

It is the opinion of the Commission that any criminal acts that may have been carried out during the course of the events should continue to be investigated. It is the opinion of the Commission that there is room for suspicion that a considerable percentage of the people gathered at the Temple Mount and their leaders apparently were involved in the obstruction of public order, causing harm to police and worshipers and endangering their lives.

Use of Force by the Police

The Commission has reached the conclusion that the lives of the police on the Temple Mount were endangered, and that they feared for their lives, and for the lives of thousands of worshipers who were at the Western Wall.

The firing of tear gas and rubber bullets by the police, which came following the massive barrage of stones and other objects, was intended to deter the rioters and to repel them from the vicinity of the Western Wall. In light of the injuries which they sustained, the police were forced to retreat from the Temple Mount through Mughrabi Gate, and the barrage continued over the Western Wall, the Mughrabi Gate and the Ophel Road.

The breaking into the Temple Mount came as a result of the continuation of the rioting and the barrage of stones, and of the fear for the lives of two police officers who remained caught in the Temple Mount police station. There was also a concern that the weapons and ammunition in the station would fall into the hands of the rioters. Since communications were cut off, the police commanders did not know that the policemen trapped in the station succeeded to escape on their own....

The Functioning of the Senior Command Level of the Israel Police

... The police had advance information on the possibility of rioting. The method of thinking and attitudes of the commander of the southern district and of the commander of the Jerusalem area were routine and even mistaken. There was no consideration of the special sensitivity of the Temple Mount and there was no advance preparation for a wide variety of possible situations. The supervision concerned itself with one element only, "the laying of a cornerstone for the Third Temple," and, when that was cancelled, they took routine measures.

Area and district commanders did not take into account the accumulated influence of the intifada, the environment created by terrorist elements and their attitude towards the Gulf crisis, and calls for incitement by the muezzin and the preachers on the Temple Mount on the Friday before the events. These phenomena required the presence of initiative and suspicion that did not exist in this case. The police, further, did not have files on preparations for possible contingencies and, therefore, they were not tested.

In the opinion of the Commission, the situation that was created on the Temple Mount required the presence of commanders, of the most senior levels, on the Temple Mount. The situation also required the presence of area and district commanders and, as the situation intensified, there was room for the summoning of the commissioner. The activating of an emergency situation for the security of the Temple Mount, the setting up of a forward command post, the concentration of forces and the establishment of positions, could have deterred the frenzied masses from rioting. Following other events, the command posts were not staffed by senior commanders, the communications between different points on the Mount did not function properly and neither the commissioner nor the minister of police were briefed early on regarding developments in the situation.

There are no sharp or uniform definitions regarding responsibility for command on the Mount. The Commission is of the opinion that the uniformity of command must be kept and that all the forces working in the Old City must report to the Old City command. . . .

An elite force must be permanently allotted to the Temple Mount and its vicinity to work under uniform supervision with defined jurisdictions and responsibilities. . . .

Intelligence

Difficulties exist in the gathering of information, its analysis, in issuing warnings and in assisting in preventing disruptions of public order. The Commission is of the opinion that the division of labor between the GSS and the police is basically correct and should not be changed.

The GSS has assumed upon itself the gathering of information on the organization of disruptions of order and the police has taken upon itself the gathering of information in the street, in connection to developments that are characterized as spontaneous.

. . . Concerning the incident on the Temple Mount, there was no lack of advance information: general warnings by the GSS [Israeli intelligence agency], and, above all, there was clear information—the calls of the preachers, leaflets and the multiplicity of groups of masked assailants that called for gathering on the Temple Mount.

The mistake of the commissioner, the commander of the southern district and the Jerusalem area commander was in the evaluation of the information and in focusing on the assumption that, if the "laying of the cornerstone" could be prevented, everything would settle down peacefully—as in the past. . . .

Ban on Demonstrations in the Area of the Old City

The national interest of the State of Israel and the special situation in the Old City require re-evaluation of what can or cannot be permitted in respect to gatherings and demonstrations which may lead to disturbances.

The Commission recommends preventing gatherings for the purpose of demonstrations on the Temple Mount, the Western Wall, and throughout the Old City. The freedom of worship of all religions in their holy places should be preserved. Only official State events may be permitted in the vicinity of the Western Wall.

Use of Technological Means

The use of live ammunition on the Temple Mount under the prevailing conditions was justified by the Commission. It is also clear that it is the policy of the police to use live ammunition only as a last resort, and only if lives are endangered. It is necessary to develop technological means whose efficiency would be greater than that of the use of gas and rubber bullets. The Commission emphasizes the immediate need to develop alternatives to the use of live ammunition. The Commission recommends the immediate establishment of a techno-defense crew that will evaluate possibilities for solving the problem of protecting the Temple Mount and the Western Wall. . . .

Chapter 3: The Temple Mount from a Legal, Historical and Political Perspective

The Legal Situation

The Temple Mount falls under the sovereignty of the State of Israel and, therefore, it is subject to all the laws of the State. Following the Six-Day War, Israeli sovereignty was extended to the eastern part of Jerusalem, including the Old City, in which the Temple Mount is situated. The extension of sovereignty was entailed in a Knesset law—the Amendment of the Law and Administrative Ordinance (5748/1948). Furthermore, in the Protection of the Holy Places Law (5767/1967), the freedom of access to the holy places of all religions is guaranteed. Paragraph 1 of this law, because of its importance, also appears in the Basic Law: Jerusalem— Capital of Israel, that was passed in 1980.

The Jews and the Temple Mount

The Temple Mount has been considered holy by Israel since the time of

David. Even when the people had been uprooted from the land, its interest in the holy site was maintained. After the Jordanian conquest, in 1948, the Jordanian government did not allow free access to the site for Jews, even though that had been ensured in the armistice agreement between Israel and Jordan in 1949. Observant Jews are prohibited from entering the Temple Mount, according to the command of the sages of Israel and of the Chief Rabbis, and their prayers are held at the Western Wall. Non-observant Jews enter the Temple Mount as visitors only. Freedom of access to the Temple Mount is anchored in the laws of the State and in the judgments of the High Court of Justice.

The Muslims and the Temple Mount

Since the Arab conquest of Jerusalem in 638, the Temple Mount has been a Muslim religious center. The High Court of Justice recognized the Temple Mount as a holy place for Muslims and it functions as a center of Muslim prayer. Given the exceptional sensitivity surrounding this holy place, former Prime Minister of Israel Levi Eshkol said, as early as 27 June 1967, to the heads of all religions that "... the holy places in Jerusalem are open to all religions. Everyone is welcome to visit and pray at the holy places, according to his religion and without discrimination. ..."

In accordance with the principle, the internal administration of matters relating to the Temple Mount, including the mosques thereon, has been given to the authority of the Muslim Waqf.

The Responsibility for the Security of the Temple Mount

The responsibility for the security of the Temple Mount has been placed on the civilian authorities, whether during the days of the British Mandate or during the time of Jordanian rule. That is to say, the maintenance of public order is a state matter. The government of Israel, which holds sovereign jurisdiction over the Temple Mount, is, therefore, responsible for security on the site. Even Waqf authorities have not seen themselves as responsible for security matters.

In the report by an Arab "commission of investigation"—signed by Anwar al-Khatib, Anwar Nuseibeh and Ba'id Alla al-Adin—which was published following the fire at Al-Aqsa mosque in 1989, it was stated, inter alia, that "... the occupation authorities, being as they are, cannot escape their security responsibilities. The guardians of the Muslim shrines have no security jurisdiction or function. ..."

The Application of Criminal Law at the Holy Places

The High Court of Justice (HCJ 267/68) determined that criminal law, in its entirety, applies to the "holy places," but the state authorities have acted with caution in all matters concerning the enforcement of the law on the Temple Mount, owing to the sensitivity of the place and to a desire to prevent any outbursts of a religious nature.

Freedom of Religion—the Adjudicative Angle

Freedom of religion for Jews on the Temple Mount, as opposed to freedom of access, has been dealt with in many judgments of the High Court of Justice. In these judgments, criticism has been directed at the police decision to refuse permission to Jews who wish to pray on the Temple Mount. The majority of the appeals have been rejected by the Court, and, in most cases, an opinion has been expressed that the Temple Mount matter must be approached with great sensitivity, preferable to "... the hard-line and non-flexible approach of the law...." (see HCJ 222/86).

[Chapters 4, 5, 6 omittted]

SENTENCING OF
WASHINGTON'S MAYOR
October 26, 1990

After a long and controversial case, Marion Barry, the black, three-term mayor of Washington, was sentenced to six months in prison October 26 for cocaine possession. Only a higher court's reversal of Barry's conviction, which he appealed, would spare him from imprisonment. His trial captivated the city— indeed much of the nation—with the prosecution depicting him as a high-living drug user and womanizer who neglected his official duties. The defense portrayed him as the victim of racially motivated federal prosecutors who spent millions to entrap him. Opinion about Barry's verdict tended to split along racial lines in Washington, creating community tensions and sharp controversies throughout the case.

FBI agents and local police arrested Barry January 18 in a downtown Washington hotel room where he was lured by a former girlfriend, Hazel Diane "Rasheeda" Moore, who was cooperating with the agents. At her urging, the mayor smoked crack cocaine, while a hidden videotape camera recorded the scene.

The videotape provided the dramatic highlight of the trial when it was shown to jurors June 29, and repeatedly thereafter on television newscasts. Barry was shown inhaling from a pipe, his head held back, facing a mirror as Moore sat on a bed. Moments later armed men burst into the room, shouting "Police!" "FBI! FBI! You're under arrest," another said. As FBI agent Ronald Stern attempted to read the startled mayor his rights, Barry muttered, "This was a setup, goddamn it. It was a [expletive] setup." Looking toward Moore, he said, "Bitch set me up."

Five days after his arrest, Barry appeared with his wife and young son

*at a church and appealed to Washingtonians for their love and under-
standing as he sought a way "to heal my body, soul and mind." While he
did not specify his affliction, Barry entered a Florida treatment center
for alcoholism the following day. The mayor left the job of running the
city to an assistant until he returned March 13, speaking of his "alcohol
dependency" and vowing to complete a course of treatment.*

*In the meantime, a federal grand jury had indicted him on eight counts
of drug possession and perjury. It filed six more charges before his trial
began June 4. Perjury charges arose from his denials to a grand jury in
January 1989 that he had given drugs to an acquaintance, Charles Lewis,
or had received drugs from Lewis or had any knowledge that Lewis used
drugs. Lewis, convicted in the Virgin Islands on drug charges in April
1989, later told police investigators he had smoked cocaine with Barry in
a Washington hotel in December 1988. City police detectives had traced
Lewis to the hotel on that occasion but did not pursue their investigation
when they learned that the mayor was in Lewis's room.*

Barry's Trial and Sentencing

*After a trial of more than three months, a federal district court jury of
District of Columbia residents—nine women and three men (ten black
and two white)—found Barry guilty August 11 on one charge of cocaine
possession, acquitted him on another, and could not agree on the
remaining twelve charges, all alleging drug possession or perjury. The
prosecution later said it would not seek to retry Barry on the dozen
deadlocked issues. His chief counsel, R. Kenneth Mundy, conceded to the
jury that the mayor had been an occasional cocaine user but contended
that the government never proved cocaine possession beyond a reasonable doubt. Barry did not testify.*

*The single conviction was not on the matter that got the most
attention, the videotaped hotel tryst; rather it stemmed from the testimony of another woman acquaintance, Doris Crenshaw, who said she had
used cocaine with Barry at a Washington hotel in November 1989.*

*Barry and followers were jubilant that he had been convicted on only
one count, a misdemeanor charge, which often draws only a fine; if a jail
term is attached to the sentence, it is often suspended in favor of the
defendant's doing community service work. Many of Barry's detractors
bitterly criticized the verdict, contending that the evidence was sufficient
to convict him on several charges. The sentence of six months in prison,
however, drew the ire of his remaining supporters.*

*Judge Thomas Penfield Jackson explained the reasoning behind the
sentence. "His breach of public trust alone warrants an enhanced
sentence." Jackson spoke of the mayor's "subterfuge and false testimony" to avoid exposure and prosecution. "Having failed as the good
example he might have been to the citizens of Washington, D.C.—and, in
particular, to the young who are so much more likely to respond to
example than to admonition—the defendant must now become an*

example of another kind." The judge concluded that Barry's conduct "represented a willful attempt at obstruction of justice."

At the same time, Jackson noted that Barry, a "compulsive user of cocaine," was not only a criminal but a victim and deserving of "as much compassion as anyone so afflicted." The judge recommended drug treatment for Barry during his imprisonment. He fined the mayor $5,000 and ordered him to pay the cost of his confinement and postrelease supervision, which would continue for one year. Federal officials estimated that cost at about $10,000. The maximum sentence for the offense was a year in prison and a fine of $5,000.

Defeat in November Election

The conviction appeared to doom Barry's political career. He did not seek a fourth term as mayor, an office he had held since 1978, but two days after the verdict he quit the Democratic party and announced he would run as an independent for an at-large seat on the D.C. Council. He suffered defeat in the November 6 election, and his successor as mayor, Sharon Pratt Dixon, was his most vocal critic in the political arena. Promising to "clean house" if elected, she won an upset victory in the city's Democratic primary election in September and then went on to a landslide triumph in the general election over her Republican opponent.

Barry left behind a city in bad financial shape and, according to a blue-ribbon commission, a demoralized, inefficient government. The commission, headed by economist Alice Rivlin, former director of the Congressional Budget Office, presented a report in November depicting an overstaffed and cumbersome city government facing huge budget deficits and potential bankruptcy.

> *Following is the sentencing memorandum and order read by U.S. District Court judge Thomas Penfield Jackson at his sentencing of Washington mayor Marion Barry October 26 for possession of cocaine:*

Section 3553 (c) of Title 18, U.S.C. [United States Code], requires the Court to state its reasons upon the record in open court for imposing a particular sentence. Of greatest significance to me in sentencing this defendant is the high public office he has at all relevant times occupied. He was at the time of his offense, the time of his conviction, and is now at the time of his sentencing, the elected head of government, as Mayor the chief public official and personage of the City of Washington, D.C., the capital of the United States.

His breach of public trust alone warrants an enhanced sentence. By his own unlawful conduct the defendant rendered himself beholden to, and thus vulnerable to influence from, anyone who had first-hand knowledge of it. Whether that vulnerability was ever exploited is immaterial for present purposes. Moreover, the prevalence of the public rumors of defendant's frequent and conspicuous drug use—never dispelled, and now unfortunately shown to have been true—has given aid, comfort, and encouragement to the drug culture at large, and contributed to the anguish that illegal drugs have inflicted on this city in so many ways for so long. His prominence inspired others to emulate him and to behave as they believed he did. Having failed as the good example he might have been to the citizens of Washington, D.C.—and, in particular, to the young who are so much more likely to respond to example than to admonition—the defendant must now become an example of another kind.

There are, in addition, other aggravating circumstances to be taken into account. First, although the verdict represents the defendant's first conviction, and is of what some might call a minor crime, the Court finds that the offense of which he stands convicted was neither his first nor his last such offense. Second, I find from the evidence that the defendant employed subterfuge and false testimony—his own and that of others—in an attempt to avoid exposure and prosecution altogether. The Court concludes the defendant's conduct in that regard represented a willful attempt at obstruction of justice.

I am ignoring, for purposes of sentencing, what I perceive to have been the defendant's efforts, once prosecution had commenced, to induce the jury to disregard the law and the evidence. The jurors will have to answer to themselves and to their fellow citizens for the way in which they discharged their duty.

The cocaine the defendant used with Ms. [Doris] Crenshaw in November 1989 was procured from some third person. It is not unlikely that that person was someone like the 35-year-old small-time drug dealer who was convicted in this court and sentenced, in January, 1990, to a mandatory minimum prison term of 35 years without parole. It might also have been a person like the 22-year-old Howard University student who began serving a mandatory minimum sentence of 12 years, seven months, in July of 1989, also without parole, for distributing drugs on and around the University campus.

These people were, of course, part of the drug supply network. There would, however, be no people like them—and also no drug crisis—if there were no consumers to make a market for their illicit drugs. The defendant was such a consumer, not only in November of 1989, but on numerous occasions before and since. Proportionate justice would seem to call for some fairly comparable penalty for him.

I find, however, that there is evidence of mitigating circumstances operating in the defendant's favor, and I believe he is entitled to their benefit despite his persistence, until the moment of his sentencing, in a formal attitude of denial. He has admitted to being an alcoholic. I find, from the evidence I have heard and his attorney's judicial admission, as well as the defendant's belated acknowledgment, that he is also a compulsive user of cocaine. He is, thus, in a sense a victim as well as a perpetrator and deserving of as much compassion as anyone so afflicted, however he may have come to it. It appears, moreover, that at the moment he is making significant and sustained progress at self-rehabilitation, and that he enjoys the support of his family, his true friends and his church as he endeavors to do so.

It is, therefore, this 26th day of October, 1990, ORDERED, that the defendant Marion S. Barry, Jr., is hereby committed to the custody of the U.S. Bureau of Prisons for a term of six (6) months, with a recommendation for drug treatment during his confinement, and fined the sum of $5,000, payable to the United States. The defendant shall also, as required by the Sentencing Reform Act of 1984, pay the cost of his confinement and post-release supervision to the United States. The defendant may remain at liberty on his personal recognizance until his place of confinement is designated, and shall then report voluntarily thereto as directed by the Bureau of Prisons. Upon his release from confinement, the defendant shall be placed on supervised release for a period of one (1) year, subject to the standard conditions of probation promulgated by the Sentencing Commission, and upon the further conditions that he submit to periodic, unscheduled urinalysis and to drug treatment and/or aftercare when and as directed by the Probation Office; that he pay the fine hereby imposed within the period of supervised release; and that he pay a mandatory special assessment of $25.00; and it is

FURTHER ORDERED, that the Court hereby makes the necessary findings under 18 U.S.C. [U.S. Code] § 3143(b). The defendant is released on his personal recognizance, and, unless defendant otherwise requests, the execution of sentence is stayed pursuant to Fed.R.Crim.P. 38(b) [appeal designation] pending completion of proceedings on a timely appeal taken herefrom.

November

PRESIDENT BUSH ON
CLEAN AIR ACT REVISIONS
November 15, 1990

President George Bush November 15 signed into law a major revision of the 1970 Clean Air Act, marking the end of a decade-long political stalemate in Washington over how to rewrite it. Crafted during America's first great wave of environmental awareness and last revised in 1977, the Clean Air Act commanded a central position among federal environmental laws.

The original act created the Environmental Protection Agency (EPA) to set antipollution standards and regulate specified industries, such as automobile manufacturers, that were national in scope. The states were required to draft and enforce plans to reduce air pollutants in large urban areas. Although generally acclaimed by the public and politicians from the start, the act was ill-suited to deal with later concerns such as acid rain.

To reduce acid rain, the new legislation sought to achieve 40 percent fewer sulfur dioxide emissions by the year 2000. Other amendments mandated tighter standards for tailpipe emissions, a clean-fueled vehicles program, and new controls on sources of industrial pollution in cities where air quality violated federal standards. Chemicals that deplete the protective ozone layer high above the Earth were scheduled to be phased out, and industries faced stricter standards on toxic air pollution.

Industry lobbyists blocked or softened some of the more stringent provisions during the legislation's long journey through Congress, but nearly all sides agreed that it still promised considerably cleaner air by early in the next century. In 1990, as in 1977, debate focused on economic versus health and environmental considerations.

Regulatory costs, including new technologies to reduce pollutants, are borne largely by business and industry—and ultimately by consumers. They amounted to $250 billion in the 1980s, according to the EPA's estimate. But the fear of economic disruption discouraged the EPA and state governments from being as strict as the law allowed or required. Moreover, business owners and others complained that the law's provisions were too detailed and complex. William H. Rehnquist, then an associate justice, agreed in a 1980 Supreme Court opinion, saying that they "virtually swim before one's eyes."

The 1977 debate shaped the political landscape on the clean air issue for more than a decade. Rep. John D. Dingell, D-Mich., emerged as perhaps the most powerful member of Congress on the issue and as a protector of midwestern industries, including Detroit-based auto makers. Rep. Henry Waxman, D-Calif., became the leading advocate of stringent standards favored by environmentalists. In the Senate, Democratic leader Robert C. Byrd of West Virginia sought to protect his state's high-sulfur coal mines; as an industrial fuel, this type of coal was a prime source of industrial air pollution.

Congress took up clean air legislation again in 1982, the deadline established under the 1977 amendments for most metropolitan areas to meet air quality standards. With Congress deadlocked on the issue, the EPA extended the deadline to 1987. Since 1981, when Ronald Reagan entered the White House, federal support for clean air had weakened. With little initiative coming from either Capitol Hill or the EPA, enforcement of the Clean Air Act in the 1980s fell largely to environmental groups, which tried with some success to force compliance through lawsuits.

As President Reagan left office, however, political pressure was growing for cleaner air. This pressure was attributed to publicity about acid rain, global warming, and the failure of several urban areas to meet the 1987 deadline for reducing ground-level ozone—smog's main ingredient—and carbon monoxide. About 75 million Americans then lived in areas that violated federal standards for ground ozone, and 40 million lived in areas where carbon monoxide levels were too high. Some parts of the Northeast detected record high levels of ozone during the hot, smoggy summer of 1988.

Bush's Clean Air Plan

George Bush, vowing to be the "environmental president," appointed a respected conservationist, William K. Reilly, as EPA director. Byrd had stepped down as the Senate's Democratic leader, and his successor, George J. Mitchell of Maine, was an environmentalist. In June 1989 Bush announced support for a revision of the Clean Air Act.

When the specifics of Bush's proposal were revealed the following month, however, environmentalists were disappointed. Bush wanted to tighten auto emission standards but let the manufacturers "average" the emissions among all models in a single model year. Moreover, any maker who reduced emissions below required levels could "bank" the extras for future expansion or sell them to a polluter. Auto makers welcomed the plan. On acid rain, Bush proposed extending compliance deadlines into the first decade of the next century.

"Unfortunately, the president stepped up to the problem, blinked, and stepped back," said Max Baucus, D-Mont., chairman of the Senate Environmental Protection Subcommittee. But if Democrats criticized Bush's plan, they nevertheless praised his initiative for breaking a legislative logjam. While alienating many environmentalists, Bush won a powerful ally in Dingell, who introduced Bush's plan in the House. Later Dingell compromised with Waxman to erase several of the Bush provisions. The Dingell-Waxman agreement set the stage for the legislation's passage in the House.

Congressional Action: Key Features

The House approved the new legislative package (HR 3030) May 23, 1990, on a 410-21 vote. The Senate, 89-11, had passed a separate bill (S 1630) April 3 after extensive bargaining with the White House to prevent a filibuster. The two chambers negotiated into the fall over which version would prevail. The White House offered a set of new proposals September 26, but by then it was too late to make much difference. Senate conferees, for example, had already given in to House provisions requiring much more stringent urban smog controls on businesses ranging from dry cleaners to oil refineries. Industry lobbyists counted that as their worst loss.

The conferees felt free, in part, to opt for stronger controls because of skepticism that Bush would veto the bill in the waning days of an election year session. They agreed, for example, that the government should give income assistance and retraining to coal miners and others facing unemployment due to an expected shift from the use of high-sulfur to low-sulfur coal. The House had approved income assistance despite a veto threat, but the Senate had not. To avert a western rebellion, the conferees balked at mandating cleaner air over the Grand Canyon and other national parks and opted to finance a study of the issue. Environmentalists suffered other defeats in accommodations to delay certain new antipollution controls on automobiles and fuels until late in the 1990s and on the steel industry until 2020.

At last on October 22 the conferees pieced together a complete bill that did not draw the active opposition of environmentalists and industry lobbyists, despite their complaints. Among the lawmakers, old rivalries dissolved into a festival of bipartisan back-patting. All sides seemed to consider the legislation too important an election-year trophy to let slip away. The House voted approval October 26 and the Senate October 27, as the 101st Congress entered its final hours.

President Bush, too, seemed caught up in the same congratulatory *spirit. At the White House bill-signing ceremony, he declared with rhetorical exuberance: "This legislation isn't just the centerpiece of our environmental agenda. It is simply the most significant air pollution legislation in our nation's history."*

Following are excerpts from remarks by President George Bush at the White House November 15, 1990, as he signed into law legislation revising the Clean Air Act of 1970:

... Today we add a long-awaited and long-needed chapter in our environmental history, and we begin a new era for clean air.... I am very proud on behalf of everyone here to sign this clean air bill—Clean Air Act of 1990.

This landmark legislation will reduce air pollution each year by 56 billion pounds—that's 224 pounds for every man, woman, and child in America. It will go after the three main types of air pollution: acid rain, smog, and toxic air pollutants. This bill will cut emissions that cause acid rain in half and permanently cap them at these new levels. It will reduce pollutants that cause smog in our cities by 40 percent, so that by the year 2000, over 100 major American cities with poor air quality will have safer, healthier air. And it will cut dangerous air toxics emissions by over 75 percent, using new technologies. And by the next decade, its alternative fuel provisions will help reduce our dependence on foreign oil. This bill means cleaner cars, cleaner power plants, cleaner factories, and cleaner fuels; and it means a cleaner America. Virtually every person in every city and every town will enjoy its benefits.

This legislation isn't just the centerpiece of our environmental agenda. It is simply the most significant air pollution legislation in our nation's history, and it restores America's place as the global leader in environmental protection.

Nineteen ninety is now a milestone year for the environment. I also hope that it will be remembered as an important year for environmental cooperation. There were several members of my administration who saw to it, through thick and thin, that this bill got to my desk: Bill Reilly, the EPA Administrator; Jim Watkins, the Secretary of Energy. From my own staff, our Chief of Staff worked tirelessly—John Sununu. Roger Porter did an outstanding job, working day in and day out with the Members of Congress. Boyden Gray—the same thing. Bob Grady and so many others. And they did a great job on this.

And I also want to thank once again the Senators and Members of Congress from both sides of the aisle. Many of you are with us today, and as I mentioned earlier, others couldn't be with us today. But it isn't because of lack of interest. Congress is out; many are scattered to the winds. But the list is too long to single out everybody from the Hill that worked on this. But again, I just want to thank you that are here today and the others who couldn't be with us for your commitment and dedication—

as well as the Governors, the Governors and the experts from local governments who were also instrumental in building true bipartisan support for this legislation.

We met with business leaders who saw stewardship to the environment as a key to long-term economic growth. And we met with academics and innovative problem-solvers from every side who have helped build the foundation for this legislation.

I want to commend the environmental groups that we've met with, like the Environmental Defense Fund, under the leadership of Fred Krupp, for bringing creativity to the table to end what could have been a hopeless stalemate.

We all had tough choices to make. Some said we went too far; others said we didn't go far enough. But despite our differences, we all agreed on the goal: clean air for all Americans. We agreed on the means: a new Clean Air Act.

And we all agreed it was time to take a new approach. This bill is both ambitious in its goals and innovative in its methods. For the first time, we've moved away from the red tape bureaucratic approach of the past. The old tradition of command and control regulation is not the answer. By relying on the marketplace, we can achieve the ambitious environmental goals we have as a country in the most efficient and cost-effective way possible. We'll have to take advantage of the innovation, energy, and ingenuity of every American, drawing local communities and the private sector into the cause. It's time for a new kind of environmentalism, driven by the knowledge that a sound ecology and a strong economy can coexist.

The approach in this bill balances economic growth and environmental protection. The approach is comprehensive, cost-effective; and most of all, it will work. The first major pollution reductions are where we need them most. It offers incentives, choice, and flexibility for industry to find the best solutions, all in the context of continued economic growth. The bill is balanced: It will stimulate the use of natural gas from the wells of Texas and Louisiana; and fuels made from the farms of Iowa, Illinois, the great Midwest; and cleaner, low-sulfur coal from the hills of West Virginia to the Rocky Mountain States. This bill can make America the global leader in developing a new generation of environmental technologies to which the world is now turning.

But it does more. The legislation sets reasonable deadlines for those who must comply; but once deadlines go by, once they pass, the penalties are severe. American heritage is precious. We will not turn our backs or look the other way. That means polluters must pay. And so, there is a new breeze blowing, a new current of concern for the environment. Today marks a great victory for the environment, a day when we have strengthened our clean air statutes, already the world's toughest. This legislation is not only in America's interest; like so many of the environmental issues that we are working on, this bill is in the interest of people all over the world.

And the new environmental ethos is growing. We see it in community efforts and in school involvement across America, and we're seeing it in the innovative response of private industry—in alternative fuel service stations, electric vehicles. These companies understand we must pioneer new technology, find new solutions, envision new horizons if we're to build a bright future and a better America for our children.

There's an old saying: "We don't inherit the Earth from our parents. We borrow it from our children." We have succeeded today because of a common sense of global stewardship, a sense that it is the Earth that endures and that all of us are simply holding a sacred trust left for future generations. For the sake of future generations, I again thank each and every one of you for your commitment to our precious environment. I am now honored to sign this clean air bill into law.

Thank you all who have worked so hard for this day to become possible. Thank you, and God bless all of you. . . .

LEGAL DISPUTE OVER BROADCAST OF NORIEGA PHONE CALLS

November 18, 1990

While awaiting trial on federal drug charges, Gen. Manuel Antonio Noriega, the deposed Panamanian dictator, became embroiled in a legal question over whether he could receive a fair trial. The case arose over two Cable News Network (CNN) broadcasts of snippets from telephone calls the general had made from the Metropolitan Correction Center near Miami. All prisoners at the medium-security facility were permitted to make phone calls within prescribed rules.

The television network reported November 8 it had tapes of some Noriega phone calls that had been recorded by prison authorities, but without revealing where or how it obtained the tapes. CNN proceeded to broadcast barely audible segments from two conversations, both in Spanish. One call was from Noriega to the Cuban Embassy in Panama and the other to a former Panamanian official, whom Noriega called "Lucco," at an undisclosed place. Network officials had first played the recordings privately for Noriega's chief attorney, Frank Rubino, who confirmed they were authentic.

Rubino quickly obtained a temporary court order to bar further broadcasts to prevent the disclosure of privileged attorney-client information. While such monitoring of prisoners' phone calls is considered standard practice, courts have held that prison authorities have no right to record a prisoner's conversation with his or her attorney. Prison rules require that inmates be informed that their calls may be monitored unless they advise authorities they are calling legal counsel. Noriega contended he was never informed his calls were wiretapped.

In issuing the restraining order, Judge William H. Hoeveler of the U.S.

District Court in Miami asked CNN to let him review the tapes to determine if their contents would jeopardize Noriega's legal defense. The network refused, saying his order amounted to an unconstitutional prior restraint of publication or broadcast in this situation. The next day, November 9, the network broadcasted a portion of a tape containing a conversation in Spanish between Noriega and a translator at his lawyer's office in Miami.

Hoeveler declared CNN officials in contempt of court and asked the FBI to find out who had leaked the tapes to the network. Unidentified investigators soon were quoted as saying Jose Blandon, a former Noriega aide who became a prosecution witness, was a suspect. He denied any wrongdoing. Rubino argued that a violation of client-attorney confidentiality already had occurred and was sufficient to have the case dismissed.

Supreme Court on Prior Restraint

The U.S. Court of Appeals for the Eleventh Circuit, in Atlanta, upheld the judge's restraining order November 9. CNN then took its appeal to the Supreme Court, and a score of news organizations filed friend-of-the-court briefs in support of the network. The Court issued an unsigned order November 18 refusing to lift the ban or call the case for review.

As is customary in such orders, the Supreme Court did not explain its reasoning. However, Justices Thurgood Marshall and Sandra Day O'Connor issued a brief dissenting opinion. They said the restraining order could not be reconciled with past Court decisions declaring prior restraint unconstitutional. Although the Court ruled on a procedural question rather than the merits of the case, several legal scholars expressed belief that the ruling possibly indicated the Supreme Court's thinking about the basic question of prior restraint.

Over the years the Court had upheld prior restraint against the press only occasionally on a temporary basis, as in 1979 when it refused an emergency request to lift a federal judge's order temporarily barring Progressive magazine from publishing an article on how to make a hydrogen bomb. The case became moot before the justices could address it on its merits.

The Noriega case likewise became moot soon after the Supreme Court upheld Judge Hoeveler's order. In compliance, CNN submitted five tapes—including about thirty conversations—to him for review. On November 28 he lifted the ban, saying the recorded material would not harm Noriega's legal defense. CNN declined to broadcast any more of the tapes. Rubino said the only lawyer-client conversation in CNN's possession was the one it had already broadcast November 9. He said, however, that the government may have taped other conversations between Noriega and his law office that CNN never obtained. The attorney vowed to continue with his attempt to have the case dismissed.

Noriega's Courtroom Plea

Noriega made a similar plea at a hearing Judge Hoeveler conducted November 16. It was the general's first public appearance since he surrendered January 3 to U.S. military forces that invaded Panama the previous month and overthrew his government. Without delay, he was flown to a U.S. prison to await trial on charges that resulted from indictment by federal grand juries in Miami and Tampa, Florida, in February 1988.

The indictments named him and sixteen associates, accusing them of extensive federal narcotics violations, including drug smuggling and racketeering. Noriega was charged with participation in a conspiracy to smuggle drugs into the United States and with taking $4.6 million in bribes to arrange the safe movement of U.S.-bound cocaine from Medellin, Colombia. The indictments depicted an intimate business relationship between Noriega and the notorious Medellin drug cartel. (Grand Jury Indictments of General Noriega, Historic Documents of 1988, p. 81; Bush Announces Invasion of Panama, Historic Documents of 1989, p. 701)

Noriega's attorneys long had challenged the right of the United States to put him on trial. The prosecution conceded in court hearings that Noriega was a prisoner of war but argued that nothing in international treaties prevented him from being tried for criminal offenses committed prior to hostilities. The defense further contended that his status as head of Panama's military forces and as the country's "Maximum Leader" equivalent to head of state gave him immunity from prosecution.

At the November 16 hearing, Noriega claimed that he was a political prisoner who had been deprived of the right to a fair trial. "They have taken my money, deprived me of my lawyers, videotaped me in my cell, wiretapped my telephone calls with my lawyers and even given them to the Endara government and the press," he said. He referred to Guillermo Endara, who became president of Panama after the invasion. Endara's government sued Noriega in a U.S. court October 24 on racketeering charges to recover $6.5 billion that it said he had stolen from the nation. In addition, Panama requested that Noriega be returned to his homeland to face a murder charge.

Trial's Delay

The trial, twice postponed, was scheduled to start June 24, 1991. One cause of delay centered on payments for Noriega's attorneys. They argued that he had been deprived of funds to pay for their services and refused to accept the top rate ($75 an hour) set for court-appointed public defenders. The U.S. government froze Noriega's assets, which it estimated at about $20 million and others said amounted to much more. His attorneys asked for the release of some $11 million, which they said the U.S. government had paid Noriega for acting as an informant to U.S. drug agents and the Central Intelligence Agency (CIA) before he fell from Washington's favor during the late 1980s.

The Justice Department refused to provide the court a listing of Noriega's assets and their sources because it might subject U.S. intelligence officials to defense-team questioning. The department sought instead to unfreeze $6 million for his legal fees. But department officials said they were obstructed by foreign banks where the money was held. The banks or their governments would presumably claim the money if it was officially determined that Noriega had acquired it illegally.

> *Following is the Supreme Court's order of November 18, 1990, upholding a federal district court's ban on Cable News Network broadcasts of taped telephone calls that former Panamanian dictator Manuel Antonio Noriega made from an American prison:*

<u>No. 90-767 (A-370)</u>

Cable News Network, Inc., et. al. v. Manuel Antonio Noriega and United States

On petition for writ of certiorari to the United States Court of Appeals for the Eleventh Circuit and on application to stay restraining orders issued by the United States District Court for the Southern District of Florida.

[November 18, 1990]

The application to stay restraining orders of the United States District Court for the Southern District of Florida presented to JUSTICE KENNEDY and by him referred to the Court is denied.

The petition for a writ of certiorari is denied.

JUSTICE MARSHALL, with whom JUSTICE O'CONNOR joins, dissenting.

The issue raised by this petition is whether a trial court may enjoin publication of information alleged to threaten a criminal defendant's right to a fair trial without *any* threshold showing that the information will indeed cause such harm and that suppression is the only means of averting it. The District Court in this case entered an order enjoining petitioner Cable News Network (CNN) from broadcasting taped communications between respondent Manuel Noriega, a defendant in a pending criminal proceeding, and his counsel. The court entered this order without any finding that suppression of the broadcast was necessary to protect Noriega's right to a fair trial, reasoning that no such determination need be made unless and until CNN surrendered the tapes for the court's inspection. The Court of Appeals affirmed this conclusion.

In my view, this case is of extraordinary consequence for freedom of the press. Our precedents make unmistakably clear that " '[a]ny prior restrain[t] of expression comes to this Court bearing a "heavy presumption" against its constitutional validity,' " and that the proponent of this drastic remedy " 'carries a heavy burden of showing justification for [its] imposition.' " *Nebraska Press Assn.* v. *Stuart* (1976), quoting *Organization for a Better Austin* v. *Keefe* (1971); accord, *New York Times Co.* v. *United States* (1971) *(per curiam)*. I do not see how the prior restraint imposed in this case can be reconciled with these teachings. Even more fundamentally, if the lower courts in this case are correct in their remarkable conclusion that publication can be *automatically* restrained pending application of the demanding test established by *Nebraska Press,* then I think it is imperative that we re-examine the premises and operation of *Nebraska Press* itself. I would grant the stay application and the petition for certiorari.

ARMS REDUCTION AND
EUROPEAN COOPERATION TREATIES
November 19 and 21, 1990

President George Bush, Soviet president Mikhail S. Gorbachev, and leaders of the twenty other NATO and Warsaw Pact countries signed a treaty November 19 that would strip much of the nonnuclear weaponry from the European continent and greatly diminish the massive Soviet army that fostered Europe's division and militarization for four decades. Some statesmen and commentators viewed the signing as codifying the end of the Cold War. The pact was also likened to the 1815 Treaty of Vienna, which ushered in a century of peace for most of Europe. The signatory countries also issued a joint declaration that they would "build new partnerships and extend to each other the hand of friendship."

The arms pact was the highlight of an eventful three-day summit meeting in Paris of the Conference on Security and Cooperation in Europe (CSCE), a loose-knit association of thirty-four member nations, including the United States, Canada, and every European state except Albania. The association was touted as the embryo of Europe's new political framework, although the Bush administration remained skeptical about permitting it to expand at the expense of NATO.

Nevertheless, the United States joined with the other CSCE members on November 21 in signing the Charter of Paris for a New Europe, a lengthy agreement proclaiming a new order of peaceful relations. "The era of confrontation and division of Europe has ended," the charter proclaimed. "We declare that henceforth our relations will be founded on respect and cooperation." The charter established a permanent secretariat in Prague, a center in Vienna for conflict prevention, and an office in

Warsaw for monitoring elections. It also called for the creation of a CSCE parliamentary assembly.

Division Amid Euphoria

"The Cold War is over," said President Bush, who previously had refrained from making that statement. "In signing the Charter of Paris we have closed a chapter of history." President Francois Mitterrand of France ended the conference by declaring that all members "share a common vision of the world and a common set of values."

But amid the euphoria there were harbingers of potential disruptions of Europe's new order. At the French government's invitation, foreign ministers of Estonia, Latvia, and Lithuania, Baltic republics seeking their independence from the Soviet Union, went to Paris as unofficial observers. Gorbachev vetoed their participation in the conference. He warned that ethnic unrest and "mindless separatism" could halt progress toward European cooperation. Several Western European governments, facing actual or potential separatist movements, stymied discussion of a Swiss proposal to protect minorities. But Bush insisted that any new international system would have to safeguard minority rights.

CSCE Arises from Helsinki Accords

The CSCE was created in Finland fifteen years earlier by the leaders of thirty-five nations (East Germany, then a separate nation, was the thirty-fifth) who signed what came to be known as the Helsinki Accords. In return for tacit recognition of the European boundaries determined by World War II, the Soviet Union and its Warsaw Pact partners promised greater respect for human rights in their countries.

The document gave hope to dissidents even if the Communist governments sought to evade the Helsinki promises. President Jimmy Carter had made human rights a keystone of his foreign policy, and Ronald Reagan followed that course during the later years of his presidency. Bush continued to pursue it, but the critical factor was Gorbachev's decision in the late 1980s to seek cooperation rather than confrontation with the West. CSCE provided the basic framework and process for bringing about evolutionary political change in Europe. The reduction talks on conventional arms, under way in Vienna since March 1989, were conducted within the CSCE framework.

Arms Treaty Provisions

The arms treaty would require roughly 100,000 of the 250,000 tanks, cannons, and other weapons to be scrapped or removed from the European continent. Most of them would be taken from the Soviet arsenal. Calling it "the farthest-reaching arms agreement in history," Bush said in Paris that the treaty "signals the new world order that is emerging." Ratification by the Senate was expected without difficulty after the 102nd Congress convened in January 1991.

In large measure, the treaty merely ratified an unraveling of Soviet military power. Since 1988 Moscow had retrenched militarily as it faced political convulsions and economic stagnation at home. The contraction was so fast that once-major provisions, such as a limit on troop levels in Europe, were removed from the treaty. Soviet troop strength already had diminished in Eastern Europe as the Soviet Union's former satellite states regained political control.

The arms treaty and separate joint declaration were signed by Belgium, Bulgaria, Britain, Canada, Czechoslovakia, Denmark, France, Germany, Greece, Hungary, Iceland, Italy, Luxembourg, the Netherlands, Norway, Poland, Portugal, Romania, Spain, Turkey, the Soviet Union, and the United States. Signers of the Charter of Paris were, in addition to those countries: Australia, Cyprus, Finland, Ireland, Liechtenstein, Malta, Monaco, San Marino, Sweden, Switzerland, the Vatican, and Yugoslavia.

> *Following are texts of the "Treaty of Conventional Armed Forces in Europe" and the "Joint Declaration of Twenty-Two States," both signed November 19, 1990, and the "Charter of Paris for a New Europe," signed November 21, all at the Paris meeting of the Conference on Security and Cooperation in Europe:*

TREATY ON CONVENTIONAL ARMED FORCES IN EUROPE

Declaration of the States Parties to the Treaty on Conventional Armed Forces in Europe with Respect to Personnel Strength

In connection with the signature of the Treaty on Conventional Armed Forces in Europe of November 19, 1990, and with a view to the follow-on negotiations referred to in Article XVIII of that Treaty, the States Parties to that Treaty declare that, for the period of these negotiations, they will not increase the total peacetime authorized personnel strength of their conventional armed forces pursuant to the Mandate in the area of application.

Declaration of the States Parties to the Treaty on Conventional Armed Forces in Europe with Respect to Land-Based Naval Aircraft

To promote the implementation of the Treaty on Conventional Armed Forces in Europe, the States Parties to the Treaty undertake the following political commitments outside the framework of the Treaty.

1. No one State will have in the area of application of the treaty more

than 400 permanently land-based combat naval aircraft. It is understood that this commitment applies to combat aircraft armed and
equipped to engage surface or air targets and excludes types designed
as maritime patrol aircraft.

2. The aggregate number of such permanently land-based combat naval
   aircraft held by either of the two groups of States defined under the
   terms of the Treaty will not exceed 430.

3. No one State will hold in its naval forces within the area of
   application any permanently land-based attack helicopters.

4. The limitations provided for in this Declaration will apply beginning
   40 months after entry into force of the Treaty on Conventional
   Armed Forces in Europe.

5. This Declaration will become effective as of entry into force of the
   Treaty on Conventional Armed Forces in Europe.

WHITE HOUSE FACT SHEET [ON CFE TREATY]

Today the 22 members of NATO and the Warsaw Pact signed a
landmark agreement limiting conventional armed forces in Europe (CFE).
The CFE treaty will establish parity in major conventional armaments
between East and West in Europe from the Atlantic to the Urals. The
treaty will limit the size of Soviet forces to about one third of the total
armaments permitted to all the countries in Europe. The treaty includes
an unprecedented monitoring regime, including detailed information exchange, on-site inspection, challenge inspection, and monitoring of
destruction.

East-West Limits

The treaty sets equal ceilings from the Atlantic to the Urals on key
armaments essential for conducting surprise attack and initiating large-
scale offensive operations. Neither side may have more than:

20,000 tanks
20,000 artillery pieces
30,000 armored combat vehicles (ACV's)
6,800 combat aircraft
2,000 attack helicopters

To further limit the readiness of armed forces, the treaty sets equal
ceilings on equipment that may be with active units. Other ground
equipment must be in designated permanent storage sites. The limits for
equipment each side may have in active units are:

16,500 tanks
17,000 artillery pieces

27,300 armored combat vehicles (ACV's)

In connection with the CFE treaty, the six members of the Warsaw Pact signed a treaty in Budapest on November 3, 1990, which divides the Warsaw Pact allocation by country. The members of NATO have consulted through NATO mechanisms and have agreed on national entitlements. These national entitlements may be adjusted.

Country Ceilings

The treaty limits the proportion of armaments that can be held by any one country in Europe to about one third of the total for all countries in Europe—the "sufficiency" rule. This provision constrains the size of Soviet forces more than any other in the treaty. These limits are:

13,300 tanks
13,700 artillery pieces
20,000 armored combat vehicles (ACV's)

5,150 combat aircraft
1,500 attack helicopters.

Regional Arrangements

In addition to limits on the number of armaments in each category on each side, the treaty also includes regional limits to prevent destabilizing force concentrations of ground equipment.

Destruction

Equipment reduced to meet the ceilings must be destroyed or, in a limited number of cases, have its military capability destroyed, allowing the chassis to be used for nonmilitary purposes. After the treaty enters into force, there will be a 4-month baseline inspection period. After the 4-month baseline period, 25 percent of the destruction must be complete by the end of 1 year, 60 percent by the end of 2 years, and all destruction required by the treaty must be complete by the end of 3 years. Parties have 5 years to convert limited amounts of equipment.

Large amounts of equipment will be destroyed to meet the obligations of the CFE treaty. The Soviet Union alone will be obliged to destroy thousands of weapons, much more equipment than will be reduced by all the NATO countries combined. NATO will meet its destruction obligations by destroying its oldest equipment. In a process called "cascading," NATO members with newer equipment, including the U.S., have agreed to transfer some of this equipment to allies with older equipment. Cascading will not reduce NATO's destruction obligation. Under the cascading system, no U.S. equipment must be destroyed to meet CFE ceilings. Some 2,000 pieces of U.S. equipment will be transferred to our NATO allies.

Verification

The treaty includes unprecedented provisions for detailed information exchanges, on-site inspections, challenge inspections, and on-site monitoring of destruction. At the initiative of the U.S., NATO has established a system to cooperate in monitoring the treaty. Parties have an unlimited right to monitor the process of destruction.

The CFE treaty is of unlimited duration and will enter into force 10 days after all parties have ratified the agreement.

JOINT DECLARATION OF TWENTY-TWO STATES

The Heads of State or Government of Belgium, Bulgaria, Canada, the Czech and Slovak Federal Republic, Denmark, France, Germany, Greece, Hungary, Iceland, Italy, Luxembourg, the Netherlands, Norway, Poland, Portugal, Romania, Spain, Turkey, the Union of Soviet Socialist Republics, the United Kingdom and the United States of America

- greatly welcoming the historic changes in Europe,
- gratified by the growing implementation throughout Europe of a common commitment to pluralist democracy, the rule of law and human rights, which are essential to the lasting security on the continent,
- affirming the end of the era of division and confrontation which has lasted for more than four decades, the improvement in relations among their countries and the contribution this makes to the security of all,
- confident that the signature of the Treaty on Conventional Armed Forces in Europe represents a major contribution to the common objective of increased security and stability in Europe, and
- convinced that these developments must form part of a continuing process of co-operation in building the structures of a more united continent,

Issue the following Declaration:

1. The signatories solemnly declare that, in the new era of European relations which is beginning, they are no longer adversaries, will build new partnerships and extend to each other the hand of friendship.
2. They recall their obligations under the Charter of the United Nations and reaffirm all of their commitments under the Helsinki Final Act. They stress that all of the ten Helsinki Principles are of primary significance and that, accordingly, they will be equally and unreservedly applied, each of them being interpreted taking into account the others. In that context, they affirm their obligation and commitment to refrain from the threat or use of force against the territorial integrity or the political independence of any State, from seeking to change existing borders by threat or use of force, and from acting in any other manner inconsistent with the principles

and purposes of those documents. None of their weapons will ever be used except in self-defense or otherwise in accordance with the Charter of the United Nations.

3. They recognize that security is indivisible and that the security of each of their countries is inextricably linked to the security of all the States participating in the Conference on Security and Co-operation in Europe.

4. They undertake to maintain only such military capabilities as are necessary to prevent war and to provide for effective defense. They will bear in mind the relationship between military capabilities and doctrines.

5. They reaffirm that every State has the right to be or not to be a party to a treaty of alliance.

6. They note with approval the intensification of political and military contacts among them to promote mutual understanding and confidence. They welcome in this context the positive responses made to recent proposals for new regular diplomatic liaison.

7. They declare their determination to contribute actively to conventional, nuclear and chemical arms control and disarmament agreements which enhance security and stability for all. In particular, they call for the early entry into force of the Treaty on Conventional Armed Forces in Europe and commit themselves to continue the process of strengthening peace in Europe through conventional arms control within the framework of the CSCE. They welcome the prospect of new negotiations between the United States and the Soviet Union on the reduction of their short-range nuclear forces.

8. They welcome the contribution that confidence- and security-building measures have made to lessening tensions and fully support the further development of such measures. They reaffirm the importance of the "Open Skies" initiative and their determination to bring the negotiations to a successful conclusion as soon as possible.

9. They pledge to work together with the other CSCE participating States to strengthen the CSCE process so that it can make an even greater contribution to security and stability in Europe. They recognize in particular the need to enhance political consultations among CSCE participants and to develop other CSCE mechanisms. They are convinced that the Treaty on Conventional Armed Forces in Europe and agreement on a substantial new set of CSBMs, together with new patterns of co-operation in the framework of the CSCE, will lead to increased security and thus to enduring peace and stability in Europe.

10. They believe that the preceding points reflect the deep longing of their peoples for close co-operation and mutual understanding and declare that they will work steadily for the further development of their relations in accordance with the present Declaration as well as

with the principles set forth in the Helsinki Final Act.

The original of this Declaration of which the English, French, German, Italian, Russian and Spanish texts are equally authentic will be transmitted to the Government of France which will retain it in its archives. The Government of France is requested to transmit the text of the Declaration to the Secretary-General of the United Nations, with a view to its circulation to all the members of the United Nations, indicating that it is not eligible for registration under Article 102 of the Charter of the United Nations. Each of the signatory States will receive from the Government of France a true copy of this Declaration.

In witness whereof the undersigned High Representatives have subscribed their signatures below.

CHARTER OF PARIS

A New Era of Democracy, Peace and Unity

We, the Heads of State or Government of the States participating in the Conference on Security and Co-operation in Europe, have assembled in Paris at a time of profound change and historic expectations. The era of confrontation and division of Europe has ended. We declare that henceforth our relations will be founded on respect and co-operation.

Europe is liberating itself from the legacy of the past. The courage of men and women, the strength of will of the peoples and the power of the ideas of the Helsinki Final Act have opened a new era of democracy, peace and unity in Europe.

Ours is a time for fulfilling the hopes and expectations our peoples have cherished for decades: steadfast commitment to democracy based on human rights and fundamental freedoms; prosperity through economic liberty and social justice; and equal security for all our countries.

The Ten Principles of the Final Act will guide us towards this ambitious future, just as they have lighted our way towards better relations for the past fifteen years. Full implementation of all CSCE commitments must form the basis for the initiatives we are now taking to enable our nations to live in accordance with their aspirations.

Human Rights, Democracy and Rule of Law

We undertake to build, consolidate and strengthen democracy as the only system of government of our nations. In this endeavour, we will abide by the following:

Human rights and fundamental freedoms are the birthright of all human beings, are inalienable and are guaranteed by law. Their protection and promotion is the first responsibility of government. Respect for them is an essential safeguard against an over-mighty State. Their observance and full exercise are the foundation of freedom, justice and peace.

Democratic government is based on the will of the people, expressed regularly through free and fair elections. Democracy has as its foundation respect for the human person and the rule of law. Democracy is the best safeguard of freedom of expression, tolerance of all groups of society, and equality of opportunity for each person.

Democracy, with its representative and pluralist character, entails accountability to the electorate, the obligation of public authorities to comply with the law and justice administered impartially. No one will be above the law.

We affirm that, without discrimination, every individual has the right to:

freedom of thought, conscience and religion or belief,
freedom of expression,
freedom of association and peaceful assembly,
freedom of movement;

no one will be:

subject to arbitrary arrest or detention,
subject to torture or other cruel, inhuman or degrading treatment or punishment;

everyone also has the right:

to know and act upon his rights,
to participate in free and fair elections,
to fair and public trial if charged with an offence,
to own property alone or in association and to exercise individual enterprise,
to enjoy his economic, social and cultural rights.

We affirm that the ethnic, cultural, linguistic and religious identity of national minorities will be protected and that persons belonging to national minorities have the right freely to express, preserve and develop that identity without any discrimination and in full equality before the law.

We will ensure that everyone will enjoy recourse to effective remedies, national or international, against any violation of his rights.

Full respect for these precepts is the bedrock on which we will seek to construct the new Europe.

Our States will co-operate and support each other with the aim of making democratic gains irreversible.

Economic Liberty and Responsibility

Economic liberty, social justice and environmental responsibility are indispensable for prosperity.

The free will of the individual, exercised in democracy and protected by the rule of law, forms the necessary basis for successful economic and social development. We will promote economic activity which respects and upholds human dignity.

Freedom and political pluralism are necessary elements in our common objective of developing market economies towards sustainable economic growth, prosperity, social justice, expanding employment and efficient use of economic resources. The success of the transition to market economy by countries making efforts to this effect is important and in the interest of us all. It will enable us to share a higher level of prosperity which is our common objective. We will co-operate to this end.

Preservation of the environment is a shared responsibility of all our nations. While supporting national and regional efforts in this field, we must also look to the pressing need for joint action on a wider scale.

Friendly Relations among Participating States

Now that a new era is dawning in Europe, we are determined to expand and strengthen friendly relations and co-operation among the State of Europe, the United States of America and Canada, and to promote friendship among our peoples.

To uphold and promote democracy, peace and unity in Europe, we solemnly pledge our full commitment to the Ten Principles of the Helsinki Final Act. We affirm the continuing validity of the Ten Principles and our determination to put them into practice. All the Principles apply equally and unreservedly, each of them being interpreted taking into account the others. They form the basis for our relations.

In accordance with our obligations under the Charter of the United Nations and commitments under the Helsinki Final Act, we renew our pledge to refrain from the threat or use of force against the territorial integrity or political independence of any State, or from acting in any other manner inconsistent with the principles or purposes of those documents. We recall that non-compliance with obligations under the Charter of the United Nations constitutes a violation of international law.

We reaffirm our commitment to settle disputes by peaceful means. We decide to develop mechanisms for the prevention and resolution of conflicts among the participating States.

With the ending of the division of Europe, we will strive for a new quality in our security relations while fully respecting each other's freedom of choice in that respect. Security is indivisible and the security of every participating State is inseparably linked to that of all the others. We therefore pledge to co-operate in strengthening confidence and security among us and in promoting arms control and disarmament.

We welcome the Joint Declaration of Twenty-Two States on the improvement of their relations.

Our relations will rest on our common adherence to democratic values and to human rights and fundamental freedoms. We are convinced that in order to strengthen peace and security among our States, the advancement of democracy, and respect for and effective exercise of human rights, are indispensable. We reaffirm the equal rights of peoples and their right to self-determination in conformity with the Charter of the United Nations and with the relevant norms of international law, including those relating to territorial integrity of States.

We are determined to enhance political consultation and to widen co-operation to solve economic, social, environmental, cultural and humanitarian problems. This common resolve and our growing interdependence will help to overcome the mistrust of decades, to increase stability and to build a united Europe.

We want Europe to be a source of peace, open to dialogue and to co-operation with other countries, welcoming exchanges and involved in the search for common responses to the challenges of the future.

Security

Friendly relations among us will benefit from the consolidation of democracy and improved security.

We welcome the signature of the treaty on Conventional Armed Forces in Europe by twenty-two participating States, which will lead to lower levels of armed forces. We endorse the adoption of a substantial new set of Confidence- and Security-building Measures which will lead to increased transparency and confidence among all participating States. These are important steps towards enhanced stability and security in Europe.

The unprecedented reduction in armed forces resulting from the Treaty on Conventional Armed Forces in Europe, together with new approaches to security and cooperation within the CSCE process, will lead to a new perception of security in Europe and a new dimension in our relations. In this context we fully recognize the freedom of States to choose their own security arrangements.

Unity

Europe whole and free is calling for a new beginning. We invite our peoples to join in this great endeavour.

We note with great satisfaction the Treaty on the Final Settlement with respect to Germany signed in Moscow on 12 September 1990 and sincerely welcome the fact that the German people have united to become one State in accordance with the principles of the Final Act of the Conference on Security and Co-operation in Europe and in full accord with their neighbours. The establishment of the national unity of Germany is an important contribution to a just and lasting order of peace for a united, democratic Europe aware of its responsibility for stability, peace and co-operation.

The participation of both North American and European States is a fundamental characteristic of the CSCE: it underlies its past achievements and is essential to the future of the CSCE process. An abiding adherence to shared values and our common heritage are the ties which bind us together. With all the rich diversity of our nations, we are united in our commitment to expand our co-operation in all fields. The challenges confronting us can only be met by common action, co-operation and solidarity.

The CSCE and the World

The destiny of our nations is linked to that of all other nations. We support fully the United Nations and the enhancement of its role in promoting international peace, security and justice. We reaffirm our commitment to the principles and purposes of the United Nations as enshrined in the Charter and condemn all violations of these principles. We recognize with satisfaction the growing role of the United Nations in world affairs and its increasing effectiveness, fostered by the improvement in relations among our States.

Aware of the dire needs of a great part of the world, we commit ourselves to solidarity with all other countries. Therefore, we issue a call from Paris today to all the nations of the world. We stand ready to join with any and all States in common efforts to protect and advance the community of fundamental human values.

Guidelines for the Future

Proceeding from our firm commitment to the full implementation of all CSCE principles and provisions, we now resolve to give a new impetus to a balanced and comprehensive development of our co-operation in order to address the needs and aspirations of our peoples.

Human Dimension

We declare our respect for human rights and fundamental freedoms to be irrevocable. We will fully implement and build upon the provisions relating to the human dimension of the CSCE.

Proceeding from the Document of the Copenhagen Meeting of the Conference on the Human Dimension, we will co-operate to strengthen democratic institutions and to promote the application of the rule of law. To that end, we decide to convene a seminar of experts in Oslo from 4 to 15 November 1991.

Determined to foster the rich contribution of national minorities to the life of our societies, we undertake further to improve their situation. We reaffirm our deep conviction that friendly relations among our peoples, as well as peace, justice, stability and democracy, require that the ethnic, cultural, linguistic and religious identity of national minorities be protected and conditions for the promotion of that identity be created. We declare that questions related to national minorities can only be satisfactorily resolved in a democratic political framework. We further acknowledge that the rights of persons belonging to national minorities must be fully respected as part of universal human rights. Being aware of the urgent need for increased co-operation on, as well as better protection of, national minorities, we decide to convene a meeting of experts on national minorities to be held in Geneva from 1 to 19 July 1991.

We express our determination to combat all forms of racial and ethnic hatred, antisemitism, xenophobia and discrimination against anyone as well as persecution on religious and ideological grounds.

In accordance with our CSCE commitments, we stress that free movement and contacts among our citizens as well as the free flow of information and ideas are crucial for the maintenance and development of free societies and flourishing cultures. We welcome increased tourism and visits among our countries.

The human dimension mechanism has proved its usefulness, and we are consequently determined to expand it to include new procedures involving, *inter alia,* the services of experts or a roster of eminent persons experienced in human rights issues which could be raised under the mechanism. We shall provide, in the context of the mechanism, for individuals to be involved in the protection of their rights. Therefore, we undertake to develop further our commitments in this respect, in particular at the Moscow Meeting of the Conference on the Human Dimension, without prejudice to obligations under existing international instruments to which our States may be parties.

We recognize the important contribution of the Council of Europe to the promotion of human rights and the principles of democracy and the rule of law as well as to the development of cultural co-operation. We welcome moves by several participating States to join the Council of Europe and adhere to its European Convention on Human Rights. We welcome as well the readiness of the Council of Europe to make its experience available to the CSCE.

Security

The changing political and military environment in Europe opens new possibilities for common efforts in the field of military security. We will build on the important achievements attained in the Treaty on Conventional Armed Forces in Europe and in the Negotiations on Confidence- and Security-building Measures. We undertake to continue the CSBM negotiations under the same mandate, and to seek to conclude them no later than the Follow-up Meeting of the CSCE to be held in Helsinki in 1992. We also welcome the decision of the participating States concerned to continue the CFE negotiation under the same mandate and to seek to conclude it no later than the Helsinki Follow-up Meeting. Following a period for national preparations, we look forward to a more structured co-operation among all participating States on security matters, and to discussions and consultations among the thirty-four participating States aimed at establishing by 1992, from the conclusion of the Helsinki Follow-up Meeting, new negotiations on disarmament and confidence and security building open to all participating States.

We call for the earliest possible conclusion of the Convention on an effectively verifiable, global and comprehensive ban on chemical weapons, and we intend to be original signatories to it.

We reaffirm the importance of the Open Skies initiative and call for the successful conclusion of the negotiations as soon as possible.

Although the threat of conflict in Europe has diminished, other dangers threaten the stability of our societies. We are determined to co-operate in defending democratic institutions against activities which violate the independence, sovereign equality or territorial integrity of the participating States. These include illegal activities involving outside pressure, coercion and subversion.

We unreservedly condemn, as criminal, all acts, methods and practices of terrorism and express our determination to work for its eradication both bilaterally and through multilateral co-operation. We will also join together in combating illicit trafficking in drugs.

Being aware that an essential complement to the duty of States to refrain from the threat or use of force is the peaceful settlement of disputes both being essential factors for the maintenance and consolidation of international peace and security, we will not only seek effective ways of preventing, through political means, conflicts which may yet emerge, but also define, in conformity with international law, appropriate mechanisms for the peaceful resolution of any disputes which may arise. Accordingly, we undertake to seek new forms of co-operation in this area, in particular a range of methods for the peaceful settlement of disputes, including mandatory, third-party involvement. We stress that full use should be made in this context of the opportunity of the Meeting on the peaceful settlement of disputes which will be convened in Valletta at the beginning of 1991. The Council of Ministers for Foreign Affairs will take into account the Report of the Valletta Meeting.

Economic Co-operation

We stress that economic co-operation based on market economy constitutes an essential element of our relations and will be instrumental in the construction of a prosperous and united Europe. Democratic institutions and economic liberty foster economic and social progress, as recognized in the Document of the Bonn Conference on Economic Co-operation, the results of which we strongly support.

We underline that co-operation in the economic field, science and technology is now an important pillar of the CSCE. The participating States should periodically review progress and give new impulses in these fields.

We are convinced that our overall economic co-operation should be expanded, free enterprise encouraged and trade increased and diversified according to GATT rules. We will promote social justice and progress and further the welfare of our peoples. We recognize in this context the importance of effective policies to address the problem of unemployment.

We reaffirm the need to continue to support democratic countries in transition towards the establishment of market economy and the creation of the basis for self-sustained economic and social growth, as already undertaken by the Group of twenty-four countries. We further underline the necessity of their increased integration, involving the acceptance of disciplines as well as benefits, into the international economic and financial system.

We consider that increased emphasis on economic co-operation within the CSCE process should take into account the interests of developing participating States.

We recall the link between respect for and promotion of human rights and fundamental freedoms and scientific progress. Co-operation in the field of science and technology will play an essential role in economic and social development. Therefore, it must evolve towards a greater sharing of appropriate scientific and technological information and knowledge with a view to overcoming the technological gap which exists among the participating States. We further encourage the participating States to work together in order to develop human potential and the spirit of free enterprise.

We are determined to give the necessary impetus to co-operation among our States in the fields of energy, transport and tourism for economic and social development. We welcome, in particular, practical steps to create optimal conditions for the economic and rational development of energy resources, with due regard for environmental considerations.

We recognize the important role of the European Community in the political and economic development of Europe. International economic organizations such as the United Nations Economic Commission for Europe (ECE), the Bretton Woods institutions, the Organisation for Economic Co-operation and Development (OECD), the European Free Trade Association (EFTA) and the International Chamber of Commerce (ICC) also have a significant task in promoting economic co-operation, which will be further enhanced by the establishment of the European Bank for Reconstruction and Development (EBRD). In order to pursue our objectives, we stress the necessity for effective co-ordination of the activities of these organizations and emphasize the need to find methods for all our States to take part in these activities.

Environment

We recognize the urgent need to tackle the problems of the environment and the importance of individual and co-operative efforts in this area. We pledge to intensify our endeavours to protect and improve our environment in order to restore and maintain a sound ecological balance in air, water and soil. Therefore, we are determined to make full use of the CSCE as a framework for the formulation of common environmental commitments and objectives, and thus to pursue the work reflected in the Report of the Sofia Meeting on the Protection of the Environment.

We emphasize the significant role of a well-informed society in enabling the public and individuals to take initiatives to improve the environment.

To this end, we commit ourselves to promoting public awareness and education on the environment as well as the public reporting of the environmental impact of policies, projects and programmes.

We attach priority to the introduction of clean and low-waste technology, being aware of the need to support countries which do not yet have their own means for appropriate measures.

We underline that environmental policies should be supported by appropriate legislative measures and administrative structures to ensure their effective implementation.

We stress the need for new measures providing for the systematic evaluation of compliance with the existing commitments and moreover, for the development of more ambitious commitments with regard to notification and exchange of information about the state of the environment and potential environmental hazards. We also welcome the creation of the European Environment Agency (EEA).

We welcome the operational activities, problem-oriented studies and policy reviews in various existing international organizations engaged in the protection of the environment, such as the United Nations Environment Programme (UNEP), the United Nations Economic Commission for Europe (ECE) and the Organisation for Economic Co-operation and Development (OECD). We emphasize the need for strengthening their co-operation and for their efficient co-ordination.

Culture

We recognize the essential contribution of our common European culture and our shared values in overcoming the division of the continent. Therefore, we underline our attachment to creative freedom and to the protection and promotion of our cultural and spiritual heritage, in all its richness and diversity.

In views of the recent changes in Europe, we stress the increased importance of the Cracow Symposium and we look forward to its consideration of guidelines for intensified co-operation in the field of culture. We invite the Council of Europe to contribute to this Symposium.

In order to promote greater familiarity amongst our peoples, we favour the establishment of cultural centres in cities of other participating States as well as increased co-operation in the audio-visual field and wider exchange in music, theatre, literature and the arts.

We resolve to make special efforts in our national policies to promote better understanding, in particular among young people, through cultural exchanges, co-operation in all fields of education and, more specifically, through teaching and training in the languages of other participating States. We intend to consider first results of this action at the Helsinki Follow-up Meeting in 1992.

Migrant Workers

We recognize that the issues of migrant workers and their families legally residing in host countries have economic, cultural and social aspects as well as their human dimension. We reaffirm that the protection and promotion of their rights, as well as the implementation of relevant international obligations, is our common concern.

Mediterranean

We consider that the fundamental political changes that have occurred in Europe have a positive relevance to the Mediterranean region. Thus, we will continue efforts to strengthen security and co-operation in the Mediterranean as an important factor for stability in Europe. We welcome the Report of the Palma de Mallorca Meeting on the Mediterranean, the results of which we all support.

We are concerned with the continuing tensions in the region, and renew our determination to intensify efforts towards finding just, viable and lasting solutions, through peaceful means, to outstanding crucial problems, based on respect for the principles of the Final Act.

We wish to promote favourable conditions for a harmonious development and diversification of relations with the non-participating Mediterranean States. Enhanced co-operation with these States will be pursued with the aim of promoting economic and social development and thereby enhancing stability in the region. To this end, we will strive together with these countries towards a substantial narrowing of the prosperity gap between Europe and its Mediterranean neighbours.

Non-governmental Organizations

We recall the major role that non-governmental organizations, religious and other groups and individuals have played in the achievement of the objectives of the CSCE and will further facilitate their activities for the implementation of the CSCE commitments by the participating States. These organizations, groups and individuals must be involved in an appropriate way in the activities and new structures of the CSCE in order to fulfill their important tasks.

New Structures and Institutions of the CSCE Process

Our common efforts to consolidate respect for human rights, democracy and the rule of law, to strengthen peace and to promote unity in Europe require a new quality of political dialogue and co-operation and thus development of the structures of the CSCE.

The intensification of our consultations at all levels is of prime importance in shaping our future relations. To this end, we decide on the following:

> We, the Heads of State or Government, shall meet next time in Helsinki on the occasion of the CSCE Follow-up Meeting 1992. Thereafter, we will meet on the occasion of subsequent follow-up meetings.
>
> Our Ministers for Foreign Affairs will meet, as a Council, regularly and at least once a year. These meetings will provide the central forum for

political consultations within the CSCE process. The Council will consider issues relevant to the Conference on Security and Co-operation in Europe and take appropriate decisions.

The first meeting of the Council will take place in Berlin.

A Committee of Senior Officials will prepare the meetings of the Council and carry out its decisions. The Committee will review current issues and may take appropriate decisions, including in the form of recommendations to the Council.

Additional meetings of the representatives of the participating States may be agreed upon to discuss questions of urgent concern.

The Council will examine the development of provisions for convening meetings of the Committee of Senior Officials in emergency situations.

Meetings of other Ministers may also be agreed by the participating States.

In order to provide administrative support for these consultations we establish a Secretariat in Prague.

Follow-up meetings of the participating States will be held, as a rule, every two years to allow the participating States to take stock of developments, review the implementation of their commitments and consider further steps in the CSCE process.

We decide to create a Conflict Prevention Centre in Vienna to assist the Council in reducing the risk of conflict.

We decide to establish an Office for Free Elections in Warsaw to facilitate contacts and the exchange of information on elections within participating States.

Recognizing the important role parliamentarians can play in the CSCE process, we call for greater parliamentary involvement in the CSCE, in particular through the creation of a CSCE parliamentary assembly, involving members of parliaments from all participating States. To this end, we urge that contacts be pursued at the parliamentary level to discuss the field of activities, working methods and rules of procedure of such a CSCE parliamentary structure, drawing on existing experience and work already undertaken in this field.

We ask our Ministers for Foreign Affairs to review this matter on the occasion of their first meeting as a Council.

Procedural and organizational modalities relating to certain provisions contained in the Charter of Paris for a New Europe are set out in the Supplementary Document which is adopted together with the Charter of Paris.

We entrust to the Council the further steps which may be required to ensure the implementation of decisions contained in the present document, as well as in the Supplementary Document, and to consider further efforts for the strengthening of security and co-operation in Europe. The Council may adopt any amendment to the supplementary document which it may deem appropriate.

The original of the Charter of Paris for a New Europe, drawn up in

English, French, German, Italian, Russian and Spanish, will be transmitted to the Government of the French Republic, which will retain it in its archives. Each of the participating States will receive from the Government of the French Republic a true copy of the Charter of Paris.

The text of the Charter of Paris will be published in each participating State, which will disseminate it and make it known as widely as possible.

The Government of the French Republic is requested to transmit to the Secretary-General of the United Nations the text of the Charter of Paris for a New Europe which is not eligible for registration under Article 102 of the Charter of the United Nations, with a view to its circulation to all the members of the Organization as an official document of the United Nations.

The Government of the French Republic is also requested to transmit the text of the Charter of Paris to all the other international organizations mentioned in the text.

Wherefore, we, the undersigned High Representatives of the participating States, mindful of the high political significance we attach to the results of the Summit meeting, and declaring our determination to act in accordance with the provisions we have adopted, have subscribed our signatures below.

RESIGNATION OF
PRIME MINISTER THATCHER
November 22, 1990

After ten and a half years as Britain's prime minister, Margaret Thatcher bowed to pressure within her Conservative party and declared November 22 she would resign. She did so six days later, after the party named John Major to replace her as its leader, thus conferring on him the prime ministership. Thatcher had held the office since May 4, 1979, for the longest continuous tenure in this century.

Thatcher, at age sixty-five, appeared as combative as ever. But her popularity suffered with wage-earners from her introduction of a much-reviled tax on municipal services and with business for her resistance to Britain's involvement in a European union. Some political commentators suggested that the public had simply grown weary of Thatcherism.

The word "Thatcherism" embraced a political agenda that emphasized self-reliance and disdain for government assistance. Its key features were the promotion of capitalism, removal of state controls on industry, and a reduction of elaborate social welfare programs. Thatcher's efforts in Britain were only partly successful. She denationalized much of Britain's industry but failed to make it more productive. She trimmed but did not dismantle the welfare system. National prosperity seemed as elusive when she left office as when she entered it. Unemployment remained high, and in 1990 inflation ran at about 10 percent—double the European average.

The prime minister's plain speech and straightforward style won her grudging support among voters who opposed her policies. She soon earned the nickname "Iron Lady" and became a national hero in 1982 when she sent an armed force to recapture the Falkland Islands, which

Argentina had claimed and seized. Politically, Thatcher heaped scorn on her foes—in her own party and the Labor opposition. She invariably spoke with great certainty, leaving little room for argument, doubt, or reconsideration. To a complaining electorate, she was wont to say, "I never promised you a rose garden."

Party Revolt

Thatcher showed a remarkable ability for political survival during those often-contentious years. No other prime minister had led a British party to victory three consecutive times, as she had with the Conservatives in 1979, 1982, and 1987. Ultimately it was a Conservative leadership revolt that unseated her. Seizing on a widely held belief that Thatcher had overstayed her welcome with the electorate, the Conservatives openly challenged her as party leader in mid-November for the first time in fifteen years. She had won that leadership post by defeating former prime minister Edward Heath in a contest February 11, 1975.

Michael Heseltine, who had resigned as defense minister in 1986 in disagreement with Thatcher, directed the challenge. Heseltine drew strong assistance in the final days of the dump-Thatcher campaign from Sir Geoffrey Howe, whom Thatcher had removed as foreign minister in July 1989 after a disagreement over monetary strategy. She gave him the largely honorary post of deputy prime minister, from which he resigned November 1, 1990, in reaction to her resistance to a European monetary and political union. Four days earlier, Chancellor of the Exchequer Nigel Lawson also had resigned for similar reasons.

In the House of Commons November 13, Howe bitterly accused the prime minister of jeopardizing British interests in Europe and dividing the government. The next day Heseltine presented himself as a candidate in opposition to her reelection to the Conservative leadership post. In the initial balloting by Conservative members in the House of Commons on November 20, she outpolled him but not with enough margin to prevent a second round of voting later. Thatcher vowed to continue with the race, but, according to press reports, a group of advisers persuaded her that she was losing support and should resign.

Resignation and Election

A government announcement was released in London at 9:34 a.m., November 22, saying: "The Prime Minister ... has informed the Queen that she does not intend to contest the second ballot of the election for leadership of the Conservative Party and intends to resign as Prime Minister as soon as a new leader of the Conservative Party has been elected." Thatcher appended a personal statement saying: "I have concluded that the unity of the party and the prospect of victory in a general election would be better served if I stood down to enable Cabinet colleagues to enter the ballot."

When the Conservative members of the House of Commons voted again

November 27, the leadership race had expanded to three candidates: Heseltine, Major, and Foreign Secretary Douglas Hurd. Major, a Thatcher loyalist whom she had groomed as a successor, won 185 votes to Heseltine's 131, and Hurd's 56. The following morning, Thatcher submitted her resignation to Queen Elizabeth II, who asked Major to form a new government.

Major's Background

Major, at age forty-seven, became the youngest British prime minister in this century. Like Thatcher, eighteen years his senior, he came from a lower middle class background. But his background drew even a sharper contrast than hers to the British establishment of wealth and privilege.

Major grew up in a poor London district and left school at age sixteen. He worked at various jobs and spent a year on welfare before finding employment with a commercial bank. He moved up swiftly in his banking career and involved himself in local Conservative party politics, winning a seat in Parliament in 1979.

Major's rise in politics was as swift as it was in banking. According to British political lore, Thatcher began grooming him as a successor in the mid-1980s, moving him steadily upward through key government posts—from a junior minister in Social Security, to chief Treasury secretary, to foreign secretary, and—last—to chancellor of the exchequer, where he presided over monetary policies.

Quest for Party Unity

"Our job now I think is quite clear," Major said upon assuming the party leadership position. "We're going to unite ... and win the next general election." As a step toward restoring party unity, he retained Hurd as foreign secretary and brought Heseltine into the cabinet. The Conservative majority in Commons rejected an attempt by Labor leader Neil Kinnock to call a general election immediately. By law, the election must be held by mid-year 1992.

Only hours after Thatcher announced she was resigning, she went before Commons for a last Question Time, a practice of Parliament that requires the prime minister to appear periodically to answer questions. There she heard praise from several members, Labour and Conservative, but also the accusation from Labour member Greville Janner that "she has left the place in such a shambles."

> *Following are excerpts from Prime Minister Margaret Thatcher's final Question Time in the House of Commons, November 22, 1990, hours after she had announced her resignation:*

PRIME MINISTER MARGARET THATCHER
BEFORE THE BRITISH HOUSE OF COMMONS

PRIME MINISTER THATCHER: Mr. Speaker, this morning I chaired a meeting of the cabinet. A quarter to one, I had an audience with Her Majesty the Queen. Later this afternoon, I shall lead for the government against the motion put down in the name of the leader of the opposition [to require an immediate general election].

SPEAKER [BERNARD WEATHERILL]: Tony Marlow.

MARLOW: Would my right honorable friend—would my right honorable friend, excepting those of us on this side who share her objectives, whatever our roles may have been in recent weeks, but this is a day—this is a time of sadness and happiness. Sadness—sadness—sadness for her—sadness for her from the great well of affection that exists throughout the House. Happiness in celebration of what has been, is and will remain the greatest peacetime political reign of this century, and a day of dedication to sustain and build on the massive achievements of Prime Minister Margaret Thatcher.

THATCHER: Mr. Speaker, may I thank my honorable friend. The same person in a slightly different capacity will be available to serve Britain in whatsoever way it happens.

SPEAKER: Mr. Neil Kinnock [Labour Party opposition leader].

KINNOCK: Mr. Speaker, may I pay tribute to the Prime Minister and to her decision this morning. She showed by that that she amounts to more than those who have turned upon her in recent days. Mr. Speaker, the right honorable lady, I know, considers the principle of choice to be extremely important and that is rightly so. Does she agree with me that the people of Britain should now be given the power of choice in a general election?

THATCHER: Mr. Speaker, may I thank the right honorable gentleman for his earlier comments. In reply to his later question, the answer is no. No more than we had an election when Mr. [Harold] Wilson changed to Mr. [James] Callaghan.

SPEAKER: Mr. [Winston] Churchill.

CHURCHILL: Is my right honorable friend aware that she deserves the gratitude of the entire nation for her—for her part in bringing to an end the Soviet's part in the arms race and burying once and for all the Cold War between the superpowers. It is in that capacity that she will be remembered as the greatest peacetime prime minister this country has ever had.

THATCHER: I'm grateful to my honorable friend for his staunchness in defense and for his remarks. It was a great privilege to attend the CSCE [Conference on Security and Cooperation in Europe] conference in Paris and to sign some of the disarmament agreements and for the new CSCE, which merely ushers in a new order in Europe, and I hope, a very successful peaceful one.

SPEAKER: Mr. [Joe] Ashtown.

ASHTOWN: Mr. Speaker, may I say to the Prime Minister that many of us recognize that she had to take a very tough decision this morning and we believe she took the right decision and took it with great dignity.

May I also say to her that however wide our political divisions, and they are, of course, very wide, no one can doubt the special style she's brought to that dispatch box, nor her courage, conviction, and determination which she has brought to her premiership.

Mr. Speaker, perhaps I might ask her to use this opportunity to offer to the House any advice she might have for her successor.

THATCHER: Mr. Speaker, I thank—apart from the last bit, may I thank the right honorable gentleman for his kindness. May I remind the House that I expect to be here on Tuesday afternoon, and possibly even on Thursday afternoon—laughter—so I hope the House will be as kind then as it is today. [Laughter]

SPEAKER: Mr. Greville Janner.

JANNER: Mr. Speaker, may I be permitted to thank the Prime Minister for many personal kindnesses which she has given over many years to back benches on both sides of the House? May I at the same time say how deeply concerned my constituents are that she has left the place in such a shambles? Is she aware that they are desperately worried about poll tax, about the deepening recession, about the health problems, and they are worried about the educational system and about the whole poor shambles. Will the Prime Minister indicate who she thinks should take a share in the blame for what is, after all, a conservative mess?

THATCHER: Well, the honorable gentlemen always was quite a good advocate. He could speak to any brief and I don't believe he believed a word of that. [Laughter]

SPEAKER: Sir John Stokes.

STOKES: Does my right honorable friend not agree that the age of chivalry is gone and has been succeeded by those economists with calculators? Does she further not look back with pride and satisfaction at all those years when she was leader of this country and a world statesman?

THATCHER: I think, Mr. Speaker, the age of chivalry will not have gone so long as my honorable friend is a member of this house. And yes, in response to his question, I do look back with some pride and some satisfaction of our achievements for our country over the last 11-1/2 years. . . .

MR. AITKEN: Has my right honorable friend considered that the voice of a great former prime minister could be extremely influential on great issues of state such as our future role in Europe? Will she assure her many friends in the House and the country that she will continue to champion— that she will— [Laughter]

THATCHER: Order! [Laughter]. Order! [Laughter]. Mr. Aitken.

AITKEN: My question, Mr. Speaker, was directed to a great former prime minister. Will she assure her many friends in the House and the country that she will continue to champion the causes for which she has fought so valiantly?

THATCHER: Mr. Speaker, what my honorable friend says had, in fact, secretly occurred to me, that one's voice might be listened to after. I believe we now have a policy for the future of Europe, behind which we can all unite. And I believe that many people in other countries in Europe, believe in a Europe of nation-states and in cooperation between those nations. . . .

HUBBLE TELESCOPE FLAWS, NASA'S FUTURE DIRECTION

November 27 and December 10, 1990

Separate studies issued within two weeks of each other centered on the troubled National Aeronautics and Space Administration (NASA). The first, released November 27, inquired into the spectacular failure of the $1.5 billion Hubble Space Telescope, the largest and most complex scientific instrument ever put into orbit. The second was a report on December 10 by a twelve-member panel of scientists, corporate executives, and former NASA officials. In recommending significant changes in NASA's direction, they said, among other things, that it should redesign and simplify the planned space station and rely less on a manned space shuttle.

The inability of the Hubble Space Telescope to focus properly was NASA's most prominent failure since the shuttle Challenger *exploded after liftoff in January 1986 and plunged into the Atlantic, killing all seven persons aboard, before a global television audience. NASA's review of the telescope project depicted costly design changes and delays caused by frequent clashes between the Marshall Space Flight Center in Huntsville, Alabama, and the Goddard Space Flight Center in Greenbelt, Maryland. Ultimately, inadequate testing prevented the agency and a key contractor from detecting the telescope's disabling flaw.*

The telescope, within a cylindrical spacecraft forty-three feet long and weighing more than twelve tons, was released from the space shuttle Discovery *high above the Earth on April 24. After vain attempts by ground-control operators to obtain clear images of the heavens from the telescope, NASA announced June 27 that one of the mirrors was flawed.*

Light from distant objects strikes a primary mirror, then bounces to a

753

secondary mirror, and funnels through a hole to recording instruments. The light is thus concentrated to sharpen the image. The mirrors must be polished to a precise smoothness so that the light is reflected at exactly the proper angles without distortion. The Hubble mirrors were tested separately but not together, and the flaw was not detected until too late.

"It's a tragedy; it's incredibly disappointing," said Sidney C. Wolff, director of the National Optical Astronomy Observatories in Tucson, Arizona. Other astronomers also expressed dismay that their high expectations for seeing the universe from above the Earth's distorting atmosphere had been shattered.

Investigators concluded that both NASA and its main contractor, the Perkin-Elmer Corporation in Danbury, Connecticut (now Hughes Danbury Optical Systems), failed to monitor in any detail the manufacture of the mirrors. They traced the error to the improper positioning of a simple measuring rod. It gave incorrect readings during optical testing.

"Why was the problem not detected?" asked Lew Allen, Pasadena, California, who headed a six-member board of investigation. "The answer to that question is not a particularly happy one," he said in announcing the board's findings. The company's technicians had never before made such a large mirror, yet it denied access to outside experts and overseers, the report said. Even NASA's single quality-control officer at the contractor's facility was not allowed to witness key tests. Moreover, the report added, Perkin-Elmer's leading optical expert was never told about the tests that revealed the flaws. "There were at least three cases where there was clear evidence that a problem existed," Allen said. "And they were dismissed."

The board did not attempt to assess blame for the flaw other than determine how it occurred. NASA officials said that to correct the telescope's focus would require a space shuttle flight, and it would be unlikely to occur before 1993.

Redirecting NASA's Goals

A collection of problems beset the U.S. space program in 1990. The fleet of space shuttles was grounded for months by fuel leaks, and a proposed $20 billion space station was plagued by design problems. In the summer, the National Space Council, headed by Vice President Dan Quayle, designated an Advisory Committee on the Future of the U.S. Space Program and asked it to recommend what changes should occur in the space programs. Norman R. Augustine, chairman of the Martin Marietta Corporation, headed the committee.

In its report, the panel recommended that the agency shift its emphasis from manned space shuttles to unmanned spacecraft. It said NASA should give scientific research priority over "space stations, aerospace planes, manned missions to the planets and many other major pursuits which often receive greater visibility." In particular, the panel recommended a two-pronged approach for science activities: (1) studying the Earth's environment from space with satellites and probes in a

"Mission to Planet Earth," and (2) using manned and unmanned missions to explore space in a "Mission from Planet Earth."

In a news briefing after releasing the report, Augustine said it was statistically probable that the United States would lose another shuttle before the decade was over. An alternative launcher would prevent such an accident from grounding the space program for years, as happened after the Challenger disaster in 1986. The advisory committee said construction of space shuttles should end with the one that was under construction.

Criticism of NASA was "deserved and occasionally even self-inflicted," the report said. It added that the agency was trying to do too many things on a limited budget. However, the panel opposed a total revamping of the nation's space operations. "NASA, and only NASA, realistically possesses the essential critical mass of knowledge and expertise upon which the nation's civil space program can be sustained. . . ."

Generally Favorable Reaction

The committee's recommendations were endorsed by Quayle and NASA Administrator Richard Truly. "[T]his report clearly points out the need for fundamental changes in our civil space program," Quayle said. "We will make changes." The vice president called on the committee to meet again in June 1991 to assess progress on the implementation of its recommendations. "NASA and I intend to take each of these recommendations seriously," Truly said.

"Clearly times have changed," said Augustine. "The heavy driver for the space program used to be competition with the Soviets. Today, there is not that clear competition, but the fundamental values of exploration that drive us . . . are less tangible but no less important."

Scientists generally seemed pleased with the recommendations for increased emphasis on scientific exploration. "This could be the dawn of a second golden age," predicted Bruce C. Murray of the California Institute of Technology. "This is a realistic set of recommendations rather than a pie-in-the-sky wish list," commented John E. Pike, a space policy analyst for the Federation of American Scientists.

> Following is the "Executive Summary" of "The Hubble Telescope Optical System Failure Report," issued November 27, 1990, by the NASA board of investigation, and excerpts from the "Summary and Principal Recommendations of the Advisory Committee on the Future of the U.S. Space Program," released December 10:

HUBBLE TELESCOPE

The Hubble Space Telescope (HST) was launched aboard the Space Shuttle Discovery on April 24, 1990. During checkout on orbit, it was discovered that the telescope could not be properly focused because of a flaw in the optics. The HST Project Manager announced this failure on June 21, 1990. Both of the high-resolution imaging cameras (The Wide Field/Planetary Camera and the Faint Object Camera) showed the same characteristic distortion, called spherical aberration, that must have originated in the primary mirror, the secondary mirror, or both.

The National Aeronautics and Space Administration (NASA) Associate Administrator for the Office of Space Science and Applications then formed the Hubble Space Telescope Optical Systems Board of Investigation on July 2, 1990, to determine the cause of the flaw in the telescope, how it occurred, and why it was not detected before launch. The Board conducted its investigation to include interviews with personnel involved in the fabrication and test of the telescope, review of documentation, and analysis and test of the equipment used in the fabrication of the telescope's mirrors. The information in this report is based exclusively on the analyses and tests requested by the Board, the testimony given to the Board, and the documentation found during this investigation.

Continued analysis of images transmitted from the telescope indicated that most, if not all, of the problem lies in the primary mirror. The Board's investigation of the manufacture of the mirror proved that the mirror was made in the wrong shape, being too much flattened away from the mirror's center.... The error is ten times larger than the specified tolerance.

The primary mirror is a disc of glass 2.4 m[eters] in diameter, whose polished front surface is coated with a very thin layer of aluminum. When glass is polished, small amounts of material are worn away, so by selectively polishing different parts of a mirror, the shape is altered. During the manufacture of all telescope mirrors there are many repetitive cycles in which the surface is tested by reflecting light from it; the surface is then selectively polished to correct any errors in its shape. The error in the HST's mirror occurred because the optical test used in this process was not set up correctly; thus the surface was polished into the wrong shape.

The primary mirror was manufactured by the Perkin-Elmer Corporation, now Hughes Danbury Optical Systems, Inc., which was the contractor for the Optical Telescope Assembly. The critical optics used as a template in shaping the mirror, and reflective null corrector (RNC), consisted of two small mirrors and a lens. The RNC was designed and built by the Perkin-Elmer Corporation for the HST Project. This unit had been preserved by the manufacturer exactly as it was during the manufacture of the mirror. When the Board measured the RNC, the lens was incorrectly spaced from the mirrors. Calculations of the effect of such displacement on the primary mirror show that the measured amount, 1.3 mm, accounts in detail for the amount and character of the observed image blurring.

No verification of the reflective null corrector's dimensions was carried out by Perkin-Elmer after the original assembly. There were, however, clear indications of the problem from auxiliary optical tests made at the time, the results of which have been studied by the Board. A special optical unit called an inverse null corrector, designed to mimic the reflection from a perfect primary mirror, was built and used to align the apparatus; when so used, it clearly showed the error in the reflective null corrector. A second null corrector, made only with lenses, was used to measure the vertex radius of the finished primary mirror. It, too, clearly showed the error in the primary mirror. Both indicators of error were discounted at the time as being themselves flawed.

The Perkin-Elmer plan for fabricating the primary mirror placed complete reliance on the reflective null corrector as the only test to be used in both manufacturing and verifying the mirror's surface with the required precision. NASA understood and accepted this plan. This methodology should have alerted NASA management to the fragility of the process and the possibility of gross error, that is, a mistake in the process, and the need for continued care and consideration of independent measurements.

The design of the telescope and the measuring instruments was performed well by skilled optical scientists. However, the fabrication was the responsibility of the Optical Operations Division at the Perkin-Elmer Corporation (P-E), which was insulated from review or technical supervision. The P-E design scientists, management, and Technical Advisory Group, as well as NASA management and NASA review activities, all failed to follow the fabrication process with reasonable diligence and, according to testimony, were unaware that discrepant data existed, although the data were of concern to some members of P-E's Optical Operations Division. Reliance on a single test method was a process which was clearly vulnerable to simple error. Such errors had been seen in other telescope programs, yet no independent tests were planned, although some simple tests to protect against major error were considered and rejected. During the critical time period, there was great concern about cost and schedule, which further inhibited consideration of independent tests.

The most unfortunate aspect of this HST optical system failure, however, is that the data revealing these errors were available from time to time in the fabrication process, but were not recognized and fully investigated at the time. Reviews were inadequate, both internally and externally, and the engineers and scientists who were qualified to analyze the test data did not do so in sufficient detail. Competitive, organizational, cost, and schedule pressures were all factors in limiting full exposure of all the test information to qualified reviewers.

NASA'S FUTURE

The United States' civil space program was rather hurriedly formulated some three decades ago on the heels of the successful launch of the Soviet Sputnik. A dozen humans have been placed on the moon and safely returned to earth, seven of the other eight planets have been viewed at close range, including the soft landing of two robot spacecraft on Mars, and a variety of significant astronomical and other scientific observations have been accomplished. Closer to earth, a network of communications satellites has been established, weather and ocean conditions are now monitored and reported as they occur, and the earth's surface is observed from space to study natural resources and detect sources of pollution.

Problems and Perspectives. In spite of these virtually unparalleled achievements, the civil space program and its principal agent, the National Aeronautics and Space Administration, are today the subject of considerable criticism. The source of this criticism ranges from concern over technical capability to the complexity of major space projects; from the ability to estimate and control costs to the growth of bureaucracy; and from a perceived lack of an overall space plan to an alleged institutional resistance to new ideas and change. The failure of the *Challenger*, the recent hydrogen leaks on several Space Shuttle orbiters, the spherical aberration problem encountered with the Hubble Space Telescope, and various launch processing errors such as a work platform left in an engine compartment and discovered during launch preparations, have all heightened this dissatisfaction.

Some of the concern is, in the view of the Committee, deserved and occasionally even self-inflicted. For example, the practice of separately reporting the cost of space missions according to accounting categories (which for bookkeeping purposes allocates launch services to a distinct account) results in confusion as to what is the actual cost of a mission.

Yet, in spite of recognized current problems, care must also be taken not to impose potentially disruptive remedies on today's NASA to correct problems that existed in an earlier NASA. The much publicized spherical aberration problem of the Hubble Space Telescope encountered this past year is in fact a consequence of an assembly error left undiscovered in tests conducted a decade age—in 1980. The decision to launch the Challenger in cold weather, when the seals between rocket motor segments would be most suspect, took place five years ago and has spurred NASA to many management changes. Since the Challenger accident, NASA has increased the emphasis on safety, and has borne the burden of delaying launches when reasonable questions arose over the readiness to launch safely. On the other hand, processing incidents during launch preparation continue to occur in NASA operations, and to be the cause of justifiable concern.

Because of the intense interest in—and scrutiny of—America's commendably open and visible civil space program, it is sometimes easy to overlook the fact that technical problems such as hydrogen leaks, faulty seals and erroneous assembly procedures are not unique to today's space activities, or even to NASA. Although problems of any sort are most emphatically not to be condoned, when comparing today's space program with the successes of the past, it must also be recalled that America's first attempt to launch an earth satellite using the Vanguard rocket ended in failure. By the end of 1959, 37 satellite launches had been attempted: less than one-third attained orbit. Ten of the first eleven launches of unmanned probes to the moon to obtain precursor data in support of the Apollo mission failed. Three astronauts were lost in a fire aboard the Apollo capsule during ground testing. A fuel cell exploded during the mission of Apollo XIII en route to the moon, seriously damaging the spacecraft. During the few months surrounding the Challenger accident, a Delta, an Atlas-Centaur, two Titan 34-D's, a French Araine-2 and a Soviet Proton were all lost.

Space missions, whether manned or unmanned, are fundamentally difficult and demanding undertakings that depend upon some of the world's most advanced technology. The Saturn V rocket required the integration of some six million components manufactured by thousands of separate contractors. Voyager 2 arrived at Neptune a mere one second behind its final updated schedule after a 12-year, 4.4 billion mile flight, approaching within 3,000 miles of the plant's surface. The information to be gathered by the Earth Observing System could approach 10 trillion bits of information—about one Library of Congress—per day. The matter of human frailty is perhaps of even greater import: in the case of the Apollo program, some 400,000 people at some 20,000 locations were involved in its design, test and operation.

Concerns. Nonetheless, given the cost of space activities, in both financial and human terms, and their profound impact on America's prestige throughout the world, no goal short of perfection is acceptable. The Committee finds that there are a number of concerns about the civil space program and NASA which are deserving of attention.

The first of these is the lack of a national consensus as to what should be the goals of the civil space program and how they should in fact be accomplished. It seems that most Americans do support a viable space program for the nation—but no two individuals seem able to agree upon what that space program should be. Further, those immediately involved in the program often seem least inclined to compromise for the common good. Some point out that most space missions can be performed with robots for a fraction of the cost of humans, and that, therefore, the manned space program should be curtailed. Others point out that the involvement of humans is the very essence of exploration, and that only humans can fully adapt to the unexpected. Some point to the need for accelerated commercialization of space while others argue the benefits of fundamental science—only to be challenged in turn to prove, say, the tangible value of studies in astronomy—and so on.

Second, and closely related to this contentious yet fundamental matter, our Committee believes that NASA is currently over-committed in terms of program obligations relative to resources available—in short, it is trying to do too much, and allowing too little margin for the unexpected. As a result, there is the frequent need to revamp major programs, which in turn sometimes results in forcing smaller (scientific) pursuits to pay the bill for problems encountered in larger (frequently manned) missions. Of major importance, in our view, is the fact that margins needed to provide confidence in maintaining cost, schedule, performance, and especially reliability, too often are minimal or absent.

Third, continuing changes in project budgets, sometimes exacerbated by actions needed to extricate projects from technical difficulties, result in *management inefficiencies.* These demoralize and frustrate the individuals pursuing those projects—as well as those who must pay the bills.

Fourth, there is the matter of institutional aging and the concern that NASA has not been sufficiently responsive to valid criticism and to the need for change.

Fifth, the personnel policies embodied in the civil service system are, in the opinion of the Committee, hopelessly incompatible with the long-term maintenance of a leading-edge, aggressive, confident, and able work force of technical specialists and technically trained managers that will be needed by NASA in the years ahead.

Sixth, it is a natural tendency for projects to grow in scope, complexity, and cost. Deliberate steps must be taken to guard against this phenomenon if programs are not to collapse under their own weight—often, as already noted, taking a toll on the smaller projects that must share in the budget.

Seventh, the material foundation of any major space project is its "technological base." It is this base that produces the key building blocks, or "enablers," that make major missions possible—new materials, electronics, engines and the like. The technology base of NASA has now been starved for well over a decade and must be rebuilt if a sound underpinning is to be regained for future space missions.

Eighth, space projects tend to be very unforgiving of any form of neglect or human failing—particularly with respect to engineering discipline. Spacecraft incorporating flaws are not readily "recalled" to the factory for modification. It is this category of problem that has evoked much of the criticism directed at NASA in recent years, although with new technology there are growing opportunities for systems that are "self-healing."

Finally, ninth, the civil space program is overly dependent upon the Space Shuttle for access to space. The Space Shuttle offers significant capabilities to carry out missions where humans are uniquely required—as has been the case on a number of occasions. The Shuttle is also a complex system that has yet to demonstrate an ability to adhere to a fixed schedule. And although it is a subject that meets with reluctance to open discussion, and has therefore too often been relegated to silence, the statistical evidence indicates that we are likely to lose another Space Shuttle in the next several years ... probably before the planned Space Station is completely established on orbit. This would seem to be the weak link of the civil space program—unpleasant to recognize, involving all the uncertainties of statistics, and difficult to resolve.

The Space Shuttle differs in important ways from unmanned vehicles—on the positive side it provides the flexibility and capability attendant to human presence and it permits the recovery of costly launch vehicle hardware which would otherwise be expended. On the negative side, it tends to be complex, with relatively limited margins; it has not realized the promised cost savings; and should it fail catastrophically, it takes with it a substantial portion of the nation's future manned launch capability and, potentially, several human lives.

The Committee recognizes the important role of the Space Shuttle for missions where there is the need for human involvement, and notes that the Space Shuttle is absolutely essential to America's civil space program for the next decade or more. Necessary steps to assure the viability of Space Shuttle operations this decade should therefore proceed. Nonetheless, the Committee believes in hindsight that it was, for example, inappropriate in the case of Challenger to risk the lives of seven astronauts and nearly one-forth of NASA's Launch assets to place in orbit a communications satellite.

Agency Responsibilities. Against the backdrop of these and other concerns, the Committee was asked to consider whether some altogether new form of management structure should be established to pursue portions of the nation's civil space program, as has been recommended by various observers. Such a model might include an altogether separate agency patterned after, say, the Strategic Defense Initiative Organization of the Department of Defense, which would be established to pursue major new initiatives such as the Mars exploration program. Another possibility occasionally proposed is to separate the Space Shuttle's operation from NASA so as to permit the space agency to focus upon the pursuit of advanced technology and new leading-edge missions.

The conclusion of the Committee is that changes of such sweeping scope are inappropriate. First, in spite of imperfections, by far the greatest body of space expertise in any single organization in the world resides within NASA. Further, in the case of Space Shuttle operations, the maturity of the system is neither compatible with a (potentially disruptive) shift to a new operator nor, in the opinion of the Committee, is it ever likely to be— even though in principle we favor private sector operations over government operations whenever practicable. NASA and its predecessor, NACA, have followed this practice with regard to the aeronautics program— producing unmatched technology that helped make America's commercial aircraft industry preeminent in the world. A similar effort is needed with respect to space activities—but the Space Shuttle is not, in our opinion, the correct mechanism for accomplishing this objective.

Briefly stated, the Committee believes that NASA, and only NASA, realistically possesses the essential critical mass of knowledge and expertise upon which the nation's civil space program can be sustained—and that the task at hand is therefore for NASA to focus on making the self-improvements that gird this responsibility.

A Space Agenda. The question then arises: "What should be the U.S. space program?" Although it may be tempting to lay out an accelerated plan to accomplish the unaccomplished and to attack the unknown, to do so in the absence of fiscal and technical realism would be a disservice, and would only magnify the problem of management "turbulence" that already has been so costly to the space effort—both in money and morale.

The question thus becomes one of what can and should the U.S. afford for its civil space endeavors in the time of unarguably great demands right here on earth, ranging from reducing the deficit to curing disease and from improving education to eliminating poverty. The answer to this question is made all the more difficult because the space program touches so many aspects of our lives and contributes to the accomplishment of goals ranging from improving education to enhancing our standard of living and from assuring national security to strengthening communications among the peoples of the world. The space program produces technology that enhances competitiveness; the largest rise and subsequent decline in the nation's output of much-needed science and engineering talent in recent decades coincided with, and some say may have been motivated by, the build-up and subsequent phase-down in the civil space program.

Global understanding has been enhanced through the establishment of widespread satellite telecommunications. Countless lives and considerable property have been saved through advanced weather forecasting and the use of spaceborne search and rescue systems. Basic scientific knowledge has been obtained that addresses such important questions as why one planet evolves to become altogether uninhabitable, while another nurtures life.

It can be argued that at least some of these benefits can be reaped by other more direct means. If the objective is to stimulate education, then why not give the money being spent on space to our schools? If the objective is to study the stars, then why not build more and better telescopes here on earth? To ease poverty, give aid to those in need. Yet perhaps the most important space benefit of all is intangible—the uplifting of spirits and human pride in response to truly great accomplishments—whether they be the sight of the single human orbiting freely around the earth at 18,000 miles per hour, or a picture of Uranus' moon Miranda transmitted 1.7 million miles through space, and taking some 2-1/2 hours merely to arrive at our listening stations even when traveling literally at the speed of light. Such accomplishments have served to unite our nation, hold our attention, and inspire us all, particularly our youth, as few other events have done in the history of our nation or even the world.

Our Committee concludes that America does want an energetic, affordable and successful space program, a predilection to which we as individuals unabashedly confess. This support has been evidenced in the gradual growth in space funding for nearly two decades. The question remains, however, "What should we afford?" In this regard, a historical perspective is helpful. At its peak, during the Apollo years, America spent 0.8 percent of its gross national product on its civil space program. This level amounted to about 4.5 percent of federal spending at the time and, perhaps more importantly, about 6 percent of the discretionary portion of the federal budget. Today, we as a nation are spending about one-third of the Apollo peak spending as a portion of the GNP ... and the fraction of the increasingly pressured total discretionary budget has declined to 2.5 percent.

Presumably reflecting public support, both the Executive Branch and the Congress have recently shown a willingness to increase civil space spending on the order of 10 percent per year (real growth) for a well-executed program. This, therefore, is the baseline selected by this Committee to assure at least a first order fiscal test in our proposals.... Our specific assumption is that the civil space budget will grow by approximately 10 percent per year in real dollars throughout most of this decade, leveling out at about 0.4 percent of the GNP. This is a budget that can enable a strong space program—but only if funding is predictable and programs are carefully managed and consistently executed. As a reference, civil space spending recently approved for 1991 represented 8.5 percent real growth over the prior year's spending.

In defining a space agenda we believe it is not sufficient merely to list a collection of projects to be undertaken in space, no matter how meritorious each may be. It is essential to provide a logical basis for the structure of the program, including a sense of priorities.

A Balanced Space Program. It is our belief that the space science program warrants highest priority for funding. It, in our judgment, ranks above space stations, aerospace planes, manned missions to the planets, and many other major pursuits which often receive greater visibility....

Having thus established the science activity as the fulcrum of the entire civil space effort, we would then recommend the "mission-oriented" portion of the program be designed to support two major undertakings: a Mission to Planet Earth and a Mission from Planet Earth. Both, we believe, are of considerable importance. The Mission to Planet Earth, as we would define it, is the undertaking that in fact brings space down to earth—addressing critical, everyday problems which affect all the earth's peoples. While we emphasize the need for a balanced space program, it is the Mission to Planet Earth which connotes some degree of urgency. Mission to Planet Earth, as we would define it, comprises a series of earth-observing satellites, probes and related instruments, and a complementary data handling system aimed at producing a much clearer understanding of global climate change and the impact of human activities on earth's biosphere. This effort will provide us with a much better understanding of our environment, how we may be affecting it, and what might be done to restore it.

The Mission from Planet Earth is principally, but not exclusively, focused upon the exploration of space. This is where most of the manned space undertakings are to be pursued and as such this tends to be the most costly aspect of the civil space program.

Today, America's manned space program is at a crossroads. The Committee believes that a focus must be given to this program now if it is not merely to drift through the decade ahead. Although there is no particular timetable that can in good conscience be assigned to this pursuit, it nonetheless sorely needs agreement as to direction.

At least in part because of its cost, the manned space program has been at the very hub of controversy swirling around the nation's civil space activity. It can be argued that much of what humans can perform in space could be conducted at less cost and risk with robotic spacecraft—and in many instances we believe it should be.

But are there not activities in space which properly should be the province of human intelligence, flexibility and being? The Committee found it instructive in this regard to ask whether we would be content with a space program that involved no human flight. Our answer is a resounding "no." ...

But if there is to be a manned space undertaking, what should it be? Surely the goal is not merely to provide routine transportation of cargo to and from space. In this regard, we share the view of the President that the longterm magnet for the manned space program is the planet Mars—the human exploration of Mars, to be specific. It needs to be stated straightforwardly that such an undertaking probably must be justified largely on the basis of intangibles—the desire to explore, to learn about one's surroundings, to challenge the unknown and to find what is to be found. Surely such an endeavor must be preceded by further unmanned visits, and by taking certain important steps along the way, including returning for extended periods to the moon in order to refine our hardware and procedures and to develop the skills and technologies required for long-term planetary living.

The Committee offers what we believe to be a potentially significant new approach in the planning of human space exploration. Although we appreciate the arguments for setting a "date certain" for many or even most of our space goals, as did President Kennedy with respect to going to the moon, we believe that a program with the ultimate, long-term objective of human exploration of Mars should be tailored to respond to the availability of funding, rather than to adhering to a rigid schedule....

Using this management approach, the Committee believes that a sound, long-term human exploration program can be pursued....

But fundamental uncertainties remain with respect to the feasibility of long duration human spaceflight, uncertainties that revolve around the effects of solar flares, muscle deterioration due to weightlessness, the loss of calcium in human bone structure, and the impact of galactic cosmic radiation. These basic issues need to be resolved before undertaking vast projects—by means of long-duration operations involving humans in space. We thus arrive at what we believe is the fundamental reason for building a space station: to gain the much needed life sciences information and experience in long duration space operations. Such information is vital if America is not to abdicate its role in manned spaceflight.

We do not believe that the Space Stations Freedom, as we now know it, can be justified solely on the basis of the (non-biological) science it can perform, much of which can be conducted on earth or by robotic spacecraft for less cost. Similarly, we doubt that the Space Station will be essential as a transportation node—certainly not for many years. However, the Space Station is deemed essential as a life sciences laboratory, for there is simply no earthbound substitute.....

... [W]e believe the justifying objectives of the Space Station Freedom should be reduced to two: primarily life sciences, and secondarily microgravity experimentation. In turn, we believe the Space Station

Freedom can be simplified, reduced in cost, and constructed on a more evolutionary, modular basis that enables end-to-end testing of most systems prior to launch. . . .

. . . [T]here remain two vital elements of space infrastructure to which attention must be devoted. This infrastructure underpins the nation's ability to actually undertake advanced space missions, and is addressed in two parts: first, the technology base, and second, the earth-to-space transportation system. . . .

First and foremost in this foundation-laying effort is the technology base which absolutely must be replenished. America has not initiated development of a new main rocket engine—the muscle of any space pursuit—in nearly two decades. Work on advanced space power systems has been modest; on very high specific simple propulsion devices even more limited, on advanced concepts such as aerobraking only formative. In fact, the overall technical base underpinning the space program has been permitted to languish in terms of funding for several decades. . . .

The second element of space infrastructure concerns the provision of high-confidence, reasonable-risk transportation to space. In this regard, the U.S. will be unalterably committed to the Space Shuttle for many years hence. Thus, NASA simply must take those steps needed to enhance the Shuttle's reliability, minimize wear and tear, and enhance launch schedule predictability. Cost reductions also are desirable but secondary to the preceding objectives.

We further conclude that NASA should proceed immediately to phase some of the burden being carried by the Space Shuttle to a new unmanned (but potentially man-rateable) launch vehicle that offers increased payload capacity and is derivable wherever practicable from existing components to save time and cost. . . .

It should be recognized that the substantial near-term cost of developing any new heavy-lift launch vehicle make a purely financial argument for its existence not particularly compelling. Rather, the objective is to attain a reliable, unmanned vehicle that complements the Space Shuttle and that can be used for routine space trucking, saving the Space Shuttle for those missions requiring human presence. . . .

Over the longer term, the nation must turn to new and revolutionary technologies to build more capable and significantly less costly means to launch manned and unmanned spacecraft, including those that one day will travel to the moon and Mars. However, the type of launch vehicle and the specific operational concept that will be needed to propel spacecraft from the earth's surface to orbit and on to the moon and Mars will depend on the results of mission architecture studies now under way. In the meantime, while we await the definition of the future spacecraft and launch vehicle requirements, the nation must maintain a vigorous Advanced Launch System technology program. . . .

International Pursuits. We emphasize that international cooperation should continue to be an integral part of the U.S. civil space program. But we also emphasize that the U.S. should retain management control for critical in-line program elements in certain long-term undertakings such as human space exploration, and that the U.S. must continue to have a fully competitive stance in areas such as the access to space itself, i.e., launch vehicles which have broad impact on the fundamental viability of America's civil and commercial space programs. . . .

DEADLINE PRESSURE ON SADDAM HUSSEIN

November 29, 30, and December 5, 1990

The United Nations Security Council on November 29 authorized "all necessary means" to remove Iraq's occupying forces from Kuwait if they remained there after January 15, 1990. The council's Resolution 678—the twelfth resolution condemning Iraq since its August 2 takeover of Kuwait—set the deadline weeks ahead to give Iraqi president Saddam Hussein "one final opportunity" to avoid war. A large military force of massive firepower faced him in Saudi Arabia and the Persian Gulf. In all, twenty-eight countries provided some degree of support for this UN-sponsored buildup, but it was overwhelmingly American and under U.S. command.

President George Bush, vowing to "go the extra mile for peace," announced to a White House news conference November 30 that he would invite Iraqi foreign minister Tariq Aziz to Washington and was willing to send Secretary of State James A. Baker III to Baghdad in search of a peaceful solution to the Persian Gulf crisis. Hussein's government accepted Bush's invitation to talk and, in what was interpreted as a gesture of good will, soon allowed several thousand Westerners to leave Iraq and Kuwait.

Many others, mostly workers from other Arab countries and Asia—but also a few Westerners—had been permitted to leave earlier. All foreigners unable to flee at the war's onset were detained as "guests" of the Iraqi government. The West considered them hostages seized by Hussein for bargaining power with the United States. Some were housed at likely military targets in an effort to deter American air attacks. On December 11 the State Department said all the Americans had been brought out except for some 500 who chose to stay. Many of them held dual citizenship and had family ties in Iraq or Kuwait.

But the diplomatic initiative soon was bogged down in a dispute over meeting dates. Iraq insisted on starting no sooner than January 12, and Washington saw the delay as a ploy to extend the deadline. Baker never went to Baghdad; he did meet with Aziz in Geneva on January 9, 1991, but to no avail. Hussein remained defiant. UN secretary general Javier Perez de Cuellar undertook a final peace mission to Baghdad as the deadline approached. He returned empty-handed. War followed on January 16, 1991, with U.S.-led air attacks on Iraqi positions in Iraq and Kuwait.

Importance of Resolution 678

Resolution 678 set the stage for the first use of UN-sponsored force against a member nation since the Korean War in 1950. Baker, in urging the council to act November 29, declared it a "watershed" event. Bush, in his news conference the next day, called the resolution "historic." The United States had lobbied hard for Security Council approval, and won twelve of the fifteen votes cast; Cuba and Yemen voted no, and China abstained. Voting yes were the United States, Soviet Union, Britain, and France, all permanent council members wielding veto power. They were joined by eight rotating (temporary) members—Canada, Colombia, Ethiopia, Finland, Ivory Coast, Malaysia, Romania, and Zaire.

China, a permanent member, objected to an explicit mention of military force, according to press accounts. It reportedly consented to abstain rather than cast a veto only after the document's sponsors substituted the phrase "all means necessary." However, there was never any doubt that the meaning was the same. All prior resolutions condemning Iraq had been cast in terms of using nonmilitary force, even though economic sanctions invoked by the council required a shipping blockade enforced by warships.

Switch to Offensive Action

The Bush administration had cast the allied military buildup in Saudi Arabia in terms of defending that kingdom against the threat of an Iraqi invasion. But on several occasions Bush expressed impatience with the boycott as a means of choking Iraq into submission. In a surprise move November 8, the president ordered that U.S. troop strength in the Persian Gulf be nearly doubled to give it an "adequate offensive option." Defense officials later indicated they had scrapped previous troop-rotation plans. The troops would remain until they were no longer needed. This shift of emphasis in the administration's thinking stirred uneasy concern in Congress and among several West European governments. Antiwar protests began in the United States and Europe. Sen. Sam Nunn, D-Ga., chairman of the Senate Armed Services Committee, criticized the size of the troop buildup. Some leading Senate Republicans requested a special session of Congress to discuss troop deployments, and forty-five Democratic members of Congress brought suit in federal court to compel Bush to seek congressional approval before committing the nation to war. They lost the suit, but the president requested and received such approval after the new 101st Congress met in January.

Question of Economic Sanctions

A critical question in the prewar debate was whether the economic sanctions were effective. There seemed to be uncertainty within the administration itself. In testimony before the House Armed Services Committee on December 5, Director William H. Webster of the Central Intelligence Agency (CIA) predicted that mounting shortages in Iraq were likely to close its energy-related and military industries by spring. But Baker, testifying the same day before the Senate Foreign Relations Committee, said that "none of our efforts have yet produced any sign of change in Saddam Hussein."

At that time Baker still thought he would go to Baghdad to talk to Hussein, as Bush had proposed. But there would be no give-and-take in the talks, Baker explained. "Put simply," he told the committee, "my mission to Baghdad will be to attempt to explain to Saddam the choice he faces: Comply with the Security Council or risk disaster for Iraq."

Following are the remarks of Secretary of State James A. Baker III to the UN Security Council November 29, 1990; the text of Resolution 678; a summary of all Security Council resolutions condemning Iraq's takeover of Kuwait; President Bush's remarks at a White House news conference November 30; excerpts from CIA director William H. Webster's December 5 testimony before the House Armed Services Committee; and excerpts from Baker's testimony the same day to the Senate Foreign Relations Committee:

BAKER'S UN REMARKS

Today's vote marks a watershed in the history of the United Nations. Earlier this week, members of this council heard testimony of crimes committed against the citizens of Kuwait. There can be no doubt that these are crimes incompatible with any civilized order. They are part of the same pattern that includes the taking of innocent hostages from many nations.

The entire international community has been affronted by a series of brutal acts.

- Iraqi forces have invaded and seized a small Arab neighbor.
- A once prosperous country has been pillaged and looted.
- A once peaceful country has been turned into an armed camp.
- A once secure country has been terrorized.

The nations of the world have not stood idly by. We have taken political, economic, and military measures to quarantine Iraq and to contain its aggression. We have worked out a coordinated international effort involving over 50 states to provide assistance to those nations most in need as a consequence of the economic embargo of Iraq. And, military forces from over 27 nations have been deployed to defend Iraq's neighbors from further aggression and to implement UN resolutions. The 12 resolutions passed by the Security Council have established clearly that there is a peaceful way out of this conflict: the complete, immediate, unconditional Iraqi withdrawal from Kuwait; the restoration of Kuwait's legitimate government; and the release of all hostages.

I do not think all of this could have taken place unless most nations shared our vision of what is at stake. A dangerous man has committed a blatant act of aggression in a vital region at a critical moment in history. Saddam Hussein's actions, the vast arms he possesses, the weapons of mass destruction he seeks, indicate clearly that Kuwait was not only not the first but probably not the last target on his list. If he should win this struggle, then there will be no peace in the Middle East; only the prospect of more conflict and a far wider war.

If Saddam should come to dominate the resources of the gulf, his ambitions will threaten all of us here and the economic well-being of all nations. Finally, if Iraq should emerge from this conflict with territory or treasure or political advantage, then the lesson will be clear: aggression pays. As I said earlier today, we must remember the lesson of the 1930s: aggression must not be rewarded.

Since August 2, many nations have worked together to prove just that. Many unprecedented actions have been taken. The result is a new fact: a newly effective UN Security Council, free of the constraints of the Cold War. Yet, the sad truth is that the new fact has not yet erased the old fact of Iraqi aggression, and that, and that alone, is the ultimate test of success.

We must ask ourselves why Saddam Hussein has not recoiled from his aggression. We must wonder why he does not understand how great are the forces against him and how profound is the revulsion against his behavior.

The answer must be that he does not believe we really mean what we say. He does not believe that we will stand united until he withdraws. He thinks that his fact of aggression will outlast our fact: an international community opposed to aggression.

We are meeting here today, therefore, first and foremost, to dispel Saddam Hussein's illusions. He must know from us that a refusal to comply peacefully with the Security Council resolutions risks disaster for him.

Members of the council, we are at a crossroads. Today, we show Saddam that the sign marked "peace" is the direction he should take.

Today's resolution is clear. The words authorize the use of force, but the purpose—I truly believe—is to bring about a peaceful resolution. No one here has sought this conflict. Many nations here have had good relations with the people of Iraq. But the Security Council of the United Nations cannot tolerate this aggression and still be faithful to the principles of the UN Charter.

With passage of today's resolution, we concur with other council members that this should lead to a pause in this council's efforts, assuming no adverse change in circumstances. We do so while retaining our rights to protect our foreign nationals in Iraq and mindful of the terms of the Fourth Geneva Convention and the Geneva Protocol of 1925, should Saddam Hussein use chemical or biological weapons.

By passing today's resolution—a pause for peace—we say to Saddam Hussein: "We continue to seek a diplomatic solution. Peace is your only sensible option. You can choose peace by respecting the will of the international community. But if you fail to do so, you will risk all. The choice is yours."

If we fail to redress this aggression, more will be lost than just peace in the Persian Gulf. Only recently, in Europe, the nations party to the Cold War assembled to bury that conflict. All the peoples of Europe and North America, who had nothing to look forward to except an unending, twilight struggle, now have a fresh start, a new opportunity. Conflict and war are no longer the watchwords of European politics.

Members of the council, we meet at the hinge of history. We can use the end of the Cold War to get beyond the whole pattern of settling conflicts by force, or we can slip back into ever more savage regional conflicts in which might alone makes right. We can take the high road toward peace and the rule of law, or Saddam Hussein's path of brutal aggression and the law of the jungle. Simply put, it is a choice between right and wrong.

I believe we have courage and the fortitude to choose what's right.

UN RESOLUTION 678

The Security Council,

Recalling and reaffirming its resolutions 660 (1990), 661 (1990), 662 (1990), 664 (1990), 665 (1990), 666 (1990), 667 (1990), 669 (1990), 670 (1990) and 674 (1990),

Noting that, despite all efforts by the United Nations, Iraq refuses to comply with its obligation to implement resolution 660 (1990) and the above subsequent relevant resolutions, in flagrant contempt of the Council,

Mindful of its duties and responsibilities under the Charter of the United Nations for the maintenance and preservation of international peace and security,

Determined to secure full compliance with its decisions,

Acting under Chapter VII of the Charter of the United Nations,

1. *Demands* that Iraq comply fully with resolution 660 (1990) and all

subsequent relevant resolutions and decides, while maintaining all its decisions, to allow Iraq one final opportunity, as a pause of goodwill, to do so;

2. *Authorizes* Member States cooperating with the Government of Kuwait, unless Iraq on or before 15 January 1991 fully implements, as set forth in paragraph 1 above, the foregoing resolutions, to use all necessary means to uphold and implement Security Council resolution 660 (1990) and all subsequent relevant resolutions and to restore international peace and security in the area;

3. *Requests* all States to provide appropriate support for the actions undertaken in pursuance of paragraph 2 of this resolution;

4. *Requests* the States concerned to keep the Council regularly informed on the progress of actions undertaken pursuant to paragraphs 2 and 3 of this resolution;

5. *Decides* to remain seized of the matter.

VOTE: 12 for, 2 against (Cuba and Yemen); 1 abstention (China)

THE GULF CRISIS: UN SECURITY COUNCIL ACTIONS

- **August 2—Resolution 660** Condemns invasion. Demands unconditional and immediate withdrawal. *Vote:* 14 for, 0 against, 1 abstention (Yemen).
- **August 6—Resolution 661** Imposes economic sanctions. Authorizes non-military measures to enforce trade sanctions. *Vote:* 13 for, 2 abstentions (Yemen and Cuba).
- **August 9—Resolution 662** Declares Iraq's annexation of Kuwait null and void. *Vote:* Unanimous (5-0).
- **August 18—Resolution 664** Condemns Iraq for holding foreign nationals hostage and demands their immediate release. *Vote:* Unanimous (15-0).
- **August 25—Resolution 665** Outlaws all trade with Iraq by land, sea, and air. Bars financial dealings with all UN members. *Vote:* 13 for, 2 abstentions (Yemen and Cuba).
- **September 13—Resolution 666** Establishes guidelines for humanitarian food aid to Iraq and occupied Kuwait. *Vote:* 13 for, 2 opposed (Yemen and Cuba).
- **September 16—Resolution 667** Condemns Iraq for violence against foreign embassies and diplomats in Kuwait. Demands protection for diplomatic and consular personnel. *Vote:* Unanimous (15-0).
- **September 24—Resolution 669** Agrees to consider exceptions to Resolution 661 for shipment of humanitarian supplies and authorizes examination of requests for economic assistance under Article 50.

Vote: Unanimous (15-0).

- **September 25—Resolution 670** Tightens embargo on air traffic and authorizes detention of Iraq's merchant fleet. *Vote:* Unanimous (15-0).
- **October 29—Resolution 674** Holds Iraq responsible for all financial losses resulting from invasion and seeks evidence of human rights abuses by Iraqi troops in Kuwait. Calls for the release of third-country nationals and the provision of food to those being held against their will. *Vote:* 13 for, 2 abstentions (Yemen and Cuba).
- **November 28—Resolution 667** Condemns Iraqi attempts to alter the demographic composition of Kuwait and to destroy the civil records maintained by the legitimate government of Kuwait. Mandates Secretary General to take custody of a copy of the Kuwaiti population register. *Vote:* Unanimous (15-0).
- **November 29—Resolution 678** Authorizes "member states cooperating with the government of Kuwait" to use "all necessary means" to uphold the above resolutions, while giving Iraq "one final opportunity, as a pause of good will" to abide by the resolutions by January 15, 1991. *Vote:* 12 for, 2 against (Yemen and Cuba), 1 abstention (China).

BUSH STATEMENT

We're in the gulf because the world must not and cannot reward aggression; we're there because our vital interests are at stake; and we're in the gulf because of the brutality of Saddam Hussein. We are dealing with a dangerous dictator all too willing to use force, who has weapons of mass destruction and is seeking new ones, and who desires to control one of the world's key resources—all at a time in history when the rules of the post-Cold War world are being written.

Our objectives remain what they were since the outset. We seek Iraq's immediate and unconditional withdrawal from Kuwait; we seek the restoration of Kuwait's legitimate government; we seek the release of all hostages and the free functioning of all embassies; and we seek the stability and security of this critical region of the world.

We are not alone in these goals and objectives. The United Nations, invigorated with a new sense of purpose, is in full agreement. The UN Security Council has endorsed 12 resolutions to condemn Iraq's unprovoked invasion and occupation of Kuwait, implement tough economic sanctions to stop all trade in and out of Iraq, and authorize the use of force to compel Saddam to comply.

Saddam Against the UN

Saddam Hussein has tried every way he knows to make this a fight between Iraq and the United States—and clearly, he has failed. Forces of 26 other nations are standing shoulder to shoulder with our troops in the gulf. The fact is that it is not the United States against Iraq; it is Iraq against the world. There has never been a clearer demonstration of a world united against appeasement and aggression.

Yesterday's UN Security Council resolution was historic. Once again, the Security Council has enhanced the legitimate peacekeeping function of the United Nations. Until yesterday Saddam may not have understood what he's up against in terms of world opinion. I'm hopeful that now he will realize that he must leave Kuwait immediately.

I'm continually asked how effective are the UN sanctions that were put into effect on August 6. I don't know the answer to that question. Clearly, the sanctions are having some effect, but I can't tell you that the sanctions alone will get the job done. Thus, I welcome yesterday's UN action.

Damage to the Nations of the World

The fledgling democracies in Eastern Europe are being severely damaged by the economic effects of Saddam's actions. The developing countries of Africa and in our hemisphere are being victimized by this dictator's rape of his neighbor, Kuwait. Those who feel that there is no downside to waiting months and months must consider the devastating damage being done every day to the fragile economies of those countries that can afford it the least.

As [Federal Reserve Board] Chairman Alan Greenspan testified just the other day, the increase in oil prices resulting directly from Saddam's invasion is hurting our country, too. Our economy, as I said the other day, is at best in a serious slowdown, and if uncertainty remains in the energy markets, the slowdown will get worse.

I've spelled out once again our reasons for sending troops to the gulf. Let me tell you the things that concern me most.

- First, I put the immorality of the invasion of Kuwait itself. No nation should rape, pillage, and brutalize its neighbor. No nation should be able to wipe a member state of the United Nations and Arab League off the face of the earth.
- I'm deeply concerned about all hostages—innocent people held against their will in direct contravention of international law. Then there's this cynical and brutal policy of forcing people to beg for their release—parceling out human lives to families and traveling emissaries like so much chattel.
- I'm deeply concerned about our own embassy in Kuwait. The flag is still flying there. A handful of beleaguered Americans remain inside the embassy unable to come and go. This treatment of our embassy violates every civilized principle of diplomacy. It demeans our people; it demeans our country. And I am determined that this embassy, as called for under Security Council Resolution 674, be fully replenished and our people free to come home.
- What kind of precedent will these actions set for the future if Saddam's violation of international law goes unchallenged? I'm also

deeply concerned about the future of Kuwait itself. The tales of rape and assassination, of cold-blooded murder and rampant looting, are almost beyond belief. The whole civilized world must unite and say this kind of treatment of people must end, and those who violate it. The Kuwaiti people must be brought justice.

- I'm deeply concerned about Saddam's efforts to acquire nuclear weapons. Imagine his ability to blackmail his neighbors should he possess a nuclear device. We're seen him use chemical weapons on his own people. We've seen him take his own country, one that should be wealthy and prosperous, and turn it into a poor country—all because of an insatiable appetite for military equipment and conquest.

Getting the Job Done

I've been asked why I ordered more troops to the gulf. I remain hopeful that we can achieve a peaceful solution to this crisis. But if force is required, we and the other 26 countries who have troops in the area will have enough power to get the job done. In our country, I know that there are fears about another Vietnam. Let me assure you, should military action be required, this will not be another Vietnam. This will not be a protracted, drawn-out war.

The forces arrayed are different. The opposition is different. The resupply of Saddam's military would be very different. The countries united against him in the United Nations are different. The topography of Kuwait is different. And the motivation of all our volunteer force is superb.

I want peace. I want peace, not war. But if there must be war, we will not permit our troops to have their hands tied behind their backs. I pledge to you there will not be any murky ending. If one American soldier has to go into battle, that soldier will have enough force behind him to win, and then get out as soon as possible, as soon as the UN objectives have been achieved.

I will never—ever—agree to a halfway effort. Let me repeat: We have no argument with the people of Iraq; indeed, we have only friendship for the people there. Further, I repeat that we have no desire to keep one single American soldier in the gulf a single day longer than is necessary to achieve the objectives set out above.

No one wants to see a peaceful solution in this crisis more than I do. And, at the same time, no one is more determined than I am to see Saddam's aggression reversed.

Lastly, people now caution patience. The United States and the entire world have been patient. I will continue to be patient. But yesterday's UN resolution, the 13th by the Security Council, properly says to Saddam Hussein: Time is running out. You must leave Kuwait, and we've given you time to do just exactly that.

The Extra Mile for Peace

Many people have talked directly to Saddam Hussein and to his foreign minister, Tariq Aziz. All have been frustrated by Iraq's ironclad insistence that it will not leave Kuwait. However, to go the extra mile for peace, I will issue an invitation to Foreign Minister Tariq Aziz to come to Washington at a mutually convenient time during the latter part of the week of December 10th to meet with me. I'll invite ambassadors of several of our coalition partners in the gulf to join me at that meeting.

In addition, I'm asking Secretary Jim Baker to go to Baghdad to see Saddam Hussein. I will suggest to Iraq's president that he receive the Secretary of State at a mutually convenient time between December 15th and January 15th of next year.

Within a mandate—within the mandate of the UN resolution, I will be prepared, and so will Secretary Baker, to discuss all aspects of the gulf crisis. However, to be very clear about these efforts to exhaust all means for achieving a political and diplomatic solution, I am not suggesting discussions that will result in anything less than Iraq's complete withdrawal from Kuwait, restoration of Kuwait's legitimate government, and freedom for all hostages.

WEBSTER TESTIMONY

... At the technical level, economic sanctions and the embargo against Iraq have put Saddam Hussein on notice that he is isolated from the world community and have dealt a serious blow to the Iraqi economy. More than 100 countries are supporting the U.N. resolutions that impose economic sanctions on Iraq.

Coupled with the U.S. government's increased ability to detect and follow up on attempts to circumvent the blockade, the sanctions have all but shut off Iraq's exports and reduced imports to less than 10 percent of their pre-invasion level.

All sectors of the Iraq economy are feeling the pinch of sanctions, and many industries have largely shut down. Most importantly, the blockade has eliminated any hope Baghdad had of cashing in on higher oil prices or its seizure of Kuwaiti oil fields.

Despite mounting disruptions and hardships resulting from sanctions, Saddam apparently believes that he can outlast international resolve to maintain those sanctions. We see no indication that Saddam is concerned at this point that domestic discontent is growing to levels that may threaten his regime or that problems resulting from the sanctions are causing him to rethink his policy on Kuwait.

The Iraqi people have experienced considerable deprivation in the past. Given the brutal nature of the Iraqi security services, the population is not likely to oppose Saddam openly. Our judgment has been and continues to be that there is no assurance or guarantee that economic hardships will compel Saddam to change his policies or lead to internal unrest that would threaten his regime....

The blockade and embargo have worked more effectively than Saddam probably expected. More than 90 percent of imports and 97 percent of exports have been shut off. Although there is smuggling across Iraq's borders, it is extremely small relative to Iraq's pre-crisis trade.

Iraqi efforts to break sanctions have thus far been largely unsuccessful. What little leakage has occurred is due largely to a relatively small number of private firms acting independently, and we believe that countries are actively enforcing the sanctions and plan to continue doing so.

Industry appears to be the hardest hit so far. Many firms are finding it difficult to cope with the departure of foreign workers and with the cutoff of imported industrial inputs, which [made up] nearly 60 percent of Iraq's total imports prior to the invasion.

These shortages have either shut down or severely curtailed production by a variety of industries, including many light industrial and assembly plants, as well as the country's only tire manufacturing plant.

Despite these shutdowns, the most vital industries, including electric power generation and refining, do not yet appear to be threatened. We believe they will be able to function for some time, because domestic consumption has been reduced, because Iraqi and Kuwaiti facilities have been cannibalized and because some stockpiles and surpluses already existed.

The cutoff of Iraq's oil exports and the success of sanctions have also choked off Baghdad's financial resources. This, too, has been more effective and more complete than Saddam probably expected. In fact, we believe that a lack of foreign exchange will, in time, be Iraq's greatest economic difficulty. The embargo has deprived Baghdad of roughly $1.5 billion of foreign exchange earnings monthly. . . .

We believe Baghdad's actions to forestall shortages of food stocks, including rationing, encouraging smuggling and promoting agricultural production, are adequate for the next several months. The full harvest of fruits and vegetables is injecting new supplies into the market and will provide a psychological as well as tangible respite from mounting pressures.

The Iraqi population in general has access to sufficient staple foods. Other foodstuffs, still not rationed, also remain available. However, the variety is diminishing, and prices are sharply inflated. For example, sugar purchased on the open market at the official exchange rate went from $32 per 50-kilogram bag in August to $580 per bag last month. . . .

Looking ahead, the economic picture changes somewhat. We expect Baghdad's foreign exchange reserves to become extremely tight, leaving it little cash with which to entice potential sanctions busters. At current rates of depletion, we estimate Iraq will have nearly depleted its available foreign exchange reserves by next spring.

Able to obtain even a few key imports, Iraq's economic problems will begin to multiply as Baghdad is forced to gradually shut down growing numbers of facilities in order to keep critical activities functioning as long as possible. Economic conditions will be noticeably worse, and Baghdad will find allocating scarce resources a significantly more difficult task.

Probably only energy-related and some military industries will still be functioning by next spring. This will almost certainly be the case by next summer. Baghdad will try to keep basic services such as electric power from deteriorating.... The regime will also try to insulate critical military industries to prevent an erosion of military preparedness. Nonetheless, reduced rations, coupled with rapid inflation and little additional support from the government, will compound the economic pressures facing most Iraqis.

By next spring, Iraqis will have made major changes in their diets. Poultry, which is a staple of the Iraqi diet, will not be available. Unless Iraq receives humanitarian food aid, or unless smuggling increases, some critical commodities such as sugar and edible oils will be in short supply.

Distribution problems are likely to create localized shortages. But we expect that Baghdad will be able to maintain grain consumption, mainly wheat, barley and rice, at about two-thirds of last year's level until the next harvest in May. The spring grain and vegetable harvest will again augment food stocks, although only temporarily. To boost next year's food production, Baghdad has raised prices paid to farmers for their produce and decreed that farmers must cultivate all available land. Nonetheless, Iraq does not have the capability to become self-sufficient in food production by next year. ...

Although sanctions are hurting Iraq's civilian economy, they are affecting Iraq's military only at the margins. Iraq's fairly static defensive posture will reduce wear and tear on the military equipment and, as a result, extend the life of its inventory of spare parts and maintenance items.

Under non-combat conditions, Iraqi ground and air forces can probably maintain near current levels of readiness for as long as nine months. We expect the Iraqi air force to feel the effects of sanctions more quickly and to a greater degree than the Iraqi ground forces because of its greater reliance on high technology and foreign equipment and technicians.

Major repairs to sophisticated aircraft like the F-1 will be achieved with significant difficulty, if at all, because of the exodus of foreign technicians. Iraqi technicians, however, should be able to maintain current levels of aircraft sorties for three to six months.

The Iraqi ground forces are more immune to sanctions. Before the invasion, Baghdad maintained large inventories of basic military supplies, such as ammunition, and supplies probably remain adequate.

The embargo will eventually hurt Iraqi armor by preventing the replacement of old fire-control systems and creating shortages of additives for various critical lubricants. ...

While we can look ahead several months and predict the gradual deterioration of the Iraqi economy, it is more difficult to assess how or when these conditions will cause Saddam to modify his behavior. At present, Saddam almost certainly assumes that he is coping effectively with the sanctions. . . .

Saddam's willingness to sit tight and try to outlast the sanctions, or in the alternative, to avoid war by withdrawing from Kuwait, will be determined by his total assessment of the political, economic and military pressures arrayed against him.

BAKER TESTIMONY

. . . We have to face the fact that four months into this conflict none of our efforts have yet produced any sign of change in Saddam Hussein. He shows no signs of complying with any of the Security Council resolutions. Instead, he appears to be doubling his bets.

He has tried to make Kuwait part of Iraq, systematically looting and dismembering a sovereign Arab state. He has been terrorizing the population, his soldiers committing unspeakable crimes against innocent Kuwaitis. He has called for the overthrow of King Fahd of Saudi Arabia and president [Hosni] Mubarak of Egypt, he has threatened to rain terror and mass destruction on his Arab neighbors as well as on Israel, and he has been playing the cruelest of games with hostages and their families and with our diplomats in Kuwait.

After serious and sobering consultations, the United Nations Security Council last Thursday passed by an overwhelming majority a 12th resolution, one that authorizes all necessary means, including the use of force, to eject Iraq from Kuwait after Jan. 15, 1991.

In passing this resolution, the international community is giving Saddam yet another chance—indeed, one last chance—to come to his senses. In passing Thursday's resolution, the international community sends the following clear message:

We continue to seek a diplomatic solution. Peace is your only sensible option. You can choose peace by respecting the will of the international community, but if you fail to do so, you will risk all. The choice is yours.

To ensure, Mr. Chairman, that he understands this choice, the president has invited the foreign minister of Iraq to Washington and has directed me to go to Baghdad. Put bluntly, this is the last, best chance for a peaceful solution.

If we are to have any chance of success, I must go to Baghdad, Mr. Chairman, with the full support of the Congress and the American people behind the message of the international community.

Let me be clear: This meeting will not be the beginning of a negotiation over the terms of the United Nations resolutions. Those terms are clear — complete, immediate and unconditional withdrawal from Kuwait, a restoration of the legitimate Kuwaiti government and the release of all foreign nationals.

Nor is this the beginning of a negotiation on subjects which are unrelated to Iraq's brutal occupation of Kuwait. I will not be negotiating the Palestinian question or the civil war in Lebanon. Saddam Hussein did not invade Kuwait to help the Palestinians. He did it for his own self-aggrandizement, and as Eduard [A.] Shevardnadze, [the Soviet foreign minister], has said, Mr. Chairman, you do not enslave one people to free another.

Put simply, my mission to Baghdad will be an attempt to explain to Saddam the choice he faces: Comply with the objectives of the Security Council or risk disaster for Iraq. To give substance to these words, the president has directed the secretary of Defense, the chairman of the Joint Chiefs and me to work with the other members of the international coalition to reinforce the multinational force in the gulf and to coordinate its efforts. Our aim is to ensure that if force must be used, it will be used suddenly, massively and decisively.

Do the troop reinforcements and the Security Council resolution mean that war is inevitable? Surely not. There is a peaceful solution possible, one that does not reward aggression, and everyone, including Saddam Hussein, knows what that is. He can choose peace by withdrawing unconditionally from Kuwait and by releasing all hostages.

He will not make that peaceful choice, however, in our opinion, unless he understands that the alternative to peaceful compliance is that he will be forced to comply. That is the message that we are trying, in every way we know how, to send him. That is the meaning of the steps the international community has taken over the past month. It is not a new strategy but rather a continuation and reinforcement of the strategy that we have been pursuing since August.

Now, I know that some here and throughout the country are very uneasy about the prospects of war. Mr. Chairman, no one wants war — none of us. Not you, not the president, not me — none of us. None of us, though, have sought this conflict, and we are making every attempt possible to resolve it peacefully. To resolve it peacefully without appeasing the aggressor.

I know the arguments of those who believe that time and the economic embargo alone will work to resolve this conflict peacefully, but I think we have to face some very hard facts. If sanctions are to succeed, they have got to do more than simply hurt Iraq economically. They must hurt Iraq so much that Saddam Hussein changes his behavior and withdraws from Kuwait. That is the criteria by which sanctions must be judged.

In considering the role of sanctions in our strategy, we need to ask ourselves, can economic sanctions alone compel a dictator like Saddam Hussein to make the politically difficult choice of withdrawing from Kuwait? Absent a critical military threat, will he take the Security Council's actions seriously? Is there anything in Saddam Hussein's history that could lead us to believe that sanctions alone would get him out of Kuwait?

Mr. Chairman, if I might, let me try to answer these questions based on the results so far.

After four months of a stringent embargo, no one doubts that sanctions are having some effect on the Iraqi economy. But we have to face the difficult fact, I think, that no one can tell you that sanctions alone will ever be able to impose a high enough cost on Saddam Hussein to get him to withdraw.

So far, all available evidence suggests that they have had little, if any, effect on his inclination to withdraw. That is in part because Saddam, to a considerable extent, can decide who in Iraq gets hurt by the sanctions. And you can bet the Iraqi people will feel the pain first and most deeply, not the Iraqi military and not the government of Iraq itself. . . .

So we need to remember who it is we are trying to get out of Kuwait. He is a ruthless dictator. He has an inflated sense of Iraq's leverage and a very high pain threshold. He undoubtedly believes he can endure economic sanctions. However, surely he understands more acutely the consequence or the consequences of military force. Waiting not only gives him time to break the sanctions, but waiting, Mr. Chairman, imposes costs on us.

As we wait, Saddam will continue torturing Kuwait and continue killing it as a nation. As we wait, he will continue manipulating hostages, attempting to break the coalition.

As we wait, he will continue to fortify Kuwait. He will continue to build chemical and biological weapons. And he will continue his efforts to acquire a nuclear weapons capability.

As we wait, he expects other issues to deflect our attention, to weaken our resolve and to dissolve the international coalition. . . .

While not prejudging any decision whether force should be used sometime after Jan. 15, I can state unequivocally that failure to continue preparations now has at least three dangerous consequences:

First, it would undercut our diplomatic leverage by removing the other alternative to a peaceful withdrawal, which is use of force. It would send Iraq exactly the wrong message, that is, continue to play for time: You will have lots of it because the Security Council resolution is just a bluff. . . .

Second, the failure to prepare a credible offensive military option would only tend to reaffirm the status quo and to legitimize to some the brutal occupation that he is now carrying out against Kuwait and its people.

Third, the failure to prepare adequately now would mean that should conflict come, we would be irresponsibly risking greater casualties, putting the lives of those young Americans already on the front lines in the Persian Gulf at greater risk then they need to be.

The president will not stand for that. And neither, Mr. Chairman, I submit, will the American people. . . .

It is often said that there has been no clear answer given to the question of why we are in the gulf. Much of this, I think, results from the search for a single cause for our involvement, a single reason the president could use to explain why the lives of American men and women should be put in harm's way in the sands of Arabia, on the seas around it or in the air above it.

Mr. Chairman, let us stop this search and let us be honest with ourselves and with each other. There are multiple causes, there are multiple dangers, there are multiple threats and standing alone, each is compelling. But you put them all together and the case is overwhelming. Put very bluntly, a very dangerous dictator, armed to the teeth, is threatening a critical region at a defining moment in history. It is the combination of these reasons, that is: who is threatening our interest, what capabilities he has and is developing, where he is carrying out his aggression and when he has chosen to act that make the stakes so very high for all of us.

Let me explain. Strategically, this man is a capricious dictator whose lust for power is as unlimited as his brutality in the pursuit of it. He has invaded two neighbors, is harboring terrorists and now is systematically exterminating Kuwait. He used poison gas even against his own people. He develops deadly toxins. And he seeks relentlessly to acquire nuclear bombs. . . .

Geographically, Saddam's aggression has occurred in a political tinder-box that is crossroads to three continents. His success would only guarantee more strife, more conflict and eventually a wider war. . . .

Economically, his aggression imperils the world's oil lifelines, threatening recession and depression here and abroad, hitting hardest those fledgling democracies that are least able to cope with it.

His aggression is an attempt to mortgage the economic promise of the post-Cold War world to the whims of a single man.

Morally, we must act so that international laws, not international outlaws, govern the post-Cold War world. We must act so that right, not might, dictates success in the post-Cold War world. We must act so that innocent men and women and diplomats are protected, not held hostage.

In the post-Cold War world, historically, we must stand with the people of Kuwait so that the annexation of Kuwait does not become the first reality that mars our vision of a new world order. We must stand with the world community so that the United Nations does not go the same way as the League of Nations.

Politically, Mr. Chairman, finally, politically, we must stand for American leadership. Not because we seek it but simply because no one else can do the job. And we did not stand united for 40 years to bring the Cold War to a peaceful end in order to make the world safe for the likes of Saddam Hussein.

So these then are the stakes, Mr. Chairman. . . . Now, more than at any time during this conflict, it is important that we stand united with the world community in full support of the United Nations Security Council resolutions. Simply put, it is a choice between what's right and what's wrong.

December

SUPREME COURT ON
MIRANDA DECISION
December 3, 1990

The Supreme Court handed down a decision December 3 upholding and possibly expanding the rights of criminal suspects during police questioning. The Court, generally believed to be unsympathetic to expanding the rights of the accused, decided in favor of such rights by a surprisingly large 6-2 vote. In Minnick v. Mississippi *the Court reaffirmed the so-called Miranda rule on police interrogation by a larger majority than had voted for it initially. It was set forth in 1966 by a bare five-member majority led by Earl Warren, then the chief justice. To protect a suspect's Fifth Amendment right against self-incrimination, Warren said, the suspect must be informed before police questioning that he has a right to remain silent, that anything he says may be used as evidence against him, and that he is entitled to have a lawyer present during questioning.*

In further defining that rule, Justice Anthony M. Kennedy wrote the majority opinion and placed himself in the unusual position of being on the opposite side from Chief Justice William H. Rehnquist and Justice Antonin Scalia. Normally the three were like-minded in criminal cases. Scalia wrote the dissenting opinion, in which Rehnquist joined. Justices Byron R. White, Thurgood Marshall, Harry A. Blackmun, John Paul Stevens, and Sandra Day O'Connor endorsed Kennedy's opinion. Justice David H. Souter did not participate in the case, which was argued the week before he joined the Court. (Judge Souter's Testimony to Senate Judiciary Committee, p. 615)

The decision overturned a 1988 ruling by the Mississippi Supreme Court, which held that the police could begin a new round of questioning if the suspect's lawyer was not present but had previously been consulted.

Kennedy held on behalf of the Court that the Mississippi decision did not adequately protect a suspect from "coercive pressures" to talk to the police.

Robert S. Minnick was sentenced to death in Mississippi, where he was convicted of committing a murder when he and another escapee from a local jail broke into a mobile home in search of weapons. The homeowner and a friend surprised them during the burglary and were killed. The two fugitives fled and later split up. Four months later, Minnick was arrested in Lemon Grove, California, on a Mississippi warrant, and jailed in San Diego.

Minnick requested a lawyer, with whom he spoke more than once during a weekend. On the following Monday, jail officials ordered Minnick to talk to a Mississippi sheriff who had arrived to question him. In the absence of the lawyer, Minnick gave an incriminating statement. Mississippi courts held that the statement was admissible as evidence of guilt.

Kennedy said that the Mississippi court did not properly interpret the Supreme Court's ruling in a 1981 case, Edwards v. Arizona, *which elaborated on Miranda. In* Edwards *the Court said that once a suspect requests a lawyer, police questioning cannot continue "until counsel had been made available" to the suspect. Kennedy said the fact that Minnick had previously talked to a lawyer did not fulfill the "made available" stipulation. "A single consultation with an attorney does not remove the suspect from persistent attempts by officials to persuade him to waive his rights, or from the coercive pressures that accompany custody and may increase as custody is prolonged," he wrote. The Court's decision would not prevent Mississippi from retrying Minnick for murder but it would eliminate the incriminating statement as evidence.*

Scalia assailed the majority's view as "a veritable fairyland castle of imagined constitutional restrictions upon law enforcement." He added that "the Constitution's proscription of compelled testimony does not remotely authorize this incursion upon state practices; and even our recent precedents are not a valid excuse."

> *Following are excerpts from the majority and dissenting opinions issued December 3, 1990, in* Minnick v. Mississippi, *which upholds and elaborates a suspect's right to counsel during police questioning:*

No. 89-6332

Robert S. Minnick, Petitioner *v.* Mississippi	On writ of certiorari to the Supreme Court of Mississippi

No. 89-6332

[December 3, 1990]

JUSTICE KENNEDY delivered the opinion of the Court.

To protect the privilege against self-incrimination guaranteed by the Fifth Amendment, we have held that the police must terminate interrogation of an accused in custody if the accused requests the assistance of counsel. *Miranda* v. *Arizona* (1966). We reinforced the protections of *Miranda* in *Edwards* v. *Arizona* (1981), which held that once the accused requests counsel, officials may not reinitiate questioning "until counsel has been made available" to him. The issue in the case before us is whether *Edwards'* protection ceases once the suspect has consulted with an attorney.

Petitioner Robert Minnick and fellow prisoner James Dyess escaped from a county jail in Mississippi and, a day later, broke into a mobile home in search of weapons. In the course of the burglary they were interrupted by the arrival of the trailer's owner, Ellis Thomas, accompanied by Lamar Lafferty and Lafferty's infant son. Dyess and Minnick used the stolen weapons to kill Thomas and the senior Lafferty. Minnick's story is that Dyess murdered one victim and forced Minnick to shoot the other. Before the escapees could get away, two young women arrived at the mobile home. They were held at gunpoint, then bound hand and foot. Dyess and Minnick fled in Thomas' truck, abandoning the vehicle in New Orleans. The fugitives continued to Mexico, where they fought, and Minnick then proceeded alone to California. Minnick was arrested in Lemon Grove, California, on a Mississippi warrant, some four months after the murders.

The confession at issue here resulted from the last interrogation of Minnick while he was held in the San Diego jail, but we first recount the events which preceded it. Minnick was arrested on Friday, August 22, 1986. Petitioner testified that he was mistreated by local police during and after the arrest. The day following the arrest, Saturday, two FBI agents came to the jail to interview him. Petitioner testified that he refused to go to the interview, but was told he would "have to go down or else." The FBI report indicates that the agents read petitioner his *Miranda* warnings, and that he acknowledged he understood his rights. He refused to sign a rights waiver form, however, and said he would not answer "very many" questions. Minnick told the agents about the jail break and the flight, and described how Dyess threatened and beat him. Early in the interview, he sobbed "[i]t was my life or theirs," but otherwise he hesitated to tell what happened at the trailer. The agents reminded him he did not have to answer questions without a lawyer present. According to the report, "Minnick stated 'Come back Monday when I have a lawyer,' and stated that he would make a more complete statement then with his lawyer present." The FBI interview ended.

After the FBI interview, an appointed attorney met with petitioner. Petitioner spoke with the lawyer on two or three occasions, though it is not clear from the record whether all of these conferences were in person.

On Monday, August 25, Deputy Sheriff J. C. Denham of Clarke County, Mississippi, came to the San Diego jail to question Minnick. Minnick testified that his jailers again told him he would "have to talk" to Denham and that he "could not refuse." Denham advised petitioner of his rights, and petitioner again declined to sign a rights waiver form. Petitioner told Denham about the escape and then proceeded to describe the events at the mobile home. According to petitioner, Dyess jumped out of the mobile home and shot the first of the two victims, once in the back with a shotgun and once in the head with a pistol. Dyess then handed the pistol to petitioner and ordered him to shoot the other victim, holding the shotgun on petitioner until he did so. Petitioner also said that when the two girls arrived, he talked Dyess out of raping or otherwise hurting them.

Minnick was tried for murder in Mississippi. He moved to suppress all statements given to the FBI or other police officers, including Denham. The trial court denied the motion with respect to petitioner's statements to Denham, but suppressed his other statements. Petitioner was convicted on two counts of capital murder and sentenced to death.

On appeal, petitioner argued that the confession to Denham was taken in violation of his rights to counsel under the Fifth and Sixth Amendments. The Mississippi Supreme Court rejected the claims. With respect to the Fifth Amendment aspect of the case, the court found "the *Edwards* bright-line rule as to initiation" inapplicable. Relying on language in *Edwards* indicating that the bar on interrogating the accused after a request for counsel applies " 'until counsel has been made available to him,' " the court concluded that "[s]ince counsel was made available to Minnick, his Fifth Amendment right to counsel was satisfied." The court also rejected the Sixth Amendment claim, finding that petitioner waived his Sixth Amendment right to counsel when he spoke with Denham. We granted certiorari, and, without reaching any Sixth Amendment implications in the case, we decide that the Fifth Amendment protection of *Edwards* is not terminated or suspended by consultation with counsel.

In *Miranda* v. *Arizona,* we indicated that once an individual in custody invokes his right to counsel, interrogation "must cease until an attorney is present"; at that point, "the individual must have an opportunity to confer with the attorney and to have him present during any subsequent questioning." *Edwards* gave force to these admonitions, finding it "inconsistent with *Miranda* and its progeny for the authorities, at their instance, to reinterrogate an accused in custody if he has clearly asserted his right to counsel." We held that "when an accused has invoked his right to have counsel present during custodial interrogation, a valid waiver of that right cannot be established by showing only that he responded to further police-initiated custodial interrogation even if he has been advised of his rights." Further, an accused who requests an attorney, "Having expressed his desire to deal with the police only through counsel, is not subject to further interrogation by the authorities until counsel has been made available to him, unless the accused himself initiates further communication, exchanges, or conversations with the police. . . ."

The merit of the *Edwards* decision lies in the clarity of its command and the certainty of its application. We have confirmed that the *Edwards* rule provides "'clear and unequivocal' guidelines to the law enforcement profession...." (*Arizona v. Roberson*, 1988)

The Mississippi Supreme Court relied on our statement in *Edwards* that an accused who invokes his right to counsel "is not subject to further interrogation by the authorities until counsel has been made available to him...." We do not interpret this language to mean, as the Mississippi court thought, that the protection of *Edwards* terminates once counsel has consulted with the suspect. In context, the requirement that counsel be "made available" to the accused refers to more than an opportunity to consult with an attorney outside the interrogation room.

In *Edwards,* we focused on *Miranda's* instruction that when the accused invokes his right to counsel, "the interrogation must cease until an attorney is *present,*" agreeing with Edwards' contention that he had not waived his right "to have counsel *present* during custodial interrogation...."

Our emphasis on counsel's *presence* at interrogation is not unique to *Edwards.* It derives from *Miranda,* where we said that in the cases before us "[t]he presence of counsel ... would be the adequate protective device necessary to make the process of police interrogation conform to the dictates of the [Fifth Amendment] privilege. His presence would insure that statements made in the government-established atmosphere are not the product of compulsion." Our cases following *Edwards* have interpreted the decision to mean that the authorities may not initiate questioning of the accused in counsel's absence....

We consider our ruling to be an appropriate and necessary application of the *Edwards* rule. A single consultation with an attorney does not remove the suspect from persistent attempts by officials to persuade him to waive his rights, or from the coercive pressures that accompany custody and that may increase as custody is prolonged. The case before us well illustrates the pressures, and abuses, that may be concomitants of custody. Petitioner testified that though he resisted, he was required to submit to both the FBI and the Denham interviews. In the latter instance, the compulsion to submit to interrogation followed petitioner's unequivocal request during the FBI interview that questioning cease until counsel was present. The case illustrates also that consultation is not always effective in instructing the suspect of his rights. One plausible interpretation of the record is that petitioner thought he could keep his admissions out of evidence by refusing to sign a formal waiver of rights. If the authorities had complied with Minnick's request to have counsel present during interrogation, the attorney could have corrected Minnick's misunderstanding, or indeed counseled him that he need not make a statement at all. We decline to remove protection from police-initiated questioning based on isolated consultations with counsel who is absent when the interrogation resumes.

The exception to *Edwards* here proposed is inconsistent with *Edwards'* purpose to protect the suspect's right to have counsel present at custodial interrogation. It is inconsistent as well with *Miranda,* where we specifically rejected respondent's theory that the opportunity to consult with one's attorney would substantially counteract the compulsion created by custodial interrogation. We noted in *Miranda* that "[e]ven preliminary advice given to the accused by his own attorney can be swiftly overcome by the secret interrogation process. Thus the need for counsel to protect the Fifth Amendment privilege comprehends not merely a right to consult with counsel prior to questioning, but also to have counsel present during any questioning if the defendant so desires." (citation omitted)

The exception proposed, furthermore, would undermine the advantages flowing from *Edwards'* "clear and unequivocal" character. Respondent concedes that even after consultation with counsel, a second request for counsel should reinstate the *Edwards* protection. We are invited by this formulation to adopt a regime in which *Edwards'* protection could pass in and out of existence multiple times prior to arraignment, at which point the same protection might reattach by virtue of our Sixth Amendment jurisprudence, see *Michigan* v. *Jackson* (1986). Vagaries of this sort spread confusion through the justice system and lead to a consequent loss of respect for the underlying constitutional principle.

In addition, adopting the rule proposed would leave far from certain the sort of consultation required to displace *Edwards*. Consultation is not a precise concept, for it may encompass variations from a telephone call to say that the attorney is in route, to a hurried interchange between the attorney and client in a detention facility corridor, to a lengthy in-person conference in which the attorney gives full and adequate advice respecting all matters that might be covered in further interrogations. And even with the necessary scope of consultation settled, the officials in charge of the case would have to confirm the occurrence and, possibly, the extent of consultation to determine whether further interrogation is permissible. The necessary inquiries could interfere with the attorney-client privilege. . . .

Both waiver of rights and admission of guilt are consistent with the affirmation of individual responsibility that is a principle of the criminal justice system. It does not detract from this principle, however, to insist that neither admissions nor waivers are effective unless there are both particular and systemic assurances that the coercive pressures of custody were not the inducing cause. . . .

Edwards does not foreclose finding a waiver of Fifth Amendment protections after counsel has been requested, provided the accused has initiated the conversation or discussions with the authorities; but that is not the case before us. . . . Petitioner's statement to Denham was not admissible at trial.

The judgment is reversed and the case remanded for further proceedings not inconsistent with this opinion.

It is so ordered.

JUSTICE SCALIA, with whom THE CHIEF JUSTICE joins, dissenting.

The Court today establishes an irrebuttable presumption that a criminal suspect, after invoking his *Miranda* right to counsel, can *never* validly waive that right during any police-initiated encounter, even after the suspect has been provided multiple *Miranda* warnings and has actually consulted his attorney. This holding builds on foundations already established in *Edwards* v. *Arizona*, but "the rule of *Edwards* is our rule, not a constitutional command; and it is our obligation to justify its expansion." *Arizona* v. *Roberson* (1988). Because I see no justification for applying the *Edwards* irrebuttable presumption when a criminal suspect has actually consulted with his attorney, I respectfully dissent.

I

Minnick was ... extradited and tried for murder in Mississippi. Before trial, he moved to suppress the statements he had given the FBI agents and Denham in the San Diego jail. The trial court granted the motion with respect to the statements made to the FBI agents, but ordered a hearing on the admissibility of the statements made to Denham. After receiving testimony from both Minnick and Denham, the court concluded that Minnick's confession had been "freely and voluntarily given from the evidence beyond a reasonable doubt," and allowed Denham to describe Minnick's confession to the jury.

The Court today reverses the trial court's conclusion. It holds that, because Minnick had asked for counsel during the interview with the FBI agents, he could not—as a matter of law—validly waive the right to have counsel present during the conversation initiated by Denham. That Minnick's original request to see an attorney had been honored, that Minnick had consulted with his attorney on several occasions, and that the attorney had specifically warned Minnick not to speak to the authorities, are irrelevant. That Minnick was familiar with the criminal justice system in general or *Miranda* warnings in particular (he had previously been convicted of robbery in Mississippi and assault with a deadly weapon in California) is also beside the point. The confession must be suppressed, not because it was "Compelled," nor even because it was obtained from an individual who could realistically be assumed to be unaware of his rights, but simply because this Court sees fit to prescribe as a "systemic assuranc[e]" that a person in custody who has once asked for counsel cannot thereafter be approached by the police unless counsel is present. Of course the Constitution's proscription of compelled testimony does not remotely authorize this incursion upon state practices; and even our recent precedents are not a valid excuse.

II

In *Miranda* ... this Court declared that a criminal suspect has a right to have counsel present during custodial interrogation, as a prophylactic assurance that the "inherently compelling pressures" of such interrogation will not violate the Fifth Amendment. But *Miranda* did not hold that these "inherently compelling pressures" precluded a suspect from waiving his right to have counsel present. On the contrary, the opinion recognized that a State could establish that the suspect "knowingly and intelligently waived ... his right to retained or appointed counsel." For this purpose, the Court expressly adopted the "high standar[d] of proof for the waiver of constitutional rights," set forth in *Johnson* v. *Zerbst* (1938).

The *Zerbst* waiver standard, and the means of applying it, are familiar: Waiver is "an intentional relinquishment or abandonment of a known right or privilege"; and whether such a relinquishment or abandonment has occurred depends "in each case, upon the particular facts and circumstances surrounding that case, including the background, experience, and conduct of the accused." We have applied the *Zerbst* approach in many contexts where a State bears the burden of showing a waiver of constitutional criminal procedural rights. . . .

Edwards, however, broke with this approach, holding that a defendant's waiver of his *Miranda* right to counsel, made in the course of a police-initiated encounter after he had requested counsel but before counsel had been provided, was *per se* involuntary. The case stands as a solitary exception to our waiver jurisprudence. It does, to be sure, have the desirable consequences described in today's opinion. In the narrow context in which it applies, it provides 100% assurance against confessions that are "the result of coercive pressures." . . . But so would a rule that simply excludes all confessions by all persons in police custody. . . . "Admissions of guilt," we have said, "are more than merely 'desirable'; they are essential to society's compelling interest in finding, convicting, and punishing those who violate the law."

III

. . . Most of the Court's discussion of *Edwards* . . . is beside the point. The existence and the importance of the *Miranda*-created right "to have counsel *present*" are unquestioned here. What *is* questioned is why a State should not be given the opportunity to prove (under *Zerbst*) that the right was *voluntarily waived* by a suspect who, after having been read his *Miranda* rights twice and having consulted with counsel at least twice, chose to speak to a police officer (and to admit his involvement in two murders) without counsel present.

Edwards did not assert the principle that no waiver of the *Miranda* right "to have counsel *present*" is possible. It simply adopted the presumption that no waiver is *voluntary* in certain circumstances, and the issue before us today is how broadly those circumstances are to be defined. They should not, in my view, extend beyond the circumstances present in *Edwards* itself—where the suspect in custody asked to consult an attorney, and was interrogated before that attorney had ever been provided. In those circumstances, the *Edwards* rule rests upon an assumption similar to that of *Miranda* itself: that when a suspect in police custody is first questioned he is likely to be ignorant of his rights and to feel isolated in a hostile environment. This likelihood is thought to justify special protection against unknowing or coerced waiver of rights. After a suspect has seen his request for an attorney honored however, and has actually spoken with that attorney, the probabilities change. The suspect then knows that he has an advocate on his side, and that the police will permit him to consult that advocate. He almost certainly also has a heightened awareness (above what the *Miranda* warning itself will provide) of his right to remain silent. . . .

Under these circumstances, an irrebuttable presumption that any police-prompted confession is the result of ignorance of rights, or of coercion, has no genuine basis in fact. . . .

One should not underestimate the extent to which the Court's expansion of *Edwards* constricts law enforcement. Today's ruling, that the invocation of a right to counsel permanently prevents a police-initiated waiver, makes it largely impossible for the police to urge a prisoner who has initially declined to confess to change his mind—or indeed, even to ask whether he has changed his mind. . . .

It seems obvious to me that, even in *Edwards* itself but surely in today's decision, we have gone far beyond any genuine concern about suspects who do not *know* their right to remain silent, or who have been *coerced* to abandon it. . . . The procedural protections of the Constitution protect the guilty as well as the innocent, but it is not their objective to set the guilty free. That some clever criminals may employ those protections to their advantage is poor reason to allow criminals who have not done so to escape justice.

Thus, even if I were to concede that an honest confession is a foolish mistake, I would welcome rather than reject it; a rule that foolish mistakes do not count would leave most offenders not only unconvicted but undetected. More fundamentally, however, it is wrong, and subtly corrosive of our criminal justice system, to regard an honest confession as a "mistake." While every person is entitled to stand silent, it is more virtuous for the wrongdoer to admit his offense and accept the punishment he deserves. . . . Today's decision is misguided, it seems to me, in so readily exchanging, for marginal, *super-Zerbst* protection against genuinely compelled testimony, investigators' ability to urge, or even ask, a person in custody to do what is right.

PAZ'S ACCEPTANCE
OF NOBEL LITERATURE AWARD
December 10, 1990

Octavio Paz received the 1990 Nobel Prize for Literature from King Carl Gustaf XVI of Sweden in an elaborate ceremony in Stockholm on December 10. The Swedish Academy of Letters, in announcing the award two months earlier, said it was bestowed on the Mexican writer for works characterized by "sensuous intelligence and humanistic integrity." More than two dozen of his books of poetry and prose had been translated from Spanish into other languages. The seventy-six-year-old Nobel laureate was first published as a teenager and was probably best known to foreign readers as a poet, essayist, critic, and philosopher. In Mexico, he was also an influential political commentator who sometimes described himself as a "disillusioned leftist."

Paz insisted, however, that he was not a political activist or even a member of any political party. Some saw him as a "celebrity intellectual" who recorded and interpreted the aspirations and foibles of humankind. After four decades his 1950 essay El laberinto de la soledad *("The Labyrinth of Solitude") remained an oft-consulted and quoted analysis of modern Mexico and the Mexican personality. Paz was the first Mexican to win the Nobel literary award, but for the second year in a row—and for the third time within a decade—the prize went to a writer of Spanish. Camilo José Cela of Spain was the winner in 1989 and Gabriel García Márquez of Colombia in 1982.*

In 1981 Paz received the Cervantes prize, the highest for literature offered in the Spanish-speaking world and in 1982 captured the prestigious American Neustadt Prize. He had been a visiting professor at Harvard, Cambridge, and Texas universities. When his Nobel award was announced, he was in New York for the opening of the Metropolitan Museum of Art's exhibit, "Mexico: Splendor of Thirty Centuries." He had contributed an essay to the exhibit's catalogue.

From his Manhattan hotel suite, Paz conducted news interviews in English and Spanish, saying on one occasion that he thought his selection was evidence that Europe and North America had come to appreciate Latin American literature. Asked if he thought the Nobel prize was for him or for Mexico, he was quoted as saying: "To me, a poet represents not only a region but the universe. Writers are the servants of language. Language is the common property of society, and writers are the guardians of language. A writer has two loyalties. First, he belongs to a special tribe of writers. Then he belongs to a culture, to his own country. Mine is Mexico."

Background

Paz was the grandson of a novelist-journalist-politician who espoused the cause of Mexican peasants and, Paz said, instilled in him a love for literature. His father was a lawyer and liberal politician of Indian and Spanish heritage. His Spanish-born mother encouraged him to study and travel broadly. In his twenties, Paz witnessed the Spanish Civil War, and upon returning to Mexico in 1938, helped to found an influential literary journal, "Taller"—meaning workshop.

In 1943 Paz received a Guggenheim Fellowship and spent two years studying in the United States, where he delved deeply into English and American literature. He then entered the diplomatic service and later served as Mexico's ambassador to France, Switzerland, Japan, and India. Paz resigned from the government in 1968 to protest police repression of student demonstrations during that summer's Olympic Games in Mexico City.

As is customary at the acceptance of a Nobel Prize for Literature, Paz delivered a lengthy address to his audience of Swedish and foreign dignitaries in Stockholm. Also honored were nine other winners of 1990 Nobel prizes: Richard E. Taylor of Canada, Jerome I. Friedman of Chicago, and Henry W. Kendall of Boston, for physics; Elias J. Corey of Cambridge, Massachusetts, for chemistry; Harry M. Markowitz of New York, Merton H. Miller of Chicago, and William F. Sharpe of Stanford University for economics; and Joseph E. Murray of Milford, Massachusetts, and E. Donnall Thomas of Seattle, for medicine.

The Stockholm gathering tended to overshadow a companion ceremony in Oslo for the awarding of the 1990 peace prize by the Norwegian Nobel Committee. Its recipient, Soviet president Mikhail S. Gorbachev, had to remain in Moscow to deal with economic and political problems in the Soviet Union. Anatoly G. Kovalev, the Soviet first deputy foreign minister, collected the award. Kovalev read a message from the Soviet leader to the audience of 900 in Oslo Town Hall, including Crown Prince Harald of Norway, saying that there was a "unique opportunity for reason and the logic of peace to prevail over that of war and annihila-

tion." However, Gorbachev warned that "there are some very grave threats that have not been eliminated. . . ."

The annual Nobel awards, bearing the name of the late Swedish industrialist Alfred Nobel, were first made in 1901 except for economics, which originated in 1969. Each award consists of a diploma, gold medal, and four million in Swedish kronor, the equivalent of about $700,000 in late 1990. Because Norway was once a part of Sweden, awards ceremonies are held in both Stockholm and Oslo, the two capitals.

Following is an address, in translation, by Mexican writer Octavio Paz, winner of the 1990 Nobel Prize for Literature, upon his acceptance of the award at ceremonies in Stockholm on December 10:

I begin with two words that all men have uttered since the dawn of humanity: thank you. Grace is gratuitous; it is a gift. The person who receives it, the favored one, is grateful for it, and if he is not base, he expresses gratitude. That is what I do now, at this moment, with these weightless words. I hope my emotion compensates for their weightlessness. If each of my words were a drop of water, you would see through them and glimpse what I feel: gratitude, acknowledgment, and also an indefinable mixture of fear, respect, and surprise at finding myself here before you, in this place that is the home of both Swedish learning and world literature.

Languages are vast realities that transcend the political and historical entities that we call nations. The European languages that we speak in the Americas illustrate this. The special position of our literatures, when compared with the literatures of England, Spain, Portugal, and France, depends precisely on this fundamental fact: they are written in transplanted tongues. Languages are born in, and grow from, the native soil; they are nourished by a common history. Some of the European languages were rooted out from their native soil and their own tradition, however, and planted in an unknown and unnamed world. They took root in the new lands, and as they grew within the societies of America, they were transformed. They are the same plant, and yet a different one. Our literatures did not possibly accept the changing fortunes of the transplanted languages; they participated in the process, even accelerated it. Soon they ceased to be merely trans-Atlantic reflections. At times, our literatures have been the negation of the literatures of Europe. More often, they have been a reply.

In spite of these oscillations, however, the link has never been broken. My classics are those of my language, and I consider myself a descendant of Lope de Vega and Quevedo, as any Spanish writer would. Yet I am not a Spaniard. I think that most writers of Spanish America, as well as those from the United States, Brazil, and Canada, would say the same about the English, Portuguese, and French traditions. To understand more clearly the special position of writers in the Americas, we might recall the dialogue that has been conducted by Japanese, Chinese, or Arabic writers with the different literatures of Europe. It is a dialogue that cuts across multiple languages and civilizations. Our dialogue, on the other hand, takes place within the same language. We are Europeans, yet we are not Europeans. What are we, then?

It is difficult to define what we are, but our works speak for us. In the field of literature, the great novelty of the present century has been the appearance of the American literatures. The first to appear was the English-speaking one, and then, in the second half of the twentieth century, the Latin American literature in its two great branches, Spanish America and Brazil. Although they are very different, these three literatures have a common feature: the conflict, which is more ideological than literary, between cosmopolitanism and nativism, between Europeanism and Americanism.

What is the legacy of this dispute? The polemics have disappeared; the works remain. Apart from this general resemblance, the differences between the three literatures are many and profound. One of them belongs more to history than to literature: the development of Anglo-American literature coincided with the rise of the United States as a world power, whereas the rise of our literature coincides with our political and social misfortune, with the upheavals of our nations. This proves, once again, the limitations of social and historical determinism: the decline of empires and social disturbances sometimes coincide with moments of artistic and literary splendor. Li-Po and Tu Fu witnessed the fall of the Tang dynasty; Velázquez painted for Felipe IV; Seneca and Lucan were contemporaries and also victims of Nero.

The other differences are of a literary nature. They apply more to particular works than to the character of each literature. But can we say that literatures have a character? Do they possess a set of shared features that distinguish them from other literatures? I doubt it. A literature is not defined by some fanciful, intangible character; it is a society of unique works, which is united by relations of opposition and affinity.

The first fundamental difference between Latin-American literature and Anglo-American literature lies in the diversity of their origins. Both began as projections of Europe—in the case of North America, the projection of an island; in our case, the projection of a peninsula. The two regions are geographically, historically, and culturally eccentric. The origins of North America are in England and the Reformation; ours are in Spain, Portugal, and the Counter-Reformation. About the case of Spanish America, I should briefly mention what distinguishes Spain from other European countries, giving it a particularly original historical identity. Spain is no less eccentric than England, but its eccentricity is of a different kind. The eccentricity of the English in insular, and is characterized by isolation: it is an eccentricity that excludes. Hispanic eccentricity is peninsular, by contrast, and consists of the coexistence of different civilizations and different pasts. It is an inclusive eccentricity. In what would later be Catholic Spain, the Visigoths professed the heresy of Arianism, and we might note also the centuries of domination by Arabic civilization, the influence of Jewish culture, the Reconquest, and other characteristic features of Spanish history.

Hispanic eccentricity was reproduced and multiplied in America, especially in countries such as Mexico and Peru, where ancient and splendid civilizations had existed. In Mexico the Spaniards encountered history as well as geography. That history is still alive; it is a present rather than a past. The temples and gods of pre-Columbian Mexico are a pile of ruins, but the spirit that breathed life into that world has not disappeared. It speaks to us in the hermetic language of myth, legend, forms of social coexistence, popular art, customs. Being a Mexican writer means listening to the voice of that present, that presence. Listening to it, speaking with it, deciphering it, expressing it.

Perhaps we may now perceive more clearly the peculiar relation that binds us to, and separates us from, the European tradition. This consciousness of being separate is a constant feature of our spiritual history. Separation is sometimes experienced as a wound that marks an internal division, as an anguished awareness that invites self examination. At other times it is a challenge, a spur that incites us to action, to go forth and encounter others and the outside world.

It is true that the feeling of separation is universal, not peculiar to Spanish Americans. It is born at the moment of our birth: as we are wrenched from the Whole, we fall into an alien land. This experience becomes a wound that never heals. It is the unfathomable depth of every man; all our ventures and exploits, all our acts and dreams, are bridges designed to overcome the separation and reunite us with the world and our fellow beings. Each man's life, and the collective history of mankind, can be seen as an attempt to reconstruct the original situation. An unfinished and endless cure for our divided condition. But it is not my intention to provide yet another description of this feeling. I wish simply to stress that for us this existential condition expresses itself in historical terms. It becomes an awareness of our history.

How and when does this feeling appear, and how is it transformed into consciousness? The reply to this double-edged question can be given in the form of theory or in the form of personal testimony. I prefer the latter: there are many theories, and none is entirely convincing. The feeling of separation is bound up with the oldest and vaguest of my memories: the first cry, the first scare. Like every child, I built emotional bridges in the imagination to link me to the world and to other people. I lived in a town on the outskirts of Mexico City, in an old dilapidated house that had a jungle-like garden and a great room full of books. First games and first lessons. The garden soon became the center of my world; the library, and enchanted cave. I used to read and play with my cousins and schoolmates. There was a fig tree, a temple of vegetation; and four pines trees, three ash trees, a nightshade, a pomegranate tree, wild grass, and prickly plants that produced purple grazes. Adobe walls. Time was elastic, space was a spinning wheel.

All time, past or future, real or imaginary, was pure presence. Space transformed itself ceaselessly. The beyond was here, all was here: a valley, a mountain, a distant country, the neighbors' patio. Books with pictures, especially history books, eagerly leafed through, supplied images of deserts and jungles, palaces and hovels, warriors and princesses, beggars and kings. We were shipwrecked with Sinbad and Crusoe, we fought with D'Artagnan, we took Valencia with the Cid. How I would have liked to stay forever on the Isle of Calypso! In summer the green branches of the fig tree would sway like the sails of a carvel or a pirate ship. High up on the mast, swept by the wind, I could make out islands and continents, lands that vanished as soon as they became tangible. The world was limitless, yet it was always within reach; time was a pliable substance that weaved an unbroken present.

When was the spell broken? Gradually, rather than suddenly. It is hard to accept that a friend has betrayed you, that a woman you love has deceived you, that the idea of freedom is the mask of a tyrant. What we call "finding out" is a slow and tricky process, because we ourselves are the accomplices of our errors and our deception. Still, I can remember rather clearly an incident that was the first sign, though it was quickly forgotten. I must have been about six when one of my cousins, who was a little older, showed me a North American magazine with a photograph of soldiers marching along a huge avenue, probably in New York. "They've returned from the war," she said. This handful of words disturbed me, as if they foreshadowed the end of the world, or the Second Coming of Christ. I vaguely knew that somewhere far away a war had ended a few years earlier, and that the soldiers were marching to celebrate their victory. That war had taken place, however, in another place and in another time, not here and now. The photograph refuted me. I felt literally dislodged from the present.

From that moment, time began to fracture. And there appeared a plurality of spaces. The experience repeated itself more and more frequently. Any piece of news, a harmless phrase, a headline in a newspaper: everything proved the outside world's existence, and my own unreality. I felt that the world was splitting, that I did not inhabit the present. Real time was elsewhere. My time, the time of the garden, the fig tree, the games with friends, the drowsiness among the plants under the afternoon sun, a fig torn open (black and red like a live coal, but sweet and fresh): this was a fictitious time. In spite of what my senses told me, the time from over there, that belonged to the others, was the real one, the time of the real present. I accepted the inevitable. I became an adult.

That was how my expulsion from the present began. It may seem paradoxical to say that we have been expelled from the present, but it is a feeling we have all known. Some of us experienced it first as a punishment that we later transformed into consciousness and action. The search for the present is the pursuit neither of an earthly paradise nor of a timeless eternity; it is the search for a real reality. For us, as Spanish Americans, the real present was not in our own countries. It was the time lived by others, by the English, the French, the Germans. It was the time of New York, Paris, London. We had to go and look for it and bring it back home. Those were the years of my discovery of literature.

I began to write poems. I did not know what made me write them; I was moved by an inner need that is difficult to define. Only now have I understood that there was a secret relationship between my expulsion from the present and my writing of poetry. Poetry is in love with the instant, and seeks to relieve it in the poem. Thus it separates the instant from sequential time and transforms it into a fixed present. In those years, though, I wrote without wondering why I was doing it. I was searching for the gateway to the present; I wanted to belong to my time and to my century. A little later this obsession became a fixed idea: I wanted to be a modern poet. My search for modernity had begun.

Modernity is an ambiguous term. There are as many types of modernity as there are societies. Each has its own. The word's meaning is uncertain and arbitrary, like the name of the period that preceded it, the Middle Ages. If we are modern compared with medieval times, are we the Middle Ages of a future modernity? Is a name that changes with time a real name? Modernity is a word in search of its meaning. Is it an idea, a mirage, or a moment of history? Are we the children of modernity or its creators? Nobody knows for sure. It doesn't matter much: we follow it, we pursue it. For me, in those early years as a writer, modernity was fused with the present, or rather produced it: the present was its final supreme flower.

My case was not exceptional. Since the Symbolist period, modern poets have chased after that magnetic and elusive figure that fascinates them. Baudelaire was the first. He was also the first to touch her, to discover that she is nothing but time that crumbles in one's hands. I am not going to relate my adventures in pursuit of modernity; they are not very different from those of other twentieth-century poets. Modernity has been a universal passion. Since 1850 she has been our goddess and our demoness. In recent years there has been an attempt to exorcise her with talk of "postmodernism." But what is postmodernism, if not a more modern modernity?

For us, as Latin Americans, the search for poetic modernity runs historically parallel to the repeated attempts to modernize our countries. This tendency began at the end of the eighteenth century, and it included Spain, too. The United States was born into modernity, and by 1830 it was already, as Tocqueville observed, the womb of the future; but we were born at a moment when Spain and Portugal were moving away from modernity. That is why there was frequent talk of "Europeanizing" our countries: the modern was outside, it had to be imported.

In Mexican history, this process began just before the War of Independence. Later it became a great ideological and political debate that passionately divided Mexican society throughout the nineteenth century. One event was to call into question not the legitimacy of the reform movement, but the way in which it had been implemented: the Mexican Revolution. Unlike its twentieth-century counterparts, the Mexican Revolution was not really the expression of a vaguely utopian ideology. It was, rather, the explosion of a reality that had been historically and psychologically repressed. It was not the work of a group of ideologists intent on introducing principles derived from a political theory, but a popular uprising that unmasked what was hidden. For this reason, it was more of a revelation than a revolution. Mexico was searching for the present outside only to find it within, buried but alive. The search for modernity led us to discover our antiquity, the hidden face of the nation. I am not sure that this unexpected historical lesson has been learned by all—that between tradition and modernity there is a bridge. When they are mutually isolated, tradition stagnates and modernity vaporizes. When they are joined, modernity breathes life into tradition, while the latter responds with depth and gravity.

The search for poetic modernity was a Quest, in the allegorical and chivalric sense that this word had in the twelfth century. I did not find any Grail, although I did cross several wastelands, visiting castles of mirrors and camping among ghostly tribes. Still, I discovered the modern tradition. For modernity is not a poetic school, it is a lineage, a family dispersed over several continents, which for two centuries has survived many changes and misfortunes: indifference, isolation, and tribunals in the name of religious, political, academic, and sexual orthodoxy. Because it is a tradition and not a doctrine, it has been able to survive and to change at the same time. This is also why it is so diverse: each poetic adventure is distinct, each poet has sown a different plant in the miraculous forest of speaking trees.

If the works are diverse and each route is distinct, what is it that unites all these poets? Not an aesthetic, but a search. My own search was not fanciful, even though the idea of modernity is a mirage, a bundle of reflections. One day I discovered that I was returning to the starting point instead of advancing, that the search for modernity was a descent to the origins. Modernity led me to the source of my beginning, to my antiquity. Separation became reconciliation. Thus I discovered that the poet is a pulse in the rhythmic flow of generations.

The idea of modernity is a byproduct of our conception of history as a unique and linear process of succession. The origins of this conception are in the Judeo-Christian tradition, but it breaks with Christian doctrine. In Christianity, the cyclical time of pagan cultures is supplanted by unrepeatable history, which has a beginning and will have an end. Sequential time was the profane time of history, an arena for the actions of fallen men, yet still governed by a sacred time that had neither a beginning nor an end. And after Judgment Day, there will be no future either in heaven or in hell. In the realm of eternity there is no succession, because everything is. Being triumphs over becoming.

The new time, our concept of time, is linear like that of Christianity, but it is open to infinity, it makes no reference to Eternity. Ours is the time of profane history, an irreversible and perpetually unfinished time that marches toward the future and not toward its end. History's sun is the future. Progress is the name of this movement toward the future.

Christians see the world, or what used to be called the *seculum* or worldly life, as a place of trial: in this world, souls can be lost or saved. In the new conception, by contrast, the historical subject is not the individual soul but the human race, sometimes viewed as a whole and sometimes through a chosen group that represents it: the developed nations of the West, the proletariat, the white race, or some other entity. The pagan and Christian philosophical tradition had exalted Being as changeless perfection overflowing with plenitude, but we adore change; it is the motor of progress and the model for our societies. Change articulates itself in two ways, as evolution and revolution. The trot and the leap. Modernity is the spearhead of historical movement, the incarnation of evolution or revolution, the two faces of progress. And progress takes place by means of the dual action of science and technology, applied to the realm of nature and to the use of her immense resources.

Modern man has defined himself as a historical being. Other societies chose to define themselves in terms of values and ideas different from change: the Greeks venerated the *polis* and the circle, yet they were unaware of progress. Like all the Stoics, Seneca was much exercised by the eternal return; St. Augustine believed that the end of the world was imminent; St. Thomas constructed a scale of being, linking the smallest creature to the Creator; and so on. One after the other, these ideas and beliefs were abandoned. It seems to me that the same decline is beginning to affect our idea of Progress—and, as a result, our vision of time, of history, of ourselves. We are witnessing the twilight of the future.

The decline of the idea of modernity, and the popularity of a notion as dubious as "postmodernism," are phenomena that affect not only literature and the arts. We are experiencing the crisis of the essential ideas and beliefs that have guided mankind for over two centuries. First, the concept of a process open to infinity and synonymous with endless progress has been called into question. I need hardly mention what everybody knows: that the resources of nature are finite and will run out one day. We have inflicted what may be irreparable damage on the natural environment and our own species is endangered. Science and technology, the instruments of progress, have shown with alarming clarity that they can easily become destructive forces. The existence of nuclear weapons is a refutation of the idea that progress is inherent in history—a refutation that can only be called devastating.

Second, we must reckon with the fate of the historical subject, mankind, in the twentieth century. Seldom have nations or individuals suffered so much: two world wars, tyrannies spread over five continents, the atom bomb, the proliferation of one of the cruelest and most lethal institutions known to man: the concentration camp. Modern technology has provided countless benefits, to be sure, but it is impossible to close our eyes to slaughter, torture, humiliation, degradation, and all the other wrongs inflicted on millions of innocent people in our century.

And third, the belief in the necessity of progress has been shaken. For our grandparents and our parents, the ruins of history—the spectacle of corpses, desolate battlefields, devastated cities—did not invalidate the underlying goodness of the historical process. The scaffolds and tyrannies, the conflicts and savage civil wars, were the price to be paid for progress, the blood money to be offered to the god of history. A god? Yes, reason itself was deified and was prodigal in cruel acts of cunning, according to Hegel. But now the alleged rationality of history has banished. And in the very domain of order, regularity, and coherence (in pure sciences like physics), the old notions of accident and catastrophe have reappeared. This disturbing resurrection reminds me of the terrors that marked the advent of the millennium, of the anguish of the Aztecs at the end of each cosmic cycle.

The last in this hasty enumeration of the elements of our crisis marks the collapse of all the philosophical and historical hypotheses that claimed to reveal the laws governing the course of history. The believers, confident that they held the keys to history, erected powerful states over pyramids of corpses. These arrogant constructions, destined in theory to liberate men, were quickly transformed into gigantic prisons. Today we have seen them fall, overthrown not by their ideological enemies, but by the impatience and the desire for freedom of the new generations. Is this the end of all utopias? It is, more precisely, the end of the idea of history as a phenomenon whose outcome can be known in advance. Historical determinism has been a costly and bloodstained fantasy. History is unpredictable, because its agent, mankind, is the personification of indeterminacy.

Thus we are very probably at the end of one historical period and at the beginning of another. The end of the Modern Age, or just a mutation? It is difficult to tell. In any case, the collapse of utopian schemes has left a great void, not in the countries where this ideology has been proved to have failed, but in those countries where many embraced it with enthusiasm and hope. For the first time in history, mankind lives in a sort of spiritual wilderness, no longer in the shadow of the religious and political systems that consoled us even as they oppressed us. All societies are historical, but every society has lived under the guidance and the inspiration of a set of metahistorical beliefs and ideas. Ours is the first age that is ready to live without a metahistorical doctrine.

Whether they be religious or philosophical, moral or aesthetic, our absolutes are not collective, they are private. This is a dangerous experience. It is also impossible to know whether the tensions and the conflicts unleashed in this privatization of ideas, practices, and beliefs that belonged traditionally to the public domain will end up destroying the social fabric. Men could become possessed once more by ancient religious fury or by fanatical nationalism. It would be terrible if the fall of the abstract idol of ideology were to foreshadow the resurrection of the buried passions of tribes, sects, and churches. The signs, unfortunately, are disturbing.

The decline of the ideologists whom I have called metahistorical, by which I mean those that assign to history a goal and a direction, implies a tacit abandonment of global solutions. With good sense, we tend more and more toward limited remedies for concrete problems. It is prudent to abstain from legislating about the future. Still, the present requires much more than attention to its immediate needs. It demands a more rigorous global reflection. For a long time I have firmly believed that the twilight of the future heralds the advent of the now. And to think about the now requires, first of all, a recovery of critical vision. For example: the triumph of the market economy (a triumph that is owed to its adversary's default) cannot be only a cause for joy. As a mechanism the market is efficient, but like all mechanisms it lacks conscience and compassion. We must find a way of integrating it into society so that it expresses the social contract and becomes an instrument of justice and fairness. The advanced democratic societies have reached the enviable level of prosperity, but at the same time they are islands of abundance in the ocean of universal misery.

The question of the market is intricately related to the deterioration of the environment. Pollution affects not only the air, the rivers, and the forests, it also affects our souls. A society possessed by the frantic need to produce more in order to consume more tends to reduce ideas, feelings, art, love, friendship, and people themselves to consumer products. Everything becomes a thing to be bought, used, and thrown on the rubbish heap. No other society has produced so much waste, material and moral, as ours.

Reflecting on the now does not imply relinquishing the future or forgetting the past: the present is the meeting place for the three directions of time. Neither can it be confused with facile hedonism. The tree of pleasure does not grow in the past or in the future, but at this very moment. Yet death is also a fruit of the present. It cannot be denied, for it, too, is a part of life. Living well implies dying well. We have to learn to look death in the face. The present is alternately luminous and somber, like a sphere that unites the two halves of action and contemplation. Thus, just as we have had philosophies of the past and of the future, of eternity and of the void, we shall have a philosophy of the present. The poetic experience could be one of its foundations. What do we know about the present? Nothing, or almost nothing. Yet poets do know at least one thing: that the present is the source of presences.

In my pilgrimage in search of modernity, I lost my way in many places, only to find myself again. I returned to the source and discovered that modernity is not outside us, but within us. It is today and the most ancient antiquity; it is tomorrow and the beginning of the world; it is a thousand years old and newborn. It speaks in Nahuatl, draws Chinese ideograms from the ninth century, appears on the television screen. This intact present, recently unearthed, shakes off the dust of centuries, smiles, and suddenly starts to fly, disappearing through the window. A simultaneous plurality of time and presence: modernity breaks with the immediate past only to recover an age-old past, and to transform a tiny fertility figure from the Neolithic age into our contemporary.

We pursue modernity in her incessant metamorphoses, but we never trap her. She always escapes; each encounter ends in flight. We embrace her, and she disappears immediately: it was just a little air. It is the instant, that bird that is everywhere and nowhere. We want to capture it alive, but it flaps its wings and vanishes in the form of a handful of syllables. We are left empty-handed. And then the doors of perception open slightly and the other time appears, the real time, the one that we were searching for without knowing it: the present, the presence.

U.S. FOOD AID TO SOVIET UNION
December 12, 1990

Saying that the Soviet Union "is facing tough times, difficult times,"
President George Bush on December 12 extended it federally guaran-
teed credits to buy $1 billion worth of American farm goods. The food
would alleviate shortages that had compelled several large Soviet cities
to impose rationing. At Bush's side for the announcement in the White
House Rose Garden was Soviet foreign minister Eduard A.
Shevardnadze, who did not attempt to gloss over his country's condi-
tion. "[T]here is a certain instability in the Soviet Union,"
Shevardnadze said in response to a reporter's question, "and we are
worried about that, that's a fact."

Bush said he was acting "to help the Soviet Union stay the course of
democratization and to undertake market reforms." He obviously wanted
to help the author of those reforms, Gorbachev, retain control in a time of
economic and political crisis in the Soviet Union. The European Eco-
nomic Community took a similar step December 14 by approving $2.4
billion in emergency food, medical, and technical assistance for the Soviet
Union. The community's twelve national leaders who met in Rome were
intent on helping Gorbachev rebuff Communist hard-liners who wanted
to sabotage his policies.

However, Gorbachev's resolve to move ahead with reforms was soon
thrown in doubt by puzzling events in the Soviet Union. Shevardnadze's
remarks about instability seemed prophetic, for only eight days later he
abruptly resigned as foreign minister with a dramatic but cryptic
warning that "reactionaries" were pushing his country toward dictator-
ship. (Soviet Foreign Minister Shevardnadze Resigns, p. 825)

Gorbachev's Hard-Liner Support

Shevardnadze's departure appeared to weaken Gorbachev's already diminishing support among reformers who wanted to move faster and farther than he had. The Soviet leader's political survival appeared increasingly dependent on Kremlin conservatives, including orthodox Marxists, who had opposed both his domestic and his foreign policies. A number of them had complained that to receive Western economic aid was humiliating. Vladimir A. Kryuchkov, chief of the Soviet secret police agency KGB, went a step further on December 22 by suggesting that this aid was also sinister.

Speaking to the Congress of People's Deputies, the national legislature, Kryuchkov warned that spying would be conducted under the pretext of economic contacts. Moreover, he insisted that Westerners would cheat their Soviet partners and impose an alien capitalist outlook on the country. His speech was made at the request of deputies who wanted to hear how the KGB was carrying out its orders to crack down on black marketeering and economic sabotage. In that regard, he complained that "self-seekers" took advantage of liberalized economic rules to enrich themselves.

Other Trade Restrictions Intact

Although Shevardnadze's resignation and Kryuchkov's comments cast a pall over U.S.-Soviet relations, at year's end the Bush administration had not withdrawn the offer of food aid. To make credits available to the Soviet Union, Bush used statutory authority to lift portions of a trade-restriction law for six months. The law, the so-called Jackson-Vanik Act of 1974, banned export credits until the Soviet Union permitted free emigration. Specifically, Bush lifted the law's restriction on loans issued under the auspices of the Commodity Credit Corporation, an agency of the Agriculture Department, and authorized up to $1 billion in federally guaranteed loans.

Gorbachev eased Soviet controls on emigration, permitting 150,000 Soviet Jews to move to Israel and 50,000 to the United States in 1990. In response to freer emigration, Bush joined Gorbachev in signing a trade treaty in June 1990 that would lift nearly all U.S. restrictions on its Soviet trade.

However, Bush said he would not send the treaty to Congress for approval until the Soviet Union enacted a law that codified its liberalized emigration practices. That law had not been enacted when Bush suspended the export-credit ban, so other restrictions on trade with the Soviet Union, some dating from 1951, remained in effect.

However, Bush took another step to aid the Soviet Union by saying he would ask the International Monetary Fund (IMF) and the World Bank to grant it "special association," a status short of full membership but giving Moscow access to the economic and financial expertise of the two international lending institutions.

Following is the text of President George Bush's announce-
ment of food assistance for the Soviet Union and of a news
conference also attended by Soviet foreign minister Eduard
A. Shevardnadze and Secretary of State James A. Baker III,
December 12, 1990:

PRESIDENT BUSH: Mr. Minister, welcome. I have a brief statement, and then I will turn the conference here, press conference, over to Minister [Eduard A.] Shevardnadze and Secretary of State [James A.] Baker to respond to questions.

But I have just had an opportunity to discuss with Foreign Minister Shevardnadze a number of issues of U.S.-Soviet relations, including our cooperation in the gulf, and I am pleased with the great progress that we made on START [Strategic Arms Reduction Treaty] and hopeful that we will be ready to sign a treaty at a summit in Moscow on February 11th through 13th.

We also talked, at length, about the situation in the Soviet Union and the response of the United States to the economic problems there.

I asked Minister Shevardnadze to convey to President [Mikhail S.] Gorbachev my desire to respond both to the short-term needs of the Soviet Union and to contribute to fundamental economic reform, long supported, *perestroika* and continue to—

We discussed, frankly, the relationship of economic change in the Soviet Union to the critical task of democratization, and I reiterated our strong desire to see both political and economic reform continue because they are inextricably linked.

I outlined specific and important steps that we're willing to take in support of reform. And after consulting closely with [Agriculture] Secretary [Clayton] Yeutter as well as secretaries Brady [Treasury Secretary Nicholas F. Brady] and Baker, I told Minister Shevardnadze that I am prepared to respond to a Soviet request for credit guarantees for a purchase of agricultural commodities through a waiver of the Jackson-Vanik amendment.

While I've taken this step, I still look forward to a passage of Soviet emigration law, codifying the generally excellent practices of the past year.

And this, then, will permit us to make further progress toward the normalization of the U.S.-Soviet economic relationship.

In addition, we've proposed to the Soviets a special technical assistance project to help in assessing their food distribution problem and to support market reforms. I will also authorize a joint public-private medical assistance effort to help the Soviet Union cope with immediate shortages of pharmaceuticals and basic medical supplies.

In the longer term, only steps that the Soviet Union itself takes can ensure the economic health there. Thus, to promote fundamental economic reform, I will propose that the World Bank and the IMF [International Monetary Fund] work out with the Soviet Union a special association to give the U.S.S.R. access to the considerable financial and economic expertise of those institutions.

I have asked Secretary of the Treasury Nick Brady, as U.S. governor of both institutions, to pursue this proposal with them and also with our other allies, who I'm sure will be in accord.

As I've said before, I want *perestroika* to succeed. The Soviet Union is facing tough times, difficult times. But I believe that this is a good reason to act now, in order to help the Soviet Union stay the course of democratization and to undertake market reforms.

The United States has an interest in a Soviet Union able to play a role as a full and prosperous member of the international community of states. And I am hopeful that these initiatives will further that goal.

Mr. Minister, we're delighted you're here, and I'll turn this over to you and Jim Baker.

Q: Mr. President, does that mean the START treaty has been completed?

BUSH: The question will be handled by the secretary of State.

BAKER: Let me answer your question about a START treaty by saying that we made some very good progress, I think, in Houston.

There are still some issues that remain, and I think beyond that the president's statement speaks for itself. We would hope very much that the treaty would be ready—would hope that it would be ready for signature over the February 11th to 13th date in Moscow.

Q: What are the remaining issues? What issues were resolved that hadn't been resolved before Shevardnadze came to Houston?

BAKER: The issues are very technical issues, involving a number of different—some verification issues, issues respecting monitoring of solid-rocket facilities or missile-assembly facilities.

I'm sure you're quite familiar with the perimeter-portal monitoring concept, Jim. It's those kind of issues we're still struggling with, and we still have quite a few of those to deal with.

Now, the minister said inside that he thought it would be useful if we had an in-depth discussion in here of telemetry encryption and the problem of the shroud that's involved in that. But we decided not to do that. But those are the kind of issues that we're dealing with.

Q: How much export credits? Mr. Secretary, how much should we consider the steps taken today to be a payoff for the Soviets' cooperation on the gulf crisis?

BAKER: You shouldn't consider any of the steps taken today to be a payoff or a payback for the cooperation that we've seen on the gulf crisis.

We see that cooperation across a broad range of issues.

We've talked about our cooperation with respect to settling regional conflicts, our cooperation with respect to arms control, and this pattern and spirit of cooperation developed many years ago and has been improving as we move along.

So none of the issues today — I mean none of the measures announced today are in any sense a payback.

It is very much in the national interests of the United States to see the Soviet Union succeed in their efforts to reform politically and to move to a free market economic system.

Q: Mr. Secretary, did the minister make specific economic requests? And if so, was there anything that you turned down?

BAKER: There was nothing that was turned down. The only request had to do with a request not for grant assistance or gifts, if you will, but for credits that would permit the purchase of food supplies under our commodity credit program, and the president's decision to waive Jackson-Vanik will permit that.

Q: How much? Can I ask about your opinion of the Soviet Union?

BAKER: Five hundred million to a billion, somewhere in that—in that range.

Q: Immediately available or do they have to be subject to USDA [Department of Agriculture] review of creditworthiness, or are they available immediately?

BAKER: The mechanics of implementing that will be up to the folks that run the Commodity Credit Corporation program. It's my understanding that within certainly the lower end of that range there is some flexibility in the program, but that's up to them to determine.

The president has made it possible through waiving Jackson-Vanik.

Q: Is it bulk grain or value-added? Mr. Secretary, was your decision [inaudible] repeatedly that the problem that's concerned U.S. officials has been the distribution of food within the Soviet Union?

How will this effort by the United States assist in that problem, which U.S. officials have said is at the heart of the matter?

BAKER: One of the things the president announced was a technical economic assistance program to assist with the problems of distribution. The problems that exist today, I think—and we discussed this in Houston—have been and are being considered by the Soviet leadership in terms of making sure that the supplies which are purchased on the basis of these credits get where they want them to go. Now, they know exactly where they expect to see shortages during the course of this winter, as they move toward a market economy.

Q: Mr. President, was your decision driven by any fear that the Soviet Union is unstable?

And if I may also direct that question to Minister Shevardnadze. Sir, do you consider in any respect your country on the brink of civil war?

SHEVARDNADZE [through interpreter]: Let me just say a few words in connection with President Bush's remarks. I believe that he has made a very important statement, particularly as regards President Bush's visit to the Soviet Union.

We understand that during the visit of President Bush to the Soviet Union, very important agreements will be signed. First of all, the first treaty reducing strategic offensive arms, a treaty that the whole world is interested in seeing.

And in addition to that, a very important package of other agreements is emerging, and it will be signed, as regards our cooperation in trade and the economy, in science and technology, and specifically I would like to mention the investment treaty.

And secondly, the president has made a very important statement about his support for the changes happening in the Soviet Union. And I am referring to his decision to waive the Jackson-Vanik amendment, and that will make it possible to give credits for the supplies of food to the Soviet Union.

I know that it was not easy for the president to make that decision, and therefore we very much appreciate the president's decision, and I am sure that everyone in the Soviet Union will welcome and appreciate that decision.

I also believe that it is very important that the president has decided to favor a special status of association for the Soviet Union with the International Monetary Fund and the World Bank.

A question has been asked here whether this was some kind of payoff or payback for some cooperation from the Soviet Union, or this means that we are in a new relationship, a new full-scale relationship with the United States.

I think what the president has just announced and what the secretary of State, and the secretary of State's remarks show that we are indeed in a very new phase of our relations.

There was no crisis in the Persian Gulf when our two presidents met at Malta, and then there were other talks and discussions between them, and I am also referring to our ministerial meetings at Wyoming and at Irkutsk where we spoke about cooperation and partnership.

And all the other things, such as the Persian Gulf crisis and our cooperation on the Security Council resolutions, that was after those important events.

And let me say how profoundly I am gratified that we, indeed, are witnessing a new relationship, a new kind of cooperation between our two countries.

Let me express my gratification and my appreciation to the people of the United States, to the president and the secretary of State for the support of your country at this very difficult time for us.

Q: Is your country unstable? Mr. Minister, is your country unstable?

Mr. Shevardnadze, you could have been free of the Jackson-Vanik provisions a long time ago if your country had passed an emigration law.

Why wasn't that done so that you wouldn't have been put in this bind? And, Secretary Baker, what assurances do you really have that these promises will be met?

SHEVARDNADZE [through interpreter]: Well, I agree with you. But, as you might know, the draft emigration law has been prepared. The Soviet foreign ministry is one of the authors of that legislation. That legislation has been adopted in first reading by the Supreme Soviet. And I have no doubt that very soon there will be a final vote and that legislation will become law.

BAKER: Charles, let me simply say that we have received assurances from the minister and the government of the Soviet Union that the pattern of emigration that has pertained over the past months and even years, where there has been a great increase in the ability of people to emigrate from the Soviet Union, will be maintained and will be continued.

And you heard the minister say that they will continue to press the Supreme Soviet to pass the emigration legislation.

Let me make sure that everyone understands here we are talking about a waiver of Jackson-Vanik that permits the Soviet Union to purchase from private sources in the United States food products, primarily grains which — the repayment of which will be guaranteed by the U.S. government. This is not the equivalent of the granting of most-favored-nation trading status. That of course has not been done, and that takes the conclusion of a trade agreement.

Q: Have you seen the IMF study on the Soviet Union yet? Have you seen the IMF study? Do you think the Soviet Union is unstable, and is this decision driven by that calculation?

BAKER: Are you asking me or the minister?

Q: First you. Well, I'd like the minister to address that as well.

SHEVARDNADZE [through interpreter]: The fact that there is a certain instability in the Soviet Union and we are worried about that, that's a fact.

But I will not say that we are on the verge of a [inaudible], that we are on the verge of a civil war; I have no doubt that the Soviet people will cope with our problems.

And I would like to support what the president has just said, and that is, it is up to the Soviet people — above all, it is up to the Soviet people to cope with our problems. And we certainly very much appreciate the U.S. support.

Q: Mr. Secretary, have you seen the trade treaty that—how long is the waiver to be in place?

BAKER: The waiver will have to be reviewed. It's my understanding that the law requires a review in July of 1991.

Q: What about the previous question? What about the instability question, Mr. Secretary?

BAKER: The previous question—you heard the—you heard the minister, foreign minister of the Soviet Union give you an answer with respect to the question of stability. Let me simply say that instability in the Soviet Union is very definitely not, in my view, in the interests of the United States of America, and instability in the Soviet Union is not, in my view at least, in the interests of the world.

SHEVARDNADZE [through interpreter]: Let me add something to what the secretary just said.

It would be a terrible thing if we were unable to assure stability at this time.

It would be a terrible thing for Europe and for the world. It would mean negating the very important treaties signed in Paris, the historic treaties signed in Paris. Let me assure you that we're aware of our responsibility to our people and to the world.

BANK FAILURES' TOLL ON
DEPOSIT INSURANCE FUNDS
December 16, 1990

Huge losses incurred by savings and loan institutions in the 1980s triggered a wave of bankruptcies and compelled the government to begin pumping tens of billions of tax dollars into a depleted deposit insurance fund. Ultimately the fund may require hundreds of billions to protect individual depositors. Even as the Bush administration and Congress devised this bailout, the biggest ever undertaken by the government on behalf of an industry, federal regulators were clearly concerned that the crisis would spill over into banking.

Reports of financial trouble in the banking system grew during 1990, culminating soon after the year's end in the collapse of the Bank of New England, the region's dominant bank. As the situation was portrayed December 16 by L. William Seidman, chairman of the Federal Deposit Insurance Corporation (FDIC), federally insured banks were failing faster than had been expected, and for the third year in a row would draw down a separate fund for insuring bank depositors. Some $4 billion probably would be drained from the fund in 1990 and $5 billion in 1991, moving it perilously close to insolvency, Seidman said in a televised interview on the NBC program "Meet the Press."

However, Seidman insisted that banks generally were in far better shape than the S&Ls—or thrifts, as savings and loan institutions are called. Treasury Secretary Nicholas F. Brady, who appeared on the same television program, agreed. However, Brady said "the banks are not as healthy as we would want them." Seidman foresaw about 180 bank failures in 1991, involving assets of $70 billion. They represented the worst among about 1,000 financially troubled banks.

Seidman thought that the bank fund could be replenished by the 12,000 federally insured banks, without assistance from the Treasury. "We think they have plenty of resources to do that," he said. Effective January 1, 1991, the banks were required to pay into the fund 19.5 cents on each $100 of deposits they held, an increase from the previous level of 12 cents. Seidman favored further increases until each bank paid the equivalent of 1 percent of its deposits, which he estimated would add $20 billion to $25 billion to the fund. Many bankers objected that higher assessments reduce a bank's ability to attain profitability. The question was expected to be considered by Congress in 1991 as part of a fuller look at the structure of the banking business.

Banks' Financial Troubles

Many of Seidman's remarks appeared to be in response to a study prepared for the House Subcommittee on Financial Institutions by economists James R. Barth, R. Dan Brumbaugh, and Robert E. Litan. They calculated that even a mild economic recession in 1991 could swamp the banks' deposit insurance fund and force a rescue with taxpayers' money, as was done with the S&Ls. They noted that banking was far less profitable than it once had been.

Several of the biggest American commercial banks suffered from defaults on foreign loans they made in the 1970s, and many banks were hurt by a decline in real estate prices in the late 1980s. Their lending in both markets was spurred by deregulation of financial markets in that decade, which tended to blur the distinction between banks, S&Ls, and other types of financial institutions.

It was deregulation in the form of lax oversight and enforcement in the mid- to late 1980s, critics say, that was chiefly responsible for an avalanche of S&L failures in the second half of the decade. As insolvency took its toll, the number of operating thrifts fell from 3,993 at the beginning of the decade to 2,878 at the end. More than 500 of those still in business were reported to be technically insolvent—the government could not yet afford to close them down—and more than 100 others were operating on perilously low capital reserves.

Inadequacy of 1989 S&L Legislation

In February 1989, nearly a decade after the first casualties of the S&L crisis appeared, the Bush administration submitted legislation to Congress for closing the insolvent thrifts and selling their assets. The initiative led to passage of the Financial Institutions Reform, Recovery, and Enforcement Act of 1989, which President George Bush signed into law August 9, 1989. The new law earmarked $114 billion to close or merge the bankrupt S&Ls. (President Bush's Remarks on Signing S&L Bailout Bill, Historic Documents of 1989, p. 463)

The law also reorganized the federal deposit insurance structure, setting up the Savings Association Insurance Fund for S&L depositors

*and the Bank Insurance Fund for commercial banks—both under control
of the FDIC—replacing agencies that had gone bankrupt. Seidman
directed the overall bailout effort. He remained as FDIC director and was
placed in charge of the new Resolution Trust Corporation (RTC). Its
functions were to "resolve," that is close, the bankrupt thrifts and sell off
their assets, or merge them with healthy institutions.*

*The bailout legislation assumed that the government would take over
about 400 S&Ls. But conditions in the industry worsened during 1989,
and the year ended with record losses of $19.2 billion in the industry. As
losses mounted, estimates of the bailout cost soared. Federal Reserve
chairman Alan Greenspan and General Accounting Office director
Charles A. Bowsher said on separate occasions during the early months of
1990 that a final price tag of $500 billion was possible.*

*Brady told Congress in May that 1,000 savings institutions— about 40
percent of the total—were endangered. Two months later, Seidman said
the S&L bailout fund would need a new infusion of $100 billion from the
government in 1991. Congress recessed in October without making any
more money available; the RTC was expected to tap $18.8 billion in
disputed borrowing authority during the early months of 1991 to stay in
business.*

"Keating Inquiry" in Congress

*The savings and loan scandal left Congress with additional problems.
The Senate Ethics Committee spent much of 1990 looking into allegations that five senators exerted improper influence on behalf of Charles
H. Keating, Jr., to try to keep federal regulators from closing his Lincoln
Savings and Loan Association in California. The delayed closing occurred
in April 1989, at an expected cost to the government of $2 billion. The
committee recessed its hearings until 1991 without deciding whether any
of the accused members had violated Senate rules. The five were Alan
Cranston, D-Calif.; Dennis DeConcini, D-Ariz.; John Glenn, D-Ohio;
John McCain, R-Ariz.; and Donald W. Riegle, Jr., D-Mich.*

*Together the senators' reelection campaigns and their other political
causes received $1.3 million from Keating. They acknowledged they had
acted in his behalf, but protested that they did not do so for his money
but because he was a friend or constituent. Publicity focusing on the
Keating case made it a symbol of the entire costly debacle of S&L
failures. Keating was the best-known "S&L kingpin," as he was sometimes characterized in the press.*

*While the ethics question was before Congress, Keating served a month
in jail following his arrest on a California criminal fraud indictment, and
he faced civil racketeering charges. Attorney General Dick Thornburgh
told the Senate Judiciary Committee in July that significant fraud had
been detected in about 25 percent to 30 percent of the savings institutions
that collapsed. He said the Justice Department was looking into about
18,000 criminal referrals involving about 310 thrifts.*

*In another development, the FDIC filed a civil lawsuit September 21
against President Bush's son Neil and ten other directors or officers of
the Silverado Banking Savings and Loan Association in Denver, charging
them with attempting to conceal Silverado's bad financial condition and
consequently making the government's takeover of Silverado more costly.
The government sought $200 million in damages. Bush, a Denver oil man,
served on Silverado's board of directors for three years, until August 1988.
The government seized the thrift six months later. In a separate action in
September, Bush appeared before an administrative law judge in Denver
to deny charges that he violated conflict-of-interest rules in handling
Silverado's transactions with his business partners.*

> *Following are excerpts from an NBC News transcript of its
> "Meet the Press" program televised December 16, 1990, in
> which Treasury Secretary Nicholas F. Brady and Federal
> Deposit Insurance Corporation chairman L. William
> Seidman discussed bank failures with interviewers Irving R.
> Levine of NBC News, Alan Murray of the* Wall Street
> Journal, *and moderator Garrick Utley of NBC News:*

...**MR. UTLEY:** Many big banks are feeling the pains of this recession;
many of them are in trouble.

How worried are you about the banking system, particularly the major
banks in this country?

SECRETARY BRADY: Well, I think that, as Bill Seidman will tell
you later in the program, the banks are not as healthy as we would want
them. But I think a very important distinction ought to be made between
what went on in the S&L industry and what's going on in the banking
industry.

The banks have $200 billion worth of capital with another $60 billion in
reserves. When the S&L industry got into trouble, it had $10 billion—10
billion then when they got into trouble, $200 billion plus reserves now.
That's a vast difference.

MR. UTLEY: But there's also a difference now because the FDIC has
fewer funds to cover deposits that have to be compensated for. Mr.
Seidman is going to say he's going to have to come to somebody for more
funds in the next couple of years.

Should he come to the public funds, to the Treasury?

SECRETARY BRADY: Well, wait for Bill Seidman's answer. But I
think what he's going to tell you is that there are plans afoot which are
satisfactory plans, plans that will work, whereby the buttressing up of the
bank insurance fund, which I think he believes in, can be accomplished
through private sources alone, i.e., the banking community.

MR. MURRAY: Mr. Secretary, a decade ago when the savings and loan
industry first got into trouble, the Reagan administration said the way
we're going to deal with this is to give the savings and loan industry new

powers to go into new businesses.

Now, right now your department is working on a plan to deal with the banking industry and its troubles, saying that one of the ways we're going to deal with this is give banks new powers to go into new businesses. Why shouldn't the taxpayer be grabbing his wallet?

SECRETARY BRADY: Good question, Alan, but, as I mentioned, it's totally different. It's one thing to have the powers to go into new businesses if you have the capital. And I think that the plan that we're going to come forward with will ensure that the banks do have the capital. We simply have to—with regard to what's going to happen to the banking industry, we have to realize this is a different world. You have an 800—you can call an 800 number and make a purchase any place in the United States. If you go to North Dakota or California, even though you have a bank in Virginia, all you have to do is pull out your credit card.

Things are different. We should adapt our banking system to the changes that are taking place in the world, and put it back on the map as number one.

MR. MURRAY: The public has gotten a little bit of a mixed message on these banking issues from the administration lately, partly because White House chief of staff John Sununu and some others in the administration are criticizing regulators for being too tough on banks—cutting back credit.

Can you clear that up for us? Why are we getting this mixed message about whether regulators are being too tough on banks or not being tough enough?

SECRETARY BRADY: Yes, I sure can. I don't think there is a difference in Governor Sununu's point of view, certainly not in the president's point of view, not in my point of view. What we've said is quite clear. Let's use common sense. Regulators should not over-regulate, and commercial bankers ought to fulfill their obligations to longstanding customers to lend them the money they need for good and constructive projects which will create jobs and investment. . . .

MR. UTLEY: Final quick question, Mr. Secretary, in terms of individual bank accounts and the FDIC insurance. It's $100,000 per account. Do you think that's too expensive? Do you think it should be cut back or limited under future legislation?

SECRETARY BRADY: Garrick, again, that is—it's a good question that's right at the center of our study. We haven't made a conclusion. We haven't had a chance to talk to the president who—I'm, again, old-fashioned: I believe he deserves the information from Cabinet members first so he can make his mind up. We're going to do that; you'll have the answer shortly.

MR. UTLEY: Mr. Secretary, Secretary Brady, thank you very much for being with us this morning here on "Meet the Press."

Next, we'll get some answers about that and other questions. Our guest will be William Seidman—chairman of the Federal Deposit Insurance

Corporation—as we continue. . . .

MR. UTLEY: Mr. Seidman, your reserves at the FDIC are now at the lowest level in terms of accounts across the nation in the 56-year history of the FDIC. Aren't you very concerned about that?

MR. SEIDMAN: Well, we are concerned, and we think we have to do something about it. That's why [we] are working with the Treasury Department and the secretary to develop a recapitalization plan for the fund.

MR. UTLEY: Who pays for that?

MR. SEIDMAN: The bankers are going to pay for that. We think they have plenty of resources to do that. And we expect that they will agree that that's what ought to be done.

MR. UTLEY: About three months ago you said the FDIC would have to be paying about $3 billion this year to cover some of these accounts that have gone bust. This week you upped that to $4 billion. Is that the top, or is this open-ended?

MR. SEIDMAN: Well, predicting the future is always uncertain. And since my record is not too good this year, I don't want to be nailed down with any particular number. But we think right now that $4 billion is probably the right number for 1990. And we just have our new forecast for 1991, which looks like another $5-billion loss.

MR. UTLEY: So it's going up?

MR. SEIDMAN: We will be down to $4 billion reserves at that time. That's clearly not sufficient, and that's why we need a recapitalization plan.

MR. LEVINE: The extent of the problem is indicated in a report that the Congress will receive tomorrow which indicates that over the next three years the fund may be short some $63 billion to cover bank failures. . . .

MR. SEIDMAN: Well, that report is trying to forecast, you know, three years ahead. Really, no one's record is very good. We may be in an economic boom by that time, so I don't take too seriously the three-year forecast because I don't think anybody can do that.

I think the report is useful, and it shows—as our own numbers show— that we're under stress and that we need more funds.

MR. LEVINE: From the taxpayer point of view, does this mean that we're headed for an S&L-scale type bail-out for the nations' banks?

MR. SEIDMAN: No, it doesn't. Our own figures show that, even if we took their highest number, which is $60-some billion, with the recapitalization we'll have over $50 billion in hand to meet that. So at worst there would be a small additional amount needed to be borrowed from the Treasury.

MR. LEVINE: Now, a lot depends on what happens in the economy, of course. How would you describe the state of the economy at present?

MR. SEIDMAN: Well, I think we're in a downturn. We're in the beginning of what may be a recession. We'll have to wait and see.

MR. LEVINE: I spoke to you the other day, Mr. Seidman, and you said, "I'd say it's probably a recession. The real question is not, 'is it a recession,' but how deep and how long it will be."

Do you still hold to that view?

MR. SEIDMAN: Well, that's always the question when you're starting a downturn. Is it going to be mild and short, or steeper or longer? And I don't think anybody knows.

Right now, everything we can see is there's strong, underlying strength, particularly in the export area. But no one knows for sure.

MR. MURRAY: Mr. Seidman, the report that Irving referred to earlier also puts out that one of the problems in the banking industry is that banks continue to pay dividends to their stockholders to keep their stockholders happy, even when they aren't making much money.

Why haven't you stopped that? Why can't you and your regulators crack down on that practice?

MR. SEIDMAN: Well, I think we should stop it. We in the insurance fund—since we pick up the bill when the dividends are too high—have been strong advocates of cutting back on dividends. There are a lot of market considerations that have to be a part of any decision.

But I am certainly for reducing dividends, unless they're paid out of earnings.

MR. MURRAY: So you will be doing that in the future?

MR. SEIDMAN: Well, we'll be working with the other regulators to develop new controls in that area, yes.

MR. MURRAY: Mr. Chairman, some people—including some current members of the Bush administration—think that one of the reasons we're in a recession right now is because of some overzealous regulation by people in your organization at the Comptroller of the Currency and so forth.

Do you think that has anything to do with the economic problems we have right now?

MR. SEIDMAN: Well, it could have something to do with it. I mean, we're all human, and we know that we had a bad experience in the S&L industry; and we're trying to avoid that by making sure our supervision is strong and appropriate.

But that clearly is not in my mind the basic problem. The basic problem is that we have had a period of very high building, very high levels of debt, and we're going to have to live through an adjustment.

MR. UTLEY: Talking about the major banks and the recession, I imagine in your office, in the bottom drawer of your desk, you have a list of major banks on your endangered species list—whatever may happen to them.

Could you share what's on that list? How many banks are you really worried about, and how do they get out of the problem?

MR. SEIDMAN: Well, we do have a list. We have about a thousand banks on that list now. That's down from 1,500 a couple of years ago.

MR. UTLEY: How may of these really important, leading banks, would you [sentence unfinished]

MR. SEIDMAN: Well, I don't want to identify individual banks, but every bank that we think is in trouble is on that list; and every bank that's on that list gets special attention from us to see if we can take them off the list and put them in the recovery room.

MR. UTLEY: Is part of that recovery treatment going to mergers that you would be encouraging or look favorably upon?

MR. SEIDMAN: I think that that will be something that we will be looking at. We will be looking at what kind of actions we can help them take to regain their strength.

MR. UTLEY: There was a bit of a tension this past week when it was discovered or disclosed publicly that about a billion dollars in public funds, Treasury funds, were put in the Bank of New England which has been having some difficulty. That's triple the level of earlier in this year.

Is that the kind of move that, in your view, the public can feel safe and confident about? . . .

MR. SEIDMAN: Well, I think that was kind of much ado about nothing. It was simply put in the Treasury account instead of the Fed account. It was all secured. And I really think it was just something that would help the bank at the moment.

MR. LEVINE: Now, Mr. Seidman, in order to try and recoup for the taxpayers some of the money that's needed for the bail-out of the S&Ls, you're trying to sell property, real estate, which has been acquired from failed S&Ls. You're having trouble selling that property in a depressed market.

And now you plan to give financing of some 85 percent, in some cases, to people who want to buy that property. Doesn't that simply expose the taxpayers to probably greater cost, if these borrowers default on that?

MR. SEIDMAN: Well, the answer to that is no. If they're going to buy property from us, they're going to have a down payment, so we're ahead of the down payment. Hopefully, they'll stay in there on account of that. At worst, we'll get the property back and we'll have their down payment.

MR. LEVINE: The cost of the S&L bail-out varies from month to month. If it is financed over a 10-year period, how much will it cost? And if it's over a 30-year period, how much will it cost?

MR. SEIDMAN: Well, I think the numbers that the secretary gave in the past are still valid for the up-front costs. And when you add in the '88 deals and everything, you're somewhere between $175 and $200 billion. Add to that whatever interest you think is appropriate.

MR. MURRAY: Mr. Seidman, your detractors in the White House—of which there are a few—breathed a sigh of relief earlier this year when you said you were going to be stepping down from your job. But here we are in December and you're still here. Can you tell us something about your plans?

MR. SEIDMAN: Well, I'll certainly be reviewing them as kind of a New

Year's resolution. I haven't really found a good, you know, quiet time when I can slip away. But I'll be thinking about what I ought to do and make a New Year's resolution in that regard.

MR. UTLEY: William Seidman, we'll wait to see what that resolution is so you can come back and tell us in January.

MR. SEIDMAN: Thank you.

RESIGNATION OF
SOVIET FOREIGN MINISTER
December 20, 1990

Soviet Foreign Minister Eduard A. Shevardnadze, the principal archi-tect of president Mikhail S. Gorbachev's policy of friendship with the West, abruptly resigned December 20 with a warning that "dictatorship is coming" to the Soviet Union. Shevardnadze's surprise announcement stunned his audience, the Congress of People's Deputies, which included Gorbachev. "I cannot reconcile myself to what is happening in my country," the foreign minister said in his brief, impassioned speech. However, Shevardnadze did not say precisely what so troubled him about Soviet affairs that he perceived a dictatorship in the making. Nor did he make clear whether he thought Gorbachev himself was about to impose iron rule or was telling Gorbachev and liberal legislators to beware of "reactionaries" intent on doing so.

Shevardnadze went to the podium in the Kremlin Palace of Congresses because members of the congress, the partly elected national legislature, insisted that he justify his record as foreign minister. He had come under attack for negotiating disarmament treaties that reduced Soviet military power, for the collapse of Communist governments in Eastern Europe, for Moscow's consent to the reunification of Germany, and—most recently—for cooperation with the United States in opposition to Iraq.

Instead of reading a detailed rebuttal, the foreign minister handed his prepared remarks to Gorbachev and turned to the hushed audience, saying "I have perhaps the shortest and most difficult speech of my life." He went on, red-faced and obviously angry, alluding to but not naming a host of critics who he said were personally insulting and "hounding" him. Shevardnadze spoke of "reactionaries" menacing the country and men-

tioned "boys in colonel's epaulets," an obvious reference to two outspoken army colonels whose barbed criticism of him and his foreign policy was condoned by their military superiors.

Shevardnadze contended that his attackers sought to undermine Gorbachev's course of reconciliation with the West. Gorbachev was quick to assert that his foreign minister's departure did not signal a change in foreign policy. The same day Shevardnadze spoke, the congress voted overwhelmingly to restate its support of that policy.

Gorbachev appeared hurt and perplexed by Shevardnadze's speech. Several hours later the Soviet leader went to the same podium and accused his former colleague and confidant of deserting him in a time of crisis. "Now, perhaps, is our most difficult time, and to leave at this time is unforgivable," Gorbachev said. "This must be condemned." Nevertheless, he recalled that the two had worked closely together for a decade to bring about perestroika, the restructuring of Soviet society, and he referred to Shevardnadze as "Eduard Amvrosievich"—using a form of address that connotes friendship or intimacy. Shevardnadze, in turn, addressed Gorbachev as Mikhail Sergeyevich, calling him a "friend" and "fellow thinker" to whom "I express profound gratitude."

What "hurts most," Gorbachev said, was that Shevardnadze did not speak to him in advance about resigning. Moreover, he did not "let me fully assess the reasons for his decision" during two phone conversations they held after Shevardnadze's speech, Gorbachev added. The Soviet leader revealed that he had planned to recommend his foreign minister for the new position of vice president.

One week later, at Gorbachev's insistence, the congress approved Gennadi I. Yanayev, an undistinguished apparatchik, for the job. Yanayev, age fifty-four, had spent most of his career in the Communist Youth League and the trade-union organization. He could not obtain the required two-thirds vote of the congress until a second round of balloting, and then only after Gorbachev pleaded that he needed a trusted aide as vice president. Legislators from non-Russian Soviet republics were critical that Gorbachev had chosen a Russian, and reform-minded deputies insisted that the vice president should have been a reformer with a broad background.

Gorbachev's Rightward Tilt

Shevardnadze's resignation, Yanayev's election, and recent anti-Western speeches by Vladimir Kryuchkov, director of the KGB secret police agency, "contributed to the sense that Soviet politics had veered off in a new direction," wrote Soviet affairs specialist Robert Cullen in the New Yorker. "In the conversations I had with friends and acquaintances before and during the Congress, it was taken for granted that the country was entering a period of reaction." Other correspondents in the Soviet Union filed similar reports.

Political observers noted that progressives who had once strongly backed

Gorbachev now accused him of timidity—even backtracking—on matters of political reform, and indecisiveness in dealing with a faltering national economy. Some were turning for leadership to Boris Yeltsin, the Soviet leader's populist rival. Ousted from the Kremlin's inner circle in 1987, Yeltsin made a remarkable comeback in 1989 by defeating Gorbachev's candidate for the presidency of Russia, the biggest of the Soviet republics. Frustrated by Gorbachev's reluctance to commit the Soviet Union to a Western-style market economy, Yeltsin defected from the Communist party during its 28th congress in July 1990 to form and head an opposition party. (Documents from 28th Communist Congress, p. 439)

U.S. Reaction to Shevardnadze Resignation

With his support on the left weakening, Gorbachev was perceived to be seeking support from his former foes on the right, who had opposed his political reforms at home and his hand of friendship to the West. Shevardnadze's resignation and warning reinforced that belief. Washington's reaction to the Soviet foreign minister's departure was cautious, but clearly American officials found the news disquieting. "We would obviously be foolish not to take the warning in Minister Shevardnadze's resignation statement seriously," Secretary of State James A. Baker III said in the first official U.S. response. "But we are pleased President Gorbachev has said that there will be no change in Soviet foreign policy," he added at a State Department news conference.

Baker clearly regretted Shevardnadze's leaving. "On a personal note," the secretary of state said, "let me say that I've known Eduard Shevardnadze to be a man of his word, a man of courage, conviction and principle." They had met seventeen times since March 1989 and were reported to have developed a harmonious working relationship. Shevardnadze, like Baker, was not a career diplomat. And each had developed a close working relationship with his boss. Baker had won the reputation of a loyal and trusted adviser to Bush; Shevardnadze claimed a similar status with Gorbachev.

Born January 28, 1928, Shevardnadze was reared in a Georgian village, the son of a schoolteacher. Intent on a political career, he studied at a Communist party school and rose quickly in Komsomol, the organization of young Communists. As the minister of internal affairs for the Georgian republic in 1966-1972, he was noted for zealously prosecuting high party officials for corruption and racketeering. Then as the Georgian party secretary in 1972-1986 he drew Gorbachev's attention for using opinion polls to guide his policies and promoting quasi-capitalist experiments to invigorate the republic's economy. In July 1985, four months after assuming power in the Kremlin, Gorbachev named Shevardnadze to replace the aging Andrei A. Gromyko as foreign minister.

In that position, Shevardnadze often related the new Soviet foreign policy to the country's needs to lure Western investments and ease the central government's restraint on restive republics. He reportedly told

Foreign Ministry officials that they should be guided by the "common interests of mankind" rather than a "class war."

> *Following are excerpts from Eduard A. Shevardnadze's speech to the Congress of People's Deputies in Moscow, December 20, 1990, announcing his resignation as Soviet foreign minister, and from President Mikhail S. Gorbachev's response from the same podium later that day, as transcribed and translated by the U.S. Foreign Broadcast Information Service (Shevardnadze's speech) and the Soviet press agency Tass (Gorbachev's):*

SHEVARDNADZE SPEECH

Comrade deputies: I have perhaps the shortest and the most difficult speech of my life....

I would like to make a short statement, comprising two parts.

The first part: Yesterday there were speeches by some comrades—they are our veterans—who raised the question of the need for a declaration to be adopted forbidding the president and the country's leadership from sending troops to the Persian Gulf. That was the approximate content, and this was not the first or the second occasion. There are many such notes and items in the press, on television, and so on.

These speeches yesterday, comrades, overfilled the cup of patience, to put it bluntly. What, after all, is happening with the Persian Gulf? On about 10 occasions both within the country and outside the country's borders I have had to speak and explain the attitude and the policy of the Soviet Union toward this conflict. This policy is serious, well considered, sensible, and in accordance with all standards, present standards, of civilized relations between states. We have friendly relations with the state of Iraq. They have been built up over years. These relations are being preserved, but we have no moral right at all to reconcile ourselves to aggression and the annexation of a small, defenseless country. In that case we would have had to strike through everything that has been done in recent years by all of us, by the whole country, and by the whole of our people in the field of asserting the principles of the new political thinking. This is the first thing.

Second, I have been repeatedly explaining—and Mikhail Sergeyevich [Gorbachev] spoke of this in his speech at the Supreme Soviet—that the Soviet leadership does not have any plans—I do not know, maybe someone else has some plans, some group—but official bodies, the Defense Ministry—and they are now accusing the foreign minister of having such a plan, a plan to land troops in the Persian Gulf, in that region. I have been explaining and saying that there are no plans like this, they do not exist in practice. Nobody is planning to send even one serviceman in a military uniform, even one representative of the Armed Forces of the Soviet Union.

This was said. But someone needed to raise this issue, this problem again. I know what is happening in the corridors of the congress.

The third issue. I said there and I confirm and state it publicly that if the interests of Soviet people are encroached upon, if just one person suffers—wherever it could happen, in any country, not just in Iraq but in any other country—yes, the Soviet Government, the Soviet side will stand up for the interests of its citizens. I think that deputies should back up, should back up the Soviet leadership in this. [applause] I would like to raise another question. Excuse me, is it all accidental? Is it an accident that two members of the legislature made a statement saying that the minister of internal affairs was removed successfully and the time has come to settle accounts with the foreign minister?

This statement has been circulated literally throughout the world press and in our newspapers. Are they such daredevils, these lads—I will call them that, age permits me to because they are really young, in a colonel's shoulderboards—to address such statements to a minister, to a member of the government? Look in the newspaper, I will not name a single name today. What is surprising, I believe one must think seriously about this: Who stands behind these comrades, and what sort of thing is this? Why does no one deny it and say that this is not so, that there are no such plans? Perhaps there are such plans?

In this connection permit me to say a few words about the personal worth of the man, about his personal sufferings, because many people think that the ministers who sit there or the members of the government or the president or someone else are hired, are being hired and that they can do what they like with them. I think that is impermissible. In this connection I remember that party congress. Was this really a chance phenomenon? Because at the congress a real struggle developed, a most acute struggle, between the reformers and—I will not say conservatives, I respect the conservatives because they have their own views which are acceptable to society—but the reactionaries, precisely the reactionaries. [applause] Furthermore, this battle, it must be stated bluntly, was won with merit by the progressive section, by the progressive members, delegates, by the progressively-minded delegates to the congress. I would like to recall that it was against my will, without being consulted, that my name, I, my candidacy, was included for secret voting, and I had 800 against; 800 delegates voted against. What then: Is this random, or on purpose? Is the Foreign Ministry's policy not good enough? Or am I personally undesirable? This is a serious matter, more than serious. I say that, all the same, this is not a random event. Excuse me, I am now going to recall the Supreme Soviet session. At Comrade Lukyanov's initiative, literally just before the start of the sitting, a serious matter was included on the agenda about the treaties with the German Democratic Republic. As it happened, I was on my travels, and they called in deputies, and people found themselves in an utterly stupid position, and the issue was a flop. I myself had to speak the following week. How did it turn out? Those same people who are now speaking as the authors came out with serious accusations against the foreign minister, of unilateral concessions, of incompetence, lack of skills, and so on and so forth. Not one person could be found, including the person in the chair, to reply and say simply that this was dishonorable, that this is not the way, not how things are done in civilized states. I find this deeply worrying.

Things went as far as personal insults. I endured that, too. Comrades, a hounding is taking place. I will not name the publications, all manner of publications, the Pamyat society—I add the Pamyat society to these publications—what expressions: Down with the Gorbachev clique! They also add Shevardnadze and several other names. Who are they, the so-called reformers? I will put it bluntly, comrades: I was shaken; I was shaken by the events of the first day, the start of the work of our congress. By the pressing of a button, the fate not only of the president but of perestroyka and democratization was decided. Is that normal? Democrats, I will put it bluntly: comrade democrats, in the widest meaning of this word, you have scattered. The reformers have gone to seed. Dictatorship is coming; I state this with complete responsibility. No one knows what kind of dictatorship this will be and who will come—what kind of dictator—and what the regime will be like.

I want to make the following statement: I am resigning. Let this be—and do not respond, and do not curse me—let this be my contribution, if you like, my protest against the onset of dictatorship.

I express profound gratitude to Mikhail Sergeyevich Gorbachev. I am his friend. I am a fellow thinker of his. I have always supported, and will support to the end of my days, the ideas of perestroyka, the ideas of renewal, the ideas of democracy, of democratization. We have done great things in the international arena. But, I think that it is my duty, as a man, as a citizen, as a Communist; I cannot reconcile myself to the events taking place in our country and to the trials awaiting our people. I nevertheless believe, I believe that the dictatorship will not succeed, that the future belongs to democracy and freedom.

Thank you very much. [applause]

GORBACHEV REMARKS

I would not like to either simplify the situation or dramatize it excessively. The main thing is not to panic, not to grow hysterical or engage in indictments for which we will feel sorry tomorrow.

This very serious situation has indeed reached a climax. We must try to sort it out. We found it possible and advisable for speeches by Ryzhkov, Kryuchkov and Shevardnadze, we agreed to grant twice the time for them to be able to set out their assessments and proposals at this congress. All this seemed to fit into the normal process as envisaged by us.

But Eduard Shevardnadze's statement of his resignation came as a surprise to me. Frankly speaking, this is what hurts most.

My telephone conversations with him—we've had two already—do not let me fully assess the reasons for his decision. We have agreed to meet, sit down and discuss everything.

I would not dot all i's, would not pass a judgment such as an unequivocal condemnation of Shevardnadze's move. Or, on the other hand, ask him, despite and regardless of what has happened, to revoke his statement. I believe that we need to think it over, to think it through. I will tell you why.

What he said here and to me over the telephone testifies to the fact that Eduard Amvrosiyevich made this move to protest against those seeking to take advantage of the difficulties and undermine perestroika policy, its main directions for the renewal of society.

He believes that this assault has acquired a planned character as a series of attacks. He found it necessary to resort to the most acute forms to disrupt this assault and stop those who want to exploit the situation to draw us away from the line we are pursuing. These are the reasons he set out here and to me. It is not his personal interest.

I share his conviction in the sense that we must defend perestroika—I proclaimed this thesis from the outset as the principal task to be accomplished by this congress.

The actual situation in which this, our fourth congress, is taking place is that we all, all of our society, have reached the limit. We must either reconfirm our choice or change our strategy. This, essentially, is the question.

Differences in decisions on tactics, in the pace of perestroika are, after all, details of the process of life, search and coordination. I said in my report: we need to protect this strategy, despite all the losses, miscalculations and mistakes, which engendered heavy consequences and for which we have to take responsibility.

I am not seeking to evade responsibility, but I see that my responsibility lies above all in taking this policy to its logical end in order to make it yield positive results for all of society.

That Comrade Shevardnadze acted the way he did without having talked to the President, I personally disapprove. Moreover I will tell you squarely, now that we have come to this point: I had plans to nominate him for Vice President. This is the way it is. And if I were to dot all the i's—it was not for nothing that I arrived at this decision. This man made his choice long ago regarding the impossibility for us to go on living in the society we all lived in.

Ten years ago, in the well-known situation he began to struggle against certain forces. We knew about it, and those who were close know it all very well.

Like myself, he—when working locally and here—came to the conclusion that, even with the degree of power we had at our disposal, we were unable to fully develop renovation processes. Life called for us to go through all tests and all heated debates in order to arrive at an under-standing that we must use the chance to start changing everything in society. He belongs to this kind of people. . . .

And even after everything I said, I do not want you and me to think now that Shevardnadze is being written off, that he is going down in history. . . .

Now, perhaps, is our most difficult time, and to leave at this time is unforgivable. This must be condemned and the demand should be voiced—to continue the struggle. Whatever the turns, the road we have embarked upon is here to stay and we shall follow it. This is the main thing.

Today, we must confirm before our people and before the world community what we did during the first congress, when we asserted our state's foreign policy, our strategy to normalize international relations, our approaches which are already bearing fruits for all of the present civiliza-tion, having opened the way towards a lengthy peaceful period. . . .

All this calls for urgent measures to establish order, tighten discipline and impart stability to society, measures without which transformations cannot be moved forward.

We have entered the critical stage of these transformations. Dozens of states covered such stages at some or other point of their historical development, and always such transitions called for strong power. . . .

At issue is strong power rather than a dictatorship. One should not blend the two notions. This would be supplanting one notion with the other. As President, I do not have information—and I possess vast information—to prove that somewhere someone has already hatched a junta or another dictatorship of this kind for us. I do not have this information in my possession.

But if we are irresponsible, thoughtless, if we do not feel the pulse of society and let the chance to solidify power and give new dynamic to it pass us by, the time may come when society will be looking for a way out, using any variants. We should also know this. Such are the laws and lessons of history.

I was utterly frank with you. In this connection, I reject Comrade Shevardnadze's thesis as one also senses in it the feeling of panic. I hope you will support the proposal that was put forward by two deputies, patriarchs of our culture. Let's decide that we will not go too far in our suppositions and accusations and will not impute to our society and the country what is non-existent. I think we should reject emotionally charged invectives concerning separate strata. We must do without them.

CUMULATIVE INDEX, 1986-1990

A

Abortion. *See also* Birth control
Economic Summit Meeting (Paris), 430 (1989)
Parental Consent for Teenage Abortions, 387-407 (1990)
Presidential Debates on, 722, 723, 736-738, 766-767 (1988)
Republican Party Platform on, 642 (1988)
Souter Confirmation Hearing, 624-627 (1990)
State of the Union, 65 (1988)
State Restrictions
    Florida Bill Defeated, 217 (1990)
    Idaho Bill Vetoed, 215-219 (1990)
Supreme Court Decisions
    Parental Consent Cases, 387-407 (1990)
    Thornburgh Case, 559-580 (1986)
    Webster Case, 365-389 (1989)

Acquired immune deficiency syndrome (AIDS)
AMA Report, 817-832 (1987)
Democratic Party Platform on, 564 (1988)
FDA Approval of AZT (azidothymidine), 327-330 (1987)
Institute of Medicine Report, 887-908 (1986)
PHS Report on Aids Education, 319-326 (1987)
Presidential Commission Report, 415-446 (1988)
Presidential Debates on, 730-731 (1988)
Reagan's Budget Message, 9 (1987); 150, 155 (1988)
Republican Party Platform on, 638 (1988)
Supreme Court on Victims of Contagious Disease, 245-252 (1987)
Urban League Report, 55-58 (1987)

Adams, Robert McCormick
Smithsonian Agreement on Indian Bones and Burial Artifacts, 539-543 (1989)

Adoption
House Report on Discarded Children in America, 671-686 (1989)
Republican Party Platform on, 635-636 (1988)

Affirmative action
Black America Report, 58 (1987)
Kerner Report Updated, 189-190, 193 (1988)
Supreme Court Decisions, 321-332 (1989)
    Minority Broadcasters, 419-435 (1990)
    Reverse Discrimination, 651-678 (1986); 331-349 (1987)
    Tenure Review Disclosure, 23-34 (1990)

Afghanistan
Amnesty International Human Rights Report, 607 (1989)
Negotiated Settlement Agreements, 257-266 (1988)
Reagan-Gorbachev Summit Meeting, 991, 993 (1987); 356, 358, 361 (1988)
State of the Union, 66 (1988)
UN Report on Human Rights, 919-936 (1986)

Africa. *See also* specific countries
Democratic Party Platform on, 68 (1988)
Republican Party Platform on, 685-686 (1988)

African National Congress (ANC), 65-80, 140 (1990)

Aged. *See also* Medicaid and Medicare
Republican Party Platform on, 639-640 (1988)

Agriculture. *See also* Food supply
Bishops' Report on Economic Justice, 1002-1005 (1986)
Democratic Party Platform on, 564-565 (1988)
Economic Report, 124, 126-127 (1987)
Farm Subsidies
    Economic Summit (Houston), 469, 471-473, 480 (1990)

833

B

N

O